Critical Acclaim for *The Head Start Debates*

"A tremendous contribution to a longstanding debate affecting the future of Head Start; a dialogue that is imperative to the lives of so many of our nation's most deserving children and families. By rigorously presenting the many, sometimes competing, perspectives about Head Start outcomes, goals, and future direction, editors Zigler and Styfco have done a great service to this debate.

This book encourages long-needed dialogue and collaboration among educators, clinicians, and investigators, and will significantly inform policy at this critical juncture in the progress of Head Start programs."

—T. BERRY BRAZELTON, M.D.,
PROFESSOR EMERITUS, PEDIATRICS, HARVARD MEDICAL SCHOOL

"Our children represent our nation's future. That's why this book is so important. It provides a thoughtful look at early childhood development and school readiness. It brings together a wide array of experts with insightful analyses and commentary about the evolution and future of the Head Start program as well as the future of early intervention geared toward the promotion of school readiness in this country."

—SENATOR CHRISTOPHER DODD,
CONNECTICUT

"With this book, Edward Zigler and Sally Styfco have made another crucial contribution to the ongoing national conversation on Head Start—a discussion that has enormous implications for millions of America's most vulnerable children. Read it!"

—MARIAN WRIGHT EDELMAN,
PRESIDENT, CHILDREN'S DEFENSE FUND

"Zigler and Styfco have given us a national treasure...another landmark volume on Head Start. Steeped in scholarship and abundant with diverse perspectives, the Head Start Debates is a powerful, balanced, provocative analysis of the most trenchant and durable issues facing our nation's pioneer and most promising social program. Not Pollyanish or capricious, this is the first no-nonsense compendium of articles that is audacious enough to speak truth to policy. It is tough love for Head Start...crisp, caring, concerned, compassionate, and right on target. Urgently needed today and, unequivocally, a classic for tomorrow."

—SHARON LYNN KAGAN, ED.D.,
COLUMBIA UNIVERSITY

"*The Head Start Debates* brings into clear focus the significant impact of Head Start on our nation's pre-school population. It is truly a *tour de force* for those policymakers and educators who want to make a major difference in insuring the development of our nation's most important resource—its youngest children!"

—GERALD N. TIROZZI, PH.D.,
EXECUTIVE DIRECTOR,
NATIONAL ASSOCIATION OF SECONDARY SCHOOL PRINCIPALS

The Head Start Debates

The Head Start Debates

Edited by

Edward Zigler, Ph.D.

and

Sally J. Styfco

Yale Center in Child Development and Social Policy
Yale University, New Haven, Connecticut

·P·A·U·L·H·
BROOKES
PUBLISHING CO®

Baltimore • London • Sydney

Paul H. Brookes Publishing Co.
Post Office Box 10624
Baltimore, MD 21285-0624

www.brookespublishing.com

"Paul H. Brookes Publishing Co." is a registered trademark of
Paul H. Brookes Publishing Co., Inc.

Typeset by Integrated Publishing Solutions, Grand Rapids, Michigan.
Manufactured in the United States of America by
Sheridan Books, Inc., Fredericksburg, Virginia.

Library of Congress Cataloging-in-Publication Data

The Head Start debates / edited by Edward Zigler and Sally Styfco.
    p.   cm.
    Includes bibiographical references and index.
    ISBN 1-55766-775-6 (hbk.)—ISBN 1-55766-754-3 (pbk.)
    1. Head Start programs—United States. I. Zigler, Edward, 1930– II. Styfco, Sally J.
LC4091.H438 2004
372.21—dc22   2004040756

British Library Cataloguing in Publication data are available from the British Library.

Contents

Impact on Health

Impact on Families

Research Must Be Better

Debate III: The Future of Head Start

Quality

Models for the Future

About the Editors

Edward Zigler, Ph.D., Yale University, 310 Prospect Street, New Haven, Connecticut, 06511

Dr. Zigler is Sterling Professor of Psychology, Emeritus, at Yale University and Director of the Yale Center in Child Development and Social Policy. He was one of the planners of Project Head Start and was the federal official responsible for administering the program when he served as the first director of the U.S. Office of Child Development (now the Administration on Children, Youth and Families). He was also Chief of the U.S. Children's Bureau. He regularly testifies as an expert witness before congressional committees and has served as a consultant to every presidential administration since that of Lyndon Johnson. Dr. Zigler has conducted extensive research on topics related to child development, psychopathology, and mental retardation and has authored hundreds of scholarly publications.

Sally J. Styfco, B.A., Yale University, 310 Prospect Street, New Haven, Connecticut, 06511

Ms. Styfco is Research Associate at the Child Study Center and in the Psychology Department at Yale University and Associate Director of the Head Start Section at the Yale Center in Child Development and Social Policy. She is a writer and policy analyst specializing in issues pertaining to children and families, particularly early childhood and later educational intervention. Her work spans the topics of Head Start, child care, children with disabilities, federal education initiatives, the effects of poverty on child development, and the historical progression of government policies in these areas.

Contributors

W. Steven Barnett, Ph.D.
Director
National Institute for Early Education Research
Rutgers, The State University of New Jersey
120 Albany Street, Suite 500
New Brunswick, New Jersey 08901

Delores Baynes
Parent
Willimantic, Connecticut 06226

Douglas J. Besharov, LL.M., J.D.
Joseph J. and Violet Jacobs Scholar in Social
    Welfare Studies
American Enterprise Institute for Public
    Policy Research
1150 17th Street NW
Washington, D.C. 20036
Professor
University of Maryland School of Public Affairs
Van Munching Hall
University of Maryland
College Park, Maryland 20742

Helen Blank, M.U.P.
Senior Fellow
National Women's Law Center
11 Dupont Circle NW, Suite 800
Washington, D.C. 20036

Barbara T. Bowman, M.A.
Professor
Erikson Institute
420 North Wabash Avenue
Chicago, Illinois 60611

John T. Bruer, Ph.D.
President
James S. McDonnell Foundation
1034 South Brentwood Boulevard
St. Louis, Missouri 63117

Judith A. Chafel, Ph.D.
Professor
Indiana University
7th and North Rose Avenue
Bloomington, Indiana 47405

David B. Connell, Ph.D.
Senior Analyst
Dimock Community Health Center
55 Dimock Street
Roxbury, Massachusetts 02119

Amy Stephens Cubbage, M.S., J.D.
Early Career Education Consultant
West Hartford, Connecticut 06107
Adjunct Faculty
Wheelock College
200 The Riverway
Boston, Massachusetts 02215

Arthur J. Frankel, Ph.D.
Professor and Director
Center for Social Work Research and Practice
University of North Carolina, Wilmington
601 South College Road
Wilmington, North Carolina 28403

Walter S. Gilliam, Ph.D.
Associate Research Scientist
Yale University
Child Study Center
230 South Frontage Road
New Haven, Connecticut 06520

Polly Greenberg
Child/Parent/Staff Development Specialist
4914 Ashby Street NW
Washington, D.C. 20007

Sarah M. Greene, M.A.
President and CEO
National Head Start Association
1651 Prince Street
Alexandria, Virginia 22193

James Griffin, Ph.D.
Senior Research Analyst
Institute of Education Sciences
U.S. Department of Education
555 New Jersey Avenue NW
Washington, D.C. 20208

Carolyn Harmon, Ph.D.
Consultant
Washington, D.C. 20003

Christopher C. Henrich, Ph.D.
Assistant Professor of Psychology
Georgia State University
University Plaza
Atlanta, Georgia 30303

John Hood, B.A.
Chairman and President
John Locke Foundation
200 West Morgan Street, #200
Raleigh, North Carolina 27601

Wade F. Horn, Ph.D.
Clinical Child Psychologist
Laytonsville, Maryland 20882

Alfred J. Kahn, D.S.W.
Professor Emeritus Social Policy and Planning
Columbia University
School of Social Work
622 West 113th Street
New York, New York 10025

Sheila B. Kamerman, D.S.W.
Compton Foundation Centennial Professor
Columbia University
School of Social Work
622 West 113th Street
New York, New York 10025

Jane Knitzer, Ed.D.
Acting Director
National Center for Children in Poverty
215 West 125th Street, 3rd Floor
New York, New York 10027

Robin Gaines Lanzi, M.P.H., Ph.D.
Assistant Professor of Human Science
Georgetown University
3700 Reservoir Road NW
Washington, D.C. 20057

Joan Lombardi, Ph.D.
Director
The Children's Project
5006 50th Place NW
Washington, D.C. 20016

Paul J. Lombroso, M.D.
Professor
Yale University
Child Study Center
230 South Frontage Road
New Haven, Connecticut 06520

Greta M. Massetti, Ph.D.
Research Assistant Professor of Psychology
    and Pediatrics
Center for Children and Families
University at Buffalo, SUNY
318 Diefendorf Hall
3435 Main Street
Buffalo, New York 14214

John Merrow, Ed.D.
President
Learning Matters
Host and Executive Producer, *The Merrow
    Report* (PBS)
6 East 32nd Street
New York, New York 10016

Gwen Morgan
Wheelock College
200 The Riverway
Boston, Massachusetts 02215

Robert W. O'Brien, Ph.D.
Senior Research Analyst
The CDM Group, Inc.
5530 Wisconsin Avenue
Chevy Chase, Maryland 20815

Mariela M. Páez, Ed.D.
Assistant Professor
The Carolyn A. and Peter S. Lynch School of
    Education
Boston College
Campion Hall 126
Chestnut Hill, Massachusetts 02467

Deborah A. Phillips, Ph.D.
Professor
Department of Psychology
Georgetown University
37th and O Streets NW
Washington, D.C. 20057

Chaya S. Piotrkowski, Ph.D.
Professor
Graduate School of Social Service

Fordham University
113 West 60th Street
New York, New York 10023

Peggy Daly Pizzo, Ed.M.
Senior Scholar
School of Education
Stanford University
485 Lasuen Mall
Stanford, California 94305

Nicole Oxendine Poersch, B.A.
Consultant
Chevy Chase, Maryland 20815

Gregg Powell, Ph.D.
Senior Associate
R & P Associates
116 South Lee Street
Alexandria, Virginia 22314

Kyle D. Pruett, M.D.
Clinical Professor of Psychiatry and Nursing
Yale University
Child Study Center
230 South Frontage Road
New Haven, Connecticut 06520

Craig T. Ramey, Ph.D.
Distinguished Professor of Health Studies
Director
Georgetown University Center on Health and
    Education
3700 Reservoir Road NW
Washington, D.C. 20057

Sharon Landesman Ramey, Ph.D.
Susan H. Mayer Professor of Child and Family
    Studies
Director
Georgetown University Center on Health and
    Education
3700 Reservoir Road NW
Washington, D.C. 20057

Arthur J. Reynolds, Ph.D.
Professor of Social Work, Human
    Development, and Educational Psychology
Waisman Center
University of Wisconsin–Madison
302 School of Social Work Building
1350 University Avenue
Madison, Wisconsin 53706

Julius B. Richmond, M.D.
John D. MacArthur Professor of Health Policy,
    Emeritus
Department of Social Medicine
Harvard Medical School
641 Huntington Avenue
Boston, Massachusetts 02115

Carol H. Ripple, Ph.D.
Senior Research Associate
Casey Family Services
127 Church Street
New Haven, Connecticut 06510

Loretta Sanchez, M.B.A.
Congresswoman
U.S. House of Representatives
1230 Longworth House Office Building
Washington, D.C. 20515

Rebecca D.A. Schrag, M.A.
Doctoral Candidate (Clinical Psychology)
University of Virginia
102 Gilmer Hall
Charlottesville, Virginia 22904

Irving E. Sigel, Ph.D.
Distinguished Research Scientist, Emeritus
Educational Testing Service
Rosedale Road
Princeton, New Jersey 08541

Catherine E. Snow, Ph.D.
Henry Lee Shattuck Professor of Education
Harvard Graduate School of Education
Larsen 3
Cambridge, Massachusetts 02138

Jule M. Sugarman, B.A.
Retired, Associate Director
Head Start
Port Republic, Maryland 20676

Heather L. Sugioka, M.A.
Personnel Coordinator
Chestnut Hill Benevolent Association
1450 Worcester Road
Framingham, Massachusetts 01702

Elizabeth Edwards Tufankjian, M.S.
Education Consultant
Judge Baker Children's Center
3 Blackfan Circle
Boston, Massachusetts 02155

David P. Weikart, Ph.D.
(Deceased December 2003)
President Emeritus
High/Scope Educational Research
    Foundation
600 North River Street
Ypsilanti, Michigan 48198

Sheldon H. White, Ph.D.
Professor
Department of Psychology
Harvard University
William James Hall
33 Kirkland Street
Cambridge, Massachusetts 02138

Grover J. Whitehurst, Ph.D.
Director
Institute of Education Sciences
U.S. Department of Education
555 New Jersey Avenue NW
Washington, D.C. 20208

Martin Woodhead, Ph.D.
Professor of Childhood Studies
Faculty of Education and Language Studies
The Open University
Briggs Building
Milton Keynes, MK76AA
United Kingdom

Foreword

I have been a close observer of Head Start since the moment of its inception. In October 1964, the ink still wet on President Johnson's signature of the Economic Opportunity Act, I was trying to enlist in the new federal commitment to fight a war on poverty. Having worked for the previous dozen years in efforts aimed at improving health services for disadvantaged Americans, I assumed that when the formalities were over I would be taking responsibility for parts of the Office of Economic Opportunity's health-based mission—as I ultimately did. But before those arrangements were completed, the freshly minted director of the Community Action Program suggested I look in on a meeting to consider a new possibility designed to improve the long-term prospects of disadvantaged preschool children.

At that meeting, I became witness not only to the naming of the initiative as "Head Start" but also to the enunciation of a grand vision, based on a clear and simple idea: The federal government would enable local communities to provide poor and minority children with the early experiences that would equip them to start school on par with their middle-class peers. No longer would they arrive at school with their lifetime chances already stunted.

Astonishingly, that vision has withstood the test of time and has continued to serve as the touchstone of one of the most successful federal programs in the nation's history. In its particulars, it has continued to evolve to reflect the radical changes of the last decades: in the nature of poverty and family structure, in the rapid escalation of mothers entering the workplace, in our demands that formal education keep pace with new economic conditions, and in our understanding of the importance of the earliest years.

The Head Start Debates comes at a critical time in the evolution of the Head Start idea. With luck, this collection will help to avert one of those swings of the pendulum that could demolish hard-won gains on one front in the struggle to redistribute resources to achieve greater triumphs on another.

I am convinced that a careful reading of this book offers persuasive evidence that we can reconcile superficially opposing views by applying what we have learned about "what works" rather than focusing on ideological differences. We no longer need to argue whether our goal should be "school readiness" or "social competence," child care for working parents or family literacy. Nor whether "parent involvement" or links to a "medical home" are better investments than "teacher quality." These goals are not trade-offs in a zero-sum game; they are essential complementarities in a new century's responses to the challenge of assuring equal opportunity at the very beginning of life.

Three conclusions seem to me to emerge from these pages:

1. A clear focus on school readiness, even reading readiness, is fully compatible with both the original goals *and* the current operations of Head Start.

2. School readiness is a many-splendored thing, which requires attention to children's physical, cognitive, and interpersonal development as well as attention to family and neighborhood surroundings.

3. Enhancing the nation's capacity to achieve these goals requires systematic learning from research and from experience to identify what works and to apply that knowledge to improve outcomes for young children in the widely varied settings in which they spend their days.

Drawing on the observations in the following chapters, here is how I see the implications of these conclusions:

1. A clear focus on school readiness, even reading readiness, is fully compatible with both the original goals and the current operations of Head Start.
We have known from the beginning that poor children are at significant risk of failing in school, that school problems begin early, and that initial reading failure is difficult to overcome and can lead to snowballing deficits in acquiring content knowledge. Head Start's goal has always been to act on all we know to provide disadvantaged young children—and their families—with the boost they need to help children succeed in school and in life.

Now that we know in much greater detail than we did 35 years ago about the specifics of what it takes to achieve that goal, Head Start, and all programs for young children and families, must continue to add to the early childhood toolbox. We have always known we need hammers and nails and screwdrivers and wrenches and saws to build this solid early childhood house, not just a single tool. Now we know more than we used to about how to assure that each of those tools will do their job ever more effectively.

2. School readiness is a many-splendored thing, which requires attention to children's physical, cognitive, and interpersonal development as well as attention to family and neighborhood surroundings.
This means immersing young children, including infants and toddlers, in environments that are safe, nurturing, stimulating, responsive, knowledge-centered, and rich in language. It means cultivating children's natural curiosity and eagerness to learn. It means putting in place whatever it takes to strengthen family and community capacity to support children's developing competence.

The chapters that follow show clearly that all aspects of development affect one another. What goes into making children ready for school is far more than flash cards. Their teachers must be trained and supported in offering enriched language and literacy environments and practiced in using language for extended discourse. Their parents' capacity must be expanded so that they can act more effectively on their commitment to their children's education. In families in which parents are impaired in caring for their children due to depression, substance abuse, personality disorders, or domestic violence, programs must be able to mobilize prompt and competent help.

Both research and experience demonstrate the importance of the early years for developing trust in relationships and the desire for mastery and for learning to manage one's impulses, to listen, take turns, and get along with others. "Reading readiness" is not a narrow notion of knowing the alphabet; recognizing shapes, colors, and numbers; or reciting the days of the week. Efforts to link children and families with the health care, nutrition, and other services they need cannot be allowed to compete with providing opportunities for parent involvement, for children to acquire the concepts that enable them to make sense of the world, or for encouraging children in the dramatic play that contributes to literacy and a rich vocabulary. Curiosity and cognition will flourish when they are shared and jointly enjoyed.

3. *Enhancing the nation's capacity to achieve these goals requires systematic learning from research and from experience to identify what works and to apply that knowledge to improve outcomes for young children in the widely varied settings in which they spend their days.*
Few of the contributors to this book would challenge the notion that we now know that Head Start, and other comprehensive early childhood programs designed on the Head Start model, *can* work. Nor would any disagree that not all Head Start programs, nor all Head Start strategies, are equally effective in achieving agreed-upon goals.

In the earliest days of Head Start and the Great Society, the growth of social programs was accompanied by demands from policy makers for systematic data to determine the efficacy of policies and programs, especially those serving populations without a lot of political clout. The assumption of the time was that the results of "scientific" research and evaluation would ultimately be so precise as to allow social scientists to determine which programs and policies were worthy of the investment of public funds and citizen energies. Proven models would be described, disseminated, and ultimately cloned.

But this approach to social change could not endure. The evaluation results never arrived in time, and the research couldn't provide sufficiently precise answers about what works, when, in what dosages, and for whom in order to predetermine program, policy, and investment choices. Especially when the researchers were trying to use traditional methods (based on randomly assigned experimental and control groups) to assess complex, interactive, community-based programs, they couldn't solve the problems of selection bias, attrition, small sample sizes, or the importance of "unobservables." They couldn't solve the ethical problems of withholding effective interventions from some or the pesky tendency of good programs to change as they were adapted over time and in response to varying local circumstances.

Even more important, we belatedly learned that models crafted centrally—whether in universities, think tanks, or legislatures—and imposed from outside without provision for local adaptation were unlikely to work. Without local ownership and input, simple replications of centrally devised solutions were often less effective than the original model. We learned that unless the local implementers *believe in* what they are doing, the models are unlikely to be successful.

Now we are finally at the stage where we are achieving a balance. We may not be able to promulgate a single best model—not for Head Start, not for Early Head Start—but we do recognize that there is substantial generalizable wisdom about what works that should inform community efforts—in the form of performance standards, in the form of technical assistance, and in the form of information to draw on.

Thus, the challenge is not to keep designing more and more elegant experiments to determine whether Head Start "works." Rather, the challenge is to learn all we can about everything that works to achieve the outcomes we seek and to keep learning. We must get better at understanding how the most effective programs work, the practices and strategies that make them effective, and how these are best combined and continually improved. We must get better at identifying the attributes of effectiveness and high quality wherever they occur and the elements of the infrastructure that sustain and support these attributes. We must zero in on reconciling local flexibility and community embeddedness with accountability for a few, carefully selected, face-valid measures, including how Early Head Start participants do when they enter Head Start and how Head Start children do in kindergarten. And, we must construct the mechanisms whereby these insights can be spread and systematically applied and refined.

The editors and contributors to this book deserve our deep appreciation. They have assembled the lessons of the past 35 years that can help to assure that communities throughout the nation will have the tools and resources available to realize the long-standing dream that all the nation's children, regardless of race, income, or ethnic background, will arrive at school with a realistic chance of succeeding in both school and life.

—Lisbeth B. Schorr

Preface

Head Start is the nation's largest and oldest early intervention program for young children and families in poverty. For most of its nearly 40 years, Head Start has enjoyed strong—but far from universal—popularity. It has weathered its share of criticism—some targeted and deserved, some arising from ideology or a hostile political agenda. Yet, the program remains alive and well, counting among its strongest supporters the approximately 20 million children it has graduated and sent on their way to elementary school. Their families, too, have been consistent and forceful advocates for a program they see as their own.

Head Start was conceptualized before there was an established knowledge base on the potential of intervention to promote young children's development. In fact, practical experience with the project was an important force in the accrual of this knowledge. As a path-breaking program, mistakes were understandably made. Head Start's original goal statement was vague, allowing multiple interpretations of what the effort was supposed to accomplish. There were some errors in program design and operations. Quality control was an afterthought. Evaluations of program effectiveness were often misguided. Policy makers expected too much and appropriated too little. All of these circumstances ignited controversies that continue to this day.

New arguments are being raised over the direction of Head Start's future. These go far beyond President George W. Bush's criticism of the program as not doing enough to promote language and preliteracy skills and his desire to devolve Head Start to the states. The fact is that times have changed since the program began. A lot has been learned about intervention, but some of this knowledge has been slow to work into daily practice. The children and families who attend Head Start today are different in significant ways from that first cohort in 1965: Their cultural and language backgrounds are more diverse; the children's parents are younger and more likely to be single and employed; and the poverty they experience has grown uglier, with welfare reform adding new stresses. The political and social landscapes have also evolved since Head Start began. The War on Poverty is over, as are prolonged welfare and the custom for most mothers to stay at home with their children. The public education establishment is beginning to welcome preschoolers, and group care for even younger children has grown in acceptance and by necessity. While most agree that Head Start must change in response to these developments, debates rage over what course of action is wisest.

Fortunately, decisions concerning the future of Head Start can be based on a broad knowledge base. Because Head Start is a comprehensive service program, it is rightfully the province of many disciplines. Thus, scholars in a host of fields have devoted a great deal of energy and thought to modifications in the Head Start approach. Unfortunately, these ideas often do not travel over academic fences. Generally, educators, administrators, developmental psychologists, medical and mental health professionals, social workers, and others talk more among themselves than with one another. Their work—and Head

Start itself—would surely be enriched by more integration and collaboration, or at least recognition of what is going on in different domains.

The tragedy of this situation is that policy makers get at best an incomplete and at worst a narrow view of the evidence and expert opinions surrounding Head Start. While policy makers need and want to weigh the merits of the various positions to make sound legislative decisions, they have more than once been swayed by one side or the other because they did not know much about alternative choices. The fragmentation of the literature thus stymies the formation of social policies based on the best available knowledge.

We assembled this book in an effort to pull together the competing views on many contentious issues surrounding Head Start. Yes, one purpose is to enable policy makers to have a balanced perspective before they mandate change. Another is to give professionals in various fields access to the thinking in other areas. Our ultimate hope is to encourage all of those who care about Head Start and who may carry strong opinions about its proper course to stop and listen to what the other side is saying. Whether this strengthens or moderates each individual's resolve, the positions formed in the future will at least be more enlightened.

The flavor of the controversies we chose to cover will be familiar to anyone acquainted with the history of early intervention: Does Head Start work? Do its ascribed benefits fade away or are they lasting? Should we expect them to last? What exactly is the program supposed to do? Should it make children smarter or improve their social competence and school readiness, or is child development really secondary to the "original" implied goal of empowering poor adults to rise out of poverty? And what about the future? Should Head Start offer or in fact become a child care service where children eligible for the program are tended so that their parents can go to work? Who should be eligible for Head Start? At what age should Head Start begin, and how long should it last? And what should we do about those nagging problems with service quality? Finally, is Head Start's unique federal-to-local structure worth revitalizing, or should the program be bequeathed to the states to run in the best interests of their own residents?

We asked noted spokespersons on various sides of these issues to contribute their opinions. Although the book is titled *The Head Start Debates*, the format is not a one-to-one confrontation. Rather, we grouped the points that are under debate, and the authors prepared chapters to state their particular views. Most topics have several respondents, although in a few cases, invitees became unable to participate. In these and a few other instances, we reprinted or excerpted already published works to balance the discussion.

We admit that at times the diversity of opinions our contributors delivered challenged our promise for editorial neutrality. Aware of our reputation as fans (albeit not uncritical ones) of Head Start, we are especially grateful to those in opposite camps who joined the debate. We hope we succeeded in allowing their views to be presented just as strongly as those of authors whose opinions are more aligned with our own.

Actually, even those authors we originally expected to pen "friendly" analyses surprised us with some harsh criticisms of Head Start as it is currently delivered. We hope that means we succeeded in achieving the point of this collaborative effort. We want this book to challenge the status quo and to influence Head Start services, quality, and administration during a future of rapid change. We hope the opinions presented here will be useful to decision makers who, for some time, have been wrangling with such issues as

Head Start expansion, program accountability, what the new interests in early brain development and early literacy mean for Head Start's preschool and birth to 3 versions, the demise of welfare and rise in demand for child care, and the gathering call to devolve Head Start to the states. And, because Head Start is a national laboratory for developing effective means of intervention, the ideas our contributors present about its future also have valuable implications for theory and practice in a wide range of child and family services.

Acknowledgments

The efforts of Mackenzie Lawrence, Heather Shrestha, and many others at Paul H. Brookes Publishing Co. enabled this book to be transformed from a complicated draft to a finished product with amazing speed. They thought of every detail, large and small, and managed the entire publication process with skill and professionalism.

To the memory of H. Smith Richardson, Jr.,
a truly great American who had a special concern
for those of our children at risk of not living our nation's dream

The Goals of Head Start

Is Head Start a success or a failure? Opinions vary depending on what one expects the program to accomplish. This section covers disagreements over three goals that historically have been attached to Head Start.

The first argument concerns the appropriate developmental target of early intervention efforts. Craig and Sharon Ramey present the view that cognitive development, which they define broadly, should be the focus of Head Start. We join lead author Rebecca Schrag to argue that Head Start was designed to affect school readiness, which involves far more than cognition, and take the opportunity to explain how the term "school readiness" is the modern rendition of what was long called "social competence."

The second argument is whether Head Start should be judged on the basis of the progress children have made when they begin elementary school or whether benefits derived from preschool should carry through the school years and beyond. Martin Woodhead, in an adaptation of his classic expository, warns that promising anything beyond short-term effects from Head Start programs that vary enormously in quality and communities served is a sure way for psychologists to disillusion policy makers and taxpayers with the value of early intervention. Irving Sigel argues that the overriding purpose of social intervention is to alter the developmental trajectories of children raised in poverty and that programs such as Head Start cannot succeed unless they enlist all relevant professional disciplines, heed the desires and changing circumstances of participants, and evolve better theories and assessment techniques that allow for individual outcomes and program guidance.

The third argument brings us to the roots of Head Start as a weapon in the War-on-Poverty arsenal. Polly Greenberg describes Head Start as an original Community Action Program created to empower impoverished citizens to share equally in our nation's resources and governance. Carolyn Harmon counters that Head Start was conceived as a child development program with objectives linked to—but not identical with—those of the antipoverty war. Julius Richmond, the first director of Head Start, describes a less contentious, quite productive affiliation between Head Start and Community Action during his administrative tenure.

—Edward Zigler and Sally J. Styfco

CHAPTER 1

Early Educational Interventions and Intelligence

Implications for Head Start

CRAIG T. RAMEY AND SHARON LANDESMAN RAMEY

Intelligence is a complex, undeniably important, and controversial topic, especially within the arena of Head Start policy and practice. Considering intelligence from an historical perspective and in light of emerging scientific evidence is informative for future deliberations about the direction of Head Start programs, their performance standards, and evaluation of their success. To what extent can Head Start programs contribute positively to the development of intelligence in young children and increase the likelihood of their academic and social success in school?

Reviews of the research evidence agree that *when children from low-income, multirisk families and communities participate in intensive, high-quality preschool programs, the children show benefits.* These benefits are apparent in their developmental competence, most notably in the areas of general intelligence and language development (Barnett, 1995; Bryant & Maxwell, 1997; Guralnick, 1997; Haskins, 1989; Karoly et al., 1998; S.L. Ramey & Ramey, 1999a, 2000; Yoshikawa, 1995). In studies that have followed children's development through the primary grades—and sometimes far beyond—continued benefits often are documented. These include improved test scores on standardized assessments of reading and mathematics, markedly reduced rates of grade retention (grade repetition), and lowered rates of placement in special education (Barnett, 1995; C.T. Ramey & Ramey, 1998).

In this chapter, we first make the case that improving children's intelligence is an important program goal for early intervention programs, especially for Head Start in the 21st century. Second, we present a review of the key findings from evaluations of the Abecedarian Project conducted since the 1970s, which has provided evidence of multiple, practical developmental benefits that last into adulthood. The Abecedarian Project is the first randomized, controlled trial of early educational intervention that started when chil-

3

dren were infants and provided continuous supports to children and families for at least the first 5 years of life. Thus, this project provides an exceptional opportunity to understand the extent to which an intensive, multiyear, educational, and health support program can make a lasting difference in children's intelligence and overall well-being. Third, we summarize the principles of effective early intervention programs—that is, the factors that appear to be essential in order for children to benefit from their participation. Fourth and finally, we discuss key issues for policy and decision making in the arenas of Head Start, education, child care, and parent and family support programs.

HEAD START IN THE EARLY YEARS: A COMMITMENT TO IMPROVING CHILDREN'S EVERYDAY INTELLIGENCE

When Head Start began in 1965, its national vision was to improve children's everyday or real-world intelligence prior to entering kindergarten or first grade. The method for achieving this goal was to offer children from economically impoverished homes some of the wealth of learning opportunities that their more advantaged peers had prior to entering public school. Educators and developmental psychologists who had worked with low-income children in preschool settings already knew how quickly and eagerly children from all walks of life learn when they are in a safe and supportive setting with adults they can trust. They also saw firsthand the tremendous inequities in the lives of many economically poor children compared with economically advantaged children in terms of home-based learning and developmental encouragement. These inequities led to later developmental delays in those who had restricted learning opportunities and were readily noticed in children's speech and vocabulary, their everyday problem-solving abilities, and their tested intelligence (IQ scores). For many children who lived in extreme poverty, their most apparent delays related to their knowledge about the larger world and were pronounced in the areas of language and reading readiness (preliteracy skills), numbers and numeracy, and reasoning abilities. Without a doubt, the founders and leaders of Head Start in the 1960s, along with many middle-class volunteers who eagerly helped with Head Start programs throughout the country, believed that Project Head Start would increase children's everyday intelligence and their subsequent academic success in school.

Intelligence Defined: Everyday versus Academic Definitions

In the everyday sense, intelligence is widely accepted to be an indicator of a person's broad array of skills and knowledge. More (rather than less) intelligence is viewed quite positively—with only slight skepticism from some segments of society about the value of having extremely high levels (that is, genius-range intelligence). Intelligence is not considered a hidden trait but rather something that shows itself actively. Examples include how well a person handles real-life issues, such as planning, analyzing, information gathering, decision making, and generating new ideas and solutions.

In the academic and scientific world, however, the definition of intelligence is far from resolved. There are numerous competing theories and many hotly debated issues about how best to measure intelligence and whether intelligence itself is a stable lifelong trait versus something that can be modified by experience or affected by the testing situation itself (Ceci, 1991; Zigler & Butterfield, 1968). Many of the superb academic treatises about the nature of intelligence are laden with terminology from statistics, learning theory, genetics, and developmental and evolutionary biology. Some of the most celebrated new theories promote an exciting vision of intelligence as a multifaceted representation of diverse human talents. Howard Gardner (1993) proposed a theory that there are "multiple intelligences," including interpersonal, linguistic, logical-mathematical, bodily-kinesthetic, spatial, musical, and intrapersonal. Robert Sternberg (1995), in his "triarchic theory of intelligence," posited three distinct types of intelligence: creative, practical, and academic. Academic intelligence, of course, is the one primarily measured by traditional standardized tests of intelligence. Critics complain that such all-encompassing ideas about intelligence are not testable or refutable, whereas fans appreciate the recognition of multiple pathways to success in life that cannot be reduced to just what is taught and tested in traditional school settings.

We endorse the view that children benefit immensely when they have school readiness skills related to reading, writing, and arithmetic, as well as a solid language foundation and general knowledge about many things in the world. We know that standardized tests of intelligence and school achievement are important indicators of children's developmental progress but are woefully inadequate to tap the full range of their skills and learning. Ideally, there will be major advances in how to assess children's skills and knowledge more fully and fairly. Improved assessment techniques should also help educators realize their goals of providing the best *individualized* instruction to each child at each stage of development and increasing the opportunities for children's multiple types of intelligence to shine in the school setting.

The Heated Controversies Surrounding the Use of Standardized Intelligence Tests in Head Start

To understand why the Head Start community has been so strongly divided about whether intelligence should remain an important outcome goal for Head Start programs, or whether it should even be measured at all, it is informative to consider the use and misuse of intelligence tests in our country. (See Gould, 1996, for a highly readable and far more extensive history.) In the early 20th century, formal intelligence tests were developed as a way to help predict which children would do better (or worse) in a formal school setting. These standardized tests evaluated children's skills in many different areas that were closely associated with the kinds of tasks encountered in school, such as following a sequence of instructions, listening to stories and retaining key details, performing basic number operations, and detecting similarities and differences among objects. These "intelligence tests" were never intended to measure the full range of human talents and skills.

Further, any careful historical or current analysis of the content of the items on the most widely used intelligence tests reveals that children with an increased fund of knowledge and more learning experiences were more likely to earn higher scores. Indeed, this is why these tests have been so good at predicting how well groups of children would perform in school. The predicative power of the tests eventually was treated as much stronger than ever intended.

All too often, the scores a child "earned" based on his or her responses to the items on a standardized intelligence test, known as an intelligence quotient or IQ score, were considered to be a true and valid indicator of the child's real intelligence—both current and future. As a result, educators often used children's IQ scores to decide many matters related to what, where, and how children were taught. Many teachers trusted that the IQ test could accurately measure a child's "true potential" and "innate ability" for learning and later school success. Further, the test manuals that provided guidelines for professionals about how to interpret the IQ score implied that a child's intellectual potential could *not* be fundamentally changed. Thus, until the passage and enactment of the Education for All Handicapped Children Act of 1975 (PL 94-142), many children were doomed to a label of "less intelligent" and were excluded from many interesting and important academic learning opportunities, all because of their performance on a single standardized test of intelligence.

Regardless of the fact that the IQ test scores of *large groups* of school-age children can predict their *general* school performance, many educators, psychologists, and parents have long realized that there are many individual exceptions. Some children with low or average IQ scores seem to soar academically; such children often have been labeled as "overachievers." Children with high IQ scores who do not do well in school have been called "underachievers." Other children with very low scores, below 70 or 75, are labeled as having mental retardation, even though some of these children seem to function reasonably well in their everyday worlds. These seeming mistakes in judging a child's intellectual competence may be rare, but the consequences for individual children and their families are, unfortunately, severe and often lifelong.

Another seriously disturbing aspect of intellectual assessment is that children from lower socioeconomic classes consistently perform below children from middle- and upper-income families. Further, there almost always have been significant ethnic and racial differences in test scores. These differences among groups of children have been interpreted by many scientists, policy makers, and the general public as representing genetic or inherited qualities, thereby constituting evidence that some children are destined, by their genes, to be either inferior or superior. A simplistic and once widely held view was that these qualities were inherently unalterable.

In the 1970s, McCall, Appelbaum, and Hogarty (1973) provided compelling evidence that IQ scores of individual children do fluctuate dramatically over the preschool and school-age years: ages 3 to 17. Individual children typically have IQ test scores that differ, on average, by 28 points—more than the amount needed to place a child in the gifted versus average IQ range or the average versus mental retardation range. Although this important longitudinal study could not pinpoint all of the reasons for these fluctuations in IQ scores at different test occasions, the investigators did show that parenting practices were likely to be a significant influence on the children's intelligence growth patterns.

One of the most controversial and highly publicized scientific papers on intelligence appeared in the same decade that Head Start was launched. In a 1969 monograph in the *Harvard Educational Review,* Arthur Jensen reported that African Americans had average IQ scores about 15 points lower than Caucasians and strongly implied that this difference was a trait that could not be altered. This paper appeared in the midst of our country's vigorous Civil Rights Movement, which drew attention to the extreme disparity in how African Americans were treated in all areas of life, including education, housing, employment, health care, recreation, and citizenship rights. The reality of long-term, systematic racial discrimination was undeniable—and its consequences were far-reaching. In academic and political circles, there was an outcry against Jensen and the potential harm that was likely to result from his monograph.

Scholarly analysis and criticism of Jensen's position continue. The essence of his early ideas was reenacted and expanded in a highly popular book in 1994, *The Bell Curve: Intelligence and Class Structure in American Life,* by Richard Herrnstein and Charles Murray. They claimed that they were academic mavericks, unfairly rejected and criticized by liberal colleagues who refused to face up to the "true facts" that confirmed that some people are fundamentally and unalterably less capable than others. Their book had the aura of a scholarly tome, with hundreds of pages and numerous, highly detailed scientific tables and graphic displays of data. Despite the fact that the scientific community, once again, found serious flaws with statistical analyses and the reasoning in this book, as well as the fact that the authors systematically excluded published evidence contrary to their thesis, their central ideas received tremendous public attention. To a large extent, Herrnstein and Murray affirmed the belief of many laypeople, politicians, and scholars—namely, that differences in intelligence are real, inevitable, and in line with the social order of the world. That is, people on the top of the ladder earn this right largely because of their natural superiority, whereas those at the bottom are truly inferior and their performance cannot be much raised.

Not surprisingly, such a nativist position is at odds with the Head Start program's intent to give children early opportunities to learn, which in turn are expected to increase their readiness for school and their later life achievements. About two thirds of the children served by Head Start are from ethnic minorities, and almost all are economically impoverished. Thus, the position of unalterable innate abilities places the majority of Head Start children and families in a negative light as being permanently less capable. At best, proponents of the nativist view of intelligence see the Head Start program as a "token effort" that is doomed to achieve only minimal and short-term benefits. Needless to add, these groups consider efforts to improve the quality or intensity of Head Start a waste of tax dollars.

The old Westinghouse Report (Cicirelli, 1969), which presented the findings from an evaluation of Head Start programs conducted when most were only offered for a few weeks during the summer, also had a devastating effect that many still remember to this day. The report's authors argued that Head Start did *not* succeed in boosting children's intelligence for very long—with the "fade-out" of benefits apparent after a few years in elementary school. The Consortium for Longitudinal Studies later reported similar findings (Lazar, Darlington, Murray, Royce, & Snipper, 1982), a group that pooled data from 11 experiments designed to test efficacy of early education programs for impoverished children. The Consortium reported that the IQ score benefits observed in the preschool years were much reduced in magnitude by about third grade. Interestingly, this same group found significant positive benefits in terms of children's actual school performance on a variety of real-world measures (multiple school performance indicators) that lasted beyond elementary school.

Over the decades, as the Head Start program broadened to include more health and nutrition initiatives, social services, and parent involvement activities, it was reasonable that increases in children's tested intelligence not be used as the program's central outcome measure. Indeed, given the strong controversies and racial overtones surrounding the use of intelligence tests (which have been criticized as being culturally biased in what they measure), the Head Start Bureau's decision to *de*-emphasize the development of children's intelligence and academic skills seemed politically and socially understandable.

Along with the broadening of services provided by Head Start programs, children's social and emotional skills were identified as important goals. It is noteworthy, however, that there was not strong evidence that low-income children were noticeably lagging or delayed in these areas. In contrast, literally hundreds of studies continued to document that there were large disparities between children from low- and middle-income families in their academic readiness for school, their IQ scores, and their subsequent academic achievement in school (C.T. Ramey & Ramey, 1998; S.L. Ramey & Ramey, 2000).

Why Intelligence Should Not Be Overlooked as a Goal of Head Start Programs

Despite tremendous sensitivity around the use of standardized tests to measure the intelligence of low-income and minority children and despite the acknowledged misuses and abuses of IQ test scores in the past, there are excellent reasons why improving children's intelligence should be recognized as a central goal for Head Start programs. Among these reasons are the following:

1. The compelling evidence from laboratory studies in the field of developmental neurobiology that demonstrates large and lasting effects of early experience and the early rearing environment on brain development and learning (Sackett, Novak, & Kroeker, 1999; Shonkoff & Phillips, 2000; Shore, 1997): Children who learn better and learn more are truly more intelligent and capable. This increased intelligence translates into a greater ability to solve everyday problems in school, at home and at play, and later in work situations. When children are not provided with optimal amounts and quality of early learning and language experiences, it is highly likely that their brain development and their corresponding behavioral skills will be insufficiently developed, which in turn will hinder their success in school and life.

2. The mounting evidence from studies of infants and young children that associates particular types of experiences with increases in particular skills and learning strategies: These studies include both experimental and naturalistic studies and essentially are in agreement with the neurobiology findings that direct experiences influence the expression of genetic and biological propensities as well as a child's eventual everyday competencies, motivation, and success. (For examples of summaries of this research, see parent-oriented publications by Diamond & Hopson, 1999; C.T. Ramey & Ramey, 1999; Your Child, 2000.)

3. Theories about intelligence and improved ways of assessing multiple aspects of a child's emerging skills that relate to later school achievement (Ceci & Williams, 1997; Gardner, 1993; Sternberg, 1996): Although these theories are not without controversy, they are based on sound evidence about the multifaceted nature of human competencies. They are exciting to early childhood educators and parents alike because they open the possibility of new ways to enhance many different types of human talent. Children in Head Start, like all children, display early interests and skills that go beyond the realm of traditional academic subjects of reading, writing, and arithmetic. Increasingly, our nation's best teachers and best schools are discovering ways to recognize and cultivate a

wider range of children's abilities, which we believe are truly part of human intelligence (S.L. Ramey & Ramey, 1999b, 2000).

4. The findings from more than five decades of research about early interventions and child care, which indicate that children's tested intelligence and real-world indicators of success in school and in young adulthood can be improved by participation in high-quality, intensive, educationally oriented programs (C.T. Ramey et al., 2000; S.L. Ramey & Ramey, 1999a, 2000; Reynolds, 2000).

Collectively, these scientific advances are directly germane to the future of Head Start programs and public education. To the extent that Head Start programs can vigorously and consistently incorporate this increased knowledge about the factors that improve children's early development and performance, these programs will better serve the children, their families, and society as a whole. The original goal of Head Start remains as important and challenging today as it was in 1965—namely, to improve the odds for success among children who historically have entered school without age-appropriate intellectual and language skills. To succeed in school and in life, children undeniably need good health, good learning experiences, and ongoing social and intellectual supports to perform their best.

THE ABECEDARIAN PROJECT: A CASE STUDY IN EARLY CHILDHOOD EDUCATION

The Abecedarian Project was launched in Chapel Hill, North Carolina, in 1971, and its evaluation continues. The name for this project—Abecedarian—came from Latin roots and means "one who learns the fundamentals, such as the alphabet." The project began with one primary goal, shared with Head Start: to improve the school readiness and later school performance of children from very low-income, multirisk families. The investigators were aware that early evaluations of Head Start had allegedly demonstrated only modest benefits that seemed to fade out over the early elementary school years. Accordingly, the investigators planned the Abecedarian Project as a *preventive effort* (C.T. Ramey & Campbell, 1984; C.T. Ramey, MacPhee, & Yeates, 1982) that had the following features:

1. It began much earlier in the children's lives (ages 3–6 months).

2. It provided much greater amounts of intervention time than the typical Head Start program. Specifically, children in the Abecedarian Project received a full day (at least 6 hours and up to 10 hours) of the education program, 5 days per week, for 50 weeks each year, compared with the usual half-day Head Start program often provided fewer days per week, for 7 or 8 months per year.

3. It continued for 5 years until children entered public school (and for some groups, an extra 3 years of support in elementary school and summer enrichment programs were provided). Most Head Start children receive less than 1 year of additional supports.

4. It utilized a new educational and developmental curriculum specifically developed to promote the intellectual (cognitive), language, emotional, social, and physical development of infants, toddlers, and young children—known originally as *Learningames* (Sparling & Lewis, 1979, 1984) and later revised and renamed *Partners for Learning* (Sparling,

Lewis, & Ramey, 1997). It included a specific language curriculum (above and beyond *Learningames*) that emphasized language development and early conversational skills (C.T. Ramey, McGinness, Cross, Collier, & Barrie-Blackley, 1981).

5. For both the language and general education curricula, all teachers and teacher assistants received extensive training and weekly in-service training, coupled with active supervision of teachers' classroom interactions with children.

6. The study was designed to measure multiple aspects of children's development, not just their IQ scores, as well as the quality of stimulation in their home environments, parent–child interactions and attachment, and the adult development of their mothers.

The Abecedarian Project effort was designed specifically to prevent developmental delay and mental retardation (defined by performance below 85 and 70, respectively, on standardized tests of development and intelligence); to reduce grade retention, which almost always was attributable to substandard academic and social performance; to lower rates of special education placement, largely associated with poor learning and classroom performance; and to prevent extremely low levels of academic achievement in the critical areas of reading and mathematics (defined as performing below the 25th percentile nationally). Although the project was framed in terms of prevention, we also expected that the intellectual and academic achievement of all participating children would be improved by this intensive educational intervention and that the families would benefit from receiving the supports the Abecedarian Project provided, including health and social services.

The Abecedarian Project did *not* have the usual *untreated* control group, because we recognized that factors such as poor early nutrition, lack of adequate pediatric care and immunizations, and the need for social services in these families were likely to harm children's development and could not ethically be withheld. Accordingly, we provided the following supports and services to children in both the control and treatment groups:

*   Free and unlimited fortified formula for infants (prior interview data indicated none of the mothers chose to breast-feed their infants) and disposable diapers

*   Reduced cost or free health care (as appropriate) for the first 5 years of life

*   Ongoing family support services and, when needed or requested, outside referrals to community social and health service providers

In essence, the Abecedarian Project was a true comparison of different types of supports to low-income, multirisk families rather than the traditional treatment versus no treatment study. Both groups received stable, high-quality health and social services, but only the intervention group received the formal center-based program for the first 5 years of life. Families in the control group were never prevented from seeking and obtaining other supports, including enrolling their children in other preschool programs. (*Note:* The positive results of other preschool programs for these children are described by Burchinal, Lee, & Ramey, 1989.)

In contrast to Head Start, the designers of the Abecedarian Project did not assume that all low-income children were at risk for poor intellectual development or below average school performance. Based on a large published literature (Birch & Gussow, 1970) about the relationship of social and economic indicators in the family to children's later intellectual and academic performance, multiple risk variables were used to create a High Risk Index (C.T. Ramey & Smith, 1977) to identify which children were most likely to benefit from this program. These risk factors included maternal or paternal education less than high school graduation, low maternal intelligence (IQ score below 90), family income substantially below the federal poverty line, single parent, no close maternal relatives in the community, older siblings with mental retardation or poor school performance, receiving public assistance in the form of welfare and/or public housing, contact with social services agencies (including prior child abuse and/or neglect), and parental mental health problems. Almost all of the women were recruited during the last trimester of their pregnancy. More than 95% of those invited to participate in this research project chose to do so, even knowing that they would be randomly assigned to one of the two treatment groups.

In this section, we highlight what we consider to be the major outcomes of participation in the Abecedarian Project. We have grouped these findings into three broad areas: 1) children's intelligence and cognition, 2) children's reading and math achievement in the school years and early adulthood, and 3) general life adjustment in the adolescent and early adulthood years.

Children's Intelligence and Cognition Benefited from Early Educational Intervention

The results for children's test scores on many different types of developmental, cognitive, and intelligence tests, administered from 3 months through 21 years of age, have shown a clear and consistent pattern. During the first 12 months of life, children in both the treatment and control groups showed age-typical patterns of development, with no significant effects of the treatment apparent during these early months. Beginning at 18 months, however, the children in the early education treatment group scored significantly higher at every 6-month interval up to 54 months (seven tests in all). At age 4, for example, 40% of the children in the control group earned IQ scores of 85 or below, compared with only 5% of the children in the Abecedarian program (C.T. Ramey & Campbell, 1984).

When children entered public school, typically at age 5, they continued to be assessed with intelligence tests administered individually by trained psychologists at ages 5, 6½, 8, 12, and 15 years. At every one of these ages, the children in the intervention group again performed at significantly higher levels. (See C.T. Ramey et al., 2000, for a detailed presentation of these findings.) The children's IQ scores showed the largest differences during their earlier preschool years, with differences being somewhat smaller as the children got older. The groups differed during the school years an average of approximately 5 points on each test occasion (whereas the amount averaged about 10 points between 18 months and 4½ years). Even at age 21, the individuals who participated in the Abecedarian educational program continued to score 5 points higher (with an average IQ score of 90) compared with those in the control groups (Campbell, Ramey, Pungello, Sparling, & Miller-Johnson, 2002).

In addition to the general tests of development and intelligence, children's cognitive abilities were evaluated in laboratory settings where the children's abilities to learn new tasks was measured. For example, when toddlers were exposed to a task in which they

learned to identify small differences between shapes, those in the intervention group performed this discrimination-learning task significantly better (C.T. Ramey & Smith, 1977).
Another example involved a Piagetian battery of tasks in which children's emerging concepts about relationships between objects were measured. The results showed that the
Abecedarian children performed at significantly higher levels (Campbell & Ramey, 1990).

In summary, children's learning and intelligence appear to be significantly enhanced
when they receive continuous, high-quality early education. These benefits appear above
and beyond those that may be attributed to improved social and health services and nutrition. The benefits are also in addition to possible benefits that the control children received in other community preschool programs (Burchinal, Lee, & Ramey, 1989). As
shown in the next section, the benefits of the Abecedarian early education program appear to be even more impressive when more practical measures of children's developmental and educational progress are considered.

Reading and Mathematics Test Scores Significantly Higher

The Woodcock-Johnson Psycho-Educational Battery, Part 2 (Woodcock & Johnson, 1977)
was administered at ages 6, 8, 12, 15, and 21 years. The children who participated in the
Abecedarian early education program consistently scored significantly higher in their
reading and math achievement. On average, the magnitude of these benefits was clearly
enough to make a difference in their classroom performance. Further, the results from the
standardized test scores were corroborated separately by teacher ratings, with classroom
teachers rating the children who received the Abecedarian program as significantly more
verbally skilled. At age 21, the children's reading skills in the intervention group were almost two grade equivalents higher than those in the control group. Specifically, the young
adults who received the Abecedarian treatment were reading, on average, at the eleventh-
grade level, whereas those in the control group read at about the ninth-grade level. In
math achievement, the Abecedarian program participants performed at an average grade
level of 9.2, whereas those in the control group scored at 7.9 (Campbell et al., 2002).

Success in School and Young Adulthood

Several real-world indicators of adjustment and success support the conclusion that providing high-risk, low-income children with early, continuous, and educationally sound
enrichment programs yields long-term benefits (C.T. Ramey et al., 2000; S.L. Ramey &
Ramey, 2000). Among children who received the 5 preschool years of the Abecedarian
educational program, only 12% were placed in special education (essentially the national
average) compared with 48% of the children in the control group. Rates of grade retention were also markedly lower in the treated group (30%) compared with the control
group (55%). The costs of special education placement and repeating a grade are high, in
terms of both taxpayer dollars and personal psychological costs to the children and their
families.

One of the most encouraging findings focuses on the activities of these individuals
as young adults (Campbell et al., 2002). At age 21, significantly more of the individuals
who attended the Abecedarian preschool program were enrolled in higher education programs, working in jobs rated at higher skill levels, and less likely to have had a child.

Thus, increased reading and math skills do matter in seeking and maintaining employment and making informed choices about continued education and training opportunities. It is likely they also contribute, in part, to decisions individuals make about where and how to live and when to start a family. These indicators of adult adjustment are understandably of great interest to policy makers.

KEY FEATURES OF EARLY INTERVENTIONS AND HOME ENVIRONMENTS ASSOCIATED WITH LARGE BENEFITS FOR CHILDREN

Not all early intervention or two-generation family support programs achieve their well-intentioned goals of improving the lives of young children and their families (C.T. Ramey, Ramey, Gaines-Lanzi, & Blair, 1995). We summarized principles of effective early intervention—that is, the key features we conclude make a difference in whether an early intervention program succeeds in improving children's development, especially in the areas vital for general intelligence, language skills, and school readiness (C.T. Ramey & Ramey, 1998). These principles include the timing, intensity, duration, and extensiveness of the intervention supports provided; the degree of direct child engagement and the cultural appropriateness of the intervention; and the extent to which children continue to have highly supportive environments after the intervention. In essence, we think there is ample evidence that programs for high-risk, low-income children must fulfill the following conditions in order to produce significant cognitive benefits:

1. They must directly engage the child so that very young children actually receive the types of stimulation and learning appropriate for their developmental progress.

2. They must be of high quality, with an emphasis on education and language development. The quality of preschool programs is repeatedly shown to depend on the education and skill levels of the caregivers. Ideally, high-quality programs have a well-developed curriculum; a clear philosophy of early childhood education; adequate staffing for the number of children served; and plenty of supplies, materials, and space for providing children with a safe, interesting, and varied set of learning activities.

3. They have a good parent education program so that parents become more knowledgeable and positive parenting behavior is strongly supported. Note, however, that parent education programs alone (that is, without a center-based program for children) have seldom demonstrated any positive effects for high-risk children in terms of their cognitive development or school readiness (C.T. Ramey & Ramey, 1998).

4. They begin when children are younger than 3 years of age (we think infancy is the ideal time) and continue at least through school entry. Multiyear programs are especially vital for the most vulnerable children who typically begin to show developmental delays in the second year of life. Additional supports during the early elementary school years are likely to be most needed by children who enter poor-quality public schools and who do not have access to educationally oriented after-school and summer programs (see Chapter 28).

5. The programs provide full-day education and enrichment for the children on a year-round basis. This intensity factor is important because many high-risk children living in poverty do not receive adequate supports and are not provided with sufficient amounts of

crucial learning opportunities outside the program. A poor-quality full-day program for young children is morally indefensible because it cannot promote gains and may actually harm development (NICHD, 1997). Similarly, a high-quality program offered only a few days a week, a few hours per day, and/or for just part of the year is simply unlikely to be sufficient to produce significant and lasting benefits. Given that the majority of mothers with young children are now in the workforce for at least 30 hours per week, including mothers leaving welfare, it is imperative that *all forms of child care* be evaluated in terms of their impact on children as well as their convenience and support for parents.

As in almost all matters concerning children and parents, there are many differences of opinion and philosophy. The previous principles and recommendations are not based solely on ideology or hope. Rather, these reflect more than four decades of rigorous research and program evaluation about what differentiates the more and less successful programs for children in poverty. At the same time, it is important to recognize that there are many different ways to ensure that children in poverty receive the continuously high-quality early care and education that they (like all children) need. Many low-income parents are well educated, have positive and readily available social support, are employed in stable and desirable jobs, and have excellent parenting knowledge and skills. Their children are not at very high risk, although it is still important for their children to receive high-quality nonparental child care if the family needs it. In contrast, for those low-income families who do not have multiple positive supports and are plagued by other stressors (e.g., crime, substance abuse, mental health problems, low parental intelligence) or who are especially vulnerable (e.g., teen parents), additional child care supports are *essential* to prevent negative effects on their children and to improve their children's intelligence, language skills, and school readiness.

These features that distinguish the most successful early interventions are ones that can feasibly become part of the Head Start endeavor, especially when Head Start programs develop collaborations with local child care providers, agencies, and groups to ensure that all children and families have a good start in life and the needed supports when children transition to school (S.L. Ramey & Ramey, 2000).

POLICY DELIBERATIONS AND PROMISING
SOLUTIONS FOR HEAD START IN THE 21ST CENTURY

This is an ideal time to enact widespread policy reform, based on sound scientific evidence, to improve the health and education of our nation's most vulnerable children. It is ideal because the knowledge base for what young children truly need is well developed; there is strong bipartisan commitment to Head Start and its continued improvement; unemployment is relatively low, at the same time that welfare-reduction goals are being met; and the national concern about the quality of child care and education is at an all-time high. Recognizing the need for an increasingly well-educated workforce and citizenry essential to a strong, competitive democracy, there is increasing federal and state interest in assuring that all children are ready for school.

Our recommendations are straightforward and achievable with the current resources available to our nation. Collectively, these policy changes, if enacted, can contribute immensely to the strength of our country.

Recommendation 1: Build on the long-standing bipartisan support for Head Start and early childhood education programs.

Recommendation 2: Enforce the new program standards for Head Start and for Early Head Start in a manner that is vigorous and consistent.

Recommendation 3: Provide a new kind of technical assistance that is more individualized, sustained, and "hands on" regarding classroom incorporation of strong language and literacy programs and appropriate learning activities to maximize all children's school readiness skills.

Recommendation 4: Allow for new competition and alternative types of early education programs in the free market to serve low-income and other at-risk families, with adequate safeguards for quality and accountability.

Recommendation 5: Offer effective incentives for collaborative and partnership programs that combine funding streams and increase the continuity of supports for children, particularly between Head Start and education programs (including special education) and subsidized child care. The fragmentation and complexity of federal, state, and local programs of services and supports for poverty families are staggering, inefficient, and demoralizing. National leadership in creating more efficient and effective child and family programs is needed and will necessitate major changes.

Recommendation 6: Decrease the excessive red tape and administrative surveillance that are not associated with documented benefits to providers and program participants.

Recommendation 7: Increase the ongoing monitoring and formal evaluation of Head Start programs and other federal and state early intervention programs, including those for children with special health care needs, disabilities, and risk conditions.

Recommendation 8: Create a stable and open peer review system (consistent with the well-respected model used by the National Institutes of Health) to ensure greater equity in the review and award of grants and contracts related to Head Start and other early childhood programs.

Recommendation 9: Develop a mechanism for the timely review and public release of relevant information collected by federal agencies regarding programs for young children and their families. Excessive caution and control have dominated the release of many critical reports about government programs; this has eroded public and professional confidence in the quality of the research and evaluation and the accuracy of the results. A new era of openness and willingness to consider "failures" in large-scale initiatives, perhaps including aspects of Head Start itself, is essential in order to realize direct benefits for children.

Among the worst consequences of program realities is that children themselves often suffer when serious compromises are made for the sake of political popularity or administrative expediency. A truly effective set of programs and policies to eradicate social inequities associated with poverty must go beyond a superficial solution that currently contains programs of uneven quality. The tremendous progress of the national Head Start program must be continued and strengthened in new, innovative, and effective ways. With certainty, children's intelligence can be improved in the first 5 years of life when they receive the types of daily stimulation, learning, and responsible care they need (C.T. Ramey & Ramey, 1999). Effective early intervention can provide lasting benefits well into adulthood that will improve individual lives as well as our country as a whole.

REFERENCES

Barnett, W.S. (1995). Long-term effects of early childhood programs on cognitive and school outcomes. *Future of Children, 7*(3), 25–50.

Birch, H.G., & Gussow, J.D. (1970). *Disadvantaged children: Health, nutrition, and school failure.* New York: Grune and Stratton.

Bryant, D., & Maxwell, K. (1997). The effectiveness of early intervention for disadvantaged children. In M.J. Guralnick (Ed.), *The effectiveness of early intervention* (pp. 23–46). Baltimore: Paul H. Brookes Publishing Co.

Burchinal, M., Lee, M., & Ramey, C.T. (1989). Type of day care and preschool intellectual development in disadvantaged children. *Child Development, 60,* 128–137.

Campbell, F.A., & Ramey, C.T. (1990). The relationship between Piagetian cognitive development, mental test performance, and academic achievement in high-risk students with and without early educational experience. *Intelligence, 14,* 293–308.

Campbell, F.A., Ramey, C.T., Pungello, E., Sparling, J., & Miller-Johnson, S. (2002). Early childhood education: Outcomes as a function of different treatments. *Applied Developmental Science, 6,* 42–57.

Ceci, S.J. (1991). How much does schooling influence general intelligence and its cognitive components? A reassessment of the evidence. *Developmental Psychology, 27,* 703–720.

Ceci, S.J., & Williams, W.M. (1997). Schooling, intelligence, and income. *American Psychologist, 52*(10), 1051–1058.

Cicirelli, V.G. (1969). *The impact of Head Start: An evaluation of the effects of Head Start on children's cognitive and affective development.* Athens, OH: Westinghouse Learning Corporation.

Diamond, M., & Hopson, J. (1999). *Magic trees of the mind.* New York: Plume.

Education for All Handicapped Children Act of 1975, PL 94-142, 20 U.S.C. §§ 1400 *et seq.*

Gardner, H. (1993). *Frames of mind: The theory of multiple intelligences.* New York: Basic Books.

Gould, S.J. (1996). *The mismeasure of man.* New York: Norton.

Guralnick, M.J. (Ed.). (1997). *The effectiveness of early intervention.* Baltimore: Paul H. Brookes Publishing Co.

Haskins, R. (1989). Beyond metaphor: The efficacy of early childhood education. *American Psychologist, 44,* 274–282.

Herrnstein, R.J., & Murray, C. (1994). *The bell curve: Intelligence and class structure in American life.* New York: Free Press.

Jensen, A.R. (1969). How much can we boost IQ and scholastic achievement? *Harvard Educational Review, 39,* 1–123.

Karoly, L.A., Greenwood, P.W., Everingham, S.S., Hoobe, G., Kilburng, M.R., Rydell, C.P., et al. (1998). *Investing in our children: What we know and don't know about the costs and benefits of early childhood interventions.* Santa Monica, CA: Rand.

Lazar, I., Darlington, R., Murray, H., Royce, J., & Snipper, A. (1982). Lasting effects of early education: A report from the Consortium for Longitudinal Studies. *Monographs of the Society for Research in Child Development, 47*(2–3, Serial No. 195).

McCall, R.B., Appelbaum, M.I., & Hogarty, P.S. (1973). Developmental changes in mental performance. *Monographs of the Society for Research in Child Development, 38*(3, Serial No. 150), 1–84.

NICHD Early Child Care Research Network. (1997). Poverty and patterns of child care. In G.J. Duncan & J. Brooks-Gunn (Eds.), *Consequences of growing up poor* (pp. 100–130). New York: Russell Sage.

Ramey, C.T., & Campbell, F.A. (1984). Preventive education for high-risk children: Cognitive consequences of the Carolina Abecedarian Project. *American Journal of Mental Deficiency, 88,* 515–523.

Ramey, C.T., Campbell, F.A., Burchinal, M., Skinner, M.L., Gardner, D.M., & Ramey, S.L. (2000). Persistent effects of early childhood education on high-risk children and their mothers. *Applied Developmental Science, 4,* 2–14.

Ramey, C.T., MacPhee, D., & Yeates, K.O. (1982). Preventing developmental retardation: A general systems model. In J.M. Joffee & L.A. Bond (Eds.), *Facilitating infant and early childhood development* (pp. 343–401). Hanover, NH: University Press of New England.

Ramey, C.T., McGinness, G., Cross, L., Collier, A., & Barrie-Blackley, S. (1981). The Abecedarian approach to social competence: Cognitive and linguistic intervention for disadvantaged preschoolers. In K. Borman (Ed.), *The social life of children in a changing society* (pp. 145–174). Mahwah, NJ: Lawrence Erlbaum Associates.

Ramey, C.T., & Ramey, S.L. (1998). Early intervention and early experience. *American Psychologist, 53,* 109–120.

Ramey, C.T., & Ramey, S.L. (1999). *Right from birth: Building your child's foundation for life.* New York: Goddard Press.

Ramey, C.T., Ramey, S.L., Gaines-Lanzi, R., & Blair, C. (1995). Two-generation early intervention programs: A child development perspective. In I. Sigel (Series Ed.) and S. Smith (Vol. Ed.), *Two-generation programs for families in poverty: A new intervention strategy. Vol. 9. Advances in applied developmental psychology* (pp. 199–228). Norwood, NJ: Ablex.

Ramey, C.T., & Smith, B.J. (1977). Assessing the intellectual consequences of early intervention with high-risk infants. *American Journal of Mental Deficiency, 8,* 318–324.

Ramey, S.L., & Ramey, C.T. (1999a). Early experience and early intervention for children "at risk" for developmental delay and mental retardation. *Mental Retardation and Developmental Disabilities Research Reviews, 5,* 1–10.

Ramey, S.L., & Ramey, C.T. (1999b). *Going to school: How to help your child succeed.* New York: Goddard Press.

Ramey, S.L., & Ramey, C.T. (2000). Early childhood experiences and developmental competence. In J. Waldfogel & S. Danziger (Eds.), *Securing the future: Investing in children from birth to college* (pp. 122–150). New York: Russell Sage.

Reynolds, A.J. (2000). *Success in early intervention: The Chicago child-parent centers.* Lincoln: University of Nebraska Press.

Sackett, G.P., Novak, M.F., & Kroeker, R. (1999). Early experience effects on adaptive behavior: Theory revisited. *Mental Retardation and Developmental Disabilities Research Reviews, 5,* 30–40.

Shonkoff, J.P., & Phillips, D. (Eds.). (2000). *From neurons to neighborhoods: The science of early child development.* Washington, DC: National Academy Press.

Shore, R. (1997). *Rethinking the brain: New insights into early development.* New York: Families and Work Institute.

Sparling, J., & Lewis, I. (1979). *Learningames for the first three years: A guide to parent-child play.* New York: Walker & Co.

Sparling, J., & Lewis, I. (1984). *Learningames for threes and fours: A guide to adult and child play.* New York: Walker & Co.

Sparling, J., Lewis, I., & Ramey, C.T. (1997). *Partners for learning.* Lewisville, NC: Kaplan.

Sternberg, R. (1995). *A triarchic approach to giftedness.* Storrs, CT: National Research Center on the Gifted and Talented.

Sternberg, R.J. (1996). *Successful intelligence.* New York: Simon & Schuster.

Woodcock, R.W., & Johnson, M.B. (1977). *Woodcock-Johnson Psycho-Educational Battery: Part 2: Tests of academic achievement.* Boston: Teaching Resources Corporation.

Yoshikawa, H. (1995). Long-term effects of early childhood programs on social outcomes and delinquency. *Future of Children, 5*(3), 51–75.

Your child: Birth to three. (2000, Fall/Winter). *Newsweek* [special edition].

Zigler, E., & Butterfield, E.C. (1968). Motivational aspects of changes in IQ test performance of culturally deprived nursery school children. *Child Development, 39,* 1–14.

CHAPTER 2

Familiar Concept, New Name

Social Competence/School Readiness as the Goal of Head Start

REBECCA D.A. SCHRAG,
SALLY J. STYFCO, AND EDWARD ZIGLER

S ince the implementation of Head Start in 1965, researchers and policy makers have been struggling with the question of whether the program works. Although ostensibly the question may seem simple, it has repeatedly been obscured by changing expectations of Head Start and by differing perceptions of the program's goals. In order to evaluate accurately the success of a social program such as Head Start—whether it works—there must be a standard by which to judge, a goal or ideal against which the reality of the program can be measured. Only with the clear presentation of such a goal or set of goals will the evaluation of Head Start prove productive and worthwhile.

Head Start's goals have been steeped in confusion and controversy since its inception. For much of its history, there has been a general misconception that the program's main objective is to enhance children's cognitive development; for a long time, both researchers and policy makers looked almost exclusively at IQ scores and achievement test scores as the indices of Head Start's success. Although cognitive development is certainly a priority of Head Start, it is only one piece in a comprehensive set of program goals, goals that—for a variety of reasons—have not been easy to specify or measure.

There are two general paths that led interpreters astray as they culled the purpose of Head Start. One stems from its identity as a social program, which, logically, should have some benefit to the society that pays for it; the second stems from the language used by the planners of Head Start to describe the program, which was both cumbersome and difficult to understand. Head Start was born out of a campaign to end poverty, so it seemed fair to expect it to have some impact on socioeconomic disadvantage. In the 1970s and 1980s, social problems such as juvenile delinquency, teen pregnancy, and drug use became the maladies du jour, and people looked to Head Start to set its young charges on the right path, away from these evils. In the 1990s, the nation bemoaned the lack of preparation among young adults entering the workforce. The problem was projected to worsen: High numbers of young children were seen entering school without the basic skills to master the curriculum, placing them in the costly track of grade retention, special education, unemployment, and welfare. Eyes again turned to Head Start, this time to reduce educational expenditures and boost the productivity of the labor force.

All of these dreams were made possible by Head Start's planners, who unwittingly cleared the second path leading to general misunderstanding of the program's goals. The original planning document was quite vague in terms of what Head Start should accomplish. There was no straightforward goal statement or even a summarizing paragraph stating what this program aimed to do. Instead, there was a list of seven objectives (quoted in the following paragraph) that described what children living in poverty needed to begin formal schooling. Each objective began with a gerund, suggesting that Head Start would be a process rather than a means to an end. The planners were being realistic. Their project was supposed to last 6–8 weeks during the summer, right before children entered school. The planners knew they could not give their young students everything they needed to succeed in school in this short time. The planners therefore conceptualized Head Start as a step, not as the journey's end.

The initial goals of Head Start very much reflected the "whole child" philosophy endorsed by the planning committee. The committee members understood that school readiness was abetted by multiple systems of child development and thus required a comprehensive services program. In their own words, the focus of such a program should be

- Improving the child's physical health and physical abilities

- Helping the emotional and social development of the child by encouraging self-confidence, spontaneity, curiosity, and self-discipline

- Improving the child's mental processes and skills with particular attention to conceptual and verbal skills

- Establishing patterns and expectations of success for the child, which will create a climate of confidence for his future learning efforts

- Increasing the child's capacity to relate positively to family members and others while at the same time strengthening the family's ability to relate positively to the child and his problems

- Developing in the child and his family a responsible attitude toward society, and fostering constructive opportunities for society to work together with the poor in solving their problems

- Increasing the sense of dignity and self-worth within the child and his family (*Recommendations for a Head Start Program by a Panel of Experts,* 1965, pp. 1–2)

The committee believed that each of these objectives were needed to provide a head start on school for children from disadvantaged families. They explained in the planning document that the early childhood years are the most critical period in the poverty cycle, due to the rapid pace at which children develop learning patterns and form individual expectations and aspirations. For children living in poverty, they continued, "there are clearly observable deficiencies in [these] processes which lay the foundation for a pattern of failure—and thus a pattern of poverty—throughout the child's entire life" (p. 1). Thus, Head Start was viewed as a way to interrupt this pattern of failure and poverty, as a means by which disadvantaged children would be able to begin school on par with their middle-class peers.

At no point in the planning document was Head Start cited as an ultimate cure for poverty; rather, its overall mission extended only so far as to help to ensure that disadvantaged children did not begin school already behind.

The numerous goals set forth by the planning committee were both comprehensive and complex, which is not surprising given the scope and depth of the program's over-arching mission. Nevertheless, it is not hard to see how researchers found it difficult to establish a method of evaluation that could adequately measure the success of Head Start in realizing these rather vague goals. For this, among other reasons, much of the initial research focused almost exclusively on Head Start's intellectual component, specifically on how many IQ points the program added to children's intelligence test scores. Despite all of the work the original Head Start planners put into applying their "whole child" philosophy, somehow academic success became the key focus of nearly every program evaluation, and the findings were rarely in Head Start's favor (Cicirelli, 1969).

IN SEARCH OF SOCIAL COMPETENCE

It was not until the early 1970s that the Office of Child Development (OCD)—the government agency then responsible for Head Start—began a concerted effort to redefine ways to measure Head Start's success. Launching from the original goals of the planning committee, OCD formally adopted *social competence* as a suitable term for the overarching goal of Head Start and, therefore, as the critical dependent variable for any future evaluations. Social competence was interpreted to mean the qualities and abilities children need to succeed in an academic environment. Of course, the children must be at a certain level of cognitive development, but they must also be physically healthy (How can children learn if they are sick or malnourished?), socially apt (How can they concentrate on lessons if they cannot get along with their teacher or peers?), and have families who are involved in their education (How will they value their own schooling if it exists in isolation from their primary role models?). With the adoption of social competence as Head Start's primary goal, psychologists and educators hoped that program evaluations would begin finally to assess these various outcomes instead of focusing on cognitive development alone.

In some senses, one might expect that the adoption of one official objective for Head Start would allay the confusion surrounding the program's purpose; in actuality, this was hardly the case. The task of devising a formal definition of the construct, as well as appropriate outcome measures, still remained. For the ensuing 10 years, three different groups (the Educational Testing Service, the Rand Corporation, and Mediax Associates) worked on formulating an operational definition of social competence for use in program evaluations. The project, however, ran into several political and academic barriers. For example, the Educational Testing Service initially assembled a conference of child development experts who eventually identified 29 variables as "facets" of social competence (Anderson & Messick, 1974), bringing the OCD no closer to an operating definition that could be used in evaluations. Although progress was made, funding for the project came to an abrupt halt in the early 1980s. It is difficult to pinpoint exactly why funding halted, but one reason is that the new Reagan Administration felt that the development of competence measures for Head Start was of little value and should be cut from the budget. Ironically, the only part of the project salvaged was devoted to cognitive measures. Not only did such measures already exist but also their use had yielded little in previous Head Start evaluations. Early childhood specialists were frustrated, not only because they still had no tool to assess social competence but also because so much concern for children's physical, social, and emotional development had been abandoned (Raver & Zigler, 1991).

In spite of the significant amount of work put into the development of measures of social competence, no practical instrument was forthcoming; the goals and, consequently, the success of Head Start remained difficult to quantify. In 1978, Zigler and Trickett warned, "the hour grows late, and unless the social sciences develop a practical and coherent measure, social competence will never replace the IQ as our primary measure of the success of intervention programs" (p. 797). Unfortunately, their prediction has come true for Head Start. The program's failure to produce permanent increases in IQ scores has been proven over and over again, but the possibility that it has positive effects in other areas has been largely ignored.

Although the absence of a formal definition and assessment tools continued for years, there was nonetheless a growing consensus among early childhood professionals as to the meaning of social competence. In 1978, Zigler and Trickett published a paper that gave impetus to the development of that consensus. They argued that early childhood intervention programs should be regarded as efforts to prepare children for school and that social competence is the best standard by which to judge whether such preparation has been achieved. They presented a list of specific features that should enter into social competence, as well as generally accepted ways to measure them. These features included

1. Physical health (assessed by measures such as growth rates and immunization histories)

2. Cognition (tapped by standardized intelligence tests)

3. Achievement (also indicated by standardized tests)

4. Socioemotional factors (clustered around motivation, self-image, attitudes, and social relationships; evaluated using a variety of measures with established reliability and validity)

Changing Terminology

The gist of the definition of social competence established by Zigler and Trickett has become widely accepted and has been seen in an increasing number of early intervention evaluations. The terminology, however, has shifted. The shift became apparent in 1989 when President George H.W. Bush and the nation's governors adopted national education goals; these goals were signed into law in March 1994 as the Goals 2000: Educate America Act (PL 103-227). Goal 1 reads, "By the year 2000, all children in America will start school ready to learn." Using the new catch phrase, Congress adopted school readiness as Head Start's official goal in the 1998 reauthorization act. Congress did not, however, nullify the goal of social competence adopted in the 1970s. In fact, they did not change the basic program at all. They did not have to because for a preschooler, being socially competent is synonymous with being ready to start school.

Unfortunately, the construct of school readiness faces many of the same challenges as that of social competence. In 1990, Kagan commented that, "conceptually, readiness remains poorly defined and variously interpreted. Practically, it is mired in confusion with practitioners and policy makers advancing widely differing positions regarding it and related issues . . ." (p. 272).

One primary point of contention is whether school readiness develops as a function of biological maturation or as the result of specific influences in a child's environment. Each of these conflicting views leads to the support of different types of policies and practices (Kagan, 1990). Those who adhere to the maturationist view of readiness believe that children should not be placed in school until they reach a certain developmental level; rather, they should be placed in an extra year program to allow for the natural occurrence of biological maturation. Those who support the environmental notion of readiness believe that remedial interventions, such as additional hours of school attendance, can enhance a child's readiness (Powell, 1995). Other sources of confusion in the discussion of readiness include the difference between readiness for school and readiness to learn, as well as the question of whether readiness is a uniform child characteristic or a distinguishing characteristic of a local community (Powell, 1995).

Goals and Measures Projects Define School Readiness

The National Education Goals Panel, a group of scholars and policy makers responsible for documenting America's progress in meeting the eight National Education Goals, has identified five dimensions of early learning and development that most effectively prepare a child to enter school (Goal 1). These dimensions were chosen because they "reflect a multifaceted conception of early learning and development" (Powell, 1995, p. 19). The dimensions are

- Physical well-being and motor development

- Social and emotional development

- Approaches toward learning

- Language usage

- Cognition and general knowledge (National Education Goals Panel, 1992, p. 19)

Like those assessing America's progress in meeting its educational goals, Head Start too has made advancements in developing more concrete program performance measures to evaluate service quality and effectiveness. These measures deliberately represent all of the dimensions set forth by the National Education Goals Panel and reflect the same multifaceted approach to school readiness. The Program Performance Measures Initiative, intended to serve as "an outcome-oriented accountability system" (U.S. Department of Health and Human Services, 1998, p. 1), maintains that social competence is the primary program goal, supported by five objectives:

1. Enhancing children's healthy growth and development

2. Strengthening families as the primary nurturers of their children

3. Providing children with educational, health, and nutritional services

4. Linking children and families to needed community services

5. Ensuring well-managed programs that involve parents in decision-making

Each of these objectives is measured by specific indicators such as, "Head Start children demonstrate improved positive attitudes toward learning" and "Head Start children receive meals and snacks that meet their daily nutritional needs" (U.S. Department of Health and Human Services, 1998, p. 2). The similarity of Head Start's performance measures to the indices for Goal 1 provides evidence that the terms *social competence* and *school readiness* actually describe a singular construct, at the very least for the purposes of program evaluation.

ANOTHER ANGLE ON MEASURING SUCCESS

Although clarifying the goal of Head Start is the first and certainly most critical step toward accurately measuring its success, questions that arise during actual program evaluation are equally important in order to understand what the program has accomplished. One of these questions was raised and examined by Hebbeler (1985), who conducted research on the long-term educational attainments of Head Start graduates in the public schools of Montgomery County, Maryland. Although extremely high attrition rates invalidate many of her results, Hebbeler's attempt to address the complexity of the research issue at hand merits special attention. Specifically, she examined not only how well Head Start graduates perform in school when compared with a similar control group but also how well they perform in absolute terms. She drew attention to the fact that in studies of Head Start's effect on educational attainment, the control groups are often comprised of children from family and economic backgrounds similar to those of the preschool groups but quite dissimilar to those of the average preschooler. She explained,

> While this approach to examining impact is well grounded in the traditions of program evaluation, it has left unanswered, or at least undiscussed, the second question: just how well did the children in the experimental group do? This is not the same as asking whether they do better than a group that by all available indicators is likely to do poorly. (p. 207)

To find out how well Head Start graduates really do, Hebbeler not only examined the differences between them and a control group of similar socioeconomic background but also compared their performance with that of other students in the Montgomery County public schools, the majority of whom were from middle- to upper-class families. Hebbeler found that most of the Head Start cohorts she followed into high school had poor school performance compared with their classmates from wealthier families.

From a theoretical standpoint, Hebbeler's study raises the question of how to employ appropriate standards by which to judge the effectiveness of a program such as Head Start. As Hebbeler herself notes, "Improved performance is a possible program goal, but so is attainment of an absolute level of performance" (1985, p. 214). In other words, should graduates of Head Start be expected to achieve a standard level of school readiness that is somehow predetermined or merely to achieve more than they would have in the absence of the program's influence? This question of how to determine program success is a complex one that must be kept in mind when analyzing Head Start research, particularly that which relates to cognitive outcomes.

CONCLUSION

We posit that school readiness has always been—and should continue to be—the primary goal of Head Start. The program was designed to give impoverished children an actual head start, a chance to catch up to their middle-class peers so that all of the nation's children can enter school at the same level, ready for school and ready to learn. Head Start's mission has remained the same since its inception, despite shifting terminology, arguments over definitions, and the overemphasis on intelligence in the research. The National Education Goals testify to the fact that America's aspirations for its children have come to match those of Head Start. If Head Start is fulfilling its purpose, then America has a proven model and is one step closer to achieving the first goal of nationwide school readiness.

REFERENCES

Anderson, S., & Messick, S. (1974). Social competency in young children. *Developmental Psychology, 10,* 282–293.

Cicirelli, V.G. (1969). *The impact of Head Start: An evaluation of the effects of Head Start on children's cognitive and affective development.* Report presented to the Office of Economic Opportunity (Report No. PB 184 328). Washington, DC: Westinghouse Learning Corporation.

Goals 2000: Educate America Act of 1994, PL 103-227, 20 U.S.C. §§ 5801 *et seq.*

Hebbeler, K. (1985). An old and a new question on the effects of early education for children from low-income families. *Educational Evaluation and Policy Analysis, 7,* 207–216.

Kagan, S.L. (1990). Readiness 2000: Rethinking rhetoric and responsibility. *Phi Delta Kappan, 72,* 272–279.

National Education Goals Panel. (1992). *The national education goals report: Building a nation of learners.* Washington, DC: U.S. Government Printing Office.

Powell, D.R. (1995). *Enabling young children to succeed in school.* Washington, DC: American Educational Research Association.

Raver, C.C., & Zigler, E. (1991). Three steps forward, two steps back: Head Start and the measurement of social competence. *Young Children, 46,* 3–8.

Recommendations for a Head Start program by panel of experts. (1965). Washington, DC: U.S. Department of Health, Education and Welfare, Office of Child Development.

U.S. Department of Health and Human Services. (1998). *Head Start Performance Measures, 2nd Progress Report.* Washington, DC: Author.

Zigler, E., & Trickett, P. (1978). IQ, social competence, and evaluation of early childhood intervention programs. *American Psychologist, 33,* 789–798.

CHAPTER 3

When Psychology
Informs Public Policy
The Case of Early Childhood Intervention

Martin Woodhead

A nalyses of the potential for psychological research to inform public policy are now perennial, especially when the welfare and development of young children are at issue. Frequently, discussion centers on the problem of how to communicate research, what dissemination modes to use, and so forth. But effective dissemination is not always a problem. Occasionally, social scientists reap rewards for their determined efforts when their research captures the attention of policy makers, politicians, and the public at large and is generally accepted as having made a tangible contribution to the development of policy. On such occasions, attention turns away from problems of communication to issues of responsibility—psychologists' responsibility to ensure the validity not only of their research findings but also of inferences that are drawn for policy.

A most relevant illustration comes from a series of reports published between 1977 and 1983 by the Consortium for Developmental Continuity, later renamed the Consortium for Longitudinal Studies. The group convincingly demonstrated for the first time that well-planned preschool programs could have a lasting effect on the fortunes of socially disadvantaged (especially African American) young children into adult life (Consortium for Developmental Continuity, 1977; Consortium for Longitudinal Studies, 1978, 1983; Darlington, Royce, Snipper, Murray, & Lazar, 1980; Lazar, Darlington, Murray, & Snipper, 1982). These reports were the product of collaboration among investigators representing 11 projects, each a well-planned and carefully researched preschool intervention, adopting an experimental or at least quasi-experimental design and involving young children born between 1958 and 1968. By conducting a joint follow-up study in 1976, and again in 1980, the Consortium was able to provide a comprehensive picture of the extent of long-term effects. Several of the projects within the Consortium also reported follow-up data independently (Clement, Schweinhart, Barnett, Epstein, & Weikart, 1984; Gray, Ramsey, & Klaus, 1982). Table 3.1 lists the 11 projects in the Consortium. For simplicity, they are identified in the following discussion by the name of their lead investigator.

Data from the Consortium and its constituent projects served an important function in strengthening public support for early childhood programs for disadvantaged children, notably Head Start. These studies were also cited in broader debates about the case for extending public education to 4-year-olds (discussed by Zigler, 1987). They also made up part of the evidence that shaped the Education of the Handicapped Act Amendments of 1986 (PL 99-457), mandating public services including education for children with disabilities from birth to age three. The lessons for policy were also discussed for other western countries (Woodhead, 1985) and for third world countries (Halpern & Myers, 1985; Liddell, 1987; Myers & Hertenberg, 1987).

This chapter reviews the implications for public policy that have been claimed from this body of early intervention data, focusing particularly on projects within the Consortium. This review was written in the mid-1980s and is based on research available at that time. Although these studies were published some time ago, their influence lingers in policy discussions. Further, issues concerning generalizability and interpretation of the Consortium findings echo in current debates over the effectiveness of Head Start and the wisdom of universal preschool.

Table 3.1 Preschool evaluations in the Consortium for Longitudinal Studies

Projects	Lead investigator
The Early Training Project, Tennessee	Susan W. Gray
Perry Preschool Project, Ypsilanti, Michigan (often referred to as the High/Scope study)	David Weikart
Parent Education Infant and Toddler Programme, Florida	Ira J. Gordon/R. Emile Jester
Comparison of Five Approaches for Educating Young Children from Low Income Homes, Illinois	Merle B. Karnes
The Louisville experiment: Comparison of four programs, Kentucky	Louise B. Miller
The Harlem Study, New York	Francis H. Palmer
Verbal Interaction Project (Mother-child home program), New York	Phyllis Levenstein
The Micro-social Learning Environment project, New Jersey	Myron Woolman
The New Haven Project, long-term effects of Head Start and Follow-Through, Connecticut	Edward Zigler
The Philadelphia Study, impact of preschool on intellectual and socioemotional development, Pennsylvania	E. Kuno Beller
The Institute for Developmental Studies (IDS) Experiment in Early and Sustained Enrichment, New York	Martin Deutsch

Source: Consortium for Longitudinal Studies, 1983

THE POLITICAL STATUS OF EARLY CHILDHOOD INTERVENTION

Few areas of social and educational policy are ever evaluated on such an extended time frame as has been applied to intervention studies. One major reason why researchers have been motivated to carry out such long-term evaluations lies in the relatively marginal status of early childhood programs on the policy agenda. Although universal schooling is taken as a sine qua non of Western civilization, governments have remained ambivalent about the desirability of providing a comprehensive pattern of services to support families with young children. Even when preschool services have been developed, the goals of enhancing children's welfare and their development per se have frequently been subsumed within a more compelling political priority, be it the release of women into the labor force (e.g., as in Britain during two world wars; Tizard, Moss, & Perry, 1976); the furtherance of equal opportunities for working parents (e.g., postwar Swedish day care provision; Berfenstam & William-Olsson, 1974); or, as in this case, the pursuit of social egalitarian goals (e.g., through the War on Poverty during the 1960s; Zigler & Berman, 1983; Zigler & Valentine, 1979). By and large, these are the priorities that have shaped the direction of research programs. So, in the case of Head Start, the broad range of potential concurrent benefits to children and families has received relatively little attention compared with the search for empirical support for the political ideals of the War on Poverty in measurable long-term effects (especially cognitive effects) throughout schooling and into adult life (Kotelchuck & Richmond, 1987; Zigler, 1976). It was this search, continued over 2 decades, that culminated in the Consortium's apparently unequivocal evidence that early childhood programs might, after all, live up to the promise cherished by the president who initiated the first Head Start program in 1965—"that no American child shall be condemned to failure by the accident of his birth" (President Johnson, quoted in Zigler & Valentine, 1979, p. 20).

Harnessing the credibility of early childhood programs to broad social goals, which on the face of it are far removed from immediate priorities for young children, has had one other consequence. Early childhood advocates have displayed considerable ingenuity in framing their case to address the political imperatives of the day. When Head Start was initiated in the early 1960s, claims about the long-term value of early intervention were sufficient to justify expenditure by an administration committed to reduce social and educational inequalities. By contrast, in the late 1970s and early 1980s, even data as strong as those offered by the Consortium would not have had great political significance if the implication appeared to be simply one of increased public expenditure. In this context, the impact of long-term effects data has been greatly enhanced by the presentation of policy conclusions that appear not only to be justified by scientifically derived data but also are politically expedient. Particularly significant have been the use of "real-life" measures (e.g., employment and delinquency) that, when combined with a cost-benefit approach, have led to dramatic claims that, far from being a burden on the public purse, preschool is a sound financial investment. This induced the *Wall Street Journal* to review a follow-up of the High/Scope Perry Preschool Project children at 19 years of age (Clement et al., 1984) with a feature titled "A Head Start Pays Off in the End" (Crittenden, 1984). The article began, "If ever there was a program for the 1980s, a program that addresses the needs for greater productivity and the needs of women and the problem of poverty, it is—are you ready?—preschool education."

Media coverage is only the first indicator of the successful communication of a message. Arguably, it was no coincidence that the year after the first report from the Consortium for Developmental Continuity (1977) saw the first substantial increase in Head Start's budget since publication of the Westinghouse report nearly a decade earlier. More remarkable is the fact that steady increases in Head Start's budget were maintained in the unfavorable public-spending climate of the mid-1980s, topping $1 billion by 1985 (Administration on Children, Youth and Families, 1985). One commentator argued that the decision to include Head Start as one of the social "safety-net" measures was due, at least in part, to the Consortium investigators' assiduous efforts to convey the message of their evidence to influential politicians of the day (Datta, 1983a).

In short, reports from the Consortium and its constituent projects certainly count as having been highly successful in having an impact on public policy, and the conclusions they drew were, on the face of it, well founded in their data. Yet despite the widespread attention paid to this research, many questions remained inadequately answered that could have had a strong bearing on the implications for policy. This chapter centers on three questions in particular that retain timeliness and relevance to subsequent findings:

1. What causal processes could have produced effects over such a long period?

2. What significance does an understanding of possible causal processes have for policy?

3. How valid are the implications that have commonly been inferred from the data?

EVIDENCE OF LONG-TERM EFFECTS

The longest-term evidence of effectiveness offered in the Consortium reports was based on data collected in 1980. By that time, children in four of the projects (those directed by Beller, Gray, Karnes, and Weikart) were old enough to have completed high school. In each case, the program group had higher completion rates, a finding that proved to be significant when the data were pooled. Taken together, there was a 15% difference in high school completion rates (Royce, Darlington, & Murray, 1983). These effects were matched by evidence of higher occupational aspirations and expectations among the children and their parents. In view of the numerous other influences on children's progress during the intervening dozen or more years, the discovery of significant effects on these measures seems, on the face of it, fairly convincing evidence that early intervention has a lasting impact, at least until the end of schooling.

The Consortium did report one measure after children had left school: children's success in obtaining employment. For the three projects for which participants were old enough to make the criterion relevant (Beller, Gray, and Karnes), no direct effects could be discerned on their success in the job market (Royce et al., 1983).

Since the final Consortium report was published in 1983, children in the project directed by David Weikart were followed up again at 19 and 27 years of age (Clement et al., 1984; Schweinhart, Barnes, & Weikart, 1993). Indeed, the High/Scope Perry Preschool Project still takes much of the limelight when it comes to arguing the policy implications of early intervention research. Unlike the other Consortium projects, the High/Scope study demonstrated that preschool had a significant effect on employment rates for the participants at age 19 and on earnings as adults. The preschool group also completed more schooling and relied less on social services, such as welfare. Also, this was a rare study that showed clear though diminishing effects on scholastic attainment during the school years (Schweinhart & Weikart, 1980). In addition, there were significant effects on levels of juvenile and adult crime and arrests. These "real-life" measures are what most often captured the public imagination. Preschool intervention was no longer seen as an issue for debate solely among psychologists and educationists; it came to take a spotlight in the debates about maternal and child welfare, youth unemployment, and the prevention of delinquency (Farrington, 1985). Publication of such clear-cut findings on a whole series of salient measures, which have been converted into cost-benefit analyses, combined with the indefatigable efforts of the High/Scope team to communicate their findings, account for the substantial public attention that has been paid to this single project.

A PROMISE FOR SOCIAL POLICY

Taken together, these findings seem to translate readily into major policy implications for the development of early childhood programs both in the United States and abroad. It is tempting to let the matter rest there, with an apparently watertight case for investment in the early years that promises not only to reduce the incidence of educational failure throughout schooling but also to have a measurable impact on many of the social ills that beset advanced industrial countries. There has certainly been a great deal of media discussion of this tantalizing possibility, but—at the time of writing, 1988—there was remarkably little published academic review of the findings, either in terms of research adequacy or in terms of implications for policy (also noted by Datta, 1983b; Haskins & Gallagher, 1984). Exceptions include an article by Zigler (1987), in which he challenged the misapplication of preschool intervention data in debates about extending kindergarten programs to all 4-year-olds, and one of my earlier articles in which I attempted to define the limits on generalizability (Woodhead, 1985).

The fact that the academic community has paid relatively little critical attention to this research may, in part, stem from an understandable reluctance to appear to be challenging the scientific base for politically precarious social and educational programs that achieve a great deal for children and families in poverty. The consequence, however, is that tacit endorsement is given to conclusions about the power of early intervention that emerge from simplistic interpretation of the message in the data. This may appear politically expedient in the short term, but in the long run it carries inherent dangers. In the first place, it reinforces the political preference to urge single strategy and (relatively) inexpensive educational solutions to complex social and economic problems (Lazerson, 1970). Second, it risks perpetuating the idea that the impact an educational intervention has on an individual can be understood in isolation from the context in which it occurs. Third, it fails to recognize that there may be features of experimental projects that are difficult, even impossible, to reproduce in a national social program (including the fact of being experimental and by definition only being available to a particular group of children). Fourth, as Zigler's article reemphasized, it encourages advocates to overstate the case, courting a political backlash if the program does not turn out to fulfill the promises made for it (Zigler, 1987).

These dangers were well illustrated by the media coverage surrounding publication of High/Scope's monograph, *Changed Lives* (Clement et al., 1984). The *Wall Street Journal* feature has already been mentioned. The national and local press throughout the United States consistently reported data from the High/Scope Perry Preschool Project under dramatic headlines, including, for example, "Head Start Saves Children and Money" (1984) and "Head Start Gets a High Grade" (1984). Such reports fudged several, by no means trivial, issues about the relationship between one carefully planned and maintained experimental project and the 1,200 diverse community-run programs collectively known as Head Start (Besharov & Hartle, 1987; Kotelchuck & Richmond, 1987).

One way of approaching these issues is by asking questions about generalizability. What were the features of the successful programs, and how far are they, could they be, and need they be replicated on a wider scale for early intervention to be effective? Such questions have been examined by Woodhead (1985) and Zigler (1987). As a general summary, the data suggest that, at least for extremely disadvantaged children, a wide range of early intervention strategies may be effective. This does not necessarily mean, however, that all strategies are effective. Far from it. There are certain distinctive shared features of the Consortium projects that were not systematically tested but that may have accounted for their success. All were carefully planned and implemented, staff were well supported, there were low child-to-adult ratios (averaging 5:1), and all had a carefully designed program applied within a clear framework of aims. All involved parents actively in the learning process, and some required their active participation in parent programs and home visiting. In the absence of further systematic research specifically examining the impact of these variables, a cautious conclusion for policy would acknowledge that assured effectiveness among the general run of preschool programs may necessitate implementation of minimum standards in some or all of these respects.

MODELS OF EARLY INTERVENTION EFFECTIVENESS

As noted previously, this chapter focuses on trying to explain how a moderate intervention during the early years could result in a long-term change in prospects for adult life. What is an appropriate explanatory model? What are its implications for deriving policy both for early childhood and for the rest of the education system through which the former preschool child must progress? One way of approaching these issues is by asking what the policy maker is expected to make of the data, an interpretation that could differ depending on the explanatory model chosen.

The simplest model for explaining the evidence would assume early intervention has *direct effects*. According to this model, children who have attended preschool cope more effectively with school and stay on longer because they are more able: Preschool has made them smarter. This view of early intervention is implicit in the catchphrase "an inoculation against failure," although arguably that particular expression has always been more a part of the folklore of early intervention than a serious attempt to understand the process (Klaus & Gray, 1968). In any case, Head Start has never been solely concerned with cognitive goals: "Improving the child's mental processes and skills with particular attention to conceptual

and verbal skills" was only *one* of the seven objectives for Head Start set by the original planning committee (Richmond, Stipek, & Zigler, 1979, p. 137). The other objectives covered
physical, emotional, and social development; self-concept; relationships with parents; and
patterns and expectations of school success. Even so, the prospects of causing a permanent
change in children's cognitive functioning became the principal criterion of many early
evaluations, not least because of the ready availability of well-proven psychometric measures in this area (Zigler & Trickett, 1978). The broad educational goals of the War on
Poverty were "easily translated into 'becoming smarter,' particularly in a nation as infatu-
ated with intelligence test scores as the United States" (Zigler & Berman, 1983, p. 896).

On the face of it, a direct effects model has a number of virtues that might commend
it to those responsible for formulating policy. It is easy to comprehend and simple to present in public debate; it is clear-cut, lacking the vagaries and uncertainties that can hinder
decision making; it makes for straightforward, apparently scientifically based policy
choices between strategies according to their relative effectiveness; and it appeals to a cultural preference for social interventions targeted to effect individual change. Yet, there is
very little in the evidence to suggest that the long-term effects identified in the Consortium meta-analysis came about because of marked permanent changes in children's cognitive competencies as a direct result of their attendance at a preschool program. Although
the superiority of experimental groups in measured intelligence remained significant and
robust (on the stringent criterion of deleting the project with the most significant effect
and recalculating the result) for up to 2 years after completion of the program, the effects
rapidly weakened in subsequent years (Lazar et al., 1982). In this respect, the message of
the data on IQ scores was not substantially altered since Bronfenbrenner's earlier conclusion that despite promising short-term effects,

> By the first or second year after completion of the program . . . the children began to
> show a progressive decline, and by the third or fourth year of follow-up had fallen back
> into the problem range of the lower 90s and below. (1974a, p. 52; see also Bronfenbren-
> ner, 1979, p. 168)

The implication for an explanatory model is that a direct effect via IQ score is clearly
not the answer. If the cognitive effects of early intervention wash out during the early
grades, then they cannot be directly responsible for children's later school progress. One
explanation that appealed initially to the Consortium investigators (reported by Lewin,
1977) was that there might be a sleeper effect—although the effects on IQ score were no
longer manifest, they had not disappeared but were lying dormant until some process of
maturational change or environmental triggering stimulated their reawakening during
the later school years. On closer scrutiny, this interpretation seems somewhat implausible
(Clarke & Clarke, 1981, 1982; Seitz, 1981), although this does not mean that cognitive
abilities do not have a place in an explanatory model, as will become apparent. This discussion, however, must turn to other variables in the search for processes that might account for transmission of long-term effects, variables that are less about permanent change
in the child's psychological functioning and more about changes in the child's relationship to significant features of the social environment, both at school and at home.

One group of variables in particular can be singled out as offering evidence that an
enduring change had taken place in the relationship of program children to the school sys-

tem. These were referred to by the Consortium as measures of "school competence," comprising "retention in grade" and "referral to special education classes." The general pattern was that children who had experienced a preschool program were less likely to be referred to special education and less likely to be retained in grade. Meta-analysis of both variables for all the projects with equivalent data produced effects that were significant and robust for the projects with more nearly randomized designs (Lazar et al., 1982). Most important, the effect on special education actually became stronger as children progressed through school, right up to the twelfth grade (Royce et al., 1983).

How did early intervention affect these indicators of school competence? The Consortium authors themselves offered a plausible explanation:

> When the children entered first grade, they had positive attitudes toward classroom activities, were able to adapt to classroom procedures, and were able to learn and do the schoolwork. The public school experience, in short, was also positive. The children's positive attitudes toward school were reinforced; they felt competent. In all probability, their teachers identified them as competent and treated them as such. Once set in motion, success tended to breed success, resulting in the program/control differences in school performance. (Lazar et al., 1982, p. 64)

Data from two of the Consortium projects endorsed this interpretation, with evidence that children who had attended preschool received higher teacher ratings for social development, attitudes toward learning, and conduct (Beller, 1974; Schweinhart & Weikart, 1980). It must be emphasized that these children's performance was still quite poor, even after preschool. Many program group children were referred to special education (Gordon, 23%; Gray, 3%; and Weikart, 14%). But without preschool, referral to special education became a very common experience indeed for control group children (Gordon, 54%; Gray, 29%; and Weikart, 28%; see Lazar et al., 1982, p. 32). Presumably, the children who had attended preschool escaped that potential failure trap because they projected a more positive image to their teachers and to the school psychologists responsible for referral.

This is where the short-lived cognitive effects may have come in. Bearing in mind Zigler and Berman's (1983) warning, if during the early grades these children were seen as smarter as well as more adjusted to the demands of school, this could have been sufficient to trigger a more positive cycle of achievement and expectation (or perhaps more realistically, help prevent the worst aspects of the negative cycle of failure). This effect could carry the child through the later grades, long after the initial cognitive benefits had washed out. The Consortium authors acknowledged the potential significance of these processes as part of the explanation for the transmission of long-term effects:

> Assignment to special classes in itself *affects* children. They are labeled in their own eyes and the eyes of others. Labels such as 'emotionally disturbed' or 'mildly retarded' have a life of their own, remaining on children's records for years and potentially affecting each new teacher's expectations for and treatment of a child. (Lazar et al., 1982, p. 58; italics added)

Some other implications of this line of reasoning have been much less widely acknowledged—namely, that a characteristic of the school context into which children moved *after* participating in a preschool program may have played a significant part in explaining the apparent power of that program to modify those children's fortunes in the long term.

To summarize the analysis so far, early intervention appears to have been effective not because in itself it fundamentally altered children's psychological functioning. Rather, in the short term it appears to have rendered them better able to cope with the demands of schooling at a critical time when their identities within the education system were being established. To use a metaphor from the world of athletics, the process of long-term effectiveness does not appear to be like a marathon 15-year test of the stamina of a single runner. Rather, it resembles a relay race, in which the burst of superior performance in the first runner (e.g., cognitive abilities and social adjustment) soon fades but not before the baton has been passed to later runners on the team (e.g., parent and teacher expectations, avoidance of referral to special classes), each of which transmits and even increases that initial superiority.

To put it another way, within the school system at that time, special education referral and retention in grade appear to have functioned as gateways that steered many disadvantaged children down a path of low expectations and achievement. There is nothing inevitable about special education serving these functions. It is nonetheless salutary to note that the originator of one of the IQ tests that has been widely applied as the gatekeeper in this process, Binet harbored no illusions about the consequences of referral, noting that "it will never be to one's credit to have attended a special school" (quoted in Lazerson, 1975, p. 50). Arguably, preschool intervention was effective because in the short term it acted on gatekeeper variables such as IQ score.

The significance of gatekeeper variables can be clarified by analogy with a British educational practice that was common during the decades following World War II. At that time, most children took to an examination at 11 years old (the 11+ examination) on which basis high scorers were selected to attend a grammar school while the majority of children went on to a secondary modern or technical school. During the weeks and months leading up to the 11+ examination, it became common for teachers to coach their children on tasks similar to those in the examination. If a systematic experiment had been set up to evaluate the long-term effects of preexamination coaching for 11 year olds, then it is reasonable to expect that experimental group children would have gone on to perform better throughout schooling and in the final examinations, more frequently gained access to universities, and even been more successful in adult life, compared with control group children who had no particular preparation. What would be the appropriate conclusion from such findings? Would it be that the last few months of primary (elementary) school are a sensitive or critical period in the formation of children's competencies? A more plausible explanation would recognize that the primary school program only appeared to have such a profound impact because of its proximity to the 11+ examination gateway, which would fundamentally shape their future.

The process of early intervention effectiveness is not as straightforward as this example, but the implication is that the evidence of long-term effects is the product of a complex and more subtle process than any simple reading of the data would suggest. A good deal of attention has been paid here to the potential importance of referral to special education and retention in grade as transmission pathways that could have transformed short-term effects into long-term outcomes. Many other important transmission pathways are probably unknown because they have not been measured. Those that were identified in the Consortium studies and that appear to be significant pathways include the self-concept and educational attitudes of the children, as well as the attitudes and aspirations of their parents. From interview data collected in 1976, it became clear that children who had attended preschool were significantly more achievement oriented, and their parents were more satisfied with their children's progress, even after controlling for their actual progress (Lazar et al., 1982). In short, preschool intervention was affecting children, their teachers, and their parents, both directly (e.g., children were more competent) and indirectly (e.g., the children projected a more positive impression that modified parental aspirations as well as teachers' decision making).

The perspective that emerges from this analysis recognizes that no social action affects an individual in isolation. The long-term effects of an early intervention cannot be understood without reference to the social context within which that intervention is introduced and within which an individual's subsequent development is enmeshed. The importance of this perspective was increasingly being advocated by developmental theorists beginning in the 1970s. In his review of the relationship between developmental research and public policy, Bronfenbrenner appealed for "the study of human development in context" (1974b, p. 5) and subsequently proposed an "ecological" framework for research, of which his hypotheses 48–50 are especially pertinent to this analysis (Bronfenbrenner, 1979). Another influential example of this general perspective is particularly suited to the study of intervention effects. A *transactional model* (Sameroff, 1975; Sameroff & Chandler, 1975) has the virtue of not only recognizing that effects are the result of a complex interaction of variables in home and school, throughout the school years and beyond, but also that the children themselves play an active part in the process through the images they project and the self-concept they acquire of themselves, either as competent and motivated or pathetic, problematic, and unwilling.

POLICY IMPLICATIONS OF LONG-TERM EFFECTS

The potential power of a transactional model to explain the process of long-term effects has been acknowledged by a number of authors of intervention research (Lazar et al., 1982; Schweinhart & Weikart, 1980). The implications that adoption of such a model might have for policy have received much less attention, however. As already noted, if a direct effects model were supported by the data, it could provide a clear message for policy. Policy makers would be quite justified in drawing a general conclusion about the value of quality preschool programs in disadvantaged children's development, their power to reduce the need for special education services, and the enduring quality of their effect right through into adulthood. By contrast, in the case of a transactional model, the significance of intervention as the cause of greater competence in school and adult life is not nearly as clear cut. The long-term significance of any impact it has on the child depends on the mediation of other processes in family and school. The importance, and even existence, of these transmission pathways will undoubtedly vary from one culture to another and one school system to another. They may even vary between one experimental setting and another, between an experimental project and an individual community Head Start, and between one birth cohort and another. Trying to establish the potential of early intervention becomes a little like trying to establish the contribution of heredity. Policy makers push for an absolute figure, but in social scientific terms, this makes little sense. As Campbell put it,

> Too many social scientists expect single experiments to settle issues once and for all. This may be a mistaken generalization from the history of great crucial experiments in physics and chemistry. . . . Because we social scientists have less ability to achieve "experimental isolation," because we have good reason to expect our treatment effects to interact significantly with a wide variety of social factors many of which we have not yet mapped, we have much greater need for replication experiments than do the physical sciences. (1969, pp. 427–428)

Arguably, one should not even expect results of replication experiments to settle the issue once and for all either. Such is the nature of human development that an identical early experience may be found to result in quite different outcomes according to the cultural context in which it occurred. Cultural context includes not only the constellation of other situational variables that interact with the impact of a specific experience but also the different meanings ascribed to the experience by participants as well as by those who influence their development.

If this general principle is applied to early intervention data, then the central issue for policy becomes whether contextual conditions are in fact similar between the site of data (in this case, preschool programs experienced by children growing up in the 1960s) and the site for policy (whether contemporary Head Start or school kindergarten or preschool programs in the United States or preschool in other industrialized or third world countries). If so, it may be reasonable to assume that the magnitude of initial early intervention effects would be as great and that there would be transmission pathways sufficient to transform short-term effects into long-term outcomes. If these conditions were not satisfied, however, serious questions must be raised about the validity of drawing general conclusions for policy. Hypothetically, the magnitude of preschool intervention effects might be attenuated in a setting where one transmission pathway was missing. Of course, they might also actually be amplified if different conditions generated an even stronger transmission pathway.

The case of Latin American countries provides a clear illustration of this. Halpern and Myers noted that both the more acute effects of poverty on development and the very different context of schooling might well modify the effects of preschool intervention:

> The conditions of schooling in the developing countries—large classes, few instructional resources, often poorly trained teachers, an inadequate number of "places" in each grade—are such that the newly acquired skills that preschool participants bring to the primary school may be less influential than in the U.S. in shaping the course of children's school careers. When *promotion policies are only loosely tied to children's abilities, when there is no special education to be "avoided," and when there are resources for only 10 or 20% of primary school participants to complete secondary school,* positive long-term effects on the course of children's school careers found in the U.S. may not be replicated in developing countries. (1985, p. 16; italics added)

The lesson from this analysis is that acceptance of a transactional model to account for long-term effects modifies the messages for policy. The Consortium data yielded valuable information not only about the impact of preschool interventions but also indirectly about the impact of school practices on children's educational progress. Although it provided good evidence of the power of early intervention to alter children's life chances, it also pointed to other strategies that could have been employed to achieve this end, notably the modification of school practices that contribute to the process of failure.

It is worth remembering that for many of those who set up experimental preschool projects in the United States in the 1960s, a belief in the potential of preschool was only part of the motive. The way poor children—especially poor, low ability, African American children—were treated within the school system was a source of deep frustration. For example, in 1962, David Weikart was responsible for psychological services in Ypsilanti, Michigan, where he set up the Perry Preschool Project, and later High/Scope. He and colleagues observed,

> Children unable to learn at the standard rate were seen simply as failures. The major remedy of choice was to require students to repeat grades until they learned the necessary skills. This practice produced, in Ypsilanti, the outlandish result of approximately 50% of all ninth-graders being from one to five years behind in grade, and a 50% dropout rate with legal school-leaving occurring for some youngsters as early as seventh grade. (Weikart, Bond, & McNeil, 1978, p. 2)

It is notable that Head Start was established in 1965 to provide federal funds directly to local community agencies (and it still does). Perhaps bypassing practices common in the public school system was viewed as an important first step in helping disadvantaged children. In short, preschool was being justified not only because it could compensate for presumed deficiencies in children's home life but also because it could modify the undesirable effects of deficiencies in the school system. There's an important lesson here. Insofar as special education and grade retention practices played a significant role in the transmission of long-term effects, then any changes in those practices might alter, and possibly weaken, the measurable long-term effects of preschool intervention. This is not a hypothetical claim. Concern about the experience of disadvantaged children in the school system that was part of the rationale for establishing Head Start in the 1960s was translated during the 1970s into widespread litigation over the inadequacies of educational opportunity for children with disabilities, culminating in the implementation of the Education for All Handicapped Children Act of 1975 (PL 94-142; Abeson & Zettel, 1977). The requirement of this law that children with disabilities receive education in the "least restrictive environment" discouraged school authorities from widespread use of special education classes and, for a time, sparked a wave of research designed to establish the relative educational merits of special classes versus inclusion for children with various disabilities (e.g., Heller, 1982). If these reforms have been effective, then the school context in which contemporary preschool interventions are embedded will be different. The implication is that school procedures prevalent in the 21st century may no longer be reproducing the function that 1960s special education and grade retention practices served in the transformation of initial preschool effects into long-term outcomes. Consequently, the effect of preschool intervention on the long-term fortunes of disadvantaged children who border on having mental retardation might well be weaker than a literal interpretation of data from the Consortium projects would predict.

The school procedures discussed here represent only one type of transmission pathway identified in Consortium analyses, and the policy significance of the research does not rest on this set of variables alone. Another major pathway is via family attitudes to their

children's schooling and prospects. The same considerations about deriving policy implications apply to these as well. Clearly, family attitudes have not been subject to such readily discernible shifts as the reforms in policy affecting special education. However, there
is some reason to believe that family and community processes may have been particularly
sensitively attuned to preschool effects at the time the Consortium projects began their
work. Gray, Ramsey, and Klaus (1983) came closest to acknowledging this. The early
1960s was a special time for disadvantaged African Americans and their families. It was
a period of desegregation and civil rights legislation, when the voice of Martin Luther
King, Jr., rang in the ears not just of African Americans but also of the world. For African American parents, it was a time of hope, which they focused on their children. Of
course, for preschool workers, it was also a time of great optimism; they were initiating
their project against the political background of the War on Poverty and the psychological background of optimism about the power of early experience (Bloom, 1964; Hunt,
1961). Faith, hope, and optimism are difficult qualities to measure, but that does not
mean that they should be forgotten when judging the implications of these studies. As
Gray (1985) put it, "the times were on our side." Whether they are still so decades later
could have an important bearing on the legitimacy of assuming that what has been
achieved through preschool interventions with children born in the early 1960s would be
reproduced in the same degree or kind if the experiments were repeated with children
born in the 1990s and later.

   In short, interpreting the early intervention evidence for policy requires more than
recognition of questions about the internal validity of the data (although these also have
to be addressed). The focus of this chapter has been on a different set of issues that arise
out of acknowledgement that the effects of early intervention come about as a result of a
complex set of interactions between the initial effects of the preschool program and a set
of mediating variables in the family and school. Variations in the context of family and
school may have a significant impact on the extent of measurable long-term effects of preschool intervention. Consequently, generalizations about the potential of any particular
educational or social strategy risk being misleading unless they take full account not only
of the features of the strategy itself but also of the cultural and educational system in which
that potential is embedded. That lesson applies both within national systems, which vary
geographically and are subject to continuous evolution, and across national systems, in
which the organization of schooling varies, as do the economic and cultural bases on which
it is founded.

CONCLUSION

In a frequently quoted analysis of the potential for research-based policy development,
Campbell argued for "an experimental approach to social reform, an approach in which
we try out new programs . . . and in which we retain, imitate, modify, or discard them on
the basis of apparent effectiveness on the multiple imperfect criteria available" (1969,
p. 409). The pioneering studies reviewed in this chapter (and numerous others that followed) have considerable potential to inform the policy process in the terms in which
Campbell anticipated, provided it is recognized that where human development is con-

cerned even an experimental approach can rarely yield definitive, universally applicable statements about the extent to which a program is effective.

Even if it were possible to identify unequivocal messages in this area of research, Campbell's is still a very optimistic view of the relationship that might be established between research and policy. Granted that American politicians and administrators have been reported to be more attuned to the messages of research than their counterparts in other countries such as Britain (Sharpe, 1978), but these messages are nonetheless rarely translated directly into reforms. More frequently, they are drawn into a complex web of sometimes inconsistent and frequently competing lines of argument, public pressure, and political priority. This process was illustrated by Zigler (1987) during the 1980s movement to extend public education to 4-year-olds. He argued that the evidence of early intervention research was applied, and in some respects misapplied, as part of an educational case for reform that also sprang from concern about the failings of secondary schools. These educational lines of argument have now also been overlaid by a quite different issue, namely, the problem of responding to parental demands for more adequate child care services in the early years, which might be partly but not completely resolved by increased preschool provision.

Arguably, social scientists have never been as remote from the process of informing public policy as is implied by conventional images of dispassionate scientific inquiry. In the 1980s, however, the relationship between the impartiality of research and the partiality attached to the solutions that are inferred from that research was extensively reappraised (Hatch, 1982; Howard, 1985; Robinson, 1984). But this time, psychologists were increasingly being drawn into the policy arena. They were no longer content to merely illuminate social problems or offer solutions to be implemented by others but were actively campaigning for public policies that appear to have been demonstrated by the research to be effective. For instance,

> Equity is still an obtainable goal of social policy in the United States. To achieve this goal we may have to use some of the strategies that proved successful in the past and discard others that were not useful. In the realm of child and family policy, this could mean *new roles for scientists* and experts *as advocates*. (Valentine & Zigler, 1983, p. 279; italics added)

The strenuous efforts of the Consortium authors to communicate their findings to influential policy figures clearly illustrate this role (Datta, 1983a), as do the carefully coordinated dissemination efforts of the High/Scope "Voices for Children" project (Haskins & Gallagher, 1984; High/Scope Educational Research Foundation, 1984).

In the short term, these advocacy efforts certainly served an important political function in strengthening the lobby for increased expenditure and further development of early childhood programs. They were offered as powerful empirical support to the popular sentiment that experiences in the early years are formative of personal fortunes in adult life. In this chapter, however, I have argued that in the long run, the scientific value of this body of research lies in its power to illustrate the inadequacy of such an appealing view of the role of early childhood intervention in attaining the goals of social policy. On the one hand, that view places unrealistic emphasis on the early years as a period for effecting permanent individual change through educational and social programs. On the other hand, it distracts attention from other concurrent and subsequent processes in community and school that interact with experiences in the early years to determine long-term patterns of development. Accordingly, a first responsibility of social science advocacy is to avoid perpetuating and indeed to actively seek to counteract the tendency in public debate to adopt simple deterministic views of the scope for intervention in human development.

The evidence of long-term effects needs to be introduced into public debate within the context of a model of human development that recognizes many other factors besides the preschool program that contributed to the transmission of its effects and that need to be taken into consideration when interpreting the evidence for policy. In some settings, these factors might not be present, whereas in others, the particular network of influences on child development might suggest an alternative focus for intervention that might prove more fruitful than a preschool program.

One of the problems in communicating the messages of this research is that experimental design in itself encourages disproportionate attention to be directed toward the critical manipulated variable as *the* cause of observed differences between experimental and control groups, no matter how remote in time or nature the outcome measures are from the intervention. Yet, failure to communicate a more sophisticated understanding of long-term effects carries certain risks. At the time of writing (1988), public expectations are becoming narrowly focused on the apparent power of early intervention to tackle social problems single-handedly. Such expectations are unlikely to be realized in practice. In the long run, this could undermine public sympathies toward early childhood programs, as well as diminish the credibility of experimental research as a tool of social reform.

REFERENCES

Abeson, A., & Zettel, J. (1977). The end of a quiet revolution: The United States Education for All Handicapped Children Act. *Exceptional Children, 44,* 115–128.

Administration on Children, Youth and Families. (1985). *Project Head Start: Statistical fact sheet.* Washington, DC: Department of Health, Education, and Welfare.

Beller, E.K. (1974). Impact of early education on disadvantaged children. In S. Ryan (Ed.), *A report on longitudinal evaluations of preschool programs* (Vol. 1, pp. 15–48). Washington, DC: Department of Health, Education, and Welfare.

Berfenstam, R., & William-Olsson, I. (1974). *Early child care in Sweden.* London: Gordon & Breach.

Besharov, D.J., & Hartle, T.W. (1987). Head Start: Making a popular program work. *Pediatrics, 79,* 440–441.

Bloom, B.S. (1964). *Stability and change in human characteristics.* New York: John Wiley & Sons.

Bronfenbrenner, U. (1974a). *Is early intervention effective?* Washington, DC: Department of Health, Education, and Welfare.

Bronfenbrenner, U. (1974b). Developmental research public policy, and the ecology of childhood. *Child Development, 45,* 1–5.

Bronfenbrenner, U. (1979). *The ecology of human development.* Cambridge, MA: Harvard University Press.

Campbell, D.T. (1969). Reforms as experiments. *American Psychologist, 25,* 409–429.

Clarke, A.M., & Clarke, A.D.B. (1981). Sleeper effects in development: Fact or artifact? *Developmental Review, 1,* 344–360.

Clarke, A.M., & Clarke, A.D.B. (1982). Intervention and sleeper effects: A reply to Victoria Seitz. *Developmental Review, 2,* 76–78.

Clement, J.R.B., Schweinhart, L.J., Barnett, W.S., Epstein, A.S., & Weikart, D.P. (1984). *Changed lives: The effects of the Perry Preschool Program on youths through age 19* (Monograph No. 8). Ypsilanti, MI: High/Scope.

Consortium for Developmental Continuity. (1977). *The persistence of preschool effects*. Washington, DC: Department of Health, Education, and Welfare.

Consortium for Longitudinal Studies. (1978). *Lasting effects after preschool*. Washington, DC: Department of Health, Education, and Welfare.

Consortium for Longitudinal Studies. (1983). *As the twig is bent: Lasting effects of preschool programs*. Mahwah, NJ: Lawrence Erlbaum Associates.

Crittenden, A. (1984, November 29). A Head Start pays off in the end. *The Wall Street Journal*.

Darlington, R.D., Royce, J.M., Snipper, A.S., Murray, H.W., & Lazar, I. (1980). Preschool programs and later school competence of children from low-income families. *Science, 208,* 202–204.

Datta, L. (1983a). A tale of two studies: The Westinghouse/Ohio evaluation of Project Head Start and the Consortium for Longitudinal Studies report. *Studies in Educational Evaluation, 8,* 271–280.

Datta, L. (1983b). We never promised you a rose garden but one may have grown anyhow. In Consortium for Longitudinal Studies, *As the twig is bent: Lasting effects of preschool programs* (pp. 467–480). Mahwah, NJ: Lawrence Erlbaum Associates.

Education for All Handicapped Children Act of 1975, PL 94-142, 20 U.S.C. §§1400 *et seq.*

Education of the Handicapped Act Amendments of 1986, PL 99-457, 20 U.S.C. §§1400 *et seq.*

Farrington, D. (1985). Delinquency prevention in the 1980s. *Journal of Adolescence, 8,* 3–16.

Gray, S. (1985, August). *The early training project*. Paper presented at the annual meeting of the American Psychological Association, Toronto, Canada.

Gray, S.W., Ramsey, B.K., & Klaus, R.A. (1982). *From 3 to 20: The Early Training Project*. Baltimore: University Park Press.

Gray, S.W., Ramsey, B.K., & Klaus, R.A. (1983). The Early Training Project: 1962–1980. In Consortium for Longitudinal Studies, *As the twig is bent: Lasting effects of preschool programs* (pp. 33–70). Mahwah, NJ: Lawrence Erlbaum Associates.

Halpern, R., & Myers, R. (1985). *Effects of early childhood intervention primary school progress and performance in the developing countries*. Ypsilanti, MI: High/Scope–U.S. Agency for International Development.

Haskins, R., & Gallagher, J.J. (1984). *The Voices for Children Project: A Report to the Carnegie Foundation*. Chapel Hill: University of North Carolina, Bush Institute for Child and Family Policy.

Hatch, O. (1982). Psychology, society and politics. *American Psychologist, 37,* 1031–1037.

Heller, K.A. (1982). Effects of special education placement on educable mentally retarded children. In K.A. Heller, W.H. Holtzman, & S. Messick (Eds.), *Placing children in special education: A strategy for equity* (pp. 262–299). Washington, DC: National Academy Press.

High/Scope Educational Research Foundation. (1984). *Response to the Haskins and Gallagher report on the Voices for Children Project*. Ypsilanti, MI: Author.

Howard, G.S. (1985). The role of values in the science of psychology. *American Psychologist. 40,* 255–266.

Hunt, J.McV. (1961). *Intelligence and experience*. New York: Ronald Press.

Klaus, R.A., & Gray, S.W. (1968). The Early Training Project for disadvantaged children. *Monographs of the Society for Research in Child Development. 33*(4, Serial No. 120).

Kotelchuck, M., & Richmond, J.B. (1987). Head Start: Evolution of a successful comprehensive child development program. *Pediatrics, 79,* 441–445.

Lazar, I., Darlington, R.B., Murray, H.W., & Snipper, A.S. (1982). Lasting effects of early education: A report from the Consortium for Longitudinal Studies. *Monographs of the Society for Research in Child Development. 47*(195, serial No. 2–3).

Lazerson, M. (1970). Social reform and early childhood education: Some historical perspectives. *Urban Education, 5,* 84–102.

Lazerson, M. (1975). Educational institutions and mental subnormality: Notes on writing a history. In M.J. Begab & S.A.R. Richardson (Eds.), *The mentally retarded and society: A social science perspective* (pp. 38–52). Baltimore: University Park Press.

Lewin, R. (1977, March 3). Head Start pays off. *New Scientist,* 508–509.

Liddell, C. (1987). Some issues regarding the introduction of preschool enrichment programmes for black South African children. *International Journal of Educational Development, 7*(2), 127–131.

Myers, R.G., & Hertenberg, R. (1987). *The eleven who survive: Toward a re-examination of early childhood development program options and costs* (World Bank Education and Training Report No. EDT 69). Washington, DC: World Bank.

Richmond, J.B., Stipek, D.J., & Zigler, E.F. (1979). A decade of Head Start. In E.F. Zigler & J. Valentine (Eds.), *Project Head Start: A legacy of the war on poverty* (pp. 135–152). New York: Free Press.

Robinson, D.N. (1984). Ethics and advocacy. *American Psychologist, 39,* 787–793.

Royce, J.M., Darlington, R.B., & Murray, H.W. (1983). Pooled analysis: Findings across studies. In Consortium for Longitudinal Studies, *As the twig is bent: Lasting effects of preschool programs* (pp. 411–460). Mahwah, NJ: Lawrence Erlbaum Associates.

Sameroff, A.J. (1975). Early influences on development: Fact or fancy? *Merrill-Palmer Quarterly, 21*(4), 267–294.

Sameroff, A., & Chandler, M. (1975). Reproductive risk and the continuum of caretaking casualty. In F. Horowitz (Ed.), *Review of child development research* (Vol. 4, pp. 187–244). Chicago: University of Chicago Press.

Schweinhart, L.J., Barnes, H.V., & Weikart, D.P. (1993). *Significant benefits: The High/Scope Perry Preschool study through age 27.* Ypsilanti, MI: High/Scope Educational Research Foundation.

Schweinhart, L.J., & Weikart, D.P. (1980). *Young children grow up* (Monograph 7). Ypsilanti, MI: High/Scope.

Seitz, V. (1981). Intervention and sleeper effects: A reply to Clarke and Clarke. *Developmental Review, I,* 361–373.

Sharpe, L.J. (1978). The social scientist and policy-making in Britain and America: A comparison. In M. Bulmer (Ed.), *Social policy research* (pp. 303–312). London: MacMillan.

Tizard, J., Moss, P., & Perry, J. (1976). *All our children.* London: Temple Smith/ New Society.

Valentine, J., & Zigler, E. (1983). Head Start: A case study in the development of social policy for children and families. In E. Zigler, S.L. Kagan, & E. Klugman (Eds.), *Children, families and government: Perspectives on American social policy* (pp. 260–288). New York: Cambridge University Press.

Weikart, D.P., Bond, J.T., & McNeil, J.T. (1978). *The Ypsilanti Perry Pre-School Project: Pre-school years and longitudinal results through fourth grade* (Monograph 3). Ypsilanti, MI: High/ Scope.

Woodhead, M. (1985). Pre-school education has long term effects: But can they be generalized? *Oxford Review of Education, 11*(2), 133–155.

Zigler, E.F. (1976). Head Start: Not a program but an evolving concept. In J.D. Andrews (Ed.), *Early childhood education: It's an art? It's a science?* (pp. 1–14). Washington, DC: National Association for the Education of Young Children.

Zigler, E.F. (1987). Formal schooling for four-year olds? No. *American Psychologist, 42,* 254–260.

Zigler, E.F., & Berman, W. (1983). Discerning the future of early childhood intervention. *American Psychologist, 38,* 894–906.

Zigler, E.F., & Trickett, P.K. (1978). IQ, social competence and evaluation of early childhood intervention programs. *American Psychologist, 33,* 789–798.

Zigler, E.F., & Valentine, J. (Eds.). (1979). *Project Head Start: A legacy of the War on Poverty.* New York: Free Press.

CHAPTER 4

Head Start—Revisiting a Historical Psychoeducational Intervention

A Revisionist Perspective

IRVING E. SIGEL

In 1990, I wrote a paper in which I addressed some critical issues pertaining to Head Start. The paper was titled "Psychoeducational Intervention: Future Directions" and in it I presented the basic argument that

> Educational intervention should be part of a conceptualization that places education in a developmental context which links preschool education to later schooling. In addition, attention is directed to the adoption of a more effective ecologically valid evaluation approach rather than the traditional analyses of data aggregation. (p. 159)

I argue that these issues are as relevant in 2004 as they were in 1990. One might justifiably ask how that can be the case when parent satisfaction with Head Start programs is so great. This conclusion is based on a poll of parents that found virtually 90% were satisfied with their child's Head Start program. In fact, Head Start is rated higher in consumer satisfaction than any other government program. Does this finding indicate that the program is effective and has done an optimal job in fulfilling its mission? My argument is, not necessarily. Chances are parents' satisfactions are based on different criteria than professionals, but parents' opinions should be recognized and valued even though they may differ from professional opinions. Such testimonials, gratifying as they may sound to the parents and teachers, are not sufficient evidence for the critics of Head Start who argue that such testimonials are not valid evaluations. The only evidence that would be sufficient would be based on randomized design experiments.

Portions of this chapter are reprinted from Sigel, Irving E. "Psychoeducational Intervention: Future Directions," *Merrill-Palmer Quarterly* 36(1), (January 1990), with permission of the Wayne State University Press.

Haskins and Sawhill (2003) claimed, however, that no well-designed studies have been done. They wrote, "After nearly forty years of operation, there is not a national random assignment evaluation of the long term impacts of Head Start" (p. 3). They do not deny that children who leave Head Start for kindergarten show cognitive gains as compared with children in other programs, "but that the effects faded within a year or two of the time children entered the schools" (p. 3). So, the gains are short-lived, and by the second or third grade, the Head Start graduates are not distinguishable from their peers.

In this chapter, I want to focus on the naïve expectation that gains made in preschool should persist in subsequent grades. Before taking on this issue, I accept the evidence that Head Start programs are in need of repair. For example, Head Start needs increased teacher qualifications, especially recognizing the increased diversity in language groups served by Head Start programs. The demands placed on the teaching staffs are becoming increasingly complex by virtue of different needs of urban and rural groups. It is argued that the Head Start program in its current form does not fulfill its obligations to the children, their families, and society as a whole. I take issue with this argument; it overlooks or ignores the difficulties in remediating complex social problems that are inextricably linked in the real world. I then proceed to offer some ideas for changing the Head Start program.

CONCERNS ABOUT HEAD START EVALUATION

Ever since the beginnings of Head Start evaluations, I have asked why there was such an extensive and intensive set of evaluations of this innovative program when we do not have such evaluations of educational programs in the elementary schools. Public education was already established and accepted as a social good; however, to embark on preschool interventions as a compensatory effort to give children a head start in getting ready for school was a novel and radical suggestion. In fact, we are still in the process of learning how to carry out such a massive undertaking. But the history of the Head Start program has continued to be controversial, with critics claiming that the jury is still out as far as Head Start is concerned. The ongoing evaluation of Head Start, it is argued, will help resolve some of the issues about program effectiveness.

Establishing Head Start was the beginning of a new era in early childhood education. Preschool education in 1965 was not viewed as remedial but as an opportunity for enhancing social-emotional development. Nursery schools were typically the province of university teacher training programs and catered to elite populations. Preschool educators rejected academic programs, believing they were the province of kindergarten teachers. Poor children were usually enrolled in child care centers that were essentially custodial, caring for children of working parents. These agencies rarely focused on school readiness. Thus, the Head Start initiative had little in the way of established programs to serve as the model for remediation or advancing the children's readiness for kindergarten.

Critics of Head Start argue that in spite of the billions of dollars spent on preschool programs their effectiveness is marginal, with no clear statement of "why." They point out that it is possible to create programs whose graduates maintain gains over long periods of time, identifying three exemplary programs: the Abecedarian project in North Carolina, the Perry Preschool project in Michigan, and one conducted by Arnold Reynolds at the

University of Wisconsin. Haskins and Sawhill considered these successful because they reduced grade retention and placement in special education, increased high school graduation rates and college attendance, and produced a host of related effects (2003, p. 3). These programs are very particular with highly controlled environments and trained staff, and, in some cases, they are university based. The Abecedarian Project, for example, is described as "a carefully controlled scientific study of the potential benefits of early childhood education for poor children. Children from low-income families received full time, high quality educational intervention in a child care setting from infancy though age 5." Furthermore, the assertion is made that the "cognitive and academic benefits from this program are stronger than for most early childhood programs" (p. 3). These programs quite convincingly demonstrate that when the resources and expertise are available and the population served is relatively small, early childhood education pays off.

To compare a typical Head Start classroom to any of the programs Haskins and Sawhill describe is an unfair comparison. It is like comparing a second-hand car to a Cadillac. Rather then criticize Head Start, critics should be more judicious in evaluating the constraints of Head Start classrooms (e.g., poorly trained and underpaid teachers, limited funding for innovative programming).

The increase in cultural diversity among the urban poor is another issue that complicates the educational programs. The number of languages spoken in some urban centers is so varied that there are not enough qualified teachers to provide adequate instruction. Haskins and Sawhill's advocacy for state agencies assuming the responsibility for Head Start is an unreasonable suggestion because of the need for a more uniform consistent national educational program to assure quality education for all eligible poor children. It is difficult to believe that states that have marginal resources (e.g., Mississippi, Alabama) can mount a program of quality, even with some federal help, when their own educational resources are limited.

Head Start does need improvement and may be suffering from entrenched commitments to program philosophy. I contend that improvements require a rethinking of the Head Start philosophy rather than restructuring the existing agency, which has a long history of creating intervention programs. Critics of Head Start should consider the gains that have been made by vast numbers of children in spite of the oft-stated limitations in trained personnel and limited community support.

The effects of Head Start seem to be short-lived; after first and second grade, academic performance levels off and Head Start children are indistinguishable from children who have not had preschool experience. These results should not be surprising for at least three major reasons. The first, there is no vertical integration between most Head Start programs and public kindergartens that would support the gains the children may have made. Changes in the physical classroom environment, from a relatively small intimate classroom to a more crowded large space with different teacher–child ratios, create new adjustment tasks for the children. Second, the quality of the Head Start experiences may be compromised by the relatively low level of financial support and educational background of Head Start teachers. Third, the families of these children usually live in substandard environments with the usual accompaniment of poverty. In other words, expecting the Head Start experience to ameliorate the effects of poverty requires considerable effort on the part of parents and teachers to support the uphill fight that these children face. The children's gain from their preschool experience can only be solidified by quality support from kindergarten teachers and beyond.

It is essential that critics of Head Start be cognizant of the fragility of the gains these children make unless sustained support is forthcoming from family members. The schools are not usually equipped to provide the necessary ancillary support services needed to sustain gains (e.g., tutoring for literacy). So, will the children be prepared intellectually, socially, and psychologically to make and maintain their accomplishments achieved in Head Start? There is continued evidence that the transition to kindergarten and to subsequent schooling has not lived up to expectations for school performance, especially in the long run (Bickel & Spatig, 1999).

SOME SUGGESTIONS FOR HEAD START EVALUATION

I believe a more rational assessment is required of the entire Head Start funding for program efforts, teacher qualifications, teacher salaries, and a commitment to vertical integration between preschool and public school. Concurrently, the administration, curriculum developers, and teachers have to become partners in this enterprise. Teachers in the coming years will be challenged with new and complex sets of issues, especially those dealing with cultural diversity. It is a major challenge for the 21st century.

There is a need for greater specificity of the particulars within Head Start that are linked to academic outcomes in the short term and the long term (Hinde, 1992). Such information would enable precise calibration of the curriculum to the anticipated outcomes. There is a dearth of longitudinal studies identifying these particulars as efforts are made to explain educational achievements.[1] I believe even in 2004 there is no indication that an overall research strategy is being pursued. This was the case in 1990, and it is the case in 2004 (U.S. Department of Health and Human Services, 1990).

Proposed Research Agenda

The research agenda should incorporate specific attention to how Head Start goals are translated into teaching strategies, materials, classroom organization, parenting programs, and in partnering with necessary community resources. To create the context for my basic argument for an overall research strategy, let me remind the reader of the basic mission of Head Start as initially stated in 1965. The program was set up to provide impoverished and marginalized children from 3 to 5 years of age with comprehensive developmental services to ensure that they would be prepared to enter kindergarten and acquire the appropriate skills to be able to succeed in school. By implication only, psychologists and educators have been deemed as the appropriate group to assume the primary role of evaluation because they are the experts in assessment of children's intellectual, emotional, and social competence. Reliance on these specialists poses limitations on the quality of not only the variables being addressed but also the timing and the methods of evaluation, including the basic premise on which educational programs are built.

There is overwhelming evidence that children from any impoverished group are in danger of remaining at the poverty level unless there is some drastic change in their edu-

---

[1]There is one intervention program that comes closest to the identification of specific factors that influence outcomes (Leong, D.J., & Bodrova, E. [1996]).

cation, their parents' employment, and, above all, social acceptance by the mainstream society. Unless some enlightened political leadership emerges that will substitute action for rhetoric, no profound social changes will be made, only Band-Aid efforts. Note that the so-called welfare reform programs provide ample evidence for placing families in increasingly difficult situations by expecting them to function at work without adequate child care (Administration for Children and Families, 1999).

Children from these families are presumably at greater risk for school failure because the welfare reforms merely compound problems for impoverished minority groups. To fully comprehend and work with populations living in such marginal environments requires an interdisciplinary team of professional psychologists, economists, sociologists, and anthropologists working within a comprehensive integrative framework to address these issues. It is only workable if these varied members of these disciplines are able to establish a common, mutually acceptable discourse.

An awareness of the complexity of social problems and of the need for intervention programming is necessary before programs for intervention can be properly developed. In spite of the difficulties I describe, we have no other choice than to work in such a fashion to maximize our efforts. In effect, we do the best that we can and hopefully without compromise.

The following ideas are offered as a point of departure for beginning a dialogue to identify approaches to deal with some of the ongoing educational and social problems in the Head Start context. Let me begin by comprehensively defining intervention to guide the subsequent discussion:

Intervention is an effort to redirect the anticipated trajectory of development. This is done in our educational system from the time a child enters school to the end of his or her education. I refer to this as intervention when the goal is set for deliberately focusing efforts at poverty-level members of minority groups. We are engaging deliberately in altering their anticipated developmental trajectory because our observations of these groups, young and old, foreshadow higher levels of economic distress, anxiety, and continued social deviant behaviors such as crime, juvenile delinquency, dropping out of school, teenage pregnancy, and other negative social, cognitive, and behavioral outcomes. Their chances of rising above these life situations are not good because to create change at the individual and group level requires considerable economic and social support from within and from others such as family members or social and educational agencies. These predictions are based on demographic and census data that report that impoverished minority groups show higher levels of chronic unemployment, poor health and nutrition, premature birth, and infant mortality—among a host of other social problems—than nonminority groups (Wilson, 1987). It is believed that by intervening in the stream of ongoing behavior, the predicted direction of development for these groups can shift from the anticipated negative outcomes to healthy, positive ones (Sigel, 1972).

In addition, Schiefelbusch suggested action components implied in the intervention concept:

> The term also implies that professionals are competent to enter the life of certain individuals in order to assist them in achieving a more desirable state. The term also implies that we know when and how we should intervene. Imbedded in our assumptions is the belief that under certain circumstances intervention programs should be undertaken and, indeed, the needy individual has a right to such intervention. (1981, p. 373)

These assertions are based on social analysis of the consequences of poverty, irrespective of race and ethnicity. Further, there are theoretical links between types of current negative life experiences and long-term outcomes that need to be specified. Finally, a body of knowledge that has been accumulated over the past decades clearly demonstrates both the positive and negative effects of various types of early experience (Kagan & Zigler, 1987). So, the particular type of intervention that can alter the life course of children and families enables them to redirect their lifestyle in a comprehensive way to a socially acceptable and positively functional life.

To achieve this, we need to devise a well thought out, mutually acceptable, and integrated developmental model based on explicit and implicit knowledge. This model must articulate in detail the anticipated linkages, whether linear or circuitous, between the early experiences and their sequelae. The social interest in such redirections does not rest on sheer altruism (except perhaps for the dedicated individuals who devote their lives to such social action) but on pragmatic objectives to enable individuals to become active, social, responsible citizens contributing to society instead of draining economic and service resources. Wilson (1987) addressed these questions, bemoaning the fragmented approach evidenced in intervention programs in the 21st century. One underlying issue that is implicit in such interventions is the lack of cultural sensitivity. Respect for and acceptance of cultural differences is a basic requirement for every intervention program. In practical terms this means developing appropriate strategies for working within the constraints of cultural differences while still engaging in necessary intervention activities. This requires that highly trained curriculum educators work within these programs.

ASSUMPTIONS UNDERLYING INTERVENTION EFFORTS

Five assumptions that shaped our intervention efforts over the years are still viable, although modified somewhat in light of recent thoughts (see Assumption 2):

   1. *A tenet for programming for successful intervention is that such basic characteristics as intelligence and personality are modifiable to some degree.* As Blair (1999) so aptly stated, "tailoring educational experiences to the individual needs of each learner is a laudable goal and one likely to greatly improve educational practices."

   2. *To improve the probability that an intervention program will not only succeed but also enable us to understand why it accomplished its goal, a two-step program of research is recommended the likes of which have not been done in the Head Start program.* The requirement is to differentiate between efficacy and efficiency:

In efficacy trials, a decision regarding whether a given treatment works is paramount. The object is to utilize a research design that gives as clear an indication as possible of whether a treatment worked with the target population. In a controlled efficacy trial, variables related to differential effects must be identified in the design stage of the trial, incorporated into the sampling plan, and controlled in the analysis stage of the trial.

An effectiveness trial is related to differential treatment outcome. It differs from an efficacy trial in that it must utilize a therapeutic regimen (read educational program) of known efficacy (Blair, 1999).

   3. *Optimizing the ongoing environment, which in turn could affect future actions, can modify an individual's developmental trajectory.* Derived from the modifiability assumption, the ear-

lier the intervention is begun, the better the chances are for effecting positive growth. This belief, however, must be tied to the particular domain in question. Learning to read at the age of 6 months is not better, it is just earlier (Sigel, 1986, 1987).

4. *We have the theory and the necessary technology needed to effect change or change illusions (a conviction that change has occurred even when the facts are otherwise).* For example, despite the fact that little scientific evidence was available to support the idea that preschool education could, in fact, alter the developmental trajectory of impoverished children, this country embarked on a massive preschool project with optimism. The Head Start program began with the naive assumption that a summer program would be adequate to effectively help children and then realized that a 2-year program was needed. As of 2004, we are still not certain what programming in the early preschool years ensures a successful kindergarten experience (Benasich, Brooks-Gunn, & Clewell, 1992; Lee, Brooks-Gunn, & Schnur, 1988; Zigler & Valentine, 1979).

5. *The assumption that the targeted populations are willing to become sincere and committed partners in the intervention efforts is taken for granted.* To check this assumption, it is necessary to reflect on a few questions: Will the poor see this intervention effort as a way to improve their lot in life or as a way to be co-opted? Are minority members interested and willing to enter the mainstream of American life? What price do the poor minorities have to pay in terms of their self-respect, cultural identity, and heritage if they enter the program? Participants in an intervention program may be unwilling to surrender some of their cultural practice. For example, Latino parents may be encouraged to speak English with their children at home but may not wish to do this because they are afraid their children will lose their Spanish fluency.

ADDITIONAL QUESTIONS

These assumptions form the basis by which intervention efforts can be pursued. From these assumptions, we are led to further relevant questions:

1. *What professionals should be involved in psychoeducational intervention efforts and why?* Intervention requires an interdisciplinary team, or at least an interdisciplinary perspective, to come to terms with the manifold problems in identifying relevant social, economic, and psychological factors. Further, this team, in conjunction with the target group, should be able to set priorities for what and how change might be affected. No one discipline or federal, state, or municipal agency has a monopoly on the answer. Social and behavioral scientists should be involved. For example, knowledge should help specify linkages between the prerequisites for enabling the child and those for enabling his or her family to reduce their risk of developing malfunctions. This is the conceptual phase in the intervention process, to be followed by the operational phases—the translation of the knowledge into workable programmatic operational plans. These two steps must be integrated in an interactive feedback system so that operations inform theory and theory may change as needed to keep the program effective. This requires openness and willingness to accept necessary changes on the part of theory and/or program builders. The nature of the feedback suggested here is comparable to Blair's (1999) notions of efficacy and effectiveness. The conceptual aspect is analogous to the efficacy notion, whereas the operational phase is analogous to effectiveness.

2. Who are the target populations? Risk factor is the basic criterion for determining who is to be involved in intervention efforts. The target populations are those designated as at risk for developmental delays or developmental dysfunction. Premature infants in general are usually considered to be at risk, especially those from impoverished families. No doubt, other groups can be designated at risk by virtue of age (older adults), illness (families with psychotic members), or minority or poverty status. In this discussion, I focus on infants and preschoolers because early intervention can create the basis for redirecting the negative predicted developmental trajectory and reducing the probability of later problems.[2]

3. What are the goals of intervention? The goals of the intervention program have to be considered at both a general and a specific level. On the general level, the goal for all at-risk populations is the same—shifting the projected trajectory from negative to positive, thereby enhancing the chances of success and the quality of living (Evans, 1971). On the specific level, goals will vary with the particular population. Initially, the goals should be defined relative to the relationship between the ongoing situation and the predicted outcome. From the perspective of a trajectory model, the defined intervention variables must be linked with the desired outcome. The goals may vary depending on how far in the future the trajectory is planned (e.g., whether the intervention goals are short term or long term). The timeline should depend on the targeted behavioral changes. For example, intervening in preschool with the objective of reducing the risk of having difficulty in kindergarten will have a different strategy than intervention targeted to prevent illiteracy or school drop-out years later.

Goals may change with the changing times and changing nature of the participants. At times, outcomes are difficult to define a priori since they are subject to developmental changes in the life span of the individual as well as to changing values and expectations for the children in the broader society. Further, new knowledge may alter the goals as well as the feasibility of achieving them. Goal determination and contingent operations are dynamic processes in a state of movement.

In the past, the main goal of preschool programs for children at the poverty level was to enhance cognitive skills and prevent cognitive impairments, particularly with the intent of raising children's IQ scores or cognitive competence (see Chapter 1; Kagan et al., 1969; Spitz, 1986). The objective of raising cognitive competence and the belief that such change would alter children's developmental trajectory via school functioning and subsequent employment are simplistic and naive. Although cognitive change as a criterion of program effectiveness is appealing in its simplicity, it is the wrong objective for program effectiveness. No intervention program was (or is) singularly cognitively oriented. To assume that providing children with a variety of cognitive experiences in a benign environment would automatically improve cognitive development, and the improvement would be maintained, does not have a sound theoretical or empirical base. Further, changes, when found, mostly have superficial and short-lived outcomes (Spitz, 1986).

Success in school depends on continual enrichment, along with social and psychological support and, perhaps, alteration of familial milieu (i.e., maternal attitudes, beliefs,

---

[2]Advocating intervention early is not to preclude intervening at other age levels. It depends on the objectives of the program (e.g., intervention for reducing teenage pregnancy should be done when the children are old enough to understand the issues). The content and method of intervention has to be the major basis for determining when and how to intervene.

and knowledge; parental employment; parental education). We have yet to define how to alter the developmental trajectory for cognitive and social competence by creating a comprehensive approach for the task. I contend that school intervention should be accompanied by considerable specificity regarding how to complement the school activity. This is not just helping a child do his or her homework; it involves learning how to read to the child, how to use constructive teaching strategies, and what kinds of language to use. This is not an easy role for the schools to undertake at the kindergarten level. It will be suited for the preschool. Whitehurst and colleagues (1994), for example, developed a program for reading that has been shown to be effective. Other types of involvement to engender support for school performance, generating motivation to learn in order to acquire school-relevant cognitive and linguistic skills, can be taught to parents by parent educators. The use of games and different ways of watching television are among the techniques that have been found useful (Powell, 1988). To be sure, these were recognized as important for success in the past, but they were not usually built into the parent involvement models. The evaluation model assessing program success should get a good and valid picture of parent practices. Using questionnaires instead of direct observation does not provide valid information regarding success of the program (Sigel & Kim, 1996).

In sum, the criteria for program effectiveness should evaluate the child's interest in learning, motivation to achieve, and understanding of communication, among other things. These objectives need not be tied to just conventional learning in school but also to extra school learning. At the preschool level, the general intervention goals should include broad scale targets (e.g., health, enlarging the child's family environment)—in other words, they should provide the basis for general enrichment.

Particular cultural goals for intervention outcomes should be set at the preschool level. In view of the fact that intervention programs are initiated among diverse populations (e.g., African Americans, various Hispanic groups, American Indians), each having its own culture and values, goals for preschool programs should be coherent with the culture. To accomplish this, objectives should be determined in concert with members of those groups

The setting of social goals is not the purview of the social or behavioral scientist. Goal development should be based on intervention objectives developed with relevant community members, teachers, and caregivers. Consultation with social and cultural anthropologists and behavioral scientists may facilitate program development, thereby helping with the implementation by formulating questions. In this way, these professionals can provide insights that broaden the points of view of all involved in the enterprise. The specifics of the program can be derived from the common objectives and put into place by those technically competent to set up appropriate curriculum (e.g., linking program content to defined objectives). Jurgen Zimmer (1984) did program development in this way. Working with teachers and parents in West Germany, he has shown such cooperation to be effective.

The developmental psychologist has a place in such an effort because, in addition to helping to develop curriculum, he or she can help to create assessment procedures that will yield sensitive and valid understanding of children's achievement. These findings can be used for formative evaluation so that modification of the program and new ways to help the child can evolve. By incorporating relevant cultural values, the program evolves from the community and is not grafted on with few, if any, indigenous roots. Further, a community-based effort gives a sense of program ownership of the effort. This approach reflects respect for cultural diversity and ensures greater participation and acceptance of the program (Zimmer, 1984).

4. *Is there an optimum time for intervention, and how is that time determined?* In general, the optimum time for intervention for any at-risk child is assumed to be as early as possible. My argument is based on the principle, the earlier the better. Such an approach makes sense because I contend that development is an ongoing, continuous process. What evidence is there for this perspective? When it comes to influencing IQ score by preschool programming, the answer is that the data are unconvincing (Spitz, 1986). If you ask whether preschool experiences lead to eventual grade placement, then the answer is probably yes. If, however, the question is framed in terms of number of students needing special education, then the answer is that fewer preschool children need special education (Schweinhart, Weikart, & Larnar, 1986). Are children who have been to preschool less likely to be delinquent? The answer is an equivocal yes (Berrueta-Clement, Schweinhart, Barnett, Epstein, & Weikart, 1984). These and other claims, however, are of limited validity because the scientific basis for them is questionable (Spitz, 1986).

Although there is some evidence that early experience influences later development, the explanations for such outcomes are limited because there is no good developmental theory explaining these findings. The fact that those children do better later on in school, or increase in attention span or the like, does not tell us much about the linkage between early intervention and outcome. What we desperately need is a developmental theory to guide the developmental trajectory and understand how to keep it on course.

RATIONALE FOR THEORY-BASED PROGRAMS

Intervention programs must be theoretically based. To my knowledge there has never been an intervention theory relating timing of entry to a program or type of program relative to type of hoped for outcomes for the child and his or her family. There have been few attempts to carefully assess the differences among these programs on a long-term basis without any vested interest in the type of program (Miller & Bizzell, 1983a, 1983b; Miller, Bugbee, & Hybertson, 1985; Miller & Dyer, 1975). As far as I know, the extensive research by Louise Miller showing long-term differences for preschool program effects has not generated any new approaches or caused changes in existing programs. It is as though her research was solely useful as an exercise in evaluation and not intended to influence ongoing preschool programs. Part of the reason for this is, I believe, that there is a culture of territoriality and ethnocentrism among professionals that precludes changes in one's program even when research findings suggest them, such as those implied by Miller and her colleagues.

Even the Lazar, Darlington, Murray, Royce, and Snipper (1982) monograph that demonstrated that preschool education does have some long-term effects and that there is a relationship between preschool experience and some outcomes, offers little understanding of the reasons for such the outcomes. Whether these changes can be truly attributed to preschool exclusively is unclear. What types of preschool programs are the most effective is unclear. Head Start programs are diverse and varied (see Commissioner's Office of Research and Evaluation and the Head Start Bureau, 2000, for details). Whether school-based or home-based programs are equally effective is also unclear. The reason may be due to the procedure of aggregating the data from all programs. This may have been necessary to test whether overall preschool experiences have a long-term impact. Because each program has some unique qualities that contribute to the outcomes, we need to learn precisely which types of preschool programs make a difference and why. Does any preschool program make a difference? Do the policy makers working with aggregated data sets recognize the need for more individualized program development to deal with the diversity among programs (Commissioner's Office of Research and Evaluation and the Head Start Bureau, 2000).

In this way, the proposition that so many espouse—that early experience is a true head start to change the direction of children's developmental trajectory to a socially and personal positive one—can be tested in a rational way. Embedding this idea into a conceptual framework that encompasses the social reality of children and their families can contribute to the development of a differential theory in which different developmental trajectories are defined and theory operation linkage is articulated (Sigel, 1975).

TASKS FOR FUTURE INTERVENTION EFFORTS

I believe that the following four tasks must be undertaken to increase the probability of Head Start intervention efforts to be effective:

1. Create a developmental psychosocial theory. The first step in creating a psychosocial theory of intervention is to recognize that psychoeducational intervention at any level is not the province of one discipline. Minority children are embedded in a complex social and political network, so understanding the meaning of poverty requires the involvement of different disciplines such as anthropology, sociology, education, and developmental and social psychology. This is only in keeping within the behavioral science realm when the focus is psychoeducational (Laosa, 1979). In addition, it has to be made clear that success of intervention programs on a long-term basis involves the larger social and political community. This is especially true of health and nutritional care.

The parents' employment status is an ever-present reality for minority families. Economic self-sufficiency at an appropriate level is important. This entails considering changes in the welfare system, the job training program, and the like. I am talking here of a basic change in social perspective and responsibility if we really intend to create intervention programs that will make a difference now and in the future.

2. Create developmentally linked educational programs, especially relevant to transition to kindergarten with social and achievement goals. Success should be viewed in terms of long-term outcomes such as coping with elementary school and beyond. To achieve this requires articulating linking school programs vertically so that a stage-like, developmental spiral evolves. Such an educational model, theoretically grounded, has the potential for building interest and excitement in learning as prerequisite to later schooling. Of particular psychological significance concomitant with acquiring an interest in learning is the evolving image of selfhood. These marginal children live in a world that defines their marginality, irrespective of talent or competence. All social signs, including the notion of being a Head Start student, assign them to an underclass status. The general segregation of Head Start classrooms by race, ethnic group, and social class, although not by design, reinforces their marginality. Can anything be done to minimize internalization of beliefs about their own individual worth? This is a basic challenge that must be squarely faced by all of the professionals engaged with these children and their parents.

To accomplish this goal requires considerable cooperation between the preschool and the public schools. If only one could create adequate curricula that would follow an integrated vertical curriculum, chances are that early gains in academic achievement would be folded into subsequent learning. This approach is possible when curricula are built to focus on the children's growth as the centerpiece of the intervention effort; perhaps if this is done, some basic educational changes could occur.

3. *Use an individual difference strategy for program evaluation.* Current evaluation efforts are usually based on the conventional experimental research design (Lazar et al., 1982). The unit of analysis is often the program. To carry out a rigorous design in intervention research is not possible. Lack of a rigorous design does not mean that the thinking and the analysis of program outcomes cannot be rigorous. As Cicourel stated, "Traditional research methods in social science devote considerable effort to the design of studies whose instruments achieve a high level of reliability, but they seldom satisfy ecological validity conditions" (1986, p. 249).

Evaluations using programs as a unit of analysis in educational contexts minimize attention to individual differences. Not only is the program the unit of analysis but also standardized test results are dealt with as aggregates. The individual differences, however, should be the focus of the analysis because we know that wide individual differences in accrued benefits from intervention programs occur among poor children (Sigel & Perry, 1968). In fact, the chances are that there is considerable range in competence scores among most Head Start children. It may be that this very diversity precludes adequate predictions of subsequent performance and adjustment to kindergarten.

Aggregating data by classrooms or programs actually misrepresents the effects of intervention efforts. What are some of the important questions that should be addressed? Who are the children who benefited from the program? Who are the children who showed little or no change? Who are the children that regressed? The answers to such questions will be more revealing and significant than reading reports of what percentage of children gained from a program. In fact, this issue arises when any evaluation is reported indicating what percentage of children in an experimental program showed significant gains compared with a control or a comparison group. Did any of the children in the control or comparison group in another program, or even no program, show the similar quality of change as the treatment group? Can we not learn much from analyzing the experiences of the control groups? The basic question for me is, what accounts for differences and for whom? Unless we can answer this question with some degree of specificity, our evaluation efforts can misrepresent the social reality of the benefits of intervention. Evaluation should determine how many children gain, how many children do not gain, and then why some gain and others do not, irrespective of statistical findings. Then, the question is how to explain these variations. Wouldn't this kind of information be more important than knowing mean differences between control and experimental groups on some variables?

4. *Seek alternatives to traditional experimental research design.* There are other ways to evaluate intervention programs. I believe that anthropological and ethnographic studies are in order, particularly with the underprivileged populations. Briefly stated, the coping styles of the poor are many and varied. There are those families who live very disorganized lives; they are defeated by life and find themselves trapped. Other families are resilient; they struggle, refuse to surrender, and maintain a capacity to survive. There are those who are nutritionally undernourished, whose health is impaired, and who suffer from neglect. Under such conditions, how can one find adequate control groups? On what criteria does one match, especially if there is no theory guiding the activity? The need is for ecologically valid assessment procedures and research models.

Hopefully, ethnographies could yield more contextual information about performance and a more inclusive narrative of the children's actions on a variety of tasks. Then assessment can be tied to a broader and more enlightening range of outcomes. If the environments are rich enough for the child to explore and come to experience various kinds of materials, then generalization will be possible. This approach to assessment is more expensive than the usual tasks is true. But, if our intent is to have a better understanding of the child and his or her performance for subsequent educational planning, then I would prefer the ethnography as the first step in order to develop more valid outcomes.

FINAL THOUGHTS

In the foregoing discussion I focused on the issues regarding preschool intervention programs. The reason for intervening at all, however, is to alter the lifetime developmental trajectory of disadvantaged children because we are interested in life beyond preschool. I believe we should be concerned to the degree we coordinate our thinking and our research with longer term needs of these children and their families. Creating linkages, while retaining our particular focus, is needed to develop a more pragmatic and integrated view. Paul Secord (1986) voiced similar concerns:

> Applied scientists must be more than scientists; they must have considerable knowledge and experience relevant to the application and must draw upon biographical, historical, and social structural knowledge if the application is to be effective. . . . The major role in all of this for social science itself is the development of social theory as it pertains to the involvement of social structures and individuals in the process of social change. . . . Intervention work for developmental psychologists is a major challenge that demands maximum ingenuity and wisdom since the task is complex in the educational context. But, even more demanding is its place in the larger social and political arena. Progress in social science toward a better understanding of structures will eventually alleviate the situation, but applied research will inevitably and always require knowledge and experience of the particular target situation that goes beyond theoretical knowledge. (p. 219)

In fact, such approaches may provide the initial level of conceptualization for setting up the kind of efficacy studies advocated by Blair (1999).

REFERENCES

Administration for Children and Families. (1999, December 13). *Head Start bests Mercedes and BMW in customer satisfaction: Program scores highest above all government programs.* [Press Release]. Washington, DC: Author. Retrieved January 3, 2000 from http://www.acf.dhhs.gov/news/press/1999/hssatisfies.htm

Benasich, A.A., Brooks-Gunn, J., & Clewell, B.C. (1992). How do mothers benefit from early intervention programs? *Journal of Applied Developmental Psychology, 13,* 311–362.

Berrueta-Clement, J.R., Schweinhart, L.J., Barnett, W.S., Epstein, A.S., & Weikart, D.P. (1984). *Changed lives: The effects of the Perry Preschool Program on youths through age 19.* Monographs of the High/Scope Educational Research Foundation, No. 8.

Bickel, R., & Spatig, L. (1999). Early achievement gains and poverty-linked social distress: The case of post-Head Start transition. *The Journal of Social Distress and the Homeless, 8*(4), 241–254.

Blair, C. (1999). Science, policy, and early intervention. *Intelligence, 27,* 93–110.

Cicourel, A.V. (1986). Social measurement as the creation of expert systems. In D.W. Fiske & R.A. Shweder (Eds.), *Metatheory in social science: Pluralisms and subjectives* (pp. 246–270). Chicago: University of Chicago Press.

Commissioner's Office of Research and Evaluation and the Head Start Bureau. (2000). *Celebrating cultural and linguistic diversity in Head Start.* Washington, DC: U.S. Department of Health and Human Services, The Administration on Children, Youth and Families.

Evans, E.D. (1971). *Contemporary influences in early childhood education.* New York: Holt, Rinehart and Winston.

Haskins, R., & Sawhill, I. (2003). *The future of Head Start.* The Brookings Institution Policy Brief, Welfare Reform & Beyond, 27. Washington, DC: The Brookings Institute.

Hinde, R.A. (1992). Developmental psychology in the context of other behavioral sciences. *Developmental Psychology, 28*(6), 1018–1029.

Kagan, J.S., Hunt, J.M., Crow, J.F., Bereiter, C., Elkind, D., Cronbach, L.J., et al. (1969). How much can we boost IQ and scholastic achievement?: A discussion. *Harvard Educational Review, 39,* 273–356.

Kagan, S.L., & Zigler, E.F. (1987). (Eds.). *Early schooling: The national debate.* New Haven, CT: Yale University Press.

Laosa, L.M. (1979). Social competence in childhood: Toward a developmental, socioculturally relativistic paradigm. In M.W. Kent & J.E. Rolf (Eds.), *Primary prevention of psychopathology: Vol. III. Social competence in children* (pp. 253–279). Hanover, NH: University Press of New England.

Lazar, I., Darlington, R., Murray, H., Royce, J., & Snipper, A. (1982). Lasting effects of early education: A report from the Consortium for Longitudinal Studies. *Monographs of the Society for Research in Child Development, 47*(2–3, Serial No. 195).

Lee, V.E., Brooks-Gunn. J., & Schnur, E. (1988). Does Head Start work? A 1-year follow-up comparison of disadvantaged children attending Head Start, no preschool, and other preschool programs. *Developmental Psychology, 24,* 210–222.

Leong, D.J., & Bodrova, E. (1996). *Tools of the mind: The Vygotskian approach to early childhood education.* Upper Saddle River, NJ: Merrill/Prentice Hall.

Miller, L.B., & Bizzell, R.P. (1983a). Long-term effects of four preschool programs: 6th, 7th, and 8th grades. *Child Development, 54,* 725–741.

Miller, L.B., & Bizzell, R.P. (1983b). The Louisville experiment: A comparison of four programs. In Consortium for Longitudinal Study (Ed.), *As the twig is bent: Lasting effects of preschool programs.* Mahwah, NJ: Lawrence Erlbaum Associates.

Miller, L.B., Bugbee, M.B., & Hybertson, D.W. (1985). Dimensions of preschool: The effects of individual experience. *Advances in Applied Developmental Psychology, 1,* 25–90.

Miller, L.B., & Dyer, J.L. (1975). Four preschool programs: Their dimensions and effects. *Monographs of the Society for Research in Child Development, 40*(5–6, Serial No. 162).

Powell, D.R. (Ed.). (1988). *Parent education as early childhood intervention: Emerging directions in theory, research, and practice.* Norwood, NJ: Ablex (Advances in Applied Developmental Psychology Series, Vol. 3).

Schiefelbusch, R.L. (1981). A philosophy of intervention. *Analysis and Intervention in Developmental Disabilities, 1,* 373–388.

Schweinhart, L., Weikart, D., & Larnar, M. (1986). Consequences of three preschool curriculum models through age 15. *Child Research Quarterly, 1,* 15–46.

Secord, P.F. (1986). Explanation in the social sciences and in life situations. In D.W. Fiske & R.A. Shweder (Eds.), *Metatheory in social science: Pluralisms and subjectives* (pp. 197–221). Chicago: University of Chicago Press.

Sigel, I.E. (1972). Developmental theory: Its place and relevance in early intervention programs. *Young Children, 27,* 364–372.

Sigel, I.E. (1975). The search for validity or the evaluator's nightmare. In R.A. Weinberg & S.G. Moore (Eds.), *Evaluation of educational programs for young children: The Minnesota Round Table on Early Childhood Education II* (pp. 53–66). Washington, DC: The Child Development Associate Consortium.

Sigel, I.E. (1986). Early social experience and the development of representational competence. In W. Fowler (Ed.), *Early experience and the development of competence.* (*New Directions for Child Development, 32;* pp. 49–65). San Francisco: Jossey-Bass.

Sigel, I.E. (1987). Early childhood education: Developmental enhancement or developmental acceleration? In S.L. Kagan & E.F. Zigler (Eds.), *Early schooling: The national debate* (pp. 129–150). New Haven, CT: Yale University Press.

Sigel, I.E. (1990). Psychoeducational intervention: Future directions. *Merrill-Palmer Quarterly, 36,*(1) 159–172.

Sigel, I.E., & Kim, M.I. (1996). The answer depends on the question: A conceptual and methodological analysis of a parent belief-behavior interview regarding children's learning. In S. Harkness & C.M. Super (Eds.), *Parents' cultural belief systems: Their origins, expressions, and consequences* (pp. 83–120). New York: Guilford.

Sigel, I.E., & Perry, C. (1968). Psycholinguistic diversity among "culturally deprived" children. *American Journal of Orthopsychiatry, 38,* 122–126.

Spitz, H.H. (1986). *The raising of intelligence: A selected history of attempts to raise retarded intelligence.* Mahwah, NJ: Lawrence Erlbaum Associates.

U.S. Department of Health and Human Services. (1990). *Head Start research and evaluation: A blueprint for the future. Recommendations of the Advisory Panel for the Head Start Evaluation Design Project* (DHHS Publication No. ACY 91–31195). Washington, DC: Author.

Whitehurst, G.J., Epstein, J.N., Angell, A., Payne, A.C., Crone, D., & Fischel, J.E. (1994). Outcomes of an emergent literacy intervention in Head Start. *Journal of Educational Psychology, 84,* 541–556.

Wilson, W.J. (1987). *The truly disadvantaged: The inner city, the underclass, and public policy.* Chicago: University of Chicago Press.

Zigler, E., & Valentine, S. (1979). *Project Head Start: A legacy of the war on poverty.* New York: Macmillan.

Zimmer, J. (1984). Preschool curriculum development and kindergarten education based on life situations: German, Asian and Latin American experience. In L.Y. Ching, C.H Keng, & L.C.S. Men (Eds.), *Preparation for adulthood: Proceedings of the Third Asian Workshop on Child and Adolescent Development.* Kuala Lumpur, Malaysia: Department of Pedagogy and Educational Psychology, Faculty of Education, University of Malaya.

CHAPTER 5

Three Core Concepts
of the War on Poverty

Their Origins and Significance in Head Start

POLLY GREENBERG

T he Poverty Warriors versus the developmental psychologists? There was no "versus." In the fall of 1964, we on the Office of Economic Opportunity (OEO) headquarters staff in Washington, D.C., were working on putting together the national Head Start project within the Community Action Program—after Sargent Shriver, Head Start's "founding father," got the great idea of creating a massive school readiness program similar to the typical pleasant preschool of the day but with a major emphasis on health. The "Poverty Tsar" not only had the idea, but he also had

- The power (given to him by the President of the United States)

- The budget—$96 million for the first summer only (given to him by the United States Congress)

- The brilliance, will, and political skill to actualize the idea nationwide

Several months earlier, in August 1964, the Congressional appropriation made funds available to launch the Economic Opportunity Act of 1964 and, as part of it, a new federal agency (OEO—the War on Poverty's national headquarters for all components of the poverty program).

But a large number of staff people and consultants, working out of various agencies, had been doing prep work for a while. Some of my good friends and professionally allied acquaintances from the preliminary Job Corps planning we'd been immersed in for nearly a year in connection with the President's Council of Economic Advisors and the President's Task Force Against Poverty, and other interagency work I'd been doing as a staff person at the U.S. Office of Education (USOE; now called the Department of Education) on poverty-related projects, were now transferred from the USOE to OEO. Most of them

61

became Job Corps or Community Action Program senior staff. (I was *not* a senior staff person. I was in my young thirties, and, as far as I recall, there were *no* "girls" of *any* age on OEO senior staff—Lisbeth Schorr, for example, was not there yet—unless you count the brilliant Jean Camper Cahn, on loan from the Ford Foundation from November 1964 to March 1965, creator, with her husband Edgar, of OEO's Legal Services program. Jean was also one of the only African Americans originally involved in high-level work at OEO.)

Among those transferred were Wade Robinson, who had been brought in a year before from the Harvard University School of Education by Francis Keppel (its Dean, himself on leave to be President Kennedy's U.S. Commissioner of Education) to serve as Acting Director of Job Corps during its earliest formative stage (before, in the late fall of 1965, Sargent Shriver invited Otis Singletary, a university Chancellor, to serve as Job Corps Director during its first operational year) and myself as Wade's Special Assistant.

Senior staff members were hurtling through the design and launching of many nationwide programs at once. We were incredibly short staffed. The OEO telephone extension list I have *for the entire federal agency and each of its administrative offices and programs* names a tiny staff, so we were all more or less involved in everything—in some instances *less* and in other instances *more*. Soon, I was in the middle of the explosively evolving Head Start concept. (The first staff paper on as yet unnamed Head Start in the Head Start archives, dated October 31, 1964, is mine; Wade asked me to write about the preschool/parent involvement part because, at the time, I was the only staff member with an early childhood education background. I was a Sarah Lawrence graduate who had specialized in child development from a depth psychologies—currently called "dynamic" psychology—viewpoint, primary education, cultural anthropology with an emphasis on psychosocial child development in widely differing cultures, and the history of the American "Negro" family. I had taught in a publicly funded child care center for low-income families; worked in a New York City public school after-school program with low-income young Puerto Rican children and their families; worked at the residential Wiltwyck School [for 8- to 12-year-old delinquent boys who were sent there by New York City courts] and in its Harlem social work office; taught primary grades in rural Maryland for 2 years; had gotten a master's of education in developmental beginning reading; and for 7 years had the leadership roles in D.C.'s Georgetown Co-op Nursery School, which my four little children attended.)

In the winter of 1965, I became the Senior Program Analyst for the Southeast Region, charged with getting, overnight, what soon came to be called Head Start into as many counties as possible in the seven southeastern states. There were 616 counties. Of course, Sargent Shriver was working on this too, at the highest level, and so was OEO's public relations genius Holmes Brown. Thanks to Jule Sugarman—the amazing administrator who, under Shriver's leadership, directed the national Head Start program into existence virtually overnight and through its first 5 years—we also had government interns on weekends to help. Otherwise, I was it for the deep South. Grantees chosen for funding were to be announced by President Johnson in May, only 4 months away!

Of course, getting children ready for first grade was by no means a novel idea in 1964: Sixteen states already had statewide kindergarten, private kindergartens and nursery schools were plentiful in all states, and almost all states had public kindergartens, at least in their cities. It was the children who did *not* have these opportunities about whom

Sargent Shriver, a wealthy businessman from the nation's first family—not a touchy-feely fellow—who had been a member of Chicago's Board of Education, was deeply concerned.

We were aware that there were a handful of prominent pediatricians, child psychiatrists, and child development researchers/theoreticians—off in the wings, not on the staff—thinking about young children from low-income families, just as this little group of child development specialists was aware of the bigger War on Poverty out there and a Community Action Program somewhere in the OEO headquarters building. A few big name nutritionists, dentists, public health and public school people, early childhood educators, and social workers were *also* thinking in new ways about their role in helping young children from low-income families through a multiservice program that would include some informal preschool/kindergarten experiences.

We were *definitely* aware that the experts were there, all varieties of experts. In fact, Dick Boone, Director of OEO's Division of Policy and Development and one of Sargent Shriver's right-hand men, helped Shriver and Jule Sugarman think of stars in all relevant fields who might be willing to serve on a planning committee. (My contribution to Dick was the names of several well-known early childhood educators who indeed *did* become members of this committee.)

We paid "outside experts" no more mind than they paid *us*. We were enormously, exhilaratedly busy, participating in the prenatal and neonatal stages of creating a federal agency (!) that was to be devoted to coordinating, expanding, and creating programs, services, and supports for people wanting to leave living in permanent poverty behind them; we were *simultaneously* involved in the design and launching of one War on Poverty program after another. Most important, we were told by our bosses, was the Community Action Program. Also being created were Job Corps and Upward Bound (for school dropouts who were in danger of falling through the cracks en route to productive adulthood), VISTA (an attempt to create a cadre of young adults who would have a year of *direct contact* with poor individuals, their issues, and their communities all over rural, reservation, and inner-city America and would return home and sensitize the people around them to the problem of "poverty in our backyards," *to personalize* the statistics), Legal Services (as everyone knows now and knew then, people with economic disadvantages are often the victims of injustice, including execution, because—in addition to innumerable other reasons—they don't have the access to effective attorneys that affluent people do), and Foster Grandparents (older volunteers who worked warmly with children in various programs).

The "outside experts" were doing what academics usually do in government programs—although there were many more of them than is customary, hundreds of them representing all disciplines and professions (especially law, economics, and sociology), in and out and all around the various federal agencies we worked in during the famously intellectual Kennedy Administration that immediately preceded the War on Poverty and, therefore, preceded the planning of one fabulous "landing" in the war, Head Start. Sargent Shriver's style, like the Kennedy brothers', was to talk with *everyone* who might have a good idea or important information, so experts abounded around him—by mail, by telephone, in position papers, and in person. The experts, from the typical OEO staff member's point of view, were kibbutzing from afar, from ivy-covered towers and the halls of academe (with a flurry of flights to Washington, where they were paid for a day or two to "consult" or "advise").

Few doubted that the child development specialists were wise with regard to child development and *irrelevant* to the challenge of designing and making operational a thoughtful array of ways for people living in profound poverty to catch a glimpse of possible routes out of its quicksand, to feel a glimmer of hope that they might be able to change their statistically probable and personally presumed destiny, and for those not already too multiply and severely handicapped by the deprivations, punishments, anger, stuntings, violent traumas, depression, low horizons, mirage "opportunities," and dead ends that living in generations of pervasive poverty levies—those amazing survivors—to laboriously, rung by rung, move forward and upward, more likely into the group known as "the underclass" or "the working poor," in which people hover just over the poverty line for the rest of their lives, than into the middle class.

There are innumerable wonderful success stories of poor people who hurdle many hurdles and *do* make it into the blue collar or middle class without special programs. Most often, these stories involve people with only three or four strikes against them, rather than nine or ten, or people with amazing mothers or fathers, exceptional intelligence, strength, and stamina—individuals who happen to be able to overcome *much* more than people born into the middle class or into families with privilege and/or wealth are expected to overcome to "succeed." (The latter group is rarely expected to "overcome" *anything* beyond the angst of being human—typically, its members just glide through.) There's also the matter of luck—what the economy is doing, connecting (or never having a chance to connect) with a long-term mentor, inadvertently being in the right place at the right time, and so forth.

Most often there isn't *enough* (intensive enough, extensive enough, comprehensive enough) polyfaceted support for grievously disadvantaged parents to enable them to lead their children altogether out of poverty (Schorr, 1988).

The half-dozen or so internationally distinguished child psychiatrists and psychologists at elite academic institutions who talked miscellaneously with Sargent Shriver (prior to the idea of Head Start) when he was thinking about what to do for young children in the War on Poverty were knowledgeable about the critical importance of the early years, the stages of psychosocial and mental development, and the problems that can arise in this development. They were eager to find out more about children from low-income families. They were knowledgeable about how to design and implement small model projects and how to do careful, credible research on the fundamentally important subject of creating optimal circumstances in which children can grow and learn.

Although they obviously wanted to help a modest, manageable number of young children from low-income homes, no research psychologist was, originally, either a catalyst or an advocate for a huge national Head Start program.

Sargent Shriver has often said (as in Michael Gillette's 1996 book) that he asked Jerome Bruner, a famous representative of the child development experts, what he thought about a program for young children on the verge of entering school, to help them do better. Dr. Bruner wrote a paper saying that an "experiment" in early childhood "intervention" with a group as large as 2,500 would be feasible. *Experiment? Intervention?* Shriver said, "That's wonderful, but that's no good. We've got to help 5 million children get healthy and ready for the culture of school." Professor Bruner said, "Well, good luck to you, Mr. Shriver, but you can't succeed with a mass program in this field."

Martin and Cynthia Deutsch contacted me. They wanted large sums of money to expand their research. OEO sent me to New York to visit their program. They pursued funding for research from Head Start officials but never exhibited interest in a national program.

Edgar Cahn, who worked for the Department of Justice, but was on loan to Sargent Shriver as a special assistant, described his boss's relationship with the developmental psychologists this way:

> Shriver had a sense of delightful disdain for professionalism per se. That came up in the context of Head Start and child development. Martin Deutsch and others were saying you've got to have Ph.D.'s, and it's a five-year process, and I remember he asked Dick Boone to get together what amounted to the equivalent of a developmental chart about what it would take to get a child development program off the ground. . . . Shriver flew into almost a rage, saying, "If I listen to the experts, this will take 5 years and a Ph.D. for every parent in the Head Start program. People have been raising children for a long time, and they've been doing a creditable job, and some of the children have worked out well and some of them haven't. But I'm not going to take this. We need high visibility. We need impact programs. (Gillette, 1996, p. 217)

Benjamin Bloom, a distinguished research psychologist who had talked with President Johnson and testified before Congress about the importance of the early years, was at one of the few meetings we held (at the Peace Corps' building) to see which way the wind was blowing among the experts (early childhood and others). Contrary to the claim in the New York Times obituary headline, "a Leader in the Creation of Head Start" (November 15, 1999), Dr. Bloom voted against a national program, and explained that much more research had to be done before there would be enough knowledge about educating poor children for the government to go beyond small programs. (I know because I chaired the meeting. Dick Boone remembers this too.)

To the OEO staff, though, small, perfect, model programs were *not* what Head Start was to be *about*. It was to be about providing the basics of happy, healthy, childhood days and readiness for the middle-class school culture to *millions* of children and to woo their families into it, too. Parents who have had repeated humiliating failures in school often subtly sabotage their children's ability to commit to school learning as deeply as they might. When parents feel well-respected and warmly welcomed by their children's schools, the children feel emotionally free to fully engage.

Although parenting education wasn't their bag, the few developmental psychologists who were initially consulted and who later found themselves on the Head Start Planning Committee agreed that there *should be* some parenting education in a program for young children. Parent education—becoming aware of how to encourage children, help them develop self-discipline, and enrich their lives—was a standard part of all nursery schools and parent co-op preschools of the day, as was parent participation in the classroom—a pillar of the parent cooperative movement—which was at its peak during this period (Taylor, 1967).

Maybe the developmental psychologists who spoke and wrote most about Head Start in its first quarter century weren't, at the time, aware of the discipline/profession of early childhood education (e.g., Read, 1950), or maybe they didn't take this "low-status" women's field seriously or didn't notice Dr. James Hymes' contributions to Head Start de-sign. (He had a Ph.D. in parent education from Columbia University, a well-established national reputation in this specialty, and was, like Dr. Edward Zigler, a member of the Head Start Planning Committee.) I say this because they credited themselves with the "innovation" of adding parent education/participation to Head Start. (The Poverty War-riors, many of whose children were in, or had attended nursery school—or preschool in a church or neighborhood recreation center, and so forth—didn't think parenting education and parent volunteers in the classroom were clever new ideas and smiled at what they saw as the experts' conceit.)

But I don't recall that the priority of any of this group of specialists, including the few early childhood folks, was overall development, education, employment, income, and personal/political empowerment of parents so they could advocate effectively for their children, influence community services such as health clinics and schools to provide good service to their children, benefit from opportunities for themselves, create literate home environments, help their children with their homework, move to safe neighborhoods— in short, *move up to the middle class.* No one was *against* all this, but it wasn't a *priority.* Yet, I believe research and common sense say that

- Growing up in middle-class families is what most increases children's chances to avoid growing up in low-income families.

- Children who have grown up in middle-class families and have become middle-class par-ents are more likely to raise *their* children in the middle class rather than in poverty.

Said another way (and said by the Community Action staff), if we want children to grow up in blue collar or middle-class families instead of in poverty, we should do all we can *as quickly as is possible* to help families who can and *want* to become middle class when the kids are still kids (while, of course, providing programs and services to children, as well).

"How did our ideas get turned upside down like this?" wonders a perplexed origi-nal OEO staff person. "The emphasis was on enabling people to learn and earn themselves out of poverty, modeling the ability to improve and *achieve* for their kids, just like the rest of us—to become taxpayers instead of tax eaters, as Sarge used to say. We wanted to pro-vide an immediate boost for their children, too, and their dropout teenagers. But where did the laughable notion come from that 1 or 2 years of a half or even whole-day preschool with some parent participation on the periphery could be expected to work this wonder?"

"It's partly *your* fault," a grinning OEO guy replies. "You haven't written about our ideas. What gets written becomes the history and focus, regardless of the facts and origi-nal goal. And what gets written is a mixture of fading memory, ignorance of what *else* was going on, special interests, and narcissism, which combine to cause confusion about who was an expert child development researcher, and who—quite another matter—wanted to mass produce health care and pleasant readiness-building childhood experiences; about who believed that something put together from many existing sources was a good idea, and who had the power and will to implement it wholesale—hardly the same thing!"

Obviously, not all low-income people are interested in upward mobility. Notions of status and wealth don't turn them on. (As many people who have one, the other, or both can attest, status and wealth don't guarantee happiness.) But even people who aren't interested in upward mobility *do* want jobs, basic financial security, and opportunities to develop their interests and talents. If we want children to grow up in contented families, with choices for everyone and freedom from financial wretchedness, then we should do all we can to create jobs, viable opportunities of many kinds, and adequate levels of guaranteed income. In the 1960s, not many Poverty Warriors were talking about reducing disparities in earnings between the rich and the working poor, but we *were* talking about "new careers for the poor"—meaningful work with reasonable pay.

The pediatricians and public health people who were advising Sargent Shriver were knowledgeable about *physical* development, factors that foster it, and its aberrations and deprivations. Many were very disapproving of the public health system's appalling failure to attend to the needs of all poor children. The chairman of the planning committee was neither a psychologist nor an early childhood educator—he was the Shriver's pediatrician, Dr. Robert Cooke. Initially, the heaviest emphasis in Head Start was health. Dr. Julius Richmond, a distinguished pediatrician and the part-time national director of Project Head Start, had a lot to do with actualizing this.

Dr. Richmond was the perfect choice. He brought to Head Start a long history of advocacy for the all-around well-being of children from low-income families, a distinguished research background in the area of child care for early intervention purposes, wisdom, common sense, and status. Unfortunately, he had a new position at the Upstate Medical Center and could not be in Washington, D.C., full time. And when he was there, he *also* had to launch the Neighborhood Health Centers, per Sargent Shriver. If Head Start's health and mental health components aren't as good as they should be, there's no mystery about how to improve them. Those holding the purse strings don't put money into what they don't value, what they value but personally are already getting, or what the populace doesn't pressure them to make a priority. It's a choice.

In the early 1960s, members of all of these professions were discovering that disastrous nutritional deprivation and severely limited natural learning experiences—conversation, enriched play, story reading, simple outings to the zoo, and so forth—damage a child's intellectual development *so much* that he or she may be considered to have mental retardation!

In the 1990s, brain researchers reported the same thing, and both professionals and the public responded with excitement. Though research is certainly a good thing, and was built into the War on Poverty and Head Start from before the beginning, the powers that be in our society typically permit research and more research (including wrongly designed and inappropriately focused research, such as the infamous and very destructive Westinghouse/Ohio University study), and interminable debate about the research that was off-target (hence irrelevant) in the *first* place, to replace sufficient action to *solve the poverty problem* to the maximum feasible extent. We do not choose to mass produce *all* of what we already know about enormously reducing poverty and improving children's lives and express breathless excitement when the fact that we have quite a lot of programs, services, and approaches that work is pointed out by a reputable expert (e.g., Schorr, who writes about what works and urges us to do what we can to make it standard practice). How much more research is needed to determine, for example, that many of the world's children are starving and that feeding them every day from now on would "work"?

The Poverty Warriors' reaction to what one of them calls "the experts' remarkable discovery that a healthy, happy, enriched childhood is good for children" was, in today's parlance, "Duh!" Experts were immersed in another high tide of their century-long ebbing and flowing nature versus nurture debate. In the 1960s, the importance of *environment* was being rediscovered and emphasized; in the 1990s, the importance of *genetics* once again got lots of attention. (In the psychology literature of the early 1960s, there was great excitement about the work of J. McVicker Hunt and Benjamin Bloom. Hunt published papers and books about how IQ scores could be raised dozens of points with the "right experiences," whereas Bloom expounded the importance of the early years of life as a "critical period" in intellectual development.) "Who cares?" asked the Poverty Warriors, in disbelief. How do the facts that environment isn't *everything,* or that there are many important things left to be learned about child development, exempt the richest society in the world from making every effort to make life reasonably decent for each of its children *now?*

THE TRIPOD ON WHICH THE WAR ON POVERTY (INCLUDING HEAD START) WAS TO BE PREMISED

In this section, listed in the order in which they appeared historically, are the three core concepts of the War on Poverty, as defined and developed by the President's Committee on Juvenile Delinquency and Youth Crime (PCJD)—created by Attorney General Robert Kennedy and adopted by President Kennedy's Council of Economic Advisors and subsequently by President Lyndon B. Johnson—the President's Task Force Against Poverty, Sargent Shriver, and the Community Action Program/Job Corps staff within OEO. Dick Boone, an originator of these three core concepts, was on the PCJD staff. Head Start was developed in his office at OEO. Dick remembered the day "Sarge" called him into his office and then sent him away to "draft" Head Start. All three of these fundamental themes, which can be considered the head, the spine, and the guts of Head Start, were determined before Head Start was conceptualized (and therefore before five or six child development experts became involved).

Readers can decide for themselves how consistent these three pivotal principles were/are with the interests, research, writings, positions, and reward systems of the developmental psychologists who were one of many groups of specialists later involved in planning and advocating for Head Start. Wonders one Poverty Warrior, "How did this one rather low-on-the-totem-pole category of academics—child psychologists—get so much public policy clout? Each relevant type of expert should *inform* public policy, not *dominate* it. Why did other types of experts cede them this power to dwarf the discussion into the little box of 'does it, doesn't it, does it, doesn't it work' for 35 years!"

For going on four decades, Head Start's distinguished experts have consistently blown off OEO's and Head Start's community action theorists and practitioners in the customary, culturally accepted ways that rapid reform, progressive social change advocates and activists are *always* minimized in scholarly circles: Their ideas are rarely, if ever, mentioned, and they themselves are marginalized. Those who truly desire to transform an unjust social order are ignored. If indeed they are considered at all, they are glanced at askance and considered goofy kooks. (In other settings, such as northern inner-city ghettos and Mississippi in the 1960s, citizens critical of the grossly unfair socioeconomic and political status quo are called "outside agitators," or "leftists," and of course the knee-jerk mind jumps to "Communists.")

Scholars see assisting the oppressed in their efforts to achieve freedom, in contrast to benevolently bestowing services on them, as too controversial to go near or even acknowledge. The "powers that be" in most locales see this kind of collegial assistance to poor people in problem solving, and in releasing and stimulating the power to perceive their situation critically, to speak out about it, and to do something small and personally meaningful about it, as downright subversive. Poor people are supposed to be *recipients,* not *transformers* of a corner of the system that fails them. The three core concepts of Head Start defied this attitude.

1. All willing citizens and existing relevant organizations should be enlisted in an effort to fight poverty in their particular community.

This has been a central theme of Sargent Shriver's work throughout his life. There are people of good will, people with a wide variety of skills and perspectives, and people knowledgeable about one or another program and its population—and where the disconnects and gaping gaps are—working in a number of categorically funded, rigidly separated institutions, agencies, and services in every community, including, of course, job training, job placement, and jobs.

There is also *poverty* in every community. The wisdom possessed by staff in all relevant agencies, and the concern, diverse abilities, and energy of *all* willing members of each community, including residents of targeted neighborhoods, must be mobilized and united to examine needs, plan, and implement the modification, expansion, or gap-filling creation of the kinds of jobs, services, and programs that can increase opportunity and help people find escape routes from the cycle of poverty.

2. It is essential to plan and implement all efforts to help poor people WITH them, not FOR them.

Even in the dreariest, most dilapidated inner-city neighborhood or rural pocket of poverty there are people with tremendous energy, people with capable brains, and people with vast expertise about the difficulties of being born, raised, mired, and buried in pervasive poverty. (There are also stupid poor people. Experts who study this subject find that intelligence, and lack of it, are equally distributed among socioeconomic classes and races.)

If high proportions of people who've been trapped in poverty all their lives become apathetic, and some become angry or act out in antisocial ways, it's almost always because they see no exit from their situation. They feel doomed by a destiny over which they have no control. They believe in unmitigable fate. The circumstances of their upbringing and subsequent individual lives have not enabled them to develop feelings of positive personal power or a *vision* of themselves in any life except the only life they know, both of which— the feeling of having enough personal power to make positive things happen for yourself and an image of yourself in a very different life—are foundations of "mastery motivation" and motivation to "achieve." Most people's aspirations are formed in relation to what those closest to them do and *their* income. To succeed is to equal or slightly exceed parents, siblings, and others who directly surround us. Many people come to believe either

- That they are the pawns of a system not designed to offer them authentic opportunities *starting where they are* and enabling them to move forward effectively (so they quit trying, and busy themselves with the incredible effort necessary to keep their heads above water at all, and *we* label it "apathy")

OR

- That society as a whole has neither significant conscience nor sincere intentions about "equal opportunity" for *them* (e.g., enough guilt feelings and enough motivation to actualize the much lauded American ideal of equal opportunity for *all*) and, therefore, *they,* the disenfranchised, aren't obligated to participate in anything not resulting in their own immediate gratification—which may be functioning without conscience toward others, or the venting of rage, or may, most commonly, mean living generously within the extremely limited boundaries of their ethnic/racial subculture (one or another version of "the culture of poverty," subcultures which exist within, and are strongly influenced by, mainstream American culture, but which are in most ways walled off from it.)

Typically, advocates who have lived in poor communities and served as street workers, civil rights workers, VISTA or Peace Corps volunteers, ombudsmen, and so forth find that neither one of these perceptions is a delusion.

3. It is time to launch an all-out war on child poverty.

America has high ideals about equal opportunity for everyone, America is affluent, and Americans have become aware of the poverty, compounded by racism, in their midst; therefore (it was said in the 1960s and is said today by many of those who said it then, plus a cadre of concerned younger people) it is time to launch an all-out war, similar to World War II, intended to vanquish the enemy. There will always be some people—for example, people with profound mental retardation; people with medically unresponsive psychosis; people with severe disabilities from birth, illness, or accident; veterans with physical injuries or mental health disorders; or people who were so severely neglected and abused (physically and mentally) as children that they are beyond repair—who can't make it on their own. If their families can't do it, a wealthy society should take care of them at a non-poverty level. But most people *can* get out of poverty if given opportunities (including the "opportunity" to be paid decent wages for their work).

By definition, some people in a capitalist country will make much more money than others, and there will be a pyramid of socioeconomic stratifications. But that isn't synonymous with saying that people at the lowest level must live in hovels and tenements and in dangerous, dirty, ugly neighborhoods; that they must live with disabilities and illness that go untreated; that they must be unemployed (in some cases, because they're ineligible for remediations, hence unemployable); and that the young among them must attend the nation's certifiably worst schools. We can do more to improve the quality of life for people at *all* levels.

Poverty is caused by a number of factors and includes populations with very different needs. The largest group of destitute people used to be older adults, especially elderly women. Another group of underprivileged people were those with serious disabilities. In the 1930s, many decided that it was unconscionable for older adults and individuals with disabilities to be living in poverty. Social Security was established to help these two groups—and much more has been done *since* then, including the creation of Medicare and

Medicaid—and although Social Security and the other nationwide government programs have significantly reduced poverty and its problems, most humane citizens believe that substantial additional improvements in our care of these populations and in the effectiveness of these programs need to be made. The point is, it is possible, using various approaches as appropriate, to alleviate poverty for various populations, and already in the 1960s, we *knew* it. As we begin the 21st century, however, Americans haven't demonstrated a widespread will to *do* it.

A group of people who were very much on everyone's minds in the mid-1960s—and are still on everyone's minds in the year 2004, but with less of our compassion—were high school dropouts and other youth who were total strangers to all forms of taken-for-granted American privilege and faced bleak futures. Some youth, especially in urban areas, enter the criminal world because it's the only world where "success" is a sure bet—at least until prison claims them or they're murdered by their peers. Often, there's a dismal mismatch between *brains* (lots) and *chances* (few if any) to do something worthwhile. The idea was to offer *opportunity*—a more effective approach to education, job training for available jobs, and both basic and auxiliary services, such as health care, counseling, and confidence building, as needed to allow each young person to be successful in the working world.

Some Poverty Warriors' Perspectives

Although they weren't named in the Economic Opportunity Act, the War on Poverty's Chief Executive, Sargent Shriver, was alarmed to learn that young children represented a very large segment of the poverty population. He thought that health care, good nutrition, and general experiences similar to those middle-class children usually have would help underprivileged children be better able to take advantage of the wonderful opportunity that high-quality education offers—not that there's much of *that* in the slums. As the experts wrangle about whether Head Start "works" and indulge in endless expensive research, resulting in a locked embrace of fierce polemics and counter polemics (which seems to bring pleasure to the combatants or they wouldn't do it), the ordinary, kindly, middle-class parent may wonder if Head Start is quite so bizarre as the twistings of critics have tried to make it seem.

Thirteen million 3- to 5-year-olds are enrolled in preschools, and 71% of these children come from upper-income families who *voluntarily* enroll them. We know the value of preschool and happy childhoods. What do you think would happen if the general public was told that playgroups, preschool, child care, health care, and nourishing food would be taken from their children unless they could prove these things "work"? Parents, grandparents, and child-caring people of all kinds, especially people who provide their children with upscale upbringings, would create a huge hullabaloo. "What do you mean 'works'?" they would chorus indignantly. "Certainly the *absence* of all this wouldn't be optimal for children; that's how we know these things are good for children." Moreover, if middle-class and blue collar families were told that their children would only get all these things—including nutritional food—for half-a-day starting at age 4 and ending soon after, the ensuing riots would be evidence that sensible people, though they've never researched or evaluated anything, know that good care is a must from the beginning and on through the teen years.

"Why anyone would be opposed to infant/toddler Early Start for *all* babies who need it, Follow Through for all Head Start graduates (and all children who need it should *be* in Head Start or equivalently comprehensive programs), and Follow Through for all of the same kids through age 18, I can't imagine," says a former Community Action staff member. "Why do experts allow the debate to rage over either/or? Of course we should do *all* that we can to help kids become good people, good parents, good citizens. Is anyone out there pleased, or even satisfied, with the school failure and dropout rate in our country? With the semiliterateness of a fifth of the population? With the number of people addicted to drugs, on welfare, homeless on the streets, in prison, or in lives of crime? What's the matter with us? Don't we want to do everything we can for as many people as we can to create productive people and a better, stronger country for everyone?

Cost isn't the real issue. The cost would be nothing compared to many things this country spends money on. (A case in point is the Iraq attack, plus all of the follow-up billions.) I guess I *can* imagine why many people oppose thorough preventive help: The real issue is our contempt for poor people. It makes us feel superior to think there are others who are inferior. We don't want to help them get out of poverty. Without poor people, how could we feel successful? As it is, the masses—most of us—don't have to make the effort to be morally and ethically superior, or to develop our skills and gifts to our fullest potential, or give enormously of our time to community improvement projects—to feel 'successful,' all we have to do is have more possessions, privileges, opportunities, money, and social status than both welfare and working poor people."

A second rapid reformist, who had just finished reading *Lives on the Line* (Shirk, Bennett, & Aber, 1999), adds, "True. And who would cut the heads off our catfish?" (See story below.)

Here's a delightful and ever-so-typical example (from a chapter titled, "Making Ends Meet, One Catfish at a Time" [from Shirk et al., 1999]) of how, in our benevolent generosity, never-so-affluent American decision-makers "help" people avoid welfare.

Celeste, the family's matriarch, works as a band-saw operator. That's a pretty benign-sounding job title for what she does—cut the heads off of catfish. One a second. Sixty a minute. Three thousand, six hundred an hour. Twenty eight thousand, eight hundred a day. "Basically, I work in an indoor field," she says. "A *refrigerated* indoor field."

Celeste, 37, has been working in the Belzoni plant of Delta Pride Catfish, the nation's largest producer of farm-raised catfish, for about 10 years. She makes $6.20 an hour, a total of $10,855 in 1997. (The poverty threshold for a family of five was $19,380 in 1997.)

In the past week, Celeste grossed $311.25, which included $63.62 in overtime pay. Deductions reduced her take-home pay to $235.22. Most of the deductions are for mandatory contributions like Social Security and Medicare and union dues. But a few are discretionary: $2.40 a week for a cancer insurance policy that would pay Celeste $10,000 if she or a child were diagnosed with a serious cancer; $11.40 for a $53,000 term life insurance policy on her and $10,000 policies on each child; and $10 for savings. (No one can tell Celeste, who survived a life-threatening illness, that the cancer insurance is most likely a scam.) In the *best* of months, there's just $125 left over for unanticipated expenses, such as school supplies, clothes, a visit to the doctor, medicine, or a car repair. How does Celeste make it all work? "The Lord blesses me every day, and I thank him for it," she says.

Although Celeste has health insurance through her job, a substantial co-payment is required for doctors' visits and prescription drugs. Last month, when she was suffering from asthma, she went to a doctor five times, at $22 a visit. Her asthma medication cost her $200. (She buys it only when her asthma is acting up. "Paying for my drugs is like paying another rent," she says.)

Luckily, she worked a lot of overtime. "I get home at nine or ten o'clock at night and just have time to get to bed before I have to get up again," she points out. "Sometimes my kids wonder if they have a mother."

When the catfish plant cuts back its workers' hours—a virtual certainty from June through December—the family's budget is seriously squeezed. "They don't call it that, but I've really got a seasonal job," Celeste says. "We haven't had our light turned off yet," she says, "and we've never gone to the refrigerator and found nothing in it, so I can't complain." (Shirk, Bennett & Aber, 1999, pp. 202–205)

Some readers may think that the most famous Celeste in the world—Babar the elephant's wife—has it much better than Celeste the hard-working American mother. Must be that our model for lending a helping hand is Genghis Kahn.

Another Poverty Warrior comments, "And compared to the cost of *not* doing the right thing—special ed, repeating grades, serious mental health problems, crime, prison—investing in young children and their families would be a bargain."

"Tell all middle-class parents their children are going over to the worst schools in town for their entire school lives and you'll have a fight on your hands," says a fourth activist. "Blame Head Start for how our society refuses to help poor children with safe neighborhoods, decent housing, quality after school care, etc? And for what inferior schools do year after year? How conveniently this gets all us off the hook! Fade out? Huh!"

Shriver's Words

Sargent Shriver and Lyndon B. Johnson had both been in World War II and shared a common understanding of war. Shriver often discussed it. He has been discussing it for 36 years. Here is how, in 1991, he described his view of the War on Poverty:[1]

> We were thinking about a total, all out, national effort, like the effort against Hitler. We weren't thinking about a little program here and there. You have to put immense resources into winning a war. Everybody in this society understands that when you're fighting a military war, but people don't understand it when you're talking about a war on *poverty.* We never got the money to fight an all out war, like the Persian Gulf War, where everything was concentrated on it.

---

[1] The four paragraphs that follow in this extract are transcribed from Sargent Shriver's conversation with David Bradley—Executive Director of the National Community Action Foundation (NCAF), a private, nonprofit organization in Washington, D.C. that advocates and lobbies Congress for organizations serving low-income populations—in an interview by the NCAF that Dave videotaped on November 6, 1991. Do you know that as I wrote this there were still 940 Community Action Agencies located all around the country?

Of course I thought we'd be getting much more money through the second Johnson Administration to develop this program. I'd have been a fool, I'd have been ridiculous, not to have thought that. How could you possibly envision eliminating poverty even in *one country* with only a million, or 2 million, or even 10 million dollars? I'm not saying that money alone can cure poverty, but you can't cure it with peanuts, either. Human beings aren't perfect.

You're not going to totally solve poverty. *No* kind of war is going to solve all the problems involved. No matter how much you spend on a war, you won't solve all the problems. Did the [first] Persian Gulf War fix everything up? Solve that whole situation? Saddam Hussein is still there. We still have a huge problem in the Middle East. It would have been silly to have expected total success. It's equally silly to expect even a *massive* war on poverty to solve all poverty, but we never had a massive war.

In a military action, you do whatever it takes to win. There's no such thing as coming out second in winning a military war. If you go at poverty from all angles, many landings, sorties, intelligence gatherers, fight vigorously on many fronts at once, rout the enemy out of every village, you'll at least have a *chance* of winning.

THE HEAD START DEBATES: DOES HEAD START "WORK"?

There's a great deal of debate, but it doesn't always deal with the bigger picture and most important issues—in fact, frequently it *detracts* from them. How might Poverty Warriors assess Head Start? I can only conjecture.

I don't claim to know much about program evaluation, but I do know two basic principles: First, you're supposed to judge a program with reference to its goals. For starters, I'd consider the questions that follow. If I thought it necessary, I would take action as suggested below, for surely the second principle of program evaluation is to *use* its results by making every effort to improve the project in areas found to be less effective than they *should* be, not simply to carp and carp and, for nearly 40 years, harp on well-understood deficiencies, as has been done since the summer Head Start began.

All Willing Citizens Should be Enlisted in an Effort to Fight Poverty in Their Community

Are a wide variety of willing citizens, including

- All manner of relevant professionals

- Faculty members from many disciplines (e.g., sociology, cultural anthropology, economics, political science, management, in addition to the others who have hoisted their flags on this turf)

- Business leaders

- Volunteers from churches, senior and service clubs, and colleges and high schools in the community

involved, one way or another, in Head Start *in every locality* and at *the national level?* I'll bet everything I've got that they're not!

Prominent Head Start advocates have failed to mobilize the middle-class *public* as advocates. This isn't the leaders' interest. This isn't their specialty. One could say that, of course, no one is an expert on everything, and experts should limit themselves to their area of expertise. Or, one could say, as a Poverty Warrior does, "It's a well-understood ploy of elite experts—experts with national stature. They insinuate themselves into spokesman roles and the clubby confines of inner political power circles and then divert political, academic, professional, and media attention from true social change to trivia (in this case, this curriculum, that curriculum, IQ points). The *real* issue is getting the nation to fight poverty in an all-out attempt to win. But it isn't their issue. *Their* issue is protecting and promoting their status, while as they see it, doing good."

Most people are kind and compassionate if confronted with trauma or tragedy. A shooting in the neighborhood school, an earthquake in Turkey, a fire that ravages a home on a freezing night—incidents such as these arouse outpourings of money, clothing, and prayer. When Eleanor Roosevelt went to meet with people living in pockets of rural poverty (accompanied by the press), she put a *face* on poverty, and people responded. And, years later, when Lyndon Johnson traveled to a tar-papered shack on a mountainside in eastern Kentucky (with a flock of reporters) to listen to a gaunt, miserable, unemployed sawmill worker talk about his family's woes, *he* put a face on poverty, and people responded.

We're looking at a circular but semi-soluble problem. If, as the influential economist John Kenneth Galbraith wrote in 1958, one of government's chief responsibilities in a democracy is to ensure the well-being of all its citizens by balancing the needs and wishes of diverse groups, including the down and out, as best it can—if it would be in *everybody's* best interest to think big about public needs—then our federal, state, and local governments should do a much better job of ensuring that the assorted needs of the needy are met. As it is, the needs of big business dominate public policy, and "freedom" means freedom for the fortunate. To get to the roots of poverty, from which many of our society's evils stem, government at all levels should once again focus on and put a face on poverty. This is essential in enlisting the public in eliminating it, and the public *must* be enlisted because without people power behind them, elected officials can go only so far—they can lead but only so far before they lose, or are unable to enlist, any followers.

At the White House level, experts in many fields could be gathered to pull together what we know (so much!) about the causes, complexities, and *cures* that add up to very significant alleviations and sometimes solutions, with a strong emphasis on what every agency, corporation, and citizen can do to help. If the expertise of advertising and communications specialists was used and the same clever energy was put into *this* project as is put into making us want to drink beer and buy cars, the citizenry's interest in rapidly reducing poverty in America probably could be re-aroused. Facts can't gain access to minds unwilling to let them in, but we could try harder to educate the public in this area. For example, middle schools and high schools could require every student to experience many, many hours of community service in low-income homes and neighborhoods, working *with* residents. Colleges and universities could design a new degree and could train "community facilitators" to teach about poverty and engage community groups in discussing and developing solutions.

Once informed and empowered to *do* something about it, all but the most mean-spirited members of the public, the few whose hearts are just muscles, might be more likely to vote for candidates who want to wage total war on poverty in their localities and join in the war themselves as funders of helpful programs and services, volunteer providers of technical assistance, mentors for families or children, and so forth.

It Is Essential to Plan and Implement All Efforts to Help Poor People WITH Them, Not FOR Them

Do evaluations show that all of the following is happening? I've only seen it all happening in the *best* Head Start and other community action programs run largely by poor people, formerly poor people, and their political allies.

In every community, there are a wide variety of poor people, including Head Start parents and others (people on welfare or newly off-welfare, long-term working poor, youths—not just a few handpicked representatives of the poor), *regularly* recruited by peers trained as outreach workers, community organizers, and discussion facilitators to be

- *Regular* participants in ongoing and issue-oriented discussions pertaining to the personal and sociological problems of their poverty (including the fact that the low wages received by the 7.5 million working people who, *in spite of* working, live below the poverty level is a *political* problem, a changeable reality, not an act of God), obstacles in the path leading out of poverty, available programs—Head Start and others—that could be helpful in meeting their needs or those of someone they know, what the eligibility requirements are, what the eligibility requirements *should* be, how many available spaces there are in specific needed programs, how many spaces *should* there be to meet the need in the community (conversation on *this* topic should follow community research by discussants and facilitators), what services and quality of service community institutions (e.g., libraries, schools, health clinics, police, street and street light departments) offer, who should be contacted and continuingly pushed to bring about necessary changes in funding (for more slots), services offered (conventional or creative gap-fillers), quality of service (training, firing, transferring, hiring), and so on.

- *Active, constructive* advocates in appropriate places—writing letters to decision makers; getting media training; learning about funding sources and how to write proposals; learning how to link together programs, services, and the funding streams that make them possible; learning how to be community outreach workers, organizers, and discussion facilitators . . . if we do it right, what goes around comes around.

Are Head Start children's parents being heavily recruited and heartily welcomed into jobs of many kinds and *significant* decision-making roles in the program, with extensive high-quality staff development and credentialing as appropriate? The answer is an enthusiastic yes compared with the upward mobility and new careers for poor people available in most other human services programs—*especially* good is the early childhood education component, with the Child Development Associate career ladder, including linkages to community college and 4-year college degrees. But the answer is also a disappointed *no* in some of the other components of Head Start (though models exist here too) and compared with what it *could* be.

Credit for as much emphasis on jobs and new careers for poor people as there *is* goes to the powerful, insightful Head Start community itself, both the bureau within the federal government, and the National Head Start Association (e.g., past and present staff, parents), and some of their professional allies who believe that their role is to ensure the provision of ample amounts of technical assistance to parents who are moving in, up, and out of Head Start. If the educational component (for children and parents) isn't good enough, and the literacy aspect (for children and parents) is weak, let's provide more money for staff development and adult education rather than blame the victim. (Of course, education, especially literacy learning, is inadequate for this same population in our public schools; it isn't fair to hang it all on Head Start.) Training money in Head Start is absurdly scarce and has been gutted during the George W. Bush Administration. If "planned variations" in curricular approaches have been developed, let new careerist parents learn about the more significant ones and choose among them.

Children and adults alike learn, and form and reform and refine ideas, in part by talking with others, some of whom believe the goal and the means of reaching it to be what we do and some of whom strenuously *don't*.

Though sometimes invited, middle-class people often remain on the periphery of any discussion of possible solutions to poverty. They have other pressing priorities and extremely limited exposure to poor people in their own settings—if, indeed, any exposure at all. Probably, though they would deny it to avoid feeling guilty or obligated to get involved, they say there are plenty of services out there, the problem is those poor people who fail to take advantage of them. This is a typical uninformed citizen's view. There are many people in all socioeconomic groups who don't wish to take advantage of opportunities, even if they could. Take college, for example—there are all sorts of loans and ways to pay for college, yet, many middle-class people choose not to enroll. But regardless of how it looks from the top, help of many kinds doesn't exist in many places. In any given county, only a limited number of spaces in a selected number of services exist. Head Start, although it *exists* in most places, has room for only a fraction of the eligible children.

The liberal/moderate view is that we need more programs and services for "pitiful poor people," that there aren't enough, and that not all that exist are good enough. We should "do more" *for* "the poor."

The conservative view is that poor people are poor because they're lazy; why should they need special programs and services at all? All they have to do is work hard in school and get a job. There's only 3.8% unemployment, you know. (According to the Bureau of Labor Statistics, in the third week of April, in the year 2000, for instance, this translates to 5 million, 483,000 human beings, many of them parents, who were available for work but couldn't find it. This number doesn't include their children, of course, or all the discouraged jobless people, many of them with serious health or mental health problems, and many of them parents who didn't seek work in that particular week. Nor does the monthly unemployment statistic hint at the horrid economic situation of most of America's 7.5 million working poor, again, many of them parents.) Since April 2000, the numbers of unemployed people have almost doubled. In late 2003, as I write, unemployment hovers between 6.4% and 6.7%.

Except for a handful of Head Starts such as the huge Child Development Group of Mississippi (CDGM), briefly discussed on pages 79–81, and a small minority of community action organizations, we leave poor people absolutely out of the discussion—*they* aren't even invited. They would be considered too ignorant and innocent of how the world works to be included if the idea were considered at all, which it isn't, because wasting time on this seems to most experts as preposterous as would the idea of including dogs and cats in all deliberations and decisions. To Poverty Warriors, however, discussing and decision making are an essential part of personal growth—confidence building and building know-how—and the process of breaking out of the sticky cycle of poverty.

In contrast to the "do for" approach of helping individuals, as some of us who were on OEO's original staff see it, true generosity to poor people isn't merely giving charity (though that's often a kind and welcome thing to do). And it isn't even merely giving programs and services (though they are much needed and appreciatively received). We believe that the presence of poor people in the struggle for their growth, education, and liberation from the multiple psychological, educational, sociological, economic, and political traps in the pits of our society must not be child/adult participation, the grateful versus the expert, the awed versus the oracle—*pseudo*-participation. It must be the committed involvement of "equals." The disadvantaged have expertise in poverty, and, when freed from its shackles of self-doubt or learned low-aspiration, many have a degree of motivation to alter their lot that no expert will ever have. The expert, on the other hand, has essential technical assistance to offer. Together, progress can be made in solving some of the tenacious problems of poverty.

Practitioners, whether in health, mental health, social work, or education, usually do unto parents and children as academics do unto them. They present themselves to their "patients," "clients," or "students" as possessing knowledge that they are (arrogantly or graciously) giving. As they do this, they (knowingly or unknowingly) attribute ignorance—even of common sense and life-learned wisdom—to the learners.

Every developmental psychologist and educator who understands Piaget knows that the most effective learning occurs when someone

- Investigates a topic that's very meaningful to him or her

- Participates in planning and deciding how to proceed

- Bumps into new facts and ideas

- Incorporates the knowledge into his or her thinking, thus changing it

- Acts on his or her environment armed with this new understanding

"Investigate a topic that's very meaningful": Traditional education for children and parents conceals facts that are fundamental to self-improvement and the equalizing of people in our communities—classism, oppression, and racism. Traditional education for parents, even in Head Start, resists discussion of these truths and, therefore, leaves in place barriers to many individuals' total commitment and leaves their emotional energy unharnessed.

As with children, the type of education that pours knowledge into the empty vessel and writes on the blank slate of the mind not only results in learning but also, to a certain extent, inhibits and anaesthetizes both critical and creative thinking. Alternatively, the problem-solving style of education, which results in learning too, *stimulates* critical and creative thinking. Were it not for the facts briefly reviewed in the next paragraph, it would be curious that developmental psychologists, of all people, don't emphasize in their Head Start debates the importance of constructivist learning about things that are tremendously meaningful to them for Head Start parents. Learning includes analysis and action. We know this, but we don't apply it to adult learners—particularly if they're poor with little education—because it's empowering, and empowerment of others feels threatening to experts (and to almost everyone who *has* some degree of power—clout).

A paramount of any elite is to structure its kingdom to serve its political interests and preferences. This includes its education system—admissions, curriculum, credits, accreditation, degrees required for various job levels, and so forth. First, elite professors at prestigious institutions and professional organizations work to achieve collegial consensus on the issues that are important to them. Once these bastions are secure, the premiere leaders work to get the leaders of all lesser institutions marching along to the approved drummer. On the whole, the lower you go in the hierarchy of educational institutions (whether medical schools, law schools, or psychology departments) the less understanding their head honchos and ordinary faculty have of the essential issues and intricacies of their field, and the shakier they feel status-wise, so the more rigid their requirements have to be and the more strenuously they have to guard the moats of their flimsy castles from invasion by outsiders—for example, Head Start parents who have become truly empowered with knowledge and skills.

How could the experts allow Head Start parents to study alternative educational approaches, for instance, and pick the one they prefer for their program, and then get trained to implement it when the experts themselves have been unable to agree on which is "best" for more than three decades? This would *not* serve the researchers' political interests because this approach would "work" for the children as well (or not) as does (or doesn't) the *present* approach, making invalid the claim that more regression-analyses-laden research is needed. But in *my* view, and in the opinion of many progressive "rapid social change" reformers, this would be by far the best thing to do for parents and children. *All* parents, even public school parents, even Head Start parents, should have the opportunity to get educated about educational choices and should *have* choices pertaining to their children's education. *All* children should have a chance to see their parents as respected people who like to learn and who make important decisions.

"That's right," a well-known sociologist who was involved with OEO in the early years chimes in. "Then add to the mix the way academia works. A high flier in any particular department at each prestigious institution who has done work in a particular area is given the whole kingdom around that idea. The high fliers in equivalent departments at the fancy institutions defer and refer to the king. The king's graduate students, and all other graduate students in the discipline, understand that if they want a key to the kingdom, they are required to attribute all major ideas in a given domain to the king of that kingdom—their mentor or their mentor's colleagues. Lesser academics are allowed to 'discover' details, but no one may challenge what the king says. There's no room to acknowledge that non-Ph.Ds, least of all poor people, know anything crucial in a system like this."

As the years pass, this trail of attributions and citations is the only official history on the subject. Hence, for example, for the next century or so, the importance of working with a child as part of a family, and a family as part of a community, will be attributed to Cornell's Urie Bronfenbrenner, a member of the Head Start Planning Committee, although the notion that this "basic" originated with Dr. Bronfenbrenner would startle any sociologist, social psychologist, cultural anthropologist and other academics who have *always* looked at it this way and consider it odd to look only at the "mother–child dyad."

"True," laughs psychoanalyst Tom Levin, conceptualizer and founding director of the Child Development Group of Mississippi and one of the most profoundly creative, effective, and least recognized Poverty Warriors ever. "But though the developmental psychologists talk about it a lot, they don't seem to take *that* powerful relationship seriously. Because if they *did,* they'd understand why supporting mothers in strengthening themselves and in becoming effective people in their children's Head Start and in their communities is the most powerful way to ignite each child's motivation. The developmental psychologists are interested only in the superficial aspects of child development, not in complicated emotional dynamics, which are intimately entwined with parents, and make parents so powerfully influential in children's destinies. *Empowering a child's powerless parent empowers the child and is more significant than anything Head Start teachers—unless they are the children's parents or close kin—can possibly do."*

During Head Start's first summer in 1965, CDGM was the second biggest Head Start in the country (I left the government to become one of three founders and became more involved in "maximum feasible participation" of the poor), with 84 centers—organized from scratch by the poorest of the poor—dotted over 30 counties, 6,000 children, and 1.4 million dollars for community schools that people who had been earning $10 to $15 a week as sharecroppers and domestics *would run and staff themselves.* CDGM grew for the next few years after that; it had 120 centers and 12 million dollars. Parents were learning how to be health and social services coordinators, administrators, and early childhood teachers in a state that did not even have public kindergarten, and in a *part* of the state where 51% of the people earned less than $1,000 per year.

Sargent Shriver still considers CDGM the Head Start program that has done the most from then until now (though it has had three different names since the 1960s) to galvanize *extremely* poor people to *act* on behalf of their young children and to earn by learning new human services "careers" that help the children of their own economically impoverished communities.

Dick Boone, who brought the "maximum feasible participation of the poor" concept into Head Start and was its staunchest defender, has always considered CDGM the best and best publicized example ever of this philosophy in action. (The philosophy, details, dynamics, politics, and people of CDGM are documented in my 1969 book, *The Devil Has Slippery Shoes,* the first book published about Head Start, originally by MacMillan, the same publisher that published the Zigler/Valentine *Project Head Start* book 10 years later.)

I learned from Dick Boone, Tom Levin, and the impoverished people at CDGM that it's a fundamental **first** ingredient of *enabling people who do not believe that they can change their fate in any way, so do not try, to take advantage of any of the available opportunities* that allow them to inch out of poverty. This, along with an assortment of direct services to each child, is unarguably the best way to get their *children* out of poverty. As Tom Levin (1967) has written,

> Head Start must be an instrument for social change. Preschool education for communities of the poor which prepares the child for a better life without mobilizing the community for social change is an educational and sociological "fraud." New approaches to the solution of the problems of poverty are growing out of the increased awareness of self-power developing within the poverty communties. Professionals must be prepared to reject traditional donor-donee relationships which perpetuate loss of self-worth and consequent resignation to powerlessness.
>
> The child cannot be redeemed without redeeming the community. The community cannot be redeemed without application of the vigorous community organization and so-

cial action principles which are needed to achieve an imaginative, creative, and effective
Head Start program—or any other program that is addressing itself to the education, social, or health needs of the poor. (p. 880)

To insist that parent income and the multidimensional developmental opportunities
that many deprived parents guzzle up and greatly grow from are essential if lifting young
children permanently from poverty is the overarching goal, **is in no way to deny** the urgent importance of providing *high quality comprehensive* services to the children themselves.
Pitting the two goals and their proponents against one another would seem to be a subtle,
societally acceptable and probably subconscious strategy for further fracturing unity among
Head Start supporters, the media, and the public and deflecting effort from action to more
mere discussion, thus neglecting to do enough for either parents or children.

And, I learned from Sargent Shriver that good people in all walks of life would help
if faced with "the faces of poverty." (Part of my role in CDGM was to awaken northerners
to the plight of Mississippi's destitute and disenfranchised African Americans. Marian
Wright Edelman, who was on CDGM's Board of Directors, did this, too. We got an extraordinary response.)

It Is Time to Launch an All-Out War on Child Poverty

If, as a Poverty Warrior rather than as a developmental psychologist, I were evaluating
Head Start, I'd study the literature in disciplines relevant to reducing poverty—and the
tangle of problems that are both its cause and its result—for young children while they're
still young children and the literature relevant to ensuring that all American children *really*
have the "equalest" opportunities possible to grow up into a socioeconomic strata above
poverty and near-poverty levels. (Opportunities will never be completely equal unless, in
addition to everything else, we do genetic engineering, plus raise all children from birth
on in a kibbutz-type environment, which probably wouldn't work perfectly either, and neither of which I'm advocating.) Then I would investigate whether, across the nation, *every
piece* of the picture—each of which contributes a small but *only* a small amount to creating
lives safely above a poverty level, plus opportunities for quality of life improvements and/or
upward mobility (which are not synonymous)—is *all in place.* There isn't space here to discuss or even list all of them, but things like tempting options for teens other than proving
they're "successful" and adult by getting pregnant, such as family planning education and
services; prenatal care; nourishing food and complete health/ mental health care for all children up to 18 years and their parents; at least a year of parental leave and a child allowance
to supplement income for each child born; parent– child centers in all neighborhoods; adequate child neglect and abuse prevention and intervention; adequate infant/toddler, preschool, and school-age child care programs with adequately paid staff; child support payments in cases of divorce; job training; jobs; worthy wages for one and all; a progressive
income tax system; earned income tax credits; income insurance when hard times hit;
equally funded and developmentally appropriate schools that focus on "growing" the attributes of good character; practicing the virtues and values that make democratic communities work; and developing each child's interests and gifts.

When evaluating a child's learning in an educational setting, one must first evaluate what learning opportunities the child is being offered and how *well.* When evaluating

Head Start, I would first assess the quality of the support that the community is giving Head Start parents, staff, and children—the sorts of things mentioned just above and earlier in this chapter. Second, I would assess how effectively Head Start staff are offering *each individual child* learning experiences that emphasize the feelings of self-worth and the kinds of competencies and social skills that create a sense of well-being (America's preeminent social philosopher and educational philosopher, John Dewey, wrote dozens of books and articles about why and how to do this) and make good marriage partners, parents, employees, and citizens for a democracy; I would *not* freak out about academic skills and test scores. (Actually, there's even little correlation between *high school* test scores and adult income, never mind *preschool* test scores; there's also little correlation between cognitive skills and adult income, or cognitive skills and the feeling that one has a good life, or cognitive skills and being a contributing citizen. Over the years, I've looked for studies that prove any connections, but haven't found any.)

If I were evaluating Head Start, I would examine it as a tiny part of a total poverty eradication effort, as an effort to alter the current situation in which, from conception onward, some children get the gold and some get the shaft. What goes on in the classroom is a small part of what goes on in a terrific Head Start program.

CONCLUSION

The editors of this book asked me to write about the developmental psychologists *versus* the Poverty Warriors. To OEO staff, there was no "versus"; at the expense of sounding profoundly disrespectful, I've tried to illustrate that we were just on entirely different wavelengths and gave little or no thought to each other.

Many Poverty Warriors thought that parents *and* professionals would work with Head Start children, each learning from the other. Parents care more about their own children than any professional ever could. Parents have more influence on their children throughout their children's lives than any professional—who is here today, during school hours only, for a year or two, and then gone—ever could. Parents with paychecks can do more for their children than penniless parents. Professionals have a degree of expertise to offer, either in the form of modeling and discussing, or technical assistance, or connecting with movers and shakers. We thought that children *and* parents *and* professionals (e.g., early childhood teachers, social workers, health personnel) would develop (as would the developmental psychologists' research opportunities).

There would be health services *and* social services *and* generic, "developmentally appropriate" learning experiences through which children would grow physically, emotionally, socially, intellectually, and in preparedness for the joltingly different school culture they were about to enter. Remember, early childhood educators' primary goal since the 1920s has been whole-child development.

In general, we think Americans seem to be moving slowly from being mere human beings toward becoming more *humane* beings, and little by little, with some scary setbacks, our country is becoming a more humane place. We've given up owning slaves and wives, for example. We've even begun to face racism, ageism, and gender bias.

But some past and present Poverty Warriors of all ilks believe that, so far, we have avoided tackling the biggest problem of all—the gigantic disparities in power, privilege, and income between our top and bottom social classes and between our "comfortable" middle class and miserable "underclass." We believe it urgently necessary—in order to prevent the increasing unrest that surrounds us, and in order to make truer our words about equal opportunity, including equal opportunity to achieve *happiness*—that in all types of arenas, certainly including the Head Start community and the affluent *friends* of Head Start community, we begin a dialogue about the government's role in income distribution, preferably pretax via income caps and floors. If we want to eliminate poverty we can. America is extraordinarily wealthy.

Head Start, a comprehensive program for young children and families, shouldn't be judged by whether it catapults kids from the poorest of the poor to the top of the class, to corporate executives' desks, or to Congress. Head Start should be judged for what it was designed to be. With that in mind, we say: 1) All components can be improved, and 2) the basic concept, which is sometimes implemented beautifully, is right as rain on a thirsty cornfield.

REFERENCES

Dewey, J. (1900). *The child and the curriculum.* Chicago: University of Chicago Press.

Dewey, J. (1902). *The school and society.* Chicago: University of Chicago Press.

Galbraith, J.K. (1958). *The affluent society.* Boston: Houghton Mifflin.

Gillette, M.L. (1996). *Launching the War on Poverty: An oral history.* New York: Twayne.

Given a Chance. (1995). Produced by Dante J. James for Blackside as part of the PBS series, *America's War on Poverty.* Video available at many public libraries and for sale to institutions through the PBS catalog.

Greenberg, P. (1990). *The devil has slippery shoes: A biased biography of the Child Development Group of Mississippi.* Washington, DC: Youth Policy Institute. (Original work published 1969, Toronto, Ontario: MacMillan)

Levin, T. (1967). Preschool Education and the Communities of the Poor—A Report on the Child Development Group of Mississippi (pages 863–881, an appendix). Hearings before the Subcommittee on Employment, Manpower, and Poverty of the Committee on Labor and Public Welfare. Ninetieth Congress. First Session on Examining the War on Poverty. Part 2. Jackson, Mississippi. April 10, 1967. (Copies available from Polly Greenberg, 4914 Ashby Street, NW, Washington, DC 20007.)

Read, K. (1950). *The nursery school: A human relationships laboratory.* Philadelphia: W.B. Saunders.

Schorr, L.B. (1988). *Within our reach: Breaking the cycle of disadvantage.* New York: Doubleday.

Shirk, M., Bennett, N.G., & Aber, J.L. (1999). *Lives on the line: American families and the struggle to make ends meet.* Boulder, CO: Westview Press.

Taylor, K.W. (1967). *Parents and children learn together.* New York: Teachers College Press.

Zigler, E., & Valentine, J. (Eds.). (1979). *Project Head Start: A legacy of the War on Poverty.* New York: MacMillan.

CHAPTER 6

Was Head Start a Community Action Program?

Another Look at an Old Debate

CAROLYN HARMON

There is widespread agreement on these basic facts about the circumstances that led to the creation of Head Start:

- The Economic Opportunity Act of 1964 (PL 88-452), Title II—Urban and Rural Community Action Programs—established local nonprofit antipoverty agencies (later known as "the CAPs") to be operated with "maximum feasible participation" of the poor. Each CAP was expected to develop its own programs to reduce or eliminate poverty.

- By autumn of 1964, it was clear to Office of Economic Opportunity (OEO) Director Sargent Shriver that the CAPs would not be able to develop enough initiatives of their own to spend their fiscal year 1965 appropriation. For this reason—and to counteract mounting Congressional opposition to the Community Action Program—Shriver decided to fill the gap with a preschool program for poor children.

At this point, the battle over Head Start's true identity begins.

Ever since the publication of *The Devil Has Slippery Shoes,* Polly Greenberg's self-described *Biased Biography of the Child Development Group of Mississippi (CDGM)* in 1969, the notion has been making the rounds that Head Start was diverted from its true purpose as a community action program by craven liberal politicians, elitist academic developmental psychologists, and an American political system that would not tolerate true reform. In this version of history, the original Head Start Planning Committee (the Cooke Panel) proposed a limited experimental program, based on a deficit model of the poor, which was to provide compensatory education and other services to disadvantaged preschool children. The role of their parents, in this scenario, was primarily to be "improved" by

85

middle-class experts (Ellsworth & Ames, 1998; Greenberg, 1969/1990, 1998; Valentine & Stark, 1979). It was only through the intervention of unnamed planners in OEO and/or spontaneous efforts by Head Start parents that the program became a vehicle for empowering the disadvantaged to challenge oppressive social institutions, as exemplified by CDGM; but in the end, conservative forces triumphed, and Head Start was redirected to changing individual parents and children, rather than society.

A brief history of Head Start, titled *A Lost Legacy: Head Start's Origins in Community Action* (Kuntz, 1998), carries on this tradition. Kuntz argued that,

> In the beginning, Head Start was not simply a program for children. Initially, Head Start aimed at improving whole communities by giving parents and community members new opportunities to participate in the nurturing and education of their children. In its early years the program showed considerable promise as a community action effort. . . . Indeed, Head Start might have become one of the most significant community-level efforts at institutional reform in the second half of the twentieth century had it not retreated from community action. (p. 1)

Like the other critical historians,[1] Kuntz identified this retreat with Edward Zigler's actions as Director of the Office of Child Development, to which Head Start had been transferred from OEO in 1969. Specifically, Kuntz cites the 1970 restriction on use of parent activity funds for certain types of political action and new parent involvement policies that clearly established and expanded the authority of Head Start Policy Councils but required that half of their membership be reserved for *parents* of Head Start children rather than local residents in general. Her comments on the latter rule summarize the essential conflict between "poverty warriors" and child developmentalists:

> This rule ensured that councils were not filled with activists who, in Zigler's view, cared more about systemic change than the opportunities provided to a particular group of young children. Perhaps more than any other change, this one signaled that Head Start would focus on *specific children,* rather than the broader communities. (p. 29; italics added)

Kuntz conceded, as do the other critical historians, that this action was probably politically necessary for Head Start's survival, however much they deplore the fact.

It is indeed true that Zigler intended to ensure that the program's primary focus would be on improving the lives of participating children and families and that he also sought to protect Head Start from the tidal wave of criticism that threatened to engulf it by 1970. (Full disclosure: I worked as Zigler's Executive Assistant at the Office of Development, and we have been good friends for 35 years.) Otherwise, however, the critical historians' account of Head Start from its origins through the early 1970s is open to challenge on a number of grounds. In particular, these writers gloss over the inherent conflict between Head Start and community action theory, confuse statutory authority under which the program was created with specific program requirements, and ignore the well-documented disdain with which Head Start was regarded by ideologically committed staff of the Community Action Program within OEO—a disdain that was reflected to some extent at the local level. Although these writers suggest that many local Head Starts

---

[1] The writers referred to here as "critical historians" actually represent a variety of social science disciplines and professional activities, but begin from similar premises and reach similar conclusions.

were community action programs, as they loosely define the term, they rely chiefly on Greenberg's (1969/1990) account of CDGM to make the case—and then ignore the complex and nuanced story she tells about the conflicts that arise when concern for children is forced to compete with adult agendas. These conflicts, and how they led to the 1970 revisions in Head Start parent involvement policy, are the subject of this chapter.

THE THEORY OF COMMUNITY ACTION

How "community action" became the centerpiece of the War on Poverty is cogently discussed by Lemann (1988, 1989), whose conclusions are supported by published recollections of participants in the two task forces that developed antipoverty policy under Presidents Kennedy and Johnson (Gillette, 1996). In essence, neither group seriously considered the obvious ways to attack poverty—public jobs programs or direct money payments to the poor—for political and cost reasons. Thus constrained, they adopted the theory of community action, which had been introduced to the discussion by Dave Hackett, the Executive Director of the President's Committee on Juvenile Delinquency (PCJD).

This theory, which had its origins in the work of sociologists Richard Cloward and Lloyd Ohlin (1960), had been the basis of a few urban projects sponsored by the Ford Foundation and the PCJD. Essentially, it held that

- Existing government programs aimed at alleviating poverty were uncoordinated at the point of delivery.

- These programs did not address unique local circumstances because the poor were not consulted about their needs and how best to meet them.

The solution, in Lemann's summary, was that

> What poor people needed were new neighborhood-based organizations. . . . Under community action the government would set up a kind of planning board in the neighborhood, the board would consult with the poor people there, and, eventually, a mission would emerge. In principle, a community-action agency could do ANYTHING—it was not an anti-poverty program so much as a mechanism through which new anti-poverty programs would be invented. . . . The only rule was that the solution to the neighborhood's problems could not be imposed from above (that is, from Washington). (1988)

President Johnson accepted this approach to combating poverty in December 1963, and named Sargent Shriver to head the War on Poverty in February 1964, with a mandate to plan legislation. During this process, Dick Boone, a staff member of Shriver's group, introduced the famous phrase "maximum feasible participation" to ensure consultation with the poor in the direction of local community action agencies. This phrase represented Boone's addition to Community Action theory, namely: The cause of poverty was a lack of power as well as money; therefore, the cure for poverty must include *empowerment*.

In effect, "maximum feasible participation" would be the means of turning the local community action agencies into a power base from which the poor would learn to organize themselves to get what they wanted from the power structure (Lemann, 1989).

By all accounts, including Shriver's own (Gillette, 1996), the majority of participants in the War on Poverty Task Force did not intend participation of the poor to mean "control," nor did they equate "community action" and "empowerment" with encourag-

ing class warfare. The group, however, did not attempt to hammer out a precise definition of any of these terms among themselves or in the legislation presented to Congress;
they expected that experience would show what was and was not effective over time
(Lemann, 1988, 1989). The Congress that passed the Economic Opportunity Act of 1964
also did not attempt to specify exactly what was meant by "community action" or "maximum feasible participation" of the poor, thereby leaving the way clear for unending dispute. Lemann suggested an intriguing parallel:

> In 1964, when the enabling legislation for it was passed, community action was not a
> widely agree-upon cure for poverty. It stood in relation to mainstream liberalism as supply-
> side economics would to conservatism in 1981; it was an untested idea championed by a
> small group of thinkers who seized an opportunity to make it government policy. Just as
> supply-side tax cuts have never been clearly shown to do what they're supposed to do—
> increase government revenues—community action never demonstrably reduced poverty in
> a neighborhood. (1989)

He also noted—as did Kenneth B. Clark and Jeanette Hopkins (1970) in their early evaluation of local Community Action Program agencies—the perversity of expecting the ghetto
poor to end their own poverty without reference to national economic and social forces
and observed that fairly quickly the antipoverty claims for community action were scaled
back to "developing a new generation of black leaders" (Lemann, 1989).

The principle that community action programs should be locally originated to meet
local needs, however, was never really abandoned by the most ardent proponents of community action theory, which proved to be a problem for Head Start.

Head Start, the Economic Opportunity Act, and the
Community Action Program at the Office of Economic Opportunity

Sargent Shriver utilized discretionary authority available to him under Title II of the Economic Opportunity Act of 1964 to create and fund Head Start as a "Program of National
Emphasis." In 1966, Title II was amended to formally establish Head Start. Thus, Head
Start was, by statute, a "community action program." But, it is simply fatuous to claim,
as some critical historians do, that Head Start and the local CAP agencies, therefore, had
identical missions (however defined) or that adult empowerment must *by definition* have
had higher priority than comprehensive services to preschool children and their families.
Setting aside the question of what else the CAP agencies were to do, the law clearly intended that they would have service program components "to meet the needs of low-income
individuals and families" (Sec. 205[a]). (It may be useful to recall that Foster Grandparents and Upward Bound—neither of which have been cited as mighty engines of social reform—were community action programs under Title II as well.) As Sargent Shriver
has repeatedly made clear, he saw Head Start as focused on children first and interpreted
its community action dimension as parent involvement in all aspects of the program
(Shriver, 1979). The people he selected to run the program—pediatrician Dr. Julius Richmond, career administrator Jule Sugarman—and the senior staff they selected to work in
it shared this view (Gillette, 1996; Orton, 1979; Richmond, 1979; Sugarman, 1979).

The Community Action Program within OEO attracted many people who were ideologically committed to Dick Boone's more radical interpretation of community action,

however. These "CAP purists" believed that Head Start, as a "packaged service" from Washington, D.C., violated the community action principle that all CAP programs be developed locally by the poor. Sugarman stated that some CAP staff went so far as to advise local CAP agencies not to take Head Start (Gillette, 1996, pp. 230–231). Both Sugarman and Head Start staff director Richard Orton (1979) recalled that CAP staff never lost their hostility for the program. Some CAP staff seemed to have accepted Head Start as a necessary evil; Greenberg (1998) quoted a senior OEO staff member as saying that "Head Start was a temporizing measure to 'run cover' for the *real* poverty program, the one that was being mounted to break the cycle of poverty, the Community Action Program, while it converted theorizing and demonstrations into a nationwide program" (p. 57).

At the same time, a few true believers among the OEO staff were enthusiastic about the program's potential and reasoned that, even though Head Start did not *originate* at the local level, it could be made a legitimate community action program by requiring substantial parent involvement in running it. The source of the idea that Head Start was "rooted in community action" is Polly Greenberg (1969/1990, 1998), who was a mid-level staff person at OEO at the time. Greenberg, an early childhood educator who had been involved with nursery schools and community development in low-income neighborhoods, was attracted to community action theory through connections to the PCJD while employed at the U.S. Department of Education (see Chapter 5). Although she saw the preschool program proposed by Shriver as a cynical attempt to get votes, it is clear that she also cared deeply about children and saw an opportunity to achieve both community action and child development goals through a greater amount of parent involvement than she believed the Cooke Panel had recommended. In her accounts of this period, Greenberg and other OEO staff—referred to variously as "we," "rapid reformists," or "CAP people" (only Dick Boone and two others are ever mentioned by name)—"wrote into the Head Start plan requirements for heavy parent participation at every program level." She went on to state that "*Head Start would not have had its remarkable parents-as-employees-leaders-and-activists emphasis had only the Kennedy Foundation people* [i.e., members of the Cooke Panel who had previously worked with the Kennedy Foundation on mental retardation issues] *Shriver selected, and the other scholars and leaders added mainly by Jule Sugarman, been making decisions*" (1969/1990, p. 779) and accused Sargent Shriver of "removing the community action facet of Head Start's origins and intentions from history because it wasn't something *he* believed was so important" (1969/1990, p. 781).

Those assertions are best addressed by others who were there at the time. In any event, Greenberg elsewhere appears to say that the community action character of the Head Start did not outlast her personal tenure at OEO, which she left in April of 1965 to work with CDGM in Mississippi: "except for the nine-month period between Head Start's conception (October, 1964) and first center openings (June, 1965), few people at the national leadership level were interested in anything more than training parents to parent better and help staff more" (Greenberg, 1998, p. 51). (This must have been very dispiriting reading for the many Head Start staff who remained with the program and helped to develop both the first Parent Involvement Policy Guidelines in 1967 and the 1970 revisions.)

Valentine and Stark (1979) did not give OEO staff even this much credit; unlike other critical historians, they acknowledged that the Cooke Panel felt that parents should play a very important role—including decision making—in Head Start, although the panel did not attempt to spell out that role in detail. They asserted, however, that by calling for *participation* rather than *control* by the poor of programs such as Head Start, OEO fell short of the original conception of community action theory. These writers claimed that the community action character of Head Start developed only spontaneously in practice.

To summarize: Although Head Start was originally funded under the Community Action Program title of the Economic Opportunity Act, it was not considered a legitimate community action program by CAP staff at OEO. A small group of OEO staff attempted to adapt community action theory to include Head Start by emphasizing parent involvement in program decisions, but Greenberg asserted that there was no support for community action principles within the national Head Start program by the first summer of operation. Other critical historians fault "parent involvement" as insufficient to conform to the principles of community action and claim grass-roots origins for Head Start's later development into a true community action program. On the evidence, we might conclude that Head Start's "roots" in community action were rather shallow.

Community Action and the Child Development Group of Mississippi

It took enormous courage and dedication for Polly Greenberg to go to Mississippi to work with poor African Americans in the summer of 1965, to persist as she did in the face of the many obstacles she encountered there, and then to immortalize that experience with such remarkable candor. Without doubt, the very existence of CDGM was enormously valuable to the cause of freedom and equality for the viciously oppressed Black population of Mississippi. Because, however, her account of CDGM is the principle source for later claims that early Head Start was a parent-run community action program, later "stolen" from poor parents by opponents of social change (Ellsworth & Ames, 1998; Greenberg, 1998; Kuntz, 1998; Valentine & Stark, 1979), what she has to say about the theory and practice of community action within CDGM demands careful scrutiny. The following discussion relies entirely on Greenberg's *The Devil Has Slippery Shoes: A Biased Biography of the Child Development Group of Mississippi (CDGM)—A Story of Maximum Feasible Poor Parent Participation* (1969/1990) and all page citations refer to it.

The Theory   The first point to be made is that CDGM's founders—New York psychoanalyst and social activist Dr. Tom Levin, Delta Ministry Executive Director Art Thomas, and Polly Greenberg—did not envision the program as only a vehicle through which poor people would pursue abstract social change goals. In a refinement of community action theory, they saw poor African Americans of Mississippi, adults and children alike, as needing psychological empowerment in order to achieve political empowerment and social change:

> The children who were about to enter our CDGM centers tended toward passivity and individual resignation. The economic reality of their families played the major part in this. . . . Passiveness and limited aspirations were appropriate adaptations to the frustration and deprivation imposed on children by mothers who had no other choice. Mothers were also being frustrated and depressed, and also had developed passive qualities and limited aspirations. Thus the children's passivity was expected and encouraged by adults. (p. 98)

CDGM would help individual parents and children overcome these limitations by giving parents and their peers in the community the confidence-building experience of controlling the Head Start centers that served their children and also by reserving Head Start jobs exclusively for parents and members of the local poor community. The quality of services for the children was accorded great importance as well, although it would come at a slower pace to accommodate the empowerment objectives for parents. As Greenberg put it,

> CDGM was an experiment in reversing the usual Head Start procedure of classroom quality first, then attempting to work toward involving parent and community; CDGM was to begin with parents and the community—and then work toward quality in the classroom. (pp. 102–103)

This approach was believed to be most beneficial for children in the long run for several reasons: First, community action efforts by empowered parents would eliminate barriers to their children's optimal development; second, empowered parents would be better role models for their children; and third, parent control of the program would enhance its beneficial effect on children by ensuring greater continuity between program and home. As Greenberg said,

> In CDGM, the goal and efforts were primarily directed toward lifting the lid off children by prodding their parents and others in poor communities toward recognizing and developing the latent power they have, to cope with ceilings cramping their children, not by adjusting to them . . . but by cutting into them so as to provide children with a "place in the sun." (p. 40)

And with parent control:

> Children would go to people selected from their families by committee members elected by their families, where they would find reinforcement of the potential and worth of their people. CDGM children wouldn't leave homes in which parents had no opportunity for planning about the lives of their children, and no opportunities to learn and grow themselves; and go to "ideal" classrooms; and return to homes where they found parents as excluded as ever from the educational process. Instead, CDGM children would go to less "ideal" classrooms in which their parents were working out educational philosophies and techniques appropriate for changing their total lives. (p. 100)

In reality, this approach posed serious problems for Greenberg, an experienced nursery school teacher with extensive training in early childhood education. Attentive reading of *The Devil Has Slippery Shoes* reveals a great deal about how difficult it is to take the long view required by CDGM's adult empowerment and social change priorities when confronted with the immediate needs of real children in real Head Start centers.

The Practice   Greenberg was not a romantic on the subject of the poor and expected that training and (unobtrusive) guidance by experts such as herself would be required to achieve both the adult empowerment and program quality goals she had for CDGM. She is at pains to point out that CDGM was not created or managed by the poor themselves. In her words,

> Freedom requires a framework. Many of the poor of course are able to discuss and decide what programs they want . . . but many of the poor have not evidenced that ability yet, for reasons which must be corrected, to outline the procedures, propose the schemes, and

make the comprehensive schedules that will free them to pursue their goal; and *this* is a fact frequently skirted by Movement workers. We who wanted so much for CDGM to be what it was because of the poor alone, sometimes let our prejudices and needs edit our perceptions and memories so that we quite sincerely believed that the poor alone *did* create CDGM. This was not true. Somebody had to think about these administrative things for CDGM. (pp. 44–45)

Local poor African American parents of preschool children and other poor people from the community did indeed, by all accounts, form committees to hire staff, get facilities, and enroll children in Head Start centers for the summer of 1965, and the centers were operated through these committees thereafter. In her later writing, Greenberg (1998) has stated that during the life of CDGM, more than 900 parents served on committees that operated more than 140 centers, and more than 2,200 people were employed at some time by the centers. However, from its inception through its defunding and reorganization by OEO in 1967, CDGM policy and budgets were controlled by a board that was not elected by local communities. Founders of the group intended to create a community-elected Council of Neighborhood Centers to counterbalance the board and to hold elections for community seats on the board itself, but this did not come to pass for reasons to be discussed next. Greenberg's job was Director of Teacher Development and the Program for Children, and she frequently expressed frustration at the lack of interest in the content of the program on the part of the CDGM board and its second Executive Director, John Mudd (pp. 340; 366–367; 480–482; 497–498), even to the point of agreeing with OEO critics that "under John Mudd the education part of CDGM was a stepchild" (p. 498).

Greenberg's most significant struggles in developing a quality program, however, were with most of the CDGM staff and their allies in the community who were more radical than she. In a telling comment, she describes these "Movement" people as "people with strong civil rights backgrounds, mostly from out of state, to whom the project's importance *wasn't its nursery school activities but rather its long range political significance*" (pp. 268–269; italics added). It is clear from her narrative that Greenberg was constantly struggling against those who saw her desire for program quality as a violation of the community action principle of self-determination by the poor. The conflict between these competing perspectives arose over and over again. Some examples include

1. The use of Standard American English in curriculum materials—Greenberg felt that ease with use of Standard American English was essential for Head Start children's success in school and in the wider society; she was challenged by staff who believed that materials should reflect "the people's language" (p. 169); in this case she prevailed.

2. Teacher qualifications and training—Although CDGM has become a virtual icon for some critical historians' belief that warm, local community people needed no other qualifications to work with Head Start children, Greenberg fought bitterly against this view within CDGM. She clearly rejected as "uninformed" the notion that when it comes to teaching little kids "anybody can do it" and wanted to establish training and performance criteria for advancement of Head Start classroom staff beyond entry-level jobs. For this, she says, her colleagues at CDGM saw her as "against jobs for the needy, and in favor of absurdly unnecessary nuances and abilities—'unnecessary' because not understood in relation to freedom goals" (p. 480). She quickly found that local Head Start committees

had not always chosen teachers wisely, and she wanted to weed out the worst of these teachers, whom she found to be "incorrigibly cruel, dull, or selfish" (p. 480). However, she never won staff or board support for the proposed personnel standards and merit-based teacher salary scale needed to ensure that Head Start classroom staff would be competent to work with young children. Even during the second CDGM grant (1965–1966) "The ruiners continued to teach with the inspirers. . . . I was the culprit, because, as Mrs. S put it: 'You likes some to teach bad, and you stamps it with approval, because you pays them the same, no matter what they does'" (pp. 480–481).

3. Establishing and enforcing minimum quality standards—Greenberg and her staff were extremely hesitant to insist on minimum standards for the children's program, partly because of their own beliefs and partly due to opposition. Staff argued about "where to let standards . . . sag in order to allow communities to develop their own common-sense standards" (p. 143), but when they did insist on changes "because of the distress we felt for the children suffering through the program or because of the anxiety we felt lest OEO shut down the sad center" (p. 230), they were resented by the local Head Start committee and did so only in extreme cases. Indeed, Greenberg estimated that, at the end of the first summer, more than 20% of the centers were "pretty terrible" (p. 241).

Ultimately, Greenberg felt that her opponents questioned the legitimacy of nonpoor professional staff doing anything at all (which is, it could be argued, a logical extension of her frequently expressed disdain for experts):

> Is it a lack of confidence in the poor to provide information? Insult to admit that the poor don't know everything yet? Condescending to teach as well as to be friends and coequals? Intimidating to introduce choices and alternatives? Most of the CDGM central and mid-level staff answered YES. I answered NO. (p. 248)

A more specific clash arose between interests of the Community Organization staff of CDGM and (let's call it) the child developmentalist group. Greenberg said that the organization's first Director of Community Organization actively undermined her efforts in the community by telling local Head Start hiring committees that "no qualifications were required to teach, parents knew best, and so on" (p. 60). At a workshop to orient newly hired Area Administrators and Community Organizers—where she was given only 1 hour of a 2-day agenda—Greenberg observed that

> There was little evidence that they saw any sense of linking these interests with a kindergarten program. Those that didn't consider the Head Start altogether irrelevant to their purposes saw it as "a good thing"; primarily because of the food, and secondarily because it would be sort of fun for the children. (p. 436)

And during a later workshop in March 1966,

> Community organizers seemed very resentful of any emphasis on the preschool part of CDGM. Somehow, someone, somewhere, had failed to promote the fact that this was what Head Start was all about, and that we were, in effect, "getting away with" anything else. (p. 489)

Adding to her grievance, after the summer of 1965, there were twice as many staff for community organizing than field staff for teacher development and the children's program (p. 594).

Surprisingly, the *Community Organization* component of CDGM never developed. The Director of Community Organization/Social Services was responsible for organizing and training Head Start parents and others in their community to identify problems and resources to address them—"including all things preventing communities from growing or available to aid them in doing so" (p. 428). The examples Greenberg provides—welfare laws, FHA loans, legal aid, credit unions, health clinics, and so forth—could have been provided by Sargent Shriver and suggest that CDGM's leaders had a much less confrontational view of community action activities than came to define the concept later on. However, the first Director of Community Organization—a veteran of the Southern Nonviolent Coordinating Committee, which in the summer of 1965 was already moving toward Black Separatism—opposed CDGM at the outset "because he claimed to be interested in organizing communities," (p. 24) and his employment there was essentially a bribe to prevent him from mobilizing his allies to oppose it. Greenberg said that this individual organized desegregation sit-ins and other civil rights activities in the community independently of CDGM but did no work for the program and actively undermined the professional staff during his summer of employment there (pp. 60–61, 290–291). No effective person was subsequently found for the job; as a result, the Community Organizers in the field received no training or direction and became alienated from the central staff (pp. 594–595). Because that function was not performed, Greenberg said, Head Start parents were not given the tools for effective community action as envisioned by CDGM's originators. She also cited the failure of the Community Organization staff for lack of progress toward more significant control of CDGM by the local poor—specifically, the local Head Start Committees never took the opportunity to become directly involved in writing proposals for funding, and a planned process for election of representatives to the Board of CDGM and creation of a Council of Neighborhood Centers never materialized (pp. 290, 367, 426). One significant instance of organized political action did take place in 1966, when CDGM parents and children went to Washington, D.C., to protest the threatened loss of funds to their program (pp. 437–457)—the type of activity that Head Start parents from all over the nation have engaged in from the beginning to this day.

So it seems that whatever CDGM did to so antagonize Senator Stennis and the white political establishment of Mississippi, it wasn't the kind of community action that the critical historians seem to have in mind—at least according to Greenberg. Sargent Shriver says that it was CDGM's role as a spearhead of the civil rights movement—of which he was quite supportive—that provoked the wrath of Stennis and others and eventually jeopardized the continued existence of OEO and all its programs (Zigler & Valentine, 1979, p. 62). Greenberg is curiously elusive about CDGM's civil rights activities, although she did make the claim that CDGM was more effective at mobilizing poor African Americans statewide than the Freedom Democratic Party (pp. 674–681).

Parent involvement also did not develop as Greenberg had hoped. She had pushed for parent involvement in the "actual children's program" but reports that, "Although some parents taught, were on committees, in on policy decisions, many parents were still *sending their children* to the center" (p. 498). Greenberg wanted to insist that any child attending the program must have a family member willing to be scheduled to serve as a regular volunteer while the children were in session so the family member could get

"some of the feeling of a freedom program" (p. 499) and learn more about educational possibilities with which to push the public schools toward improvement. Although she
"wasn't for requirements," Greenberg believed that parents should be more formally pres-
sured to participate, a position that the Board of CDGM did not accept. In summing up
this problem, Greenberg sadly concluded that, "In many communities there was far less
involvement than CDGM liked to admit; some of it inevitable; some correctable, had we
concentrated on it" (p. 490). Part of the problem, she claimed, was that the Community
Organizers felt parents were their property; and while they jealously guarded their turf
against encroachment by Greenberg and her staff, they did nothing to increase parent involvement in their children's classrooms. But, problems with involving overburdened
poor parents in Head Start on a regular basis are all too common everywhere; there is no
doubt that the CDGM program was much loved and a great source of pride among the
impoverished African American population of Mississippi, many of whom are movingly
quoted in *The Devil Has Slippery Shoes*.

Greenberg's struggles to balance her belief in community action principles with her
child developmentalist objectives became acute when, in early 1966, she made a decision
that was seen as usurping the authority of the local Head Start committees and area staff
members (pp. 502–505). In the ensuing uproar, Greenberg's decision was overridden
(pp. 534–539), and she left CDGM in June 1966 "shrouded in [a] cloud of suspicious
hostility" (p. 658). It is good to be able to report that 25 years later she received a certificate of appreciation from CDGM for her contributions (p. 707).

To summarize: Although CDGM is cited by all critical historians (including Greenberg herself) to make the case that Head Start was a community action program controlled by the poor and dedicated to changing society, a close reading of her lengthy account presents a more complicated and instructive picture. The founders of CDGM
assumed that parent control of the program at the center level would produce changes in
individual confidence and motivation needed for political empowerment and social
change; parents and their community peers were *not* involved in CDGM's centralized
administration, budgeting, policy making, or proposal writing. The founders of CDGM
believed that a *quality preschool program,* developed through a *collaboration* of parent-
employees and professionals, and with regular volunteer parent involvement, was very
important for the present and future life of each child enrolled in the program, but fewer
parents were directly involved with the program than Greenberg desired or than critical
historians seem to believe. Efforts to achieve empowerment and child development objectives clashed when put to the test; the conflict was greatly exacerbated by CDGM staff
who held more radical views than Greenberg of the community action principle of self-
determination and who saw the children's program as only incidental to their system
change goals. As a result, quality of services at some centers was very poor, but, according to Greenberg, so was community organizing for system change. Training and organizing the poor to make existing social institutions more responsive to their needs did not
take place as planned, although CDGM children and families did participate in an effort
to restore funding for the program. Despite these problems, CDGM was still an important source of pride, material improvement, and the beginnings of empowerment for
many poor African Americans in Mississippi.

If this is a fair reading of Greenberg's account, then CDGM was less an icon of community action, as the critical historians understand it, than a caution against placing abstract social change ideologies above the interests of children and families. In many respects, CDGM presents a microcosm of the conflicts over Head Start that Zigler sought to resolve in 1970.

HEAD START, 1970: COMMUNITY ACTION, THE CAPS, AND PARENT INVOLVEMENT

It seems amazing today that there were no systematic efforts to identify the actual extent and types of conflicts concerning Head Start at the local level between 1965 and 1970 (although it is less amazing when we stop to consider the enormous demands placed on national and regional program administrators, the pressures to focus on outcomes, and the difficulty of collecting and analyzing data before the existence of networked personal computers); but as a result, any generalizations about these conflicts must be offered with the understanding that now, as at the time, we can only try to do the best we can with the information available.

Background

In 1969, Head Start was transferred to the Office of Child Development (OCD), a new agency within the Department of Health, Education and Welfare. Zigler became director of OCD in 1970. The program was still authorized and funded under Title II of the Economic Opportunity Act, and local CAP agencies were the presumptive first choice as Head Start grantees. The CAPs could "delegate" program operations to a local nonprofit organization or public school system, and most did so; the "delegate agencies" then operated one or more Head Start centers in the area served by the CAP. Because a Head Start grant application required CAP approval, CAPs had considerable power over program operations if they chose to use it. Every center had its own Parent Advisory Committee, and there were comparable Policy Advisory Councils (PACs) at the Delegate Agency and CAP level. Fifty percent of the members of each of these groups were to be Head Start parents, with the remainder made up of representatives of various public and private organizations or professionals who had a concern for children. (This arrangement often posed the sticky question of "who *really* speaks for the poor?" Kuntz [1998] examined a 1971 case in which a hiring dispute between the Milwaukee CAP and Head Start parents was resolved by federal administrators in favor of the CAP and concluded that this signaled a *retreat* from community action.)

The responsibilities of PACs and other policies concerning parent involvement in the program were first set forth in 1967 policy guidelines developed under the leadership of Bessie Draper, who had joined Head Start as its first Parent Involvement Specialist in 1966. As Zigler has noted (Zigler & Muenchow, 1992), it was Draper more than anyone else who gave operational meaning to the idea of parent involvement. Draper was neither an early childhood educator nor a "CAP person" and brought a common-sense approach to the issue that parents and professionals alike welcomed, namely because poor people generally do not possess the skills needed to run the program alone, parent involvement necessarily meant *participation* in partnership with professionals, rather than *control;* but she also believed that Head Start had an affirmative responsibility to ensure opportunities for participation in decision making and to help parents develop skills with which to capitalize on these opportunities within the program and throughout their lives. To this end, parents were encouraged to develop their own projects, and Parent Activity funds were available to support them.

Major Conflicts

Not surprisingly, there were many conflicts and much competition for control of various aspects of Head Start between CAPs and Delegate Agencies, between Head Start program staff and parents, among parents, and in endless other combinations and permutations. The most significant conflicts mirrored those Greenberg described at CDGM, with some CAPs and their allies on Head Start Advisory Committees taking the role played by the "movement workers" in her account.

First, although many Head Start parents wanted a greater voice in personnel decisions, some Parent Advisory Councils—primarily from large, urban communities—were demanding "control" of the program. Whereas to some this meant an expansion of their authority into more aspects of program operation, at the extreme such demands seemed to call for ejection of professionals altogether and a free hand to run the program with no outside standards or oversight (Valentine & Stark, 1979). The implications of the latter position for minimally adequate children's services were seen in Greenberg's account. (On the other hand, Head Start programs operated by school boards were more often resistant to the level of parent involvement prescribed in the 1967 Head Start policy guidelines. This situation demanded more assertiveness and persistence than parents unaccustomed to dealing with professionals as equals could always bring to bear.) Despite Bessie Draper's best efforts, the 1967 parent involvement guidelines did not provide enough detail to be clearly enforceable, and conflicts of both types were difficult to resolve.

Second, there were conflicts between Head Start programs, both staff and parents, over CAP interference in personnel decisions. Some CAPs, whether for ideological or purely practical political reasons, treated Head Start as a jobs program. Like the Movement workers at CDGM, they did not believe that any special qualifications were required to work with young children in groups and insisted that delegate agencies hire individuals who were unqualified or, at worst, unsuited to work in a children's program in any capacity (Zigler & Muenchow, 1992). Parents' preferences concerning personnel could be ignored by the CAPs (or any Head Start delegate agency) because parents had only an advisory role in staff selection at that time.

The third conflict involved the use of Head Start's name and funds for confrontational social activism by local CAPs and their allies on Head Start Policy Advisory Councils and paralleled the competition between system change and quality children's services agendas that run through Greenberg's account of CDGM. As Lemann observed of the CAPs, there were many—both urban and rural—that led a "relatively quiet existence" (1989). It was a smaller group of CAPs located mainly in large urban ghettoes that engaged in the militant confrontational tactics and threatening rhetoric that gave CAPs the radical image that alienated much of the public and Congress. By 1970, Zigler was alarmed to find that many members of Congress had come to believe the Community Action Program funds—including Head Start's—were supporting militant efforts to disrupt society and made it clear that they wanted this to stop (Zigler & Muenchow, 1992).

To the extent that local Head Start funds were actually used for confrontational protest tactics, this did not have unanimous and enthusiastic support from parents. Indeed, many parents of children enrolled in such programs complained to their Congressmen, who in turn complained to Zigler at an informal meeting early in 1970. For example, parents were upset that Parent Activity funds needed for other purposes had been consumed by the cost of protest activities with which they disagreed. Another allegation concerned CAP use of Parent Activity funds to pay for a controversial form of interpersonal skills training known at the time as "T-Groups." (Unsurprisingly, parents could find no relationship between this activity and Head Start, nor did individual Congressmen; E. Zigler, personal communication, November 15, 2000). However representative or accurate these complaints may have been, their credibility was enhanced by Bessie Draper's observations concerning the actual composition of the 50% parent membership on Parent Advisory Councils. In the course of extensive visits to local programs as national Head Start Parent Involvement Specialist, Draper had discovered many cases in which "parent" members were in fact social activists who had no children in Head Start and who were occupying a seat on the Council to advance their own agendas (Zigler & Muenchow, 1992). Although they had no stake in the program, they were in a position to exert considerable influence on the use of Parent Activity funds.

Concerned about Head Start's survival (having recently learned that the Nixon administration was considering the elimination of Head Start within 3 years), Zigler rather quickly issued a directive forbidding the use of Parent Activity funds for demonstrations, sit-ins, and other "disruptive" forms of protest. This decision was not universally popular, but it did not engender concerted opposition among Head Start parents either. They were not silenced, as evidenced by numerous mass meetings and delegations that year to protest what concerned them most—threatened cuts in the Head Start budget. Their response suggests that "changing the system," however much some might have desired it, was not seen by parents as the highest priority for the program. By contrast, some CAPs were outraged by Zigler's limitations of the use of Parent Activity funds, which led to a meeting in Washington, D.C., at which they presented him with several "nonnegotiable demands." It was at the conclusion of this meeting that one CAP delegate declared his willingness to "sacrifice a generation of children" in order to achieve systemic change (Zigler & Muenchow, 1992, p. 111). It is doubtful that many parents of the children to be sacrificed would have shared this view, and it confirmed Zigler's belief that parents—not CAP activists—were the best advocates for their own children. Strengthening the role of Head Start parents in decision making was, therefore, the next step.

Parent Involvement Policy Changes

Zigler has presented his own thoughts about poor parents and their role in Head Start in publications too numerous to mention here, without impressing those critical historians who continue to assert that he (and academic psychologists in general) believed that "bad parents" were the problem to which Head Start was the solution. As a point of personal privilege, I want to state for the record that Zigler—whose own parents were poor and powerless immigrants—has always had the highest respect for poor parents and their determination to do the best for their children under incredibly difficult circumstances. Having witnessed countless meetings between Zigler and Head Start parents, I am confident that all of them—including those with whom he strenuously disagreed—felt that respect and returned it. Moreover, like any good psychologist, he has always appreciated the enormous effect of parents as role models for their children and (much like Greenberg, actually) believed that experiences that promote feelings of self-worth and personal effectance in the parent are therefore good for their children as well. These beliefs were shared by the many members of the Head Start community who collaborated in the effort to strengthen the role of parents in the program.

Zigler asked Bessie Draper to develop a revised parent involvement policy for Head Start that would address the conflicts described previously. Under Draper's extraordinarily deft leadership, Head Start Policy 70.2 was created and issued in 1970. To signal the enhanced role of parents in the program, PACs were renamed Head Start Policy Councils. Key provisions of the new policy that strengthened the hand of Head Start parents included the following:

- Policy Councils were formally included in personnel decisions at the delegate agency and grantee (CAP) level, with power to approve or disapprove hiring and firing of the Head Start director at each level.

- Policy Councils were given new authority to approve or disapprove program budgets.

- Policy Council membership was modified to require that at least 50% of the members be parents of Head Start children currently enrolled in the program. The intended effect of this requirement was to avoid dilution of parent influence by people who had no direct stake in the program and also to ensure that each generation of Head Start parents would have the same opportunities to develop their leadership skills as those who preceded them.

- The policy also included a chart detailing the respective roles of delegate and grantee agency boards, policy committees, and Head Start directors; it made clear those areas in which parents must be consulted, where they had operating responsibility, and where they had power to approve or disapprove. This had the effect of making parent involvement policy both more coherent and enforceable.

Contrary to the assertions of the critical historians (e.g., Kuntz, 1998), parents were *not* discouraged from using Parent Activity funds to address community problems. The policy explicitly mentions their use for "common concerns, such as health, education, welfare, and housing" (Zigler & Muenchow, 1992, p. 113). It did, however, require that Head Start program proposals make a specific request for parent activity funds and provide a general explanation of how they would be used.

It was less than some parents had wanted but created opportunities that had not been available to many. The fact that some school boards resisted so strongly—and more than one major school-operated Head Start grant was defunded—testifies to that fact. The question for the critical historians to answer is: Did parents—or society—actually lose something in the process?

CONCLUSION

Community action theory and "CAP purists" at OEO had no use for Head Start; that much seems clear. That a Head Start which was identified with radical activism—in plain English, the Black Power Movement—would not have survived in the political climate of the early 1970s seems to be accepted even by the critical historians. But what of the critical historians' belief that Head Start was a community action program, run by the poor with the goal of changing society? Exhibit A—CDGM—does not really bear them out in many important respects. According to Greenberg, at least, the primary goals of CDGM were subtle and developmental—to bring about psychological empowerment among poor African Americans in Mississippi through a quality developmental preschool program in which parents played a central role. The child development goals of the program were rejected by "Movement" staff and their allies who took the more radical system change view espoused by the critical historians, to the detriment of program quality; but they did not do any community organizing or training with local poor people. The only political activism by CDGM community members Greenberg reports was in defense of the Head Start program.

To ask the question another way: Did the 1970 parent involvement policy actually end parent activism where it had existed before? If anyone knew how much actual "community action" by Head Start parents that was not directly related to the program itself occurred before and after 1970, it would be helpful, but systematic information is not available. Parents' activism around Head Start certainly continued unabated and was given the structure needed for even more effectiveness with the formation of the National Head Start Association in the 1970s. But, were they activists for Head Start because they couldn't be activists for system change? The critical historians almost seem to say that the only avenue of protest, organizing, and power for the poor was Head Start—but it wasn't, and isn't.

Certainly, many poor people have had more power to act in their children's behalf, and improve their own lives, through participation in Head Start than they had before. Everyone who worked to transform parent involvement from an idea to a reality, however different his or her perspectives, deserves our respect. Whether Head Start today is as effective as it could be in ensuring meaningful parent involvement and responding to the very different challenges facing the families served in the 21st century, and what it should try to do in the future, are questions that should engage everyone who cares about children. The major lesson we can take from the evidence available to us now is that when adult ideologies compete with children's needs, society rarely gains but children almost certainly lose. Perhaps it's time to end the community action/child development debate and move on.

REFERENCES

Clark, K.B., & Hopkins, J. (1970). *A relevant war against poverty: A study of Community Action Programs and observable social change.* New York: Harper & Row.

Cloward, R.A., & Ohlin, L.E. (1960). *Delinquency and opportunity: A theory of delinquent gangs.* New York: Free Press.

Economic Opportunity Act of 1964, PL 88-452, 42 U.S.C. §§ 2701 *et seq.*

Ellsworth, J., & Ames, L.J. (Eds.). (1998). *Critical perspectives on Project Head Start: Revisioning the hope and challenge* (Introduction, pp. vii–xvii). Albany: State University of New York Press.

Gillette, M.L. (Ed.). (1996). *Launching the War on Poverty: An oral history.* New York: Twayne/Simon and Schuster Macmillan.

Greenberg, P. (1990). *The devil has slippery shoes: A biased biography of the Child Development Group of Mississippi (CDGM)—A story of maximum feasible poor parent participation.* Washington, DC: Youth Policy Institute. (Original work published 1969, Toronto, Ontario: MacMillan)

Greenberg, P. (1998). The origins of Head Start and the two versions of parent involvement: How much parent participation in early childhood programs and services for poor children? In J. Ellsworth & L.J. Ames (Eds.), *Critical perspectives on Project Head Start: Revisioning the hope and challenge.* Albany: State University of New York Press.

Kuntz, K.R. (1998). A lost legacy: Head Start's origins in community action. In J. Ellsworth & L. J. Ames (Eds.), *Critical perspectives on Project Head Start: Revisioning the hope and challenge* (pp. 1–48). Albany: State University of New York Press.

Lemann, N. (1988, December). The unfinished war [Electronic version]. *The Atlantic Monthly, 262*(6). Available from http://www.theatlantic.com/politics/poverty/lemunf1.htm

Lemann, N. (1989, January). The unfinished war [Electronic version]. *The Atlantic Monthly, 263*(1). Available from http://www.theatlantic.com/politics/poverty/lemunf2.htm

Orton, R.E. (1979). [Editorial introduction in] Head Start, a retrospective view: The founders. In E. Zigler & J. Valentine (Eds.), *Project Head Start: A legacy of the War on Poverty* (pp. 129–134). New York: Free Press.

Richmond, J.B. (1979). [Editorial introduction in] Head Start, a retrospective view: The founders. In E. Zigler & J. Valentine (Eds.), *Project Head Start: A legacy of the War on Poverty* (pp. 120–128). New York: Free Press.

Shriver, S. (1979). [Editorial introduction in] Head Start, a retrospective view: The founders. In E. Zigler & J. Valentine (Eds.), *Project Head Start: A legacy of the War on Poverty* (pp. 49–67). New York: Free Press.

Sugarman, J. (1979). [Editorial introduction in] Head Start, a retrospective view: The founders. In E. Zigler & J. Valentine (Eds.), *Project Head Start: A legacy of the War on Poverty* (pp. 114–120). New York: Free Press.

Valentine, J., & Stark, E. (1979). The social context of parent involvement in Head Start. In E. Zigler & J. Valentine (Eds.), *Project Head Start: A legacy of the War on Poverty* (pp. 291–313). New York: Free Press.

Zigler, E., & Muenchow, S. (1992). *Head Start: The inside story of America's most successful educational experiment.* New York: Basic Books.

Zigler, E., & Valentine, J. (Eds.). (1979). *Project Head Start: A legacy of the War on Poverty.* New York: Free Press.

CHAPTER 7

An Early Administrator's Perspective on Head Start

JULIUS B. RICHMOND[1]

The early months of the War on Poverty created by the passage of the Economic Opportunity Act of 1964 (PL 88-452) were exciting. The civil rights revolution and the aftermath of President Kennedy's assassination and President Johnson's election in 1964 generated a political will and deep social commitment to equity and social justice.

Greenberg's chapter (Chapter 5) describes one "Poverty Warrior's" perception of what took place in those early months. Greenberg is at her best in describing the impact of poverty on young children and their families. Indeed there was a national consensus that this was an important national problem. Mr. Sargent Shriver, as the first Director of the Office of Economic Opportunity (OEO), seized the opportunity to propose a nationwide early childhood program targeted at children from low-income families, which came to be known as Head Start. Although Greenberg's perceptions of how this was implemented are important for the historical record, it is fair to say that no person knew how all the pieces fit together, although Mr. Shriver and Richard Boone, his Director of the Division of Policy and Development, had a better grasp than most. But the impetus for an early childhood program came from a great many people including Mary Bunting, then President of Radcliff College, and Susan Gray of Peabody College for Teachers. In October of 1964, Polly Greenberg sent a staff memo to Mr. Shriver encouraging OEO to establish an early childhood program.

Based on dozens of similar recommendations, Mr. Shriver asked Jule Sugarman, Deputy Associate Director of OEO, to work with Robert Cooke, M.D., to formulate recommendations for such a program. Cooke was then Chairman of Pediatrics at the Johns Hopkins Medical School and an active member of the President's Commission on Mental Retardation. Greenberg was not involved in the work of the Planning Committee but later became involved in Head Start operational issues, first as the Senior Program Ana-

---

[1]See pp. 108–109 for commentary by Jule M. Sugarman.

lyst for the Southeast Region and shortly thereafter as one of the founders of the very creative Child Development Group of Mississippi.

The Planning Committee included individuals with professional backgrounds in medicine, public health, nursing, social services, psychology, civil rights, education, and teacher training. Dr. Edward Zigler was an active member who, 5 years later, became the Director of the Office of Child Development, the agency responsible for Head Start. Jule Sugarman served as the Executive Director of the Planning Committee and later became the Associate Director in charge of operations for Head Start. The committee was vigorous, courageous, resourceful, and innovative. It began its work in December, 1964, and, after eight meetings over a 6-week period, had a report completed by early February, 1965.

Indeed, the report of the committee is a refutation of Greenberg's repetitive theme that professionals in the field of early childhood development—especially academics—were opposed to the program. Although it was true that a few people she mentions (Professors Bruner and Bloom and Cynthia and Martin Deutsch) may have been cautious about proceeding on a large scale, the 15 members of the planning committee and the many professionals across the country, as well as I, felt we knew enough about young children and their families to move forward on a program for all disadvantaged children. It is unfortunate that Greenberg misses the feelings of optimism and exhilaration in the academic community. How else could we explain the willingness of the American Academy of Pediatrics to mobilize its members—on short notice—to provide consultation across the country to develop sound health programs or the resourcefulness with which university extension services established intensive training programs in early childhood education during the spring of 1965 to ensure an adequate supply of early childhood teachers for the first summer program?

But we can hear this best from the historic papers of the Planning Committee:

> There is considerable evidence that the early years of childhood are the most critical point in the poverty cycle. During these years the creation of learning patterns, emotional development, and the formation of individual expectations and aspirations take place at a very rapid pace. For the child of poverty there are clearly observable deficiencies in the processes, which lay the foundation for a pattern of failure—and thus a pattern of poverty—throughout the child's entire life.
>
> Within recent years there has been experimentation and research designed to improve opportunities for the child of poverty. While much of this work is not yet complete there is adequate evidence to support the view that special programs can be devised for these four-and five-year-olds that will improve both the child's opportunities and achievements.
>
> It is clear that successful programs of this type must be comprehensive, involving activities generally associated with the fields of health, social services and education. Similarly, it is clear that the program must focus on the problems of child and parent and that these activities need to be carefully integrated with programs for the school year. . . . The Office of Economic Opportunity should generally avoid financing programs that do not have at least a minimum level and quality of activities from each of the three fields of effort.
>
> The need for and urgency of these programs is such that they should be initiated immediately. Many programs could begin in the summer of 1965. These would help provide a more complete picture of national needs for use in future planning. (U.S. Department of Health, Education and Welfare, 1965)

Perhaps the most noteworthy aspect of the report was its emphasis on a "comprehensive child development program." This was especially significant because of the many disciplines represented among the committee members. Their sophistication was such that they recognized that no single approach would be adequate to meet the needs of these children. They were solidly in support of requiring health services, nutrition, social services, and parent participation as well as the more traditional developmental activities. In retrospect, these initial emphases have had an enduring impact, and they prevail in spite of many efforts over the years to cast Head Start exclusively as an early education or cognitive stimulation program. The committee was well aware of the importance of the first 3 years of life but felt that not enough was known about programs that might meet their needs. In 1967, 36 Parent and Child Centers were funded to address these age levels.

Although I had been aware of the work of the Planning Committee because I had friends on the committee, it came as a surprise to me when Mr. Shriver, in early February 1965, asked me to become the first director. Along with Mr. Shriver and members of the Planning Committee, I recognized the historic opportunity before us. Even though it meant disrupting my academic pursuits, because the commitment was made for a nationwide summer program only 5 months away, I dropped what I was doing and went to Washington, D.C.

Although it may appear to be defensive, I must disagree with Greenberg that I was the "nominal" director of the program. For the first 18 months I was director, I spent every waking hour to help launch Head Start along with OEO's Neighborhood Health Center Program. Those efforts were interrupted by a bout of pulmonary tuberculosis.

I was extremely fortunate to find on the scene Jule Sugarman, one of the most creative and talented managers I have ever known. Because I had little knowledge of the federal bureaucracy, Sugarman's knowledge, experience, and talents proved indispensable. As a career civil servant, he had always sought assignment to innovative programs, and he was deeply committed. Having an aversion to usual governmental titles such as "deputy," I designated him "associate director" of the program. The early days of the Head Start Program involved much decision making that would have impacts on its long-term evolution. Once a decision had been made to implement the recommendations of the Advisory Committee, by then called the Steering Committee, the questions arose: How soon? How large? How comprehensive? How feasible?

At the suggestion of Holmes Brown and Herb Kramer, successively OEO's Directors of Public Affairs, we launched a massive campaign to encourage communities to apply. This brought forth a remarkable response. Because diversity of auspices at the local level was believed to be desirable, applications came forth from social agencies, schools, health and welfare departments, and newly developing community action agencies. The requirement that each program needed to have a governing board of citizens from the community stimulated enthusiasm and feelings of empowerment among people who had never experienced participation in organized community programs. (It is of interest to note that former President Carter describes his first involvement in community affairs on returning to Georgia from naval service as serving on the local Head Start board.) This was an effort to implement the provision of the OEO legislation for "maximum feasible participation of the poor," which we took very seriously.

The OEO legislation also made possible the direct involvement of local community agencies with the national offices, without having to go through state agencies, a unique arrangement for federal programs. The only possible constraint at the state level was the option for a governor to veto a program. This didn't happen because governors generally wished to have the resources flow to their states. In Mississippi, where there was apprehension that the governor might veto a creative proposal for a statewide program, a college sponsor was found for the program (Mary Holmes Junior College) because the legislation exempted programs from the governor's review if they were under the auspices of an "institution of higher education."

Another feature of the OEO legislation was that technical assistance be provided to communities to help them establish programs. Jule Sugarman arranged for child development experts from the universities to team up with volunteers from the corps of civil service interns for management backup to help develop applications and capacity to organize programs. (It was not uncommon for these teams to return to us with handwritten applications.) We made a particular effort to target the 300 poorest counties in the nation; approximately 240 of them succeeded in developing a program. This outreach was facilitated by enlisting congressional spouses under the leadership of Lindy Boggs (who would later be elected to Congress to succeed her husband after his untimely death) to stimulate interest in their districts. Sugarman arranged a band of telephones (WATTS lines were a rarity in those days) to call key figures in their districts. This proved to be remarkably effective.

The timetable that had been set seemed impossible, but Jule Sugarman's creative management enabled us to solve problems sequentially. The first move was to send some 40,000 letters to public officials and to private agencies around the country describing the program and asking that an enclosed postcard be returned as an expression of community interest. As the cards were returning in large numbers, one of Mr. Shriver's executive staff who had campaigned for Senator Kefauver in the presidential primaries in 1952, in flipping through the cards said, "I haven't heard of these places since the Kefauver campaign."

We were very indebted to three early childhood educators who dropped their daily responsibilities to come to Washington, D.C., to help us. Keith Osborn, now at the University of Georgia, and William Rioux from the Merrill Palmer Institute helped us generate publications on curriculum. They also worked far into the night responding to requests for consultation on setting up programs. Their colleague, James Hymes Jr., who was a member of the Planning Committee and a professor at the University of Maryland, reviewed the standards for the program. He reminded us constantly of the need to have well-trained teachers. Because there was no possibility of having enough trained teachers, we relied on an intensive 10-day training program for elementary school teachers to provide professional guidance for the summer programs and to supervise the two teacher assistants who were to constitute the team for a group of 15 children. The Association of University Extension Programs mobilized its membership across the country to accomplish what seemed an impossible task.

Because relatively few teacher-training materials were available, we had to produce our own. Fortunately, I knew that Professor L. Joseph Stone of Vassar College had been making films of early childhood development, and I invited him to join us. He, along with a colleague on loan from IBM in Poughkeepsie, did the unbelievable job of producing 13 training films in 1 month. Stone's expertise in child development enabled him to use the "voice-over" technique. As he directed his cameraman to film aspects of child behavior, he would simultaneously provide interpretation for trainees concerning the meaning of the behavior he observed. Thus, a minimum of editing was required.

Joe Stone had a deep appreciation of the history of early childhood education and sensed that Head Start would become a major landmark. One evening—around 11 P.M.—as we were wearily reviewing some of his films, one of my assistants came into the room to ask that I sign the first authorization to release funds for Head Start (for $40 million). I signed with a government issue ballpoint pen, and Stone immediately asked if he could keep the pen. I handed it over with deep appreciation of his creativity in helping young children and their families.

As we were all working long hours, I was often asked why we didn't recruit more staff. My response generally was 1) we don't have any time to recruit more than our basic group, and 2) if we had more staff, then we would have to have meetings, and we don't have time for that. An amusing side note was that the program was initiated so quickly we didn't have any furniture. I learned that meetings could be conducted very expeditiously if everyone was standing.

While the program applications were being generated in a 6-week period, we had only 6 weeks in which to process the applications that were to arrive in large numbers. Again, Jule Sugarman's creativity came to the fore. He struck on the idea of requesting the local school board to authorize recruitment from the roll of substitute teachers to process the applications. Because we were housed in a dilapidated hotel, Jule Sugarman arranged a processing line, trained the new recruits, and met the deadline. The group worked all hours of the day and night. One night I brought Joe Reid, the Executive Director of the Child Welfare League of America, to visit the offices. As we approached and he saw lights blazing, meetings being held, and people scurrying about, he commented, "I haven't seen anything like this since World War II."

In all, we received 3,300 applications, and 2,700 programs were funded for the first summer. It is remarkable that so many communities qualified for so comprehensive a program because they had only 6 weeks to complete the application. Because we were apprehensive that a program for all children younger than school age would spread resources too thin, we made the judgment to initiate the program as an 8-week summer program for children in the year prior to school entry (a flexible provision to make allowance for the fact that only about half the states had requirements for kindergarten programs at the time). Starting as a summer program also took cognizance of the fact that there were relatively few trained early childhood educators at the time. Many elementary school teachers had a preference for teaching younger children, but there had been few career opportunities. Early childhood education programs were in university settings, settlement houses, or cooperatives organized by parents. Each of these was small. It was possible to attract teachers on summer vacations to enroll in intensive training courses. Approximately 30,000 elementary school teachers were enlisted for the first summer.

Because of the shortage of early childhood educators, universities were provided with training funds to correct the deficit. Over the next several years, a shift occurred from summer or part-time programs to full-year programs because there was a recognition that, although summer programs demonstrated improved achievement by the children, longer programs would be more effective. In 2002, more than 826,000 children are enrolled, and the fiscal year 2002 budget was passed at $6,200,000,000.

As the first summer program concluded, I presented a report titled *Communities in Action: A Report on Project Head Start* (Richmond, 1966) to the Annual Meeting of the American Academy of Pediatrics. The title suggests we valued our affiliation with the Community Action Program of OEO. We saw the program in the context of community commitment to improving the lives of poor children and their families. By 1970, it was clear that the OEO legislation would require a transfer of the program to another federal agency. Working with Wilbur Cohen, then Secretary of Health, Education and Welfare, and later the staff of Secretary Robert Finch, Jule Sugarman took the lead in arranging for the transfer of Head Start to the newly formed Office of Child Development.

CONCLUSION

Since 1965, twenty one million children have graduated from the Head Start program. Communities have been empowered and have a deep sense of ownership and pride in what Head Start does for individual children and their communities. In retrospect, it is remarkable that the planning committee was so prescient about meeting the needs of children growing up in poverty. Their work has endured.

COMMENTARY BY JULE M. SUGARMAN

Former Associate Director of Head Start

Most people who write about Head Start focus on the nature of the classroom program and its educational impact on low-income children. The story that has not received sufficient attention is the enormous impact Head Start has had on public policy at local, state, and federal levels. For example, in 1965 there were only 15 states that offered universal kindergarten and none that offered services for younger children. Head Start provided the impetus for universal programs for all 4-year-olds as well as a growing number of programs for even younger children.

Head Start connected millions of low-income children to health care, often for the first time since their birth. The results of this effort were critical to developing federal and state Medicaid financing for millions of low-income children.

Meals, often including both breakfast and lunch, provided many children with an enormous boost in the adequacy of their nutrition. These experiences were important to the development of the federal child nutrition and school lunch programs.

Similarly, the family and social service features of Head Start, although chronically under funded, showed real promise when they were actually present. Regrettably, there has been little growth in these services.

Prior to Head Start, few credentialed educators could find reasonably paid employment in preschool positions. The availability of federal funds changed that by providing higher, although not necessarily equal, funds for early childhood personnel with degrees. In addition, Head Start opened employment opportunities for thousands of individuals with little or no formal training. Many of these individuals came with inherent skills and were highly successful, especially when supportive training programs were available.

Building on these experiences, both government officials and the National Head Start Association continue to press for greater financial assistance to staff in improving their skills and achieving professional recognition.

Initially, Head Start was sponsored by a wide variety of agencies; one third being free standing nonprofit organizations, one third school systems, and one third Community Action agencies. Even today nonprofit organizations operate a substantial portion of programs, albeit sometimes under delegation for Community Action and education agencies.

Unlike most public programs, Head Start has, from day one, funded a wide variety of research and evaluation efforts. It is fair to say that many of these were less than useful, primarily because of the concentration on outcomes with little attention to inputs. For an administrator, or for that matter an evaluator, questions about input are critical. Unfortunately, many researchers applied their findings in a particular agency to the entire Head Start program, assuming they were identical when, in fact, there were and are wide differences among them.

The Head Start experience has been valuable in and of itself, but its impacts on other public policies and programs must be considered as part of its achievements.

REFERENCES

Economic Opportunity Act of 1964, PL 88-452, 42 U.S.C. §§ 2701 *et seq.*

Recommendations for a Head Start Program by a panel of experts. (1965). Washington, DC: U.S. Department of Health, Education and Welfare, Office of Child Development.

Richmond, J.B. (1966). Communities in action: A report on Project Head Start. *Pediatrics, 37,* 905–912.

Does Head Start Work?

Head Start's continued support and longevity are dependent on whether policy makers believe that taxpayers' dollars are being used effectively. Debate I proved that there is no agreement about Head Start's goals and thus no consensus about whether the program is meeting them. Our presentation of the debate about whether Head Start works is, therefore, built around the noncontroversial, written goals contained in the Program Performance Standards and in legislation: school readiness, health, and family functioning. Research and evaluation are also components of Head Start, so we include views about how these need to improve to better inform policy and programming.

Head Start's impact on **school readiness and success** would seem to be a relatively straightforward assessment. It, of course, is not, largely because the issue is framed by the context with which one defines readiness and school success. Catherine Snow and Mariela Páez present their view that language and literacy skills are basic to academic achievement. They find Head Start lacking as a good language environment and detail the changes they think are necessary to create a better educational experience. Chaya Piotrkowski takes a broad, flexible view of the elements of school readiness fostered by Head Start. She explains how individual programs can best prepare children for school by urging a consensus about what constitutes readiness among Head Start teachers, parents, and local kindergarten teachers and then aligning their service delivery with this shared vision. David Weikart argues that evidence-based models, although not perfect, are the best resource currently available to inform improvements to Head Start that foster school readiness.

Head Start's favorable impact on **children's health** is generally accepted more on faith than based on empirical data. Robert O'Brien, David Connell, and James Griffin summarize findings from the Descriptive Study of Head Start Health Services. They conclude that the program does a very good job promoting children's health, but they believe that enhancing staff skills and focusing on community resource development could further the health component. Jane Knitzer describes the inadequate response to the mental health needs of Head Start's children and families. She views sound mental health as vital to school readiness and believes that by making mental health practices part of quality improvement efforts, all aspects of the program will benefit and its mission will become more achievable.

Head Start has always been a two-generation program, but its **impact on families** has received scant attention from researchers and policy analysts. Peggy Pizzo and Elizabeth Tufankjian review the literature and report the results of five longitudinal studies of parent outcomes. They find that Head Start does improve parents' abilities to promote early learning and efforts to participate in their children's later schooling. A parent's account of the benefits of Head Start is related in Delores Baynes's congressional testimony about her journey from an unstable life to Head Start to college for both her and her children. U.S. Representative Loretta Sanchez gives her view as a former Head Start student, describing how the experience helped her mother and others to become more effective educators for all their children.

There is little debate that to understand how well Head Start works, the **research must be better.** Two chapters that attack common, data-based knowledge illustrate this point. W. Steven Barnett takes on the myth of fade-out, showing how the program's cognitive benefits are not necessarily "proven" to dissipate as children progress through school. Grover Whitehurst and Greta Massetti reexamine the positive FACES and Early Childhood Longitudinal Study results and argue that, contrary to popular spin, Head Start is doing a poor job of preparing children to read. Examining the domain of research in general, Deborah Phillips and Sheldon White look at the gaps in past efforts to evaluate Head Start and present the recommendations of the Roundtable on Head Start Research for building a new infrastructure for research and its uses.

—Edward Zigler and Sally J. Styfco

CHAPTER 8

The Head Start Classroom as an Oral Language Environment

What Should the Performance Standards Be?

CATHERINE E. SNOW AND MARIELA M. PÁEZ

I f Head Start classrooms are meant to prepare children for entry to and success at school, then such classrooms must be evaluated primarily from the perspective of how well they foster language and emergent literacy skills. Why this focus? The major challenge children face in the early elementary grades is learning to read. This challenge is currently unsuccessfully met by a very high proportion of the children Head Start is meant to serve. Furthermore, we know from a large research base that children with relatively small vocabularies, underdeveloped extended discourse skills, and little familiarity with the functions and uses of print are at higher risk of literacy failure (Snow, Burns, & Griffin, 1998). Children from underprivileged and from minority families are much more likely to perform poorly on reading and writing tasks than their mainstream peers from economically stable homes (Applebee, Langer, & Mullis, 1985, 1987, 1989). Poor literacy achievement at school is also associated with using a minority language in the home (Ammon, 1987; Garcia, 1991).

These differences between mainstream children and their less privileged or minority peers are already visible during the preschool period for skills that relate to literacy. A national study conducted interviews with parents of 2,000 4-year-olds about to start kindergarten to identify those subgroups at greatest risk for problems at school (National Center for Education Statistics [NCES], 1995). Based on parent reports, the African American and Latino children did not perform as well as the European American children, par-

The authors thank the Spencer Foundation for supporting the participation of the second author in writing this chapter through a mentorship grant.

ticularly on those accomplishments reflecting "school readiness" and "emergent literacy" skills, such as recognizing letters, counting to 20, reading or pretend reading stories, writing their own names, and writing or drawing rather than scribbling with a pencil. The percentage of children reported to have started speaking late was also greater in African American and Latino families. Other significant risk factors included having a mother who had less than a high school education, who had poverty status, and whose primary language was not English. However, although controlling for these additional risk factors eliminated any impact of being African American on the literacy/numeracy outcome cluster, being Latino constituted an additional risk not explained by its co-occurrence with poverty or poor maternal education. In other words, Latino children are at heightened risk of having inadequate school-entry skills even if they come from relatively economically stable households and their mothers have a high school education.

The lower performance of poor and minority children on school-entry skills is of particular concern because of the growing evidence that a good start on reading is associated with successful reading in the later elementary grades. Initial reading failure is difficult to overcome and can lead to a cumulative deficit, not just in reading itself, but also in acquiring content knowledge. It is crucial that children enter kindergarten with the emergent literacy and language skills that will enable them to benefit from formal reading instruction.

In fact, the Committee on the Prevention of Reading Difficulties in Young Children (Snow et al., 1998) recommended that children in high-risk groups be provided with early childhood environments that are language- and literacy-enriched. These environments should promote language and literacy growth and address a variety of skills that have been identified as predictors of later reading achievement. Do Head Start classrooms meet this exacting standard?

In this chapter, we review the role of Head Start in contributing to the literacy success of children and provide recommendations for improving Head Start classrooms as language and literacy environments. We assert that Head Start classrooms, in general (like all but the highest quality preschool environments), offer inadequate language and literacy environments. This argument is based partly on empirical findings concerning classroom quality, partly on an analysis of the particular needs of the children in Head Start programs, and partly on information about the educational levels and prior preparation of Head Start classroom personnel.

WHAT CONSTITUTES A GOOD LANGUAGE AND LITERACY ENVIRONMENT?

Literacy development and school success are most effectively promoted during the preschool period by the development of oral language skills (see Snow, 1991a, 1991b; Snow & Dickinson, 1991, for an elaboration of these ideas). Readers must integrate an array of capacities in order to learn to read: print skills, phonemic analysis skills, an understanding of the purposes of literacy, and language skills. We focus on language, which is often neglected in thinking about how preschool can contribute to the preparation for reading, because it is, of these four subdomains, the largest and thus the one that most needs persistent attention.

Reading is ultimately, of course, about understanding written language. Thus, recognizing the relationship between children's oral language skills (both production and comprehension) and their reading abilities is crucial. Oral language skills that likely relate to literacy include vocabulary, extended discourse, and genre differentiation.

Vocabulary and world knowledge are crucial to literacy achievement. In fact, the best single predictor of reading success is vocabulary size (Anderson & Nagy, 1992). Early reading texts, though largely limited to words presumed to be present in children's oral vocabularies, are written based on descriptions of the language of middle-class, standard English speakers. The early reading accomplishments of nonstandard dialect speakers and of non-English speakers are particularly susceptible to disruption if the words in the texts are unfamiliar to the reader. Later reading requires understanding many less common words and much new information, previous oral exposure to which can increase children's comprehension of such texts.

Extended discourse skills tapped by tasks such as telling or retelling stories are related to literacy because oral uses of these skills display the rules for use in literacy. These tasks require recognizing the reality (or maintaining the fiction) that

1. One's audience can be distant, unknown, and nonresponsive.

2. One cannot presume shared background knowledge with the audience.

3. Full comprehension of explicit information by the audience is the goal (De Temple, Wu, & Snow, 1991; Snow, 1990).

Considerable evidence shows that children who do well in literacy have higher levels of control over the pragmatic orientations needed for oral extended discourse (Snow, 1990; Snow, Cancino, De Temple, & Schley, 1991).

These extended discourse productions—narratives, explanations, arguments, descriptions, and definitions—conform to specific rules for sequencing and interrelating utterances within them. Children need to understand this *genre differentiation*—how to structure sequences of utterances appropriately for different communicative tasks. For example, in giving an explanation, more important information should come early, but in telling a successful story, key information needs to be reserved until the end. Evidence is accumulating that kindergartners' capacities to meet the differential demands of narration, explanation, description, and definition relate to their reading skills as early as first grade (Davidson & Snow 1995; Snow, Tabors, Nicholson, & Kurland, 1995).

What Are the Language Needs of Poor and Minority Children?

Vocabulary size varies widely across children of a given age as a function of social class for monolinguals and of stage of second-language acquisition for English language learners. Massive differences between the vocabulary sizes of young welfare or working-class children and middle-class children have been demonstrated repeatedly (Hart & Risley, 1992, 1995). Second-language learners often have smaller vocabularies than monolinguals, even when second-language learners speak fluently and correctly (Fitzgerald, 1995).

In addition to knowing fewer words, children have shallower vocabulary knowledge in their second language. Verhallen and Schoonen (1993) found that immigrant children attending school in the Netherlands knew less about simple, high-frequency Dutch words than did native speakers; they mentioned, for example, few descriptive features or functions when given words such as *nose,* whereas native speakers mentioned many (e.g., triangular, sharp, long, pointed, pug; for smelling, sniffing, breathing, blowing, pointing). Work with native Spanish speakers in U.S. schools suggests the same pattern (Ordoñez, Carlo, & Snow, 2002).

Extended discourse skills, such as vocabulary, are developed in the context of conversations that provide practice in and the opportunity for engaged, challenging talk. Kindergartners from working-class homes show poorer performance on tasks of giving word definitions and describing pictures than do classmates from middle-class homes (Dickinson & Snow, 1987). In addition, both African American and Latino children follow different rules for the organization of extended discourse in narrative than do European American children (Gee, 1985, 1989, 1996; Michaels, 1981; Uccelli, 1996). African American and Latino genre rules may be more complex and sophisticated than the mainstream rules, but stories told by such rules are difficult for mainstream teachers to understand or support. Thus, these children have two tasks—to learn to tell improved, longer stories and, perhaps, to learn as well a second set of rules for how to organize their stories.

In summary, we argue that children from poor or minority homes are likely to encounter difficulty in school because of smaller vocabularies, less practice in using the language needed for extended discourse, and/or adherence to different rules for differentiating genres. Ideally, Head Start and other preschool environments serving poor and minority children would provide children with sufficient experiences to overcome these challenges.

Can Preschool Programs Affect Children's Language and Emergent Literacy Skills?

Because preschool classrooms complement homes as sites of language learning for young children and may be the primary site of English learning for children whose first language is not English, we review research describing such classrooms as language environments. Most studies that examine the quality of preschools use broad-gauge tools that include language and literacy as one dimension of the assessment. Such studies have found that it is precisely on measures of the language environment that preschool programs serving underprivileged children are likely to be most inadequate. The North Carolina Public Preschools study (Bryant, Peisner-Feinberg, & Clifford, 1993) found lower ratings on the Language and Reasoning Subscale of the Early Childhood Environment Rating Scale (ECERS) than for other scales. Particularly low-scored items on the nonlanguage scales included dramatic play (a context for rich language use), cultural awareness, and professional opportunities, suggesting that minority children are not being served optimally and that mechanisms for improvement are unavailable. Bryant, Burchinal, Lau, and Sparling (1994) similarly found the subscale with the lowest score across 32 Head Start classrooms they studied was Language and Reasoning.

Two studies have focused on the impact of language environments in preschool classrooms. The Bermuda Day Care Study (Phillips, McCartney, & Scarr, 1987) showed that quality of conversation in the classroom and amount of one-to-one or small-group interactions children engaged in related to child language outcome measures. Also, Dickinson and Smith (1994) found that quality of group book-reading experienced by low-income 4-year-olds was correlated with their kindergarten language and literacy outcomes. This same study found that the amount of cognitively challenging conversation and use of varied vocabulary by teachers was correlated with the children's subsequent language and literacy development (Dickinson, Cote, & Smith, 1993).

Although the quality of adult–child discourse is important, the amount of such interaction is also critical. Smith and Dickinson (1994) found that the amount of cognitively challenging talk children experience is correlated with the amount of time they talk with adults. Other studies have also found an association between conversational partner and topic (Michell, 1982). Given the importance of adult–child interaction, it is disturbing that any individual child in the average preschool setting (including Head Start) may interact rather little with a teacher and may receive little or no individualized attention (Kontos & Wilcox-Herzog, 1996; Layzer, Goodson, & Moss, 1993; Wilcox-Herzog & Kontos, 1996).

Finally, intervention studies have demonstrated the potential of preschool to enhance language and literacy development. The Perry Preschool Project (Weikart, Bond, & McNeil, 1978) and the Abecedarian Project (Campbell & Ramey, 1994, 1995; Ramey, Bryant, & Suarez, 1985) both involved high-intensity care and a wide range of services, and both found positive effects that extended into the school years. More modest enhancements of the quality of classroom experiences also show positive effects on children's language development and preliteracy skills (Whitehurst, Epstein, et al., 1994).

Do Head Start Classrooms Function to Improve Children's Language and Literacy Skills?

There is general agreement that higher quality Head Start programs generate larger positive outcomes for children than programs of modest quality (Bryant et al., 1994; Phillips et al., 1987). In general, though, studies of quality in Head Start (and in other early childhood programs) do not focus on the nature of the language/literacy environment they provide as a key co-determinant of quality. More generally, teacher background and experience, features of the physical environment, children's activities, affective aspects of teacher–child interaction, group size, and adult–child ratios are taken as indicators of classroom quality, sometimes in conjunction with program quality indicators, such as parent involvement, attention to nutrition and hygiene, and community involvement (Frede, 1998). Although such indicators are not unimportant, it is entirely possible for a program to score very well on them and still provide inadequate language and literacy environments.

The few studies that have specifically focused on language and literacy environments in Head Start classrooms show mixed results regarding the effects of these classrooms in improving children's language and emergent literacy skills. Some studies have found that Head Start participation resulted in an improvement of children's emergent language and literacy skills (Bryant et al., 1994; Dickinson & Smith, 1994). In general, these studies have documented the benefits of Head Start participation for children from low-income backgrounds. Head Start programs are not doing enough, however, to remedy the gap that exists between the language skills of children from poor or low-income backgrounds and other populations. Studies have shown that children participating in Head Start programs score very low in emergent literacy and language abilities (Legislative Office of

Education of Ohio [LOEO], 1998; Robinson & Dixon, 1992). Results from these studies are not surprising given that researchers have documented the low priority Head Start teachers place on reading, writing, and other literacy-related activities and goals (LOEO, 1998; Marvin & Mirenda, 1994; Robinson, 1990).

Why Are We Pessimistic about Head Start's Language and Literacy Provisions?

Providing consistently rich and systematic language stimulation and literacy exposure in an early childhood setting, in a way that is consistent with the developmental needs of young children, requires an understanding of children's language and literacy development, knowledge of children's literature, general knowledge of conversational topics likely to capture children's interest, and excellent language and literacy skills on the part of the adults involved. We would argue, in fact, that it is very difficult to be sufficiently planful and to ensure consistently enriched language in the classroom without some solid curricular support—a set of structured themes that provide topics for conversation; that suggest related books to read, field trips, and group activities; and that allow for the planned infusion of novel vocabulary (as a weekly list of new words to be used by teachers) and group literacy experiences (e.g., constructing a shared written story about a class trip, writing a class letter).

Some curricula used in Head Start programs, such as High/Scope, do provide for systematic attention to language. A 1995 national survey (Epstein, Larner, & Halpern, 1995), however, found that only half of Head Start agencies reported using a principal curriculum model. Given the traditional anxieties about overly structured curricula in early childhood settings, many of these were probably adopting a "model" that does not define much in the way of content. Without the support of a content-rich curriculum, it is difficult to ensure lively, varied language and literacy activities integrated with classroom discourse.

Furthermore, even if such structured curricula were being used widely, they would not be equally appropriate for all segments of the changing Head Start population. Head Start is increasingly serving children of non–English-speaking families. Some families select Head Start with the expectation that their children will learn English there, whereas others expect maintenance of the home language but help with school-related skills. A standard English-language curriculum is not appropriate for either of these populations. Although Spanish-language curricula have been developed (e.g., Carpinteria [Campos & Keatinge, 1988]) for use in Head Start, these have never been widely circulated and are in any case appropriate only for a subset of the non-English speakers in Head Start classrooms.

HOW COULD HEAD START CLASSROOMS IMPROVE AS LANGUAGE AND LITERACY ENVIRONMENTS?

Fortunately, the quality of Head Start classrooms as language and literacy environments could be improved, with relatively modest investments.

Teacher Selection and Professional Development

A first point to keep in mind is that children learn the language they hear modelled, and the best predictor of speed of language acquisition is the amount of talk that children hear. Furthermore, in general, being exposed to more talk implies hearing more different words—including some that are not among the 3,000–4,000 most frequent words of English. Studies of talk in low-income households (e.g., Beals, 1993; Weizman & Snow, 2001) suggest that even parents with relatively low educational levels can produce talk that includes the more sophisticated vocabulary that falls outside of the 3,000 most common words, but they do so 1) relatively rarely and 2) only in the context of extended conversations. In addition, the range of vocabulary that middle-class, more highly educated parents use with preschool-age children is much greater than that typical even in the lexically richest working-class households (Davidson, 1993). Because many Head Start classroom personnel are drawn from among the ranks of adults with little education, we cannot expect their vocabulary use to be rich—especially if there is no structured curricular support within which extended conversations might develop. Yet, in the domain of vocabulary, as in other domains, what teachers know and do is one of the most important influences on what students learn (Darling-Hammond, 1998).

Numerous studies have shown that program quality is inextricably linked with staff educational background and training. A study using two representative samples of preschool children and classrooms found that teachers with the most advanced education were most effective (Howes, 1997). Teachers with associate of arts degrees and child development associate credential certificates were more effective than teachers with some college or just high school plus workshops. Another study by Howes, Whitebrook, and Phillips (1992) found that whereas both formal education and high levels of specialized training prepare teachers to be effective in the classroom, formal education was a better predictor of competent teaching. Yet many teachers arrive in Head Start classrooms with limited formal education and/or little specific training in child development or early childhood education. Thus, one way to improve the quality of Head Start programs would be to attract better-qualified teachers, such as college graduates with a strong background in early childhood education.

Another strategy would be to implement classroom-level interventions and/or high-quality in-service training within Head Start as a way of contributing to the quality of these programs. Whitehurst and colleagues (Whitehurst, Arnold, et al., 1994; Whitehurst & Lonigan, 1998) have demonstrated that even relatively low-intensity interventions directed at teachers can help them provide better language support during group book reading sessions and better early literacy environments. It is also encouraging that wide-scale professional development efforts aimed at Head Start personnel are being undertaken (Schweinhart, Epstein, Okoloko, Oden, & Florian, 1998)—preliminary findings have shown that high-quality in-service training is a significant predictor of program quality (Epstein, 1999).

Moreover, training of Head Start staff should target specific areas of need in the educational background of teachers. A survey of Head Start teachers (Jones, 1993) showed that although teachers were fully certified and felt well prepared to teach in preschool positions, they believed they needed more training in second-language acquisition and understanding bilingual development. More than half of the Head Start teachers in this survey reported that their early childhood education had not included information about these topics. Given the increasing diversity of the population Head Start serves, it is imperative that programs develop professional training to address issues of teaching children from culturally and linguistically diverse backgrounds. Staff training could deal with questions such as the following:

- What are the typical characteristics of children who are learning two languages?

- What are some effective strategies for supporting bilingual children's functioning in the classroom and their learning of English?

- How can Head Start teachers become role models for children who are learning a second language?

The implementation of such training could help teachers become more effective in their use of strategies for fostering language and literacy development in their classrooms.

An Appropriate Curriculum and More Literacy Resources

The word *curriculum,* as used within the field of early childhood education, typically refers to orientation to teaching rather than a specification of the material to be learned. Child-centered curricula tend to be associated with warmer, more nurturant, more responsive teacher behavior than is found in programs with a didactic or academic emphasis (Stipek, Daniels, Galluzo, & Milburn, 1992; Stipek, Feiler, Daniels, & Milburn, 1995). Thus, guidelines for developmentally appropriate practice endorsed by the National Association for the Education of Young Children (NAEYC) and widely used as a basis for evaluating preschool programs tend to downplay the importance of curricular content because of its association with directive, behavior-managing styles. We argue, though, that providing interesting curricular materials and activities that raise the intellectual and linguistic challenge of the program for the children in it enhances the benefits of a child-centered program. Such a combination of child-centeredness with linguistic enrichment and cognitive challenge may be of particular importance for children from homes where low parental education and low literacy levels are associated with little preparation for school entry.

To the extent that Head Start classrooms we have observed do maintain a curricular emphasis, it tends to be defined by a fairly narrow notion of "reading readiness" skills (e.g., knowing the alphabet; recognizing shapes, colors, numbers) and may paradoxically further reduce the availability of a rich language environment (Smith & Dickinson, 1994). We propose that standards for effective preschool curricula should be based on the potential of curricular materials to generate interesting talk characterized by extended conversations around specific topics, sophisticated vocabulary, and a variety of discourse genres. Furthermore, ample attention should be paid to the skills that are known to predict future reading achievement, such as expressive and receptive language skills, phonological awareness, letter identification, and concepts of print. Early childhood curricula are being developed by a number of publishers; any that are focused on language could be introduced to Head Start classrooms and may well improve the quality of the language interactions. Whatever the curricular support, activities in Head Start classrooms should be designed to

- Stimulate verbal interaction

- Enrich children's vocabularies

- Encourage talk about books

- Develop knowledge about print

- Generate familiarity with the basic purposes and mechanisms of reading

These recommendations are based on research that suggests that the language and literacy environment in Head Start classrooms could be improved by adopting an appropriate curriculum and increasing the number of literacy resources available in these programs. For example, efforts to infuse literacy materials into early childhood classrooms (e.g., the Books Aloud project) have demonstrably improved access to books and increased the consistency of reading aloud activities within classrooms (Neuman, 1996). In addition, children in the intervention classrooms performed significantly better on early literacy measures testing knowledge of letter names, phonemic awareness, and concepts of print. In another study, Whitehurst, Epstein et al. (1994) randomly assigned 4-year-olds attending Head Start to an intervention group receiving add-on emergent literacy instruction or to a control group receiving the regular Head Start curriculum. They found that the effects of access to the intervention were significant across all children in the domains of writing and print concepts. The authors concluded that significant increments in children's emergent literacy abilities could result from an appropriate curriculum in Head Start classrooms.

Explicit Guidelines for Second-Language Learners

Head Start was initiated before the upsurge in immigration, and planning within Head Start has not yet articulated specific policies for children whose first language is not English comparable to those, for example, that guide services to non-English speakers in elementary schools (SocioTechnical Applications Research, Inc., 1996). Even though Head Start programs have experienced an increase in the diversity of the cultural and linguistic groups they serve, the typical classroom serving a mixed-language population uses only English, and even many classrooms that serve almost exclusively speakers of a single language other than English still primarily use English. Within the Head Start community of educators and parents, developing readiness for school is often equated with learning English; indeed, progress in learning English was established as a standard for Head Start performance in the 1999 reauthorization. The emphasis on English proficiency as a desired outcome of Head Start has grown despite the evidence that a strong basis in a first language promotes school achievement in the second (Cummins, 1979; Lanauze & Snow, 1989).

Clear guidelines should be developed for serving second-language learners. For example, programs should have a set of criteria for determining the placement of bilingual or second-language students based on their language skills and parental reports regarding their language expectations for their children. Placement of students in specific classrooms should be done consciously and strategically to maximize the quality of the language environments that are created, rather than primarily for logistical reasons (bus routes), convenience, ethnic diversity within the classroom, or arbitrarily. One strategy that would automatically improve children's language environments is assigning children to particular classrooms based on the teachers' knowledge of different language(s) and/or the teachers' experience teaching second-language learners. Also, if programs are serving a large number of students who share the same language background, efforts should be made to group children for language homogeneity (e.g., grouping Spanish–English bilingual students in one classroom, Vietnamese–English bilinguals in another, and speakers of English-only in yet another classroom). If the demographics of a program are such that language-homogeneous classrooms are not possible, then even more attention is needed for the quality of the classroom language environment to ensure adequate enrichment for the native English speakers and appropriate adaptations for the English language learners simultaneously.

These recommendations are supported by research that has demonstrated that children's language backgrounds affect the type of experience they have in Head Start classrooms. For example, a study conducted by Martha Bronson (as cited in Dickinson & Howard, 1997) collected data using an observational tool for describing children's social behaviors (Bronson, 1996). She compared children from Spanish-speaking homes who were in English-medium Head Start classrooms with those in a Spanish-medium classroom and with their English-speaking classmates. The social adjustment of Spanish-speaking children in English-medium classrooms lagged behind that of English-medium children in the same classrooms, although children in the Spanish-medium classroom were greatly advanced over both groups. Given the power of preschool children's social development to predict long-range outcomes, including literacy (Cohen, Bronson, & Casey, 1995), these results are striking.

Another study by Tabors, Aceves, Bartolomé, Páez, and Wolf (2000) incorporated three ethnographic investigations, one in each of three different types of Head Start classrooms: an English-language classroom with English language learners from varied language backgrounds, a bilingual (Spanish–English) classroom serving Spanish-speaking and Spanish–English bilingual children, and a Spanish-medium classroom also serving Spanish-speaking and Spanish–English bilingual children. Their findings showed that young bilingual children have strikingly different experiences in the Head Start context depending on the language use patterns in the classrooms they attend. In particular, bilingual children in the English-language classroom spent a lot of time listening to talk that they might not understand without being able to contribute much to the talk themselves. However, bilingual children in the bilingual and Spanish-language classrooms had no trouble finding teachers or children to talk with and could, therefore, proceed to communicate actively and participate fully in the classroom experience. End-of-year results from these three classrooms showed no differences among the children in English vocabulary accomplishments—though all three groups were scoring below age expectations. More research is needed to establish the language and literacy effects of these different types of classrooms with larger populations over a longer period of time. In the meantime, Head Start programs should try to create language environments that can promote children's language and literacy development by maximising the resources found in the children and families they are serving and the staff who serves them.

Parent Consultation Around Goals, in Particular for English Language Learners

Particularly for children from non–English-speaking homes, parents' expectations concerning the effects of Head Start participation need to be taken into account. It is reasonable that parents might expect Head Start to provide their children with a solid basis in English; however, some Head Start classrooms (e.g., one of the three documented in Tabors et al., 2000) actually supported Spanish as well, whereas other classrooms in the same program provided an English-only environment. Yet, parents are not typically offered a choice between classrooms to match their own language use preferences—a gradual transition to English with Spanish support versus an all-English immersion experience.

Furthermore, parents may opt for an English-immersion experience because they are operating on the presupposition that their children will continue to develop the home language as a result of its use in the home. Although this certainly can happen, all too often children fail to continue to make age-appropriate progress in home-language development as they increasingly come to use English (Wong-Fillmore, 1991). Thus, parents should at least be informed of the possible consequences of choosing an all-English versus a bilingual Head Start environment and the need to use the home language systematically, persistently, and richly if they indeed want to ensure their children's long-term bilingualism (see chapter 8 in Tabors, 1997, for suggestions of ways to work with parents around these issues).

Another reason for parents to be offered choices concerning the language used in Head Start classrooms is the turbulence associated with exposure to all-English preschool classrooms if the local schools offer kindergarten and primary programs on a transitional bilingual model. Although there has been no systematic study of children going back and forth between English and home-language educational environments, practitioners often complain about the inadequate home-language skills of children entering bilingual programs in kindergarten and often implicate English-language exposure in Head Start or other preschool classrooms as a detriment to the development of age-appropriate skills in the native language.

Since its inception, Head Start has promoted parent involvement in the program and encouraged communication between staff and parents for the benefit of the children. This aspect of the Head Start program is important and should be expanded to focus particularly on parent involvement in choice of the language to be used with their children in Head Start classrooms. Moreover, efforts should be made to communicate with parents as they register their children in order to learn about their goals and expectations for their children in the program—in particular, to discover how much importance parents place on maintaining the home language and to alert parents to the possible consequences for the home language of choosing all-English classrooms.

CONCLUSION

Improving early childhood classrooms as language- and literacy-stimulating environments requires commitment to the importance of excellent early childhood environments for all children, as well as investment in staff who are well-trained in early childhood education (and, at least in a full-employment economy, salary rates commensurate with attracting professional staff). Professional in-service staff development that is far-reaching, coherent, intensive, and focused on methods for promoting language and literacy development is needed to upgrade the educational activities of Head Start staff.

The Head Start reauthorization recognized the importance of professional preparation for Head Start personnel by setting as a new performance standard the expectation that half of Head Start personnel would have associates degrees by 2003 (School Readiness Act of 2003 [H.R. 2210]). This ambitious goal can be met only if special prepara-

tion programs for early childhood educators are created that provide effective accommo-
dations for their own previous, often inadequate educational experiences. These programs,
as recommended by the National Academy of Sciences Panel on Preventing Reading Difficulties in Young Children (Snow et al., 1998), should require mastery of information
about the many kinds of knowledge and skills that can be acquired in the preschool years
in preparation for reading achievement in school. Their knowledge base should include at
least the following:

- Information about how to provide rich conceptual experiences that promote growth in vocabulary and reasoning skills

- Knowledge about lexical development, from early referential (naming) abilities to relational and abstract terms and finer-shaded meanings

- Knowledge of early development of listening comprehension skills and the kinds of syn-
  tactic and prose structures that preschool children may not yet have mastered

- Information on young children's sensitivity to the sounds of language and sense of story

- Information on young children's developmental conception of written language (print
  awareness)

- Information on young children's development of concepts of space including directionality

- Knowledge of fine motor development

- Knowledge about how to inspire motivation to read (p. 332)

These programs should also treat educators' skills in languages other than English
as resources rather than as educational obstacles. For example, in areas with many Spanish speakers, associate degree programs might well be designed in Spanish to capitalize on
the Spanish language and literacy skills of the degree-seekers and incorporate, in addition
to the basic information any early childhood practitioner needs, information that would be
of particular value to those working with Spanish-speaking children. For example,

- Features of the acquisition of Spanish as a first language

- Children's literature in Spanish

- Knowledge about variation in the dialects of Spanish spoken by U.S. immigrants

- Knowledge about bilingualism, code-switching, and second-language learning

- Information about songs, rhymes, poems, and phonological-awareness inducing games
  appropriate for Spanish-speakers

The level of educational preparation of a large proportion of the current Head Start
personnel will constitute a challenge in meeting the stated performance standard. Many
adults now working in Head Start programs will need remedial literacy education before
being prepared to enter associate programs, in particular if those programs are offered
only in English. Furthermore, many associate programs are rather general in content—
focusing on the basic academic skills needed for going on to a degree program in a 4-year
college. Innovative programs that use child-development related material to provide basic
reading and writing skills and focus on issues of health, nutrition, social, cognitive, and

linguistic development within the courses offered would prepare the students to teach in Head Start or similar preschool programs better than standard course offerings. Immediate payoff of knowledge relevant to the classroom is, of course, also an enormous advantage given that most Head Start personnel pursuing associate degrees will do so by attending classes in the evenings, while continuing to work.

The potential for Head Start to contribute to the literacy success of children in the United States is clear: Children who arrive in kindergarten better prepared with language and early literacy skills are more likely to experience success in learning to read. Currently, Head Start is not living up to its full potential as an educational resource for preschool children at heightened risk of school failure. Greater attention to the educational program provided by Head Start and efforts to make that educational program as central a focus of attention within Head Start as health, family involvement, and community support are necessary to fully exploit Head Start's potential.

REFERENCES

Ammon, M.S. (1987). Patterns of performance among bilingual children who score low in reading. In S.R. Goldman & H.T. Trueba (Eds.), *Becoming literate in English as a second language*. Norwood, NJ: Ablex.

Anderson, J.C., & Nagy, W.E. (1992). The vocabulary conundrum. *American Educator, 16*, 44–48.

Applebee, A., Langer, J., & Mullis, I. (1985). *The reading report card*. Princeton, NJ: Educational Testing Service.

Applebee, A., Langer, J., & Mullis, I. (1987). *Learning to be literate in America*. Princeton, NJ: Educational Testing Service.

Applebee, A., Langer, J., & Mullis, I. (1989). *Crossroads in American education*. Princeton, NJ: Educational Testing Service.

Beals, D. (1993). Explanatory talk in low-income families' mealtimes conversations. *Applied Pscyholinguistics, 14*, 489–514.

Bronson, M.B. (1996). *The Bronson Social and Task Skill Profile*. Newton, MA: EDC.

Bryant, D.M., Burchinal, L.B., Lau, L.B., & Sparling, J.J. (1994). Family and classroom correlates of Head Start children's developmental outcomes. *Early Childhood Research Quarterly, 9*, 289–309.

Bryant, D.M., Peisner-Feinberg, E.S., & Clifford, R.M. (1993). *Evaluation of public preschool programs in North Carolina: Executive summary*. Chapel Hill: Frank Porter Graham Child Development Center, University of North Carolina.

Campbell, F.A., & Ramey, C.T. (1994). Effects of early intervention on intellectual and academic achievement: A follow-up study of children from low-income families. *Child Development, 65*, 684–698.

Campbell, F.A., & Ramey, C.T. (1995). Cognitive and school outcomes for high-risk African-American students at middle adolescence: Positive effects of early intervention. *American Educational Research Journal, 32*, 743–772.

Campos, J., & Keatinge, R. (1988). The Carpinteria language minority student experience: From theory, to practice, to success. In T. Skutnabb-Kangas & J. Cummins (Eds.), *Minority education: From shame to struggle* (pp. 299–307). Clevedon, England: Multilingual Matters.

Cohen, G.N., Bronson, M.B., & Casey, M.B. (1995). Planning as a factor in school achievement. *Journal of Applied Developmental Psychology, 16*, 405–428.

Cummins, J. (1979). Linguistic interdependence and the educational development of bilingual children. *Review of Educational Research, 49*, 222–251.

Darling-Hammond, L. (1998). Teachers and teaching: Testing policy hypotheses from a National Commission Report. *Educational Researcher, 27*(1), 5–15.

Davidson, R.G. (1993). *Oral preparation for literacy: Mothers' and fathers' conversations with precocious readers*. Unpublished doctoral dissertation, Graduate School of Education of Harvard University, Cambridge, MA.

Davidson, R.G., & Snow, C.E. (1995). The linguistic environment of early readers. *Journal of Research in Childhood Education, 10*, 5–21.

De Temple, J., Wu, H.F., & Snow, C.E. (1991). Papa Pig just left for Pigtown: Children's oral and written picture descriptions under varying instructions. *Discourse Processes, 14*, 469–495.

Dickinson, D.K., Cote, L., & Smith, M.W. (1993). Learning vocabulary in preschool: Social and discourse contexts affecting vocabulary growth. In C. Daiute (Ed.), The development of literacy through social interaction. In *New Directions in Child Development* (pp. 67–78). San Francisco: Jossey-Bass.

Dickinson, D.K., & Howard, C. (1997). *Quarterly Report of the NEQRC* submitted to the Agency for Children and Families. Newton, MA: EDC.

Dickinson, D.K., & Smith, M.W. (1994). Long-term effects of preschool teachers' book readings on low-income children's vocabulary and story comprehension. *Reading Research Quarterly, 29*, 104–122.

Dickinson, D.K., & Snow, C.E. (1987). Interrelationships among prereading and oral language skills in kindergartners from two social classes. *Early Childhood Research Quarterly, 2*, 1–25.

Epstein, A.S. (1999). Pathways to quality in Head Start, public school, and private nonprofit early childhood programs. *Journal of Research in Childhood Education, 13*(2), 101–119.

Epstein, A.S., Larner, M., & Halpern, R. (1995). *A guide to developing community-based family support programs.* Ypsilanti, MI: High/Scope Press.

Fitzgerald, J. (1995). English-as-a-second-language learners' cognitive reading process: A review of research in the United States. *Review of Educational Research, 65*, 145–190.

Frede, E.C. (1998). Preschool program quality in programs for children in poverty. In W.S. Barnett and S.S. Boocock (Eds.), *Early care and education for children in poverty: Promises, programs, and long term outcomes* (pp. 77–98). Buffalo: SUNY Press.

Garcia, G.E. (1991). Factors influencing the English reading test performance of Spanish-speaking Hispanic students. *Reading Research Quarterly, 26*, 371–392.

Gee, J.P. (1985). The narrative of experience in the oral style. *Journal of Education, 167*, 9–35.

Gee, J.P. (1989). Literariness, formalism and sense making: The line and stanza of human thought. *Journal of Education, 171*, 61–74.

Gee, J.P. (1996). Signifying and schooling. *Linguistics and Education, 8*, 327–334.

Hart, B., & Risley, T.R. (1992). American parenting of language learning children: Persisting differences in family-child interactions observed in natural home environments. *Developmental Psychology, 28*, 1096–1105.

Hart, B., & Risley, T.R. (1995). *Meaningful differences in the everyday experience of young American children.* Baltimore: Paul H. Brookes Publishing Co.

Howes, C. (1997). Children's experiences in center-based child care as a function of teacher background and adult:child ratio. *Merill-Palmer Quarterly, 43*, 404–425.

Howes, C., Whitebrook, M., & Phillips, D. (1992). Teacher characteristics and effective teaching in child care: Findings from the National Child Care Staffing study. *Child & Youth Care Forum, 21*, 399–414.

Jones, T.G. (1993, November). *What do Head Start teachers know about non-English speaking children?* Paper presented at the 2nd National Head Start Research Conference, Washington, DC.

Kontos, S., & Wilcox-Herzog, A. (1996). *Influences on children's competence in early childhood classrooms.* Unpublished manuscript.

Lanauze, M., & Snow, C.E. (1989). The relation between first- and second-language writing skills: Evidence from Puerto Rican elementary school children in bilingual programs. *Linguistics and Education, 1*, 323–340.

Layzer, J., Goodson, B., & Moss, M. (1993). *Observational study of early childhood programs, Final report, Vol. 1: Life in preschool.* Washington, DC: U.S. Department of Education.

Legislative Office of Education of Ohio (LOEO). (1998). *Head Start's impact on school readiness in Ohio: A case study of Kindergarten students.* Report from the Ohio State Legislative Office of Education Oversight. Columbus: Author. (ERIC Document Reproduction Service No. ED 421 237)

Marvin, C., & Mirenda, P. (1994). Literacy practices in Head Start and early childhood special education classrooms. *Early Education & Development, 5*, 289–300.

Michaels, S. (1981). "Sharing time": Children's narrative styles and differential access to literacy. *Language in Society, 10,* 423–442.

Michell, L. (1982). Language styles of 10 nursery school children. *First Language, 3,* 3–28.

National Center for Education Statistics. (1995). *Approaching kindergarten: A look at preschoolers in the United States.* Statistical Analysis Report. Washington, DC: U.S. Department of Education, Office of Educational Research and Improvement.

Neuman, S.B. (1996). *Evaluation of the Books Aloud Project: An executive summary.* Report to the William Penn Foundation from Books Aloud. Philadelphia: Temple University.

Ordoñez, C., Carlo, M.S., & Snow, C.E. (2002). Depth and breadth of vocabulary in two languages: Which vocabulary skills transfer? *Journal of Educational Psychology, 94,* 719–728.

Phillips, D.A., McCartney, K., & Scarr, S. (1987). Child-care quality and children's social development. *Developmental Psychology, 23,* 537–543.

Ramey, C.T., Bryant, D.M., & Suarez, T.M. (1985). Preschool compensatory education and the modifiability of intelligence: A critical review. In D. Detterman (Ed.), *Current topics in human intelligence* (pp. 247–296). Norwood, NJ: Ablex.

Robinson, S.S. (1990). *A survey of literacy programs among preschoolers.* Ames: Iowa State University of Science and Technology. (ERIC Document Reproduction Service No. ED 317 293)

Robinson, S.S., & Dixon, R.G. (1992). *Language concepts of low- and middle-class preschoolers.* Ames: Iowa State University of Science and Technology. (ERIC Document Reproduction Service No. ED 345 225)

School Readiness Act of 2003, H.R. 2210, 108th Cong. (2003).

Schweinhart, L.J., Epstein, A.S., Okoloko, V., Oden, S.L., & Florian, J.E. (1998, July). *How staffing and staff development contribute to Head Start program quality and effectiveness.* Paper presented at Head Start's Fourth National Research Conference, Washington, DC.

Smith, M.W., & Dickinson, D.K. (1994). Describing oral language opportunities and environments in Head Start and other preschool classrooms. *Early Childhood Research Quarterly, 9,* 345–366.

Snow, C.E. (1990). The development of definitional skill. *Journal of Child Language, 17,* 697–710.

Snow, C.E. (1991a). Diverse conversational contexts for the acquisition of various language skills. In J. Miller (Ed.), *Progress in research on child language disorders* (pp. 105–124). New York: Little, Brown.

Snow, C.E. (1991b). The theoretical basis for relationships between language and literacy development. *Journal of Research in Childhood Education, 6* (Fall/Winter), 5–10.

Snow, C.E., Burns, S., & Griffin, P. (1998). *Preventing reading difficulties in young children.* Washington, DC: National Academy Press.

Snow, C.E., Cancino, H., De Temple, J., & Schley, S. (1991). Giving formal definitions: A linguistic or metalinguistic skill? In E. Bialystok (Ed.), *Language processing and language awareness by bilingual children* (pp. 90–112). New York: Cambridge University Press.

Snow, C.E., & Dickinson, D.K. (1991). Some skills that aren't basic in a new conception of literacy. In A. Purves & T. Jennings (Eds.), *Literate systems and individual lives: Perspectives on literacy and schooling* (pp. 175–213). Albany: SUNY Press.

Snow, C.E., Tabors, P.O., Nicholson, P., & Kurland, B. (1995). SHELL: A method for assessing oral language and early literacy skills in kindergarten and first grade children. *Journal of Research in Childhood Education, 10,* 37–48.

SocioTechnical Applications Research, Inc. (1996). *Report on the ACYF bilingual/multicultural survey.* Washington, DC: Head Start Bureau.

Stipek, D., Daniels, D., Galluzo, D., & Milburn, S. (1992). Characterizing early childhood education programs for poor and middle-class children. *Early Childhood Research Quarterly, 7,* 1–19.

Stipek, D., Feiler, R., Daniels, D., & Milburn, S. (1995). Effects of different instructional approaches on young children's achievement and motivation. *Child Development, 66,* 209–223.

Tabors, P.O. (1997). *One child, two languages: A guide for preschool educators of children learning English as a second language.* Baltimore: Paul H. Brookes Publishing Co.

Tabors, P.O., Aceves, C., Bartolomé, L., Páez, M., & Wolf, A. (2000). *Language development of linguistically diverse children in Head Start classrooms: Three ethnographic portraits.* NHSA Dialog, 3, 409–440.

Uccelli, P. (1996). *Beyond chronicity: Temporality and evaluation in Andean Spanish-speaking children's narratives.* Unpublished qualifying paper, Harvard Graduate School of Education.

Verhallen, M., & Schoonen, R. (1993). Vocabulary knowledge of monolingual and bilingual children. *Applied Linguistics, 14,* 344–363.

Weikart, D.P., Bond, J.T., & McNeil, J.T. (1978). *The Ypsilanti Perry Preschool Project: Preschool years and longitudinal results through fourth grade.* Ypsilanti, MI: High/Scope Press.

Weizman, Z., & Snow, C.E. (2001). Lexical input as related to children's vocabulary acquisition: Effects of sophisticated exposure and support for meaning. *Developmental Psychology, 37,* 265–279.

Whitehurst, G.J., Arnold, D.S., Epstein, J.N., Angell, A.L., Smith, M., & Fischel, J.E. (1994). A picture book reading intervention in day care and home for children from low-income families. *Developmental Pscyhology, 30,* 679–689.

Whitehurst, G.J., Epstein, J., Angell, A., Payne, A.C., Crone, D., & Fischel, J. (1994). Outcomes of an emergent literacy intervention in Head Start. *Journal of Educational Psychology, 80,* 542–555.

Whitehurst, G.J., & Lonigan, C.J. (1998). Child development and emergent literacy. *Child Development, 69,* 848–872.

Wilcox-Herzog, A., & Kontos, S. (1996). *The nature of teacher talk in early childhood classrooms and its relationship to children's competence with objects and peers.* Manuscript under review. West Lafayette, IN: Department of Child Development and Family Studies, Purdue University.

Wong-Fillmore, L. (1991). When learning a second language means losing the first. *Early Childhood Research Quarterly, 6,* 323–346.

CHAPTER 9

A Community-Based Approach to School Readiness in Head Start

Chaya S. Piotrkowski

For children living in poverty, school difficulties begin early. One third of high-poverty schools report that children have difficulty adjusting to the academic demands of kindergarten, and 7 of 10 public schools retain children in kindergarten, place them in special classrooms, or do both (Love & Logue, 1992). Minority males from low-income families are especially likely to be candidates for special placement (Gredler, 1992). These explicit and implicit tracking practices are one important gateway to negative "achievement trajectories" for children living in poverty (Alexander & Entwisle, 1988; Entwisle, 1995).

What a child from a low-income family brings to school influences subsequent achievement and educational attainment in a linked chain of events (Luster & McAdoo, 1996). Ultimately, educational underachievement can result in lowered occupational earnings, underemployment, and an intergenerational cycle of poverty. With the erosion of well-paid, low-skill jobs in manufacturing; the increased demand for highly skilled workers; and the 5-year limits set on the welfare safety net, school failure is a crisis for families and society. These dramatic economic and social changes underscore the importance of ensuring that children living in poverty encounter success as soon as they enter school.

HEAD START AND SCHOOL READINESS

Goal 1 of the Goals 2000: Educate America Act of 1993 (PL 103-277) states that, "By the year 2000 all children in America will start school ready to learn." In other words, we have made a national commitment—in word if not in deed—to ensure that all children will enter school prepared to succeed. This national focus on preventing educational fail-

The work detailed in this chapter was supported by a private foundation and by PR/Award Number R307F9770010–98 from the U.S. Department of Education. The contents or views expressed do not represent the positions or policies of the Department. I wish to thank the Head Start grantee and the parents and staff of the Head Start agencies who participated in the research reported, as well as staff and kindergarten teachers in local schools. Confidentiality constraints do not allow me to thank them by name.

129

ure is not new. Head Start was implemented to help children living in poverty achieve school success, based on the idea that individual educational achievement remains the major route to economic self-sufficiency. The naive environmentalism of the 1960s, however, contributed to the mistaken notion that Head Start primarily was a program designed to raise children's IQ scores (Zigler & Trickett, 1978). When early gains by Head Start children seemed to fade after several years of schooling, critics took this as evidence for Head Start's failure.

The Coats Human Services Reauthorization Act of 1998 (PL 105-285) clarified the mission of Head Start as promoting school readiness by enhancing the social and cognitive development of children from low-income homes. In addition to its traditional purposes of improving children's health and helping them feel competent and secure, the revised Head Start Performance Standards require that Head Start programs help children develop "positive attitudes toward learning" and "age appropriate literacy, numeracy, reasoning, problem-solving and decision-making skills which form a foundation for school readiness and later school success" (U.S. Department of Health and Human Services [DHHS], 1996, pp. 79, 81). This emphasis on school readiness represents an important change because it means that Head Start's effectiveness will no longer be judged unreasonably by how well Head Start children do in third grade but by how well Head Start prepares children for entry to school.

Head Start programs face numerous challenges on the way to implementing this mission. For one, the school readiness concept has been criticized for being thought of as a static attribute of children; for unduly burdening children; and for ignoring factors such as individual differences, inequities in children's experiences and opportunities, and the responsibility of schools to teach all children appropriately (Graue, 1992; National Association for the Education of Young Children [NAEYC], 1990; Willer & Bredekamp, 1990). School readiness also has been associated with pressurized preschools and kindergartens, the downward shift of academic expectations to increasingly younger children, measurement-driven instruction (Meisels, 1992), and the use of nonvalid tests of school readiness to make placement decisions for individual children (May & Kundert, 1992; Shepard & Smith, 1986). Thus, there has been considerable debate not only about what school readiness means but also whether the concept should be used at all (Kagan, Moore, & Bredekamp, 1995; NAEYC, 1990).

Does that mean Head Start's emphasis on school readiness is misplaced? Not necessarily. We will not solve the problems of improper assessments of children and inappropriate classroom practices by doing away with the term *school readiness*. Furthermore, we simply cannot ignore the fact that the playing field for young children is not level. Until all schools are ready for every child (Willer & Bredekamp, 1990), we cannot avoid our responsibility to help each child living in poverty step onto the path of success the minute he or she enters kindergarten or first grade. That is Head Start's mission.

Head Start programs face yet another challenge: Although there is broad agreement about overarching principles, there is no national consensus about what children actually should know and be able to do when they enter kindergarten (Bredekamp, 1992; Wesley & Buysse, 2003). Although experts have developed consensus regarding broad principles to guide early childhood education (Bowman, Donovan, & Burns, 2000), at the local level—where the serious business of preparing children for school occurs—parents and preschool teachers implement educational strategies based on their beliefs about what children should know and be able to do when they enter school.

In this context, how are Head Start programs to proceed? First, I offer a reconceptualization of school readiness as an essentially ecological concept that fits Head Start's philosophy. Second, I urge local Head Start programs to take leadership in developing community-based consensus regarding children's school readiness that brings Head Start teachers and parents together with local public school teachers and administrators. To explore how far Head Start must travel to achieve this goal, I present some data regarding consistencies and inconsistencies in the readiness beliefs of Head Start teachers and parents. Finally, I discuss the important challenge of developing shared readiness goals with kindergarten teachers in local schools.

RESOURCE MODEL OF SCHOOL READINESS

To avoid the pitfalls commonly associated with the school readiness concept, Head Start needs a conceptualization that

1. Does not treat readiness as a static attribute of children

2. Incorporates the multiple dimensions of children's development that are important for school success

3. Acknowledges the joint responsibilities of families, communities, and schools to help children have a successful early school experience (Kagan et al., 1995; NAEYC, 1990; National Task Force on School Readiness, 1991).

School readiness can be conceptualized as the political, social, organizational, educational, financial, and individual resources that help prepare children for school. The term *resources* is intended to indicate that school readiness is not simply an individual-level concept, that it is malleable and can be changed, and that it is influenced by a host of contextual factors beyond variations in children's experience and temperament.

At the community level, school readiness resources include affordable, high-quality child care and preschool for all; libraries that are easy to use; playgrounds and neighborhoods that are safe; ample social capital (Coleman, 1988); accessible, affordable medical care; and so forth. High-quality Head Start programs, therefore, are important school readiness resources in high-need communities. Schools that are ready for children have strong, accountable leadership; are welcoming to parents and children; provide continuity with early care and ease the transition into kindergarten; have ongoing professional development to support high quality instruction; respond to children's individual needs; provide needed intervention in a timely fashion; and partner with families and community service providers (Shore, 1998). Family readiness resources include a rich literacy environment, adequate financial resources, and social supports that help parents be nurturing caregivers and effective first teachers.

Usually, the concept of school readiness is applied to individual children. Investments in health and education create "human capital"—the knowledge, skills, and other attributes (i.e., resources) that affect our ability to do productive work (Schultz, 1961). If we think of schooling as the work children do (Piotrkowski & Katz, 1982), then programs such as Head Start help create rudimentary forms of human capital (i.e., individual resources) that help children be successful and productive in their workplace—the classroom setting.

The Technical Planning Group for Goal 1 of the National Education Goals Panel identified five dimensions of what I call *children's personal readiness resources*. The five dimensions are physical well-being and motor development; social and emotional development; approaches to learning; language use; and cognition and general knowledge (Kagan et al., 1995). Children may enter school with a range of these possible readiness resources that include

1. Health and the age-appropriate ability to care for self

2. The ability to regulate emotion and behavior, interact appropriately with adults and children, and communicate needs and feelings effectively

3. An interest and engagement in the world around them to motivate learning

4. Motor skills

5. Cognitive knowledge

6. The ability to adjust to the particular setting demands of the kindergarten classroom

A child can use these readiness resources to profit from his or her early schooling experiences and meet societal expectations of competence there.

Variations in temperament and early experience, including the quality of Head Start programs, result in variability in the individual readiness resources of children. But equally important, children vary in the extent to which they *need* these resources when they enter school. For example, consider a child from an affluent family that has multiple readiness resources and lives in a community where schools provide rich, individualized learning environments. This child is likely to succeed in school, regardless of what personal resources he or she initially brings to kindergarten, because he or she probably will be supported at school and at home.

A Head Start child entering a school system with high per-pupil expenditures may, in fact, come close to catching up with his or her peers from more affluent families (Whitehurst et al., 1999). Unfortunately, Head Start children commonly enter resource-poor schools. Consider a Head Start child who enters a school with low per-pupil expenditures, overcrowded classrooms, and children speaking many languages, some of which the teachers do not understand. This child's parent may be overwhelmed by the stresses of single parenthood and may have few educational skills so that the child's family cannot compensate for limited school resources. Moreover, this child's mother may believe she does not have a meaningful role in educating her child (Holloway, Rambaud, Fuller, & Eggers-Pierola, 1995). Under these circumstances, this child will need extraordinary readiness resources to succeed. Thus, while we work toward equitable and increased funding for education, better-trained teachers, and smaller classes, young children in low-income communities continue to shoulder a heavy burden.

There is evidence that beliefs about what children need to know and be able to do when they enter kindergarten vary with local readiness resources. Kindergarten teachers in high-poverty schools are more likely than other teachers to stress academic skills as necessary for school readiness (Heaviside & Farris, 1993) and to use instructional practices

(Love & Logue, 1992). Graue (1992) found different conceptions of readiness applied to different children in the same school. Among white, middle-class children, lack of readiness was attributed to immaturity, so children were kept out of kindergarten an extra year. Among poor, Hispanic children, lack of readiness was attributed to insufficient skills, so earlier schooling was seen as the solution. Thus, as long as the playing field is not level, school readiness goals and strategies that are viewed as appropriate for middle-class children may not be viewed as appropriate for children living in poverty.

A COMMUNITY-BASED APPROACH TO CHILDREN'S SCHOOL READINESS

Head Start takes on a Sisyphean task if it assumes lone responsibility for helping young children who live in poverty become prepared for school, leaving itself in the vulnerable position of being blamed for children's school difficulties. Even with high-quality programming, Head Start cannot achieve the goal of school readiness alone because there are multiple determinants of children's readiness, particularly family characteristics and the characteristics of kindergarten classrooms (Maxwell & Eller, 1994; Zill et al., 1998). Communities are more likely to succeed in preparing children for school if the key educators in children's lives agree on what "school readiness" is (i.e., what children should know and be able to do when they enter kindergarten). At minimum, local Head Start programs need to build consensus regarding school readiness with three constituencies— Head Start parents, Head Start teachers, and public school kindergarten teachers—so that everyone can work toward the same goals. A community-oriented collaborative approach to achieving children's school readiness is especially appropriate for Head Start, which is rooted in community-based organizations.

Head Start Parents' and Teachers' Views of Children's School Readiness

The mandate to develop a shared educational philosophy with parents already exists. Head Start programs are required to collaborate with parents in developing an educational philosophy "shared by the program and the parents," and staff are encouraged to work with parents "to support the goals of the curriculum in the home" (DHHS, 1996). This mandate is important, for there is evidence that children's school readiness skills are enhanced when Head Start staff and parents implement complementary interventions in the classroom and at home (Singer & Singer, 1999; Whitehurst et al., 1994).

How great is the distance between Head Start parents and teachers regarding their beliefs about what children should know and be able to do when they enter kindergarten? To explore this question, I conducted a secondary analysis of survey data gathered in 1998 for a study of school readiness beliefs in an ethnic minority, low-income, urban community on the East coast (Piotrkowski, Botsko, & Matthews, 2000). The analysis reported here is limited to 29 Head Start lead teachers in 11 Head Start centers and 156 parents/guardians of children in seven Head Start centers.[1] Almost all parents were African American or English-speaking Hispanic.

---

[1] Most were parents of the Head Start children, so "parent" is used throughout. The sample of parents in the school district was augmented by data from parents in a Head Start center just outside the school district. Parents in four Head Start centers that also received funding from state day care funds were excluded because fee-paying day care parents could not be differentiated from Head Start parents, although teachers in these four centers were included.

Developed for this study, the survey of Community Attitudes on Readiness for Entering School (CARES) asks respondents, "Think about a child who will BEGIN kindergarten in the Fall. For each item below, enter one number to indicate how IMPORTANT or NECESSARY it is for a child starting kindergarten." Respondents are then presented with 46 behaviorally anchored items and asked to rate each item as "not too important" (1), "somewhat important" (2), "very important, but not essential" (3), or "absolutely necessary" (4). Factor analysis was utilized to create eight internally consistent subscales. Four items were retained as individual items, and one ("Is interested in books and stories") was dropped from further analysis. (For a complete description of sampling and scale development, see Piotrkowski et al., 2000.)

Several limitations of this data set should be noted. First, findings may not generalize to other Head Start communities. Second, by aggregating findings across Head Start centers, important similarities or differences between parents and teachers *within* centers may be obscured. Third, parents who completed Spanish CARES surveys were excluded from the analysis (see Piotrkowski et al., 2000, for a discussion of this issue), and they may differ in important ways from those who completed English surveys. Fourth, to make the CARES survey items understandable for Head Start parents, we did not ask about more complex readiness constructs such as prenumeracy and emerging literacy skills. Finally, we cannot be sure how well the responses to the survey reflect actual beliefs.

Due to space limitations, an overview of findings is presented in Tables 9.1 and 9.2. In addition to average ratings, the percentage of respondents endorsing each item as "absolutely necessary" and results of statistical tests (t-tests) comparing Head Start teachers and parents are presented.

Readiness beliefs were divided into two domains. In the first domain were seven General Readiness Resources that pertain to a child's everyday life: health, playing well with other children, communicating needs and feelings in one's own language, emotional maturity, self-care, interest and engagement, and motor skills. In this domain, there were no significant differences in the views of Head Start parents and teachers (see Table 9.1). The findings indicate that resources traditionally emphasized by Head Start were highly valued by parents and teachers alike: health, social competencies and maturity, and being able to communicate needs and feelings. A majority of parents endorsed 20 of 21 items as "absolutely necessary" for kindergarten; a majority of teachers endorsed 17 items as "absolutely necessary." Overall, "interest and engagement" and "motor skills" were the least valued among the General Readiness Resources.

In the second domain were five Classroom-Related Readiness Resources especially pertinent to the classroom setting: communicating needs and feelings in English, compliance with teacher authority, compliance with classroom routines, basic knowledge, and advanced knowledge. Here there were significant differences of opinion between Head Start parents and teachers (see Table 9.2). A majority of parents endorsed 18 of these 24 items as "absolutely necessary," whereas only 9 items were viewed as essential by a majority of Head Start teachers. Although Head Start parents and teachers did agree that being able to comply with teacher authority was essential,[2] Head Start parents rated the

---

[2] In the broader community study, parents rated compliance with teacher authority more highly than preschool teachers did (Piotrkowski et al., 2000), but this difference did not achieve statistical significance with this smaller sample of teachers.

Table 9.1. Beliefs of Head Start parents and teachers regarding children's General Readiness Resources

General Readiness Resources	Head Start parents		Head Start teachers		
	Mean	(SD)	Mean	(SD)	p
Is rested and well-nourished, health care needs are met	3.81	(.52)	3.69	(.66)	NS
	87%		79%		
Plays well with other children, shares	3.73	(.57)	3.66	(.55)	NS
	78%		69%		
Can express feelings/needs in primary language	3.65	(.71)	3.69	(.60)	NS
	75%		76%		
Emotional maturity	3.71	(.44)	3.64	(.45)	NS
Does not hit/bite, has self-control	86%		76%		
Has sense of right and wrong	84%		61%		
Is self-confident, proud of his or her work	77%		76%		
Takes turns	70%		72%		
Shows independence	69%		72%		
Self-care	3.62	(.58)	3.59	(.46)	NS
Feeds self with fork	76%		72%		
Buttons own clothes	74%		59%		
Finds own belongings	72%		69%		
Zips own jacket	66%		52%		
Interest and engagement	3.44	(.57)	3.47	(.56)	NS
Asks a lot of questions about how and why	61%		48%		
Is curious	56%		48%		
Is interested in world around him or her	62%		59%		
Starts things on his or her own	51%		66%		
Is eager to learn	79%		76%		
Likes to solve puzzles	36%		48%		
Motor skills	3.41	(.63)	3.33	(.77)	NS
Can hold pencil, can use a scissors	66%		62%		
Throws ball, skips, runs, hops, walks up/down stairs	57%		59%		
Stacks five or six blocks by him- or herself	52%		48%		

Note: Percentages indicate responses of "absolutely necessary"; NS = $p > .05$.

four other Classroom-Related Readiness Resources as significantly more important than Head Start teachers did. Substantially more Head Start parents than teachers viewed being able to express needs and feelings in English as an essential resource. (African American and Hispanic parents did not differ significantly in their endorsement of the importance of speaking English.) Parents rated being able to comply with classroom routines and basic knowledge as essential resources, but teachers viewed them on average as "very important, but not essential." Parents and teachers also disagreed with regard to advanced knowledge. On average, parents viewed this resource as "very important," but teachers rated it as significantly less important. The results of the survey were consistent with focus groups conducted with parents who expressed very strong views about the importance of academic readiness resources.

Data were gathered at the end of the program year, so—presumably—parents had time to absorb Head Start's educational philosophy. Yet, parents still had higher expectations than Head Start teachers with regard to those readiness resources especially relevant to the classroom setting. Why do Head Start parents have such heightened readiness ex-

Table 9.2. Beliefs of Head Start parents and teachers regarding children's personal Classroom-Related Readiness Resources

Classroom-Related Readiness Resources	Head Start Parents		Head Start Teachers		
	Mean	(*SD*)	Mean	(*SD*)	*p*
Can express feelings/needs in English	3.67	(.62)	3.14	(.95)	.007
	74%		45%		
Compliance with teacher authority	3.85	(.38)	3.66	(.60)	NS
Pays attention to teacher	90%		86%		
Follows the teacher's directions	92%		72%		
Listens during group discussions/stories	81%		72%		
Basic knowledge	3.78	(.39)	3.35	(.64)	.002
Knows names of body parts (eyes/nose/legs)	88%		72%		
Knows ABCs	88%		31%		
Knows basic colors such as red, blue, yellow	83%		69%		
Can count to 10 or 15	80%		52%		
Understands big/small, sorts by color/size	69%		48%		
Compliance with classroom routines	3.56	(.50)	3.15	(.57)	.0001
Uses classroom equipment correctly	70%		52%		
Cleans up work space and spills	69%		41%		
Lines up and stays in line, waits quietly	72%		31%		
Moves from one activity to the next with no problems	64%		57%		
Completes tasks on time	46%		14%		
Advanced knowledge	3.30	(.57)	2.78	(.65)	.0001
Knows own address/telephone number	80%		55%		
Writes first name, even if some letters are backwards	66%		31%		
Understands yesterday/today/tomorrow	57%		14%		
Knows days of week in correct order	53%		14%		
Cuts simple shapes with scissors, holds pencil properly	53%		48%		
Recognizes words that rhyme such as *cat, hat*	46%		14%		
Can read a few simple words	49%		10%		
Can read simple stories	36%		10%		
Can count to 50 or more	22%		7%		
Can write on a line, can color inside the lines	34%		21%		

Note: Percentages indicate responses of "absolutely necessary"; NS = *p* > .05.

pectations? West, Hausken, and Collins (1993) concluded that education increases knowledge of child development, so less educated parents have higher expectations, implying that these parents may have age-inappropriate expectations. But this view of parents reflects a deficit perspective at odds with the empowerment philosophy of Head Start, creates distance between educators and parents, and leads to misunderstanding. In the larger community study, parents' education was unrelated to their readiness beliefs (Piotrkowski et al., 2000), and in this subsample of Head Start parents, there was no clear relationship between parental education and readiness expectations. Moreover, parents and Head Start teachers agreed on the importance of many of the General Readiness Resources children need at kindergarten entry.

Elevated readiness beliefs may just as easily reflect realistic assessments of the limited resources of local schools, rather than unrealistic expectations of children. Less than 1 year after data were collected, only 30% of children in third grade scored at or above grade level on a citywide reading test in the school district where all but one Head Start center was located. A Head Start parent told me that she was teaching her 4-year-old to recognize and recite the alphabet and to write her name because her Head Start teacher was "not allowed to," and she was concerned that her daughter might get "lost" in a large kindergarten class with many high-need children. Reasonably, this parent wanted to arm her child with as many academic resources as possible, for her child was to enter a school under review by the state for poor performance.

The findings also suggest some strategies for engaging Head Start parents in shared readiness goals. To convince parents that it is not necessary for Head Start to teach 4- and 5-year-olds to know the days of the week in correct order, Head Start programs have to offer them alternative, age-appropriate curriculum models and interventions that have been shown to enhance the school readiness skills of ethnically diverse children from low-income families using rigorous research designs. Ideally, these interventions would have both home and classroom components (Klein, Starkey, & Wakeley, 1999; Singer & Singer, 1998, 1999; Starkey & Klein, 2000; Whitehurst et al., 1994). Focusing on the readiness resources parents *themselves* identify as important is a way to engage them in the home-based interventions.

The findings also indicate that we cannot assume Head Start teachers' commitment to their program's curriculum model. Among the seven General Readiness Resources, interest and engagement were among the two resources least valued by teachers (and parents). Only "Is eager to learn" received a strong endorsement from most teachers (and parents). This lack of strong emphasis on what many consider important motivational foundations for learning—such as being curious and asking a lot of questions—may reflect a not unreasonable concern with outcomes over process. Moreover, despite the relatively lower ratings given by Head Start teachers to four of the Classroom-Related Readiness Resources, a majority of teachers, nonetheless, believed that knowledge of body parts, basic colors, and addresses/telephone numbers; counting to 10 or 15; using classroom equipment properly; and having easy transitions between activities were "absolutely necessary" for children entering kindergarten. When ratings of "very important" were examined, the number of items that Head Start teachers strongly endorsed jumped dramatically. For example, only 14% of Head Start teachers thought it was "absolutely necessary" for children to know the days of the week in correct order, but an additional 52% thought such knowledge was "very important." In fact, all Classroom-Related Readiness Resources were rated as being at minimum "very important" by a majority of Head Start teachers, including being able to communicate in English.

As a first step in developing community-based consensus regarding readiness goals for children, the results suggest that Head Start administrators should ensure that their educational philosophy is aligned with the beliefs and practices of Head Start teachers and parents. As one example, to reach consensus about a new curriculum model, one Head Start program in the community held focus groups that involved parents, teachers, and all Head Start staff, including those working in housekeeping, security, and the office.

Developing Consensus Between Local Head Start Programs and Local Schools

In addition to developing a shared educational philosophy with parents, the Head Start Performance Standards also require that Head Start programs reach out to local schools to "facilitate continuity of programming" (DHHS, 1996). Although the emphasis has been on increasing communication regarding individual children and joint transition training and activities, continuity of programming implies articulation of curriculum goals between Head Start and kindergarten. This requires consensus between Head Start staff, parents, and local schools regarding what children need to know and be able to do when they enter kindergarten. Developing a collaboration with kindergarten teachers is critical because they ultimately decide if a child is "ready," and their early assessments play an important role in special education placement, ability grouping, grade retention, and subsequent achievement trajectories (Alexander & Entwisle, 1988; Entwisle, 1995; Gredler, 1992; Powell, 1995; Rist, 1970; Shepard & Smith, 1986).

Although not focused on Head Start, studies comparing the school readiness views of parents and/or preschool teachers with those of kindergarten teachers suggest that important differences of opinion exist (Foulkes & Morrow, 1989; Hains, Fowler, Schwartz, Kottwitz, & Rosenkoetter, 1989; Harradine & Clifford, 1996; Knudsen-Lindauer & Harris, 1989; Piotrkowski et al., 2000; West et al., 1993). Across the school district studied, there was considerable consensus between kindergarten teachers, parents, and preschool teachers that General Readiness Resources such as social competence and health are necessary for children entering kindergarten. But, in this community, as in others, kindergarten teachers reported significantly lower expectations than parents and preschool teachers regarding children's classroom-related resources, particularly the basic and advanced knowledge children need when they enter kindergarten (Piotrkowski et al., 2000). The challenge of reaching consensus between kindergarten and Head Start teachers is evident in interviews conducted with 8 Head Start and 12 kindergarten teachers as part of an evaluation of Head Start's impact on school readiness in Ohio. The authors concluded, "There was little consensus among or between Head Start and kindergarten teachers about the academic expectations that should be held for early childhood learning experiences" (Legislative Office of Education Oversight, 1998, p. 14). To make the challenge even greater, in general, there is relatively little or no communication between preschool and kindergarten teachers (Love, 1992).

Given the long-standing barriers to communication between many Head Start programs and local schools, schools may not take the initiative in reaching out to community-based Head Start programs. Therefore, leadership for developing consensus regarding what children should know and be able to do at kindergarten entry and how best to achieve those readiness goals rests with local Head Start programs. The self-interest of schools and the Head Start mission are closely linked, so both would gain from this strategy. Title I of the No Child Left Behind Act of 2001 (PL 107-110) requires that schools develop plans for children's transition from programs such as Head Start and coordinate services with them. If Head Start programs, parents, staff, and kindergarten teachers work toward the same school readiness goals, there is a greater probability that Head Start children will meet those goals. Children who are better prepared are more likely to succeed, which in turn improves the record of local schools at a time when administrators and principals increasingly are being held accountable for failing schools. Everyone—particularly children—gains from such a collaboration.

CONCLUDING REMARKS

Alone, Head Start cannot do justice to its mission of preparing children for school. A community-based approach to ensuring children's school readiness may begin with joint transition planning and with sharing information about particular children (Code of Federal Regulations, 2002; Head Start Bureau, 1996), but it must move on to developing agreement about educational philosophy and school readiness goals for young children and the coordination of curricula and classroom practices. A great deal can be learned from previous transition initiatives in Head Start (see Kagan & Neuman, 1998) and from successful local collaborations (Head Start Bureau, 1996). For example, Le Ager and Shapiro (1995) describe an intervention that aligned the instructional environment of Head Start programs with local kindergartens, based on an assessment of differences between them.

Calls for collaboration and partnerships are not new to Head Start (Head Start Bureau, 1966; DHHS, 1993). Unfortunately, collaboration is labor intensive and funds are scarce. Moreover, in communities with several Head Start programs, it would be impossible for school personnel to agree on different readiness goals with different Head Start centers. In those cases, a broader vision is needed that would involve multiple Head Start programs and elementary schools within communities or school districts. Several Head Start grantees or delegate agencies might pool resources with local schools to fund a transition "outreach" coordinator (Head Start Bureau, 1996) who would be responsible for developing the collaborative vision of readiness within Head Start centers, among Head Start centers, and between Head Start centers and local schools. If local Head Start programs and public schools agree on what children should know and be able to do when they start kindergarten and the Head Start curriculum is designed to achieve those goals, children's early school failure would be a *joint* responsibility to be addressed by the local educational community, not just by schools or by Head Start.

This emphasis on developing local consensus regarding school readiness does not mean that all approaches are equally appropriate or effective for Head Start children. Moreover, Head Start programs have accountability beyond the boundaries of their local communities. Local consensus, therefore, must be joined to the Head Start Performance Standards and to interventions and curricula that have been shown to be effective with Head Start children. By demonstrating their commitment to empirically tested curricula and evaluation, Head Start programs strengthen their voice in negotiating a shared school readiness philosophy with parents and with public school teachers who may believe they are the only "true" experts.

Implementing a community-based vision of children's school readiness also leads to new evaluation questions for Head Start. Is there a shared philosophy of children's school readiness among Head Start teachers, parents, and local school staff? Are Head Start curriculum models consistent with this philosophy, and are they articulated with the local kindergarten curriculum? Is there joint professional training and regular communication between Head Start staff and teachers regarding the curriculum? Do parents engage in home-learning activities that support the common readiness goals? As partners, kindergarten teachers also can provide informal feedback to local Head Start programs about the effectiveness of their curriculum models, even absent formal evaluations.

The data presented here suggest that there already exists some local consensus regarding the resources children need at school entry that can serve as a foundation for a community-based vision. But there is still considerable distance to travel. More specifically, the challenge for local Head Start programs will be to build consensus with parents and school teachers regarding the types and extent of general knowledge and numeracy and emerging literacy skills children need at kindergarten entry and the best practices to achieve them. The task of building and implementing a community-based vision of school readiness is daunting, but the cost of failing to do so may be too great.

REFERENCES

Alexander, K.L., & Entwisle, D.R. (1988). Achievement in the first 2 years of school: Patterns and processes. *Monographs of the Society for Research in Child Development, 53*(2).

Bowman, B., Donovan, S., & Burns, M.S. (Eds.). (2000). *Eager to learn: Educating our preschoolers.* (Executive Summary.) Washington, DC: National Academy Press.

Bredekamp, S. (1992). Discussion. Assessment alternatives in early childhood. In F. Lamb Parker, et al. (Eds.), *New directions in child and family research: Shaping Head Start in the 90's. Conference proceedings* (pp. 310–312). Washington, DC: Administration on Children, Youth and Families, U.S. Department of Health and Human Services.

Coats Human Services Reauthorization Act of 1998, PL 105-285, 42 U.S.C. §§ 9801 *et seq.*

Code of Federal Regulations, Title 45, Vol. 4. Revised October 1, 2002. Washington, DC: U.S. Government Printing Office.

Coleman, J.S. (1988). Social capital in the creation of human capital. *American Journal of Sociology, 94,* S95–S120.

Entwisle, D.R. (1995). The role of schools in sustaining early childhood program benefits. *The Future of Children, 5*(3), 133–144.

Foulkes, B., & Morrow, R.D. (1989). Academic survival skills for the young child at risk for school failure. *Journal of Educational Research, 82*(3), 158–165.

Goals 2000: Educate America Act of 1993, PL 103-227, 20 U.S.C. §§ 5801 *et seq.*

Graue, M.E. (1992). Social interpretations of readiness for kindergarten. *Early Childhood Research Quarterly, 7,* 225–243.

Gredler, G.R. (1992). *School readiness: Assessment and educational issues.* Brandon, VT: Clinical Psychology Publishing Company.

Hains, A.H., Fowler, S.A., Schwartz, S.S., Kottwitz, E., & Rosenkoetter, S. (1989). A comparison of preschool and kindergarten teacher expectations for school readiness. *Early Childhood Research Quarterly, 4,* 75–88.

Harradine, C.C., & Clifford, R.M. (1996). *When are children ready for kindergarten? Views of families, kindergarten teachers and child care providers.* (ERIC Document Reproduction Service No. ED399044)

Head Start Bureau. (1996). *Effective transition practices: Facilitating continuity. Training guides for the Head Start community.* Washington, DC: Administration on Children, Youth and Families, U.S. Department of Health and Human Services.

Heaviside, S., & Farris, E. (1993). *Public school kindergarten teachers' views on children's readiness for school.* Washington, DC: U.S. Department of Education. (NCES 93410)

Holloway, S.D., Rambaud, M.F., Fuller, B., & Eggers-Pierola, C. (1995). What is "appropriate practice" at home and in child care?: Low-income mothers views on preparing their children for school. *Early Childhood Research Quarterly, 10,* 451–473.

Kagan, S.L., Moore, E., & Bredekamp, S. (Eds.). (1995). *Reconsidering children's early development and learning: Toward common views and vocabulary. National Education Goals Panel. Goal 1 Technical Planning Group.* Washington, DC: U.S. Government Printing Office.

Kagan, S.L., & Neuman, M.J. (1998). Lessons from three decades of transition research. *The Elementary School Journal, 98*(4), 365–379.

Klein, A., Starkey, P., & Wakeley, A. (1999). *Enhancing pre-kindergarten children's readiness for school mathematics.* Paper presented at the annual meeting of the American Educational Research Association, Montreal, Canada.

Knudsen-Lindauer, S.L., & Harris, K. (1989). Priorities for kindergarten curricula: Views of parents and teachers. *Journal of Research and Child Education, 4*(1), 51–61.

Le Ager, C., & Shapiro, E.S. (1995). Template matching as a strategy for assessment of and intervention for preschool students with disabilities. *Topics in Early Childhood Special Education, 15*(2), 187–218.

Legislative Office of Education Oversight. (1998). *Head Start's impact on school readiness in Ohio: A case study of kindergarten students.* Columbus, OH: Author.

Love, J.M., (1992). Connecting with preschools: How our schools help (and fail to help) entering kindergartners. In J. McRobbie, J. Zimmerman, & P.L. Mangione (Eds.), *Links to success: New thinking on the connections between preschool, school, and community. A regional symposium, proceedings paper.* San Francisco: Far West Laboratory for Educational Research and Development.

Love, J.M., & Logue, M.E. (1992). *Transitions to kindergarten in American schools. Executive Summary of the National Transition Study.* Washington, DC: U.S. Department of Education, Office of Policy and Planning.

Luster, T., & McAdoo, H. (1996). Family and child influences on educational attainment: A secondary analysis of the High/Scope Perry Preschool data. *Developmental Psychology, 32,* 26–39.

Maxwell, K.L., & Eller, S.K. (1994). Children's transition to kindergarten. *Young Children, 49*(6), 56–63.

May, D.C., & Kundert, D.K. (1992). Kindergarten screenings in New York State: Tests, purposes, and recommendations. *Psychology in the Schools, 29,* 35–41.

Meisels, S.J. (1992). Doing harm by doing good: Iatrogenic effects of early childhood enrollment and promotion policies. *Early Childhood Research Quarterly, 7,* 155–174.

National Association for the Education of Young Children (NAEYC). (1990). NAEYC position statement on school readiness. *Young Children, 1*(November), 21–23.

National Task Force on School Readiness. (1991). *Caring communities: Supporting young children and families.* Alexandria, VA: National Association of State Boards of Education.

No Child Left Behind Act of 2001, PL 107-110, 20 U.S.C. §§ 6301 *et seq.*

Piotrkowski, C.S., Botsko, M., & Matthews, E. (2000). Parents' and teachers' beliefs about children's school readiness in a high-need community. *Early Childhood Research Quarterly, 15,* 537–558.

Piotrkowski, C.S., & Katz, M.H. (1982). Indirect socialization of children: The effects of mothers' jobs on academic behavior of children. *Child Development, 53,* 1520–1529.

Powell, D.R. (1995). *Enabling young children to succeed in school.* Washington, DC: American Educational Research Association.

Rist, R.C. (1970). Student social class and teacher expectations: The self-fulfilling prophecy in ghetto education. *Harvard Educational Review, 40*(3), 411–451.

Schultz, T.W. (1961). Investment in human capital. *The American Economic Review, 52*(1), 1–17.

Shepard, L.A., & Smith, M.L. (1986). Synthesis of research on school readiness and kindergarten retention. *Educational Leadership, 44*(November), 78–86.

Shore, R. (1998) *Ready schools.* Washington, DC: National Education Goals Panel.

Singer, J.L., & Singer, D.G. (1998). *Learning through play for school readiness.* (Video). New Haven, CT: Yale University Family Television Center.

Singer, J.L., & Singer, D.G. (1999). *Learning through play for school readiness. Interim report of year two research findings.* New Haven, CT: Yale University Family Television Center.

Starkey, P., & Klein, A. (2000). Fostering parental support for children's mathematical development: An intervention with Head Start families. *Early Education and Development, 11,* 659–680.

U.S. Department of Health and Human Services (DHHS). (1993). *Creating a 21st century Head Start. Final report of the Advisory Committee on Head Start Quality and Expansion.* Washington, DC: Author.

U.S. Department of Health and Human Services (DHHS). (1996). *Head Start Program performance standards and other regulations.* Washington, DC: Author.

Vartuli, S. (1999). How early childhood teacher beliefs vary across grade level. *Early Childhood Research Quarterly, 14,* 489–514.

Wesley, P.W., & Buysse, V. (2003). Making meaning of school readiness in schools and communities. *Early Childhood Research Quarterly, 83,* 351–375.

West, J., Hausken, E.G., & Collins, M. (1993). *Readiness for kindergarten: Parent and teacher beliefs.* Washington, DC: U.S. Department of Education, Office of Educational Research and Improvement. (NCES 93257)

Whitehurst, G.J., Epstein, J.N., Angell, A.C., Payne, A.C., Crone, D.A., & Fischel, J.E. (1994). Outcomes of an emergent literacy intervention in Head Start. *Journal of Educational Psychology, 86,* 542–555.

Whitehurst, G.J., Zevenbergen, A.A., Crone, D.A., Schultz, M.D., Velting, O.N., & Fischel, J.E. (1999). Outcomes of an emergent literacy intervention from Head Start through second grade. *Journal of Educational Psychology, 91,* 261–272.

Willer, B., & Bredekamp, S. (1990). Redefining readiness: An essential requisite for educational reform. *Young Children* (July), 22–24.

Zigler, E., & Trickett, (1978). IQ, social competence, and evaluation of early childhood intervention programs. *American Psychologist, 33,* 789–798.

Zill, N., Resnick, G., McKey, R.H., Clark, C., Connell, D., Swartz, J., et al. (1998). *Head Start Program Performance Measures, Second Progress Report.* Washington, DC: U.S. Department of Health and Human Services.

CHAPTER 10

Head Start and Evidence-Based Educational Models

David P. Weikart

From the vantage point of the year 2004, it is hard to realize that Head Start was a breakthrough programming concept when it was initiated in 1965. The goal was to provide a comprehensive social, health, and family development program for poor children and improve their chances for a better life. There was an earlier time, of course, when child care was nationally provided, but the purpose differed. When the child care centers for the disadvantaged were established under the New Deal's Works Progress Administration in the 1930s, the centers were for adult purposes—to provide women with employment. When these programs were expanded during World War II, it was so mothers could be free to replace the men in factories. During these periods, child care outside of the home was accepted as a temporary necessity. With the end of the war in 1945 and the return of the soldiers to civilian life, women returned to the home and the traditional role of caring for children. Child care centers closed, and those services that remained retreated to campuses where the children of privilege were served as part of the campus school. Run by college faculty and usually staffed by undergraduate students from departments of home economics, colleges of education, or schools of nursing, the programs were limited to the general concern for social skills (e.g., sharing toys, taking turns) or health skills (e.g., self-feeding, naps, caring for bodily functions). Manuals of the day didn't mention cognitive development or academic skills (Sears & Dowley, 1963).

Professionals studying child development, however, kept an interest in the general areas of physical growth and social development. Along with a strong group of committed early childhood service providers, professionals studying child development kept the focus on the value of such services. It is tempting to portray this dedicated group as "guardians of the faith," for early childhood programming was not just a service, it was a calling. When interacting with this group of determined and purposeful graying career

143

ladies as a young male professional in the early 1960s, I often felt as if I had entered my Great Aunt Anna's formal sitting room with very dirty shoes. Their faith in their purpose and beliefs was so strong. Yet, without their dedication and maintenance of operational programs, the great historic traditions of early childhood care and education (Cleverley & Phillips, 1986) would not have been available to the nation in the 1960s. Perhaps Head Start as we know it would not have emerged from the cocoon early child care and education inhabited between World War II and the Johnson Administration's War on Poverty. It was from this group of people and the traditions they served that the social, health, and family service focus of National Head Start was captured. It is hard to stress how small this group of professionals was to serve so large a national purpose. In Michigan, for example, at a meeting in the spring of 1965 before the first summer of Head Start, the state officials gathered more than 300 teachers and administrators who would be involved in program operation. They asked how many of us worked with or had experience with preschool children. About 15 people raised their hands. A very slender reed for a national program, indeed.

My own drive to establish early childhood education programs, however, did not come from this tradition, but out of my knowledge of public school failure to successfully educate youth from poor backgrounds. The High/Scope Perry Preschool Study (Schweinhart, Barnes, & Weikart, 1993) was initiated in 1962 to determine if education before kindergarten attendance could improve both social and academic school performance. The traditions of early childhood education were so generally weak, however, that I was informed by an advisory group of professors that a plan to bring 3- and 4-year-old poor children into organized programs would be detrimental to their development. The response to this challenge was to create a study with a tight research design based on random assignment of samples and commit to a longitudinal study. The High/Scope Perry Preschool Study developed an educational approach based on the research of Piaget and the participatory learning theories of Dewey, softened by the practical experience of well-trained and experienced teachers. As I worked with Head Start, I realized that the High/Scope approach to classroom and home learning was different from what I saw developing in Head Start. They were similar but different models of education and service. Children would be served differently not only in structure but also in process.

Head Start's interest in educational models developed in 1968 with the National Planned Variation Head Start Project. Different sponsors, primarily from the National Follow Through Project at the elementary school level, were invited to provide consultation to selected Head Start programs. Included in the group of 12 models was one called the Enabler Model. The consultants for this "created" model represented the "guardians of the faith," and it was added so that the basic Head Start program model created from that point of view could be included. Aside from the obvious problems (i.e., inexperience at program operation away from homebase, lack of systematic training procedures, no assessment instruments that could fairly measure results, a whole litany of curriculum issues), the model sponsors made only five visits per year to the site. Indeed, the federal monitors of the implementation were scheduled for more. As might be expected, the results were not outstanding. High/Scope had some success as the Huron Institute (Smith, 1973) reported. For example, the High/Scope site children had a 23-point rise on the Stanford-Binet IQ test whereas all other models reported little or no change.

On the whole, the Planned Variation Head Start Project research seemed to have little immediate impact on Head Start, and the limited outcomes were certainly a factor. What the Planned Variation Head Start Project did do was raise the awareness of models and model differences in the approach to the teaching/learning context. In the late 1990s, efforts to raise the quality of Head Start programs have suggested a new look at models as a possible resource. Now, more than 30 years later, we know much more about preschool educational models. This chapter reviews information on model programs and their effects.

WHAT IS A MODEL?

Essentially, a model is a set of practices that provide a structure for program operation. The model provides a decision-making framework to guide the establishment of the physical aspects of the setting; the training of the staff; the interaction with children, parents, and the community; and the assessment of both student and program progress. Those program operators, such as myself, who subscribe to an educational model approach, believe it is the only way to produce high-quality programs with important and long-lasting outcomes. We see the failure of Head Start becoming universally successful to be the program's adherence to the concept of eclecticism drawn from the tradition of teacher theoretical and practice independence. That is, each traditionally trained teacher is expected to adjust what curriculum knowledge he or she has to the needs of each child, as required (Goffin, 1993).

But, it is the year 2004 and not 1965. What do we know after decades of research and service experience?

Model Categories

The various educational approaches used with children generally fall into four different categories (see Figure 10.1). Use of these categories permits curriculum model description and research to proceed with greater efficiency. Programs that use no model typically take a few ideas from each category. Although I first described this categorization pattern (1972), other observers have used essentially the same pattern for categorizing early childhood curricula (Kohlberg & Mayer, 1972) and parenting styles (Baumrind, 1971). The organizing principle behind this pattern is that the teacher/adult and the child in a learning situation can each take a role of either high or low initiative, depending on the intention of the curriculum theory employed.

In the *programmed* approach, which includes methods drawn from learning theory, the typical role of the teacher is to determine and then initiate the required learning activities; the role of the child is to respond and learn from what the teacher offers, not to self-initiate individual learning or activities. These centrally designed curricula include clearly defined objectives; incorporate carefully organized sequences to move children toward these objectives; and provide teachers with a script, or explicit instructions, for implementing the sequences. Content in programmed curricula usually emphasizes specific preacademic skills, learning is viewed as the acquisition of "correct" responses with respect to the programmed instruction goals, and assessment is narrowly focused on the objectives taught. It is assumed that if the behavioral objectives are specific enough, vir-

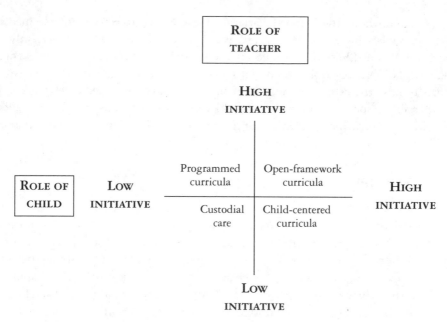

Figure 10.1. Preschool curriculum models.

tually anything can be taught to almost any child through the use of appropriate behavior-modification techniques.

In the *open-framework* approach, which is based on child development theory, it is the role of both teacher and child to initiate learning activities. The primary educational objective for the child is the development of fundamental cognitive processes and concepts, rather than specific skills (although it is assumed that specific skills will be acquired during general development). Learning results from the child's intended, direct experience in and action on the environment, followed by shared reflection on the experience. Learning is not viewed as an accumulation of specific bits of information, as in the programmed learning approach. Open-framework curricula are generally based on an explicit theory of child development (e.g., the High/Scope educational approach draws on Piagetian theory). This category provides a decision-making framework for teachers without specifying the day-to-day content of the programs. Children identify the content and interests that are of most importance to them, and learning occurs through the child's active and largely intrinsically motivated involvement in an environment structured and observed by the teacher. Children are assessed by observation (described in concrete terms) of development over time. Such a framework makes these approaches very flexible in local adaptations.

In the *child-centered* approach, which is based on social development and maturation theories, the child typically initiates learning by playing, and the teacher's role is to respond to the child's particular interests and activities. This is the traditional early childhood program, and the great majority of preschool programs around the world, if they are not eclectic, would describe themselves as being in this category (Weikart, 1999). Characterized by a focus on the development of the whole child, such programs emphasize social and emotional growth and self-expression, rather than acquisition of specific preacademic skills or cognitive development. Play is the child's work. Classroom environments are typi-cally open and, ideally, rich in stimuli. The relationship between teacher and child tends to be permissive. Content revolves around topics of interest to the child that support gen-eral socialization-enculturation, opportunities for children's independent and creative ac-tivities, and opportunities for children's exploration and development of healthy peer re-lationships. Assessment is usually a narrative story of the child's behavior.

In the *custodial* approach, which has no basis in theory, the teacher/adult provides basic care while the children entertain themselves. In some programs that focus primarily on specific health and nutrition goals, the children often remain passive in cribs or cer-tain sections of the room, waiting for the next event (e.g., toileting, snack time). Unless called for by the schedule, there is little interaction between the caregiver and the chil-dren. Often, the children undertake little activity. This approach is not recommended and, sadly, is often seen in developing countries.

STUDIES COMPARING PRESCHOOL CURRICULA

This section looks at the research undertaken to examine the differential impact of the ap-proaches (programmed, open-framework, child-centered, and custodial care) just described. Carrying out such program-comparison research is more difficult than implementing research on a single program because equality in the programs must be maintained, and random assignment of participants is essential. Few studies are able to meet these criteria.

Two Early Long-Term Studies

Two long-term preschool curriculum comparison studies that began in the 1960s—the University of Louisville study of Head Start (Miller & Bizzell, 1983) and the University of Illinois study (Karnes, Schwedel, & Williams, 1983)—focused on children living in poverty and included the Direct Instruction model (the programmed approach), the High/Scope curriculum (or another open-framework approach), and traditional nursery school programs (the child-centered approach). Both studies collected data using a variety of mea-sures of intellectual performance, as well as data from interviews and records. Both studies found that on various measures of intellectual performance, children in Direct Instruction programs initially outperformed children in child-centered and open-framework programs. But these significant differences appeared only during the program and up to a year after-ward. In other words, the widely observed pattern of IQ score improvement followed by fade-out applied to the preschool programs involved in these two long-term studies. In the Illinois study, the high school graduation rates of study participants were noticeably, if not significantly, different across program types— 70% for the child-centered program group, 48% for the Direct Instruction program group, and 47% for the study's no-program group.

The Planned Variation Head Start Study

In the late 1960s, National Head Start began a long-term study to examine the effects of using different preschool curriculum models. This 1969–1972 Planned Variation Head Start project included a dozen different preschool curriculum models at 37 sites with some 6,000 children enrolled in the model programs (Datta, McHale, & Mitchell, 1976). Among the dozen models studied were the Direct Instruction model (programmed approach); the High/Scope curriculum (open-framework approach); and an "Enabler model," which resembled a traditional child-centered approach. Although study participants were children enrolled in Head Start, they were nevertheless somewhat heterogeneous in family socioeconomic status and initial intellectual performance. Despite the national study's many design problems, two clear findings emerged. First, on the postprogram multiple choice achievement tests, children in Direct Instruction and other programmed learning programs had higher scores than did children in any of the other programs or in any of the comparison groups. Second, in intellectual performance, children in High/Scope programs had greater gains than children in any other model. High/Scope program children gained an average of 23 points on the Stanford-Binet Intelligence Scale, while children in all other models gained no more than 5 points (Smith, 1973). Because of these gains, a 20-year follow-up study including 622 children enrolled in the Head Start High/Scope programs and nonparticipating children was conducted. It found a slight though significant increase in school achievement by girls and a reduction in young adult criminal behavior. Only the High/Scope model was included in the follow-up study (Oden, Schweinhart, Weikart, Marcus, & Xie, 2000).

Short-Term Preschool Studies

A number of other early childhood curriculum comparison studies have been conducted. For example, Burts and associates engaged in a program of research based on assessing teachers' developmentally appropriate beliefs and practices (as defined by the National Association for the Education of Young Children; Bredekamp, 1987) and related child outcomes. "Developmentally appropriate practice" corresponds to the High/Scope and child-centered models, whereas "developmentally inappropriate practice" corresponds in many ways to the Direct Instruction and other programmed models. Examining a sample of 37 kindergarten children, Burts et al. found that those in a developmentally inappropriate class exhibited significantly more stress behaviors (e.g., complaints of feeling sick, stuttering, fights, tremors, nervous laughter, nail biting) than did those in a developmentally appropriate class (Burts, Hart, Charlesworth, & Kirk, 1990). They replicated this finding with a sample of 204 kindergarten children and found these curriculum group differences to be most pronounced for males and for African American children, the categories of children most likely to experience Direct Instruction classes (Burts, Hart, Charlesworth, & Kirk, 1990).

In other curriculum comparison research, DeVries and her associates systematically observed three kindergarten classes—one used a Direct Instruction model, another used an open-framework approach such as High/Scope's, and the third used an early childhood eclectic approach. Analyzing teachers' interactions with children, DeVries et al. found that the open-framework teacher significantly surpassed the other two in her use of reciprocal and collaborative negotiation strategies and shared experiences (DeVries, Haney, & Zan, 1991). Analyzing children's interactions with one another during two game-like activities, they found that compared with children in the Direct Instruction and eclectic programs, children in the open-framework program were more interpersonally interactive and had a greater number and variety of negotiation strategies and shared experiences (DeVries, Reese-Learned, & Morgan, 1991). Although *before* kindergarten and in first grade, the Direct Instruction class had significantly higher achievement test scores than did the open-framework class, these significant differences between the two classes disappeared by third grade.

Comparative curriculum research is important to the extent that the curriculum models compared represent the real choices made by early childhood teachers. Marcon (1992, 1994) identified three different preschool models actually used by teachers and operating in the Washington, D.C., public schools: teacher-directed, child-initiated, and what she called "middle-of-the-road." Marcon's research examined the development of a random sample of 295 children attending these three types of programs. The teacher-directed programs resembled the Direct Instruction model, and the child-initiated programs resembled the High/Scope curriculum. Children from the various types of classes differed significantly in their mastery of basic reading, language, and mathematics skills, with the greatest mastery being shown by children from child-initiated classes, followed by children from teacher-directed classes, then by children from "middle-of-the-road" classes. Although not statistically significant, this same differential ranking by curriculum type appeared later, in fourth grade, in children's grade-point averages overall and in most subject areas.

Other curriculum comparison findings came from the High/Scope Training of Trainers Evaluation (Epstein, 1993). She found that compared with children in nominated comparison high-quality classes not using the High/Scope curriculum, children in High/Scope classes were rated significantly higher at the end of the school year in their initiative, social relations, music and movement skills, and general development. In another study of the effects of the High/Scope curriculum, Frede and Barnett (1992) found that preschool programs throughout South Carolina that were implementing the High/Scope curriculum moderately to very well contributed more to children's school achievement at kindergarten and first-grade entry than did programs with low implementation levels. With these general findings as a base, the next section looks at a long-term study specifically designed to ask the question of model effectiveness in reaching improved education and adult productivity goals. As the only study with random assignment, it has special importance.

The High/Scope Preschool Curriculum Comparison Study

The High/Scope Preschool Curriculum Comparison study began in 1967 (Schweinhart & Weikart, 1997). The project employed a stratified random-assignment procedure to assign 68 disadvantaged 3- and 4-year-old children (both African American and Anglo) living in Ypsilanti, Michigan, to each of three curriculum models: Direct Instruction (programmed approach), High/Scope (open-framework approach), and traditional Nursery School (child-centered approach). The children attended preschool for 1 or 2 years. Children in each group attended a daily 2½-hour classroom session and received a home visit to involve their parents for 90 minutes every other week. The findings on curriculum group differences through age 23 concerning education, household, and life adjustment (particularly the number of criminal arrests) are summarized here. Comparisons can be drawn between these findings and those of the High/Scope Perry Preschool study (Schweinhart et al., 1993), because the High/Scope curriculum group's success pattern looks like that of the High/Scope Perry Study program group while the Direct Instruction group pattern looks like the no-program group.

Education   Only one significant group difference in total education-related scores took place during the study through age 23: The Direct Instruction group surpassed the traditional Nursery School group but not the High/Scope group on the Stanford-Binet Intelligence Scale at the end of the preschool program (age 5). The larger finding is the extraordinary increase in the mean IQ score of the whole sample of children, whatever curriculum model they experienced. From the age-3 baseline mean IQ score of 78, the three curriculum groups together at age 4, after 1 year of a preschool program, evidenced an improvement of 26 points. This improvement diminished by 9 points during the subsequent 6 years but held steady at 17 points above the baseline at ages 6, 7, and 10, which is a pattern of sustained improvement that contradicts the expected IQ score fade-out found in most studies.

Despite the Direct Instruction group's 2 years of intensive, carefully structured academic preparation, all three curriculum groups performed essentially the same on academic tests throughout their school years. The Direct Instruction group, however, experienced significantly more years of special education for emotional impairment or disturbance (47%); members of the other two groups experienced almost no special education (both 6%). Members of the Direct Instruction group failed almost twice as many classes as did members of the other two curriculum groups, a difference that was not statistically significant but was consistent with the Direct Instruction group's nonsignificant pattern of a lower rate of on-time high school graduation.

Household   A person in his or her early twenties is at the very beginning of adult life and is still very much in a transitional period. The striking evidence of this is that nearly half of the follow-up study's respondents (47%) were, at age 23, living with their mother and/or father—that is to say, living in their home of origin. Curriculum groups differed significantly in the percentages of members married and living with their spouses: 0% of the Direct Instruction group, as compared with 18% of the Nursery School group and 31% of the High/Scope group. This finding resembles the High/Scope Perry Preschool study finding in which 40% of program females but only 8% of nonprogram females were married at age 27 (N = 49).

Life Adjustment (Criminal Arrests)   The Direct Instruction group experienced more than twice as many *lifetime arrests,* including twice as many adult arrests, as either of the other two curriculum groups, a nearly significant finding. The Direct Instruction group averaged 3.2 lifetime arrests per person as compared with 1.5 for the High/Scope group and 1.3 for the Nursery School group. Most important, the Direct Instruction group had significantly more felony arrests than the other curriculum groups—four times as many as the other two groups combined. These differences appeared in felony arrests from ages 22 to 25, as the number of these arrests grew more substantial. Forty-three percent of Direct Instruction group members had felony arrest records, as compared with only 10% of the High/Scope group and 17% percent of the Nursery School group.

Compared with the High/Scope group, the Direct Instruction group also identified significantly more *sources of irritation* in the community (the interview item asked the respondent to identify "different types of people . . . giving you a hard time lately"). The most frequent sources of irritation identified were collection agencies, work supervisors, police, courts, and family members. The prominence of police and courts, particularly for the Direct Instruction group members, corroborates the findings of differences in numbers of felony arrests.

Finally, the Direct Instruction group reported being *suspended from work* significantly more often than did either of the other two curriculum groups—0.6 times per group member as compared with almost no work suspensions in the other groups.

CURRICULUM MODELS AND PROGRAM QUALITY

This review of a number of studies suggests that using a specific curriculum model that supports children's initiative is essential to having high-quality preschool programs that produce lasting benefits. In particular, it suggests that education officials who promote teacher-scripted instruction with young children living in poverty are pursuing a very risky path. Programs and teachers who want the effects that are found to result from a particular curriculum model must commit to following the curriculum model. Research findings regarding program effects can be generalized only to programs that are essentially the same as the programs studied. Similar research by Nabuco and Sylva (1995) in Portugal support the idea that curriculum may be more important than cultural, socio-economic, or racial factors because their findings follow the same pattern as the United States of America study outcomes. But, following a curriculum model does not require abandoning intelligent judgment, as some scholars have suggested (Goffin, 1993; Walsh, Smith, Alexander, & Ellwein, 1993). Situations in preschool programs are constantly changing; teachers must apply principles intelligently to these situations, or the principles are reduced to mindless reactions. On the other hand, while the High/Scope Preschool Curriculum Comparison study suggests that conventional early childhood wisdom is on the right track, it hardly substantiates every idea that a good early childhood educator ever had.

The High/Scope Preschool Curriculum Comparison study also should dispel any belief that home visits and teacher–parent contacts alone make the difference between programs that have lasting beneficial effects and those that do not. Bi-weekly home visits were as much a part of the Direct Instruction program as they were a part of the others. Nevertheless, this study does leave open the question of whether substantial outreach to parents is *one* of the aspects of a curriculum model that can reinforce its lasting benefits. Had the parents not been full partners in the implementation of the child-centered and open-framework curriculum models with their children, perhaps these curriculum groups would not have differed significantly from the Direct Instruction group in their average number of felony arrests at age 23.

This High/Scope Preschool Curriculum Comparison study supports advocacy of open-framework educational models over teacher-scripted instruction models for young children. It identifies the High/Scope curriculum and to some extent the traditional Nursery School approach as particular models of education that develop the decision-making capacity and social skills that children need for responsible adult life. It indicates that these approaches might help prevent crime, and it shows that choice of a curriculum model is an important factor in determining the quality of early childhood education.

What Makes an Effective Model? Selection and Use

The admonishment provided by the cluster of studies examining the issue of effective approaches to early child care and education is very specific: Use those curriculum models that are based on child-initiated learning supported by adults rather than those that consist of adult-structured lessons. Although this finding may be a little surprising, it is fortunate because it supports a desirable public policy goal: to engage professionals, families, and communities in the care and education of children in ways that allow each group to implement their own ideas and objectives. A curriculum model that emphasizes child-initiated learning best promotes this type of engagement as it is process, rather than content-focused. Because it is not scripted and therefore not closely determined by a government agency or by a textbook publisher, a curriculum incorporating child-initiated learning allows for the inclusion of local traditions, games, songs, stories, and found materials. Adults, with knowledge of the local community, can support and extend children's interests in these familiar objects and activities. This openness also permits recognition of the wide differences among children within a given classroom or center.

We know that an open-framework approach with an emphasis on child-initiation and active adult support is important. But there are even broader criteria for selecting a curriculum model that will lead to the desired results. To be effective, a high-quality preschool model needs to meet three requirements: 1) it must have a validated curriculum, 2) it must have a validated training system, and 3) it must have a validated assessment system (see Figure 10.2 on p. 155).

A Validated Curriculum   To be effective, a curriculum model must represent a coherent system based on developmentally valid theories or beliefs. Its carefully thought-through organizing principles need to form a logical system, which then becomes the basis for making decisions about day-to-day program operation and practice (e.g., setting up the learning environment, daily routine, adult–child interaction, logistics of teacher planning, nature and extent of parent involvement, organization of learning activities, resolution of conflicts, use of technology). In the High/Scope educational model, Piaget's ideas about understanding the child's development of knowledge and Dewey's educational ideas about the importance of participatory learning at all age levels serve as the organizing principles.

The theoretical basis of a model provides a discipline for both program developers and adults who apply the approach. If the teacher or caregiver can elect to introduce into the preschool program anything that is of passing interest, or if the program is simply an amalgamation of several ideas that might be described as "good practices," then there is the danger of becoming eclectic. An eclectic program lacks coherence and does not lend itself to documentation, replication, and finally, validation. Although a given eclectic curriculum may be very successful, it is essentially one of a kind and, because it cannot be replicated or validated, is of little use in planning community or nationwide early childhood services. In a national survey of 2,000 (671 responding) leaders in early childhood education, 45% reported using a mixture of model program ideas and 21% reported using no model ideas at all (Epstein, Schweinhart, & McAdoo, 1996). Few programs, even those run by the best trained, meet this first criterion for high quality.

A preschool model must be documented if it is to be understood and used by a wide range of individuals from different educational and social backgrounds. Although it is always difficult to document a program—to write down its features and practices—such a step is essential in making the program accessible to others. The process of documentation forces the developers to clarify the program's goals and methods. Once written down, it can be adapted for adults with limited skills so that community members and other paraprofessionals can participate in program operation. The process forms the basic body of knowledge for training new staff and explaining the program to parents and other interested parties, and it should be available for translation into the language of any community where the approach would be useful. It can be extended for use by others working with different groups, such as children with special educational needs or multilingual children. For the High/Scope approach, the textbook, *Educating Young Children: Active Learning Practices for Preschool and Child Care Programs* (Hohmann & Weikart, 1995) is an example of documentation. There are many other supporting print and recorded materials developed to help adapt the content of *Educating Young Children* to specific groups of adults and children. As of 2004, many of these materials are also available in Arabic, Turkish, Dutch, Portuguese, Spanish, Finnish, Chinese, French, Norwegian, and Korean.

A model system needs to be validated by research demonstrating significant effects when the model is well implemented. This absolute requirement for validation of long-term effectiveness is the one that most model approaches fail to meet. So often in education, especially with programs for young children, adults use ideas that they like. They are pronounced as valid practice because of direct and immediate experience. Yet, practices that seem logical and built on tradition often do not work to produce desired outcomes when applied in different contexts. Only well-designed, longitudinal studies can provide answers to permit the expenditure of public funds on a wide scale. Such studies are neither cheap nor quick. They are very difficult to design, fund, and carry out. But they are essential to justify the wide-scale use of specific models to solve social and educational problems. For the High/Scope approach, the long-term High/Scope Perry Preschool study offers significant validation of the model's effect throughout childhood and into adulthood. This groundbreaking study receives support from the High/Scope Preschool Curriculum Comparison study, validating the model's greater effectiveness relative to other competing models.

A curriculum model needs to be used on a wide scale and in a wide range of settings to be certain that the system actually works. By necessity, a model is developed on a selected group of young children in a limited setting. But, can a model that is well-implemented and effective on a limited scale replicate essential features on a larger scale and with different populations? It is important to try the model out in a wide range of geographical locations, different language groups, varied ethnic clusters, and selected ability groups to identify its adaptability or potential limitations when it is taken to scale. For the High/Scope approach, research on the use of the method throughout the United States and many other countries has demonstrated its capacity and robust nature to assist children. National studies in the U.S. (Epstein, 1993) have shown the model maintains its quality and fidelity in multiple replications. Other studies done in the United Kingdom by Berry and Sylva (1987) and in Portugal by Nabuco and Sylva (1995) also give strength to the original work by examining the curriculum in other cultures, program settings, and language and socioeconomic groups.

A Validated Training System   A model curriculum program needs a validated training system so that it can be transferred successfully from the model developers to a wide range of classrooms or child care settings. Like the process needed to establish the validity of the model approach, developing an effective adult training program to enable others to use the method is on the same order of difficulty. In a manner of speaking, an effective training program must recapitulate all of the previous steps. It needs to be based on a systematic model of effective adult learning. Simply disseminating the information about the model is not enough. It needs to be fully documented so that the training is consistent for all those learning the approach. If different trainers use different systems and information about the model, then the actual practice of the program will be very different. The system needs to be validated by research so that the policy makers applying the approach will know that the training component is effective. For the High/Scope approach, this validation step meant going into the field to interview High/Scope endorsed trainers, observe the individual teachers as they planned and implemented the program on a daily basis, and evaluate children in these settings to discover the extent of High/Scope curriculum impact (Epstein, 1993). Although validating the training model is difficult to undertake and complete, this final step is necessary for a model to go to scale and demonstrate its feasibility when widespread training can no longer be carried out directly by the program developers themselves.

A Validated Assessment System   A curriculum model needs an assessment system reliably indicating the growth achieved by participating children. Assessment systems are frequently selected to demonstrate child progress on dimensions that bear little or no relationship to the curriculum goals and methodology used. Typically, such systems are focused on narrow academic skills that are simple to measure, for example, using letter recognition as a measure of reading ability. In general, such assessment instruments lack validity because they are artificial and do not provide a full picture of a child's motivations and abilities. These problems are especially true when assessment of preschool children is undertaken or when there are language or cultural differences present. A good model will have an assessment plan that allows child progress to be monitored with an instrument that reflects the developmental intentions of the program. The High/Scope approach uses the High/Scope Child Observation Record (High/Scope Educational Research Foundation, 1992), an observation system that allows adults to document progress in key cognitive and social development areas. As a documentation system, the findings are based on actual examples of classroom behavior that represent the best performance the child can spontaneously produce during the natural observation period. Recording these observations allows adults to plan activities that support and extend the abilities of the children in their programs. Quantitative scores on the assessment instrument also indicate the success the approach has as it supports the child's growth.

A well-developed monitoring system must be available to ensure that the curriculum model is actually in operation when it is said to be employed. The final test of a model program is whether it is actually in use. Many times, curriculum models are more apparent in how adults describe their program than in actual application. A model that

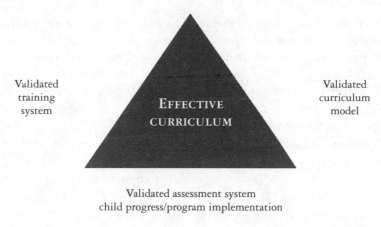

Figure 10.2. Criteria for a successful early childhood curriculum.

is used to go to scale needs a system that allows independent observers to validate the fidelity of the actual program implementation in daily operation. A well-designed program monitoring scheme will also direct attention to areas in which adults need further training. In the High/Scope approach, the High/Scope Program Quality Assessment (High/Scope Educational Research Foundation, 1998) is used for both monitoring and training purposes. Actually, this instrument allows any early education program to look at its quality of implementation, based on what is known from decades of research on best practices. As outlined in Figure 10.2, a curriculum model designed to go to scale must meet very strict standards of validation. If large public expenditures are to be made for such an effort, the model must be able to offer assurance that its curriculum, training methods, and assessment procedures are valid. Only then can policy makers be assured that the model can be broadly implemented and achieve its promised effectiveness.

MODEL PROGRAMS CONCLUSIONS

Early childhood education, like education in general, has always been a field based on belief systems, not evidence-based educational approaches. Montessori's approach to education is an outstanding representative of one such belief system. Its quaint theories and classroom materials stand in daily testimony as Montessori-trained teachers apply the system while their leaders bemoan the lack of research evidence to justify their practice. Today's attraction to the beliefs of Reggio Emilia reflect a return to Italy 100 years after Montessori. In Epstein et al.'s (1996) survey of early education usage of the 671 National Association for the Education of Young Children members who responded, 5.1% used the Creative Curriculum prepared by Dodge (Dodge & Colker, 1992). The well-written and easily accessed program in the traditional child-centered mode is appealing and obviously useful to teachers both with and without training. Yet, there is no evidence to support its use and no knowledge of its value to participating children and their families. But beliefs drive the field.

Parent education programs are another good example of the power of beliefs. The belief is by reaching parents and helping them solve family problems and improve parenting skills, the family and the child will benefit. Head Start, the High/Scope Perry Preschool study, and the High/Scope Preschool Curriculum Comparison study, among others, all had home visit components. In a careful review by the Packard Foundation (Behrman, 1999) of the six major parent home visiting programs, including such popular ones as Parents as Teachers, Healthy Families America, and Home Instruction Program for Preschool (HIPPY), the best that the authors of the report could say was, "The wide variability in the results . . . suggest that practitioners and policymakers should moderate their expectation for success of home visiting programs" (p. 22). Then, they pointed out that children and families need help and that the field is too important to ignore. We need to "craft" new approaches (p. 24).

Another belief is that we fail to spend enough money on families in need and fail to support them over a long enough period to be effective. This belief system led to the federal effort to correct both these problems through the $240 million Comprehensive Child Development Program. The program enrolled mothers and their children (either unborn or younger than 1 year of age) with a commitment for 5 years of service. Out of 24 sites, 21 participated in an evaluation of 4,410 families with random assignment of 2,213 families to the treatment group and 2,197 to no-treatment group. The cost per participating family was $35,800. Although many professionals will find problems with the services and operations in the various sites, the authors concluded that, after one of the longest and most expensive per-family service projects ever delivered to so many, "There is no evidence that providing case management by means of home visits is an effective way to improve social, education, or health outcomes for adults or children" (St. Pierre & Layzer, 1999, p. 134).

Beliefs not only drive early childhood education and parent training programs but they also affect other fields of education. Perhaps the most egregious is in drug prevention programming for preadolescents. The federally supported Drug Awareness and Resistance Education program (DARE) is famous for its almost universal presence in schools and police departments (as instructors). At more than $1 billion per year, it reaches thousands of children. Yet, carefully done research projects on the impact of the program constantly indicate that the program is not effective (Glass, 1997). The problem is that the approach has organized such a fellowship of believers that no evidence-based information is accepted. Too bad, because such commitment starves alternative models that have data to support their work.

The grand ladies who nurtured the field during its 20 years in the wilderness (1945 to 1965) represented a belief in a model that social and physical development are what children need. Further, that service can be provided by a committed adult with a general theory background, working with small groups of children in individual classrooms. When Head Start began in 1965, it was this belief system that became the basis for what is the Head Start service model. No evidence, no research validation. The ladies had scattered their labors on children of professionals whom we now know benefit not a wit from such experiences. (Of course the children responded and matured, but their peers, not enrolled, were indistinguishable when they all entered formal school.) Less is known about the children attending the few programs in settlement houses and other social services who were from less well-off families.

But evidence was building. In 1958, Kirk reported with some discouragement that, of his five experimental groups of children with disabilities, only those in the group without a specific etiology from poor families seemed to benefit from early education. And

Krech, Rosenzweig, and Bennett (1960) reported that rats reared in highly active and stimulating environments with plenty of space and opportunities to play with tunnels, wheels, high bars, balls, and so forth, were better maze solvers than their littermates who were cage-reared as per tradition. These strands lead to the creation of the High/Scope Perry Preschool study in 1962. And the 40-year work of the High/Scope Perry study, added to the work of many professionals starting from various psychological and sociological points, has supported the vast expansion of both child care and early childhood programs such as Head Start.

BUT THIS IS THE 21ST CENTURY—WHAT DO WE KNOW?

We know that there are evidence-based early childhood model programs that produce significant changes in the participating children's lives. They change their family relationships for the better: more stability and more satisfaction. They change their adult work experience for the better: improved jobs held for a longer time, more earnings. They change their social life for the better: contributory social behavior, positive relationships with peers, family, and the community. And they just may give their children a way out of poverty. They also cost the community nothing in the way of overall investment, for the evidence-based preschool model outlay is returned many times over in savings. This is the standard for Head Start to reach.

So What Is the Problem?

It's tough to work under a discipline imposed by an evidence-based model educational approach. It's more fun to have good ideas, to be free to adjust to what you think the children need, to base actions on what experience has taught, or to simply "wing it" on a daily basis. It feels better to be committed to a belief.

This approach was fine when little evidence was available to support any approach other than what experienced teachers believed. Interestingly, education is not the only field with this problem. It seems impossible for an outsider to accept, but medicine faces similar issues in spite of a common belief that it is an evidence-based profession. "The medical literature shows that physicians are often prisoners of their first-hand experience: their refusal to accept even conclusive studies is legendary. . . . [For example] despite trials showing the drug Topotecan to be effective against ovarian cancer, [gynecologic oncologist Anderson] rarely chooses it because he has never had good luck with it" (Russo, 1999, p. 36). If the issue of using evidence as a basis for decisions is a problem in medicine, we can forgive teachers in which the tradition of scientific research is less well established and certainly less well funded. Also, teacher beliefs about effective education are well established, and contrary information is hard to accept. But this is the 21st century and evidence is at hand the can help well-trained and dedicated adults to run effective programs that change children's lives. We can't, at least as yet, fix everything, or even help everyone, but with evidence-based educational model approaches we can make a significant difference. New research in education, health, neurology of the brain, pharmacology, technology, and areas not even under consideration will provide new evidence. But for now, our belief must be in the potential of all children and in their families; our practice must be drawn from evidence-based models as we build a new century.

REFERENCES

Baumrind, D. (1971). Current patterns of parental authority. *Developmental Psychology Monographs, 4*(4, Part 2).

Behrman, R.E. (Ed.). (1999). Home visiting: Recent program evaluations. *Future of Children, 9*(1).

Berry, C.F., & Sylva, K. (1987). *The plan-do-review cycle in High/Scope: Its effects on children and staff.* Oxford, England: Oxford University.

Bredekamp, S. (Ed.). (1987). *Developmentally appropriate practice in early childhood programs serving children from birth through age 8.* Washington, DC: National Association for the Education of Young Children.

Burts, D.C., Hart, C.H., Charlesworth, R., & Kirk, L. (1990). A comparison of frequency of stress behaviors observed in kindergarten children in classrooms with developmentally appropriate versus developmentally inappropriate instructional practices. *Early Childhood Research Quarterly, 5,* 407–423.

Cleverley, J., & Phillips, D.C. (1986). *Visions of childhood: Influential models from Locke to Spock.* New York: Teachers College, Columbia University.

Datta, L., McHale, C., & Mitchell, S. (1976). *The effects of Head Start classroom experience on some aspects of child development: A summary report of national evaluations, 1966–69* (DHEW Publication No. OHD-76-30088). Washington, DC: U.S. Government Printing Office.

DeVries, R., Haney, J.P., & Zan, B. (1991). Sociomoral atmosphere in direct-instruction, eclectic, and constructivist kindergartens: A study of teachers' enacted interpersonal understanding. *Early Childhood Research Quarterly, 6,* 449–471.

DeVries, R., Reese-Learned, H., & Morgan, P. (1991). Sociomoral development in direct-instruction, eclectic, and constructivist kindergarten: A study of children's enacted interpersonal understanding. *Early Childhood Research Quarterly, 6,* 473–517.

Dodge, D.T., & Colker, L.J. (1992). *The creative curriculum for early childhood* (3rd ed.). Washington, DC: Teaching Strategies.

Epstein, A.S. (1993). *Training for quality: Improving early childhood programs through systematic inservice training* (Monographs of the High/Scope Educational Research Foundation, 9). Ypsilanti, MI: High/Scope Press.

Epstein, A.S., Schweinhart, L.J., & McAdoo, L. (1996). *Models of early childhood education.* Ypsilanti, MI: High/Scope Press.

Frede, E., & Barnett, W.S. (1992). Developmentally appropriate public school preschool: A study of implementation of the High/Scope Curriculum and its effects on disadvantaged children's skills at first grade. *Early Childhood Research Quarterly, 7,* 483–499.

Glass, S. (1997, March 3). Don't you DARE. *The New Republic,* 1–12.

Goffin, S.G. (1993). *Curriculum models and early childhood education: Appraising the relationship.* New York: Merrill.

High/Scope Educational Research Foundation. (1992). *The High/Scope Child Observation Record for Ages 2½ to 6.* Ypsilanti, MI: High/Scope Press.

High/Scope Educational Research Foundation. (1998). *The High/Scope Program Quality Assessment: Preschool Version.* Ypsilanti, MI: High/Scope Press.

Hohmann, M., & Weikart, D.P. (1995). *Educating young children: Active learning practices for preschool and child care programs.* Ypsilanti, MI: High/Scope Press.

Karnes, M.B., Schwedel, A.M., & Williams, M.B. (1983). A comparison of five approaches for educating young children from low-income homes. In Consortium for Longitudinal Studies, *As the twig is bent: Lasting effects of preschool programs* (pp. 133–170). Mahwah, NJ: Lawrence Erlbaum Associates.

Kirk, S.A. (1958). Early education of the mentally retarded. Urbana: University of Illinois Press.

Kohlberg, L., & Mayer, R. (1972). Development as the aim of education. *Harvard Education Review, 42,* 449–496.

Krech, D., Rosenzweig, M.R., & Bennett, E.L. (1960). Effects of environmental complexity and training on brain chemistry. *Journal of Comparative Physiological Psychology, 52,* 509–519.

Marcon, R.A. (1992). Differential effects of three preschool models on inner-city 4-year-olds. *Early Childhood Research Quarterly, 7,* 517–530.

Marcon, R.A. (1994, November). Doing the right thing for children: Linking research and policy reform in the District of Columbia Public Schools. *Young Children, 50*(1), 8–20.

Miller, L.B., & Bizzell, R.P. (1983). The Louisville experiment: A comparison of four programs. In Consortium for Longitudinal Studies, *As the twig is bent: Lasting effects of preschool programs* (pp. 171–199). Mahwah, NJ: Lawrence Erlbaum Associates.

Nabuco, M., & Sylva, K. (1995). *Comparisons between ECERS ratings of individual pre-school centres and the results of target child observations: Do they match or do they differ?* Paper presented to the 5th European Conference on the Quality of Early Childhood Education, Paris, France.

Oden, S., Schweinhart, L.J., Weikart, D.P., Marcus, S.M., & Xie, Y. (2000). *Into adulthood: A study of the effects of Head Start.* Ypsilanti, MI: High/Scope Press.

Russo, F. (1999, May). The clinical-trials bottleneck. *Atlantic Monthly,* 30–36.

Sears, P.S., & Dowley, E.M. (1963). Research on teaching in the nursery school. In N.L. Gage (Ed.), *Handbook of research on teaching* (pp. 811–864). Chicago: Rand McNally.

Schweinhart, L.J., Barnes, H.V., Weikart, D.P. (1993). *Significant benefits: The High/Scope Perry Preschool study through age 27* (Monographs of the High/Scope Educational Research Foundation, 10). Ypsilanti, MI: High/Scope Press.

Schweinhart, L.J., & Weikart, D.P. (1997). *Lasting differences: The High/Scope Preschool Curriculum Comparison Study through age 23* (Monographs of the High/Scope Educational Research Foundation, 12). Ypsilanti, MI: High/Scope Press.

Smith, M.S. (1973). *Some short-term effects of project Head Start: A preliminary report on the second year of planned variation, 1970–71.* Cambridge, MA: Huron Institute.

St. Pierre, R.G., & Layzer, J.I. (1999, Spring/Summer). Using home visits for multiple purposes: The Comprehensive Child Development Program. *Future of Children, 9*(1), 134–151.

Walsh, D.J., Smith, M.E., Alexander, M., & Ellwein, M.C. (1993). The curriculum as mysterious and constraining: Teachers' negotiations of the first year of a pilot programme for at-risk 4-year-olds. *Journal of Curriculum Studies, 25,* 317–332.

Weikart, D.P. (1972). Relationship of curriculum, teaching, and learning in preschool education. In J.C. Stanley (Ed.), *Preschool programs for the disadvantaged* (pp. 22–66). Baltimore: Johns Hopkins University Press.

Weikart, D.P. (Ed.). (1999). *What should young children learn? Teacher and parent views in 15 countries.* Ypsilanti, MI: High/Scope Press.

CHAPTER 11

Head Start's Efforts
to Improve Child Health

Robert W. O'Brien, David B. Connell, and James Griffin

he integration of various individual and family services into a single, comprehensive plan is a prime focus in the field of human services, particularly in the field of child and family services. This interest is based on an expectation that the final result of integrating services will be greater than the sum of the parts. Given that this emphasis on integrated services heightened during the 1990s, the founders of Head Start in 1965 seem to have been well ahead of their time. Their foresight resulted in the shaping of a program that went well beyond the simple provision of an educational head start for low-income preschool children. From the beginning, the idea was for the Head Start program to become a program that would touch children and families across many domains that are recognized as critical for normal development (Zigler, Piotrkowski, & Collins, 1994). Among these domains are physical health, dental health, nutrition, and mental health. This chapter focuses on Head Start's work in the area of children's health services, specifically through these four health domains.

Typically, Head Start programs do not provide direct health services for children and families. Rather, Head Start has assumed the role of educating families and facilitating their access to appropriate health care providers in their local communities. Among the mandates for Head Start programs is responsiveness to the ongoing health needs of their local populations and an obligation to assist families within the context of local services. As someone familiar with the program might expect, the response by local programs to this mandate has manifested itself in a broad range of approaches. Some of these approaches were designed through careful planning, whereas others evolved by default. Re-

This chapter is based on the results of "A Descriptive Study of Head Start Health Services" (contract no. 105-93-1911), which was funded by the Administration on Children, Youth and Families; The Administration for Children and Families; the U.S. Department of Health and Human Services. This chapter is intended to promote the exchange of ideas among researchers and policy makers. The views expressed in it are part of ongoing research and analysis and do not necessarily reflect the position of the U.S. Department of Education.

alizing that new research was needed to understand what was taking place in the field, Head Start acknowledged its need for descriptive information on 1) how local programs provided services for families and 2) the health status of the children in these programs. This need resulted in the Descriptive Study of Head Start Health Services (Keane, O'Brien, Connell, & Close, 1996).

The health study was also a response to two federal reports that were issued in 1993. First, the Advisory Committee on Head Start Quality and Expansion issued a document called *Creating a 21st Century Head Start: Final Report of the Advisory Committee on Head Start Quality and Expansion* (1993), while the U.S. Department of Health and Human Services (DHHS) Office of the Inspector General (OIG) focused attention on Head Start by issuing a report on the implementation of expansion funds titled *Evaluating Head Start Expansion Through Performance Indicators* (1993). These reports focused on the performance of the national program within the context of an increased number of local programs serving a growing number of children. Included in their reports was a recommendation that baseline data from children's Head Start records, parent interviews, and staff interviews be collected and reviewed to increase understanding of the health problems and service needs of Head Start children and their families.

The descriptive findings of the health study were part of a long-term research strategy to meet program information needs and to provide data critical for implementing many of the Advisory Committee's recommendations. Different from studies that used the usual compilation of Head Start child health records and data from the Head Start Program Information Report (PIR), the health study's primary source of data was from individual interviews with Head Start parents (to learn about how the program helps them obtain health services for their families) and Head Start staff (to understand how local programs operate in this area).

This chapter contains 1) a summary of some study findings from the health study that shed light on how Head Start promoted child health, 2) answers regarding some critical views of Head Start health services, and 3) commentary on the adequacy of Head Start health services within the context of the current state of health programs for low-income children.

HOW DO HEALTH SERVICES FIT INTO THE HEAD START MODEL?

The Original Design of Head Start

The original intent of the creators of Head Start was to expand traditional preschool education and build a program to foster social competence—a comprehensive construct that includes health as an important component of successful, individual functioning. Head Start, therefore, promotes opportunities for society to join with low-income families in overcoming problems and/or barriers encountered in resolving these problems. In 1965, Dr. Robert Cooke and the panel of experts charged with developing this unique program laid out the basic elements of the Head Start program. Those elements included the initial emphasis on health assessments and health education:

> It is clear that successful programs of this type must be comprehensive, involving activities generally associated with the fields of health, social services, and education . . . . The

> objectives of a comprehensive program should include . . . improving the child's physical
> health and physical abilities . . . tailored to the needs of the individual community and the
> individual child. (U.S. Department of Health, Education and Welfare, 1972, p. 2)

More specifically, they noted the health-related evaluations and programs that should be integral to the Head Start program:

> Evaluation of the child should include a medical assessment (pediatric and neurological
> physical measurements, assessment of nutrition, vision, hearing and speech, and selected
> tests for TB, anemia and kidney disease), dental examination, and screening for special
> problems and special strengths in social and emotional development. (U.S. Department of
> Health, Education and Welfare, 1972, p. 3)

The foresight of the panel has been sustained as we have learned more about the associations between poverty and health status and between health status and learning (Brooks-Gunn & Duncan, 1997).

Goals of Head Start Health Services

The Head Start Program Performance Standards reflect the goals of the program by providing each local program with a set of specified objectives. How a program achieves these goals and objectives is often tied to the individual characteristics of that program. This occurs because each program operates within a unique environment, depending on such characteristics as the nature of the grantee or delegate agency (e.g., a school system versus a Community Action Agency or another type of grantee), the physical aspects of the program (e.g., the number of enrolled children, the geographic size of the designated service area), the characteristics of the target population (e.g., the primary language of the families), and the availability of community resources (e.g., the number of local service providers, local service provider acceptance of Medicaid).

Local program procedures are set up to meet the requirements that enrolled children receive health screenings and examinations, that children receive required immunizations, and that proper treatment is received for any detected health problems. Parents are expected to become actively involved in the health care of their children and become advocates for their children. Head Start assists parents who need help in a number of ways, such as identifying providers, furnishing information and transportation assistance, and securing necessary funding (Head Start is only considered as the "dollar of last resort" for direct payment for health services). Head Start staff are expected to educate and empower parents and to guide them in negotiating the health care system themselves. In reality, many primary caregivers have this skill upon enrolling their child in Head Start, but the program's objective is that *all* parents will be in a position to assume sole responsibility for these tasks by the time their children leave Head Start. In addition, educational activities designed to address preventive health issues with both children and their families have become a critical part of this health program.

Local programs each work with a Health Services Advisory Committee (HSAC) as part of their effort to be responsive to community health issues that affect the children. The HSAC consists of Head Start parents and staff as well as representatives from the local community. The establishment and expansion of such community linkages was one of the major policy recommendations of the Advisory Committee on Head Start Quality and Expansion (1993). Some Head Start programs have well-established community collaborations, and it is expected that the experiences of these programs provide valuable information for other Head Start programs and community organizations. Nationally, Head Start has been cited as an important information resource because it is the only public agency in the country that is required to report on the health needs of preschoolers from low-income homes, their access to services, and the health care resources that are available at the community level (Bell & Jones, 1993). This clearly puts Head Start in a position to make positive contributions to the health of all children, whether or not they are in Head Start.

Previous Research on Head Start and Child Health Services

Prior to the health study, only a few studies focused on the impact of Head Start on health screenings and examinations for children. Fosburg (1984) examined the Head Start health services delivery system and the outcomes it produced on the health status of the children served by Head Start, compared with the health status of non-Head Start children. Head Start children were more likely to receive a medical examination than non-Head Start children (86% versus 68%), and more Head Start children received additional preventive health services such as tuberculosis (TB) tests (67% versus 42%) and lead tests (15% versus 8%). Such findings reflect the stringent screening and examination requirements expected of every program, as operationalized through the Head Start Child Health Record.

Hale, Seitz, and Zigler (1990) examined the medical records of 40 children enrolled in Head Start, 18 low-income children on a Head Start waiting list and 20 children in a nursery school serving middle-class families. These groups of children were compared with regard to health screenings, and their medical records were examined for immunizations and pediatric checkups since birth. Children enrolled in Head Start were more likely than children on the Head Start waiting list and middle-class children to receive age-appropriate health screenings. The Head Start children were also significantly more likely than the children on the waiting list to be screened for high lead levels, anemia, TB, high blood pressure, loss of hearing, and loss of vision. The Head Start children exceeded the middle-class children in receiving TB tests, blood pressure measurements, and hearing and vision screenings. Thus, for low-income children in Head Start, the program's health services delivery system was a key difference in their receipt of preventive care (Zigler et al., 1994).

Brush, Gaidurgis, and Best (1993) examined the quality of Head Start's comprehensive services using the PIR and the findings from the on-site program reviews conducted by Head Start. Both data sources showed that most grantees deliver extensive services and meet nearly all of the Program Performance Standards in this area. Using the 1992 PIR data, Brush et al. found that, across all the reporting programs, medical treatment was provided to a mean of 97% of the children needing such services.

General Accounting Office Study on Expansion-Health Services

As one piece of its review of Head Start quality and expansion funding, OIG conducted a review of Head Start records in 1992. The review was to assess how well programs were meeting the criteria set out by the Performance Standards, including the health area. One of the study conclusions was that accurate and up-to-date record keeping by local programs seemed to be a problem, and if it was not a problem, then Head Start did not follow through with families to make sure they received necessary health services throughout the year. OIG found that the percentages of children meeting immunization requirements were generally on target in terms of the less stringent PIR reporting requirements. However, a far lower proportion of Head Start children—only 43.5% (including both 3- and 4-year-olds)—were found to be immunized at the levels required by the Performance Standards. The need to clarify the findings of the General Accounting Office (GAO) report was one reason for the initiation of the health study by the Head Start Bureau.

Summary of the Health Study Methodology

The health study findings are based on interviews of a nationally representative sample of 1,189 families with 4-year-old children. These children were enrolled in 40 Head Start programs across 23 states and Puerto Rico. The 40 programs represented a stratified random sample, drawn from approximately 1,800 Head Start programs (excluding migrant programs). The sampling plan assured broad geographic representation across four regions (East, Midwest, Southeast, and West) with appropriate distributions of urban and rural programs (based on census data) and minorities (more or less than 50%) among the enrolled populations. Two centers were randomly chosen from among those run by each program, and 15 four-year-old children were randomly selected from each center in order to develop a sample of children whose parents would be interviewed and whose Head Start health records would be reviewed.

During week-long site visits to each program, the research team conducted interviews with Head Start staff (e.g., center directors, health coordinators, mental health coordinators, parent involvement coordinators, nutrition coordinators) responsible for the administration and implementation of that program's health services. Researchers also interviewed parents about their children's health and their use of health services for their children, reviewed the Head Start health records of these children, and observed meals at each of the centers. All site visits were conducted in the spring of 1994, at the end of the Head Start academic year.

Is Head Start Responsive to Health Needs in the Real World?

In an era of increasing difficulty for low-income families in gaining access to affordable private health care, Medicaid provides valued assistance in overcoming barriers to care for families. (Federal monies providing health services to low-income children above the poverty level through the Children's Health Insurance Program [CHIP] were not available at the time of the health study.) Among the Head Start children, almost two thirds were enrolled in Medicaid at or near the time of their birth (1988–1990), although an additional one fifth signed up during the time they were enrolled in Head Start (1993–1994). Reported reasons for not enrolling in Medicaid were failure to meet eligibility requirements (income level was too high, 41.9%) or because other sources of insurance coverage were available (48.2%). By the end of the Head Start year, very few parents suggested that a lack of knowledge about Medicaid, about how it works, or about how to enroll were reasons they did not use Medicaid (or private insurance) coverage, suggesting that Head Start successfully informed parents about the benefits of and means of access to Medicaid services.

Head Start also links with health service organizations in the local community. The organization types most commonly reported as being associated with Head Start programs were public health agencies and private group providers. The most frequently reported services provided to Head Start families were medical services and screenings, vision screenings and eye care, immunizations, dental services, and nutrition services and meal planning. Commonly noted in discussions with staff about local providers was the serious lack of both specialists and general health providers who were willing or able to work with children.

Although services for low-income families may be available in many local communities, there are often serious public health risks within these same communities—the types of risks that have serious implications for the health of Head Start children and their families. The major community health risk factors that programs faced daily were reported during interviews with Head Start staff. The most frequently named public health risk factors for the communities served by these programs included substance abuse, poor parenting skills, lack of available support services for families, poor nutrition, and poverty. Child abuse and neglect and community violence are other risk factors that were mentioned, typically by staff responsible for mental health services. Virtually all of the staff noted that their Head Start programs provided parent education and community outreach activities that were designed to address specific community risk factors.

The driving question in this chapter—Is Head Start meeting its goal of empowering parents and improving the health of the children it serves?—cannot be answered until some preliminary questions are addressed.

Who Is Managing the Health Services for Local Programs?

At the time of the study, program services were under the direction of component coordinators, typically a health coordinator, a mental health coordinator, and a nutrition coordinator.[1] It was not uncommon for one person to hold one or more of these positions, particularly in smaller programs.

Health and mental health coordinators typified the dual role of health service provider/broker. Respondents from both staff positions were involved in conducting screenings and examinations, reviewing the results of these tests, and consulting with other staff in assessing the health needs of the children in their charge. When a health need was identified, health and mental health coordinators often coordinated the actual delivery of services with other Head Start staff, and the coordinators worked with local health care providers both in arranging for treatment and in following up on the treatment provided. Finally, coordinators helped parents understand the ramifications of missing screening and treatment services that may be required. Health and mental health coordinators also reported that they spent a significant amount of their time conducting health and mental health education classes for parents and teachers, as well as engaging in interagency collaborations within their communities.

---

[1] The latest revisions of the Program Performance Standards changed this configuration; however, at many Head Start programs, the former component coordinators remain involved in the same or similar tasks.

Nutrition coordinators were primarily involved in the planning, purchase, and delivery of food to the children enrolled in the program. They also conducted growth screenings and assisted with the identification of child, family, and community nutrition problems by conducting nutrition assessments, providing nutritional counseling, and conducting nutrition education classes for teachers and parents. In providing these services, the nutrition coordinators needed to work closely with other health services staff, provide training and education for staff and parents, and collaborate with other nutrition-oriented agencies in the community including the U.S. Department of Agriculture Food Service.

Given the roles these coordinators have in maintaining health standards and in educating families and other staff members, proper training and experience in the health field are very important. Many staff reported that their highest level of education was a college degree or some college; approximately 40% of the health coordinators reported that they had nursing training, and approximately one third of the mental health coordinators interviewed indicated that they had a master's degree. Larger proportions of staff respondents in programs with enrollments of 1,000 or more reported that they possessed bachelor degrees than did their counterparts in programs with enrollments under 500. This suggests that larger programs are more successful in attracting staff with higher levels of education. Higher proportions of staff from Head Start programs sponsored by school systems reported bachelor degrees than did staff from programs sponsored by other types of organizations—a likely reflection of the hiring requirements within the school systems.

Approximately one third of the center directors and half or more of each of the other staff positions associated with the health component reported performing multiple staff roles. The most frequently cited problem associated with performing multiple staff roles was the time constraint created by the additional workload. Staff in multiple roles typically expressed concerns about program-related barriers to care facing Head Start families. Identified barriers included limited Head Start budgets, particularly for health services allotments, as well as staff shortages relative to field work with families and required paperwork.

Does Head Start Get Children Required Health and Dental Health Services?

Screenings and Examinations The Program Performance Standards require that children have a complete physical examination and assessment, including vision and hearing screens, every 2 years beginning at age 3. However, children are also required to have a comprehensive health examination and dental examination no later than 45 days after enrollment. For the health study, the review of the child health records included the dates of enrollment and start of participation in Head Start services, as well as the dates and results of the most recent child health and dental examinations. To simplify comparisons across programs and centers with inconsistent start dates, July 1993 was designated as a standard reference point against which to review the recorded physical examination dates for all children. Because this date falls just before the beginning of the Head Start academic year for the participating programs, it represents a time when Head Start staff are generally working with parents to prepare children for entry into the program. It was found that the median month for children's physical examinations was July, although the modal month was August. Given the timing of most of the examinations, it was judged likely that Head Start influenced the percentage of examinations. More than 20% of those parents reporting that their children had physical examinations during the past year stated that Head Start arranged these examinations.

Using the same procedure for reviewing the dental examinations as was applied to the health examinations, July 1993 was chosen as a standard reference point for checking dental examination dates found in the health records. The median month for dental examination dates August, although the mode was September. Again, these are months in which Head Start staff are usually working with parents to ensure a smooth transition into the program, and it is likely that if Head Start had influence on the percentage of examinations completed, it would occur during these months. The impression left from these data is that Head Start likely had a positive effect on the rate of children receiving thorough dental examinations, even if it required staff to arrange the visit, provide transportation, or arrange payment to assist the children in getting examinations. The time frame was slightly behind that noted for the health examinations, but this is likely due to a shortage of dentists willing to take low-income children as patients, as well as a need to educate some parents of the need for dental examinations for preschool children.

Pre-Head Start/Post-Head Start Enrollment Comparison

One strategy used to estimate the potential impact of the Head Start health services is to look at the diagnosis of specific health conditions, both prior to or after enrollment in Head Start. By July 1, 1993, most of the families had been interviewed by Head Start and their children were enrolled for the upcoming Head Start program year. Because certain background health information was collected by Head Start from the caregiver at the initial enrollment interview, these reports were expected to provide information on health status prior to Head Start. Subsequent examination reports available in the health files were considered as having happened during the period of Head Start influence.

Although 4.8% of all children were reported to have had lower respiratory problems, 4.3% of the children had this condition noted before Head Start enrollment. Similarly, asthma, ear problems, and gastrointestinal problems were also more likely to have been detected before entry into Head Start. Conversely, several categories of health conditions were detected during health screenings or examinations that took place following entry into Head Start. These conditions—including blood disorders, speech and language problems, dental/oral health conditions, and hernias—were two to five times more likely to be detected in these later screenings and examinations. Although these findings may reflect the increased age of the children at the time of the examinations, they also clearly reflect the broad scope of the physical examination administered under Head Start's guidelines. The health examination required by Head Start is quite rigorous and much more comprehensive than typical examinations for children of this age.

Reports of Health and Dental Status

Parent reports and reviews of the child health files, both conducted in the spring of the Head Start year, indicated that 98.5% of the children received physical examinations during the previous 12 months. The health conditions most likely reported by the parents were ear problems, speech and language problems, gastrointestinal problems, lower respiratory problems, and asthma. Although the types of health conditions noted in the children's health files were similar to those reported by parents, the important point is that the frequency of the conditions noted in the records was uniformly lower than what was reported by parents. Almost 30% of the children had no mention of a health condition by their parents, whereas the child health files had no health condition listed for about three fifths of the children. Fewer than 13% of the child health files indicated that the child had multiple health conditions; however, almost one third of the parents reported multiple health conditions for their children. Approximately one tenth of the parents reported that serious injuries (typically cuts, abrasions, and stitches) had occurred to their children, whereas reports of injuries were noted in less than 8% of the child health files. These differences represent evidence for a recurring problem noted throughout the study: Head Start records are not regularly updated during the year.

The high prevalence of dental caries in Head Start children has been well documented (Barnes, Parker, Lyon, Drum, & Coleman, 1992; Edelstein, 2000; Kaste, Marianos, Chang, & Phipps, 1992), and this conclusion was supported in the health study. Overall, parent reports, combined with the review of the child health files, indicated that 96.4% of the Head Start children had received dental examinations in the previous year. More than 92% of the health coordinators reported that their programs actively provided or arranged dental examinations for enrolled children and that most of these examinations were conducted off-site. Similar to the pattern noted for health problems, although almost 42% of the parents reported that their children had identified dental conditions (more than 80% of the identified conditions were dental caries), only 11% of the health files maintained by Head Start indicated that a child had a reported dental problem. Forty two percent of the child health files had no indication of whether the child had dental problems, meaning that there was likely a record that an examination took place, but the outcome of that examination was not documented.

Reports of Immunization Status   One of the more targeted areas for focusing on Head Start health services is pediatric immunizations and the issue of whether children are up-to-date on their immunizations. There has been some confusion within the program regarding immunizations because, although Head Start immunization guidelines are consistent with—and perhaps more stringent than—the recommendations of national advisory groups, two additional sources of advice provided conflicting guidance to Head Start staff regarding complete immunizations for 4-year-old children. First, individual state requirements for entrance into kindergarten were generally less stringent than the Head Start requirements. In a survey completed by the Centers for Disease Control and Prevention in 1992, the majority of states required four or fewer Diphtheria, Pertussis, and Tetanus immunizations and three or fewer Oral Polio Vaccines for school entrance. Second, the PIR reporting requirements through 1993–1994 employed the less stringent '4–3–1–1' standard (those requirements were modified for the 1994–1995 Head Start year). Throughout the 1990s, the PIRs from all of the Head Start programs indicated that more than 85% of the children were fully immunized according to the '4–3–1–1' criterion. That standard was, and remains, consistent with national advisory group recommendations.

As noted previously, the OIG report found that although the PIR percentages were generally accurate in terms of the less stringent PIR reporting requirements, a far lower proportion of Head Start children were actually fully immunized when the 1988 Head

Start guidance was applied. Based on their reviews of child health files completed near the end of the 1992 school year, OIG found only 43.5% of all children (including both 3- and 4-year-olds) were immunized at the levels required by the Performance Standards. OIG suggested that a large number of children were not fully immunized but, in fact, almost all of these children were missing only the fifth DPT and/or the fourth OPV. These immunizations are required by Head Start for children 4 years and older before they leave the program; however, the states that require these immunizations only require them prior to entry into kindergarten.

In the health study, the immunization rates based on the children's health record review showed that more than four fifths (82%) of the 4-year-old children were fully immunized in accordance with the PIR reporting requirements, but less than one third of the 4-year-old children in the study were fully immunized according to the Head Start immunization policy ('5–4–1–1') in effect at the time. This percentage increased to more than 37% when parent-held records and the information in the health files were combined. A substantial proportion of the children had additional DPT and OPV immunizations noted on the parent records that were not recorded in their Head Start child health files. Overall, the children had more than 82% of their required immunizations, with the fifth DPT and the fourth OPV being the most likely missing shots. Our assessment was that children were being properly immunized, and that some of the variability was due to inconsistencies in requirements across the states represented in the study.

Again, the Head Start requirements are very stringent; not all states reach that level of prevention, and the states that do make '5–4–1–1' a requirement do so for kindergarten entry. This last fact may play into the timing of when shots are offered in many communities. That is, many families may simply be waiting for their children to take their kindergarten physical during the summer. Of bigger concern was the fact that fewer than one tenth of the health coordinators reported accurately that five DPT immunizations were necessary for a 4-year-old child to be considered fully immunized, and only one quarter correctly noted that four OPV vaccinations were required. An under-informed staff may actually be a more serious detriment to achieving full immunization then inadequate health services in a local service area.

Medical and Dental Treatment   Information about how children were treated for their conditions was typically thin. Parents reported that medication was the most common form of treatment. Almost one half of the parents reported their children received treatment for conditions noted at the initial health screenings or examinations with one fifth receiving treatment for conditions found during follow-up medical tests during the Head Start year. The child health files contained little documentation about whether treatments were completed or if they were in progress or ongoing. More than 80% of the health records reported a health condition with no follow-up data on the status of the recommended treatments. In the dental domain, parents reported that more than 70% of the dental treatments recommended for dental conditions were fillings. Almost 54% of the parents said that Head Start spoke to them about treatments for their children's dental conditions.

In the investigation of whether Head Start gets children the required health and dental health services, one issue became very obvious. Based on evidence noted during the scrutiny of the data on medical conditions, dental conditions, and immunizations, Head Start records generally underestimated what the parents reported and what was found on the parent-held records. Moving beyond issues regarding the validity of parental reports, the only way to truly evaluate the impact of Head Start and have an accurate picture of child health services is to gain permission to review the records of the children's health providers. However, this finding regarding the shortcomings of the record keeping system is consistent with the findings of OIG and was validated by members of the study's advisory panel, which included Head Start health staff. The parent reports do indicate that Head Start is doing its job, particularly from the parents' perspective, with regard to helping families secure proper and necessary health services.

What Services Does Head Start Offer Families Regarding Nutrition?

The positive link between good health and good nutrition is well noted in the field of child development. Poor nutrition during childhood, which is often associated with poverty, has potential lifelong effects on the health and functioning of an individual. Children from low-income families generally have lower values than other children for height, weight, and triceps skinfold thickness (Rosenbaum, 1992). However, data on low-income, school-age children and adolescents indicate that they had a greater prevalence of obesity than their counterparts in the middle-class population (Yip, Scanlon, & Trowbridge, 1993).

In Head Start, the basic nutrition requirements under the Performance Standards require screenings for children, educational activities, and, maybe most important, meals and snacks that meet one third of the nutritional needs of the children. Almost 90% of the nutrition coordinators reported that all children enrolled in Head Start received individual nutrition screenings; however, nutrition summaries were available in only some of the child health files. Approximately 5% of the children were identified as needing nutrition services. Even fewer parents (less than 5%) reported their child being obese or underweight as a health condition.

Clearly, the most successful aspect of the nutrition domain is the provision of healthful meals for the children. As part of the study, a meal (either breakfast or lunch, depending on a class's schedule) was observed at each center to determine if meals were used by staff as an opportunity for turning a routine activity into an educational activity. As a social activity, meals are generally a success, with teachers and aides using the opportunity to teach the children about proper nutrition, sharing, personal responsibility, and the importance of the meal for promoting good health. Much of this was done through teacher–child dialog, some conversational and some directive. What sometimes gets lost is that many teachers and staff also use this opportunity to role model for the children, whether it is in use of proper behavior at the table, trying and eating different foods, or cleanup and tooth brushing after the meal. It is clear that proper nutrition and nutrition education is provided in the typical Head Start classroom.

How Does Head Start Address Mental Health Issues?

Head Start uses a comprehensive mental health model, based on a positive, holistic approach that emphasizes normal child development in the context of daily living skills and social competence (Hansen & Martner, 1990). Although this model is very appealing, the data collected about mental health services and the mental health status of the children proved to be quite murky. Most of the mental health coordinators had other paid responsibilities within Head Start, and only about one quarter of their time was actually spent focusing on the mental health domain. Approximately 70% of the mental health coordinators said that all children in the program routinely received a group administered mental health or developmental screening and almost 90% reported that at least some children in their program received individual mental health screenings. Unfortunately, the outcomes of these screenings were often missing. When asked about the mental health of their children, less than 7% of the parents reported that someone from the Head Start center had suggested their children be evaluated for possible behavior problems. Mental health records maintained by Head Start were generally nonexistent, incomplete, or were maintained separate from the health files (a number of programs limited research access to the health files only). During interviews, parents seemed more inclined to list a mental health problem as a physical health problem, if they reported one at all. Facing these unexpected barriers in terms of collecting data on mental health problems (e.g., the location and access provided to files with mental health reports, lack of documentation of reports, misinterpretation of the terms used to discuss child mental health issues), the data that were returned on the mental health domain were clearly the least useful. For that reason, this is the extent to which mental health issues will be addressed here, and readers are referred to Chapter 12, which focuses solely on mental health issues.

Does Head Start Address Barriers that Prevent Families from Getting Necessary Services?

Despite Head Start's best efforts, improved child health comes from more than simply linking a family with a provider. Both parents and staff were asked about circumstances that make access to and the use of health services more difficult. These barriers to proper health services fell into two categories: barriers internal to Head Start and those that were external to the program. Internal barriers as reported by staff reflected how problems within the program, including poor communication or limited program resources, resulted in a failure to assist families. These are barriers that need to be addressed administratively by individual Head Start programs.

Reported by both parents and staff, external barriers are those that have a direct impact on families and exist independent of Head Start program policies. These included personal barriers (e.g., lack of parent understanding, lack of parent time, parent resistance, lack of child care), community barriers (e.g., lack of adequate public transportation, distance to providers), financial constraints (e.g., resistance of health care providers to accept Medicaid patients), and access to and availability of appropriate health care (e.g., lack of pediatric providers in a particular service area).

Staff reported that their local programs helped families overcome barriers by providing parent education, transportation assistance, staff education, outreach to local service providers, and assistance in establishing better scheduling for the required visits. In some cases, such as in those communities lacking adequate service providers, or in cases of families that simply function poorly, these steps were not likely to be adequate. In these instances, Head Start struggled along with the families to find a solution. Fortunately, most families do not need additional help in these areas, and of those who do, many benefit from Head Start's help and cooperation.

The findings on barriers are very similar to those noted in the GAO report on early childhood programs (1994). Insights into the efforts local Head Start programs are making to assist families in overcoming barriers shape a picture of programs actually working directly with families as well as with the local providers and other community resources. This work shows that, in many cases, local programs are heeding the recommendations of the Advisory Committee on Head Start Quality and Expansion (1993)—and in many programs they are succeeding.

How Does Head Start Educate Families Regarding Health and Prevention?

In order to promote proper preventive health services, health education activities for parents and children are critical. For children, these activities were typically presented as educational units or, more likely, integrated into the routine activities of the local program. For example, as noted previously, nutrition education and proper hygiene were usually incorporated into the classrooms' daily meal-related activities. Children also participated in learning activities designed to improve their knowledge, selection, and enjoyment of a variety of foods. Correspondingly, their parents were typically provided with educational opportunities concerning the selection of appropriate foods as well as the proper handling and preparation of foods. Parents also learned about nutrition and hygiene when they participated in Head Start activities, either at special events or in the classroom.

The health services staff is usually assisted by other local program staff to help ensure that parent health education is available to all participating families. Health education at Head Start takes place in a number of different ways, including staff to parent, parent to parent, parent to child, and child to parent. The greater the level of parent education and involvement, the more likely that parents who were previously unable to function in the health services arena are able to assume full responsibility for the health of their family by the time their children leave Head Start. Given that one of the most frequently identified health risk factors identified by Head Start staff was the lack of parenting skills, this was a common area addressed through parent workshops. Workshops reportedly were held as often as once per week (25% of the programs) to as rarely as less than once per month (10% of the programs). Although not specifically noted in this study, the frustration program staff expressed regarding the low level of parent involvement in these workshops may have affected the frequency with which they were offered.

In terms of providing health education to the children, coordinators reported that classroom discussions and role-playing activities were typically used as methods to integrate health education into the classroom. Having classroom visitors was noted as an important education activity. Because most of the Head Start staff was observed sitting and eating with the children during mealtimes, they had opportunities to encourage proper hygiene associated with meals (e.g., hand washing, maintaining a clean table, tooth brushing) and educate children about the foods and encourage them to try the foods.

Any Head Start staff member is likely to point out that proper health education is not limited to program activities. The effect of educating parents should be that they, in turn, become health educators for their children. As evidence of their role as educators, almost all of the interviewed parents stated that they discussed health topics at home with their children. Improvements in either child or adult health behaviors after entering Head Start were noted by two thirds of the parents. One tenth of the parents reported they had an increased awareness of the health behaviors of their children. More than 40% of the parents reported that their children engaged in proper health behaviors more frequently and were more aware of the impact of their own behaviors. Finally, as evidence of children becoming teachers of their parents, one tenth of the parents indicated that their children helped change the health behavior of other children or adults (including parents) in their home.

Is Head Start Meeting Its Goals of Educating Families and Improving the Health of the Children It Serves?

With the preliminary questions having been answered, it is possible to build a better answer to the basic question raised previously in this chapter. The bottom line seems to be that Head Start is doing a good job of reaching its stated goal of helping children get needed health services and teaching families about good health behaviors. Although the program does not help every enrolled family, it would be quite a remarkable venture if it did given the many constraints local programs confront in their work. Through firsthand observations of the Head Start health operations, it seems that three problem areas may ultimately mask the conclusion that Head Start is successful. These areas are 1) the availability of community resources, 2) Head Start staff training and credentials, and 3) service follow-up and record-keeping issues. What we know about these areas can serve as lessons learned for Head Start, although some of these lessons have been addressed in previous works (Bell & Jones, 1993; Zigler et al., 1994).

The Availability of Community Resources   In an era that will be increasingly noted for reforms in welfare and other public assistance programs, agencies struggling to serve low-income families face growing needs to coordinate their services with other agencies. For Head Start, the creation of useful community linkages is dependent on the active integration of their local programs with community and state-run programs (e.g., Medicaid, CHIP, child care subsidies) as well as with other federal resources, such as the United States Department of Agriculture (USDA) Nutrition Programs, the Women, Infants, and Children (WIC) program, and Temporary Assistance for Needy Families (TANF). The health study found evidence that Head Start does not work as a "stand alone" federal program. The emphasis on building community partnerships is clearly noted in the revised Program Performance Standards, which include a focus on having children linked to a "medical home" for their health services. However, for this requirement to become reality for all Head Start children, changes must come from the communities and from the families, not just from Head Start itself.

National and local efforts in this area are currently underway, as evidenced by the American Academy of Pediatrics' community outreach efforts associated with CHIP. This federally funded, state-run program is in the process of linking with various community agencies and entities, such as school systems and, in some locations, Head Start, in order to educate the public about availability and eligibility, with the ultimate goal of boosting enrollment. These efforts are showing some benefits, including secondary gains as noted in the identification of many low-income families who applied for CHIP who are actually eligible for Medicaid (Center for Medicaid and Medicare Services, 2000; Ross & Cox, 2002). Such an increase in Medicaid enrollment among low-income families means improved health services for families who are in the Head Start eligible population. This is an excellent example of how community resources can support and promote each other's goals to the ultimate benefit of the families.

One potential difficulty for Head Start in linking with community agencies is that the staff at these agencies may feel more comfortable simply cooperating with Head Start, rather than engaging in active collaboration with the local program. The Head Start programs work under the guidance of the Program Performance Standards to assure program quality, but non-Head Start agencies that work with Head Start may find these guidelines too demanding and restricting on their work. This may be particularly true for local agencies that operate on budgets tighter than that of the local Head Start program. In the health study, this problem was clearly evident through the incomplete dental reports that were returned to the program and kept in the children's health files. The result may be that an agency or provider may cooperate with Head Start on a limited basis but will hesitate to fully collaborate with the program when it becomes a drain on the resources (e.g., financial, time, staff) of that agency.

Earlier, a question was posed about how Head Start responded to the limitations or restrictions that often arise in the "real world" of health services. Part of the answer is found in how local programs take on the barriers they face in their community and among the parents and families they serve. Fitting into the real world means trying to improve families' access to existing services and attempting to identify community providers who are responsive to the unique and changing needs of the low-income population (and possibly educate those who are not responsive). One serious concern expressed by staff is that many of the families they work with only come to the program for 1 year. There are some children who attend for 2 years and some families may benefit by enrolling multiple children over a period of years, but the general feeling seems to be that families' exposure to Head Start is too limited. Consequently, staff feel that their ability to properly educate and empower some families is compromised. It then becomes important for local Head Start staff to engage local service providers in dialog about how to best serve these families, particularly after the families are no longer with Head Start.

One of the lasting legacies of Head Start on the local level should be to promote ongoing, positive relationships between providers and families. This would be reflected in relationships that give children the best advantages possible in developing the skills they need to be successful through the transition into school and beyond. Enhancing community support for low-income families also puts Head Start staff in a position to indirectly assist low-income families who do not have the opportunity to enroll. This help may come in the form of meetings with local providers to discuss the need for services among this population and how to collaborate on outreach activities to facilitate access for families in need. Such education would include discussions of language barriers, scheduling problems, and the use of Medicaid (or CHIP) funding to pay for services. It is important to understand that Head Start staff can learn from the local providers as well as teach them. Generally, the goals of Head Start and the other local agencies are similar, and the key to promoting these goals is dialog and collaboration.

The second part of the answer is that parents need to develop their own strategies for overcoming the barriers they face in seeking care for their children. Through internal training activities, Head Start is preparing staff to both help and educate those parents in need of assistance. Such interactions with these parents should at least produce short-term benefits for children in terms of accessing needed care. But, just as important, it is expected that parents acquire and maintain the skills they need to confront these barriers to care, empowering them to stand on their own when their children have completed their Head Start experiences. At this point, there is no research to verify the long-term effects on efforts to empower Head Start parents.

Head Start Staff Training and Credentials   One of the more striking findings was the number of health and mental health coordinators who reported having to serve multiple roles within their program. Although this is the likely response to limited program resources, it creates quite a burden on the staff in these positions. Data from the health study suggest that component coordinators in smaller Head Start programs are more likely to perform multiple roles. Comprehensive staff training is crucial for the provision of appropriate care and for proper education of enrolled children and their families, and such training is even more critical for staff with responsibilities for managing multiple health domains or multiple program components. This is especially true where staff people with multiple responsibilities may have been placed in their management position without the prior training or experience related to each responsibility.

Beyond the training of existing staff, the revised Performance Standards support the development of relationships with health professionals outside the program to assist center staff in carrying out specific health-related functions. Bringing in local consultants is an important strategy for supplementing the efforts of untrained health staff, particularly in small programs in which the health study data showed that component coordinators have fewer educational credentials relative to the health field. The new Program Performance Standards also raise the issue of putting people with proper credentials in appropriate positions. This step should facilitate linkages with the community and help avoid situations in which staff is not up-to-date on their knowledge and understanding of the local and programmatic regulations and requirements regarding the health of the children in their program.

Service Follow-Up and Record-Keeping Issues   One apparent weakness of the program was the lack of information on actual services provided to enrolled children. This in no way suggests that services are not being provided because parents reported that both initial and follow-up visits were completed. Rather, it seems that the problem is more likely in documentation efforts by Head Start staff. Unfortunately then, the poor documentation of health services reflects poorly on the efforts of the program in the health area. Perhaps the clearest example of the problem was in the findings related to immunizations. Although Head Start programs are required to maintain up-to-date information on the immunization status of the children they serve, 10%–15% of the children had additional immunizations noted on the parent-held immunization records that were not found in the Head Start records. In the case of the OIG report (1993), the lack of well-documented information in the children's health records cast a questionable light on the program.

Reviews of the child health files in the health study indicated that Head Start children were being properly screened for medical and dental problems; however, the health files contained relatively little documentation about whether treatments actually were completed, in progress, or ongoing, as in the case of chronic health conditions. More than 80% of the child health records indicated a health condition with incomplete or no follow-up data on the status of the recommended treatments. If Head Start is to assume the responsibility of including comprehensive health services in the program, it is necessary for staff to receive training on the importance of carefully tracking the medical progress of the children they serve. Efforts are underway to promote the use of computerized record-keeping systems, such as the Head Start Family Information System (HSFIS), but computers are not a substitute for understanding how the program is accountable for monitoring the progress of the families it serves. Staff not only have to have the tools but also they need the knowledge, motivation, and time to truly fulfill this task. The nature of the Head Start program, in which high levels of contact with children and their families are expected, does not always lend itself to integrating a highly structured, computer-based informational system to track the families. However, under the shadow of the Government Performance and Reporting Act, the Head Start program, through its local staff, is accountable for showing that it actually is helping families in the way the program is designed.

CONCLUSION

In the health study final report, it was noted that local programs engage in three levels of activities in order to serve low-income families: 1) assuring that children get screenings and needed health services, 2) assuring that children receive preventive care and establish a medical home, and 3) assuring that both children and families learn to take responsibility for their own health care. The individual interviews, both by staff and especially by parents, in conjunction with health record reviews and observations, clearly back this up. In fact, the problems in record keeping that have been inherent in Head Start for a long time may actually be hiding the fact that local Head Start programs do a very good job of this for most of the enrolled families. The work of the program is not perfect, but given the many barriers encountered along the way, it is unlikely that any program of this type could be perfect. Fortunately, not all enrolled families need Head Start's assistance in accessing health services. Local programs are designed so that those children in need of assistance can receive care and so that their families develop the skills necessary to access appropriate care independent of help from Head Start. Continued work on enhancing staff skills and on continually reviewing and improving community development will fulfill both the goals of the Program Performance Standards and the mission of Head Start to prepare children and families to face the challenges of school and move ahead to the next levels of development.

REFERENCES

The Advisory Committee on Head Start Quality and Expansion. (1993). *Creating a 21st century Head Start: Final report of the Advisory Committee on Head Start Quality and Expansion.* Washington, DC: U.S. Department of Health and Human Services.

Barnes, G.P., Parker, W.A., Lyon, T.C., Drum, M.A., & Coleman, G.C. (1992). Ethnicity, location, age, and fluoridation factors in baby bottle tooth decay and caries prevalence of Head Start children. *Public Health Reports, 107*(2), 167–173.

Bell, K.N., & Jones, J.E. (1993). *Future directions for the Head Start health component.* New York: National Center for Children in Poverty, Columbia University.

Brooks-Gunn, J., & Duncan, G. (1997). The effects of poverty on children. *The Future of Children, 7,* 55–71.

Brush, L., Gaidurgis, A., & Best, C. (1993). *Indices of Head Start program quality.* A report for the Administration on Children, Youth and Families. Washington, DC: Pelavin Associates.

Center for Medicare and Medicaid Services. (2000). *SCHIP Annual Enrollment Report (Fiscal Year 1999).* Baltimore: Author.

Edelstein, B.L. (2000). Access to dental care for Head Start enrollees. *Journal of Public Health Dentistry, 60*(3), 230–232.

Fosburg, L.B. (1984). *The effects of Head Start health services: Executive summary of the Head Start health evaluation.* A Report for the Administration on Children, Youth, and Families. Cambridge, MA: Abt Associates.

General Accounting Office (GAO). (1994). *Early childhood programs: Local perspectives on barriers to providing Head Start services. Letter Report.* Washington, DC: Author.

Hale, B.A., Seitz, V., & Zigler, E. (1990). Health services and Head Start: A forgotten formula. *Journal of Applied Developmental Psychology, 11,* 447–458.

Hansen, K.A., & Martner, J.S. (1990). *Mental health in Head Start: A wellness approach.* (DHHS Publication No. [ACF] 92–31241). Washington, DC: U.S. Department of Health and Human Services.

Kaste, L.M., Marianos, D., Chang, R., & Phipps, K.R. (1992). The assessment of nursing caries and its relationship to high caries in the permanent dentition. *Journal of Public Health Dentistry, 52*(2), 64–68.

Keane, M.J., O'Brien, R.W., Connell, D.C., & Close, N.C. (1996). *A descriptive study of Head Start services.* Prepared for the Administration on Children, Youth and Families; the Administration for Children and Families; the U.S. Department of Health and Human Services (contract no. 105-93-1911). Washington, DC. (Available at http://www.acf.hhs.gov/programs/core/pubs_reports/hshealth/hshealth_intro .html)

Rosenbaum, S. (1992). Child health and poor children. *American Behavioral Scientist, 35*(3), 275–289.

Ross, D.C., & Cox, L. (2002). *Enrolling children and families in health coverage: The promise of doing more. A report on the National Survey of Enrollment and Renewal Procedures in Medicaid and SCHIP.* Prepared for the Kaiser Commission on Medicaid and the Uninsured. Washington, DC.

U.S. Department of Health, Education and Welfare, Office of Child Development. (1972). *Recommendations for a Head Start Program by Panel of Experts.* Washington, DC: Author.

U.S. Department of Health and Human Services (DHHS) Office of Inspector General (OIG). (1993). *Evaluating Head Start expansion through performance indicators.* Washington, DC: U.S. Department of Health and Human Services.

Yip, R., Scanlon, K., & Trowbridge, F. (1993). Trends and patterns in height and weight status of low-income U.S. children. *Critical Reviews on Food Science and Nutrition, 33*(4–5), 409–421.

Zigler, E., Piotrkowski, C.S., & Collins, R. (1994). Health services in Head Start. *Annual Review of Public Health, 15,* 511–534.

CHAPTER 12

The Challenge of Mental Health in Head Start

Making the Vision Real

Jane Knitzer

From its inception, in rhetoric, Head Start has recognized the importance of promoting sound mental health. In reality, operationalizing this commitment has been problematic, as has been periodically acknowledged throughout Head Start's history (Cohen, Solnit, Wohlford, 1979; Piotrkowski, Collins, Knitzer, & Robinson, 1994; Task Force on Head Start and Mental Health, 1994; Yoshikawa & Zigler, 2000). Thus, asking the question, "Has Head Start lived up to its potential with respect to mental health," is a little like asking whether the glass is half full or half empty. The answer is yes it has . . . sort of, but no, it has not nearly addressed the original vision of the founders or the urgent challenges facing a very different Head Start population at the beginning of the 21st century. This chapter focuses on what is known about the current status of mental health in Head Start and what might enhance the depth and intensity of the policy and practice attention paid to the emotional well-being of today's Head Start population.

THE VISION

Since the beginning of Head Start in 1965, there has been a strong commitment to promoting the emotional well-being of Head Start children. This is embedded deeply in the core Head Start goal of promoting social competence. As defined by Head Start, social competence means "the child's everyday effectiveness in dealing with his or her present environment and later responsibilities in school and life" (U.S. Department of Health and Human Services [DHHS] Administration on Children, Youth and Families [ACYF] *Head Start Performance Standards*) Achieving social competence is linked to five specific objectives. The first two—to enhance children's healthy growth and development and to strengthen families as the primary nurturers of their children—have explicit mental health implications. The other three objectives are instrumental: to provide children with educational, health, and nutritional services; to link children and families to needed community services; and to ensure well-managed programs that involve parents in decision making. Although no explicit language calls attention to building relationships with the children and families to promote the children's self-confidence, engender hope, and promote parenting skills (all of which are integral to promoting emotional well-being), taken together, the five objectives frame an implicit theory of mental health. To enhance children's healthy growth, development, and school readiness, and to strengthen families as the primary nurturers of their children, it is necessary to provide educational, health (including mental health and dental), and nutritional services; link children and families with other services; and ensure well-managed programs that include a strong parental voice.

THE PRACTICE

Head Start administrators have taken the position either explicitly or implicitly that mental health issues are addressed in two ways. The first is through the overall program itself, which not only takes a comprehensive child-focused approach but also takes a comprehensive child and family approach. This, although now widely accepted and central to our understanding of both child development and good mental health practice, was quite groundbreaking at Head Start's inception. Up until 2004, however, there have been few efforts to assess specifically how the general Head Start program has affected the emotional well-being and development of young children (Yoshikawa & Zigler, 2000).

The second way in which the mental health agenda has been played out is through the program's "mental health component." Under the Performance Standards, Head Start programs are charged to 1) work collaboratively with parents on issues related to parent education; 2) secure the services of mental health professions with sufficient frequency to enable the timely identification of, and intervention in, family and staff concerns about a child's mental health; and 3) include a regular schedule of on-site mental health consultation involving the mental health professional, program staff, and parents. (See Table 12.1 for more details.) These standards provide a context for Head Start programs to develop a strong mental health approach. Ensuring that programs have access to appropriate mental health expertise, however, has not been a high priority. Data from the Program Information Report (PIR) across two time periods show a fairly consistent pattern. In 1991–1992, 45% of Head Start programs indicated that a mental health consultant was available only "on call" and did not make regularly scheduled visits (Piotrkowski et al., 1994). By 1999, there was evidence of some improvement. Thirty percent reported such professionals were "on call" as needed, and 23% reported that they had access to mental health professionals for more than 20 hours a week. However, 50% of the programs still reported access to a mental health professional for 6 or fewer hours per week (Lopez, Tarullo, Forness, & Boyce, 2000). Juxtaposed against this, in a 1993 survey, 54% of the respondents called for a full-time mental health professional *on staff* [italics added] (Piotrkowski et al., 1994). Programs also reported difficulty in finding mental health consultants who were comfortable working in low-income contexts and responsive to the ethnic and cultural diversity within Head Start.

Table 12.1. Head Start Child Mental Health Performance Standards

1) Grantee and delegate agencies must work collaboratively with parents on issues related to parent education by
  • Soliciting parental information, observations, and concerns
  • Sharing staff observations of their child and discussing issues such as separation and attachment
  • Discussing and identifying with parents appropriate response to their child's behaviors
  • Discussing how to strengthen nurturing, supportive environments and relationships in the home and at the program
  • Helping parents to better understand mental health issues
  • Supporting parents' participation in any needed mental health interventions

2) Grantee and delegate agencies must secure the service of mental health professionals on a schedule of sufficient frequency to enable the timely identification of and intervention in family and staff concerns about a child's mental health

3) Mental health program services must include a regular schedule of on-site mental health consultation involving the mental health professionals, program staff, and parents on how to:
  • Design and implement program practices responsive to identified behavioral and mental health concerns for individual and groups of children
  • Promote children's mental wellness with parent education to staff and parents
  • Assist in providing special help for children with atyptical behavior development
  • Utilize other community mental health resources, as needed

Note: Excerpted from Federal Register, 45 CFR part 1301 et al; see Appendix C 1304.24 Child Mental Health

THE MENTAL HEALTH NEEDS OF TODAY'S HEAD START CHILDREN, FAMILIES, AND STAFF

There are three sources of information about the mental health needs of today's Head Start children, families, and staff: 1) general prevalence data about emotional problems in young children, 2) data about the impact of familial risk factors on young children, and 3) research using Head Start samples and field-based studies and surveys.

Prevalence Data

Prevalence data with respect to emotional problems in young children are limited, largely due to a lack of an agreed upon classification system and methodology. A review (Lopez et al., 2000) cites two community-specific studies focused on 3-year-olds—one with a preschool population in London and the other with a rural preschool population in the United States of America. The estimated prevalence rates in the London study ranged from 6% to 7% for moderate to severe problems (with another 15% viewed as having mild problems) and from 11% to 23% in the United States study. Other research suggests that clinical level problems among young children range from 4% to 10% (Raver & Knitzer, 2002). Further, there is a growing knowledge base about the trajectory of emotional problems in early childhood, particularly with respect to conduct and attachment disorders, and most recently, anxiety disorders and depression (Shonkoff & Phillips, 2000; Webster-Stratton, 1997; Zeanah, 1999).

Risk Factors

The extensive research literature on risk and protective factors also has implications for understanding the threats to the emotional and behavioral development of Head Start children. Research confirms that poverty in the earliest years is especially harmful, and the more extreme the poverty, the more likely the negative consequences for the child (Aber, Jones, & Cohen, 2000; Duncan, Brooks-Gunn, & Aber, 1997). Other studies make clear how factors above and beyond poverty affect the emotional well-being of young children. Particularly significant are family risk factors such as parental (and particularly maternal) depression, substance abuse, family conflict, and harsh parenting practices. All have been shown, in combination or singly, to place young children at risk of later emotional and behavioral problems (Knitzer, 2000b; Moore, Zaslow, Coiro, Miller, & Magenheim, 1996; NICHD Early Child Care Research Network, 1999). This research, coupled with developments in neuroscience about early brain development, once again underscores the importance of early relationships in promoting positive emotional well-being. (Shonkoff & Phillips, 2000).

Research-Based Evidence on Risk Factors in Head Start Children and Families

Of critical importance in designing and implementing appropriate mental health strategies in Head Start is an understanding of the levels and distribution of risk in the Head Start population. Using data from the Panel of Income Survey Dynamics, Foster (2002) compared four indices of disadvantage among African American families in Head Start over two periods of time: from 1983 to 1987 and from 1988 to 1992. The indices were poverty status, welfare receipt, female headship of home, and parental joblessness—each of which has been linked to poor outcomes for children. Foster found that although poverty among African American families in Head Start decreased slightly over the two time periods, the percentage of children experiencing multiple disadvantages or extreme poverty actually increased. It could be that these data help explain why, informally, Head Start staff report that the children in Head Start now reflect more challenging behaviors and greater emotional needs that has been true in the past.

Data from the Family and Child Experiences Survey (FACES), involving a nationally representative sample of Head Start children, families, and programs followed between 1997 and 2000, are also beginning to shed new light on many aspects of the Head Start experience (DHHS, ACYF, 2002). Here too, early data point to a group of children within Head Start who are at higher risk for poor outcomes and may need more intensive mental health interventions. Thus, in 28% of the FACES family sample, the primary caregiver had less than a high school education, whereas about 40% of the sample had no employed adult. In 18% of the families, the primary caregivers were born outside of the United States. The data also paint a sobering picture of the overall extent to which depression and violence enters the world of Head Start families (recognizing that patterns vary in individual communities and programs). Close to one third of the families reported having witnessed violent or nonviolent crimes during the year before the survey, half of them more than once. Parents report that 17% of their children witnessed a crime or domestic violence, and 3% had actually been victims. Since birth, 22% of the children had their primary caregivers, other household members, or a nonhousehold biological parent arrested or charged with a crime by the police, and in 17% of the families, this had resulted in time spent in jail. Surprisingly, there are no data on issues related to substance abuse in Head Start families, at least that have been reported to date.

Also relevant to understanding the mental health challenge are the reports of high levels of maternal depression in Head Start mothers. For instance, one study that was focused on helping Head Start staff better meet the needs of " hard-to-engage" families, reported that 47% of the parents reported poverty-related sadness, demoralization, and other indices of despair (Parker, Piotrkowski, Horn, & Greene, 1995). This is consistent with emerging data from welfare-related studies involving similar populations, with levels of depression ranging from just less than 30% to more than 40% (Moore et al., 1996). A 13-state study found that in the general population, about 17% of mothers reported depressive symptoms. Among low-income women, the rate was 28% (Urban Institute, 1999). The Head Start data indicate that close to one third of the mothers reported moderate to severe depression, with no statistically significant decline over the year. Clinical and developmental knowledge has long tracked the negative impacts of maternal depression on young children (Downey, & Coyne, 1990; NICHD Early Child Care Research Network, 1999), underscoring the need to address this issue through family support, parent involvement, or sometimes, other more formal mental health treatment.

The picture of social-emotional development in children that we have from Head Start through FACES is less nuanced than the family information. Preliminary analysis indicate that among 4-year-olds, 35% do not use free time in acceptable ways (e.g., fighting while playing, talking back), 40% have difficulty following teacher's directions, and 45% have difficulty following rules and waiting their turn. These data are hard to interpret without more analysis. Other research may help to fill in the blanks. For example, a study carried out in Washington state Head Start programs reported between one quarter and one third of the children manifested aggressive behaviors that placed them in the clinical problem range (Webster-Stratton & Hammond, 1998).

With respect to the identification of serious emotional and behavioral disabilities in Head Start, the picture is complex. Since 1972, Head Start has had a mandate to serve children with disabilities, leading the way for the larger inclusion movement. But there is consistent evidence, over time, that children in Head Start with emotional and behavioral problems are either not identified, or identified as having other disabilities, particularly speech disorders. Overall, identification rates within the program have been consistently less than 1%. For instance, 1997–1998 PIR data indicated .57% of children were actually identified as having emotional and behavioral disorders (cited in Lopez et al., 2000). This is significantly below even the most conservative epidemiological estimates. As noted previously, overall prevalence rates of identifiable disorders are between 4% and 10%. In contrast, one study involving careful assessment of 151 Head Start children identified as having disabilities reported that 29% of those identified, or 5% of the total population in the program, had as the primary problem (Forness et al., 1998) emotional and behavioral disorders (Forness & Kavale, 1993; Sinclair, 1993; Sinclair, Del'Homme, & Gonzalez, 1993). As noted previously, this is closer to overall prevalence rates estimated between 4% and 10%.

It is also interesting that close to $2\frac{1}{2}$% of the parents surveyed through FACES expressed concerns about the emotional and behavioral status of their children, a rate about four times higher that the actual identification of children with emotional and behavioral problems in Head Start. At the very least, this suggests that this group of parents is having a very difficult time with their young children.

Other Data

Anecdotal and other reports from the field confirm the patterns reported in research. They suggest that Head Start, long viewed as the premier example of a preventive developmental program, is experiencing, at the ground level, increasing concern about the emotional status of their children and families (Yoshikawa & Knitzer, 1997). Most typically, staff complaints focus on the levels of provocative, inappropriate, and challenging behavior of the children. Children of concern are often described as very sad or very mad, lacking the ability to regulate their own emotions and often showing difficulty in relating to their peers or teachers. Teachers who have been in Head Start programs for many years note that, whereas they used to have one such child in a classroom, now they have three or four or even five. Even more troubling, teachers also report that when they have this many children who manifest troubling behaviors, it negatively affects the overall quality of the classroom, with too much time spent trying to manage the behaviors of this small group of children. There are even reports that such children are actually being kicked out of Head Start. Exactly how frequently this happens is not known, but it is a phenomenon also occurring in other early care and education settings (Knitzer, 2000a).

FRAMEWORKS AND CHALLENGES

The fundamental challenge that Head Start faces with respect to mental health is how to help programs develop the mental health supports they need to accomplish the overall Head Start goals. That means that mental health practice must be consistent with Head Start's core orientation: strength-based, resiliency-promoting, and family supportive. The data highlighted in previous sections also suggest that the practice strategies need to be crafted to fit multiple levels of need. These levels range from support and prevention, which are addressed most clearly in the Head Start Performance Standards, to more ecologically complex, intensive interventions, to earlier identification of and sound responses to the children who do need specialized mental health interventions. And, sadly, all programs need to have plans and protocols to deal with all-too-predictable family and community crises. Designing mental health strategies to "fit" with this range of need requires a framework for thinking about how to structure the mental health component. In an earlier article (2000a), I proposed the following four foci:

- Promoting the emotional and behavioral well-being of young children, particularly those whose emotional development is compromised by virtue of poverty or other environmental or biological risks

- Helping families of young children address whatever barriers they face to ensure that their children's emotional development is not compromised

- Expanding the competencies of nonfamilial caregivers and others to promote the emotional well-being of young children and families, particularly those at risk by virtue of environmental or biological factors

- Ensuring that young children experiencing clearly atypical emotional and behavioral development and their families have access to needed services and supports

In theory, the Head Start framework is consistent with these four foci. In reality, however, neither this, nor any other systematic, framework has been used to help individual programs assess and design intentional strategies to promote emotional well-being in staff, children, and families. Nor has such a framework been used to guide and sustain a consistent national research or technical assistance training agenda. In the hopes of moving beyond the "stuck" status of mental health in Head Start, even as its children and families are more needy, this section highlights seven conceptual and practical challenges that need to be resolved.

Challenge 1: Addressing the Ambivalence About Mental Health

To many in the Head Start community, as in the larger community, the term *mental health* carries a stigma (DHHS, Office of the Surgeon General, 1999). To some Head Start families and staff, the term *mental health* suggests "being crazy," to others, it raises fears of labeling and stereotyping the disadvantaged (Yoshikawa & Knitzer, 1997). This is not a new problem in Head Start. Yoshikawa and Zigler (2000) reported that at Head Start's inception, there was a conscious effort at the national level to avoid screening for (and thus identifying) behavioral and emotional problems. That legacy lives on. As noted previously, Head Start children with emotional and behavioral problems are under-identified. Further, even in 2004, Head Start has not played a significant role in helping local program staff assess the emotional status of their children, although some promising new tools are finally emerging (Devereux Early Childhood Assessment [DECA], 2000; Feil & Becker, 1993; Feil, Walker, & Severson, 1995). At the local level, programs report that words make a big difference. Those that have sought to engage parents by having "mental health" or "substance abuse" workshops, have often been greeted with empty rooms. Even programs with the most effective mental health strategies (sometimes developed in partnership with mental health agencies), report they avoid using the words (Yoshikawa & Knitzer, 1997). Using language that works (e.g., "emotional readiness," "emotional wellness"), engaging the Head Start community at the highest levels in a dialog about how mental health strategies could support overall goals, and clearly articulating how mental health strategies can be used to promote strengths in families, not just to pathologize them, would all help in confronting the ambivalence directly.

Challenge 2: Better Integrating What Teachers Need to Know About Emotional Development

Mental health consultants and Head Start staff report that they need help in better observing and understanding the behaviors of children, understanding the role of trauma in their lives, and becoming more careful observers of child and family strengths and weaknesses. Given the data cited earlier about the levels of risk in the Head Start population, and the fact that teachers are not always well trained in child development and behavioral principles, this assumes a new salience. If consultants can develop working partnerships with the teachers, they can play a key role, providing coaching, mentoring, and the opportunity to problem solve about classroom and individual child issues (Cohen & Kaufmann, 2000; Donahue, Falk, & Provet, 2000). Those programs that have deliberately sought to help teachers strengthen their own competencies and skills report that this serves as a powerful quality improvement strategy. Typically, however, mental health consultants are not seen as part of a quality improvement strategy. Nor, in relation to this, has mental health been seen as a tool to promote "school readiness." Yet, typically, when teachers say children are not ready to succeed in school, they usually are referring to their behaviors or their emotional development.

Challenge 3: Integrating a Family Perspective More Directly into Mental Health Services

The mental health requirements in Head Start are basically child-focused. Parents are to receive education, but the implication is that actual interventions focus on the children. This framing is not consistent with the current mental health practice, which aims to be family focused, strength-based, and culturally competent. Family members are seen as partners who participate actively in the treatment plan and strategies, interventions occur in setting most comfortable for them, and attention is paid to their needs for respite care and other supports (Friesen & Huff, 1996; Knitzer & Aber, 1995; Stroul & Friedman, 1986). These approaches are consistent with the core Head Start values, and yet, ironically, many Head Start staff members are not familiar with them (Piotrkowski et al., 1994).

The life stresses and burdens that a significant proportion of Head Start families face also means that focusing mental health strategies only on the child limits what can be accomplished. The growing understanding that family and community risk factors create the conditions that threaten the emotional development of children suggest that both the risk factors and their effects on parenting must be addressed (Knitzer, 2000a, 2000b). Yet, unless program management staff have made a conscious decision to revisit the traditional approaches, family service workers or parent involvement coordinators typically do not interact with mental health consultants. Instead, as is still relevant today, "mental health objectives and services lie within the health component of Head Start, whereas counseling of parents and other support services for families are managed though what is called the social services component" (Piotrkowski et al., 1994). At the same time, Head Start is in a powerful position to help even the most vulnerable families. Families trust Head Start and, by extension, those who are "on-site" as ambassadors from other agencies such as mental health.

Challenge 4: Building a Repertoire of Effective Practice

There are many building blocks to create a more effective mental health practice in Head Start. In 1997, my colleague, Hiro Yoshikawa, and I, in a research project growing out of a task force I chaired at the request of Dr. Edward Zigler (the then president of the American Association of Orthopsychiatry), documented field-generated mental health strategies to better meet the emerging needs of Head Start programs. Based on profiles of 14 of 73 nominated programs, the report found that mental health strategies take many forms. These range from classroom mentoring, coaching, and peer support for teachers, to cross component team meetings involving teachers, parents, and family workers facilitated by a mental health consultant, to collaborative partnerships to assess and reinvent mental health approaches (Yoshikawa & Knitzer, 1997). The report also called attention to the vexing challenge of screening and assessment in a way that promotes intervention and does not reinforce inappropriate labeling. The array of field-invented strategies we identified was impressive, addressing, in different programs, virtually all aspects of what a system of supports might look like that encompassed prevention, early intervention, treatment, and crisis intervention. In general, however, no one program focused on more than one type of intervention.

Since that report, several national research and demonstration programs have also been funded, either targeting Head Start exclusively or including Head Start as key sites. For example, in the 1997 research priority announcement, Head Start funded four mental health university partnerships. Five Head Start programs are also involved in a research endeavor known as Starting Early Starting Smart, jointly funded by the Substance Abuse and Mental Health Services Administration and the Casey Family Fund. These programs are part of a larger network of 11 health and early childhood programs developing strategies to ingrate behavioral health services into these. Most focus on linking family advocates with back-up multidisciplinary teams, but several also include broadly based preventive strategies, supplemented with more intensive efforts.

Local communities and states are also beginning to develop strategies to provide better supports to the early childhood community working with high-risk families (Knitzer, 2000c). But, there is still no national clearinghouse for information on these emerging initiatives. Nor as yet, is there a concerted policy effort to provide incentives to children's mental health agencies to develop a stronger focus on early childhood mental health in the context of either Head Start or the broader network of early childhood and learning programs.

Challenge 5: Building the Staffing and Leadership Capacity

For Head Start programs to address the mental health challenges they face, the programs will require a new level of mental health staffing and overall leadership from program directors and management teams. The current situation does not support this on a widespread basis. Supposedly, a mental health coordinator and consultant are available to every program. As noted, however, this does not always happen. Further, both the coordinator and consultant roles are ill defined, and there has been only the most rudimentary, if any, support system on their behalf through the national training and technical assistance networks. This has meant that over the years, mental health coordinators (who often play other roles as well) and mental health consultants have had little hands-on assistance in inventing coherent strategies to fit the needs of each program. In fact, many consultants report doing little but carrying out classroom observations (with few opportunities to offer feedback to staff) and making referrals. Further, program directors and senior administrators have not had much help in developing community partnerships with mental health agencies or others with appropriate expertise. Nor are there any ongoing national strategies to help orient mental health consultants to the Head Start culture or build a repertoire of best practices or practice standards (Yoshikawa & Knitzer, 1997).

Challenge 6: Addressing the Resource and Policy Gaps

Mental health has been seen as basically an "add on," not embedded, as noted previously, in a framework for quality improvement or helping achieve school readiness or welfare-related goals. As a result, there is never enough (or often, any) Head Start money for the mental health component. The emotional development of young children has simply not yet penetrated the policy radar screen, although growing policy concern with violence and violence prevention, as well as attention to the use of behavioral drugs in preschool-aged children may change this (Coyle, 2000; Zito et al., 2000). Congress has never called for a report on how Head Start might better support the emotional development of its children and families, particularly those who face the more intense risk factors, or how emotional development relates to school readiness. Mental health research initiatives in the context of Head Start have largely been isolated and short-lived, and no national institutes have helped directors understand the potential pay off of a broad-based mental health strategy. And so, in the end, it is up to the staff and the directors to make a commitment, squeezing money from somewhere. Sometimes they do. So, for instance, the director of a Head Start program with a national reputation told me that she gave her staff a choice of how to spend "discretionary" money—they could either hire a janitorial service or hire a mental health consultant. The staff opted for the later and carried out the janitorial tasks among themselves. A national program with a $6 million budget can and should do better.

Challenge 7: Strengthening the Research Agenda

There are several key directions in which more research is needed. Five seem particularly compelling. First, what do we know about the general emotional and behavioral development and well-being of young children in Head Start, or Early Head Start, either alone or in comparison to Head Start eligible children who are cared for by relatives or family child care providers, as well as those in center-based care or even prekindergarten programs.

Second, what do we know about the experience of children in Early Head Start and Head Start in families with the most risk factors? Is it possible to track changes in child and family well-being in these families? This is an area in which, despite great need, there seems to have been no research that examines children and families in Head Start by level of risk, particularly with respect to such factors as parental depression or exposure to violence. Yet, it is vital to understand whether Head Start is robust enough, intensive enough to make a positive difference with respect to family functioning, school readiness, and the transition-to-work for this subpopulation.

Third, what do the most current round of research initiatives teach us about effective prevention, early intervention, and treatment initiatives within the context of Head Start? How can such information be aggregated and disseminated to the larger Head Start community in ways that they can adapt for local conditions? What is the value of a holistic approach? Of specific interventions? Does mental health consultation really serve as a quality improvement strategy over time? Fourth, what of those children who are, or should be, identified as having emotional and behavioral disabilities? How can Head Start do a better job of the appropriate identification of the more troubled children? What happens to those relatively few children who receive mental health services from other agencies; what kind of services and support do they and their families get? How does it affect their transition to school? How can Head Start programs and the multidisciplinary teams who identify children with disabilities get more help in carrying out culturally and diagnostically sensitive assessments and in building better links with mental health agencies?

Fifth, what are the most effective training, technical assistance, and other tools to help Head Start programs develop more holistic early childhood mental health strategies that address local issues and are respectful of the ways in which different ethnic groups deal with mental health issues? In what ways can Head Start programs be encouraged to develop new partnerships with mental health agencies, substance abuse agencies, welfare agencies, and others working with their families?

In sum, what is needed is a research agenda that can help Head Start better meet the emotional needs of its diverse population, be more effective with the most high-risk children and families it serves, evaluate and disseminate information about the efficacy of specific intervention approaches, and provide new information about children with identified, diagnosable levels of disturbance.

TOWARD A STRENGTHENED HEAD START–MENTAL HEALTH CONNECTION FOR THE 21ST CENTURY

The emerging practice experience and knowledge base about the risks to young children's emotional development and the ways in which these risks can be counteracted have important implications for the future of mental health in Head Start. They suggest that it should be possible to link mental health strategies more directly to the central goals of Head Start in the 21st century: helping children enter school with the emotional, behavioral, and cognitive skills that will enable them to succeed. But moving mental health from its Cinderella status within Head Start requires designing and implementing a set of intentional practice and research strategies, along with fiscal and other incentives. The previous sections make clear that since the early 1990s some of the building blocks to develop a more holistic national strategy have been put in place. A focus on social and emotional development in young children is critical to complementing and supporting efforts promote sound early learning, particularly with respect to early reading and math literacy. There is a danger given the current emphasis on these more academic skills that efforts will be out of balance. But both common sense and research tells us that early success in school involves attention to both mind and heart. To that end, an agenda to promote more effective Head Start mental health connections in the 21st century follows.

- Develop fiscal or other incentives to ensure that local Head Start agencies and state collaboration offices, either singly or in collaboration with local resources and referral agencies, child care programs, and other parts of the early care and education systems, implement mental health strategies appropriate to program and community needs

- Increase targeted resources to realistically address the levels of mental health needs in Head Start programs

- Include strength-based early childhood mental health principles and competencies in Head Start quality improvement initiatives

- Support national and/or statewide institutes for community teams from Head Start, including directors and mental health consultants to identify effective, strength-based, family and staff-focused practices; orient new consultants to the Head Start culture; and create peer-to-peer training and support networks

- Develop a strong research agenda to test the efficacy of different types of early childhood mental health strategies in the context of Head Start, linking these school readiness and other relevant indicators

- Create ongoing mechanisms for a research consortium focused on the most vulnerable young children and families in Head Start to enhance the quality of research and to share and disseminate findings to other researchers and policy makers

- Develop and test strategies to help staff (including directors, family service coordinators and workers, classroom teachers, and home visitors) identify signs of emotional risk in young children and families, many of which are now missed

- Promote cross-agency initiatives and funding at the federal level and state levels to strengthen the ability within Head Start (including Early Head Start and other child care settings) to address families and children with multiple needs

The failure to target adequate resources and to build a vision of mental health for Head Start that can complement other efforts to improve quality in Head Start carries a cost. It hides the fact that, for some children and families, staff need more than even the best child development and family support tools. It hides the fact that staff need opportunities to talk about typically unspoken tensions of the classroom involving discipline, interethnic conflicts, and violence as part of a quality improvement strategy. It hides the fact that staff, family, and community crises are predictable and that those involved need access to emotional support. And, it hides the fact that there is a body of mental health knowledge and skill about families, groups, and children that can be used to support the larger goals of Head Start in creative, nonstigmatizing ways.

Inventing and implementing a Head Start approach to mental health that directly addresses some of the challenges that have been largely ignored since the program began is an imperative whose time has come. The children can no longer wait. The agenda is an urgent one and one that fits with the broader goals of today's Head Start.

REFERENCES

Aber, J.L., Jones, S., & Cohen, J. (2000). The impact on the mental health and development of very young children. In C. Zeanah (Ed.), *Handbook of infant mental health* (2nd ed., pp.113–128). New York: Guilford Press.

Cohen, E., & Kaufmann, R. (2000). *Early childhood mental health consultation.* Washington, DC: U.S. Department of Health and Human Services (DHHS), Center for Mental Health Services (CMHS), and Substance Abuse and Mental Health Services Administration (SAMHSA).

Cohen, D., Solnit, A., & Wohlford, P. (1979). Mental health services in Head Start. In E.F. Zigler & J. Valentine (Eds.), *Project Head Start: Legacy of the War on Poverty* (pp. 259–282). New York: Macmillian.

Coyle, J.T. (2000). Psychotropic drug use in very young children. *Journal of the American Medical Association, 283,* 1059–1060.

Devereux Early Childhood Assessment (DECA). (2000). Accessed December 6, 2003, from http://www.devereuxearlychildhood.org/about-deca.html

Donahue, P.J., Falk, B., & Provet, A.G. (2000). *Mental health consultation in early childhood.* Baltimore: Paul H. Brookes Publishing Co.

Downey, G., & Coyne, J.C. (1990). Children of depressed parents: An investigative review. *Psychological Bulletin, 108,* 50–76.

Duncan, G., Brooks-Gunn, J., & Aber, J.L. (Eds.). (1997). *Neighborhood poverty: Context and consequences for child and adolescent development.* New York: Russell Sage.

Feil, E.G., & Becker, W.C (1993). Investigation of multiple-gated screening system for preschool behavior problems. *Behavioral Disorders, 19,* 44–53.

Feil, E.G., Walker, H.M., & Severson, H.H. (1995). The early screening project for young children with behavior problems. *Journal of Emotional and Behavioral Disorders, 3*(4), 194–202.

Forness, S.R., Cluett, S.E., Ramey, C.T., Ramey, S.L., Zima, B.T., Hsu, C., et al. (1998). Special education identification of Head Start children with emotional or behavioral disorders in second grade. *Journal of Emotional Behaviors, 7,* 54–64.

Forness, S.R., & Kavale, K. (1993). Screening children in Head Start for emotional or behavioral disorders. *Severe Behavior Disorders Monograph, 16,* 6–14.

Foster, E.M. (2002). Trends in multiple and overlapping disadvantages among Head Start enrollees. *Children and Youth Services Review, 24*(12), 933–954.

Friesen, B.J., & Huff, B. (1996). Family perspectives on systems of care. In B.A. Stroul (Ed.), *Children's mental health: Creating systems of care in a changing society* (pp. 41–67). Baltimore: Paul H. Brookes Publishing Co.

Knitzer, J. (2000a). Early childhood mental health services through a policy and systems development perspective. In J.P. Shonkoff & S.J. Meisels (Eds.), *Handbook of early childhood intervention* (2nd ed., 907–956). New York: Cambridge University Press.

Knitzer, J. (2000b). *Promoting resilience: Helping young children and parents affected by substance abuse, domestic violence, and depression in the context of welfare reform.* (Children and Welfare Issue Brief No. 8). New York: National Center for Children in Poverty, Joseph L. Mailman School of Public Health, Columbia University.

Knitzer, J. (2000c). *Using mental health strategies to move the early childhood agenda.* Washington, DC: The Finance Project and The Carnegie Corporation.

Knitzer, J., & Aber, J.L. (1995). Facing the facts: Young children in poverty. *American Journal of Orthopsychiatry, 65,* 174–175.

Lopez, M., Tarullo, L., Forness, S., & Boyce, C.A. (2000). Early identification and intervention: Head Start's response to mental challenges. *Early Education and Development, 11*(3), 265–282.

Moore, K.A., Zaslow, M.J., Coiro, J.J., Miller, S., & Magenheim, E.B. (1996). *The JOBS evaluation: How well are they faring: AFDC families with preschool-aged children in Atlanta at the outset of the JOBS Evaluation.* Washington, DC: Child Trends.

NICHD Early Child Care Research Network. (1999). Chronicity of maternal depressive symptoms, maternal sensitivity, and child functioning at 36 months. *Developmental Psychology, 35,* 1297–1310.

Parker, F.L., Piotrkowski, C.S., Horn W., Greene, S. (1995). The challenge for Head Start: Realizing its vision as a two generation program. In I. Sigel (Series Ed.) & S. Smith (Vol. Ed.), *Advances in applied developmental psychology: Vol. 9, Two generation programs for families in poverty* (pp. 135–159). Norwood, NJ: Ablex Publishing.

Piotrkowski, C.S., Collins, R.C., Knitzer, J., & Robinson, R. (1994). Strengthening mental health services in Head Start: A challenge for the 1990's. *American Psychologist, 49,* 133–139.

Raver, C., & Knitzer, J. (2002). *Ready to enter: What research tells policymakers about strategies to promote social and emotional school readiness among three-and-four year old children* (Promoting the emotional well-being of children and families policy paper No. 3). New York: National Center for Children in Poverty, Columbia University.

Shonkoff, J., & Phillips, D. (Eds.). (2000). *From neurons to neighborhoods: The science of early childhood development.* Washington, DC: National Academy Press.

Sinclair, E. (1993). Early identification of preschoolers with special needs in Head Start. *Topics in Early Childhood Special Education, 13,* 184–201.

Sinclair, E., Del'Homme, M., & Gonzalez, M. (1993). Systematic screening for preschool behavioral disorders. *Behavioral Disorders, 18,* 177–188.

Stroul, B., & Friedman, R. (1986). *A system of care for severely emotionally disturbed children and youth.* Tampa: University of South Florida, Florida Mental Health Institute.

Task Force on Head Start and Mental Health. (1994). *Strengthening mental health in Head Start: Pathways to quality improvement.* New York: American Orthopsychiatric Association.

Urban Institute. (1999). *Snapshots of America's families.* Washington, DC: Author.

U.S. Department of Health and Human Services (DHHS) Administration on Children, Youth and Families (ACYF). (2002, January). *A descriptive study of Head Start families: FACES Technical Report 1.* Accessed December 8, 2003 from http://www.acf.dhhs.gov/programs/core/ongoing_research/faces/technical_report/tech_title.html

U.S. Department of Health and Human Services (DHHS) Administration on Children, Youth, and Families (ACYF). *Head Start Performance Standards.* Accessed December 8, 2003 from http://www.acf.dhhs.gov/programs/hsb/performance

U.S. Department of Health and Human Services (DHHS), Office of the Surgeon General (1999). *Mental health: A report of the Surgeon General.* Washington, DC: Author. (Also available at http://www.surgeongeneral.gov/library/mentalhealth/home.html)

Webster-Stratton, C. (1997). Early intervention for families of preschool children with conduct problems. In M.J. Guralnick (Ed.), *The effectiveness of early intervention* (pp. 429–453). Baltimore: Paul H. Brookes Publishing Co.

Webster-Stratton, C., & Hammond, M. (1998). Conduct problems and level of social competence in Head Start children: Prevalence, pervasiveness, and associated risk factors. *Clinical Child and Family Psychology Review, 1,* 101–123.

Yoshikawa, H., & Knitzer, J. (1997). *Lessons from the field: Head Start mental health strategies to meet changing needs.* New York: National Center for Children in Poverty, Joseph L. Mailman School of Public Health, Columbia University.

Yoshikawa, H., & Zigler, E.F. (2000). *Mental health in Head Start: New directions for the twenty-first century. Early education and development.* New York: Cambridge University Press.

Zeanah, C., Jr. (Ed.). (1999). *Handbook of infant mental health* (2nd ed.). New York: Guilford Press.

Zito, J.M., Safer, D.J., dosReis, S., Gardner, J.F., Boles, M., & Lynch, F. (2000). Trends in the prescribing of psychotropic medications to preschoolers. *Journal of the American Medical Association, 283,* 1025–1030.

CHAPTER 13

A Persistent Pattern of Progress

Parent Outcomes in Longitudinal Studies of Head Start Children and Families

PEGGY DALY PIZZO AND ELIZABETH EDWARDS TUFANKJIAN

From a very young child's perspective, what matters most in life are *parents.*[1] Very young children know implicitly that their well-being depends on the nature of the parent–child relationship. Head Start expansion—and particularly expansion of Early Head Start—should be designed to enhance the parent–child relationship.

Before policy makers can outline well the elements of Head Start expansion that would deeply enhance parent–child relationships, they need to know more about Head Start's influence on parents. Thus, this chapter is intended to answer the following research question: What do existing longitudinal studies of Head Start children and/or families tell us about the impact of Head Start on parents?[2]

To answer this question, 41 longitudinal[3] studies of Head Start children and families, of which 21 reported parent outcomes, were identified and reviewed. In reviewing these 21 studies, both the reported outcomes and the research design of these studies were

This chapter (and earlier reviews) benefited from the advice of several distinguished scholars and policy advisors, among them W. Steven Barnett, Ray Collins, Peter Edelman, Jim Harrell, Stuart Hauser, Gloria Johnson-Powell, Ruth Hubbell McKey, Gary Orfield, Julius Richmond, Louisa Tarullo, Carol Weiss, Lucie White, Sheldon White, and Ed Zigler. Many individuals also helped us design this review and locate and retrieve studies; these individuals are appreciatively acknowledged throughout this chapter. We are particularly grateful to Ellsworth Associates for their help in identifying and retrieving reports of unpublished studies.

In addition, we thank Michael Levine, formally of the Carnegie Corporation of New York, as well as Barbara Finberg, former Vice-President of Carnegie; a private foundation who wishes to remain anonymous; and the Merck Company Foundation, for their support.

[1]In this chapter, the term *parents* means the child's psychological parents, whether or not they are also biological parents.

[2]The review encompassed longitudinal studies of Head Start children and families rather than focusing only on long-term studies of Head Start programs. Thus, some studies investigated the impact of diverse approaches to early care and education services but included an examination of the outcomes of Head Start–participating parents.

[3]*Longitudinal* is defined as "lasting beyond the initial Head Start year" for this review. This means that some results reported by some studies reflect outcomes experienced by parents while they are still participating in Head Start. This is noted during the analysis of the studies presented later in this chapter.

analyzed, with a focus on both the strengths and weaknesses of the design and their implications for the validity of the findings.[4]

Using stringent research design criteria, five strong prospective longitudinal studies involving in total more than 2,500 families were selected for in-depth analysis. In these studies, we found a persistent pattern of Head Start parent progress in the skills needed to promote children's educational success in our school systems.

Specifically, these five large-scale longitudinal studies clearly suggest that Head Start (in either typical or demonstration forms) systematically helps parents achieve two patterns[5] of parent outcomes:

1. Improvement in parental ability to promote early learning skills (including early literacy skills)

2. Greater participation in their children's later schooling

In addition, four smaller scale longitudinal studies of Head Start children and families—involving more than 500 families—were analyzed. This analysis corroborated the findings of the larger scale studies. It is clearly noteworthy that a pattern of parent progress appears in longitudinal studies involving more than 3,000 families who participated in Head Start in different parts of the country and at different times in the program's 35-year history.

These consistent patterns suggest that Head Start, either in its regular form or in programs especially configured to focus intensively on families, may help parents acquire a range of new skills—skills that may lead to better lives for their children and themselves.

This chapter briefly summarizes parent outcome-related findings from previous Head Start research reviews. It also summarizes parent outcome-related findings from individual longitudinal studies with selected criteria for research design. Finally, it discusses the findings that converge across two or more of the studies included in this analysis.

THE RESEARCH CONTEXT

In the 35 years since its founding, Head Start has achieved national and international recognition as a successful *child* development program. Many accounts by parents, however, also attest to Head Start success, at least for some individuals, as a *parent* development program. That is to say, numerous anecdotal reports, testimonies before policy makers, journalist accounts, interviews with parents (by researchers and others), and observations by Head Start staff speak to the belief that Head Start helps parents change their lives (Greenberg, 1969/1990; Mills, 1998; National Head Start Association, 1990; Robinson & Choper, 1979; Sorenson, 1990; Zigler & Muenchow, 1992).

In contrast to this rich body of personal statements, the Head Start research literature (which is quite voluminous) seems strangely silent. When it does address Head Start's impact on parents, the conclusions are somewhat contradictory. Three major Head Start-focused research reviews have included an analysis of Head Start's impact on families. *A Review of Head Start Research Since 1969* (Mann, Harrell, & Hurt, 1977, p. 13) found "an

---

[4]This chapter is based on an earlier review, carried out by the senior author, of 39 such longitudinal studies, of which 17 reported parent outcomes (Pizzo, 1998). The senior author is indebted to Dr. Carol Weiss for encouraging her to look for broad patterns in the outcomes and for using the specific phrase "persistent patterns."

[5]For this chapter, *pattern* is defined as a finding that converged across two or more studies. In terms of the families themselves, this would mean that some aspect of parent change was found among at least 400 (or more) families participating in Head Start in different years and in different parts of the country.

increase in positive interactions between mothers and children, as well as an increase in parent participation in later programs." A 1978 review, *What Head Start Means to Families* (O'Keefe, 1978), concluded that Head Start's family effects included increased social contact for parents and strengthened understanding and ability of parents to support their child's education and development in the primary grades. *The Impact of Head Start on Children and Communities: Final Report of the Head Start Evaluation, Synthesis and Utilization Project* (McKey et al., 1985) found that actively participating parents "have high levels of psychological well-being, improve their economic and social status and have children with high levels of developmental achievement" (p. 23). The reviewers also noted that Head Start had not been successful in changing attitudes and that "mixed results" flow from "parent education programs designed to influence child-rearing practices" (p. 23).

These comprehensive research reviews provide useful insights, but the reviewers have not systematically excluded those studies of poor quality. This may limit the findings of these reviews (Gamble & Zigler, 1989). In addition, these reviews included cross-sectional as well as longitudinal studies but did not highlight the findings of the longitudinal studies, despite their greater merit. More recently, the National Research Council, in its extensive recommendations for and overview of Head Start research, also noted the trends thus far in the literature and called for more focused attention to parents in Head Start research (Phillips & Cabrera, 1996).

None of these efforts, however, have addressed in depth the particular research question around which this chapter is organized: *What do currently available longitudinal studies of Head Start children and families tell us about Head Start's impact on parents?* The following sections address this core question.

METHODS FOR THIS REVIEW

This review was conducted using the research synthesis methodologies proposed by Cooper and Hedges (1994) and Light, Singer, and Willett (1990). These methodologies include systematic

* Identification and retrieval of longitudinal studies and related documents

* Selection of longitudinal studies with parent outcomes

* In-depth analysis of those studies with significant research design strengths[6]

More than 4,100 abstracts and brief summaries of research studies (e.g., handouts at poster sessions) about Head Start children and families were identified, retrieved, and reviewed. The preliminary review screened for abstracts that reported studies described as "longitudinal" or "long-term" or as measuring the effects of Head Start in one or more of the primary grades. From this pool of studies, we identified 41 longitudinal studies of Head Start children and families, two substantial Follow-Through studies, and six site-specific Head Start-Public School Transition Demonstration studies.[7]

---

[6]To design this research review, the senior author also benefited from interactions with Gary Orfield, Shep White, Judith Singer, Terry Tivnan, John Willett, Michael Huberman, Carol Weiss, and other faculty of the Harvard Graduate School of Education.

[7]The Follow-Through studies and those site-specific evaluations of the National Head Start-Public School Transition Demonstration analyzed did not collect data during the Head Start year. Abstracts summarizing additional site-specific Transition evaluations also did not indicate data collection during the Head Start participation year. Consequently, both Follow-Through and Transition studies were not selected for in-depth analysis during this review.

Table 13.1. Longitudinal studies reviewed that report parent data

Child and Family Resource Program (Travers et al., 1982)

Disadvantaged Children and Their First School Experience (Shipman et al., 1976)

Early Learning and Early Identification Study (Marcon, 1990)

Early Learning and Early Identification Follow-Up Study: Transition from the Early to the Later Childhood Grades, 1990–1993 (Marcon, 1994b)

Predicting Parent Involvement and Its Influence on School Success: A Follow-Up Study (Marcon, 1998)

Experimental Variation of Head Start (Miller & Bizzell, 1984)

Experiments in Head Start and Early Education (Erikson et al., 1969)

Family Education and Training Program (Kagan et al., 1998)

Family Empowerment and Transitioning Program (Zeece & Wang, 1998)

The Longitudinal Head Start Family Impact Project (Peters et al., 1987)

Comparison of Long Range Effects of Participation in Project Head Start and Impact of Three Different Delivery Models (Reedy, 1991)

National Evaluation of Head Start Educational Services and Basic Educational Skills Initiative (Posante-Loro & McNeil, 1980)

National Home Start Evaluation (Love et al., 1976)

Home Start Follow-Up Study: A Study of Long-term Impact of Home Start on Program Participants (Bache, 1979)

Parent Child Development Centers (Bridgeman et al., 1981)

Parent–Child Centers (Holmes et al., 1973)

Parent Involvement in Head Start (Parker et al., 1997a, 1997b)

Planned Variation in Head Start and Follow Through (Bissell, 1972)

Project Developmental Continuity (Bond & Rosario,1982)

Relationship between Head Start Parental Involvement and the Economic and Social Self-sufficiency of Head Start Families (Oyemade et al., 1989)

Rural Child Care Project (Archambo, 1970)

Variations in Service Delivery Models in Region X (Edgar et al., 1992)

We examined the "results and conclusions" sections of these studies to ascertain whether they reported any parent data, such as changes in parent knowledge, skills, attitudes, or behaviors. If they did, we classified them as longitudinal studies that reported parent outcomes; 21 longitudinal studies that met these criteria were found (see Table 13.1).

The 21 longitudinal studies that reported parent outcomes were analyzed with criteria for research design developed from those proposed by Light, Singer, and Willett (1990). Of particular interest was how the researchers dealt with the difficult issues of formulating a central research question or two, deciding on both sample size and selection, choosing (in experimental and quasi-experimental designs) a method of comparing groups, determining an approach to measurement, and dealing with attrition. For experimental and quasi-experimental longitudinal studies, the following criteria were set for inclusion in this analysis:

- Final sample sizes of at least 200 families[8] so that the statistical analyses could be done with large samples

---

[8]The senior author initially considered choosing a final sample size of at least 80 families (40 in each comparison group). However, on reflection, she decided to concentrate on experiments with larger samples, reasoning that with this size sample, there is less chance of failing to find an effect, if most other aspects of the design are strong.

Table 13.2. Longitudinal studies selected for in-depth analysis

Early Learning and Early Identification Study (Marcon 1990, 1994b)
Child and Family Resource Program (Travers et al., 1982)
Parent Child Development Centers (Bridgeman et al., 1981)
Home Start (Love et al., 1976)
ETS-Head Start Longitudinal Study (Shipman et al., 1976)

- The use of either random assignment to treatment and control groups or the use of matching along several key family characteristics to form comparison groups

- Two or more time points for data collection relative to parent outcomes

- The use of detailed attrition analyses to rule out as much as possible the nonequivalency of groups

For nonexperimental investigations, the following criteria were set for inclusion in this analysis:

- Final sample sizes of at least 200 families

- The sample was selected from both Head Start-participating and non–Head Start-participating families

- At least 6 years of longitudinal study

- Three or more time points, including a pretest, for data collection relative to parent outcomes

- The use of detailed attrition analyses to rule out as much as possible the nonequivalency of groups.

Using these criteria, five studies were selected for further, more detailed analysis (see Table 13.2). Given the somewhat archeological nature of this review, results of this in-depth analysis are reported in chronological order, starting with the most recent study.

EARLY LEARNING AND EARLY IDENTIFICATION STUDY (1987–PRESENT)

Overview

The Early Learning and Early Identification Study, sponsored by the District of Columbia public schools (DCPS), was designed to investigate the impact of early learning programs on children's long-term school success. It is an ongoing study. Available research reports describe the basic study as a 10-year, quasi-experimental, two-cohort[9] study of an initial sample of approximately 650 children and parents—500 children randomly selected from DCPS-sponsored preschools and Head Start programs, matched in year 2 with 100 randomly selected no-preschool kindergarten children (R. Marcon, personal communication, 1995, 2000).

---

[9]Originally, three cohorts were studied, but only two cohorts were followed to Year 9 (for the kindergarten-only children) or 10 (for the preschoolers).

In the course of this extensive study of child outcomes, information about parents was collected at multiple time points in order to assess parent involvement in their children's schooling as predictors of child outcomes.[10] In two sub-studies, parent participation in their children's schooling is treated as an outcome, and the data collected is used to analyze the predictors of such involvement. Consequently, we focus on two sub-studies of an initial sample of 295 Head Start and preschool parents.[11] The first sub-study, which we refer to hereafter as the Primary Grades Study,[12] followed children and parents until the children were approximately 9 years old. The second sub-study, which we refer to hereafter as the Transition to Junior High School Study,[13] followed children and parents until the children were approximately 12 years old.

In both sub-studies, data about high versus low levels of parent involvement[14] were used, along with other data about the school, the child, and the family, in order to predict one parent outcome: subsequent participation in their children's schooling (as well as to predict child outcomes).[15]

Findings

The Primary Grades Study   This study found that "the most notable predictor of third grade involvement was parent involvement during kindergarten which was, in turn, best predicted by enrollment in Head Start" (Marcon, 1998, p. 3).

The Transition to Junior High School Study   This study found that former Head Start parents "were significantly more involved in their children's education at Year 8 or Year 9 than were parents whose children had attended PreK" (Marcon, 1998, p.5). This was particularly noteworthy because Head Start families were less advantaged than were PreK families.[16]

Strengths of the Study

The strengths of this study lie in its large sample,[17] use of sample stratification and random sampling within strata, multiple time points for data collection, and, notably, the length of time the parents were followed, particularly in view of the dispersion into ultimately more than 90 schools. For both the overall study and the sub-studies, the sample

---

[10]The reader is referred to Marcon (1989, 1990,1993a, 1993b, 1993c, 1994, 1998, 1999) and Marcon, Boldrick, & Harkins (1988) for an exceptionally detailed discussion of the overall study and its findings.

[11]Numbers are approximate, as they reflect numbers of children, rather than parents, and there were some sets of twins in the study.

[12]This sub-study investigated the predictors of parent involvement in preschool, kindergarten, first grade, and Year 6 (when most children were in third or fourth grade (Marcon, 1993c).

[13]This sub-study investigated the predictors of parent involvement in their children's education at Year 8 and Year 9, when the children were for the most part in sixth or seventh grade.

[14]As defined by a score on annual teacher ratings of parent involvement. Parents were rated as to their involvement in 1) parent–teacher conference (without which parents, by DCPS policy, could not obtain their children's report cards); 2) home visit by teacher; 3) extended class visit by parent; and 4) parental help with class activity. Parents who fulfill either none or one of these criteria are classified as "low;" parents who fulfill three or four of these criteria are classified as "high."

[15]The research paper for these sub-studies do not explicitly mention a research question (Marcon, 1993c, 1998).

[16]All findings cited here, for both sub-studies, are statistically significant at least at the $p < .05$ level.

[17]The regression analyses were not carried out on all 221 parents that comprised the Transition to Junior High School sample because the parents were classified into either low or high involvement categories based on the method described above. Thus, those parents who obtained a rating of "2"—and thus had average involvement—were not included in the regression analyses.

of initial preschool and Head Start participants was randomly selected from a stratified sample of randomly selected classrooms of three different curricular types.[18]

The stratified sampling frame was constructed by first analyzing the proportion of Head Start and prekindergarten children in the four quadrants of the District of Columbia (upper-Northwest, mid-Northwest, Northeast, and Southeast/Southwest) and then analyzing the proportion of the three preschool curricular types in each of the four quadrants. Sampling was roughly proportional to types of preschool curricula found in the four regions (Marcon, 1994; R. Marcon, personal communication, 1995, 1996).

In this study, the data about children and parents was collected at five time points for the majority of cohorts—at the end of the school year in prekindergarten, during kindergarten and first grade, during the transition from third to fourth grade ("Year 6"), and during grade six or grade seven ("Year 8 or Year 9"). The children's teachers were asked to rate parents as to their levels of involvement. The teachers were scattered proportionally throughout the District of Columbia: In Year 1, the teachers were in 39 schools; by Year 6, in 80 schools; by Year 8 or 9, in 91 schools (Marcon, 1994, 1998).

Limitations of the Study

The lack of experimental design, the focus on only one parent outcome, and the attrition from the original sample limit the study's findings. Although the comparison children are matched by sex, ethnicity, and family income level (as measured by eligibility for subsidized school lunch), there are other characteristics, preexisting the parents' decision whether to enroll their children in early childhood education, as well as the decision to choose either Head Start or another preschool, that might play a substantial role in these decisions and in later decisions about levels of parent involvement. One such characteristic might be maternal employment; another might be family size. In addition, the use of eligibility for subsidized school lunch as a measure of income level does not distinguish variation in income as well as other measures would.

The use of teacher ratings of parent involvement has merit (as compared, e.g., with parent reports of their own involvement; Marcon, 1999). However, teacher recall at the end of the school year may not always be precise or free from personal bias.

Finally, attrition between the original and final sample, although lower than found in other large-scale studies,[19] raises some questions about the study's findings. The final sample for the Primary Grade Study recovered 90% of the first-grade children and thus is reasonably representative of the parent population that uses the DCPS. A comparable figure for the Transition to Junior High School Study was not available at the time this chapter was written.

Conclusion

This study strongly suggests that 1) Head Start enrollment deeply influences later parent participation in their children's schooling and 2) this influence persists into junior high

---

[18]These different preschool curricular types (child-initiated, teacher-directed, and "middle-of-the-road" compromise) were identified through a survey of all DCPS prekindergarten and Head Start teachers of 4-year-olds (Marcon, 1994).

[19]About 28 Head Start and preschool parents could not be recovered at kindergarten and about 32 additional parents could not be recovered at Year 6, for a sub-study attrition rate in the Primary Grades Study of about 17%. The research report for the Transition to Junior High School Study does not mention an attrition rate.

school. However, possible nonequivalency of the Head Start, other preschool, and no preschool groups limits the study's findings.

CHILD AND FAMILY RESOURCE PROGRAM (1977–1982)

Overview

The Child and Family Resource Program (CFRP) evaluation investigated the impact on both children and parents of a highly family focused Head Start research and demonstration program that served pregnant women and mothers of infants (as well as the infants and toddlers) with center- and home-based activities designed to strengthen the family.

The evaluation of the infant/toddler component of CFRP was designed to be a 5-year study, across five study sites, with an initial sample of 409 low-income families with children younger than 1 year who were randomly assigned to either a treatment group (the CFRP program) or a control group.

The CFRP evaluation had four objectives: 1) to describe CFRPs and their operations, 2) to identify program models, 3) to link family outcome to participation or nonparticipation in CFRP, and 4) to link family outcome to particular aspects of the CFRP treatment and family characteristics (Travers, Nauta, & Irwin, 1982).

Findings

The CFRP evaluation found that this Head Start research and demonstration program improved parental teaching abilities (specifically those abilities that help promote early literacy in children). The most important changes occurred in the frequency of

- Overall parent child interaction

- Parent–child interaction rich in language information or involving teaching in which the child attempted mastery of some tasks.

In addition, parents participating in CFRP showed some modest differences in the degree to which they experienced frustration or irritation during a child's demand for attention, the degree to which they exercised control, and in their willingness to allow the child choice and initiative (Travers et al., 1982).

Strengths of the Study

The strengths of the study lie in the use of 1) an experimental design, including random assignment; 2) at least four data collection time points, including a pretest; 3) both quantitative and qualitative methods; 4) the length of the data collection (3 years); 5) a large sample (more than 240 families in the final sample); 6) multiple sites; 7) a multimethod approach to assessing outcomes; and 8) a variety of analytical approaches to investigating the equivalency of the groups compared.

Limitations of the Study

The flaws in the evaluation's design detract somewhat from the strengths of the findings. The lack of specific research questions guiding the CFRP and its evaluation may have contributed to an unresolved ambivalence between child and family outcomes as the primary purpose of CFRP.[20] In addition, the high level of attrition (38%) raises questions about the representativeness of the final sample. Most of the attrition was caused by family relocation. However, membership in the nonpredominant racial or ethnic group in the program was the second most common reason for dropout from the sample. In addition, the CFRP participants in the final sample differed systematically from the control group on a few other dimensions—CFRP families were smaller, had fewer wage earners, less education, and were less likely to be either enrolled in Medicaid or to interact with informal networks of support. They also had less continuous health problems. The possible systematic nature of the attrition as well as the sheer numbers of families who dropped out limit the study's findings.

Conclusion

The CFRP evaluation strongly suggests that this type of highly family focused Head Start helps parents improve both their overall interaction and their teaching interactions with their children. Despite the strong research design of this evaluation, however, the attrition constrains the findings.

PARENT CHILD DEVELOPMENT CENTERS (1970–1975; 1976–1980)

Overview

The evaluation of the Parent Child Development Centers (PCDC) is essentially the study of outcomes from three programs with similar (but not identical) approaches to the delivery of Head Start services to infants and toddlers—a primarily center-based approach intended to help "parents become more effective child-rearing agents as the primary path to reaching the goals for children" (Bridgeman et al., 1981, p. 1).

The study was a multiple-cohort, 8-year study (not including the pilot years) in three sites (Birmingham, Houston, and New Orleans) with a large initial sample of 593 pairs of parents and their children aged approximately birth to 4 years randomly assigned to program and control groups[21] (Bridgeman et al., 1981).

Neither the PCDC research design nor the analyses are guided by explicit research questions. However, both the design and analyses do directly address the aforementioned goal of the program.

Findings

Like the CFRP study, the PCDC evaluation found improved effective teaching styles among parents and in overall parent–child interactions. At the time of graduation from the program (when children were 36 months old), the overall parent pattern across the sites was positive in these two general areas (see Table 13.3).

---

[20]For example, as the ethnographic data from the study makes clear, CFRP staff were quite divided as to whether parents should participate in extensive employment and training—participation that would take mothers out of the home. Some staff felt that mothers would then be less available for interactions with their children.

[21]In Birmingham, the total final sample was 186 pairs (107 program and 79 controls); in Houston, 208 pairs (99 program and 109 controls); in New Orleans, 98 pairs (46 program and 52 controls).

Table 13.3. Selected findings from the Parent Child Development Centers at 36 months

		Program	Control	t
Birmingham				
Positive maternal interaction	N	86	70	2.47 **
(waiting room)	M	65.59	53.60	
	SD	30.78	29.52	
Effective teacher	N	84	67	4.09 **
(structured teaching)	M	12.06	10.28	
	SD	2.49	2.86	
New Orleans				
Net positive maternal language	N	42	31	2.77 **
(waiting room)	M	30.26	7.24	
	SD	27.07	39.93	
Sensitivity	N	42	31	2.28 *
(waiting room)	M	6.29	5.19	
	SD	1.62	2.30	
Effective teacher	N	11	13	2.34 *
(structured teaching)	M	10.85	9.65	
	SD	1.03	1.40	
Houston				
Positive maternal interaction	N	79	82	4.18 **
(stuctured teachings)	M	8.50	7.70	
	SD	1.00	1.38	
Home total score	N	99	108	2.61 **
(Caldwell Home Inventory)	M	36.98	33.39	
	SD	4.9	5.9	

Note: *<.05; **<.01; t = test statistic; N = number of participants; M = mean score; SD = standard deviation

In Birmingham, parents showed more positive interaction with their children[22] (e.g., participated more actively with their children, asked their children questions, had more general conversation with their children), as well as more effective teaching-type interactions with their children (e.g., used questions versus orders, used praise and encouragement). In New Orleans, parents also engaged in more positive interactions with their children (e.g., used more positive language and less controlling language) and showed greater sensitivity and more effective teaching-type interactions. In Houston, parents showed better teaching-type interactions (e.g., used more praise, encouraged the children's verbalizations more) and provided a more stimulating environment at home (e.g., more appropriate playthings, more opportunities for variety in daily routines). In addition, in structured interviews, more Birmingham and New Orleans parents in the programs supported positive means of child control (i.e., less use of punishment as a strategy to control children; Bridgeman et al., 1981, pp. 60–69).

At 48 months,[23] 1 year after graduation, the Birmingham program parents continued to show more effective teaching-styles, and there was a positive trend among these

---

[22]All results reported in this section are statistically significant at the p < .05 level, at least.

[23]The Birmingham and New Orleans samples were followed to 48 months. However, the Houston sample was only followed to 36 months.

parents for overall interaction with their children.[24] The New Orleans parents did not show this same pattern.[25]

Strengths of the Study

The strengths of this study lie in its large sample, use of random assignment, and approach to measurement. In all three sites, videotape observations were coded with varied rating systems to assess parent outcomes at least three times. In two sites (Birmingham and New Orleans), a parent questionnaire was also used. In addition, a home environment inventory was used in Houston. Although all three sites videotaped both a structured teaching and a waiting-room situation, each PCDC chose or designed its own observation instruments and questionnaires/rating scales.[26]

Limitations of the Study

The study is limited by a strikingly high attrition rate (more than 50%). However, the researchers collected baseline descriptive data on such characteristics as income per person, mother's education and age, number of children in the family, father presence, and child scores on the Bayley Mental Development Index, looking at all families as they entered the study and then again at 36 months. (It is not clear whether similar detailed attrition analysis was carried out for the 48 month sample.) They found virtually no significant differences between the dropout and final samples (Bridgeman et al., 1981).

Conclusion

The PCDC evaluation indicates that parents improved both their overall and teaching interactions with their children. These findings are bolstered by both the strong design of the study and the emergence of this finding in multiple cohorts across the three PCDC sites. The high attrition limits these findings, but the force of this limitation is diminished somewhat by the attrition analyses that showed, at least for certain demographic characteristics, that the original families did not systematically differ from the families that completed the study.

HOME START (1972–1975)

Overview

The evaluation of Home Start was intended to assess the effects of a home-based approach to the delivery of Head Start services. It was designed to be a 3-year, multisite study of an initial sample of 556 families with children ages 3–5 who were randomly assigned to either a Home Start group or a delayed-entry control group or were randomly selected from Head Start programs to form a comparison group.

---

[24]These results were statistically significant at the p < .10 level.

[25]At 48 months, the sample of parents from New Orleans was small (17 program participants and 28 controls). Consequently, statistically significant effects would be less likely detected (Bridgeman et al., 1981).

[26]In the early 1970s, when data collection first took place, the researchers reported that there were few reliable and valid ways to use observation to assess interaction between low-income mothers and such very young children. In addition, the researchers did not want to impose instruments on three programs that differed culturally.

This study has three components: summative, process, and cost-effectiveness evaluations. The analysis of the data collected was organized to answer several distinct questions. Among these was the question relevant to this review: Was Home Start effective for parents?

Findings

This study found that Home Start mothers were, after 7 months, more likely than controls to read more often to their children and to provide more books and playthings. In addition, Home Start mothers interacted more frequently with their children and used a more effective teaching-type interaction. However, once the delayed-entry control group began participating in Home Start, the differences between program and control mothers diminished (Love, Nauta, Coelen, Hewett, & Ruopp, 1976).

Strengths of the Study

The strengths of the Home Start evaluation primarily lie in its large sample, drawn from six sites, chosen from the 16 sites in which Home Start operated. Although these six were not randomly selected, the extensive descriptive data collection on family and staff characteristics, services provided to families, and financial expenditures in all 16 sites permitted analyses which concluded that "there were no major differences between the summative sites and the other ten" (Love et al., 1976, p. 42).

At each of the six sites, researchers tried to involve 120 families (40 in each of the three study groups). The pretest sample of 556 families fell a bit short of that goal but is nonetheless very substantial. The measures used to assess parent outcomes included a home inventory (High/Scope Home Environment Scale), a parent rating scale completed by the community interviewer (Mother Behavior Observation Scale), coded observation of parent–child interaction (the 8-Block Sort Task), and an extensive parent interview. Data collection took place at four time points (including a pretest) for the program, control, and Head Start groups. (In addition, new program and Head Start groups were assessed at two time points in a 7-month replication study.)

Limitations of the Study

Despite these considerable strengths, the findings of the Home Start evaluation are limited by the nature of the comparison groups as well as by substantial attrition. Use of a delayed-entry control group in a study designed to assess outcomes over a 2-year period meant that in the second program year, the control group was getting the benefits of 1 year of Home Start, making it quite difficult to obtain a clear longitudinal picture of the results of the program. In addition, using random assignment only for the Home Start and Head Start groups limited more meaningful comparisons between Head Start and a no-treatment control group or between Home Start and a no-treatment control group.

A high attrition rate of children (58% for program, 56% for control, and 57% for Head Start participants) also limits the conclusions about outcomes that might be drawn from this study. The researchers carried out analyses comparing the families at pretest with those at each of the three subsequent time points for data collection and concluded that "attrition appears not to have added any serious bias to the group comparisons" (Love et al., 1976, p. 42). Nonetheless, the high attrition rate limits the confidence with which the findings can be put forward.

Conclusion

The Home Start study strongly suggests that parents participating in this demonstration of a home-based approach to Head Start improved both their overall interaction as well as their teaching-type interaction with their children. In addition, they read more to their children and provided more playthings. These findings are underscored by the research design strengths of this evaluation, but high attrition somewhat limits these conclusions.

ETS-HEAD START LONGITUDINAL STUDY (1969–1974)

Overview

The ETS-Head Start longitudinal study was a 6-year, nonexperimental study of children in three regionally distinct communities' elementary school districts, chosen in part for their substantial populations eligible for Head Start. It was intended to be a study of child development—as it occurred between the ages of at least $3\frac{1}{2}$ (prior to any enrollment in Head Start or other preschool) and $8\frac{1}{2}$ to 9 years—among economically disadvantaged children who participated in either Head Start, other preschools, or no preschool at all.

The primary focus of the study was not to evaluate Head Start but to study child development among economically disadvantaged children, with parents studied at several time points to obtain information about background characteristics that would illumine the child-focused findings. Thus, we cannot describe the parent-related information available from this study as "parent effects." However, comparisons of characteristics of more than 1,200 parents prior to their decisions about Head Start or other preschool enrollment with those same characteristics 6 years later yield some interesting correlational parent data that are relevant to this review.

Findings

In Year 6, the study did not find an association between Head Start and the characteristics of all parents. However, in this same year, when African American mothers participating in Head Start (n = 559) were compared with African American mothers who had not enrolled their children in Head Start or any other preschool (n = 127), the study found that

> There was a consistent trend for greater involvement/interest of Head Start mothers in educational activities (i.e., helping more with the study child's homework, visiting the child's classroom more often, attending more school meetings, expressing more favorable attitudes towards the study child's school and teachers, and having the child bring more library books home). (Shipman, McKee, & Bridgeman, 1976, p. 79)

Strengths of the Study

The strengths of this study lie in its large, multisite, naturally occurring samples and the length of time the children and parents were studied.

Limitations of the Study

This study had multiple limitations. Attrition from the initial sample was substantial (more than one third) and not random. A higher percentage of final sample children came from African American, low-income families and were Head Start graduates. Attrition primarily occurred among Caucasian families, particularly in one site (Lee County, Alabama).[27] However, the attrition did not dramatically affect the racial composition of the year 6 sample as compared to the year 1 sample: 65% of the overall study children and 88% of the Head Start attendees (and therefore, presumably, approximately the same proportion of parents) were African American in year 6, as compared to 63% in year 1 (Shipman et al., 1976).

In addition, researchers used a structured parent interview to assess parent characteristics at year 6, with the consequent problems associated with parent report.[28] This limits the strength of the very substantial amount of information about parent characteristics that the ETS study retrieved.

Finally, given the very large size of the sample, it is unfortunate that non–English-speaking families were not studied (Shipman, 1971; Shipman et al., 1976).

Conclusion

The ETS-Head Start longitudinal study finding—that former Head Start parents have greater involvement with their children's primary grade schools—is important, particularly given the study's extensive database about so many low-income families in three communities. However, as in several of the previously analyzed studies, attrition limits the study's findings.

SUMMARY: CONVERGENT PATTERNS

These five large-scale prospective longitudinal studies were conducted at quite different points in Head Start's history, were conducted in markedly dissimilar parts of the country with more than 2,500 families, and used quite different approaches to measurement (see Table 13.4). Yet, persistently, two similar patterns of parent outcomes emerge. One is that parent–child interaction, particularly the type of interaction that promotes early learning and literacy, is enhanced. The second is that parents who have participated in Head Start stay more involved with their children's later schooling. These outcomes are strongly and clearly associated with Head Start, in either its typical or demonstration forms.

Parent-Related Findings in Other Longitudinal Studies

This strong persistent pattern of parent progress is corroborated in other longitudinal studies. The two patterns, however, emerge only from studies selected on the basis of quite stringent research design criteria. But other valuable information can be found, for

---

[27]The researchers explain that this attrition was primarily among Caucasian families temporarily residing in the area because of their connection with either a nearby military base or university (Shipman et al., 1976).

[28]A multimethod approach was used at year 1, combining direct coded observation with structured interview. Coded observation was also used at year 2 (the child's Head Start year) but not parent interview (Shipman et al., 1976).

Table 13.4. Measures for parent outcome patterns

Early Learning and Early Identification Study (1987–present)

Annual teacher ratings of parent involvement, defined as parent contact with teacher during the school year, in one or more of four categories:

- Parent–teacher conference
- Extended class visit by parent
- Home visit by teacher
- Parental help with class activity

Child and Family Resource Program (1977–1982)

- Structured parent interview—Fall 1978, Spring 1979, Spring 1980
- Maternal Attitude Scale—Fall 1978, Spring 1979
- Coded in-home observation—Spring 1980
- Toddler and Infant Experiences System (TIES)
- Parallel, adult-focused system developed for study
- Parent as a Teacher Inventory (PAAT)—Fall 1982
- Process/Treatment study interviews with parents and staff—Fall 1978, Spring 1979, Spring 1980
- Ethnographic study—Fall 1980, Winter 1981

Parent Child Development Centers (1970–1975; 1976–1980)

- Coded observation of a structured teaching situation and a waiting room situation
- Parent attitude questionnaires (in New Orleans and Birmingham only)
- Inventory of home environment (in Houston only)

Houston
- Site-developed observation instrument: Maternal Interaction Structured Situation (MISS)— at 12, 24, and 36 months of child age
- Home Observation for Measurement of the Environment (HOME)—at 12, 24, and 36 months of child age

New Orleans
- Site-developed observation instrument for both waiting room and teaching situation: Mother-Child Interaction scale (MCI)—at 2, 12, 24, 36, and 48 months of child age
- Site-adapted parent attitude questionnaire (adapted from the Stanford Parent Questionnaire)—at 36 months of child age, to one cohort

Birmingham
- Site-developed observation instrument for both waiting room and teaching situation—at 24, 36, and 48 months of child age
- Site-adapted observation instrument, adapted from the New Orleans Mother–Child Interaction scale—at 36 and 48 months of child age
- Site-developed parent attitude questionnaire (Birmingham Graduation Interview)—at 36 months of child age

Home Start (1972–1975)

- Coded observation: 8-Block Sort Task and Mother Behavior Observation Scale—Fall 1973, Spring 1974, Fall 1974, and Spring 1975
- Structured interview: Home Start Parent Interview—Fall 1973, Spring 1974, Fall 1974, and Spring 1975
- Inventory of the home environment: High/Scope Home Environment Scale—Fall 1973, Spring 1974, Fall 1974, and Spring 1975

ETS-Head Start Longitudinal Study (1969–1974)

- Study-developed parent interview: Year 1 and Year 6
- Observation of parent–child interaction (not specified; Year 2)

---

example, in well-designed longitudinal studies with smaller sample sizes (e.g., 80–200 families) or with *ex post facto* design, or in nonexperimental studies that involve only one sample of Head Start families over time (one group time-series). We will briefly discuss four of these types of investigations:

1. The Family Education and Training Program Study (FET), a 1998 longitudinal study conducted by Kagan, Hamilton-Lee, Marx, and Rustici (Hamilton-Lee, 1995; Hamilton-Lee & Kagan, 1994; Kagan et al., 1992; Kagan, Hamilton-Lee, Marx, & Rustici, 1998; Kagan, Neville, & Rustici, 1993; Marx & Kagan, 1994; Rustici, Kagan, & Hamilton-Lee, 1996)

2. The Parent Involvement in Head Start Study, a 1997 longitudinal study carried out by the National Council of Jewish Women (NCJW; Parker, Piotrkowski, Kessler-Sklar, & Baker, 1997a, 1997b)

3. The Family Impact Study conducted by Leik and Chalkey (Chalkley & Leik, 1995; Chalkley, Leik, Duane, & Keiser, 1996; Leik & Chalkley, 1988, 1989, 1990, 1993, 1996a, 1996b, 1997; Leik, Chalkley, & Duane, 1991; Leik, Chalkley, & Peterson, 1991)

4. Head Start Parental Involvement and the Economic and Social Self-Sufficiency of Head Start Families Study, carried out by Oyemade, Washington, and Gullo (Oyemade, Washington, & Gullo, 1989; Washington & Oyemade-Bailey, 1995)

FET was an experimental, longitudinal evaluation of a well-developed research and demonstration Head Start program. The study found that this highly parent-focused demonstration succeeded in helping parents gain employment in early care and education programs, achieve improved skills at teaching/and other interactions with their children, and increase positive perceptions of themselves[29] (Kagan et al., 1998). Involving a final sample of 81 Head Start parents in three cohorts, this study used random assignment, multiple measures (extensive demographic and employment information as well as seven different objective assessments of parent outcomes), and both a quantitative and qualitative approach. The participants (both trainees and comparisons) were recruited from parents enrolled in a New Haven Head Start program. The parents were studied at baseline and at two follow-up points.

The case studies of the parents show the deep barriers to these accomplishments that Head Start parents must move through, making the study's findings particularly important. It is also noteworthy that this most recent longitudinal investigation of parent outcomes associated with a Head Start demonstration project has similar findings to the earliest longitudinal investigations of parent outcomes linked to parent-supportive Head Start demonstration programs.

The Parent Involvement in Head Start Study yielded findings that are quite similar to those that emerged from the studies analyzed in previous sections. Controlling for demographic factors and pretest scores, the researchers found that greater parent involvement in Head Start was associated with 1) improved parent–child teaching interaction (the kind of interaction that promotes early literacy) and 2) increased later parent participation in their children's schooling[30] (Parker et al., 1997a). This nonexperimental in-

---

[29] All findings are statistically significant at the $p < .05$.

[30] Results statistically significant at the $p < .05$ level or less.

vestigation followed 119 Head Start families through both the Head Start experience and the subsequent kindergarten year. The study used a comprehensive approach to data collection. Eleven different extensive measures were used to obtain data about parent progress. Parent outcome data were collected at three time points, including a pretest that collected information about 41 variables describing family demographic contextual and personal characteristics.

The Family Impact Study was originally an exceptionally interesting cross-sectional project, transformed into a longitudinal study. The researchers did not investigate parental teaching styles or parent participation in children's later schooling but concentrated on studying overall child and family functioning. Among other important outcomes, this study found that parents who had participated in Head Start had a more positive evaluation of their own children's merits. A quasi-experimental investigation, the Family Impact Study followed 130 families (two cohorts: 1986–1987, 1989–1990) that participated in either regular Head Start, special Head Start (a family enrichment model), or a comparison group. The families were studied in both the Head Start participating year for the cohort and then again in 1993. The Family Impact Study concluded that the parents' assessment of their children's competence "increased significantly for the two Head Start groups, but no such increase occurred in the control group" (Chalkley & Leik, 1995, unpaginated). Interestingly, the NCJW Parent Involvement in Head Start Study also found that Head Start participating parents had more positive perceptions of their children after graduation from Head Start, seeing the Head Start child as more cooperative at home, for example (Parker et al., 1997a).

Oyemade, Washington, and Gullo also concentrated their study on parent outcomes other than parental teaching styles or parent participation in children's' later schooling (Oyemade et al., 1989). They were principally interested in the relationship between Head Start and parental self-sufficiency. (This is one of the few Head Start studies to significantly focus on fathers as well as mothers.) These researchers found that parent participation in Head Start was associated with increased likelihood of subsequent general parent employment (Oyemade et al., 1989), a finding for which the NCJW study also detected a positive trend[31] (Parker et al., 1997a).

Notably, the FET Study found that more parents obtained employment in early care and education programs as a result of focused Head Start parent training for this specific employment goal.

In an *ex post facto* research design, Oyemade and colleagues (1989) studied 205 Head Start-participating parents in four sites. From Head Start records, they obtained data about these parents and their degree and type of parental involvement at Head Start centers during 1978, 1982, and 1984. Assessing parent involvement at these centers, they rated them as either high-, medium-, or low-involvement programs. They also interviewed the parents a few years after the Head Start experience (The investigators did not specify how many years after the Head Start experience the parents were interviewed [Washington & Oyemade-Bailey, 1995]), using a structured survey instrument developed for the study and pilot tested in a previous study in three sites.

They found that there were no significant differences between parents at low- and high-involvement centers on "any of the socio-economic variables at the beginning of

---

[31]This result was statistically significant at the p < .10 level.

the Head Start experience" (Oyemade et al., 1989, p. 9). However, the parents at high-involvement centers showed important differences after the Head Start experience than their peers at low-involvement centers. Sixty percent of the parents from high-involvement centers were working (either full or part-time); at low-involvement centers, only 35% of the parents who had participated in Head Start were working. Specifically, with regard to fathers, 86% of the fathers from high-involvement centers were employed versus 55% from low-involvement centers.

Summary   In these four studies, encompassing more than 500 families, a strong corroborating pattern of parent progress emerges. Where parental teaching styles and later participation in children's schooling were reported, the findings are similar to those of the larger studies analyzed in the previous sections. In addition, a pattern of parent progress around evaluation of their own children's competence appears. Finally, a pattern of increased parent employment subsequent to Head Start is indicated.

CONCLUSION: DOES HEAD START HELP PARENTS?

Looking at the data carefully collected during 3½ decades of longitudinal studies involving more than 3,000 Head Start families, we conclude that Head Start systematically helps parents.

This review has identified two sets of findings convergent across two or more prospective, large-scale longitudinal studies of Head Start families: 1) that parents show more positive overall interaction and more effective teaching-type interaction with their children and 2) that parents show more involvement with their children's later schooling. In smaller longitudinal studies (or those with retrospective design), the same findings emerge. This persistent pattern of parent progress is persuasive.

Both Head Start and family focused Head Start demonstrations systematically influence parents to attain *and* sustain some type of greater engagement with their children's learning. In particular, the findings from the experimental studies analyzed here suggest that, in research and demonstration programs with a very strong family focus, Head Start parents improve skills that are associated with the promotion of early literacy in children (Connors, 1993; Dickinson, 1989; Snow, Barnes, Chandler, Goodman, & Hemphill, 1991; Whitehurst et al., 1994).

It is possible that the parents in these studies who showed this greater engagement would have done so anyway, in the absence of enrollment in Head Start. The limitations of each of these studies underscores that possibility. It is of interest, however, that systematic qualitative research on Head Start families consistently concludes that Head Start has powerful effects on parents (Ames & Ellsworth, 1997; Oden & Ricks, 1990; Oden & Ricks-Doneen, 1998; White, 1994, 1996). It is also of interest that many personal accounts by former and current Head Start parents speak of greater parental engagement in their children's education as one of Head Start's principal effects on parents (Greenberg, 1969/1990; Mills, 1998; National Head Start Association, 1990; Robinson & Choper, 1979; Sorenson, 1990; Zigler & Muenchow, 1992). In these accounts, parents attribute this change in their lives to the influence of Head Start.

In both the qualitative research and the personal narratives, Head Start parents often say that they came to Head Start with the goal of effective promotion of their children's educational success but not the knowledge (and sometimes also not sufficient confidence) to realize that goal in ways that really did help the children succeed in both preschool and later schooling. Head Start, these parents attest, helped them develop the means to reach the end—an end that each parent already sought.

Juxtaposing the strong, consistent findings from our review of 35 years of quantitative longitudinal studies with the equally consistent findings from qualitative research and with the voluminous personal statements by Head Start parents themselves, a strong persistent pattern of parent progress emerges. Although further research may be necessary, this future research should include a careful look at the cost-benefit ratios involved in Head Start programs that promote both child *and* adult developmental change.

REFERENCES

Ames, L.J., & Ellsworth, J. (1997) *Women reformed, women empowered: Poor mothers and the endangered promise of Head Start.* New York: Temple University Press.

Archambo, J.P. (1970). *Rural Child Care Project, 1969–1970 research evaluation (Final report).* Frankfort: Kentucky Child Welfare Research Foundation.

Bache, W. (1979). *Home Start follow-up study: A study of long-term impact of Home Start on program participants.* Ypsilanti, MI: High/Scope Educational Research Foundation.

Bissell, J.S. (1972). *Planned variation in Head Start follow-through* (ERIC Document Reproduction No. ED 069 335). Washington, DC: Department of Education and Welfare.

Bond, J.T., and Rosario, J. (1982) *Project Developmental Continuity Evaluation.* Ypsilanti, MI: High/Scope Educational Research Foundation.

Bridgeman, B., Blumenthal, J., & Andrews, S. (1981). *Parent child development centers* (Final evaluation report). Princeton, NJ: Educational Testing Service.

Chalkley, M.A., & Leik, R.K. (1995, April). *The impact of escalating family stress on the effectiveness of Head Start intervention.* Paper presented at the National Head Start Association's 22nd Annual Training Conference, Washington, DC.

Chalkley, M.A., Leik, R.K., Duane, G., & Keiser, K. (1996). *Enhancing resilience: The role of Head Start and cultural context in mitigating the long term impact of maternal depression on children.* St. Paul, MN: University of St. Thomas.

Connors, L.J. (1993). *Project self help: A family focus on literacy.* Baltimore: Johns Hopkins University, Center on Families, Communities, Schools and Children's Learning.

Cooper, H., & Hedges, L.V. (1994). *The handbook of research synthesis.* New York: Russell Sage.

Dickinson, D.K. (1989). Effects of a shared reading program on one Head Start language and literacy environment. In J. Allen & J. Mason (Eds.), *Risk makers, risk takers, risk breakers* (pp. 125–153). Portsmith, NH: Heinemann.

Edgar, E. et al. (1992). *Head Start research project: Variations in service delivery models in Region X.* Seattle: Washington Research Institute.

Erikson, E.L., et al. (1969). *Experiments in Head Start and early education: The effects of teacher attitude and curriculum structure on preschool disadvantaged children.* Kalamazoo: Western Michigan University, Center for Sociological Research.

Gamble, T.J., & Zigler, E. (1989). The Head Start synthesis project: A critique. *Journal of Applied Developmental Psychology, 10,* 267–284.

Greenberg, P. (1969/1990). *The devil has slippery shoes: A biased biography of the Child Development Group of Mississippi.* Washington, DC: Youth Policy Institute. (Original work published 1969, Toronto, Ontario: MacMillan)

Hamilton-Lee, M.E. (1995). Changing lives: New hope for low-income mothers. *New Schools, New Communities, 12*(1), 60–64.

Hamilton-Lee, M.E., & Kagan, S.L. (1994). *Family education and training program: Analysis of implemen-*

tation: 1993–1994. New Haven: Yale University, The Bush Center in Child Development and Social Policy.

Holmes, M.B., Holmes, D., & Greenspan, D. (1973). *The impact of the Head Start parent child centers on children.* New York: Center for Community Research.

Kagan, S.L., Costley, J., Landesman, L., Marx, F., Neville, P., Parker, S., et al. (1992). *Family education and training: Obstacles, opportunities and outcomes for low-income mothers* (Contract No. R117Q 00031, Report No. 4). Boston: Center on Families, Communities, Schools, and Children's Learning, Institute for Responsive Education.

Kagan, S.L., Hamilton-Lee, M.E., Marx, F., & Rustici, J. (1998). *Family education and training program: Final report.* New Haven, CT: Center on Families, Communities, Schools, and Children's Learning.

Kagan, S.L., Neville, P., & Rustici, J. (1993). *Family education and training: From research to practice.* New Haven, CT: Center on Families, Communities, Schools, and Children's Learning.

Leik, R.K., & Chalkley, M.A. (1988). *The Head Start family impact project* (Final report). Washington DC: Administration for Children, Youth and Families.

Leik, R.K., & Chalkley, M.A. (1989). Involving parents in Head Start. *CURA Reporter, 19*(3), 11–14.

Leik, R.K., & Chalkley, M.A. (1990). Parent involvement: What is it that works? *Children Today, May-June,* 34–37.

Leik, R.K., & Chalkley, M.A. (1993, November). *Effects of race, cohort, intervention, and family stress on the stability of parent, child and family factors.* Paper presented at the Second National Head Start Research Conference, Washington, DC.

Leik, R.K., & Chalkley, M.A. (1996a, March). *By whose standards? Assessing female headed poverty families of three races.* Paper presented at the Annual Meeting of the Pacific Sociological Association, Seattle, Washington.

Leik, R.K., & Chalkley, M.A. (1996b, June). *Findings from the longitudinal Head Start family impact project: Implications for research, practice and policy.* Paper presented at the Third National Head Start Research Conference, Washington, DC.

Leik, R.K., & Chalkley, M.A. (1997). On the stability of network relations under stress. *Social Networks, 19*(1), 63–74.

Leik, R.K., Chalkley, M.A., & Duane, G. (1991, June). *A family systems model for parent enrichment in Head Start.* Paper presented at the New Directions in Child and Family Research: Head Start in the Nineties, Arlington, VA.

Leik, R.K., Chalkley, M.A., & Peterson, N.J. (1991). Policy implications of involving parents in Head Start. In E.A. Anderson & R. Hula (Eds.), *The reconstruction of family policy* (pp. 217–235). Westport, CT: Glenwood.

Light, R.J., Singer, J.D., & Willett, J.B. (1990). *By design: Planning research on higher education.* Cambridge, MA: Harvard University Press.

Love, J.M., Nauta, M., Coelen, C., Hewett, K., & Ruopp, R.R. (1976). *The national Home Start evaluation: Final report. Findings and implications.* Ypsilanti, MI: High/Scope Educational Research Foundation.

Mann, A.J., Harrell, A., & Hurt, M., Jr. (1977). *A review of Head Start research since 1969* (DHEW Publication No. OHDS 77–31102). Washington, DC: U.S. Government Printing Office.

Marcon, R.A. (1989, March). *Parental involvement and early school success: A follow-up study of preschoolers.* Paper presented at the 35th Annual Convention of the Southeastern Psychological Association, Washington, DC.

Marcon, R.A. (1990). *Early learning and early identification: Final report of the three year longitudinal study.* Washington, DC: District of Columbia Public Schools.

Marcon, R.A. (1993a, March). *At-risk preschoolers: Early predictors of future grade retention.* Paper presented at the 39th Annual Meeting of the Southeastern Psychological Association, Atlanta, GA.

Marcon, R.A. (1993b, March). *Differential effects of preschool models on inner-city children: Following the 'class of 2000' at year five.* Paper presented at the 60th Biennial Meeting of the Society for Research in Child Development, New Orleans, LA.

Marcon, R.A. (1993c, March). *Parental involvement and early school success: Following the 'Class of 2000' at year five.* Paper presented at the 60th Biennial Meeting of the Society for Research in Child Development, New Orleans, LA.

Marcon, R.A. (1994a). Doing the right thing for children: Linking research and policy reform in the District of Columbia Public Schools. *Young Children, 50*(1), 8–20.

Marcon, R.A. (1994b). *Early learning and early identification follow-up study: Transition from the early to the later childhood grades, 1990–93.* Washington, DC: District of Columbia Public Schools.

Marcon, R.A. (1998). *Predicting parent involvement and its influence on school success: A follow-up study.* Paper presented at the Fourth National Head Start Research Conference, Washington, DC.

Marcon, R.A. (1999). Positive relationships between parent school involvement and public school inner-city preschooler's development and academic performance. *School Psychology Review, 28*(3), 395–412.

Marcon, R.A., Boldrick, E., & Harkins, C. (1988, March). *The impact of parental involvement on preschoolers' school success.* Paper presented at the 34th annual meeting of the Southeastern Psychological Association, New Orleans.

Marx, F., & Kagan, S.L. (1994). *Family education and training: From research to practice: Research design and initital findings.* New Haven, CT: Yale University, The Bush Center in Child Development and Social Policy.

McKey, R.H., Condelli, L., Ganson, H., Barrett, B.J., McConkey, C., & Plantz, M.C. (1985). *The impact of Head Start on children and communities: Final report of the Head Start evaluation, synthesis and utilization project* (DHHS Publication No. OHDS 90–31193). Washington, DC: U.S. Government Printing Office.

Miller, L.B., & Bizzell, R.P. (1984). Long term effects of four preschool programs: Ninth- and tenth-grade results. *Child Development, 55,* 1570–1587.

Mills, K. (1998). *Something better for my children.* New York: Dutton.

National Head Start Association. (1990). *Head Start: The nation's pride, a nation's challenge: Recommendations for Head Start in the 1990's.* Alexandria, VA: Author.

Oden, S., & Ricks, J. (1990). *Follow-up study of Head Start's role in the lives of children and families* (Interim report). Ypsilanti, MI: High/Scope Educational Research Foundation.

Oden, S., & Ricks-Doneen, J. (1998). Head Start remembered: The contributions of Head Start children and families. *NHSA Research Quarterly, 1*(4), 128–149.

O'Keefe, A. (1978). *What Head Start means to families.* Washington, DC: Administration for Children, Youth and Families.

Oyemade, U., Washington, V., & Gullo, D. (1989). The relationship between Head Start parental involvement and the economic and social self-sufficiency of Head Start families. *Journal of Negro Education, 58,* 5–15.

Parker, F.L., Piotrkowski, C.S., Kessler-Sklar, S., & Baker, A.J.L. (1997a). *Parent involvement in Head Start* (Final report). New York: NCJW Center for the Child.

Parker, F.L., Piotrkowski, C.S., Kessler-Sklar, S., Baker, A.J.L., Peay, L., & Clark, B. (1997b). *Parent involvement in Head Start* (Executive Summary). New York: NCJW Center for the Child.

Peters, D.L. et al. (1987). *An analysis of the effects of three modes of Head Start delivery: Head Start Delivery Modes Project.* Newark: Delaware University, College of Human Resources.

Phillips, D.A., & Cabrera, N.J. (Eds.). (1996). *Beyond the blueprint: Directions for research on Head Start's families.* Washington, DC: National Academy Press.

Pizzo, P.D. (1998). *Does Head Start help parents? A critical review of longitudinal studies of Head Start children and families.* (ERIC Report No. PS027256).

Posante-Loro, R., & McNeil, J.T. (1980). *National evaluation of Head Start educational services and basic educational skills demonstration programs.* Durham, NC: NTS Research Corporation.

Reedy, Y.E. (1991). *A comparison of long range effects of participation in Project Head Start and impact of three differing delivery methods.* Unpublished manuscript. Pennsylvania State University, Graduate School of Psychology, Harrisburg.

Robinson, J.L., & Choper, W.B. (1979). Another perspective on program evaluation: The parents speak out. In E. Zigler & J. Valentine (Eds.), *Project Head Start: A legacy of the War on Poverty* (pp. 467–477). New York: The Free Press.

Rustici, J., Kagan, S.L., & Hamilton-Lee, M. (1996). *Family education and training: Preparing for successful employment in early care and education. Integrated curriculum guide.* Baltimore: The Johns Hopkins University Center on Families, Communities, Schools and Children's Learning.

Shipman, V.C. (1971). *Disadvantaged children and their first school experiences: ETS-Head Start longitudinal study. Demographic indexes of socioeconomic status and maternal behaviors and attitudes* (Report No. PR-72–13). Princeton, NJ: Educational Testing Service.

Shipman, V.C., McKee, J.D., & Bridgeman, B. (1976). *Stability and change in family status, situational and process variables and their relationship to children's cognitive performance. Disadvantaged children and their first year experiences: ETS-Head Start longitudinal study.* Princeton, NJ: Educational Testing Service.

Snow, C., Barnes, W., Chandler, J., Goodman, I., & Hemphill, L. (1991). *Unfulfilled expectations: Home and school influences on literacy.* Cambridge, MA: Harvard University Press.

Sorenson, M. (1990). *Head Start success stories.* Washington, DC: CRS.

Travers, J., Nauta, M., & Irwin, N. (1982). *The effects of a social program: Final report of the child and family resource program's infant-toddler component* (Report No. AAI-82–31). Cambridge, MA: Abt Associates.

Washington, V., & Oyemade-Bailey, U.J. (1995). *Project Head Start: Models and strategies for the twenty-first century.* New York: Garland Publishing.

White, L. (1994). Ordering voice: Rhetoric and democracy in project Head Start. In A. Sarat & T. Kearns (Eds.), *The rhetoric of law* (pp. 185–224). Ann Arbor: University of Michigan Press.

White, L. (1996). On the vision and practice of participation in project Head Start. In G. Bellow & M. Minow (Eds.), *Law stories* (pp. 197–218). Ann Arbor: University of Michigan Press.

Whitehurst, G.J., Epstein, J.N., Angell, A.L., Payne, A.C., Crone, D.A., & Fischel, J.E. (1994). Outcomes of an emergent literacy intervention in Head Start. *Journal of Educational Psychology, 86*(4), 542–555.

Zeece, P.D., & Wang, A. (1998). Effects of the family empowerment and transitioning program on child and family outcomes. *Child Study Journal, 28*(3), 161–178.

Zigler, E., & Muenchow, S. (1992). *Head Start: The inside story of America's most successful educational experiment.* New York: Basic Books.

CHAPTER 14

A Parent's Views on Head Start

DELORES BAYNES

My name is Delores Baynes. I'm a mother of two—a boy who's 18 and a daughter who's 15. I'm presently working for the Head Start Program of the Windham Area Community Action Program, Inc. (WACAP) in Willimantic, Connecticut. I'm a social service worker who knows from experience the nightmare that many Head Start parents live. As a former Head Start parent, I'm here today to tell you my story.

I left school at the age of 14 never having completed the ninth grade. The Juvenile Court sent me to Long Lane School in Middletown, Connecticut. I was there for 4 months. When I was released, my family refused to allow me to return home. They felt I had made mistakes and needed to be punished. I was no longer allowed to visit my parents or enter their home. My brothers and sisters weren't there for me. I had no one.

I became a child of the streets and stayed where the night caught up with me. I ate whenever food was given to me. I became pregnant at 15. My son, Victor, was born on December 11, 1974. While hospitalized from his birth, the State threatened to take him away because I had no place to live. Frightened and desperate to maintain custody of my son, I agreed to stay in an apartment where trouble was destined to find me.

When my son was only a few months old, the apartment was raided. Drugs and stolen merchandise were found. The police threatened to take my child away if I didn't tell the name of the drug supplier, and the drug supplier threatened to kill me if I told anything to the police. Out of fear, I broke bond and fled to Puerto Rico.

With my son safely in Puerto Rico, I returned to the United States to face the criminal charges pending against me. Within a week of my return, I was arrested and sent to the Women's Correctional Center in Niantic, Connecticut. I was 16.

My family continued to refuse to take any responsibility for me, so I was released to the custody of friends in Puerto Rico and received 2 years probation.

This chapter is transcribed from testimony given before the U.S. Senate Subcommittee on Children, Family, Drugs and Alcoholism, July 22, 1993. Reprinted from the public domain.

My stay in Puerto Rico was not much better. I was a single parent without an education, and my self-esteem was very low. I started to live with this 18-year-old guy who was very abusive. My second child lived only moments after birth due to traumatic intrauterine brain injuries received when my boyfriend threw me up against a cement wall. My third child was born November 2, 1977. I continued to live in an abusive situation for about 4 years. But after being beaten to unconsciousness, I felt my life was going to end, and I knew I had to get out. What would happen to my children if something would happen to me?

I took my son and my daughter, and I returned to the United States. I applied for AFDC [Aid to Families with Dependent Children] and, at 23, settled into my first apartment. One day, there was a knock at the door. When I opened it, I saw two women. They presented themselves as Head Start workers and asked if they could come in. I didn't see any harm in saying yes, so we sat and talked. I was quiet and listened. They talked about the Head Start program for children of income-eligible families. From that day forward, life has been full of new and fulfilling experiences.

As I became involved in the Head Start program, I began to feel that my life was changing. The social services staff talked to me about obtaining my high school equivalent diploma. Having left high school before completing the ninth grade, I felt I couldn't do that. But, with the constant support and encouragement of the staff, I decided to go for it. It took time and effort, but I achieved it. This was my new beginning. My perspective on life was changing. I was feeling good about myself, and I was providing many hours of volunteer services to the program.

In 1983, I decided to take a bigger step. I applied for a job as assistant teacher, and I was hired. I felt somewhat intimidated at first, but with the encouragement and support of the staff, I felt capable of fulfilling this position.

Two years after becoming assistant teacher, I was still encouraged to go on and pursue my education. I enrolled in a semester of study at Hartford Community College in preparation for the child development associate credential, which I received in 1986. My position was then upgraded to teacher. But I did not stop there. I took on a new role as the social service worker for the program in 1989. I felt this was where I wanted to be. Because of my bilingual skills, I could provide support and encouragement to Head Start families. I could return the gift of caring that was shared with me as a Head Start parent.

Today, I am currently working toward an associate degree in human services. I've learned to trust, and I feel good about myself. I was fortunate to have become involved in the Head Start Program, and I am where I am now due to its existence. I can honestly say that Head Start provides for the whole family 100%. It not only provides developmentally appropriate programs for preschool children, but it provides the means by which parents can grow and become viably self-sufficient.

My Head Start story is testament to the fact that there is a substantial return for every dollar invested into the program.

I was a child of the streets, a high school drop out at age 14, a teen parent at 15, and imprisoned at 16. Today, I'm fully employed and contributing to the tax base of the U.S. economy. I'm pursuing a degree in higher education. I'm a positive role model to my children—my son Victor graduated from high school this spring and is currently in basic training with the Army Reserve. He has been accepted into Eastern Connecticut University and plans to pursue a graduate degree in law. I am involved in the social services of my community and committed to giving Head Start parents the gift of caring and concern that was given to me.

Head Start works because it looks at the whole family. It does not fragment children into parts and pieces with programs that have been developed in isolation of the parent or the community.

Yet, with all its success and all its cost-effective appropriations, Head Start continues to have many needs. In my service area of northeast Connecticut, there are over 1,900 income-eligible children, but current appropriations only allow for the service of 266. This means that 86% of those eligible for the program never receive services.

This year [1993] my program site in Willimantic, Connecticut, was extremely fortunate to receive a portion of the $1 million state appropriation for Head Start programs. This finding supports "wrap-around" services for 20 Head Start children whose parents are working or participating in job training programs, ABE, ESL or higher education. It also provides "wrap-around" for special needs children and for parents who are actively involved in treatment program. If parents are to become viably self-sufficient, and if children are to retain the positive growth provided by Head Start, then services must be expanded to provide this full-day full-year program.

CHAPTER 15

A Former Head Start Student's Views

U.S. Representative Loretta Sanchez

When I testified at a hearing commemorating Head Start's 35th birthday, I began by commending the National Head Start program for its success in ensuring that our children show up to school on the first day ready and eager to learn. I also thanked all those parents, teachers, community volunteers, health care coordinators, and others who help implement the Head Start program in their communities. In 2004, just a few years later, their numbers have only grown. It is through all their efforts to expand and extend Head Start services to families in every community that our children are getting the head start they need.

Head Start is especially important to me because I am a Head Start kid. I was one of the first in 1965. At an early age, my mother noticed I was a shy, uncommunicative child. After reading about Head Start in the daily newspaper, she was determined to get me into the new program. I must admit, the first day my mother took me to Head Start I cried. That is, until snack time, when I was too interested in new foods I hadn't experienced in my household.

After that initial experience I was ready to go to school every day, where I opened up to my social surroundings and learned. My mother also learned through the Head Start program. She began to understand the importance of her role as the primary educator of her children. Head Start also allowed my mother to learn the American way of schooling, which was different than her education in Mexico. More important, Head Start parlayed skills for my mother to be an effective parent for her children, enabling her to work on all the needs each of her subsequent children would have in the school system. Head Start educated and socialized me, but it had a multiplied effect on my six siblings. This is the true value of a Head Start education.

The experiences of a family from Santa Ana, California, exemplify the Head Start success story. These parents have three sons and one daughter. Two of their children went to Head Start as young children, and both parents are employed by Orange County Head Start.

All of their children are accomplished in their own ways. One has an undergraduate degree from San Diego State University and will receive his master's degree in public administration soon. Another is in his second year at Grossman College and will transfer to an art college next year. One more son, a Head Start graduate, attends the University of the Pacific and is majoring in pharmacology. Their daughter, also a Head Start graduate, is in her junior year of high school and is an accomplished musician and performer.

I am proud to know this wonderful family. They are living testimony to the benefits of Head Start. Local mothers have also told me how Head Start has not only put their daughters on the road to education but also has helped them develop the skills they will need to care for themselves. Our young girls have a very real need for these services. Statistics show that young women who have experienced a quality early childhood program are one third less likely to give birth out of wedlock and 25% less likely to be teen mothers.

Orange County, where my congressional district is located, has the fifth largest Head Start enrollment in California. The dedication of numerous local organizations to help bring Head Start to our disadvantaged families has made this success possible. The federal Administration on Children, Youth and Families (ACYF) was committed to serving 1 million Head Start children by 2002. In 2003, they were close to reaching that goal, although future expansion remained uncertain. It is imperative that the ACYF, the President, and Congress continue to enhance the quality of Head Start, promote school readiness and family literacy, improve staff training and credential rates, and increase the funds set aside for quality improvements. So many people—the President and members of the federal government, members of state and local agencies, and members of our communities— make Head Start successful. But, we must still fight for resources so that we can enroll more children and secure the future of Head Start.

Head Start funding is one of the wisest investments of federal or taxpayer dollars. But, proposed cuts to domestic programs could result in as many as 100,000 children and their families losing access to Head Start services. Combined with what is hoped will be an increase in enrollment for our youngest children—for whom the costs of service are higher—it is clear that appropriations for the future years must be significantly larger than before.

Perhaps more than any other federally assisted social program, Head Start serves as a symbol of hope for a better life for low-income children and families. As of 2004, there are more than 900,000 children enrolled in the Head Start program. Now more than ever, our communities are turning to early intervention to promote the well-being and safety of our families and communities. Head Start teaches families and children habits that they can carry with them for the rest of their lives. Head Start is a program that has enjoyed incredible success and bipartisan support for more than 35 years. Let us continue that tradition.

CHAPTER 16

Does Head Start Have Lasting Cognitive Effects?

The Myth of Fade-Out

W. Steven Barnett

Although Head Start is more than 3 decades old, controversy persists over the question of its long-term benefits to children's development and academic success. It is widely accepted that Head Start and other compensatory preschool programs for economically disadvantaged children can produce short-term effects, but some believe that Head Start's cognitive effects fade out during the first few years of school (e.g., Haskins, 1989; Traub, 2000). There is a long history of reports reaching this conclusion, and some have gone so far as to label Head Start a "scam" (Hood, 1992; see Chapter 36). One reason that Head Start is not funded to serve all of the eligible population may be the widespread view that Head Start is a failure, or at least irrelevant, in the long run.

Supporters of Head Start point to long-term effects found in studies of such other interventions as the Perry Preschool and Abecedarian programs. Head Start's critics respond that these programs are not Head Start and claim that evidence for positive long-term effects "almost never comes from Head Start programs themselves but from more intensive and expensive preschool interventions" (Herrnstein & Murray, 1994, p. 404). Others have questioned the ability of even these other preschool programs to produce long-term cognitive gains (Haskins, 1989; Locurto, 1991; Spitz, 1986). Herrnstein and Murray concluded that, "More intensive, hence more costly, preschool programs may raise intelligence, but both the size and the reality of the improvements are in dispute" (1994, p. 389).

This chapter seeks to clarify the issue of Head Start's long-term effects through a critical review of the literature. It goes beyond merely summarizing findings to scrutinize each study with respect to program, contextual, and methodological factors that may affect findings and produce differences in outcomes across studies. A primary goal is to attempt to resolve the apparent contradiction between findings that effects on cognitive

221

abilities fade out and findings that effects on school placements persist. The chapter begins with evidence on program implementation and short-term effects before moving on to long-term studies.

RESEARCH ON IMPLEMENTATION

A critical first step in the evaluation of any program is to determine that it has actually been implemented and assess the extent to which it delivers the services it is supposed to deliver. One reason for program failure may be that the program is never implemented or at least is not implemented as designed. A substantial body of research demonstrates that Head Start delivers a broad range of services to children and their families (Hale, Seitz, & Zigler, 1990; McKey et al., 1985; Zigler & Muenchow, 1992; Zigler & Styfco, 1994). As a comprehensive child development program, Head Start for many years has provided children with education services (typically a half-day program during the school year), health services (including medical, dental, hearing, and vision examinations and treatment), nutritional services (meals, snacks, nutrition education), and social services to children and their families through direct services or referrals.

The most recent information on the quality of educational services comes from the Head Start Family and Child Experiences Survey (FACES) conducted as part of the Head Start Bureau's efforts to enhance its program accountability system (Zill et al., 2001). The FACES study involved observations in hundreds of Head Start classrooms across the nation. The average score on the Early Childhood Environment Rating Scale (ECERS) was 4.9—a score of 3 is "minimal," 5 is considered "good," and 7 is "excellent." Head Start appears to set a floor on quality so that very few received scores of 3. These scores indicate that Head Start is higher in quality than community preschool and child care programs generally and much less likely to be of very poor quality. These findings are similar to those of Bryant, Burchinal, Lau, and Sparling (1994). And, Barnett, Tarr, and Frede (1999) found the average quality of Head Start classrooms to be substantially higher than that of other community-based early childhood programs in low-income urban areas as judged by direct observation and program director reports of classroom practices. FACES, however, also found less than 20% of the classrooms to score above 5.5 on the ECERS in 1997 and about half scored below 5 (Zill et al., 2001).

Although it is good news that Head Start classrooms are of higher quality than child care programs generally, clearly there are reasons to be concerned about Head Start quality. Head Start has been expected to replicate the results of "model" preschool programs that produced substantial long-term gains but has never been funded anywhere near the levels of the model programs (Barnett, 1998; Chafel, 1992). Moreover, with its lower budget, Head Start is asked to provide far more comprehensive services than most model programs provided (Zigler & Styfco, 1994). Inadequate funding impairs Head Start's ability to hire and retain highly qualified staff and hurts staff morale; both are likely to reduce educational quality (Chafel, 1992). Head Start is also forced to trade off teacher quality against class size and ratio. Comparison of the FACES results with data from earlier studies suggests that since the 1990s Head Start improved with respect to class size and ratio, but teacher qualifications do not appear to have improved and may have declined (Frede, 1998; Willer et al., 1991). The FACES study found that only one third of Head Start lead teachers had attained a 4-year college degree, and 20% had been with their Head Start programs for less than 2 years (Zill et al., 2001).

The educational consequences of inadequately funding Head Start are difficult to discern with precision. Frede (1998) raised many questions about the extent to which Head Start and other large-scale programs replicate the experiences provided by model programs shown to produce substantive gains for children. Ultimately, it is a matter of how high quality must be for Head Start to be good enough and what is lost when Head Start cannot produce the same amount and quality of learning experiences as the model programs. In the FACES study, few Head Start classrooms scored above 5.5 on the ECERS (Zill et al., 2001). It is doubtful that this performance is sufficiently good for most programs to produce the desired long-term benefits. Ultimately, the importance of program quality as measured by program characteristics or direct observation must be ascertained by measuring the immediate and long-term effects of variations in quality on the children.

RESEARCH ON SHORT-TERM EFFECTS

Many studies have examined the immediate and short-term effects of various types of early childhood interventions for children from low-income families. Overall, it appears that programs designed for disadvantaged children, including Head Start, on average produce immediate effects on IQ scores and achievement of about 0.5 standard deviations, or about 8 IQ points (McKey et al., 1985; Ramey, Bryant, & Suarez, 1985; White & Casto, 1985). Somewhat smaller average effect sizes were found for immediate effects on other outcomes such as self-esteem, academic motivation, and social behavior. On average, studies found that estimated effects declined over time and disappeared several years after children left the programs. Some studies (including several Head Start studies), however, found gains that persisted at least into the first few years of school for IQ score, achievement, and school outcomes such as grade retention and special education placement. The magnitude of immediate and short-term effects appears to be at least roughly related to the intensity, breadth, and amount of involvement with the children and their families (Ramey et al., 1985).

Recently, short-term results have become available from several randomized experiments with preschool programs for disadvantaged young children and their families. These studies are important because their methodology is substantially stronger than that of many earlier studies. They include Project CARE, the Infant Health and Development Program (IHDP), Even Start, and the Comprehensive Child Development Program (CCDP). Together, these studies reinforce the view that intensive and sustained high-quality early childhood programs are required to produce substantial short-term cognitive gains. Project CARE produced large gains in IQ scores through age 5 from an intensive, high-quality program from birth to five (Wasik, Ramey, Bryant, & Sparling, 1990). The IHDP provided similar services to low birth weight (LBW) infants to age 3 and had similar effects at age 3 (Brooks-Gunn, McCormick, Shapiro, Benasich, & Black, 1994). IHDP's effects disappeared by age 5 (2 years after the program ended), though modest cognitive effects may have persisted for heavier LBW children (McCarton, Brooks-Gunn, Wallace, & Bauer, 1997). The CCDP increased children's participation in center-based early childhood programs (at age 4, primarily Head Start) and mothers' participation in parenting education, mental health services, and education but produced no effects on children's cognitive development at ages 3 or 5 (St. Pierre, Layzer, & Barnes, 1998). Even Start was not found to produce any significant effects on cognitive development either (St. Pierre et al., 1998). Early Head Start was found to produce small gains for children, including 2 points on the Peabody Picture Vocabulary Test (PPVT), a test of receptive language that often is used as a quick test of intelligence, and a modest decrease in behavior problems (Love et al., 2002).

FACES and a randomized trial involving 47 classrooms provide new evidence regarding Head Start. Zill and colleagues (2001) found the median PPVT score to be 89.5 for Head Start 4-year-olds in the spring prior to kindergarten entry. They suggested that this is 4–8 points higher than expected for a typical low-income child of that age. Others have suggested that because the PPVT standard scores changed little during the 4-year-old year that Head Start has very little positive effect. Unfortunately, FACES has no control group of children who did not attend Head Start so that neither of these conclusions about the size of Head Start's effects should carry much weight.

A study by Abbott-Shim, Lambert, & McCarty (2003) provided a stronger basis for estimating effects, albeit one that does not readily generalize to all Head Start programs. In this study, 4-year-olds (n=173) who had not previously attended Head Start were randomly assigned to Head Start or a wait-list group in three participating centers with 47 classrooms. These classrooms may not be typical of Head Start; 46 of 47 classrooms were accredited by the National Association for the Education of Young Children (NAEYC). Teachers, however, had on average only 2 years of college and had taught in Head Start for less than 3 years. The study found an effect of nearly 5 points on PPVT standard scores, as well as significant effects on phonemic awareness and print concepts. Other effects included improvements in children's and parents' health habits and the percentage of children receiving health screenings, immunizations, and dental examinations. Given the quality of the participating classrooms, this study likely provides an upper bound estimate of the effects of 1 year in typical Head Start classrooms. Yet, even 4–5 points on the PPVT is considerably smaller than the initial effects of more intense interventions so that this may be more like a lower-bound estimate of the *potential* effects of Head Start (Ramey et al., 1985).

RESEARCH ON LONG-TERM EFFECTS

This review was limited to studies that met four basic criteria: 1) the program began prior to school entry, 2) the children served were economically disadvantaged, 3) at least one measure of cognitive development or academic progress was obtained at third grade or later, and 4) the research design employed a no-treatment comparison group. These criteria restricted that sample to studies of the relevant population and excluded the methodologically weakest studies (e.g., simple before-and-after comparisons with no comparison group and studies comparing "treated" disadvantaged children with "untreated" advantaged children without any statistical controls for differences in family background). The requirement for results at or beyond third grade was designed to allow sufficient time for fade-out to be observed (Caldwell, 1987).

The search for studies began with previous literature reviews including the meta-analyses. In addition, computer-assisted and manual searches of the relevant literature indexes and bibliographies were conducted (Ellsworth Associates, 1994). The search was extended with the reference lists of all studies identified as meeting the review criteria as well as the reference lists of newer preschool studies that did not meet the criteria but might cite relevant studies. Thirty-nine studies were identified that met the review criteria. This is a larger number of long-term studies than were included in previous reviews of the literature including the well-known quantitative syntheses (McKey et al., 1985; White & Casto, 1985).

Program and Sample Characteristics

The 39 studies identified fall into two categories based on the nature of the program and the research design. In 15 studies, researchers developed their own exemplary or model preschool programs. In 24 studies, researchers investigated the effects of ongoing, large-scale public programs. Of these 24, 12 studied the effects of Head Start programs, 4 studied a mix of Head Start and state or local programs, and 8 studied state or local programs including those supported by the federal Title I program.

The 15 studies of model programs are identified and described in Table 16.1. Generally, the model programs seem likely to have been of higher quality than the large-scale public programs. Reasons for this include direction and close supervision by experts, highly qualified staff, low child–staff ratios, and small group size. These advantages were made possible by much higher levels of funding per child than are available to Head Start and public school programs. In all but one study, the majority of children were African American. The Houston Parent Child Development Center (PCDC) served Hispanic American families. As might be expected, given the focus on economically disadvantaged children, the average level of mother's education was less than 12 years in all studies and less than 10 years in five studies.

Three model program studies limited their target populations in ways that might have influenced their results. The Harlem Training Project served only boys. The Perry Preschool study included children based on low IQ scores, and its sample had substantially lower IQ scores at age 3 than did children in other studies. The Milwaukee study focused on children whose mothers had low IQ scores (below 75).

As can be seen from Table 16.1, the model programs varied considerably in the ages at which children entered, number of months that services were provided, length of day, and historical context (1962–1980). Although many programs conducted home visits, only one program relied on home visits alone. One program provided one-to-one tutoring, and the others provided services in classrooms. Most of the comparison children began formal education at kindergarten. In some of the later studies, a significant percentage of the comparison group could have attended another preschool or child care program due to the introduction of Head Start and a general increase in the use of other public and private early childhood programs. In the Abecedarian study, which enrolled newborns between 1972 and 1980, two thirds of the control group attended an early childhood program for 12 months or more by age 5 (Burchinal, Lee, & Ramey, 1989).

Table 16.1 Model preschool education programs' long-term results

Program name, years program provided, and sources	Program description and ages of participation	Research design/ methodological concerns	Sample size[a]	Time of follow-up	Long-term IQ findings[a,b]	Achievement and school success[a]
1. Carolina Abecedarian 1972–1985 (Campbell, 1999; Campbell & Ramey, 1993, 1994, 1995; Carolina Abecedarian Project, 1999)	Full-day year-round educational child care Entry: 6 weeks to 3 months Exit: 5 years	Randomized	Initial E = 57 C = 54 Follow-Up Age 15 E = 48 C = 44 Age 21 E = 53 C = 51	8, 12, and 15, and 21 years	Age 12: E > C E = 93.7 C = 88.4 Age 21: E > C E = 90 C = 85	Achievement tests: E > C at ages 15 and 21 Enrolled in higher education: E > C at age 21 E = 40%, C = 20% Special education: E < C at age 15 E = 24%, C = 48% Grade retention: E < C at age 15 E = 39%, C = 59%
2. Houston Parent Child Development Center 1970–1980 (Andrews, et al., 1982; Johnson and Walker, 1991)	Full-day year-round educational child care Home visits Center-based program for parents Entry: 1 to 3 years Exit: 3 to 5 years	Randomized High attrition	Initial E = 97 C = 119 Follow-Up School data E = 50 C = 87 Achievement data E = 39 C = 78	Grades 2 to 5	Not measured	Achievement tests: E > C Grades: E = C Bilingual education: E < C E = 16%, C = 36% Special education: E = C, grades 2 to 5 E = 27% C = 31% Grade retention: E = C, grades 2 to 5 E = 16%, C = 23%
3. Florida Parent Education Project 1966–1970 (Jester & Guinagh, 1983)	Twice weekly part-day preschool (ages 2 to 3) Home visits Entry: 3 to 24 months Exit: 5 years	Initially randomized with one group, and additional control group members added at 24 months Randomization lost when new "controls" added. High attrition. School-administered tests	Initial E = 288 C = 109 Follow-Up E = 83 C = 24	Grades 4 to 7	E = C (grades 4 to 7) E = 83.1 C = 79.8	Reading achievement: E = C Math achievement: E > C Special education: E < C, grade 7 E = 23%, C = 54% Grade retention: E = C, grade 7 E = 28%, C = 29%

Program	Treatment	Design	Sample	Age/Grade	Outcome	Results
4. Milwaukee Project 1968–1978 (Garber, 1988)	Full-day year-round educational child care Job and academic training for mothers Entry: 3 to 6 months Exit: 5 years	Groups of 3 to 4 children assigned alternately to E and C groups Small sample	Initial E = 20 C = 20 Follow-Up E = 17 C = 18	Grade 4 Grade 8	E > C grade 8 E = 101 C = 91	Achievement tests: E = C, at grade 4 (E > C prior to grade 4) Grades: E = C Special education: E = C, grade 4 E = 41%, C = 89% Grade retention: E = C, grade 4 E = 29%, C = 56%
5. Syracuse Family Research Program 1969–1975 (Lally, Mangione, & Honig, 1988)	Year-round educational child care Half-day to 15 months transition and full-day from 18 months Home visits began prenatally Entry: 6 months Exit: 5 years	Matched comparison group selected at 36 months Not randomized	Initial E = 82 C = 72 Follow-Up Parents E = 52 C = 42 Children E = 49 C = 39	Grades 7 to 8	E = C, age 5 on Stanford-Binet	Teacher ratings: E > C, but for girls only Grades: E > C, but for girls only Attendance: E > C, but for girls only
6. Yale Child Welfare Research Program 1968–1974 (Seitz & Apfel, 1994; Seitz, Rosenbaum, & Apfel, 1985)	Full-day year-round educational child care Home visits Entry: Prenatal Exit: 30 months	Two comparison groups from same neighborhoods for first follow-up Matched comparison group selected for follow-up at 30 months Not randomized. School-administered tests	Initial E = 18 C = 18 Follow-Up Age 7 to 8 E = 17 C1 = 33 C2 = 31 Age 10 E = 16 C = 16	Age 7 to 8 and age 10	E = C at age 10	Achievement tests: E = C Attendance: E > C Teacher ratings: E = C Special education: E = C E = 25%, C = 50%
7. Verbal Interaction Project 1967–1972 (Levenstein, O'Hara, & Madden, 1983)	Home visits Entry: 2 to 3 years Exit: 4 years	Six groups with three matched comparison groups Not randomized	Initial E = 111 C = 51 Follow-Up E = 79 C = 49	Grade 3	E > C at grade 3 E = 101.9 C = 93.6	Achievement tests: E > C Special education: E < C, grade 7 E = 14%, C = 39% Grade retention: E = C, grade 7 E = 13%, C = 19%

(continued)

227

Table 16.1. *(continued)*

Program name, years program provided, and sources	Program description and ages of participation	Research design/ methodological concerns	Sample size[a]	Time of follow-up	Long-term IQ findings [a,b]	Achievement and school success [a]
8. Early Training Project 1962–1967 (Gray, Ramey, & Klaus, 1982, 1983)	Summer part-day preschool Home visits Entry: 4 to 5 years Exit: 6 years	Randomized School-administered tests	Initial E = 44 C = 21 Follow-Up E = 36 C = 16	Post high school	E = C at age 17 E = 78.7 C = 76.4	Achievement tests: E = C Special education: E < C, grade 12 E = 5%, C = 29% Grade retention: E = C E = 58%, C = 61% High school graduation: E = C E = 68%, C = 52%
9. Experimental Variation of Head Start 1968–1969 (Karnes, Shwedel, & Williams, 1983)	Part-day preschool Entry: 4 years Exit: 5 years	Post hoc comparison group from same communities Not randomized School administered tests	Initial E = 116 C = 24 Follow-Up E = 102 C = 19	Post high school	E < C at age 13 E = 85.0 C = 91.0	Achievement tests: E = C Special education: E = C, grade 7 E = 13%, C = 15% Grade retention : E = C, grade 7 E = 10%, C = 16%
10. Harlem Training Project 1966–1967 (Palmer, 1983)	One-to-one tutoring or child-directed play Entry: 2 to 3 years Exit: 4 years	Comparison group recruited from children born 1 to 2 months later Not randomized. School-administered tests	Initial E = 244 C = 68 Follow-Up E = 168 C = 51	Grade 7	E = C at age 12 E = 92.1 C = 88.9	Reading achievement: E < C Math achievement: E > C Grade retention: E < C, grade 7 E = 30%, C = 52%
11. High/Scope Perry Preschool Project 1962–1967 (Schweinhart et al., 1993; Weikart, Bond, & McNeil, 1978)	Part-day preschool Home visits Entry: 3 to 4 years Exit: 5 years	Randomized	Initial E = 58 C = 65 Follow-Up E = 58 C = 65	Post high school	E = C at age 14 E = 81.0 C = 81.0	Achievement tests: E > C Grades: E > C Special education: E = C, grade 12 E = 37%, C = 50% Grade retention: E = C, grade 12 E = 15%, C = 20% High school graduation: E > C E = 67%, C = 49%

Study	Treatment	Design	Sample size	Age at last measurement	IQ[b]	Other outcomes[a]
12. Howard University Project 1964–1966 (Herzog, Newcomb, & Cisin, 1974)	Part-day preschool Entry: 3 years Exit: 5 years	Comparison group from neighboring tracts Not randomized	Initial E = 38 C = 69 Follow-Up E = 30 C = 69	Grade 4	Not measured	Grade retention: E = C E = 33%, C = 47%
13. Institute for Developmental Studies 1963–1967 (Deutsch, Deutsch, Jordan, & Grallo, 1983; Deutsch, Taleporos & Victor, 1974)	Part-day preschool Home visits Parent center (K–3) Entry: 3 years Exit: 9 years	Randomized High attrition School-administered tests	Initial E = 312 C = 191 Follow-Up E = 63 C = 34	Grade 7	E = C, age 8 E = 96.7 C = 91.4	Achievement tests: E = C, grade 3 Special education: E = C E = 0%, C = 13% Grade retention: E = C E = 23%, C = 43%
14. Philadelphia Project 1963–1964 (Beller, 1983)	Part-day preschool Home visits Entry: 4 years Exit: 5 years	Matched comparison group from same kindergarten classes Not randomized School-administered tests	Initial E = 60 C = 53 Follow-Up E = 44 C = 37	Post high school	E > C at age 10 on Stanford-Binet E = 98.4 C = 91.7	Achievement tests: E = C Special education: E = C, grade 12 E = 5%, C = 6% Grade retention: E = C, grade 12 E = 38%, C = 53%
15. Curriculum Comparison Study 1965–1967 (Miller & Bizzell, 1983, 1984)	Part-day preschool program Kindergarten program Entry: 4 years Exit: 5 or 6 years	Post hoc comparison group from original pool Not randomized School-administered tests	Initial E = 214 C = 34 Follow-Up E = 134 C = 22	Post high school	Not measured	Special education: E = C, grade 12 E = 32%, C = 63% Grade retention: E = C, grade 12 E = 26%, C = 58% High school graduation: E = C E = 67%, C = 53%

[a] E refers to the experimental or intervention group, and C refers to the control or comparison group. Outcomes listed as E > C or E < C were statistically significant at the p < .05 level.

[b] IQs were measured using the WISC or WISC-R, unless otherwise noted.

229

Clearly, this "treatment" received by the control group could have produced positive effects and thus led to underestimation of the program's effects.

The 24 studies of large-scale public programs are identified and described in Table 16.2. None of the large-scale programs enrolled children before age 3, and most served children part day for one school year at age 4. As noted previously, quality is expected to be lower than in model programs, though detailed information on quality is not available in most studies, and it should be recognized that Head Start has broader services than most other programs, including improving health and nutrition. Compared with Head Start, public school programs provide much better compensation than Head Start and typically require that all teachers have appropriate 4-year degrees. However, public school class sizes tend to be larger than in Head Start. In three public school studies, preschool program participation was associated with participation in school-age programs. In the Cincinnati Title I study, most full-day kindergarten students had attended preschool and most half-day kindergarten students had not. In the two Child-Parent Center (CPC) studies, the program provided enriched education services through third grade.

Research Design

Three key aspects of research design are described in Tables 16.1 and 16.2 for model program and large-scale program studies, respectively. These include 1) the ways in which the comparison groups were formed, 2) initial and follow-up sample sizes, and 3) length of follow-up. Each of these aspects of study quality has important implications for the confidence that one can have that a study produces unbiased estimates of long-term program effects and for the interpretation of study results.

Seven of the model program studies formed comparison groups by randomly assigning children to experimental and control groups from the same pool of potential participants or by using procedures that approximated random assignment. Field studies rarely are executed perfectly, but problems with random assignment do not appear to have significantly influenced results in these studies (Barnett, 1998; Lazar, Darlington, Murray, Royce, & Snipper, 1982; Schweinhart, Barnes, Weikart, Barnett, & Epstein, 1993). The use of random assignment increases confidence that estimated effects in these studies are due to the program rather than to preexisting (and possibly unmeasured) differences between program and comparison groups. The benefits of random assignment, however, can be lost due to severe losses of study participants over time or small initial sample size, and small sample size can severely limit the power of a study to detect important effects. Only two of these experimental studies (the Abecedarian and Perry Preschool studies) began with sample sizes larger than 30 in each group and had low attrition throughout follow-up. Two other experimental studies (Milwaukee and the Early Training Project) began with extremely small sample sizes, which rendered random assignment less useful and provided little power to confidently detect even fairly large effects. The remaining four experimental studies suffered massive attrition that could have invalidated the initial random assignment.

Eight other model program studies constructed comparison groups, usually sometime after the preschool group was formed. Some of their approaches seem likely to have created control groups that differed from the program groups, often in ways that favored the program group from the start. Two studies that began as curriculum comparisons (Experimental Variation of Head Start and the Curriculum Comparison Study) formed no-treatment comparison groups after the fact by selecting children who had not attended another preschool program. This eliminated from the potential comparison pool those children whose parents sought early educational experiences for them and were most comparable to the treatment group families with respect to parental attitudes and behavior regarding education. In the Harlem Training Project, attrition during the waiting period between selection for the study and program entry at age 3 may have introduced differences favoring that later entry group, which had higher IQ scores prior to treatment than the comparison group (Lazar et al., 1982). The Yale Child Welfare Research Program study obtained a comparison group 30 months later using the same clinic records used to identify the program group. However, one group was invited to receive child care, whereas the other was invited to participate in data collection, and there was sufficient rejection of the offer in both cases to significantly influence group composition. It is disturbing that three times the number of months of clinic records was required to obtain the program group as the comparison group (Seitz, Rosenbaum, & Apfel, 1985).

All of the large-scale program studies in Table 16.2 used quasi-experimental designs. Some constructed comparison groups from waiting lists or other groups of children thought to be similar to program children. Others simply relied on natural variation in program attendance. Both strategies raise questions about the comparability of the groups due to parental choice and program eligibility requirements. Some parents exert more effort to obtain educational opportunities for their children by working hard to get them into preschool programs and moving to neighborhoods with good schools and/or preschools. The educational success of their children is unlikely to be comparable to that of other children even without the benefit of Head Start or another preschool program. The consequences of preschool program eligibility requirements, recruitment, and admission decisions are less clear. Head Start eligibility requirements limit enrollment to children living in poverty, with exceptions for children with special needs and a small percentage of those over income if there is room. The other programs serve children who are from low-income families or live in neighborhoods where a large percentage of families are poor. Within the designated population, however, programs might enroll the most needy, those with the most eager and insistent parents or who are easiest to recruit, those thought most likely to gain from the program, or some combination of these.

A lack of information on children and families prior to intervention makes it difficult to assess the extent to which various types of selection created initial differences between program and comparison groups in the large-scale program studies. Only one of the large-scale program studies identified all of the comparison children prospectively, so most of these studies do not have pretest measures of children's cognitive abilities to offer as evidence that the groups were initially the same or to use to adjust later measures. Some of the large-scale studies statistically adjusted for variations in such family background characteristics as education level of the parents in an attempt to eliminate possible biases introduced by differences between program and comparison groups. However, the extent to which these statistical approaches actually produce more accurate estimates of effects when the program and comparison groups differ on measured or unmeasured characteristics that may affect education of the child at home and decisions about preschool program participation is unknown (Campbell, 1991; Cook, 1991).

Table 16.2. Head Start and public school programs' long-term effects

Head Start

Program name, years attended, source	Ages of participation	Research design/methodological concerns	Sample size[a]	Last follow-up	Results[a]
1. Cincinnati Head Start 1968–1969 (Pinkleton, 1976)	Entry: 4 years Exit: 5 years	Compared third graders who had attended Head Start with those who had not. Not randomized. No pretest.	Initial Unknown Follow-Up Unknown	Grade 3	Achievement tests: E = C in grade 3
2. Detroit Head Start 1969–1970 (O'Piela, 1976)	Entry: 4 years Exit: 5 or 6 years	Compared children who had attended Head Start with children in Title I elementary programs. Not randomized. No pretest. School-administered tests.	Initial Unknown Follow-Up Unknown	Grade 4	Achievement tests: E > C in grade 4
3. ETS Longitudinal Study of Head Start 1969–1971 (Lee, Brooks-Gunn, Schnur, & Liaw, 1990; Shipman, 1970, 1976)	Entry: 4 or 5 years Exit: 5 or 6 years	Compared children who went to Head Start with children who went to other preschools or no preschool. Not randomized. High attrition.	Initial 1,875 Follow-Up 852	Grade 3	Achievement tests: E > C in grade 1, E = C in grades 2 and 3
4. Hartford Head Start 1965–1966 (Goodstein, 1975)	Entry: 4 years Exit: 5 years	Compared children who had attended Head Start with those who had not. Not randomized. No pretest. High attrition. School-administered tests.	Initial 293 Follow-Up E = 148, C = 50	Grade 6	Achievement tests: E = C in grade 6 Special education: E = C, E = 5%, C = 10% Grade retention: E < C, E = 10%, C = 22%
5. Kanawha County, West Virginia Head Start 1973–1974 (Kanawha County Board of Education, 1978)	Entry: 4 years Exit: 5 years	Compared children who had attended Head Start with low-income children who had not. Not randomized. No pretest. School-administered tests.	Initial Unknown Follow-Up Unknown	Grade 3	Achievement tests: E = C in grade 3
6. Montgomery County, Maryland Head Start 1970–1971; 1974–1975; 1978–1979 (Hebbeler, 1985)	Entry: 4 years Exit: 5 years	Compared children who had attended eight or nine months with those who had attended one month or less. Not randomized. No pretests. High attrition. School administered tests.	Initial E = 1,915, C = 619 Follow-Up E = 186, C = 112	Grade 11	Achievement tests: E = C, but negative trend in most grades, E > C in grade 11

Study	Entry/Exit	Design	N	Outcome age/grade	Results
7. New Haven Head Start 1968–1969 (Abelson, 1974; Abelson, Zigler, & De-Blasi, 1974)	Entry: 4 years Exit: 5 years	Compared children who attended Head Start with those who had not. Not randomized. No pretest. High attrition.	Initial E = 61, C = 48 Follow-Up E = 35, C = 26	Grade 3	Achievement tests: E > C in grade 1, E = C in grade 3 Grade retention: E < C, E = 18%, C = 35%
8. Pennsylvania Head Start 1986–1987 (Reedy, 1991)	Entry: 3 to 5 years Exit: 5 to 6 years	Compared children who attended Head Start with children who had applied but had not been admitted. Not randomized. No pretest. High attrition.	Initial E = 98, C = un-known Follow-Up E = 54, C = 18	Grade 3	Achievement tests: E = C, but positive trend in grades 2 and 3
9. Rome, Georgia Head Start 1966 (McDonald & Monroe, 1981)	Entry: 5 years Exit: 6 years	Compared children who attended Head Start with all children in first grade in disadvantaged schools in 1966. Not randomized. No pretest. School-administered tests.	Initial E = 130, C = 88 Follow-Up E = 94, C = 60	Post high school	Achievement tests: E > C in grade 5, E = C in grades 6 and above Special education: E < C, E = 11%, C = 25% Grade retention: E = C, E = 51%, C = 63% High school graduation: E > C, E = 50%, C = 33%
10. Westinghouse National Evaluation of Head Start 1965–1966 (Westinghouse Learning Corp. and Ohio University, 1969)	Entry: 4 or 5 years Exit: 5 or 6 years	Compared children who attended Head Start with those who did not (matched within grade). Not randomized. No pretest.	Initial Unknown Follow-Up 1988, 1992	Grades 1 to 3	Achievement tests: E > C in grade 1, E = C in grades 2 and 3
11. NLSCM I 1979–1989 (Currie & Thomas, 1995)	Entry: 3–5 years Exit: 5–6 years	Compared children reported to attend Head Start with siblings reported not to attend. A cross-sectional comparison, not a longitudinal follow-up. Used percentile scores. Not randomized. No pretest.	762[b]	Age varies	Achievement tests: Fade-out for African-American but not white children Grade retention: E > C, whites only
12. NLSCM II 1979–1989 (Barnett & Camilli, 2000)	Entry: 3–5 years Exit: 5–6 years	As in NLSCM I except used raw scores and analyzed white–non Hispanic and Hispanic children separately.	735[b] PPVT 668[b] PIAT	Age varies	Achievement tests: Fade-out for African-American and white children, "Fade-in" for Hispanic children

(continued)

233

Table 16.2.   (continued)

		Head Start and public schools combined			
Program name, years attended, source	Ages of participation	Research design/methodological concerns	Sample size[a]	Last follow-up	Results[a]
13. Detroit Head Start and Title I Preschool 1972–1973 (Clark, 1979)	Entry: 4 years Exit: 5 years	Compared children who had attended Head Start or Title I preschool with children who were eligible but did not attend. Not randomized. No pretest. School-administered tests.	Initial Unknown Follow-Up Unknown	Grade 4	Achievement tests: E > C in grade 4
14. DC Public Schools and Head Start 1986–1987 (Marcon, 1990, 1994)	Entry: 4 years Exit: 5 years	Compared children who attended public school preschool or Head Start with children in same kindergartens who had not. Not randomized. High attrition.	Initial E = 372 C = 89 Follow-Up E varies C varies	Grades 4 and 5	Achievement tests: E = C in grades 3 to 5 Special education: E = C, grade 4 E = 10%, C = 9% Grade retention: E = C, grade 4 E = 31%, C = 38%
15. Philadelphia School District Get Set and Head Start 1969–1971 (Copple, Cline, & Smith, 1987)	Entry: 4 years Exit: 5 years	Compared children in enriched K-3 program (follow-through) who had and had not attended preschool. Not randomized. No pretest. High attrition. School-administered tests.	Initial E = 1,082 C = 1,615 Follow-Up E = 688 C = 524	Grades 4 to 8, varies by cohort	Achievement tests: E = C Grade retention: E < C
16. Seattle DISTAR and Head Start 1970–1971 (Evans, 1985)	Entry: 4 years Exit: 5 years	Compared children who had attended Head Start and DISTAR with matched children from same school and grades. Not randomized. No pretest. High attrition. School-administered tests.	Initial E = 92 C = un- known Follow-Up E = 44 C = 20	Grades 6 and 8	Achievement tests: E = C, but positive trend, in grades 6 and 8
		Public Schools			
17. Child-Parent Center (CPC) 1965–1977 (Fuerst & Fuerst, 1993)	Entry: 3 or 4 years Exit: 9 years	Compared former CPC children with non-CPC children from same feeder schools. Not randomized. No pretest. School-administered tests.	Initial E = 684 C = 304 Follow-Up E = 513 C = 244	Post high school	Achievement tests: E > C at grade 2, E = C at grade 8 High School graduation: E > C E = 62%, C = 49%

234

Program/Citation	Ages	Design	Sample size	Follow-up	Outcomes
18. Child-Parent Center II 1983–1985 (Reynolds, 1993, 1994a, 1994b)	Entry: 4 or 5 years Exit: 9 years	Compared former CPC children with several other groups. Not randomized. No pretest. School-administered tests.	Initial Unknown Follow-Up E = 757 C = 130	Grade 7	Achievement tests: E > C for grades K to 7 Special education: E < C, E = 12%, C = 22% Grade retention: E < C, E = 24%, C = 34%
19. Cincinnati Title I Preschool 1969–1971 (Nieman & Gastright, 1981)	Entry: 4 or 5 years Exit: 6 years	Compared children who attended full-day kindergarten and mostly had preschool with children who attended half-day kindergarten and mostly had no preschool. Not randomized. No pretest. School-administered tests.	Initial E = 688 C = 524 Follow-Up E = 410 C = 141	Grade 8	Achievement tests: E > C for grades 1,5, and 8 Special education: E = C, grade 8 E = 5%, C = 11% Grade retention: E = C, grade 8 E = 9%, C = 12%
20. Maryland Extended Elementary Pre-K 1977–1980 (Eckroade, Salehi, & Carter, 1988; Eckroade, Salehi, & Wode, 1991)	Entry: 4 years Exit: 5 years	Compared attenders to nonattenders, including only children continuously enrolled in school district (kindergarten to grade 5). Not randomized. Not pretest. High attrition. School-administered tests.	Initial Unknown Follow-Up E = 356 C = 306	Grade 8	Achievement tests: E > C for grades 3, 5, and 8 Special education: E < C, grade 8 E = 15%, C = 22% Grade retention: E < C, grade 8 E = 31%, C = 45%
21. New York State Experimental Prekindergarten 1975–1976 (State Education Department, University of the State of New York, 1982)	Entry: 3 or 4 years Exit: 5 years	Compared attenders with children on waiting list and with children in other districts with no prekindergarten program. Not randomized. High attrition.	Initial 1800[c] Follow-Up E = 1,348 C = 258	Grade 3	Achievement tests: E > C in kindergarten E = C in grade 1 Special education: E = C, E = 2%, C = 5% Grade retention: E < C, E = 16%, C = 21%
22. Florida Prekindergarten Early Intervention Cohort 1 1988–89 (King, Cappellini, & Gravens, 1995)	Entry: 4 years Exit: 5 years	Compared pre-K early intervention children with children from same schools who qualified for free/reduced lunch. Not randomized. No pretest. High attrition. School-administered tests. Pre-K EI children attended schools in poorer communities. First year of program operation.	Initial Unknown Follow-Up E = 350 C = 352	Grades 3 and 4	Achievement tests: E > C in kindergarten E = C in grades 1 to 3, E < C in grade 4 Special education: E = C, E = 25%, C = 25% Grade retention: E = C, E = 3%, C = 3% Disciplined: E < C, E = 11%, C = 32%

(continued)

Table 16.2. (continued)

Public Schools

Program name, years attended, source	Ages of participation	Research design/methodological concerns	Sample size[a]	Last follow-up	Results[a]
23. Florida Prekindergarten Early Intervention Cohort 2 1989–90 (King, Cappellini, & Rohani, 1995)	Entry: 4 years Exit: 5 years	Compare pre-K early intervention children with children from same schools who qualified for free/reduced lunch. Not randomized. No pretest. School-administered tests.	Initial Unknown Follow-Up E = 983 C = 1,054	Grades 3 and 4	Achievement tests: E > C in kindergarten E = C in grades 1 to 4 Special education: E = C, E = 17%, C = 15% Grade retention: E < C, E = 9%, C = 13%
24. Florida Chapter I 1985–86 (King, Rohani, & Cappellini, 1995)	Entry: 4 years Exit: 5 years	Compared children screened into with those screened out of Chapter I pre-k based on a test (DIAL-R). Not randomized. High attrition. School-administered tests.	Initial E = 103 C = 121 Follow-Up E = 54 C = 65	Grade 8	Achievement tests: E > C in grades 1, 2, 4, 7, 8 E = C in grades 5, 6 (no data for grade 3)

[a] E refers to the experimental or intervention group, and C refers to the control or comparison group. Outcomes listed as E > C or E < C were statistically significant at the p < .05 level.
[b] The numbers of children in experimental and comparison groups were not reported separately.

Long-Term Study Findings

Findings at each study's latest follow-ups are reported in Tables 16.1 and 16.2 for outcome measures that are related to cognitive development. These include IQ test scores; achievement test scores; and the percentage of children who repeated a grade, were placed in special education, or graduated from high school.

Effects on IQ Scores   All of the model program studies found IQ score gains at some point during or after program participation. In most cases, effects were sustained until school entry at age 5 at which time 10 studies reported effects between 4 and 11 IQ points. The Milwaukee study (a randomized trial) found a gain of 25 points, and the Syracuse study (nonrandomized) reported no effect at age 5. Three studies did not measure IQ score at school entry. Findings regarding the persistence of IQ effects are remarkably consistent in one respect: All the evidence indicates that effects on IQ scores decline over time. Part of the decline in effects may be accounted for by a boost in IQ scores for comparison children as a result of kindergarten and later schooling. The two randomized trials that enrolled children in full-day programs for 5 years indicate that very early, intensive, and long-lasting intervention produces the largest early IQ score gains and that these can persist well beyond school entry. The two other studies that enrolled infants did not find persistent effects, but both were quasi-experimental and less cognitively focused, and one ceased serving children prior to age 3.

None of the large-scale program studies obtained data on such IQ tests as the Stanford-Binet or Wechsler Intelligence Scale for Children (WISC). However, several Head Start studies and the New York State Experimental Pre-K study obtained results for the PPVT, and the Westinghouse Learning Corporation (WLC) study administered the Illinois Test of Psycholinguistic Abilities (ITPA), which may or may not be comparable to other IQ tests. Only one of these studies reported positive IQ score effects that persisted after children entered school (Currie & Thomas, 1995).

Currie and Thomas (1995) found that Head Start had long-term effects on PPVT scores for white non-Latino and Latino children but not for African American children. Their conclusions are derived from a "fixed-effects" analysis of data from the National Longitudinal Survey of Youth Child-Mother file (NLSCM; Baker, Keck, Mott, & Quinlan, 1993). This approach seeks to avoid the problem of selection bias by estimating Head Start's effects from within-family comparisons in which one child attended Head Start and another did not (for this comparison, the family is "fixed"). Although an interesting effort, their approach, data, and analyses have serious limitations (Barnett & Camilli, 1999, 2000). In their analyses, Currie and Thomas combined white non-Latino and Latino children into a single "white" group. They then estimated separate fixed-effects models for the "white" group and African Americans to investigate the effects of Head Start on PPVT percentile scores. They found initial effects for both groups and long-term Head Start effects for "white" children but not for African American children.

Barnett and Camilli (2000) re-estimated the fixed-effects model using raw scores and conducting separate analyses for white non-Latino and Latino children as well as for African American children. They argued that there is no justification for treating white non-Latino and Latino children as a single population, particularly given differences in their test scores and Head Start participation rates. In addition, they pointed out that the use of percentile scores discards information contained in the raw scores on differences in ability at the low end of the distribution, and the loss of information varies among the three ethnic groups. Minimum percentile (floor) scores were obtained much more frequently for African American (15%) and Latino (10%) children than for white non-Latino children (2%).

Barnett and Camilli (2000) found small initial effects on the PPVT that did not quite reach statistical significance and significant negative coefficients on the Head Start-by-age interaction indicating a fade-out for both African American and white non-Latino children. Moreover, the estimates of Head Start's short- and long-term effects for African American and white children were nearly identical. For Latino children, they found no initial effect, but they did find a positive Head Start-by-age interaction that was statistically significant. In their view, this surprising finding for Latino children was highly implausible and suggested problems with the data or methodology. Consideration of all of the limitations of this data set (e.g., cross-sectional comparisons must be used to estimate changes over time due to the limited number of test scores for each child) and the fixed-effects model led them to conclude that it was unlikely that any valid estimates of Head Start effects could be produced using the NLSCM data.

Effects on Achievement   Estimates of long-term effects on achievement tests varied across the model program studies. Of the 12 model program studies reporting achievement test scores or grades, six found statistically significant positive effects at or beyond grade 3. The randomized trials follow the same pattern as the other studies with three of the six that measured achievement finding long-term results. The Abecedarian and Perry Preschool studies both reported effects on achievement that persisted beyond high school. The Florida study found effects through grade 4. The Milwaukee study reported effects on achievement in the early grades, but these were not statistically significant at grade 4. It bears repeating that the Milwaukee sample size was very small, and cases were lost as the children grew older so that the estimated effect can be large compared with what is found in other studies and still fail to be statistically significant.

The achievement test results of the large-scale program studies vary at least as much as those of the model program studies. Sixteen studies found evidence consistent with the belief that effects on achievement fade out over time. Sometimes, effects appear to fade out as early as first grade; in other cases, not until after third grade. Two studies present mixed evidence—effects for some children but not others, and very late effects after years of no evident effect. Six studies do not find evidence of fade-out, and some of these provide evidence of persistent effects on achievement well into middle school. Four studies reporting achievement effects beyond grade 3 (including one in which effects fade out later and one in which effects are mixed) are Head Start studies and one other includes both Head Start and public school programs.

Much of the variation in findings with respect to achievement in both the model and large-scale program studies may result from exceptionally high and nonrandom attrition for achievement test data that both reduced sample size and biased comparisons toward finding no effect. Loss of statistical significance can occur even if the estimated effect size is constant when there is a decline in sample size because participants are lost or drop out of the study over time. Moreover, all of the studies that found no effects or found that effects faded were vulnerable to either selective attrition resulting from the use of school-administered tests (which compare only the part of each group that has stayed at grade level) or a similar problem that arose because of another design flaw even when researchers administered their own tests.

Although reliance on standardized tests routinely administered by school personnel provided achievement data at low cost, it had several unfortunate consequences. First, even if no data were lost, the quality and uniformity of test administration is expected to be lower because the testing was done for entire classes by teachers (rather than specialists testing children individually) under conditions in which there may have been pressure to compromise the results. Second, some data were lost simply because the tests schools used varied making it difficult to combine scores. Third, tests are routinely administered by grade rather than by age so that children who repeat a grade are not tested with their age cohort. In many studies, these children were not included in the achievement analyses. Fourth, children expected to score poorly are most likely to not take school administered tests. Many schools do not test children in special education classes, for example. Poor students are more frequently absent and more likely to miss tests. The use of routine testing to hold schools "accountable" places pressure on school administrators to use a variety of strategies to remove poor performers from the test pool at each grade level (McGill-Franzen & Allington, 1993).

At best, studies that relied on school-administered tests have test data with lower reliability and higher rates of attrition. This reduces the ability to detect program effects, and the power to detect effects declines over time as more achievement data are lost. In addition, studies systematically lose a greater number of poorly performing students from program and comparison groups each year as the cumulative percentage of children retained in grade, placed in special education, or otherwise omitted from testing increases. The effect of this is to gradually erase any evidence of achievement differences between program and comparison groups as grade level increases.

Three Head Start studies had idiosyncratic flaws that systematically biased the achievement test results downward over time, even though researchers administered their own tests. The New Haven Head Start study individually administered achievement tests but only to children at expected grade level. As there was significantly less grade retention in the program group over time, this had the effect of gradually equating the tested program and control groups on performance as more poorly performing students were retained in grade each year. The Educational Testing Service (ETS) Head Start study tested only children in classes where at least 50% of the children were study participants, probably in order to save on the costs of testing. This eliminated from testing children who had been retained in grade or placed in special education classes. Unfortunately, there are no data on grade retention and special education for the ETS study that can be used to assess the extent of the resulting bias.

The WLC study (Westinghouse Learning Corporation and Ohio University, 1969) is one of the oldest and most widely cited studies of Head Start's effects on achievement. This study matched former Head Start children in grades 1, 2, and 3 with other children in their grade levels. This procedure automatically equates the two groups on grade level and distorts the achievement comparison to the extent that children have been differentially lost from the program and comparison groups due to grade retention and special education. Obviously, this cannot be verified directly as this procedure hides any differences in grade retention and special education between the Head Start children and their age cohort. It is possible, however, to verify that differences between the program and comparison groups increased over time due to grade repetition by looking at the ages of children in the two groups. In the first-grade data set, the Head Start and comparison groups were not significantly different in age. In the second- and third-grade data sets, the Head Start groups were significantly younger than the comparison groups. Apparently, the comparison groups contained substantial numbers of older children who had been retained in second and third grade. The age gap between Head Start and comparison groups increased across the three grades, paralleling the decline in estimated effects across grades.

For the most part, the studies that found persistent effects on achievement did not suffer from these attrition-related problems. The two experimental studies of model programs that provided strong evidence of persistent effects on achievement began with reasonable sample sizes, administered their own achievement tests, and had relatively low rates of attrition. The CPC II study obtained and analyzed test scores for children who had been retained in grade even though it relied on school administered tests. The Cincinnati Title I study can be seen as an exception that proves the rule. Although it used school-administered tests, this study had such low rates of grade retention and special education placement for all children that differences in these rates could not introduce much difference between groups.

Effects on School Progress and Placement   School progress and placement were measured by rates of grade retention, special education, and high school graduation. Across studies, the findings were relatively uniform and constitute overwhelming evidence that preschool can produce sizeable improvements in school success. All but one of the model program studies reported grade retention and special education rates, and in all of these, the rates were lower for the program group. The one model program study that did not report rates (Syracuse) simply reported that there was no statistically significant effect. In the other model program studies, estimated effects on school success were not always significant, but in most cases, they were large enough to be of practical importance. Despite small sample sizes, statistical significance on one or the other was found in five model program studies, and another, the Perry Preschool study, found significant effects on the number of years of special education received and on the classification rate for mild mental retardation.

Turning to the large-scale program studies in which sample sizes tend to be larger, statistically significant effects on grade retention or special education were found in 9 of the 12 studies that collected the relevant data. Positive results were found for both Head Start and public school programs, though relatively few of the Head Start studies looked at these outcomes. Three public school studies failed to find significant effects. The Cincinnati Title I study did not find statistically significant effects, but the base rates for retention and special education placement were relatively low. The Washington, D.C., study suggests a small effect on grade retention (not statistically significant) and no effect on special education placement, but the comparison group was more advantaged and these estimates were not adjusted for this difference between the groups (Marcon, 1993).

Table 16.3. Percentage point decreases in special education and grade retention by preschool program type.

Outcome measure	Model programs			Head Start/Public school		
	Mean	SD	N	Mean	SD	N
Special education	19.6**	14.6	11	4.7**	5.3	9
Grade repetition	14.9*	9.8	14	8.4*	5.4	10

*p < .01, two-tailed t-test with unequal variances
**p < .05, two-tailed t-test with unequal variances
Note: Does not include NLSCM estimates for grade repetition as these are available only for white and African American children separately.

The Florida study that found no effects on retention or special education did find effects on rates of disciplinary problems.

Four model program studies, one public school study, and one Head Start study assessed effects on high school graduation rates. All six estimated large effects on graduation rates, though only the four studies with least problematic sample sizes found the effect to be statistically significant. These findings are consistent with the evidence from the larger pool of studies with data on grade retention and special education placement, as both are predictive of high school graduation (Natriello, McDill, & Pallas, 1987; Schweinhart et al., 1993).

The estimated effects on grade retention and special education can be combined across studies to produce estimates for the literature as a whole and to investigate differences across studies. Table 16.3 displays estimated effects on the cumulative percentage of students placed in special education and repeating at least one grade. Thus, in this chart, an estimated effect of 20% represents a 20–percentage-point reduction in special education or grade repetition (a drop from 40% to 20%). Estimated effects are presented separately for model program studies and large-scale program studies. A simple test of statistical significance for the difference between two means indicates that effects on special education and grade repetition are larger in the model program studies. No differences in effects are apparent between Head Start and public school programs. These results are consistent with the expectation that the more intensive programs would have larger effects.

Within-Study Program Comparisons Although it would hardly be surprising if more intensive, better-funded programs produced larger effects, many things differ across studies that might also explain differences in outcomes. For example, it can be argued that by some measures the children in the model program studies were more disadvantaged than those in the large-scale program studies. Thus, it is useful to be able to look at within study comparisons of model and large-scale programs in which the context and population are the same. Two studies provide useful direct comparisons of model and large-scale programs. The Abecedarian study looked at potential effects of the comparison group's participation in community programs. Comparison group children who attended programs that (voluntarily) met federal guidelines for child care quality were found to have higher IQ scores than other comparison group children (Burchinal et al., 1989). The estimated effect on cognitive ability at school entry was roughly half the size of the effect of the Abecedarian program. This should be considered an upper bound estimate, as control group participation in child care was not random, and selection bias may inflate the estimated effect on the control group. In another study, Van de Reit and Resnick (1973) randomly assigned children to a model program or to Head Start and public school pre-school classrooms. They found that the model program students had better outcomes on IQ scores, achievement, grade retention, and special education placements.

Two studies provide information about the effects of extended elementary programs. The Abecedarian study conducted an experiment in which half of the program and control groups were randomly assigned to a special school-age program at age 5. The school-age program was provided for the first 3 years of elementary school and consisted of bi-weekly home visits in which teachers provided individualized supplemental activities in partnership with parents. The school-age program alone was largely ineffective and as an add-on had mixed effects, at best. In contrast, the CPC II study found that enriched elementary school services added substantially to the effects of the preschool program with the size of the effect increasing directly with the number of years of elementary services (Reynolds & Temple, 1998). Perhaps the extended program was more effective in the CPC II study because it significantly enhanced the elementary school experience with smaller classes, additional classroom and support staff, and an emphasis on parent involvement in the classroom. Although the CPC II study's estimated effects for the elementary program could be biased upward by selection, the results are consistent with other evidence on effective educational practices encompassed by the program, such as reducing class size (Grissmer, 1999). Moreover, analyses conducted to test for selection bias did not find it.

Some studies assessed the effectiveness of Head Start relative to public school programs (e.g., CPC II, Get Set, Detroit Title I). Public school programs might be thought to be more effective because they pay much higher salaries than Head Start and can attract better-qualified staff. Head Start might be thought more effective because it offers a broader range of services, emphasizes parent involvement, and hires many staff who are former Head Start parents. The evidence from these studies suggests smaller effects for Head Start. However, Head Start children tend to be more disadvantaged, and these within-study comparisons may be biased by preexisting differences between the populations served. As noted previously, in a cross-study comparison of grade retention and special education effects, differences are relatively small and provide no clear indication that Head Start is less effective than public school programs.

CONCLUSIONS

A substantial number of studies have investigated the long-term effects of preschool programs on disadvantaged children, but the evidence must be considered carefully because studies vary with respect to the intensity and quality of the program studied and their methodological rigor. The weight of the evidence indicates that a wide range of preschool programs including Head Start can increase IQ scores during the early childhood years, improve achievement, and prevent grade retention and special education. Evidence that Head Start and other programs can increase high school graduation rates comes from a small number of studies, but this finding is consistent with the results on grade retention and special education from a much larger number of studies. Although some studies fail to find persistent achievement effects, this null finding often can be explained by flaws in research design and follow-up procedures. A false fade-out in achievement is most likely to be found when there are substantial program effects on grade retention and special education that produce biased attrition in the achievement data (i.e., failure to test the appropriate sample). This resolves the apparent conflict between fade-out in achievement and persistently improved school outcomes.

In contrast to findings for other outcomes, it is clear that initial effects on IQ scores fade over time. With the exception of intensive, long lasting interventions that begin in infancy, the effects on IQ scores disappear. Why this occurs and how important it is are much less clear. Partly this is because it is unclear what an IQ score measures and how much what it measures changes over time (Barnett & Camilli, 2000). Obviously, IQ tests do not directly measure the same kinds of abilities at ages 3, 8, and 15, and many experts believe that intelligence is much broader than what is measured by IQ tests (Nessier et al., 1995; Sternberg & Detterman, 1986). One does have to ask how important it is to improve IQ scores if permanent improvements on broad measures of achievement can be produced without permanently increasing IQ scores.

At the same time, cross-study comparisons suggest that intensive programs beginning in the first year of life and continuing to kindergarten produce some permanent increase in IQ scores despite fade-out and larger gains in achievement and some schooling outcomes. Within-study comparisons have tended to find little long-term effect of age-at-start but were limited to small differences in age and have not involved the most intensive interventions. Research has found that similar effects on brain development result in different effects on cognitive and social development, depending on the age at which they occur (Chugani & Phelps, 1986; Chugani, Phelps, & Mazziotta, 1987; Kolb, 1989). Thus, very early interventions continuing to kindergarten could produce qualitatively different, not just larger, cognitive effects. Research on Early Head Start could contribute to our understanding of this if the programs are sufficiently intensive and continuous.

Despite the intuitive appeal of the idea that Head Start's benefits might fade out after the intervention ends because Head Start children enter schools of poor quality (Lee & Loeb, 1995), the empirical support for this view is weak. Except for IQ score, fade-out turns out to be more apparent than real. The evidence of long-term effects on achievement tests and measures of school success demonstrates that cognitive and academic effects endure without prolonged intervention. Of course, improvements in elementary education for children who attend poor quality schools would independently contribute to cognitive development as measured by achievement, school success, and, quite possibly, IQ score (Ceci, 1991; Grissmer, 1999; Husen & Tuijnman, 1991; Slavin, Karweit, & Wasik, 1994).

Although research supports the view that Head Start produces long-term improvements in cognitive abilities and school success, it also raises concerns that Head Start may have less impact than it could. Head Start programs have smaller effects than model programs, and Head Start lacks the resources to match the quality and intensity of most model programs. Some studies also suggest that Head Start is less effective than public school programs, though differences in the populations served may bias the comparisons against Head Start. Head Start probably could produce substantially larger cognitive gains for children if it had more money per child and higher standards for staff qualifications, class size, and program implementation. A higher quality Head Start also might increase its impact by delivering more hours of service. At the very least, the government ought to sponsor rigorous, large-scale randomized trials to study enhancements of quality and duration. Although it would also be satisfying to have a more definitive assessment of the effects of Head Start as it currently exists, given our present knowledge, it would be a mistake to conduct such a study that did not also seek better information about the returns to enhancing Head Start quality and duration.

Finally, policy makers and researchers should consider questions of resource allocation within Head Start and Early Head Start. Together with other reviews, the evidence presented here suggests that Head Start resources should be focused on educating the child rather than on case management and social services and services for parents (Gomby, Culross, & Behrman, 1999; St. Pierre et al., 1998). This does not mean that Head Start should discontinue relatively inexpensive and successful program elements dealing with child health and nutrition, or that socialization should be neglected (because it is an essential outcome of education), or that parents are unimportant and parent involvement should be neglected. However, the fact that parents are important in their children's lives does not guarantee Head Start and other programs working with parents success in producing significant benefits for parents or children. There is mounting evidence that many efforts directed at parents are ineffective (Boutte, 1992; Gomby, et al., 1999). Even if some parent interventions are effective in some domains (Gomby et al., 1999; Kagitcibasi, 1996; Olds & Kitzman, 1993), it may be more effective for another program to deliver these services while Head Start focuses on educating children. This is another area in which more research is vital, both because of the potential benefits from developing effective parent programs and the extent to which we currently devote substantial resources to efforts of dubious efficacy. Head Start is justifiably proud of its role as a national laboratory, but increased investments in rigorous research are required so that future studies provide clearer guidance and are not bound by the limitations that hobble many of the studies reviewed here (Zigler & Styfco, 1993).

REFERENCES

Abelson, W.D. (1974). Head Start graduates in school: Studies in New Haven, Connecticut. In S. Ryan (Ed.), *A report on longitudinal evaluations of preschool programs* (Vol. 1, pp. 1–14). Washington, DC: U.S. Department of Health, Education and Welfare.

Abelson, W.D., Zigler, E., & DeBlasi, C.L. (1974). Effects of a four-year follow through program on economically disadvantaged children. *Journal of Educational Psychology, 66,* 756–771.

Abbott-Shim, M., Lambert, R., & McCarty, F. (2003). A comparison of school readiness outcomes for children randomly assigned to a Head Start program and the program's wait list. *Journal of Education for Students Placed at Risk, 8*(2), 191–214.

Andrews, S., Blumenthal, J., Johnson, D., Kahn, A., Ferguson, C., Lasater, T., et al. (1982). The skills of mothering: A study of parent child development centers. *Monographs of the Society for Research in Child Development, 46*(6), Serial No. 198.

Baker, P., Keck, C., Mott, F., & Quinlan, S. (1993). *NLSY Child Handbook, 1993.* Columbus: Center for Human Resource Research, Ohio State University.

Barnett, W.S. (1998). Long-term effects on cognitive development and school success. In W.S. Barnett & S.S. Boocock (Eds.), *Early care and education for children in poverty: Promises, programs, and long-term outcomes* (pp. 11–44). Buffalo: State University of New York Press.

Barnett, W.S., & Camilli, G. (1999). *Estimating Head Start effects.* [Working Paper]. New Brunswick, NJ: Graduate School of Education, Rutgers University.

Barnett, W.S., & Camilli, G. (2000). Compensatory preschool education, cognitive development, and "race." In J. Fish (Ed.), *Race and intelligence: Separating science from myth* (pp. 369–406). Mahwah, NJ: Lawrence Erlbaum Associates.

Barnett, W.S., Tarr, J., & Frede, E. (1999). *Early childhood education needs in low income communities.* New Brunswick, NJ: Center for Early Education Research, Rutgers University.

Beller, K. (1983). The Philadelphia Study: The impact of preschool on intellectual and socio-emotional development. In Consortium for Longitudinal Studies (Ed.), *As the twig is bent: Lasting effects of preschool programs* (pp. 133–170). Mahwah, NJ: Lawrence Erlbaum Associates.

Boutte, G.S. (1992). *The effects of home intervention on rural children's home environments, academic self-esteem, and achievement scores—A longitudinal study.* Unpublished Dissertation, UMI Dissertation Services.

Brooks-Gunn, J., McCormick, M.C., Shapiro, S., Benasich, A.A., & Black, G.W. (1994). The effects of early education intervention on maternal employment, public assistance, and health insurance: The Infant Health and Development Program. *American Journal of Public Health, 84,* 924–930.

Bryant, D.M., Burchinal, M., Lau, L., & Sparling, J. (1994). Family and classroom correlates of Head Start Children's Developmental Outcomes. *Early Childhood Research Quarterly, 9,* 289–309.

Burchinal, M., Lee, M., & Ramey, C. (1989). Type of day-care and intellectual development in disadvantaged children. *Child Development, 60,* 128–137.

Caldwell, B.M. (1987). Sustaining intervention effects: Putting malleability to the test. In J.J. Gallagher & C.T. Ramey (Eds.), *The malleability of children* (pp. 115–26). Baltimore: Paul H. Brookes Publishing Co.

Campbell, D.T. (1991, May 6–7). *Quasi-experimental research designs in compensatory education.* Paper presented at OECD Conference on Evaluating Intervention Strategies for Children and Youth and Risk, Washington, DC.

Campbell, F.A. (1999). Unpublished analyses of Abecedarian data. (F.A. Campbell generously provided to the author unpublished analyses of the Abecedarian data reporting means for academic and school success measures by preschool treatment group and gender.)

Campbell, F.A., & Ramey, C.T. (1993, March 26). *Mid-adolescent outcomes for high risk students: An examination of the continuing effects of early intervention.* Paper presented at the biennial meeting of the Society for Research in Child Development, New Orleans.

Campbell, F.A., & Ramey, C.T. (1994). Effects of early intervention on intellectual and academic achievement: A follow-up study of children from low-income families. *Child Development, 65,* 684–698.

Campbell, F.A., & Ramey, C.T. (1995). Cognitive and school outcomes for high-risk African-American students at middle adolescence: Positive effects of early intervention. *American Educational Research Journal, 32,* 743–772.

Carolina Abecedarian Project. (1999). *Executive summary. Early learning, later success: The Abecedarian study.* Chapel Hill: Frank Porter Graham Child Development Center, University of North Carolina. (Also available from http://www .fpg.unc.edu/~abc/executive_summary.htm)

Ceci, S.J. (1991). How much does schooling influence general intelligence and its cognitive components? A reassessment of the evidence. *Developmental Psychology, 27,* 703–722.

Chafel, J.A. (1992). Head Start: Making "quality" a national priority. *Child and Youth Care Forum, 21*(3), 147–163.

Chugani, H.T., & Phelps, M.E. (1986). Maturational changes in cerebral function in infants determined by 18FDG positron emission tomography. *Science, 231,* 840–843.

Chugani, H.T., Phelps, M.E., & Mazziotta, J.C. (1987). Positron emission tomography study of human brain functional development. *Annals of Neurology, 22,* 487–497.

Clark, C.M. (1979). *Effects of the project Head Start and Title I preschool programs on vocabulary and reading achievement measured at the kindergarten and fourth grade levels.* Unpublished doctoral dissertation, Wayne State University, Detroit, Michigan.

Cook, T. (1991). Clarifying the warrant for generalized causal inferences in quasi-experiments. In M.W. McLaughlin & D. Phillips (Eds.), *Evaluation and education at quarter century* (pp. 115–144). NSSE Yearbook 1991. Chicago: NSSE.

Copple, C.E., Cline, M.G., & Smith, A.N. (1987). *Path to the future: Long-term effects of Head Start in the Philadelphia School District.* Washington, DC: U.S. Department of Health and Human Services.

Currie, J., & Thomas, D. (1995). Does Head Start make a difference? *American Economic Review, 85,* 241–364.

Deutsch, M., Deutsch, C.P., Jordan, T.J., & Grallo, R. (1983). The IDS Program: An experiment in early and sustained enrichment. In Consortium for Longitudinal Studies (Ed.), *As the twig is bent: Lasting effects of preschool programs* (pp. 377–410). Mahwah, NJ: Lawrence Erlbaum Associates.

Deutsch, M., Taleporos, E., & Victor, J. (1974). A brief synopsis of an initial enrichment program in early childhood. In S. Ryan (Ed.), *A report on longitudinal evaluations of preschool programs* (Vol. 1, pp. 49–60). Washington, DC: U.S. Department of Health, Education, and Welfare.

Eckroade, G., Salehi, S., & Carter, J. (1988). *An analysis of the midterm effects of the extended elementary education prekindergarten program.* Baltimore: Maryland State Department of Education.

Eckroade, G., Salehi, S., & Wode, J. (1991). *An analysis of the long-term effect of the extended elementary education prekindergarten program.* A paper presented at the annual meeting of The American Educational Research Association, Chicago, Illinoios.

Ellsworth Associates, Inc. (1994). *Head Start research from 1985 to 1994: An annotated bibliography.* Washington, DC: U.S. Department of Health and Human Services, Head Start Bureau.

Evans, E. (1985). Longitudinal follow-up assessment of differential preschool experience for low income minority group children. *Journal of Educational Research, 78,* 197–202.

Frede, E.C. (1998). Preschool program quality in programs for children in poverty. In W.S. Barnett & S.S. Boocock (Eds.), *Early care and education for children in poverty: Promises, programs, and long-term outcomes* (pp. 77–98). Buffalo: State University of New York Press.

Fuerst, J.S., & Fuerst, D. (1993). Chicago experience with an early childhood program: The special case of the Child Parent Center Program. *Urban Education, 28,* 69–96.

Garber, H.L. (1988). *The Milwaukee Project: Prevention of mental retardation in children at risk.* Washington, DC: American Association on Mental Retardation.

Gomby, D., Culross, R., & Behrman, R. (1999). Home visiting: Recent program evaluations—analysis and recommendations. *The Future of Children, 9*(1), 4–26.

Goodstein, H.A. (1975). *The prediction of elementary school failure among high-risk children.* Unpublished paper cited by McKey and colleagues 1985. Connecticut University.

Gray, S., Ramsey, B., & Klaus, R. (1982). *From 3 to 20: The Early Training Project.* Baltimore: University Park Press.

Gray, S., Ramsey, B., & Klaus, R. (1983). The Early Training Project, 1962–1980. In Consortium for Longitudinal Studies (Ed.), *As the twig is bent: Lasting effects of preschool programs* (pp. 33–70). Mahwah, NJ: Lawrence Erlbaum Associates.

Grissmer, D. (1999). Conclusion—Class size effects: Assessing the evidence, its policy implications and future research agenda. *Educational Evaluation and Policy Analysis, 21,* 231–248.

Hale, B., Seitz, V., & Zigler, E. (1990). Health services and Head Start: A forgotten formula. *Journal of Applied Developmental Psychology, 11,* 447–458.

Haskins, R. (1989). Beyond metaphor: The efficacy of early childhood education. *American Psychologist, 44,* 274–282.

Hebbeler, K. (1985). An old and a new question on the effects of early education for children from low income families. *Educational Evaluation and Policy Analysis, 7*(3), 207–216.

Herrnstein, R.J., & Murray, C. (1994). *The bell curve: Intelligence and class structure in American life.* New York: Free Press.

Herzog, E., Newcomb, C.H., & Cisin, I.H. (1974). Double deprivation: The less they have, the less they learn. In S. Ryan (Ed.), *A report on longitudinal evaluations of preschool programs* (Vol. 1, pp. 69–93). Washington, DC: U.S. Department of Health, Education, and Welfare.

Hood, J. (1992). *Caveat emptor: The Head Start scam. Policy Analysis, 187.* Washington, DC: Cato Institute.

Husen, T., & Tuijnman, A. (1991). The contribution of formal schooling to the increase in intellectual capital. *Educational Researcher, 20*(7), 17–25.

Jester, R.E., & Guinagh, B.J. (1983). The Gordon Parent Education Infant and Toddler Program. In Consortium for Longitudinal Studies (Ed.), *As the twig is bent: Lasting effects of preschool programs* (pp. 103–132). Mahwah, NJ : Lawrence Erlbaum Associates.

Johnson, D., & Walker, T. (1991). A follow-up evaluation of the Houston Parent Child Development Center: School performance. *Journal of Early Intervention, 15,* 226–236.

Kagitcibasi, C. (1996). *Family and human development across cultures: A view from the other side.* Mahwah, NJ: Lawrence Erlbaum Associates.

Kanawha County Board of Education. (1978). *Kanawha Count Head Start evaluation study.* Unpublished report.

Karnes, M.B., Shwedel, A.M., & Williams. M.B. (1983). A comparison of five approaches for educating young children from low-income homes. In Consortium for Longitudinal Studies (Ed.), *As the twig is bent: Lasting effects of preschool programs* (pp. 133–170). Mahwah, NJ: Lawrence Erlbaum Associates.

King, F.J., Cappellini, C.H., & Gravens, L. (1995). *A longitudinal study of the Florida Prekindergarten Early Intervention Program, Part III.* Tallahassee: Educational Services Program, Florida State University.

King, F.J., Cappellini, C.H., & Rohani, F. (1995). *A longitudinal study of the Florida Prekindergarten Early Intervention Program, Part IV.* Tallahassee: Educational Services Program, Florida State University.

King, F.J., Rohani, F., & Cappellini, C.H. (1995). *A ten-year study of a prekindergarten program in Florida.* Tallahassee: Educational Services Program, Florida State University.

Kolb, B. (1989). Brain development, plasticity, and behavior. *American Psychologist, 44,* 1203–1212.

Lally, J.R., Mangione, P., & Honig, A. (1988). The Syracuse University Family Development Program: Long-range impact of an early intervention with low-income children and their families. In D. Powell (Ed.), *Parent education as early childhood intervention: Emerging directions theory research and practice* (pp. 79–104). Norwood, NJ: Ablex.

Lazar, I., Darlington, R., Murray, H., Royce, J., & Snipper, A. (1982). Lasting effects of early education: A report from the Consortium for Longitudinal Studies. *Monographs of the Society for Research in Child Development, 47*(2–3), Series No. 195.

Lee, V., Brooks-Gunn, J., Schnur, E., & Liaw, F.R. (1990). Are Head Start effects sustained? A longitudinal follow-up comparison of disadvantaged children attending Head Start, no preschool, and other preschool programs. *Child Development, 61,* 495–507.

Lee V., & Loeb, S. (1995). Where do Head Start attendees end up? One reason why preschool effects fade out. *Educational Evaluation and Policy Analysis, 17*(1), 62–82.

Levenstein, P., O'Hara, J., & Madden J. (1983). The Mother-Child Home Program of the Verbal Interaction Project. In Consortium for Longitudinal Studies (Ed.), *As the twig is bent: Lasting effects of preschool programs* (pp. 237–263). Mahwah, NJ: Lawrence Erlbaum Associates.

Locurto, C. (1991). Beyond IQ in preschool programs? *Intelligence, 15,* 295–312.

Love, J.M, Kisker, E., Ross, C., Schochet, P., Brooks-Gunn, J., Paulsell, D., et al. (2002). *Making a difference in the lives of infants and toddlers and their families: The impacts of Early Head Start.* Washington, DC: Administration on Children, Youth and Families, U.S. Department of Health and Human Services.

Marcon, R.A. (1990). *Early learning and early identification: Final report of the three year longitudinal study.* Washington, DC: District of Columbia Public Schools.

Marcon, R.A. (1993). *Early learning and early identification follow-up study: Transition form the early to the later childhood grades 1990–93.* Washington, DC: District of Columbia Public Schools, Center for Systemic Change.

Marcon, R.A. (1994). Doing the right thing for children: Linking research and policy reform in the District of Columbia Public Schools. *Young Children, 50*(1), 8–20.

McCarton, C.M., Brooks-Gunn, J., Wallace, I.F., & Bauer, C.R. (1997). Results at age 8 years of early intervention for low-birth-weight premature infants: The Infant Health and Development Program. *Journal of the American Medical Association, 277*(2), 126–132.

McDonald, M.S., & Monroe, E. (1981). *A follow-up study of the 1966 Head Start program, Rome City Schools.* Unpublished manuscript.

McGill-Franzen, A., & Allington, R.L. (1993). Flunk 'em or get them classified: The contamination of primary grade accountability data. *Educational Researcher, 22*(1), 19–22.

McKey, R., Condelli, L., Ganson, H., Barrett, B., McConkey, C., & Plantz, M. (1985). *The impact of Head Start on children, families, and communities.* Final report of the Head Start Evaluation, Synthesis, and Utilization Project. Washington, DC: U.S. Department of Health and Human Services.

Miller, L.B., & Bizzell, R.P. (1983). The Louisville Experiment: A comparison of four programs. In Consortium for Longitudinal Studies (Ed.), *As the twig is bent: Lasting effects of preschool programs* (pp. 171–200). Mahwah, NJ: Lawrence Erlbaum Associates.

Miller, L.B., & Bizzell, R.P. (1984). Long-term effects of four preschool programs: Ninth and tenth grade results. *Child Development, 55,* 1570–1587.

Natriello, G., McDill, E.L., & Pallas, A. (1987). *Schooling disadvantaged children: Racing against catastrophe.* New York: Teachers College Press.

Neisser, U., Boodoo, G., Bouchard, T.J., Boykin, A.W., Brody, N., Ceci, S.J., et. al. (1995). *Intelligence: knowns and unknowns.* (Report of a Task Force established by the Board of Scientific Affairs of the American Psychological Association). Washington, DC: American Psychological Association.

Nieman, R.H., & Gastright, J.F. (1981). *The long-term effects of ESEA Title I preschool and all-day kindergarten: An eight-year follow-up.* Cincinnati, OH: Cincinnati Public Schools.

Olds, D., & Kitzman, H. (1993). Review of research on home visiting for pregnant women and parents of young children. *The Future of Children, 3*(3), 53–92.

O'Piela, J.M. (1976). *Evaluation of the Detroit Public Schools Head Start program, 1975–1976.* Detroit, MI: Detroit Public Schools.

Palmer, F. (1983). The Harlem Study: Effects by type of training, age of training, and social class. In Consortium for Longitudinal Studies (Ed.), *As the twig is bent: Lasting effects of preschool programs* (pp. 201–236). Mahwah, NJ: Lawrence Erlbaum Associates.

Pinkleton, N.B. (1976). *A comparison of referred Head Start, non-referred Head Start and non-Head Start groups of primary school children on achievement, language processing, and classroom behavior.* Unpublished doctoral dissertation cited by McKey and colleagues 1985. University of Cincinnati.

Ramey, C.T., Bryant, D.M., & Suarez, T.M. (1985). Preschool compensatory education and the modifiability of intelligence: A critical review. In D. Detterman (Ed.), *Current topics in human intelligence* (pp. 247–296). Norwood, NJ: Ablex.

Reedy, Y.B. (1991). *A comparison of long range effects of participation in Project Head Start and the impact of three differing delivery models.* Unpublished paper for the Graduate Program in School Psychology, Pennsylvania State University.

Reynolds, A.J. (1993). One year of preschool intervention or two: Does it matter? *Early Childhood Research Quarterly, 10,* 1–33.

Reynolds, A.J. (1994a). Effects of a preschool plus follow-on intervention for children at risk. *Developmental Psychology, 30,* 787–804.

Reynolds, A.J. (1994b, February 4). *Longer-term effects of the Child Parent Center and Expansion Program.* Paper presented at the annual meeting of the Chicago Association for the Education of Young Children.

Reynolds, A.J., & Temple, J. (1998). Extended early childhood intervention and school achievement: Age thirteen findings from the Chicago Longitudinal Study. *Child Development, 69,* 231–246.

Schweinhart, L.J., Barnes, H.V., Weikart, D.P., Barnett, W.S., & Epstein, A.S. (1993). *Significant benefits: The High/Scope Perry Preschool study through age 27.* Monographs of the High/Scope Educational Research Foundation. No. 10. Ypsilanti, MI: High/Scope Press.

Seitz, V., & Apfel, N.H. (1994). Parent-focused intervention: Diffusion effects on siblings. *Child Development, 65,* 677–683.

Seitz, V., Rosenbaum, L.K., & Apfel, N.H. (1985). Effects of family support intervention: A ten-year follow-up. *Child Development, 56,* 376–391.

Shipman, V.C. (1970). *Disadvantaged children and their first school experiences: ETS-Head Start Longitudinal Study. Preliminary description of the initial sample prior to school enrollment* (ETS Technical Report Series, PR-70–20). Princeton, NJ: Educational Testing Service.

Shipman, V.C. (1976). *Stability and change in family status, situational, and process variables and their relationship to children's cognitive performance.* Princeton, NJ: Educational Testing Service.

Slavin, R.E., Karweit, N.L., & Wasik, B.A. (1994). *Preventing early school failure: Research, policy, and practice.* Needham Heights, MA: Allyn & Bacon.

Spitz, H.H. (1986). *The raising of intelligence: A selected history of attempts to raise retarded intelligence.* Mahwah, NJ: Lawrence Erlbaum Associates.

State Education Department, University of the State of New York. (1982). *Evaluation of the New York State experimental prekindergarten program: Final report.* (ERIC Document Reproduction Service No. ED 219 123). Albany, NY: Author.

Sternberg, R., & Detterman, D. (Eds.). (1986). *What is intelligence?* Norwood, NJ: Ablex.

St. Pierre, R.G., Layzer, J., & Barnes, H.V. (1998). Regenerating two-generation programs. In W.S. Barnett & S.S. Boocock (Eds.), *Early care and education for children in poverty: Promises, programs, and long-term outcomes* (pp. 11–44). Buffalo: State University of New York Press.

Traub, J. (2000, January 16). What no school can do. *The New York Times Magazine,* 52–57, 68, 81, 90–91.

Van de Reit, V., & Resnick, M.B. (1973). *Learning to learn: An effective model for early childhood education.* Gainesville: University of Florida Press.

Wasik, B.H., Ramey, C.T., Bryant, D.M., & Sparling, J.J. (1990). A longitudinal study of two early intervention strategies: Project CARE. *Child Development, 61,* 1682–1696.

Weikart, D.P., Bond, J.T., & McNeil, J.T. (1978). *The Ypsilanti Perry Preschool Project: Preschool years and longitudinal results through fourth grade.* Ypsilanti, MI: High/Scope Press.

Westinghouse Learning Corporation and Ohio University. (1969). *The impact of Head Start: An evaluation of the effects of Head Start on children's cognitive and affective development. Vols. 1 and 2.* Report to the Office of Economic Opportunity. Athens, OH: Author.

White, K., & Casto, G. (1985). An integrative review of early intervention efficacy studies with at-risk children: Implications for the handicapped. *Analysis and Intervention in Developmental Disabilities, 5,* 7–31.

Willer, B., Hofferth, S.L., Kisker, E.E., Devine-Hawkins, P., Farquhar, E., & Glantz, F. (1991). *The demand and supply of child care in 1990.* Washington, DC: National Association for the Education of Young Children.

Zigler, E., & Muenchow, S. (1992). *Head Start: The inside story of America's most successful educational experiment.* New York: Basic Books.

Zigler, E., & Styfco, S.J. (1993). Using policy research and theory to justify and inform Head Start expansion. *Social Policy Report, 8*(2).

Zigler, E., & Styfco, S.J. (1994). Is the Perry Preschool better than Head Start? Yes and no. *Early Childhood Research Quarterly, 9*(3&4), 269–288.

Zill, N., Resnick, G., Kim, K., McKey, R., Clark, C., Shefali, P., et al. (2001). *Head Start FACES: Longitudinal findings on program performance: Third progress report.* Washington, DC: Research, Demonstration and Evaluation Branch and Head Start Bureau, Administration on Children Youth and Families, U.S. Department of Health and Human Services.

CHAPTER 17

How Well Does Head Start Prepare Children to Learn to Read?

GROVER J. WHITEHURST AND GRETA M. MASSETTI

Reading is a critical foundation for children's academic success. Children who read well read more and, as a result, acquire more knowledge in numerous domains (Stanovich, 1986). By one estimate the number of words read in a year by a middle-school child who is an avid reader approaches 10 million compared with 100,000 for the least motivated child (Nagy & Anderson, 1984). Children who lag behind in reading receive less practice in reading than other children, miss out on opportunities to develop strategies for understanding what they read, often encounter reading material that is too hard, and may come to dislike reading and school assignments that require reading. Poor readers fall further and further behind their more literate peers in reading and in other academic areas.

According to the National Center for Educational Statistics (2003), 37% of fourth graders nationally cannot read at the basic level. In other words, these children cannot read and understand a short paragraph of the type one would find in a simple children's book. This problem is strongly correlated with family income. For example, among African American and Hispanic students in the United States (two groups who experience disproportionate rates of poverty), the percentages of fourth grade students reading below the basic level in 2002 were 58% and 53%, respectively. Fifty-eight percent of fourth graders eligible for free lunch in 2002 scored below the basic level. In many urban school districts, the percentage of fourth grade students who cannot read at the basic level hovers around 70%.

Of those children who experience serious problems with reading, from 10% to 15% eventually drop out of high school, and only 2% complete a 4-year college program. Surveys of adolescents and young adults with criminal records show that about half have

This work was supported by grants to the senior author from the Administration on Children, Youth and Families. Opinions expressed herein are the authors' and have not been cleared by the grantor.

reading difficulties. Similarly, about half of youths with a history of substance abuse have reading problems (National Institute of Child Health and Development [NICHD], 2000). It is not an exaggeration to say that serious reading difficulties place a child's life at risk.

There is strong continuity between the prereading skills with which children enter school and their later academic performance. Juel (1988) reported that the probability that children would remain poor readers at the end of the fourth grade if they were poor readers at the end of the first grade was .88. The relationship between the skills with which children enter school and their later academic performance is strikingly stable. For instance, Stevenson and Newman (1986) found a correlation of .52 between the ability to name the letters of the alphabet as a child entered kindergarten and performance on a standardized test of reading comprehension in Grade 10.

LONGITUDINAL RESEARCH ON EMERGENT LITERACY IN HEAD START

Two longitudinal studies involving children in Head Start have identified important preschool predictors of elementary school reading success; one study was conducted at Florida State University (Lonigan, Burgess, & Anthony, 2000), and the other at SUNY Stony Brook (Storch & Whitehurst, 2001, 2002; Whitehurst & Fischel, 2000; Whitehurst & Lonigan, 1998). Both studies assessed an array of cognitive, linguistic, and prereading skills in children during the preschool period and followed those children into elementary school. Both studies employed sophisticated mathematical modeling techniques to identify the independent influence of various preschool abilities on reading outcomes. In both investigations, specific prereading skills such as knowledge of print (e.g., letter names), phonological awareness (e.g., being able to rhyme), and writing (e.g., being able to print one's name) were strong predictors of reading success well into elementary school.

For instance, Whitehurst and colleagues (Storch & Whitehurst, 2001) found that 55% of the differences in performance in reading ability at the end of first grade in a sample of 367 Head Start children could be predicted directly from their knowledge of print and phonological awareness at the end of kindergarten, as illustrated in Figure 17.1 (to obtain 55%, square the path weight between kindergarten prereading and first grade reading). In turn, 40% of the differences among these children in their print and phonological skills at the end of kindergarten could be predicted directly from their print, phonological, and emergent writing abilities measured at the end of Head Start. In other words, Head Start children who had begun to learn about print, sounds, and writing during the preschool period were more likely to be ready to read at the end of kindergarten and more likely to be reading successfully in elementary school. In this same sample, the influence of children's vocabulary abilities in the preschool period on their reading outcomes in elementary school was indirect compared to the effect of prereading skills in the areas of print knowledge, phonological awareness, and writing (Storch & Whitehurst, 2001).

PREREADING SKILLS

Another piece of the puzzle relating preschool abilities to reading outcomes is that experiences that develop vocabulary and conceptual skills in preschoolers are different from experiences that develop knowledge of print, phonological awareness, and emergent writ-

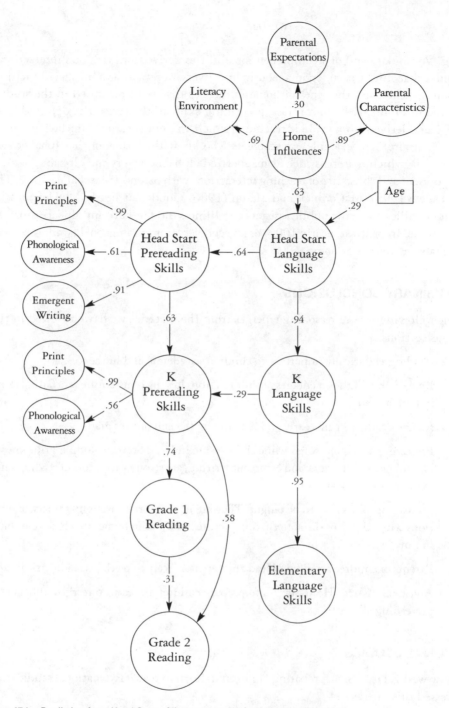

Figure 17.1. Prediction from Head Start of literacy success in elementary school

Note: This structural equation model is derived from longitudinal data on 367 children who were initially assessed when they were in Head Start at age 4 and who were followed until the end of the second grade at age 7. Each circle in the figure represents results from several independent assessments of the variables in question (e.g., Grade 1 Reading represents results from three different standardized tests of reading give to children at the end of first grade). Numbers within arrows (i.e., the path weights) represent the independent effect of one variable on another and can be interpreted in the manner one would interpret a standardized regression coefficient or a correlation coefficient. The comparative fit index (CFI) for the data in the figure is .93 (the CFI ranges from .00 to 1.00). A CFI of .93 indicates that the structural model represented in the figure fits the underlying data relatively well.

ing. Vocabulary and oral comprehension abilities derive from rich oral interactions with adults that might occur spontaneously in conversations and around shared picture book reading. These are the types of home influences that were measured in the study illustrated in Figure 17.1. In contrast, prereading skills in the categories depicted in Figure 17.1 are derived from explicit teaching (which was not measured in the study reported in the figure). For example, preschoolers who know the letters of the alphabet are from homes in which materials such as magnetized alphabet letters and alphabet name books are present and the source of teaching interactions with parents (Sénéchal, LeFevre, Thomas, & Daley, 1998). McCormick and Mason (1986) found that nearly 50% of preschoolers from families receiving public assistance in Illinois did not have any alphabet materials in the home. In contrast, nearly 100% of preschoolers from professional families played with alphabet materials at home.

PRELIMINARY CONCLUSIONS

The following line of reasoning emerges from the material we have reviewed in the previous sections:

1. Reading is critically important to children's academic and life success.

2. Remarkably high percentages of children from low-income families are failing at reading in fourth grade.

3. Reading failure begins early and is stable by the end of first grade.

4. Prereading skills measured while children are in Head Start, including print knowledge, phonological awareness, and emergent writing, are strong predictors of reading outcomes in elementary school.

5. Prereading skills have to be taught. They are not acquired through ordinary oral interactions with adults, or through sharing picture books, or in homes in which relevant teaching materials are absent.

6. Parents of children attending Head Start are not likely to teach prereading skills at home.

7. A critical task for Head Start is to prepare children to learn to read by enhancing their prereading skills.

NATIONAL STUDIES

How well is Head Start preparing children to learn to read? Two national studies have addressed this question.

The FACES Project

The Head Start Family and Child Experiences Survey (FACES), funded by Head Start and conducted by Westat, is designed to assess the changes and benefits produced by Head Start using a nationally representative sample of families and children. The FACES project attempts to establish a link between the characteristics of the Head Start program and parent and child outcomes and to assess children and families across time periods.

The FACES data reported as of this writing were derived from assessments of approximately 2,800 children in 43 Head Start centers in both the fall and spring of the Head Start year, with follow-up in the spring of the kindergarten year. With respect to emergent literacy, FACES assessed children in four areas: word knowledge (The Peabody Picture Vocabulary Test, Third Edition [PPVT-III]; Dunn & Dunn, 1997); print knowledge (Letter Word Identification from the Woodcock-Johnson Psycho-Educational Battery–Revised; Woodcock & Mather, 1989, 1990); emergent writing (Woodcock-Johnson Dictation; Woodcock & Mather, 1989, 1990); and book knowledge (nonpublished, nonstandardized measure).

FACES also collected information on the quality of the Head Start centers attended by the sample, primarily using the Early Childhood Environments Rating Scale (ECERS; Harms, Clifford, & Cryer, 1998). Data were also collected on home literacy activities (questionnaire items that were used in the National Household Education Survey of 1999). A variety of demographic data were also obtained on parents and teachers.

Initial Snapshots The first set of data provided by FACES details Head Start children's abilities at the beginning of Head Start, and provides information about the general quality of Head Start programs and the quality of Head Start classrooms.

Program Quality A positive finding from FACES is that the general program quality of most Head Start classrooms is good. No classroom observed scored below the "minimal quality" rating. By comparison with the range of quality found in nationally representative preschool and child care programs, Head Start's range was compressed, with most programs scoring in the middle range and few at either the very high or very low end of the scale (Administration on Children, Youth and Families [ACYF], 2000, 2003). ECERS, however, is a very broad measure of classroom quality not designed to capture differences in curriculum that could be quite important for emergent literacy. For example, an ECERS score will not indicate the degree to which print knowledge or emergent writing is emphasized in a classroom, and we have already seen that skills in these domains are not acquired without exposure to relevant materials and instruction. A classroom rated as excellent on the ECERS could well be inadequate for emergent literacy. This mismatch between the FACES measures, which heavily emphasize preacademic skills, and the measure of classroom environment—the ECERS—which does not capture the extent to which these skills are being taught in the classroom, makes it difficult to link Head Start classroom practices to child outcomes using the FACES data.

Entering Abilities In all three areas of emergent literacy in which FACES used standardized instruments with national norms (word knowledge, letter knowledge, and emergent writing), children were found to be substantially below average upon entry into Head Start. For example, on word knowledge, children entered Head Start one full standard deviation below the national average. Children were also delayed in letter knowledge, in which the typical child entering Head Start could identify four letters of the alphabet by name in the 2000 report (ACYF, 2003). Also in emergent writing, the typical Head Start child could not write letters of the alphabet or copy complex geometric figures, such as a star. Of course, there is nothing surprising about the finding that children from the very low-income families served by Head Start are below average in cognitive and preacademic domains. However, the degree of deficit (e.g., the inability to name or write a single letter of the alphabet) is eye-opening and of considerable concern given the predictive power of such skills. The challenge for Head Start is to move these skills upward to a point where the children served by the program are on par with children nationally.

Interpretation Dilemmas   What does FACES tell us about Head Start's success in accomplishing this goal?

Inconsistencies in Reports   Pinning down the precise results from FACES is difficult because there have been several reports, and the numbers differ somewhat across these. No explanation has been offered in later reports for the discrepancies with earlier reports. These disparities may relate to changing rules for inclusion and exclusion of children, later efforts to correct entry errors in the dataset, or changes in the variables included in multivariate analyses. The discrepancies are all small in absolute terms, but sometimes the conclusions flow in opposite directions (e.g., something is reported as a statistically significant outcome in one report but as statistically insignificant in another). We will take note of these reporting differences when they seem to bear on important conclusions.

Lack of a Comparison Group   Another challenge in interpreting the FACES data occurs because of the lack of a control or comparison group. For measures on which there are no national norms, such as the assessments of book knowledge and social skills, this is a fatal flaw because there is no way to determine or even infer that progress over the Head Start year was greater than would have been expected as a result of ordinary maturation and experiences outside of Head Start. For normed and age-standardized measures, such as the PPVT-III and the Woodcock-Johnson, the approach taken by those responsible for analyzing and interpreting the FACES data has been to assume that if standard scores were higher at exit from Head Start than at entry, then the difference is attributable to participation in Head Start. Unfortunately, regression to the mean, effects of being tested twice, and secular trends not associated with Head Start can account for some or all of the modest positive gains in standard scores that have been reported for some FACES measures. For these reasons, the FACES data are most appropriately used to describe the status of Head Start children, families, and classrooms than to suggest causal links between characteristics of the Head Start program and parent and child outcomes.

Findings for Specific Skills   The FACES reports provide detailed information regarding Head Start children's knowledge of specific emergent literary skills at entry into Head Start and growth in those skills over the Head Start year. These findings provide a snapshot of the children's entering abilities and their developmental patterns over time.

Word Knowledge   Some positive outcomes determined from FACES were for word knowledge—English-speaking children tested in both the fall and spring increased from a mean of 85.3 to a mean of 89.1 on the PPVT-III (ACYF, 2003). A 4-point gain corresponds to $\frac{1}{5}$ to $\frac{1}{4}$ of a standard deviation, which is considered small in Cohen's (1988) analysis of effect sizes. A gain of this size could easily be due to increased familiarity with the test and the assessment process on the second assessment. In this regard,

Zigler, Abelson, and Seitz (1973) long ago demonstrated that one could obtain changes of this magnitude on PPVT scores of children from low-income backgrounds simply by testing them a second time. Without a control or comparison group in FACES, it is simply impossible to attribute a ¼ standard deviation upward movement over the Head Start year to the Head Start program.

Without a control group, one could look to statistical analyses of the effects of center quality to buttress the view that changes in word knowledge over the Head Start year are due to the effects of Head Start rather than repeated testing or some other extraneous factor. Specifically, one would expect that centers with more positively rated language environments on the ECERS would house children who would show the greatest gains. Here is one of the areas in which different reports of the FACES results flow in opposite directions. Zill, Resnick, and McKey (1999) report that a two-level analysis (between-center effects vs. within-center effects) of scores in word knowledge at exit from Head Start, as well as a separate analysis of gains in these scores over the Head Start year, could identify no significant center-level predictors. Referring to the exit scores in the spring, they write that, "Once the socioeconomic characteristics of families in the programs were taken into account, the correlations between classroom quality measures and vocabulary scores were no longer significant" (p. 17). With respect to gain scores, they report that, "only three percent of the overall variation in gain scores could be attributed to differences across programs" (p. 17). In contrast, Zill and Resnick (2000) reported a statistically significant effect of child–adult ratio and ECERS language environment on word knowledge scores in the spring but still no significant effect of these program quality measures on gains across the Head Start year. Data from a 2000 ACYF progress report on FACES provide yet more inconsistent findings, indicating that 13% of the variance in language gain scores was attributable to centers, as opposed to the 6% and 3% reported in Zill and Resnick (2000) and Zill et al. (1999), respectively.

Without being able to untangle these conflicting reports of the variance accounted for and the significance of center-level effects, what can we say? Let us take the most optimistic versions of the reports, that there is an overall gain of approximately ¼ of a standard deviation in PPVT-III word knowledge scores over the Head Start year, and the most optimistic report of the amount of this gain that might be attributable to center quality, 13%. Thirteen percent of a quarter of a standard deviation is not much in practical terms or in terms of the related technical indicator, effect size.

Emergent Writing   The inconsistent reporting of the FACES results continues with the domain of emergent writing. Zill et al. (1999) reported that children could not write a letter of the alphabet at the beginning of the Head Start year, still could not write a letter at exit from Head Start, and "did not advance in comparison to national norms" (p. 7). Consistent with this report, Figure 1.3 of the ACYF (2001) progress report on FACES indicates that children gained an insignificant 1.5 standard score points (¹⁄₁₀ of a standard deviation) on the Woodcock-Johnson dictation test over the Head Start year. However, Figure 2.1 of this same document, as well as Zill and Resnick (2000), report a 4.3 standard score gain on this test. More recent FACES data report an increase of 2.0 points, or .15 of a standard deviation, on the writing task (ACYF, 2003). The reported changes over the year for both the 1997 data and the 2000 data were small, cannot be clearly attributed to Head Start for the reasons described previously for word knowledge, and appear to have been limited to the ability to copy letters, rather than more important emergent writing skills such as the ability to write letters and print one's first name.

Letter Knowledge   For letter knowledge, which is the single strongest prereading predictor of later literacy success, the typical Head Start child could not name a single letter of the alphabet at entry into Head Start in the 1997 sample and showed no significant gain in the ability to name letters by the end of the year. "In fact they showed a slight but significant decrease in average standard scores on letter identification" (ACYF, 2001, p. 19). By way of comparison, a typical middle-class child would be able to name about half the letters of the alphabet upon entry into preschool and would be able to name all the letters on entry into kindergarten. The 2000 data was more promising, indicating that children knew about four letters of the alphabet at Head Start entry, and about nine at Head Start exit (ACYF, 2003). While these changes show promising improvements in letter knowledge, Head Start children are still entering kindergarten knowing fewer letters of the alphabet than national norms.

Book Knowledge   The assessment of book knowledge, although it was not on a test with national norms, also paints a picture of very low entry skills. In the 1997 data, the typical child entering Head Start did not know that print flows from left to right and top to bottom across a page and still did not know this upon exit from Head Start. "They showed no advance in this sort of book knowledge between the fall and spring" (ACYF, 2001, p. 19). FACES 2000 showed more progress on this skill, as mean scores showed a significant increase in book and print conventions (ACYF, 2003).

Student Progress   Further information is available from FACES regarding the progress of Head Start children as they move into and through kindergarten. Assessments of participating children were conducted in the spring of the kindergarten year.

Kindergarten   Reports of kindergarten data from FACES (ACYF, 2000, 2001, 2003) have taken a more positive view, based on two findings. First, the follow-up data indicate that Head Start graduates show substantial gains in emergent literacy skills during kindergarten. For instance, by the end of the kindergarten year, children followed in the FACES sample could recognize most or all of the letters of the alphabet and were able to write letters. Their word knowledge skills, as measured by the PPVT-III, had increased to a point at which they were only about ½ a standard deviation below the national mean. The ACYF (2000) report concluded from these findings that "children leaving Head Start are indeed 'ready to learn,' because they have, in fact, learned a great deal by the end of kindergarten." An alternative interpretation is that these children were also "ready to learn" when they entered Head Start but were taught very little. That the public schools succeeded in teaching these children while Head Start did not does not seem to us to be a positive finding for Head Start. We cannot put it any better than ACYF (2001): "A probable reason why Head Start children are not learning early reading skills . . . is that many Head Start teachers are not teaching them . . . Notably, less than 4 percent of teachers specifically mention language and/or literacy as a main benefit of Head Start" (p. 19).

Low Scorers   The second finding cited by the FACES authors as supportive of significant effects of Head Start is that the children entering with the lowest skills gained most over the Head Start year: Head Start works to narrow gaps between children who begin the program at differing levels of school readiness. Gains in cognitive skills from the fall to the spring of the Head Start year were larger among children who were initially in the bottom quarter of the score distribution than among those in the middle or top quarter. (ACYF, 2001, p. 21). Of course, the lowest scorers are further from the mean of the population than the higher scorers and thus would be expected to show the most upward change because of statistical regression toward the mean. Without a control or comparison group, we cannot determine the degree to which greater gains for those who enter with lower scores represents an effect of Head Start versus a statistical artifact.

Summary   FACES divulges important information about the emergent literacy skills of children in Head Start. Namely, children enter with low levels of critical skills and show little progress over the Head Start year. In pre-post designs without control groups, such as FACES, it is difficult to make causal conclusions about pre-post gains, even if they are sizeable: These changes may be due to program effects or maturation or the effects of repeated testing or statistical regression or secular increases in performance in the population in general. However, in the absence of appreciable pre-post change, which was what was found for the emergent literacy measures in FACES, causal conclusions are possible. Specifically, Head Start nationally is having little effect on children's preparation for reading.

The Early Childhood Longitudinal Study

The lack of a control or comparison group in FACES, with the attendant difficulties in making causal inferences, is addressed in part by The Early Childhood Longitudinal Study of the Kindergarten Class of 1998–99 (ECLS-K), conducted by the U.S. Department of Education, National Center for Educational Statistics (NCES). The study followed a national sample of 22,000 children from their kindergarten year in 1998–1999 through fifth grade.

Only portions of the data collected for the kindergarten year have been reported as of this writing (West, Denton, & Reaney, 2001). With respect to emergent literacy, children were assessed on skills that overlap substantially with the measures used in FACES, including letter knowledge, book knowledge, and word knowledge. The overlap is not surprising given that the principal contractor for both FACES and ECLS-K is Westat.

Most important for the present topic, parents of children in ECLS-K were asked to indicate whether their child had attended preschool and, if so, whether the program was Head Start, child care, nursery school, or a state prekindergarten program. Parents also provided demographic data, including family income. These data allow an analysis of the effect of preschool attendance, including type of preschool, on emergent literacy skills at entry into kindergarten. After adjusting for family income, analyses indicate that beginning kindergartners with any type of preschool attendance score better in emergent literacy than children who have not attended preschool. However, the size of this gain depends on the type of preschool children attend. After adjusting for family income, children who attend state prekindergarten programs or private nursery schools are better prepared in emergent literacy (as well as math and general knowledge) than children who attend Head Start or child care programs, which did not differ in their effects (West et al., 2001).

There are important questions yet to be answered about the ECLS-K results, including whether parents accurately report the nature of their children's preschool attendance and program type and whether parents who choose nursery school or state prekindergarten programs over Head Start provide a more supportive home environment than parents who choose Head Start, even after controlling for family income. On the surface, the ECLS-K results suggest that, with respect to reading readiness, Head Start is better for a child than no preschool experience but not better than child care and not as good as state prekindergarten or nursery school. The FACES demonstration of small or no gains in emergent literacy skills over the Head Start year and the documentation of the very low priority given to emergent literacy skills by Head Start teachers are consistent with the low effectiveness of Head Start in the ECLS-K data.

THE FUTURE

This chapter is written at a time of tremendous flux in preschool education and Head Start. The entry of states on a large scale as providers of preschool education has been accompanied by reports by expert panels that emphasize the ability of preschoolers to learn about literacy and math and the importance of this knowledge for later school success (National Research Council, 2001; Snow, Burns, & Griffin, 1998). As the stakes have risen and public expenditures have increased for preschool education, so have calls for accountability.

Head Start, as the largest single provider of preschool education in the country, is necessarily caught up in these trends. This is reflected in the legislative context: The 1998 reauthorization Head Start Act called on Head Start to have qualified staff, "that can provide children with a variety of skills that have been identified, through scientifically based reading research, as predictive of later reading achievement." It also called on Head Start to ensure that participating children "know that letters of the alphabet are a special category of visual graphics that can be individually named; recognize a word as a unit of print; identify at least 10 letters of the alphabet; and associate sounds with written words" (Coats Human Services Reauthorization Act of 1998, PL 105-285). Head Start at the national level is attempting to respond to the new legislative and policy climate. They are, for example, funding a new generation of Quality Research Centers that will focus on curricula for emergent literacy and other key readiness skills; making information on emergent literacy available on the web for Head Start practitioners; launching a new Family Literacy Initiative; convening a National Leadership Institute focused on improving teaching, learning, and assessment in the areas of language development, literacy, mathematics, science, and creative arts; and acknowledging that the FACES data indicate problems that need to be addressed in the Head Start educational program.

Head Start is a very large ship whose course cannot be changed with a sudden turn of the helm. The FACES and ECLS-K data reflect the outcomes of Head Start's minimal efforts to prepare children for reading prior to the new legislative and policy emphasis on literacy. As such they represent the baseline against which Head Start's new efforts can and will be measured.

REFERENCES

Administration on Children, Youth and Families (ACYF). (2000). *FACES findings: New research on Head Start program quality and outcomes*. Washington, DC: Author.

ACYF. (2001). *Head Start FACES 1997: Longitudinal findings from the faces study: Head Start program performance measures. Third progress report*. Washington, DC: Author.

ACYF. (2003). *Head Start FACES 2000: A whole child perspective on program performance. Fourth progress report*. Washington, DC: Author.

Coats Human Services Reauthorization Act of 1998, PL 105-285, 112 Stat. 2702, 42 U.S.C. §§ 9801.

Cohen, J. (1988) *Statistical power analyses for the social sciences* (2nd ed.). New York: Academic Press.

Dunn, L.M., & Dunn, L.M. (1997). *Peabody Picture Vocabulary Test* (3rd ed.). Circle Pines, MN: American Guidance Service.

Harms, T., Clifford, R.M., & Cryer, D. (1998). *Early Childhood Environment Rating Scale*. New York: Teachers College Press.

Juel, C. (1988). Learning to read and write: A longitudinal study of 54 children from first through fourth grades. *Journal of Educational Psychology, 80,* 437–447.

Lonigan, C.J., Burgess, S.R., & Anthony, J.L. (2000). Development of emergent literacy and early reading skills in preschool children: Evidence from a latent-variable longitudinal study. *Developmental Psychology, 36, 596–613.*

McCormick, C.E., & Mason, J.M. (1986). Intervention procedures for increasing preschool children's interest in and knowledge about reading. In W.H. Teale & E. Sulzby (Eds.), *Emergent literacy: Writing and reading* (pp. 90–115). Norwood, NJ: Ablex.

Nagy, W.E., & Anderson, R.C. (1984). How many words are there in printed school English? *Reading Research Quarterly, 19, 304–330.*

National Center for Educational Statistics (NCES). (2003). *National assessment of educational progress*. Washington, DC: U.S. Department of Education.

National Institute on Child Health and Development (NICHD). (2000). *Why children succeed or fail at reading: Research from NICHD's program in learning disabilities*. Bethesda, MD: Author.

National Research Council. (2001). *Eager to learn*. Washington, DC: National Academy Press.

Sénéchal, M., LeFevre, J., Thomas, E. M., & Daley, K.E. (1998). Differential effects of home literacy experiences on the development of oral and written language. *Reading Research Quarterly, 13, 96–116.*

Snow, C.E., Burns, M.S., & Griffin, P. (Eds.). (1998). *Preventing reading difficulties in young children*. Washington, DC: National Academy Press.

Stanovich, K.E. (1986). Matthew effects in reading: Some consequences of individual differences in the acquisition of literacy. *Reading Research Quarterly, 21, 360–407.*

Stevenson, H.W., & Newman, R.S. (1986). Long-term prediction of achievement and attitudes in mathematics and reading. *Child Development, 57, 646–659.*

Storch, S.A., & Whitehurst, G.J. (2001). The role of family and home in the developmental course of literacy in children from low-income backgrounds. In P. Rebello Britto & J. Brooks-Gunn (Eds.), *The role of family literacy environments in promoting young children's emerging literacy skills: New directions in child and adolescent development* (pp. 53–71). San Francisco, CA: Jossey-Bass.

Storch, S.A. & Whitehurst, G.J. (2002). Oral-language and code-related precursors to reading: Evidence from a longitudinal structural model. *Developmental Psychology, 38, 934–947.*

West, J., Denton, K., & Reaney, L.M. (2001). *The kindergarten year: Findings from the Early Childhood Longitudinal Study, Kindergarten Class of 1998–99*. Washington, DC: National Center for Educational Statistics.

Whitehurst, G.J., & Fischel, J.E. (2000). A developmental model of reading and language impairments arising in conditions of economic poverty. In D. Bishop & L. Leonard (Eds.), *Speech and language impairments in children: Causes, characteristics, intervention and outcome* (pp 53–71). East Sussex, UK: Psychology Press.

Whitehurst, G.J., & Lonigan, C.J. (1998). Child development and emergent literacy. *Child Development, 69, 848–872.*

Woodcock, R.W., & Mather, N. (1989, 1990). WJ-R Tests of Achievement: Examiner's manual. In: R.W. Woodcock & M.B. Johnson, *Woodcock-Johnson Psycho-Educational Battery* (Rev. ed.). Chicago: Riverside.

Zigler, E., Abelson, W.D., & Seitz, V. (1973). Motivational factors in the performance of economically disadvantaged children on the Peabody Picture Vocabulary Test. *Child Development, 44,* 294–303.

Zill, N., & Resnick, G. (2000, June). *Language development and emergent literacy in Head Start: Links to program characteristics and home literacy activities.* Paper presented at the National Head Start Research Conference, Washington, DC.

Zill, N., Resnick, G., & McKey, R.H. (1999, April). *What children know and can do at the end of head Start and what it tells us about the program's performance.* Paper presented at the biennial meetings of Society for Research in Child Development, Albuquerque, New Mexico.

CHAPTER 18

New Possibilities for Research on Head Start

DEBORAH A. PHILLIPS AND SHELDON H. WHITE

Head Start has served a dual role as social intervention and research laboratory since the program was first launched in 1965. As such, it is the focus of one of the most enduring collaborations between public policy and the behavioral and social sciences to emerge from the Great Society era. Both Head Start and the scientific community have been transformed by the collaboration. This is not to say that "expert" scientists have had a deep influence on the emergence or evolution of the program. In fact, from the beginning, tensions existed between the avowed knowledge of the scientific community connected to Head Start and the experience and intuition of the localized, grass-roots players—parents, directors, teachers, community leaders—in whose hands the shape of the program has ultimately rested.

Social scientists, with developmental psychologists prominently represented, have had a complex relationship with Head Start (White & Phillips, 2001). They have straddled the hands-on role of program conceptualizer and the arms-length role of program evaluator. Some have been strong proponents of the program, while others have called its effectiveness into question. At times, the prevailing emphases within developmental psychology have bolstered the comprehensive vision of Head Start's planners, while at other times they have subverted this vision, as was the case when IQ score-modification became the primary metric by which success was judged (Zigler & Freedman, 1987; Zigler & Trickett, 1978).

By far the most salient role played by developmental scientists has been in the evaluation enterprise tied to Head Start. Head Start was established during a time of significant change in the federal management of social programs. As the War on Poverty substantially expanded the federal presence in human service programming, expectations rose regarding systematic uses of data to determine the needs of client populations and the efficacy of policies and programs established to serve them. As a result, it was assumed

263

that systematic scientific evaluations could and should be mounted to judge the value of Head Start from the moment it hit the ground. Over the past 3 decades, a great deal of thinking has been devoted to considering what it means to evaluate Head Start. These evolving views about Head Start evaluation provide the departure point for this chapter. We then turn to a discussion of the promising directions for research proposed by the Roundtable on Head Start Research, a formal initiative of the National Research Council and the Institute of Medicine aimed at guiding the broad research agenda of the Head Start Bureau.[1]

HEAD START AND EVALUATION

Evaluation has been a friend and an enemy to Head Start. The "impact" study of Head Start conducted by the Westinghouse Learning Corporation (1969), which cast doubt on the program's efficacy, ushered in both the imbalance of attention to cognitive gains as the outcome of interest and the enduring perception that short-term benefits of Head Start do not endure into the school years (White, 1971). A heated debate, which continues in 2004, about methods and measures for assessing Head Start ensued and led to a Herculean effort to define and operationalize the construct of social competence that guided the original conception of the program (Malakoff, Underhill, & Zigler, 1998; Raver & Zigler, 1997; Zigler & Trickett, 1978). This effort is ongoing and remains a central challenge to the field.

In the aftermath of the Westinghouse study, several landmark evaluations of model early intervention programs, as well as the data of the Developmental Consortium (Lazar & Darlington, 1982), re-instilled optimism about the possibility of affecting the life courses of young children growing up in poverty. Among the most prominent evaluations are those of the Perry Preschool Project (Schweinhart, Barnes, & Weikart, 1993), whose graduates have been followed up to age 27, and the Abecedarian Program (Campbell & Ramey, 1994, 1995; Vernon-Feagans, 1996), whose graduates have been followed up to age 21. The remarkable accomplishments of these children and young adults, in comparison to their peers in control groups, are well known. They span academic, economic, social, and behavioral outcomes, including many highly face-valid indicators such as avoidance of special education placements, higher educational attainment, lower rates of delinquent behavior, and lower rates of teenage childbearing (Brooks-Gunn, Berlin, & Fuligni, 2000; Currie & Thomas, 2000; Farran, 2000; Yoshikawa, 1995).

Although these results attest to what *can* be accomplished, their applicability to Head Start remains untested given the many differences between Head Start and the model programs. On the one hand, the model programs had resources of funding and personnel that are not generally available in Head Start programs. They were implemented in or near universities under the close watch of their designers and not diffused in 50,000 classrooms around the country, as is the case with Head Start. On the other hand, Head

---

[1] The Roundtable on Head Start Research of the National Research Council and the Institute of Medicine, chaired by the second author, was established in 1994 to discuss new directions for Head Start research in light of the emerging issues confronting the program. The Roundtable was founded by the Administration on Children, Youth and Families of the U.S. Department of Health and Human Services. The discussion in this chapter reflects the views of the authors and is not an official statement of the National Research Council, the Institute of Medicine, or the Roundtable.

Start typically offers a more comprehensive program than did many of these models, with components addressing health screening and immunization, child and family nutrition, direct services to parents, and referrals to social and mental health services (Zigler & Styfco, 1994). These distinctions carry important implications for efforts to credit Head Start with the achievements of these companion efforts to accomplish similar goals. One could reasonably argue that Head Start likely achieves less or more.

Of high relevance to Head Start, however, is the lesson from these long-term studies that psychometric indicators of cognitive ability and achievement are insufficient to capture the benefits that accrue to children and society from participation in early intervention. At a minimum, they need to be supplemented by credible, face-valid indicators of success in school (e.g., special education placements, absenteeism, graduation rates) and in later phases of life (e.g., teenage pregnancy rates, criminal behavior). The value of cost-benefit analyses as a highly policy-relevant vehicle for demonstrating program effects is an additional legacy of the model programs.

The stark contrast between the relatively stringent tests of long-term efficacy to which programs such as the Perry Preschool Project have been subjected and the lack of comparable, recent evidence on Head Start was partially responsible for resurfacing a serious discussion of a major Head Start evaluation in the early 1990s. The first Bush Administration convened an Advisory Panel for the Head Start Evaluation Design Project, which came to be known as the Blueprint Committee, to recommend a design for a major Head Start evaluation (U.S. Department of Health and Human Services [DHHS], 1990). The experienced researchers and administrators who comprised the advisory committee quickly dismissed the possibility of another summative study of Head Start's effectiveness akin to the Westinghouse study. This significant departure from an omnibus, long-term assessment of Head Start graduates was prompted by the committee's assessment of the contemporary realities of Head Start (White & Phillips, 2001). These realities included the following: 1) There is no one Head Start program and no solid guarantee that what is true for one is true for another; 2) only a limited number of instruments are available for use in large-scale studies and they bypass many of the legitimate and important goals of Head Start; 3) the multiple audiences for the results of Head Start evaluations, ranging from federal legislators to Head Start parents, require different kinds of information obtained in a variety of ways from a variety of sources.

The committee reached consensus that, in this context, an accurate understanding of whether and how Head Start works would involve estimation and a reconstructive process of gathering and synthesizing evidence from a range of studies. Accordingly, its members proposed the establishment of a program of studies that would systematically explore the effects of various components of Head Start's program for the multiple cultural groups and special populations being served. They further asserted two guiding questions for this program of research:

1. Which Head Start practices maximize benefits for children and families with different characteristics under what types of circumstances?

2. How are gains sustained for children and families after the Head Start experience?

The committee made a persuasive case that up-down questions about whether Head Start works (that potentially would lead to more or less funding for the program) needed to be replaced with questions focused on mechanisms of immediate and sustained change that can inform program improvement efforts. At the time, this was a significant paradigm shift from an emphasis on linking outcomes to a program to one of explaining patterns and sources of outcomes in the context of program variation. As we shall see, it convinced some but not all of those with vested interests in documenting what Head Start does and does not accomplish. Moreover, to implement the vision of the Blueprint Committee and generate a truly cumulative account of what has been and needs to be learned would require both a level of reflective planning and receptivity to results that suggest needs for change that have not traditionally been prominent in the organization of Head Start's research.

The report was, however, taken seriously by the Administration and the research field. In 1993, its fundamental message regarding the need to strengthen and lend coherence to research on Head Start was reiterated by yet another advisory committee established by the Clinton Administration that focused on issues of quality and expansion (DHHS, 1993). The 1990s were, in fact, a time of reinvigorated research on Head Start, combined with a variety of quality improvement and expansion initiatives, the most significant of which were the establishment and evaluation of Early Head Start, the initiation of a longitudinal survey of more than 3,000 Head Start families (the Family and Child Experiences Survey [FACES]) to provide descriptions of what children and their families experienced and achieved as a result of participating in Head Start, the funding of four Head Start Quality Research Centers, and the initiation of a biennial series of Head Start research conferences that is creating a community of researchers with some depth of knowledge about Head Start's activities and effects.

Alongside these department-sponsored activities, a variety of research activities grew up and added to the accumulating knowledge about Head Start. They involve both secondary data analysis and major new data collection. For example, child care surveys documented the generally higher quality of Head Start programs as compared with community-based child care (Phillips, Voran, Kisker, Howes, & Whitebook, 1994), which is now being confirmed by the FACES data (Resnick & Zill, 1999). Data from the National Longitudinal Survey of Youth documented large gains in cognitive test scores and greater access to preventive health services for white and African American children who attended Head Start over their siblings who did not, as well as sustained gains for the white children (Currie & Thomas, 1995, 1999). The Early Childhood Longitudinal Survey, funded primarily by the U.S. Department of Education, provides information on children who had been in Head Start at some point (kindergarten cohort) as well as on children who attend Head Start (birth cohort), in the context of nationally representative samples.

Despite all of this activity, Head Start remained vulnerable to prominent criticisms from the General Accounting Office (USGAO; 1997, 1998), key congressional staff (Haskins, 1989), and conservative think tanks (Hood, 1992; Olsen, 1999) that the program lacked a rigorous evaluation of its effectiveness. The prevailing climate of concern about outcomes and accountability across all government programs compounded perceptions that Head Start could no longer enjoy its exempt status from such an evaluation, the Blueprint Committee report notwithstanding.

Perhaps inevitably, the Head Start Amendments of 1998 re-ignited the discussion of a national evaluation of Head Start's impact. They called on the Secretary of Health and Human Services to appoint members to an Advisory Panel on Head Start Research and Evaluation, which met three times between April and July 1999. The debates among the panel members were reminiscent of those that characterized the Blueprint Committee and have preoccupied the early intervention evaluation community for at least 2 decades. They revolve around the big questions of what is appropriate and what is feasible and the tensions that arise at the intersection of these two issues:

- How can a balance be achieved between the need for a rigorous and credible evaluation design that will support firm causal conclusions (which would require random assignment) and the ethical issues involved in assigning children to a control group that receives no Head Start services?

- By what outcomes, and with what measures, should Head Start's effectiveness be judged?

- How can an evaluation of Head Start take into account the program-by-program variation in structure, staffing, populations served, and community contexts, while also generating results that can be generalized to the national Head Start program?

- What incentives are needed to assure program and family participation over time?

There were also some relatively new issues that had to be considered:

- How does the dramatic expansion of other child care and early childhood alternatives affect the feasibility of a randomized study design?

- How can the effects of Head Start be isolated from the effects of other early care and education programs simultaneously used by a sizeable share of enrolled children?

- How does the potential effect of Head Start on broader community child care services affect the credibility of a random assignment design?

The answers to these questions are a moving target, and those provided by the 1998 Advisory Group departed in some major ways from those of its predecessor advisory groups. Most notably, the panel recommended a national analysis of the impact of Head Start programs rather than an array of conceptually inter-connected research activities. Moreover, a hard-won consensus was reached that the analysis should rely on an experimental, longitudinal evaluation of children randomly assigned to Head Start or not Head Start and focus on program impacts on school readiness, broadly conceived. The Congressionally mandated National Head Start Impact study, with data collection ongoing through 2006, is the realization of these recommendations.

In between the advisory groups of the early 1990s and the 1998 panel, the Department of Health and Human Services funded the National Academy of Sciences to convene a Roundtable on Head Start Research. Its charge was substantially broader than those of the groups that bracketed it chronologically, namely to hold a series of discussions of new possibilities and new directions for Head Start research. It was the hope of the Department that the Roundtable would consider how research on Head Start could be better informed by and integrated into the broader repertoire of research on young children, families, and communities; address a series of carefully selected themes; and anticipate new and emerging issues that arise from the changing context of Head Start. We now turn to a discussion of this broader research agenda in which we summarize the report on the first four of the nine Roundtable meetings (National Research Council, 1996) and then discuss the substance of the five remaining meetings.

ROUNDTABLE ON HEAD START RESEARCH

The purpose of the Roundtable was to provide a systematic analysis of research needs relevant to the changing context that Head Start faces as it moves into its fourth decade. This context includes significant changes in the circumstances and expectations of families living in poverty, the growing scientific management of domestic programs, increasing recognition of the mental health needs of young children, a rapidly shifting landscape of child care and early education programs, the increasing ethnic and linguistic diversity of the early childhood population, and significant developments in the larger body of social science research that surrounds Head Start.

Members of the Roundtable on Head Start Research were drawn from government positions, universities, the medical field, Head Start organizations, family support programs, and private foundations. Collectively, they brought to the table many years of experience with Head Start, research, government, and program management. Each meeting involved the participation of additional researchers, practitioners, and policy makers who greatly expanded the expertise on which the Roundtable could draw as it considered its agenda. The Roundtable addressed itself to a series of questions about Head Start as a program, about the circumstances of the families it serves, and about state-of-the-art behavioral and social science research. Throughout its deliberations, the members of the Roundtable recognized that Head Start would face some difficult trade-offs in the years ahead and that its need for relevant data to guide future deliberations concerning the goals and scope of this long-standing, national intervention program was extremely pressing.

Research on Head Start's Families

The Roundtable's initial focus was guided by the Administration on Children, Youth and Families' conviction that research on Head Start had not given adequate attention to the program's family related services and outcomes. In response, the Roundtable's first set of deliberations considered research that takes Head Start families as the unit of analysis and explicitly addresses Head Start in the context of family and community life. The research needs that were discussed ranged from important descriptive work that captures the real lives of children and families in Head Start and oral histories that bring to life parents' own stories about how Head Start assisted their families to randomized trials of program variation.

A set of general issues regarding how to approach research on Head Start families, as well as more specific topics that warrant scientific study, emerged from the discussions. The general issues included recognition that

- The relationship between Head Start and its families is reciprocal. It is important to understand not only the ways in which parents change over the course of their involvement with Head Start but also the ways in which Head Start adapts to meet the needs of its population. Mutual adaptation between families and programs is the process of interest.

- The family–Head Start relationship takes many forms and evolves over time; it is best approached as a process rather than a discrete set of activities that operates as inputs to parent and child outcomes. As such, efforts to describe how Head Start relates to, involves, and motivates family members need to capture families' natural progressions into, through, and beyond Head Start.

- Although the primary caregiver at home is the pivotal connection to the family, the consequences of any family's encounter with Head Start extend beyond those who are directly involved, to other members of the family and the kinship and fictive kin networks in which many Head Start families are embedded.

- Given that families enter Head Start with vastly different capacities, needs, and orientations toward parent involvement, any effort to assess the effects of their engagement with the program needs to focus on trajectories of change and incremental improvements rather than outcomes measured only at a preset end point and compared with preset benchmarks. The parent who overcomes debilitating levels of depression as a result of involvement with Head Start has achieved as much as the parent who gets and keeps a paid job.

Turning to the question of "what to study," the Roundtable discussions identified three broad areas of inquiry that have not been adequately explored by research on Head Start yet have profound implications for the program and for efforts to assess its effects:

1. The challenges and opportunities posed to Head Start by the increasing ethnic, immigrant status, and linguistic diversity of the families it serves.

2. The need to embed research on Head Start within its community context, paying specific attention to the effects on Head Start and its families of violent environments.

3. The implications of the changing economic landscape and the structure of income support policies for the poor for how Head Start works with families and what it means to offer families a high-quality program.

Despite the relative inattention granted these issues by research on Head Start, the many Head Start program directors and state and local officials who became involved with the Roundtable testified to the remarkable innovations that local programs are developing to address them. This led to extensive discussions of how the wealth of information generated by these innovative programs can be more widely shared across the Head Start and early childhood community.

Recognizing the Diversity of Children and Families in Head Start   Head Start offers a natural laboratory for the study of issues that lie at the intersection of multiculturalism and development, particularly with regard to ethnicity, language, and immigration. The ethnic diversity of Head Start classrooms is well recognized. Less well known is the fact that close to three quarters of Head Start classrooms have enrollments characterized by two to three different languages (see DHHS, 2000). Moreover, Head Start is affected by the dramatic growth in first- and second-generation immigrant children well before these children enter the public schools and, in this sense, provides a harbinger of future trends affecting our nation's educational system. This affords the opportunity to study issues such as the following:

- How does the language of instruction and interactions between language learning and content learning affect young children's knowledge acquisition and first- and second-language development?

- How does language affect social interactions in Head Start? For example, how does the language mix of the children affect the social experiences of children from different linguistic groups?

- How do parents' own educational experiences shape their views of how children get ready for school and their efforts to prepare them?

- How does the immigration experience affect the needs of Head Start families and their willingness to enroll in Head Start?

- What are the implications for Head Start of the residential and economic unpredictability that characterizes the lives of migrant families?

- How do Head Start programs adjust to the shifting demographics of families served?

The Community Context of Head Start   Head Start is unique as an intervention of national scope that is carefully tailored to the needs of each local community in which it operates programs. Head Start has brought tremendous resources and vitality to the communities it serves; its effectiveness, in turn, is partly dependent on the range of services and resources that surround it. These not only include child-focused early childhood services but also the local school system; state programs; and the adult educational, training, health, and mental health systems available to parents and Head Start staff. At the same time, the United States is in the midst of both significant reform efforts—in education, health care, and social services—and significant upheaval affecting both urban and rural areas that hold major, but unclear, implications for the community contexts of Head Start in the years ahead. Pressing questions for research include the following:

- How do Head Start families' relations to other specialized services and community institutions either interfere with or contribute to Head Start's efforts to improve family well-being?

- How does involvement with Head Start affect parents' capacity to mobilize other community resources for their children?

- How do differing constellations of community resources affect what Head Start is able to offer families, how well it provides these services, and, ultimately, its effects on children and families?

- How does the presence of Head Start in a community affect the availability and quality of local resources and community institutions?

- With what prevalence and chronicity are children and staff in Head Start exposed to community and domestic violence, and what are the effects on program operations?

- What is the potential role of Head Start as a locus for violence prevention efforts? Throughout these discussions, the Roundtable members asserted that these are, in fact, community-level research issues that may be most appropriately studied at this broader level with questions about "What is and should Head Start be doing?" addressed by embedded studies.

The Changing Economic Landscape of Head Start Families   Three issues surrounding Head Start's role in the economic dimensions of poor families' lives—as employer, a site for job training, and a source of care for the children of working parents— surfaced repeatedly at the Roundtable meetings. As welfare reform affects a growing share of Head Start–eligible families, pressures on the program to articulate its relation not only to parents' childrearing responsibilities but also to their responsibilities (and requirements) to prepare for and sustain paid employment will mount. Among the issues this raises for research are

- How does Head Start affect parents' employment opportunities and career and earning trajectories, both for parents previously employed by Head Start and those who are following other routes into the labor market?

- What are effective strategies for providing for the full-time, full-year care needs of a growing share of Head Start families?

- How do parent literacy and job training initiatives within Head Start interact with the program's child development activities to affect families and children?

- How do Head Start's parent involvement strategies need to be adjusted to address the new work-related demands that characterize low-income parents' lives, as well as their motivation and capacity to get involved? How can these strategies be extended to other family members?

- Recognizing that a growing share of Head Start parents may need to rely on supplemental care arrangements, how do children's full spectrum of care arrangements interact to affect their development?

Diffusion of Local Innovation Throughout the presentations and discussions of family level research on Head Start, the Roundtable members were impressed by the high level of local innovation that characterizes Head Start's efforts to, for example, involve parents, engage fathers, address community violence, provide family literacy programs, teach in the context of multilingual classrooms, and link with other community services. They were concerned, however, about the dearth of opportunities for sharing the insights gained from innovative practices within the Head Start and early childhood service sectors. This led the Roundtable members to urge Head Start's administrators and researchers involved with the program to consider how the research community might assist with understanding the process of local innovation within Head Start and extending this experience to other programs.

Although research on Head Start is often cast in terms of its public accountability role, namely to document the activities and effects of the programs, it can also play an extremely useful role as a tool that program directors and staff can use to understand and modify their own practices. Although far from an easy task, efforts to understand what enables programs to be innovative and entrepreneurial, what would enable them to harvest and share their effective strategies and lessons learned with their colleagues in other programs, and what obstacles exist to the transfer of local innovation would be an extremely valuable addition to the portfolio of research on Head Start and to its role as a national laboratory.

Beyond Research on Head Start's Families

Following its discussions of research on Head Start's families, the Roundtable turned its attention to other priorities for future research on Head Start. Indeed, the Roundtable members were far more comfortable considering family level issues jointly with child-level issues, rather than as a discrete domain of inquiry. Along these lines, a salient theme concerned the paucity of available data on whether and how early childhood programs can affect family and parenting processes to a sufficient degree to produce measurable, positive impacts on children. The Roundtable members were surprised to discover that this complete chain of events has rarely been studied and urged those who study Head Start to embark on research that addresses this basic premise underlying early childhood intervention.

Many other topics also surfaced as deserving of support. Particularly prominent, as defined by both the researchers and practitioners on the Roundtable, were topics associated with new possibilities within Head Start for studying mental health issues, early pedagogy, and the new landscape of early childhood funding. These Roundtable discussions highlighted

- The profound influence that maternal mental health problems, such as depression, personality disorders, and substance abuse, can have on children's development and, relatedly, the importance of considering these aspects of the family context when assessing Head Start's effects on children. In general, as research on child care has amply demonstrated, it is unwise to consider "effects" of Head Start without simultaneous assessment and consideration of the developmental effects of children's home environments. The critical questions then become: How does the home environment interact with the Head Start environment to foster or undermine early development? How do caregiver–child interactions across environments affect development?

- The critical need for epidemiological research that assesses needs for and use of mental health services among the Head Start population and the need to identify effective models for linking Head Start to mental health services and professionals. A two-generation approach to these questions would be particularly useful, as would the inclusion of a component focused on the measurement of mental health problems within the Head Start population.

- The value of experimenting with Head Start-based interventions focused on, for example, children with a history of prenatal substance exposure, to ascertain the benefits of specialized versus more generic intervention strategies.

- The importance of assessing barriers at multiple system levels to inclusion of young children with developmental delays in Head Start, designing strategies for overcoming such barriers, and examining their effects. A related and important objective for research involves examining the multiple forces that influence service utilization patterns among families of children with disabilities, including utilization of Head Start, ranging from family ideology to patterns of health insurance coverage.

- The opportunity presented by Head Start to explore the difficult issues posed by integrating indigenous, nonprofessional, and professional (some of who may be from the served population) staff within a program, as well as relying on community-based professionals and paraprofessionals. With regard to a range of child outcomes, what staffing composition and structures are most beneficial for children? How can the economic well-being of indigenous staff be promoted within this context? Most generally, what are the pros and cons of different approaches given the family circumstances that confront Head Start today?

- The need to reassess, in light of new knowledge about early learning and pedagogy, the types of curricula that are most effective with children in Head Start. Is the High/Scope model appropriate for all children? How can new knowledge about early literacy and numeracy be incorporated into the Head Start curriculum? What are the implications for staff development?

- How can Head Start contribute to the computer literacy of its children and families? How can computers be more effectively used in Head Start classrooms? How can Internet technology be used more effectively to advance the goals of Head Start, including those of program collaboration, community outreach, and transfer of innovative practices? Again, what are the implications for staff development?

- The importance of conducting cost-benefit analyses of Head Start given the burden of proof now being placed on the program regarding its relatively high costs when compared with other community-based early childhood programs.

- The need to consider the implications of growing trends toward blending funding and merging programs at the local level for efforts to evaluate the discrete effects of Head Start and, more generally, for efforts to study the effects of early childhood programs on child development and family well-being. The discussion emphasized the need to design research that considers Head Start in the broader context of other early care and education programs in the same community.

Circling around and through discussions of these specific topics, the Roundtable grappled with a set of enduring, overarching issues: By what indicators should we assess Head Start given new advances in developmental psychology? How can Head Start contribute to reducing the gap between researchers and practitioners? What would it take to mount the research agenda that the Roundtable has proposed?

Assessing Head Start's Accomplishments   The task of assessing Head Start confronts a series of difficult and intertwined questions: By what criteria should Head Start be judged? Who should define these criteria? How far into the future should the program be held accountable for its graduates' outcomes? Toward which audiences should we be directing our efforts to understand what Head Start does and what it accomplishes?

One entire meeting of the Roundtable was devoted to the assessment of preschool outcomes. It was motivated by the members' keen recognition that there has been substantial growth in knowledge about early child development and the field's capability to assess child outcomes, much of which has not been translated for use by those who study social programs such as Head Start. This taps into the more general need to integrate basic research aimed at understanding developmental processes with intervention and policy research designed to influence developmental outcomes (Shonkoff & Phillips, 2000).

The Roundtable's discussions of these issues emphasized new possibilities for studying social and emotional development (e.g., assessment of peer acceptance and friendship as distinct aspects of social relationships, knowledge of social problem-solving strategies, motivational aspects of early learning, the ability to self-regulate one's emotions and behavior); the continuing need to apply new knowledge about assessing early literacy and numeracy; the importance of including behavioral observations as part of assessment toolboxes; the value of integrating assessment and intervention; and the still poorly addressed need to develop valid approaches for assessing children for whom English is not their first language, children from different cultural backgrounds, and children with disabilities. This discussion was cast, in part, in the context of growing knowledge about the important opportunities that early childhood programs provide for early detection of problems, as well as the many dilemmas that confront such efforts—not the least of which is the difficulty of distinguishing maturational delays from temporary lags from more serious and enduring developmental problems during the early childhood years. The Roundtable members were also cognizant of the fact there is still no consensus about what outcomes Head Start should be held accountable for beyond some vague agreement that they should encompass all facets of development. These include outcomes that are easily and directly measured, such as health and nutritional status, which should not be lost in the search for state-of-the-art assessments of social and cognitive outcomes.

The time frame of data collection on Head Start has generated substantial controversy, with some arguing that the investments in Head Start are warranted only to the extent that the program demonstrates effects well into the school-age years and others cautioning that Head Start cannot be held accountable for outcomes that are profoundly affected by the school environments that Head Start graduates encounter after they leave the program. Although the Roundtable did not delve into this issue in depth, there was widespread interest in enabling Head Start programs to collect a small set of highly face-valid measures of how their graduates are doing in kindergarten. This was viewed as one important mechanism for providing program directors with real-time feedback about the success with which they were preparing children for formal schooling.

Alongside these discussions of state-of-the-art child assessment, the members of the Roundtable repeatedly noted that Head Start is a well-known program about which public understanding remains shallow (National Research Council, 1996). The public at large is not familiar with what Head Start is or does, despite the program's widespread popularity. In this context, an important role for research is to inject some realism into public opinion, to inform the public about what Head Start is and what it does, as well as about what it can and cannot do. Relevant research consists not only (and perhaps not primarily) of rigorous program evaluations but also descriptive studies of what children and families experience in Head Start, oral histories from Head Start graduates, and qualitative studies of the conditions that surround and affect the efforts of Head Start staff to improve the life chances of the children they serve.

Narrowing the Researcher–Practitioner Gap   The longstanding gulf between researchers and practitioners was a theme that surfaced repeatedly at the Roundtable meetings. At every step in the research process, from defining the research agenda to applying research findings to program improvement, the researcher–practitioner relationship plays a critical role in both the validity and utility of the data that are generated. Although this gulf has been the subject of ample discussion, little has been done to build solid bridges between the research and practitioner communities.

The Roundtable felt strongly that the time has come to develop a strategic plan addressing this issue within a general research agenda for Head Start. As part of developing this plan, it will be essential to address prevailing perceptions that conducting research is antithetical, rather than integral, to serving children. Related to this is the need to provide Head Start staff with a more differentiated view of research. Although summative research can lead staff to feel evaluated and judged, qualitative and process research is inherently more user-friendly and readily adapted to the questions that are at the forefront of practitioners' concerns. Among the strategic proposals offered by the Roundtable members were the following:

- Establish ongoing forums for Head Start directors to receive training in how to read research data, interpret results, and apply them to their programs

- Provide feedback to individual programs based on their required self-assessments

- Experiment with a set of special projects that support targeted collaborations between researchers and practitioners (e.g., to develop face-valid outcome measures that can be used to follow Head Start children into kindergarten, to compare staff and researcher perceptions of the key ingredients of quality care)

- Sponsor 2-week workshops in which practitioners are introduced to the current literature on child development similar to those previously held at the University of Minnesota

- Provide greater support for practitioners to attend the Head Start Research Conferences and for researchers to become more engaged with the programs of the National Head Start Association

- Establish a program of field-initiated research that, as with the University–Head Start Partnerships, requires that researchers team up with practitioners in all phases of the proposed research project

- Connect local Head Start programs with a local researcher who becomes part of the Head Start staff team

- Support studies of research utilization by practitioners

These suggestions, in turn, have important implications for the existing technology and technical assistance program of the Administration on Children, Youth and Families.

Mounting the Agenda The Roundtable members were acutely aware of the fact that the current infrastructure supporting Head Start research is not adequate for mounting the far-reaching agenda that it developed over the course of its nine meetings. At their final meeting, they addressed the following issues: 1) What would it take? 2) Which parts of the agenda fall under Head Start's jurisdiction and what territory should be covered by others in the field? and 3) What needs to be done to sustain and extend the investments that are made in Head Start research? Their answers touched on interagency collaboration, data archiving, and the need for a stable capacity for the integrative, objective, and reflective discussions of the growing body of research on and relevant to Head Start that the Roundtable had provided.

The Roundtable members called for new forms of research organization that would build capacity for funding, guiding, assembling, and applying research on Head Start. Among the important elements were the establishment of a Head Start data archive with specific support for training and dissemination to encourage secondary data analysis and data synthesis activities; a mechanism to continuously assemble knowledge, identify new gaps, and, in general, ensure that research on Head Start is cumulative and progressive over time; efforts to facilitate interagency and public–private collaboration around the Head Start research enterprise, such as the Early Childhood Research Working Group (which periodically convenes representatives from about 30 federal agencies); specific initiatives aimed at encouraging local participation and local initiation of research activities; and the development of new capacities for dissemination of research-based knowledge about Head Start to a wider array of audiences, including the public, Head Start directors, and educators. As part of building this capacity, it will be important to consider how the vision that Head Start is developing is relevant to all low-income children and to the ever-widening spectrum of early childhood programs. The broader question of whether to invest resources in a separate infrastructure for research on Head Start or in an infrastructure that is more broadly construed (e.g., early childhood research, early intervention research) within which Head Start plays a prominent role was also debated with sound arguments for both possibilities.

CONCLUDING THOUGHTS

Situated in a book about the many debates that have surrounded Head Start, this chapter has focused on the research enterprise that has fostered both support for and criticism of the program. As we noted at the outset, the relation between Head Start and research has been and continues to be both highly salient and somewhat awkward. A sizeable share of research on the program is funded by the agency that administers it and, understandably, seeks evidence that they are doing the right thing. Increasingly, however, new pressures are bearing on this enterprise. The nation's decision makers have demanded that Head Start be subjected to a rigorous, objective, summative evaluation, which is now moving forward alongside an ongoing evaluation of the Early Head Start program. The practitioner community is seeking a stronger voice in decision-making about the focus, design, and uses of research on Head Start. They are responding to the growing demands being placed on them to collect data and accommodate broader research endeavors. Head Start program directors, in particular, are seeking new mechanisms for learning from the innovative strategies being tested by their colleagues in other communities around the country. The program itself is now surrounded by a growing array of early childhood programs, as well as by highly demanding family circumstances, leaving it vulnerable to those who ask, What is the value-added of Head Start over and above the other services now being provided to low-income families and their children? And, the number and variety of scientists and research funders who are now involved with the program has grown substantially, thus expanding the types of questions that are being posed and the range of methods that is considered appropriate for efforts to understand and evaluate Head Start.

Considering what research on Head Start ought to look like and aim to accomplish in this context is a daunting task that has been considered by a number of highly qualified advisory groups. This chapter emphasizes the work of the Roundtable on Head Start Research given that its discussions have not been widely disseminated. Its members discussed a wide range of issues that the emerging contingencies that surround Head Start raise for scientific inquiry. Perhaps its more enduring legacy, however, is the issues it raised regarding the infrastructure for research on Head Start, including:

- Its capacity for organizing research that generates a cumulative record of knowledge about the program

- Testing new strategies for fostering scientist–practitioner collaborations as a norm for research on Head Start

- Extending investments in Head Start research through data archiving and secondary data analyses

- Continuously moving back and forth between what we are learning about Head Start and what we expect the program to accomplish

- Integrating research on Head Start within the broader disciplinary research that is pertinent to the program

- Ensuring that lessons learned from local innovations are widely dispersed throughout the Head Start community

Only when a serious effort to address these profoundly challenging issues is mounted will the potential to advance the many important recommendations of the various advisory groups on Head Start research be fully realized.

REFERENCES

Brooks-Gunn, J., Berlin, L.J., & Fuligni, A.S. (2000). Early childhood intervention programs: What about the family? In J.P. Shonkoff & S.J. Meisels (Eds.), *Handbook of early childhood intervention* (2nd ed., pp. 549–588). New York: Cambridge University Press.

Campbell, F.A., & Ramey, C. (1994). Effects of early intervention on intellectual and academic achievement: A follow-up study of children from low-income families. *Child Development, 65,* 684–698.

Campbell, F.A., & Ramey, C. (1995). Cognitive and school outcomes for high risk African-American students at middle adolescence: Positive effects of early intervention. *American Educational Research Journal, 32,* 743–772.

Currie, J., & Thomas, D. (1995). Does Head Start make a difference? *American Economic Review, 85*(3), 341–364.

Currie, J., & Thomas, D. (1999). Does Head Start help Hispanic children? *Journal of Public Economics, 74,* 235–262.

Currie, J., & Thomas, D. (2000). School quality and the longer-term effects of Head Start. *Journal of Human Resources, 35,* 755–774.

Farran, D.C. (2000). Another decade of intervention for disadvantaged and disabled children: What do we know now? In J.P. Shonkoff & S.J. Meisels (Eds.), *Handbook of early childhood intervention* (2nd ed., pp. 510–548). New York: Cambridge University Press.

Haskins, R. (1989). Beyond metaphor: The efficacy of early childhood education. *American Psychologist, 44,* 274–282.

Hood, J. (1992, December). Caveat emptor: The Head Start scam. *Policy Analysis, 187.* Washington, DC: Cato Institute.

Lazar, I., & Darlington, R. (1982). Lasting effects of early education: A report from the Consortium for Longitudinal Studies. *Monographs of the Society for Research in Child Development, 47*(2–3, Serial No. 195).

Malakoff, M.E., Underhill, J.M., & Zigler, E. (1998). The effect of inner-city environments and Head Start experience on effectance motivation. *American Journal of Orthopsychiatry, 68,* 630–638.

National Research Council. (1996). *Beyond the blueprint: Directions for research on Head Start's families.* Washington, DC: National Academy Press.

Olsen, D.A. (1999, February 9). Universal preschool is no golden ticket: Why government should not enter the preschool business. *Policy Analysis No. 333.* Washington, DC: Cato Institute.

Phillips, D., Voran, M., Kisker, E., Howes, C., & Whitebook, M. (1994). Child care for children in poverty: Opportunity or inequity? *Child Development, 65,* 472–492.

Raver, C.C., & Zigler, E. (1997). Social competence: An untapped dimension in evaluating Head Start's success. *Early Childhood Research Quarterly, 12,* 363–385.

Resnick, G., & Zill, N. (1999, April). *Is Head Start providing high-quality educational services? Unpacking classroom processes.* Paper presented at the biennial meeting of the Society for Research in Child Development, Albuquerque, New Mexico.

Schweinhart, L., Barnes, H., & Weikart, D. (1993). *Significant benefits: The High/Scope Perry Preschool study through age 27.* Monographs of the High/Scope Educational Research Foundation, Number 10. Ypsilanti, MI: High/Scope Press.

Shonkoff, J., & Phillips, D. (Eds.). (2000). *From neurons to neighborhoods: The science of early childhood development.* Washington, DC: National Academy Press.

U.S. Department of Health and Human Services (DHHS). (1990, September). *Head Start research and evaluation: A blueprint for the future. Recommendations of the Advisory Panel for the Head Start Evaluation Design Project* (DHHS publication no. ACY 91–31195). Washington, DC: U.S. Government Printing Office.

U.S. Department of Health and Human Services (DHHS). (1993, December). *Creating a 21st century Head Start: Final report of the Advisory Committee on Head Start Quality and Expansion.* Washington, DC: U.S. Government Printing Office.

U.S. Department of Health and Human Services (DHHS). (2000, April). *Celebrating cultural and linguistic diversity in Head Start.* Washington, DC: Author.

U.S. General Accounting Office (USGAO). (1997). *Head Start: Research provides little information on impact of current program.* Washington, DC: Author.

U.S. General Accounting Office (USGAO). (1998). *Head Start: Challenges in monitoring program quality and demonstrating results.* Washington, DC: Author.

Vernon-Feagans, L. (1996). *Children's talk in communities and classrooms.* Cambridge, MA: Blackwell.

Westinghouse Learning Corporation. (1969, June). *The impact of Head Start: An evaluation of the effects of Head Start on children's cognitive and affective development. Executive Summary.* Ohio University Report to the Office of Economic Opportunity. Washington, DC: Clearinghouse for Federal Scientific and Technical Information (ED036321).

White, S.H. (1971). The National Impact Study of Head Start. In J. Hellmuth (Ed.), *The disadvantaged child* (Vol. 3). New York: Brunner/Mazel.

White, S.H., & Phillips, D.A. (2001). Designing Head Start: Roles played by developmental psychologist. In D.L. Featherman & M. Vinoskis (Eds.), *Social science and policy making: A search for relevance in the twentieth century* (pp. 83–118). Ann Arbor: University of Michigan Press.

Yoshikawa, H. (1995). Long-term effects of early childhood programs on social outcomes and delinquency. *The Future of Children, 5*(3), 51–75.

Zigler, E., & Freedman, J. (1987). Early experience, malleability, and Head Start. In J.J. Gallagher & C.T. Ramey (Eds.), *The malleability of children* (pp. 85–95). Baltimore: Paul H. Brookes Publishing Co.

Zigler, E., & Styfco, S.J. (1994). Is the Perry Preschool better than Head Start? Yes and no. *Early Childhood Research Quarterly, 9,* 269–287.

Zigler, E., & Trickett, P.K. (1978). IQ, social competence, and evaluation of early childhood intervention programs. *American Psychologist, 33,* 789–798.

DEBATE III

The Future of Head Start

Emanating from the different ideas about what Head Start should be and how successful it is are vastly different ideas about its future direction. We have grouped these timeless debates into five broad categories: quality improvements, child care services, expanded access, the timing of intervention (with a subcategory on early brain development), and program administration. We end the volume with two divergent models for the future.

While **quality** in Head Start has always been uneven, the problem came to the forefront around 1990 when significant program expansion began. The ensuing decade brought an unfamiliar flurry of legislation aimed at improving Head Start. Joan Lombardi and Amy Cubbage detail the political backdrop and successive laws targeting service quality, noting areas they believe require future attention. Gregg Powell describes the historical erosion of program quality and the policy shifts to investment and enforcement that he finds have produced significant enhancements. He also details the National Head Start Association's system of recognition for program excellence, showing both the potential and pitfalls of implementing quality initiatives in the field. A less optimistic view is taken by Judith Chafel and Heather Sugioka. They examine the results of legislative efforts to improve quality, finding many instances of progress but also many weaknesses and unresolved issues. All three of these chapters spotlight staff qualifications and training as critical to quality improvements in all aspects of the program. Much has been written elsewhere about the need for credentialed Head Start teachers. Here, Arthur Frankel looks at quality in the social work component, emphasizing the two-way barriers to employment of professional social workers in Head Start that, unlike the other quality issues addressed in this section, are not as amenable to legislative solutions.

The need for **child care** services has mushroomed for families eligible for Head Start. Time limits on welfare assistance and strict work requirements have proven incompatible with Head Start's traditional half-day, part-year schedule and focus on active parent involvement. Helen Blank and Nicole Poersch describe innovative collaborations and partnerships between Head Start and local child care providers that allow for longer hours of service and enhanced quality of available care. Douglas Besharov counters that the research evidence is weak regarding the effectiveness of quality child care and early childhood education programs. He argues that Head Start and other intervention efforts are too expensive for the benefits they provide and suggests that there are more cost-effective ways to support low-income parents with their child care needs.

Head Start has never been funded to serve more than about half of the eligible children, so concerns about **expanded access** have long been voiced. John Merrow goes so far as to call Head Start a "failure" because its successes have been limited to a small part of its target population. Gwen Morgan goes a step further, detailing the need for quality early education experiences for all children and explaining the changes in policy and infrastructure needed to create a universal system.

Arguments about the **timing of intervention** (both when and for how long programs should be offered) surfaced shortly after Head Start began. Some observers think the program comes too late to benefit children who have already lived their 3 or 4 years on earth in poverty; others say it comes too soon. Amidst popular hopes that a brief preschool program could boost children's performance all the way through their academic careers, others believe that intervention must last much longer. Arthur Reynolds examines findings on the optimal timing and duration of program participation and enumerates what is known and what needs to be learned about pathways through which intervention can produce long-term benefits. Sharon Ramey, Craig Ramey, and Robin Lanzi look at the importance of services during the early elementary school years, reporting the results of the Head Start Transition demonstration project. They find that program or not, school and families working together can raise the academic performance of children at least through third grade—one of the very few studies in which Head Start graduates score at national norms. Sheila Kamerman and Alfred Kahn find the Head Start model inappropriate for the circumstances of today's families and incompatible with the coming reality of universal prekindergarten. They offer compelling arguments that the program should refocus its efforts on a combined Early Head Start-Family Support intervention for infants, toddlers, and their families.

The Kamerman and Kahn chapter is a segue into a subset of the debate about the timing of intervention, namely early brain development. John Bruer argues that the scientific evidence is neither completely new nor strong enough to support social policies favoring early intervention. Paul Lombroso and Kyle Pruett examine medical research on the nature-nurture controversy and on critical periods and conclude that experiences during the early years of life are critically—but not exclusively—important to the course of human development. Finally, we present portions of Edward Zigler's classic paper, *The Environmental Mystique.* Although written during an earlier era when there were irrational beliefs in the power of the environment and plasticity of intelligence, his thesis is relevant to today's fixation on early brain development.

Head Start's **administration** is unique among federal social service programs. Federal dollars flow directly to local grantees, bypassing state governments. The arrangement made sense during the War on Poverty years but was nonetheless controversial and remains so. Wade Horn makes the case for devolving Head Start's funding mechanism to the states to allow more efficient coordination with other programs for low-income children and families. Sarah Greene explains why she believes moving Head Start to the states (or to the U.S. Department of Education) would compromise service quality, breadth, and support as well as program accountability. Walter Gilliam and Carol Ripple update their data on the implementation of prekindergartens in the states. Based on their findings that the states generally have not yet succeeded in delivering quality, comprehensive services to at-risk children, they argue against devolution at this time. Adapting an earlier article,

John Hood argues that Head Start's rationale and supporting evidence are weak, and that government should relinquish child care services to the private sector. Hood's position brings to light some common misconceptions, so with due respect to him, we use his views as a platform to contradict what has become common knowledge. We also counter his conclusion with our view that without strong, uniform standards like those governing Head Start, the private sector has generally done a poor job making quality early care and education available and affordable to all who need it.

We complete the debates with two very different **models for the future** of Head Start. Christopher Henrich relates Head Start's historical role as a national laboratory for the design and refinement of effective intervention services. He sees this work as integral to and definitive of the program's future direction and shape. Barbara Bowman takes a thoughtful look at the Head Start model in the context of the population and communities it serves today. She ponders each aspect of the model, setting aside the status quo and driving readers to rethink Head Start's goals and structure and to entertain new ways it can fulfill its vision.

—Edward Zigler and Sally J. Styfco

CHAPTER 19

Head Start in the 1990s

Striving for Quality
Through a Decade of Improvement

JOAN LOMBARDI AND AMY STEPHENS CUBBAGE

For more than 3 decades, Head Start programs have flourished from rural hillsides to city streets, from migrant communities to tribal lands. Yet, throughout Head Start's entire history, there have never been enough resources to reach the millions of children who need the service and, at the same time, protect the quality of the program. Through every phase of Head Start—from the initial start-up period in the mid-1960s, through the years of innovation in the 1970s, and into the "survival" and then "growth" period that characterized the 1980s and 1990s—there has been a debate over how best to expand the program while assuring quality.

Over the years, the focus has turned to improving the quality of Head Start only after a warning bell has sounded. The warnings have come in various forms, from evaluations to various reports requested from all levels of government. For example, during Edward Zigler's tenure as the first director of the Office of Child Development in the early 1970s, the first major Head Start research report, the Westinghouse evaluation, was released. The evaluation criteria were far too narrowly defined to adequately reflect the benefits of the program. While critical of the report, however, Zigler also took the opportunity to initiate a major quality surveillance plan (Zigler & Muenchow, 1992). The years that immediately followed were characterized as a period of improvement and innovation with the development of new programs options and the issuance of the first Head Start Performance Standards.

In 1980, as Head Start reached its 15th birthday, President Carter asked for a thorough review of the Head Start program. Dr. Zigler, who had been back at Yale for several years, agreed to lead the effort. This review seemed long overdue. Head Start funding had increased during the late 1970s; however, poverty persisted, families changed, and new challenges emerged. The 1980 report documented a number of quality issues (U.S. Department of Health and Human Services [DHHS], 1980). For example, class size had increased from 15 to 20 children, and overall expenditures per child in constant dollars had declined. With some exceptions, salaries for Head Start teachers were running about 25%–50% lower than those for comparable teaching positions. At the same time, DHHS regional office staff, charged with monitoring local programs, had declined by at least 25% percent since 1970.

The 1980 report also laid out an agenda for change including, among other recommendations, improvements in staff–child ratios and class size and assurances that at least one teacher in each class would have a Child Development Associate (CDA) credential. But a change in administrations got in the way. As the Reagan Administration took the helm in the early 1980s, the recommendations of the 1980 report were laid aside. As social services to the poor fell out of favor, advocates, inside and outside of government, moved to protect the basic program.

The early 1980s saw some limited growth in the program. Investments increased toward the later part of the 1980s, although the focus was primarily on expansion to serve more children, rather than on overall quality improvements. Over the years, Head Start training funds did not keep up with this expansion, with the percentage of the total budget dedicated to training and technical assistance decreasing throughout the 1980s. However, a number of important task force reports outlining a series of recommendations to improve education, parent involvement, social services, and health did surface during this period.

As the 25th anniversary of Head Start approached, pressures intensified to address the quality issues that had surfaced since Head Start's inception. Although earlier steps to improve and expand the program often had been taken by those within the government, by 1989, the Head Start community itself had assumed a strong leadership role. Head Start had been built on a core belief that promoted maximum participation by parents and community members. This philosophy bore fruit when Eugenia Boggus, a former Head Start parent herself, became President of the National Head Start Association (NHSA), taking an active interest in the direction of the program. In preparation for the historic anniversary, NHSA stepped up to the plate, demonstrating the courage to openly review the program. The Silver Ribbon Panel, convened in 1989, set in motion a decade of change that continues to have an impact today.

TURNING TOWARD QUALITY: THE HEAD START REAUTHORIZATION OF 1990

Head Start: The Nation's Pride, A Nation's Challenge, the report of the Silver Ribbon Panel (1990), set the agenda for the 1990 Head Start reauthorization. The panel consisted of leaders with expertise in Head Start and other early childhood programs, health services, policy, and business. The charge of the committee was to examine the key ingredients to program success and to explore how best to improve and expand services. During an intense 6-month period, the panel met to hear expert opinions and to review and discuss various task force reports and relevant policy documents. More than 70 witnesses testified at three hearings, and more than 1,400 Head Start parents and staff responded to opinion surveys. In addition, several national organizations provided input to the panel deliberations.

The panel report was organized around three key themes: ensuring quality in the provision of comprehensive services, expansion to meet the needs of changing families, and leadership to build a more coordinated system of services. The findings around quality, which were echoed throughout the decade, focused on the threats to program effectiveness. In hearings and in survey reports, the panel heard concerns about Head Start's ability to provide quality services, due to inadequate funding at a time when demands on the program were increasing. The report documented several challenges:

- Tight funding and pressure to increase enrollment threatened to weaken Head Start performance. Even with moderate inflation rates, funding per child in constant dollars had declined during the 1980s. The Head Start Bureau projected that the average federal cost per child in 1990 was $2,767, while public school costs averaged $3,456 per student. NHSA estimated the cost of Head Start should be at least $5,400.

- Local program directors reported that they were forced by financial pressures to increase efficiency through cost-cutting measures such as center consolidation, salary freezes, and reductions in services. Program administrators reported difficulty recruiting and retaining staff. Salaries were low and benefits limited. A 1988 survey found that almost half of the Head Start teachers that year earned less than $10,000 per year. The average annual beginning salary of a Head Start teacher with a bachelor's degree was $12,074, just 63% of what public school teachers were earning.

- Head Start training funds had not kept up with expansion. Moreover, the training network had suffered from disruptions in service and changes in delivery systems. Every major task force report released in the 1980s had documented the need to provide additional support to improve staff qualifications in all component areas.

- More staff was needed, particularly family support workers, who could respond to the rapidly changing needs of disadvantaged families. Furthermore, facilities, transportation, and other nonpersonnel costs were having an effect on program quality.

Response to the panel's work was overwhelming. In March of 1990, before the final report was complete, a subcommittee of the Committee on Labor and Human Resources in the U.S. Senate heard testimony from the President of NHSA regarding quality and expansion (Boggus, 1990). In addition, a House subcommittee requested a summary of issues emerging from the Silver Ribbon Panel (Lombardi, 1990). When the report was finally released, it outlined a set of recommendations that helped set the direction for the future of the program.

Funds Set Aside for Quality

One of the primary recommendations of the Silver Ribbon Panel report was to target a certain percentage of funds for quality improvements. Following this recommendation, one of the most far-reaching provisions in the 1990 Head Start Expansion and Quality Improvement Act was the establishment of the quality set-aside. (All references to the 1990 Head Start reauthorization can be found in the 1990 Head Start Expansion and Quality Improvement Act [PL 101-501].) Specifically, the legislation required that 10% of the entire fiscal year (FY) 1991 Head Start appropriations and 25% of any increase in appropriations in subsequent years be reserved for quality enhancement. This was the first time in Head Start's history that funds were reserved specifically to improve quality.

The legislation required that at least half of the quality improvement funds be used to improve staff compensation, including the provision of benefits to staff in local Head Start programs. Strengthening this compensation provision further was an amendment requiring the Department to encourage Head Start agencies to provide compensation according to salary scales that are based on training and experience. In addition, the legislation provided for a cost-of-living adjustment (COLA) for all Head Start programs.

According to the new law, the remainder of the quality set-aside allowed for a range of improvements including, among others

- Hiring more staff, including additional staff to reduce the child–staff ratio and to coordinate Head Start with other services

- Supplementing other training funds to improve staff qualifications to support staff training, child counseling, and other services that meet the needs of participating children, including those from dysfunctional families or those faced with substance abuse in their families and/or violence in their communities

- Making minor facility improvements, including the acquisition and installation of equipment, to expand the availability or improve the quality of Head Start programs

- Improving transportation, enabling eligible children to participate in Head Start

Staffing and Monitoring

In addition to the quality set-aside, the 1990 law set forth other quality improvements, including provisions that addressed monitoring and staff qualifications. With regard to monitoring, the Department was now required to conduct a full, on-site review of each Head Start agency at least once during each 3-year period to ensure compliance with the Head Start Performance Standards.

Furthermore, the reauthorization created new staffing requirements for teachers in center-based Head Start programs. Specifically, by September 30, 1994, each classroom was required to have a teacher with a CDA credential appropriate to the age of the children being served; state certificate for preschool teachers meeting or exceeding the requirements for a CDA; an associate, bachelors, or advanced degree in early childhood education; or a degree in a field related to early childhood education with expertise teaching preschool children and a state certificate for preschool teachers. This was the first time a specific staff qualification requirement was included in the actual law.

STEPPING UP THE COMMITMENT TO QUALITY AND EXPANSION: THE 1994 HEAD START REAUTHORIZATION

Bill Clinton came to the presidency in 1993 with a strong background in and support for education in general and, more specifically, with knowledge and experience of early childhood education issues. A few years earlier, in his role as governor, Clinton had been active in the establishment of the national education goals. Moreover, in the early 1990s, he had chaired the National School Readiness Task Force sponsored by the National Association of State Boards of Education. From the earliest days of his administration, Clinton made a strong commitment to invest in Head Start.

The Head Start Advisory Committee on Quality and Expansion

Just as the young administration was getting underway, new reports surfaced from the Department of Health and Human Services (DHHS) Office of the Inspector General (1993a, 1993b), documenting quality concerns. Donna Shalala, Secretary of DHHS, took immediate action. Before moving forward with new plans, the Secretary put in place a high-level bipartisan advisory committee to thoroughly review the entire Head Start program. On June 16, 1993, when announcing the formation of the Advisory Committee on Head Start Quality and Expansion, Secretary Shalala said, "We want every Head Start program to offer the comprehensive family services and high quality early childhood experience that are the core of the Head Start vision" (Advisory Committee on Head Start Quality and Expansion, 1993, p. iii).

The Secretary named Mary Jo Bane, Assistant Secretary of the Administration for Children and Families, to lead this bold initiative. The 47 members appointed to the committee reflected diverse backgrounds and perspectives and included representatives from the Head Start community, staff to members of Congress, administration officials, representatives from the public and private sector, and experts in children's health and education.

The Advisory Committee activities took place over a 6-month period and included input from hundreds of people concerned with and affected by the Head Start program. A series of focus groups on various aspects of the program was held with experts and representatives of the Head Start community, internal program data and past reports were reviewed, and outreach meetings were held with various national organizations and other interested parties. Finally, a public hearing took place with parents and staff testifying before committee members and some 1,500 people attending the National Head Start Parent Involvement Institute held in Washington, D.C. The Advisory Committee met three times and held seven subcommittee meetings to review and discuss all materials and to develop a set of recommendations. The Advisory Committee (1993) had five overall findings:

1. Head Start had been successful in improving the lives of many low-income children and families and serving as a national laboratory for early childhood and family support.

2. Most Head Start programs were offering quality services; however, the quality of programs was uneven across the country.

3. Head Start needed to be better equipped to serve the diverse needs of families.

4. There continued to be a large unmet need for services.

5. In many communities and states, Head Start, public schools, and other early childhood programs and providers responsible for young children and families were operating in isolation from one another without adequate resources, planning, and coordination.

Looking more closely at the findings on quality, the report indicated that results from on-site reviews conducted in the several years prior to the Advisory Committee showed that most programs were in compliance with program regulations and were delivering quality services. More than 30% of the grantees monitored in 1993 had fewer than 6 of 222 items out of compliance. Nationally, grantees had on average demonstrated success in more than 200 of the 222 items examined in program reviews.

Yet, the report went on to note that the picture was uneven. Slightly more than 11% of grantees monitored in 1993 were found out of compliance in 50 or more of the 222 items reviewed. Another 18% needed improvement in 26–50 areas. The report noted that it was not just the number of areas but the importance of many of the items that were cited as needing improvements, including establishing written procedures for program planning and for developing, reviewing, and revising budgets and work plans based on objectives; following up to assure the delivery of needed social services; providing staff and parent training in child development; and securing treatment for health problems. Many of the issues programs were facing were not new; they were well documented in the 1980 report. Once again, expansion without adequate resources and without adequate time for planning had strained some Head Start programs. Furthermore, community resources had often not kept up with changing family needs.

As indicated in earlier reports (DHHS, 1980; Silver Ribbon Panel, 1990) staffing across components was often a problem. Nearly 40% of the programs were reporting difficulty in hiring adequate staff. With the exception of the education component, there were no minimum education requirements for Head Start staff. Staff salaries were low. For example, Health and Social Service coordinators, often responsible for hundreds of children and families, were paid an average salary of $18,000. The most tenured teachers in 1992 averaged $15,039. Furthermore, management issues threatened program quality. One third of the grantees surveyed by the DHHS Inspector General considered management issues to be their biggest challenge for future expansion. Moreover, the capacity of the federal oversight needed to be strengthened. Finally, programs were experiencing difficulties securing and maintaining adequate facilities and transportation.

The Advisory Committee laid out an exhaustive list of recommendations for expansion, improvement, and better coordination. Along with recommendations to expand the program to younger children and ensure more full-day, full-year services, the report detailed the most extensive set of recommendations ever made. These included a number of steps to improve staffing and strengthen the availability of training and career development opportunities, expand management training, support strategic planning, update the Performance Standards, and develop performance measures.

The final report of the Advisory Committee was released in December 1993 and work began immediately on the reauthorization. Working with administration officials, staff of both Democratic and Republican members held an intense series of meetings that led to an unprecedented level of bipartisan support for passage when a final bill emerged. On May 18, 1994, President Clinton signed the reauthorization, marking the beginning of a new chapter in the history of the program—one that would finally attempt to balance quality with expansion. (All references to the 1994 Head Start reauthorization can be found in the Head Start Act Amendments of 1994 [PL 103-252].)

The 1994 Reauthorization

Following the recommendations of the Advisory Committee, in the Head Start Act of 1994, Congress continued some of the provisions in the 1990 law while stepping up efforts to ensure quality. There was a clear message in the new law that fiscal and programmatic oversight should be addressed and that more attention should be given to improving staff qualifications and training. The final bill included, among others, provisions related to the quality set-aside, staff qualifications, training and technical assistance, performance standards and measures, and monitoring.

Quality Set-Aside   The quality set-aside, the cornerstone of quality improvement in the 1990 law, was continued. The legislation required the Department to reserve 25% of any increase in funds from the adjusted prior year appropriation as "quality improvement funds." Provisions to assure funds for salaries were maintained. In addition to the activities listed in 1990, the 1994 law identified goals for the quality improvement funds, emphasizing compliance with the Performance Standards, improvements in staff qualifications and training, staff compensation, communitywide strategic planning and needs assessments, and improvements in the physical environments of Head Start programs.

Staff Qualifications   The new law reauthorized the requirements for classroom staff contained in the 1990 legislation and also contained new provisions regarding a range of staffing issues. For example, the legislation required the Department to assist Head Start agencies in establishing mentor teacher positions. In addition, the new law required the Department to review and revise, if necessary, the regulations governing qualifications of family service workers; promote the development of model training curricula; and promote a credential for family service workers. Finally, for the first time, the law authorized a "fellows" program to encourage emerging leaders from the early childhood community.

Training and Technical Assistance   Congress strengthened the training and technical assistance section of the Head Start Act in the 1994 legislation. Focusing on the needs of local Head Start agencies, the Department was required to give highest priority in the allocation of training and technical assistance resources to programs with deficiencies identified in monitoring reviews. It also required the Department to assist Head Start agencies and programs with staff training and career development, strategic planning and needs assessment at the community level, development of and transition to full-day and full-year programs based on community needs, expansion of services to families with infants and toddlers, development of sound management practices, efforts to secure and maintain adequate facilities, and development of innovative program models.

Performance Standards and Measures   One of the most critical provisions of the 1994 law was the requirement to review and revise the Head Start Program Performance Standards for the first time in 20 years. In addition, the new law required the Department to develop Performance Measures designed to measure the quality and effectiveness of Head Start programs. Specifically, the measures were to be used to identify strengths and weaknesses in the operation of Head Start programs nationally and by region and to identify problem areas that might require additional training and technical assistance.

Monitoring   The law continued the practice established in 1990 of monitoring Head Start programs every 3 years. However, several new requirements were added to strengthen the monitoring provisions. For example,

- All new grantees were to be reviewed after their first year of operation.

- The Department was required to conduct follow-up reviews and prompt return visits to any agency failing to meet the Performance Standards.

- Procedures for corrective action steps were detailed, including the development of quality improvement plans (QIP).

- The Department was required to publish a summary report on the findings of the monitoring reviews no later than 120 days after the end of the fiscal year.

Accomplishments The Clinton Administration took the new law very seriously. Associate Commissioner Helen Taylor held numerous meetings with the Head Start community, sending a clear message that "this was not business as usual" and setting in motion an unprecedented number of quality improvements. Four years after the reauthorization, Olivia Golden (1998), the Assistant Secretary for Children and Families in DHHS, testified before the corresponding subcommittees of the Senate Labor and Human Resources Committee and the House Education and Workforce Committee. The list of accomplishments was impressive. The program had expanded to serve more than 800,000 children, keeping on track to achieve the President's goal of serving 1 million children by 2002. In addition, the administration had launched Early Head Start, serving 22,000 children younger than age 3 and had successfully promoted partnerships with child care in communities all across the country.

Perhaps most important, this successful expansion had taken place at the same time as unprecedented improvements in the quality of programs. For example, the administration

- Initiated a tough stance whenever on-site reviews found serious deficiencies, replacing 90 grantees that were not able to correct performance promptly (In many other programs, substantial progress had been made to improve management and program practices.)

- Completed the final revision of the Head Start Performance Standards, for the first time in 20 years

- Completed the design of a new system of Head Start Performance Measures to track, for the first time, the outcome of Head Start services in key areas

- Established four quality research centers to develop a system of measures and track outcomes through a national random sample of Head Start children

- Provided funding for locally designed quality improvement initiatives, including efforts to hire additional family services workers

In addition, local programs implemented steady improvements in salaries and benefits for the more than 145,000 staff members. For example, staff salaries for Head Start teachers increased from $14,600 in 1992 to approximately $17,800 in 1997. The proportion of Head Start grantees providing retirement benefits increased by 24%, and virtually all agencies were providing comprehensive health insurance. These investments helped Head Start maintain an annual staff turnover rate of less than 8%, much lower than the estimated 33% in child care centers that lack adequate resources (Golden, 1998).

CONTINUING IMPROVEMENTS AND TARGETING
EDUCATION: THE 1998 HEAD START REAUTHORIZATION

By the time Head Start had to be reauthorized in 1998, there was a Republican majority in Congress. Again working in the spirit of bipartisanship, congressional staff members met with administration officials to work out the details of the bill. By this time, education reform was clearly focused on standards and improvements that would encourage literacy, particularly for at-risk children. The administration was interested in continuing the improvements started in 1994, and many members of Congress wanted to step up quality enhancements, particularly in the education component. The final bill, the Head Start Act of 1998, passed by Congress and signed by the President in the fall of 1998, contained the following new provisions to address these issues. (All references to the 1998 Head Start reauthorization can be found in the Head Start Amendments of 1998 [PL 105-285].)

Increasing the Quality Set-Aside

The 1998 law increased the quality set-aside from 25% of any additional funding from the adjusted prior year appropriation, as required in 1994, to 60% of the excess funding in FY 1999, 50% in FY 2000, 47.5% in FY 2001, 35% in FY 2002, and 25% in FY 2003. In addition, the list of goals for quality improvement funds was supplemented to enhance staff development and training.

As in the prior two reauthorizations, half of the quality set-aside was reserved for staff compensation; however, a provision was added requiring agencies to give preference in awarding of salary increases to staff who acquire additional work-related training or education. Furthermore, from the remainder of the set-aside, priority was to be given to staff training to comply with education performance standards, particularly activities to promote language and literacy development; English language acquisition for non-English background children and families; school readiness skills; training to improve staff qualifications; and staff training, child counseling, and other services to address problems of children participating in Head Start. Finally, now that the Early Head Start program was established and expanding, Congress mandated that the Department reserve no less than 5% and no more than 10% of the annual Early Head Start appropriation for training and technical assistance.

Staff Qualifications

Qualifications for classroom teachers were strengthened in 1998 by adding a set of competencies and amending the degree requirements. At least one teacher in every classroom in center-based had to demonstrate competency to

* Plan and implement learning experiences that advance the intellectual and physical development of children, including improving the readiness of children for school

* Establish and maintain a safe, healthy learning environment

* Support the social and emotional development of children

* Encourage the involvement of families in a Head Start program and support the development of relationships between children and their families

In addition, the provision governing the degree requirements of classroom teachers was also amended. Instead of requiring a CDA or higher degree for each teacher in center-based programs, at least 50% of all Head Start teachers in the nation were required to have a college degree (either associate, bachelors, or advanced) in early childhood education or a degree in a related field with experience in teaching preschoolers by September 1, 2003. All classrooms without such teachers were required to have a teacher with a CDA, a preschool teacher certificate from the state that meets or exceeds CDA requirements, or a degree in a related field with preschool teaching experience and a state preschool teacher certificate. Furthermore, Head Start agencies were required to demonstrate progress toward the goal of attaining more teachers with college degrees each year.

Education Performance Standards, Measures, and Monitoring

The new law created a new provision on education performance standards to ensure school readiness, and at a minimum, to ensure that children

- Develop phonemic, print, and numeracy awareness

- Understand and use language to communicate for various purposes

- Understand and use increasingly complex and varied vocabulary

- Develop and demonstrate an appreciation of books

- In the case of non-English background children, progress toward acquisition of the English language

In addition, the 1998 law amended Performance Measure requirements to ensure that children

- Know that letters of the alphabet are a special category of visual graphics that can be individually named

- Recognize a word as a unit of print

- Identify at least 10 letters of the alphabet

- Associate sounds with written words

Taken together, these provisions reflected a new emphasis on language and literacy that had emerged as part of education reform efforts.

Soon after the passage of the 1998 law, the Clinton Administration began issuing program guidance to implement the new provisions. Efforts were made to reach out to the community and to a wide range of experts in literacy and performance measurement.

In August 2000, the Administration on Children, Youth and Families issued an Information Memorandum to provide guidance to programs on the Head Start Outcomes Framework. The framework was intended to guide Head Start programs in their ongoing assessment of the progress and accomplishments of children in their efforts to analyze and use data on child outcomes in self-assessment and continuous improvement. The framework was composed of eight domains including language development, literacy, mathematics, science, creative arts, social and emotional development, approaches to learning, and physical health and development. The framework also included 27 domain elements and 100 examples of more specific indicators of children's skills, abilities, knowledge, and behaviors.

The framework was to guide agencies in selecting, developing, and adapting an instrument or set of tools for ongoing assessment of children's progress. It was not intended to be used directly as a checklist for assessing children. The goal was to use outcome data as an additional tool to strengthen the quality of every local Head Start program, not to create a national test for Head Start or a national assessment system of Head Start teachers.

In the closing months of the Clinton Administration, extensive training and materials were provided to Head Start staff on curriculum and assessment. More than 3,500 Head Start managers attended a National Child Development Institute held in December of 2000. The goal of the Institute was to increase the knowledge and leadership skills of local program managers in order to support school readiness and positive child outcomes in Head Start.

As the management of the Head Start program changed hands following the Presidential election of 2000, the new administration provided additional training on literacy, mentoring, and a much more targeted and controversial focus on assessment. The issues surrounding outcomes and assessment of Head Start children would become one of the most heated debates in the 2003–2004 reauthorization process.

NEW CHALLENGES AHEAD

Looking across these three waves of legislative activity, we see an increasing focus on quality concerns—all of which reflect issues that were current at the time. In 1990, after the Silver Ribbon Panel report documented quality problems, we see the emergence of the first quality set-aside with funds targeted to increased compensation. In 1994, as concerns around management and standards predominated in the Advisory Committee, changes in the law addressed these issues. Finally in 1998, as the nation faced poor test scores, particularly in literacy levels of at-risk children, the law targeted improvements in the education component.

All of these legislative changes resulted in a much stronger, more responsive, and more successful Head Start program. Moreover, the expansion not only reached hundreds of thousands of poor children who would not have otherwise had a preschool experience but also began to address two other key issues: the need for full day and the need to serve younger children. At the same time, we see unprecedented progress throughout the decade on the quality improvements, although the focus of the specific provisions changed with the times. In the early 1990s, efforts were made to make up for years of inattention to quality by providing additional resources targeted to quality improvements that reflected the needs of the grantees in a number of key areas. By the mid-1990s, the strong focus on standards and monitoring resulted in a much stronger core management system that can now respond to overall accountability issues. Finally, in the closing years of the century, we saw a renewed focus on the core early education issues facing an increasingly diverse group of children entering Head Start classrooms.

Although it will take additional time before we can evaluate the impact of the more recent efforts on classroom practice and overall child development, data from the Head Start Family and Child Experience Survey (FACES) show promising results from this decade of quality improvements. Launched in 1997, the FACES initiative is an ongoing, national longitudinal study of the development of Head Start children, the characteristics of their families, and the quality of Head Start classrooms. FACES involves a nationally stratified random sample of 3,200 children and families in 40 Head Start classrooms. The findings from FACES indicate that the quality of most Head Start classrooms is good, and that Head Start narrows the gap between disadvantaged students and all other children in key components of school readiness (DHHS, 2001). The areas that needed improvement correspond to those areas that were directly addressed in the 1998 law. New targeted efforts around language and literacy hold promise in continuing to help Head Start children get ready for school.

Yet, the history and strength of Head Start is that it is continuously improving. As Head Start moves into the future, we see at least four issues on the horizon.

First, Head Start will need to continue to focus on the quality of the education component. This will mean additional resources for training and technical assistance, as well as a renewed focus on assuring that all classrooms have teachers with appropriate college degrees in early childhood education, and stepped-up efforts to improve curriculum, assessment, and supervision. Given teacher shortages in public schools, this will mean that teacher salaries will have to increase in order to recruit and retain qualified staff. Programs will need continued resources to make this happen. In addition, programs will need additional information and support to better serve the needs of the growing number of non–English-speaking children. Although Head Start should continue to focus on school readiness, such a focus should reflect the critical importance of all domains of development.

Second, there needs to be a renewed focus on health services and parent involvement. These two components received less attention in the last reauthorization, yet poor families are facing serious health and human service needs. As in education, programs need resources to offer salaries and benefits to attract qualified health and family support staff. In the area of health, programs must be able to help families navigate a complex array of new health services. With regard to families, programs must be able to respond to an increasingly diverse population and address the intense needs of extreme poverty and families with multiple risks. Furthermore, parent involvement faces new challenges as programs move to full-day schedules to respond to the needs of families transitioning from welfare to work.

Third, Early Head Start should be expanded and programs allowed to serve more expectant families and infants and toddlers. Given the promising results of the Early Head Start evaluation and the expansion of state prekindergarten programs, the Head Start of the future should serve an increasing number of children younger than 3 years and their families. This will call for additional resources for specialized training and technical assistance to help prepare staff to work with younger children. Moreover, additional resources will be needed to keep pace with rising costs per child as more full-day and full-year services are provided.

Finally, training, technical assistance, and additional resources will be needed to promote effective collaboration. Head Start in the 21st century is not a program working in isolation in a community. All across the country, Head Start programs are partnering with community-based child care centers and family child care homes to help provide quality comprehensive services where children may already be enrolled. New roles are emerging within Head Start as programs add staff to work directly with the child care community in their neighborhoods. Quality funds will be needed to ensure that these new ways of organizing services meet the Head Start Performance Standards and that staff are trained and supported along the way.

The legacy of the 1990s is that Head Start thrived and remained the nation's pride. Yet, as the title of the 1990 report noted, it is also the nation's challenge. Safeguarding this legacy will depend on whether policy makers continue to invest in a balanced approach to expansion—one that serves more children while addressing emerging quality issues facing children, families, and staff.

REFERENCES

Administration on Children, Youth and Families. (2000, August 8). *Using child outcomes in program self-assessment* (Information Memorandum HS-00–18). Washington, DC: U.S. Department of Health and Human Services.

Advisory Committee on Head Start Quality and Expansion. (1993). *Creating a 21st Century Head Start: Final Report of the Advisory Committee on Head Start Quality and Expansion.* Washington, DC: U.S. Department of Health and Human Services.

Boggus, E. (1990, March). Testimony before the United States Senate, Subcommittee on Children, Family, Drugs and Alcoholism of the Committee on Labor and Human Resources.

Golden, O. (1998, March 26). Testimony before the Children and Families Subcommittee of the Senate Labor and Human Resources Committee, and the Early Childhood, Youth and Families Subcommittee, of the House Education and Workforce Committee.

Head Start Act Amendments of 1994, PL 103-252, 42 U.S.C. §§ 9831 *et seq.*

Head Start Amendments of 1998, PL 105-285, 42 U.S.C. §§ 9831 *et seq.*

Head Start Expansion and Quality Improvement Act, 1990, PL 101-501, 42 U.S.C. §§ 9831 *et seq.*

Lombardi, J. (1990, March 2). Testimony before the Subcommittee on Human Resources of the House Education and Labor Committee.

Office of the Inspector General. (1993a). *Examining Head Start experiences according to performance indicators.* Washington, DC: U.S. Department of Health and Human Services.

Office of the Inspector General. (1993b). *Head Start expansion: Grantees experiences.* Washington, DC: U.S. Department of Health and Human Services.

Silver Ribbon Panel. (1990). *Head Start: The nation's pride, a nation's challenge.* Alexandria, VA: National Head Start Association.

U.S. Department of Health and Human Services (DHHS). (2001, January). *Head Start Program Performance Measures, Third Progress Report.* Washington, DC: Author.

U.S. Department of Health and Human Services (DHHS). (1980, September). *Head Start in the 1980s: A report requested by the President of the United States.* Washington DC: Author.

Zigler, E., & Muenchow, S. (1992). *Head Start: The inside story of American's most successful educational experiment.* New York: Basic Books.

CHAPTER 20

Quality in Head Start

A Dream within Reach

Gregg Powell

In the early 1990s, a synergy occurred for the Head Start program bringing together the effects of investment, enforcement, and recognition to provide the impetus for a major shift in focus to quality in the nation's largest program for preschool children. The federal government provided some of the largest increases in history for the program with specific targets for using the money for improvements while also increasing efforts to monitor programs and enforce performance. At the same time, the National Head Start Association (NHSA) launched its "Quality Initiative" as an effort to recognize programs performing at higher levels than the national norms. In this chapter, the results of this synergy are discussed, both in the context of Head Start and in the context of our nation's need to prepare our children for school and beyond.

In the face of increasing evidence for the effectiveness of early childhood programs in improving the lives of children, there remains considerable opposition to funding these programs at the federal and state level (Haskins, 1989; Hood, 1992). It is argued that large, publicly funded programs such as Head Start cannot achieve the same results as model programs whose effectiveness has been established (Besharov, 1992; Haskins, 1989). On the other side, proponents for the programs point out that the differences in funding level affecting quality make it difficult, but not impossible, to achieve the same results (Barnett, 1993, 1995; Zigler & Styfco, 1994a, 1994b). Proponents further suggest that quality is difficult to maintain during periods of rapid expansion (United States General Accounting Office [USGAO], 1994a, 1994b; Zigler, Styfco, & Gilman, 1993). It appears that both sides agree that quality is the key difference between model programs and large, publicly funded programs. They differ in the belief that something can—or should—be done to eliminate this difference.

In 1990, the United States Congress passed the Head Start Expansion and Quality Improvement Act (Congressional Record, 1990), which, for the first time in the program's history, made a significant commitment to addressing quality issues. In short, the Act required that 10% of all appropriations for 1991 be earmarked to address quality concerns rather than expansion and that 25% of all new funding in subsequent years be set aside for the same purpose. The act specified that at least half of the set-aside be reserved for improving staff compensation, with the remainder available for training, technical assistance, facilities, transportation, and program enhancement. There is growing evidence that this investment in quality is achieving the desired results (Brush, Gaidurgis, & Best, 1993; Powell, 1998; Powell, Brush, & Gaidurgis, 1998). However, studies thus far have focused on specific proxies for quality. For the most part, these measures have been *structural* features of classroom-based preschool programs (i.e., group size, staff–child ratios, staff qualifications, staff retention rates).

Also included in the legislation was language requiring the Secretary of Health and Human Services to strengthen performance standards and increase the department's efforts to monitor and enforce these standards. Concurrent with these federal efforts, in 1993, NHSA introduced a Quality Initiative designed both to recognize those programs whose policies and practices go beyond minimum standards and to learn from those programs about the strategies that promote and increase quality. The initiative was divided into two levels:

- *Programs of Achievement:* This level involved identifying Head Start grantees and delegates whose policies and practices met more than 100 NHSA Quality Indicators in 10 program areas. A panel of people from the immediate and extended Head Start family carefully reviewed their documentation.

- *Programs of Excellence:* This level identified Programs of Achievement as those demonstrating short- and long-term impact on the children and families served. They also must have implemented special projects to meet the unique needs of their communities. In addition to a review of documentation, Programs of Excellence received a site visit from panel members.

Although each of these efforts is important, this chapter focuses on how their synergy came about, what effect it may be having, and what we have learned about quality in the process.

RENEWED INTEREST IN PRESCHOOL PROGRAMS

Public policy affecting children has had a checkered past in the United States. Since the early 1990s, we have seen an unprecedented interest in the area of early childhood education and development at all levels of government. Chafel (1992) attributed this newfound interest to increased knowledge of the importance of the early years to later development, research indicating the effectiveness of early intervention, the documented increase in the numbers and proportion of young children living in less than optimal conditions, and the increased desire on the part of educational policy makers to improve the chances for these children.

Results from longitudinal research on the effectiveness of preschool intervention for low-income children are widely accepted as promising and thus have played a major role in the current resurgence of interest in Head Start and other early childhood education models. Further impetus for investing in early childhood programs has come from a more pragmatic view. Economic analysis has been brought to bear on the study of early intervention with findings implying that, for every dollar invested in early education, significant returns accrue from reduced costs for later education services, crime, and welfare dependency (Barnett, 1995). Proponents for continued investment argued a decade ago that the national cost of failing to provide these services would range between $70,000 and $100,000 per child (Barnett, 1993, 1995)—significant amounts that have only risen with inflation.

These findings of the potential effectiveness and projected savings have come primarily from the study of model programs and cannot, the critics say, be generalized to large, publicly funded programs such as Head Start, Title I preschools, or even state-funded programs. It is easy to understand this reluctance when one compares the costs of the model programs with the cost of Head Start. For example, per-child cost of the Perry Preschool, in inflation-adjusted dollars, was estimated to be thousands of dollars more than the average Head Start expenditure (Zigler & Styfco, 1994b). It has been suggested by critics and supporters alike that the costly quality of the model programs forming the basis for these findings is not, and cannot, be replicated in public programs, thus raising doubts regarding the ability of public programs to achieve the same results.

As suggested by McCall (1993), these are two separate questions. First, does Head Start (or other early childhood programs) have the potential to produce improved outcomes for children and families? Second, do current programs operated for large numbers of children and families actually achieve these outcomes? The answer to the first question would appear to be a resounding yes if one accepts the large body of evidence from model early intervention programs (see, e.g., Chapters 16 and 27). The answer to the second question has yet to be provided, but logic would suggest that if Head Start were to achieve the same levels of quality (both structural and process) as those model programs, we would see similar results (Powell, 1995).

HISTORICAL CONTEXT OF HEAD START AND QUALITY

Since its founding in 1965, the Head Start program has been charged with providing comprehensive child development and family support services to some 20 million low-income preschool children and their families. Given the broad objectives of the program, any effort to assess quality merely on the basis of some classroom characteristics or teaching strategies misses the point. Zigler and Styfco (1994b), in discussing the relative value of Head Start versus the Perry Preschool, make it clear that adaptability to the changing conditions of poverty is clearly a plus for the Head Start program. Additional attempts (Washington & Greene, 1995; Washington & Oyemade-Bailey, 1995; Zigler & Styfco, 1994b) to discuss quality in the program have pointed to the many innovations over the years as evidence of successful programming.

In more than three decades, Head Start has grown from a 6-week summer program with a budget of $96 million to a 9-month school-year program (a small number now operate year round) with a $6.7 billion allocation in fiscal year 2003 (U.S. Department of Health and Human Services [DHHS], Administration on Children, Youth and Families [ACYF], 2003). The growth, however, has been uneven, often failing to keep up with inflation, let alone providing funding to maintain or improve quality (Zigler & Muenchow, 1992). Reviewing the actual funding level for the program, as compared with that of the "high quality" experimental programs with which it has been compared, has led some to question the existence of a commit-ment to developing a quality program at the national level (NHSA, 1996; Washington & Oyemade-Bailey, 1995).

Given its hasty beginnings, it is not surprising that even many of the founders of Head Start and early researchers (Harmon & Hanley, 1979; Zigler & Muenchow, 1992) questioned the ability of the program to achieve an appropriate level of quality. However, it was uneven quality that was, and remains, the most serious area of concern (DHHS, 1993). Starting off in such an ambitious fashion may have led the program managers to ignore quality controls (Harmon & Hanley, 1979). In fact, it was not until 1975 that the Head Start Program Performance Standards were fully implemented.

Era of Quality Erosion

Although the program gained widespread support from diverse communities—(e.g., local organizations, businesses, school districts, politicians, and parents) it spent the 1970s and 1980s suffering through a series of indifferent and, at times, hostile federal adminis-trations (NHSA, 1990; Washington & Oyemade-Bailey, 1995). The dual impact of infla-tion and funding cutbacks had made it increasingly difficult for Head Start agencies to provide quality services to communities in stress. As noted in a study by DHHS, Office of the Inspector General (1989), 84% of the Head Start agencies surveyed reported that the combined impact of substance abuse, domestic violence, lack of parenting skills, and crime-infested inadequate housing resulted in increased demands on staff time for indi-vidual counseling and working with troubled children in the classroom. Researchers at-tempting to measure the impact of Head Start longitudinally further supported these conclusions. Lee, Brooks-Gunn, Schnur, and Liaw (1990) made it clear that the risks re-lated to poverty in the 1990s were qualitatively different from those of the 1960s.

Expansion of Head Start in the early 1980s may have compounded existing quality problems and sent the program into a dangerous downhill slide (Zigler & Styfco, 1997). After initial plans to eliminate the program, public support convinced incoming Presi-dent Reagan that the program should be a part of the social "safety net." (See Zigler & Muenchow, 1992, for a full discussion of this period.) Under the frugal guidance of David Stockman (Budget Director), a plan was set into motion to increase enrollment while trimming the budget. This, coupled with inflation and cuts to ancillary programs, had a devastating effect on the ability of programs to maintain previous service levels (Rovner, 1990; Zigler & Styfco, 1997).

The impact of benign neglect was forcefully demonstrated by an analysis from the High/Scope Foundation (Schweinhart, 1990) showing that real funding per child, ad-justed for inflation, declined by 13% from 1981 to 1989. NHSA (1996), assuming a con-stant inflation rate of 2.5% (which is extremely conservative), estimated how years of neg-lect, followed by an emphasis on expansion and 5 years of investing in quality, brought the program back to the funding level of 1971. In the face of such sobering realities, Head Start programs were under increased pressure to serve more children with fewer dollars and, consequentially, quality suffered.

The impact of these conditions strikes at the very heart of the program's ability to maintain quality. Staff salaries, which had never been competitive, fell further behind, making it even more difficult for programs to attract and maintain qualified staff. In many cases, critical component positions were combined to cut personnel (NHSA, 1990). Finally, as other federal programs were being cut, Head Start agencies found themselves having to pay for services that used to be free or having to pay more for items that previously had been subsidized. For example, reductions in the Child Care Food Program resulted in a loss of $20 million in 1982 alone (Washington & Oyemade-Bailey, 1995). This author recalls that in the late 1970s, while director of a Migrant Head Start program in Idaho, we had the luxury of having the services of a full-time Public Health Service doctor. In addition to this, there were two nurse practitioners, four VISTA workers with advanced degrees, and the support of a CETA program for parent job training. By the mid-1980s, virtually all of this support was gone.

In the 1990s, programs reported that staff turnover rates were continuing to climb, and funds were not available to replace outdated materials, equipment, and buses (NHSA, 1990). This was compounded by the administration's push to expand Head Start at the expense of quality. Many program directors complained that they were receiving expansion funds at roughly 80% of the ongoing funding per child at the time (NHSA, 1990, 1993). Furthermore, with this rapid expansion came problems with facilities. Many communities simply had no more space to be rented at any cost. In some areas, news of Head Start funding increases led opportunistic landlords to increase previously reasonable rents (NHSA, 1990).

Quality Improvement Initiatives

As a part of the reauthorization act of 1994, the Head Start Bureau was charged with the responsibility of developing specific performance measures to evaluate the Head Start program as a whole, rather than individual programs. The goal was to provide information to be used for national reporting and charting trends over time, setting goals and measuring progress toward these goals, highlighting areas that might need federal attention, and targeting resources. The measures are organized according to the component areas: health, education, social service, parent involvement, and program management (DHHS, ACYF, 1995). Among the key structural indices included are group size, staff–child ratio, staff qualifications, and staff salaries. In developing the measures, careful consideration was also given to assessing the actual objectives of Head Start (DHHS, ACYF, 1995).

Prior to the measures project, very little work had been done utilizing the available data in Head Start for the purpose of measuring quality or outcomes in any consistent manner. The data were there but, with the exception of periodic reports, they were not being used. A report prepared for DHHS (Brush et al., 1993) took a comprehensive look at the available data and made comments regarding program quality. In preparing this report, the authors concluded that there were indeed some measures in the data that could be used to track quality. These were for the most part the usual structural indicators.

Since the implementation of the Head Start Program Performance Standards in 1975, the primary means of measuring quality and monitoring programs was through a combination of program self-assessment and Head Start Bureau on-site reviews. Over time, this process has become more formalized, and now one third of all programs receive an on-site review each year. The results of these reviews have been used by the Head Start Bureau to make decisions regarding corrective action ranging from the provision of technical assistance to defunding of grantees. Since 1990, more than 150 programs have either been defunded or have voluntarily given up their grants for performance related reasons. This represents an enormous increase over all prior years.

In addition to these improvements, the Head Start Bureau has also developed a new monitoring system that will eventually provide more useful information for decision making. Training and procedures are being put into place to reduce early problems related to regional interpretation about compliance and noncompliance with various standards. In 1993, it was found that one of the largest sources of variability on compliance was the geographic region (Brush et al., 1993).

Finally, in developing its Quality Initiative, NHSA took into consideration multiple areas typically left out by other types of ratings. These relate to the comprehensive nature of the Head Start program. It was decided that compliance with all Head Start Performance Standards was price of entry—these were considered to be minimum standards and that programs to be recognized for either Achievement or Excellence had to meet those and beyond. Working with a committee of experts (e.g., practitioners, researchers, policy makers) in all component areas (e.g., education, health, social services, parent involvement), NHSA developed specific indicators of quality services or program implementation to be addressed by applicants for Achievement. These indicators were originally organized according to the Head Start Program Performance Standards. During the revision to the process (1999), the indicators were streamlined and organized by functional areas (i.e., organizational development, parent involvement, public relations and advocacy, cultural competence, program enrichment, innovation), with a total of 77 indicators.

RESULTS OF THE SYNERGY

With a decade behind us, it is reasonable to ask what this three-pronged (investment, enforcement, and recognition) effort has managed to achieve with respect to quality in Head Start. The attempts to study the impact of each of these are spotty, but there is beginning to be a pattern developing that is worthy of discussion and further investigation.

Policy Shift to Investment

In the Head Start Reauthorization Act of 1994 (Congressional Record, 1994), the quality improvement initiative was continued by again setting aside 25% of all new money for this purpose. For the year 1995, an additional $35 million was allocated for these improvements. Summing up, the total for the first 5 years was $532.2 million allocated for investment in quality. At the same time, the enrollment in the program increased by about 80%. The bipartisan effort of Congress and two administrations finally began to turn the tide on dwindling resources for Head Start programs that had created a quality crisis during the 1980s.

In addition, this was an opportunity for the more than 2,000 Head Start grantees and delegate agencies to enrich the services delivered to more than 3.4 million children and their families between 1991 and 1995. In 1990, the average per child funding was $2,803. By 1995, this average had climbed to $4,534 (DHHS, ACYF, 1992, 1995). This translates to roughly $1,500 (after inflation) extra per child served during the 5-year period.

Given this level of investment by Congress, it is appropriate to ask whether the desired impact (i.e., improvement of the performance of Head Start programs) was achieved. Attempts to study this issue (Powell, 1998; Powell, et al., 1998) have addressed the impact of the public policy shift that occurred in 1990.

First and foremost, is whether quality, as measured by nine structural variables, improved from 1990 to 1995. The studies found significant improvement:

*   Center-based child–adult ratio decreased from a mean of 10.4 to 9.8.

*   Home-based child–adult ratio decreased from a mean of 10.8 to 9.8.

*   Child group size decreased from a mean of 18.1 to 17.8.

*   Percentage of year-to-year staff turnover decreased from 8.2 to 7.3.

*   Health staff caseload decreased from 162.7 to 144.8.

*   Family service staff caseload decreased from 42.5 to 37.8.

*   Percentage of classroom teachers with qualifications (degree or CDA) increased from 82.4 to 85.3.

*   Percentage of home visitors with qualifications (degree or CDA) increased from 59.3 to 63.3.

Secondly, in an attempt to address the "unevenness" issue, the studies measured changes on each of these measures among those programs at the lowest level of quality in 1990. The studies found significant (and stronger) improvement for these programs:

*   Center-based child–adult ratio decreased from a mean of 12.7 in 1990 to 10.9 in 1995.

*   Home-based child–adult ratio decreased from 11.2 to 10.2.

*   Child group size decreased from a mean of 18.7 to 18.1.

*   Percentage of year-to-year staff turnover decreased from 12.8 to 8.7.

*   Health staff case load decreased from 193.1 to 161.9.

*   Family service staff case load decreased from 50.4 to 42.2.

*   Percentage of classroom teachers with qualifications (degree or CDA) increased from 70.4 to 82.4.

*   Percentage of home visitors with qualifications increased from 53.6 to 61.5.

Finally, was change in individual program quality affected by initial (1990) size of the program and/or the rate of growth? Regression analyses showed that, holding constant the percentage increase in enrollment, the size of enrollment in 1990 did not appear to be related to the ability of the grantee to improve the quality over time. Smaller and larger grantees seem to have struggled to a similar degree with expansion.

However, the regression analyses did show that the percentage increase in enrollment tended to adversely affect quality improvement. Grantees with larger percentage increases did not improve as much over time as those with smaller increases in five of the areas studied: center-based child–adult ratio, home-based child–adult ratio, health staff caseload, family services staff caseload, and percentage of classroom teachers with qualifications. That is, grantees whose enrollment increased more over the 5-year period showed less improvement than others, holding constant the size of enrollment in 1990.

These investigations of the impact of quality investment in Head Start provide us with mixed results using the data currently available. There are inherent weaknesses in the data, but the findings make it clear that improvement has occurred and the "unevenness" of Head Start quality has decreased over the period of investment. These results should be able to inform public policy on improvement of government services and data collection.

Development and Implementation of a System for Recognition

For the period of the NHSA's Quality Initiative reported on here, 85 programs applied for the first level of recognition—Achievement—with only 22 successfully making it through the process. Of those 22, nine programs went on to become Programs of Excellence. Although this is not a large sample, there were enough programs in this group to begin getting a picture of what quality (as defined by the initiative) looks like in a Head Start program.

The final sample in the reporting period included 12 Programs of Achievement and 9 Programs of Excellence. Although the analysis of the characteristics, practices, and procedures of these programs will be ongoing, several trends about the profiles and service design of high-quality programs emerged.

Earlier research suggested that a number of characteristics might be predictive of quality (e.g., territory size, auspices, enrollment). Interestingly, we found reason to question these findings by what was ruled out in our initial analysis:

- Quality *does not* appear to be linked with size of program. The mean enrollment for these 21 programs was 880 with the median of 852. Seven of the programs served less than 500 children, with total staff ranging from 27 to almost 400. Yet, all found effective ways to ensure staff-to-family, staff-to-staff, and staff-to-management communication. All were characterized by a high degree of staff involvement in planning.

- Quality *does not* appear to be linked with size of territory served. While six of the programs serve only one county each, the others serve between 3 and 17 counties. These latter programs developed strategies to ensure that management staff regularly visit and monitor all the centers.

- Quality *does not* appear to be linked with grantee sponsorship. The 21 programs were equally divided among school districts, community action agencies, local government, and private nonprofit organizations, with one under a university sponsorship.

- Quality *does not* appear to be linked to program option. The programs ranged from full day/full year to half day/9 month, with many of them offering both center and home visiting options along with various forms of locally designed options. This is an important finding, as Head Start directors investigate changing their program options to better meet community needs.

During the application and on-site reviews, NHSA collected a wealth of information on both Achievement and Excellence programs over the years. Some of the more individual (and more difficult to document) characteristics, however, were not readily available. Management staff at five of the nine Programs of Excellence was interviewed to determine some of these more personal characteristics. Although these interviews were meant to be open-ended and informal, there were some standard questions that were asked of each member of the management teams.

First, basic background information—educational background, past employment, years with the program (and in the position)—was collected on each member of the team. Then, time was spent assessing some of the more philosophical aspects related to their feelings about the program. Interviewees were asked about the management style of the director (and the director was asked to describe their style). They were also asked about what motivated them to participate in the rather intensive process and what they got out of it. Finally, they were asked to describe the single most important aspect of their program that made it a Program of Excellence. A number of trends become apparent from these nine programs:

- Quality *does* appear to be linked to consistent and inspirational leadership at the top. All programs had the same director for 5 or more years, in most cases for more than 10 years. They had an average of 5–6 years of postsecondary education. All directors were perceived as leaders in their local, state, and regional communities. Ten were Johnson & Johnson/ UCLA Fellows, three were Head Start state or regional presidents, and most served on the boards of other local human service and education agencies.

- Quality *does* appear to be linked to the ability to see creative solutions to local challenges. Each of the programs had numerous efforts underway to meet a special need, often in collaboration with other community groups.

- Quality *does* appear to be linked with specific attention to management systems, both human and technological. The program directors were vigilant about maintaining and improving the mid-management capacity and the sense of total staff involvement. These management teams met formally at least once a month and in smaller groups to do joint problem solving. Making effective use of the options available through computerization was another characteristic.

- Quality *does* appear to be linked with a shared vision of the future. Virtually all staff interviewed emphasized this when questioned about characteristics leading to high quality in their programs.

In addition, all nine programs had some form of tracking progress of children and families throughout the Head Start year and into the public schools. Although varied in the amount of information collected and the time period, all appeared to track basic developmental information on both child and primary caregiver. Programs consistently used this information for planning and revising their operations.

The teaching staff at each of these programs was highly qualified and in many cases far beyond the upcoming requirements of an associate's degree in early childhood. Centers and classrooms were well organized, state of the art, and extremely conducive to learning. More than half of the centers operated by these nine programs were NAEYC accredited.

Collaboration was completely integrated into the operations of these programs, and they were each seen as leaders in their communities with respect to young children and their families. Management, staff, board, and parents were consistently involved in the development and maintenance of these collaborations. This emphasis on collaboration was evident within the agency as well, with those programs having Early Head Start (six of the nine) fully integrating the programs into a seamless birth to 5 approach.

Recommendations

Given this knowledge, we can now begin the process of sharing what we know about quality and making recommendations to other administrators that should eventually lead to further closing the quality gap between strong and weak programs.

Organization   Although no single organizational chart or structure appeared to be dominant with these programs, they do lead us to some general conclusions about what constitutes efficient operations. Each program head paid close attention to organizational design and regularly revisited its development. All nine programs were among the first to reorganize based on the revised performance standards. All continually adjusted their structures based on community and service requirements. They had periodic reviews of program operations and responsibilities accomplished with the input of all players (i.e., board, management, staff, and parents). This process included charting all activities and matching them to position descriptions and roles to ensure that no task fell off the radar. Regardless of agency type (e.g., school, CAP, nonprofit), the operation of the Head Start program was fully integrated into the operation of the overall agency. This included joint planning, constant communication, and sharing of resources. Program management was decentralized as much as possible so that each unit was capable of making timely changes to service delivery as conditions changed. However, all other divisions were included in the decision-making process to the extent that those changes might impact them.

Staffing   Much like the organizational structure, no single staffing pattern stood out—some programs used center managers while others assigned this task to members of the management team. There was, however, a commitment to maintaining highly qualified staff with reasonable workloads. Constant emphasis was placed on training and on-going education for staff at all levels. Each of these programs managed to garner resources beyond Head Start funding for this purpose. An individual plan was developed and regularly monitored for each staff member. Mentoring was used by a number of these programs, with senior staff given incentives to mentor newer staff.

Planning   Some very concrete findings about program planning come from our review of the materials supplied by both the Programs of Achievement and the Programs of Excellence. It is clear that each of these programs paid close attention to planning as a tool rather than a document required by the funding agency. Planning, implementation, monitoring, and assessment were all one seamless process. For example, data collected (e.g., Program Information Report [PIR], needs assessment, monitoring reports, child and family assessments) were regularly reviewed to identify potential trends for the ongoing planning process. All staff were kept informed about the data to be collected, why, and how it was to be used. Regular discussions were held to ensure staff understood and supported the process. Policies and procedures were regularly reviewed in light of the monitoring and assessment activities.

CONCLUSION

After 10 years of Head Start, Hunt observed,

> If our impatient society—and the reasons for this impatience are all too obvious—does not lose hope and faith too soon, it is conceivable that we of these United States of America could bring a major share of the children of the persistently poor into the mainstream of our society (but it may take a bit longer than a generation). (1975, p. 283)

After 35 years of Head Start, we have come to realize that it will also take a lot more than a brief preschool experience. Huston put it succinctly: "The problems of poverty need be attached at several levels ranging from the individual to the society as a whole" (1991, p. 293). Although Head Start is only one flake of the massive multifaceted effort that will be required to alleviate the effects of poverty in our society, it is a more significant part of attempts to reduce the achievement gap between poor and wealthy children. Our "impatient society" has relatively late come to realize that it is not just preschool but quality preschool experiences that can foster school readiness. Efforts to boost quality in the Head Start program are showing meaningful results and yielding information about the content and assessment of quality. Quality in Head Start has been lackluster and uneven for so long that it will take "a bit longer" to fix than policy makers might like. But the information presented in this chapter should encourage them that they are definitely on the right track and eventually put to rest claims that large national programs such as Head Start can never be as good as so-called model programs.

REFERENCES

Barnett, S. (1993). Benefit-cost analysis of preschool education: Findings from a 25-year follow-up. *American Journal of Orthopsychiatry, 63,* 500–508.

Barnett, S. (1995). Long-term effects of early childhood programs on cognitive and school outcomes. *The Future of Children, 5*(3), 25–50.

Besharov, D. (1992). New directions for Head Start. *The World and I, 7,* 515–531.

Brush, L., Gaidurgis, A., & Best, C. (1993). *Indices of Head Start program quality.* Washington, DC: DHHS/Administration on Children, Youth and Families, Head Start Bureau.

Chafel, J. (1992). Head Start: Making quality a national priority. *Child and Youth Care Forum, 21,* 147–173.

Congressional Record. (1990). *Head Start Expansion and Quality Improvement Act.* Washington, DC: U.S. Government Printing Office.

Congressional Record. (1994). *Head Start Reauthorization Act.* Washington, DC: U.S. Government Printing Office.

Harmon, C., & Hanley, E. (1979). Administrative aspects of the Head Start program. In E. Zigler & J. Valentine (Eds.), *Project Head Start: A legacy of the War on Poverty.* New York: Free Press.

Haskins, R. (1989). Beyond metaphor: The efficacy of early childhood education. *American Psychologist, 44,* 274–282.

Hood, J. (1992). Caveat emptor: The Head Start scam. *Policy Analysis, 187.* Washington, DC: Cato Institute.

Hunt, J.M. (1975). Reflections on a decade of early education. *Journal of Abnormal Child Psychology, 3*(4), 275–330.

Huston, A.C. (1991). Antecedents, consequences, and possible solutions for poverty among children. In A.C. Huston (Ed.), *Children in poverty: Child development and public policy* (pp. 282–315). Cambridge, MA: Cambridge University Press.

Lee, V.E., Brooks-Gunn, J., Schnur, E., & Liaw, F. (1990). Are Head Start effects sustained? A longitudinal follow-up comparison of disadvantaged children attending Head Start, no preschool, and other preschool programs. *Child Development, 61*(2), 495–507.

McCall, R. (1993). *Head Start: Its potential, its achievements, its future—A briefing paper for policy makers.* Pittsburgh, PA: University of Pittsburgh, Office of Child Development, Center for Social and Urban Research.

National Head Start Association. (1990). *Head Start: The nation's pride, A nation's challenge.* Alexandria, VA: Author.

National Head Start Association. (1993). *Investing in quality: The impact of the Head Start Expansion and Improvement Act of 1990.* Alexandria, VA: Author.

National Head Start Association. (1996). *Investing in quality revisited: The impact of the Head Start Expansion and Improvement Act of 1990 after five years of implementation.* Alexandria, VA: Author.

Powell, C.G. (1995). *A cost-benefit approach to understanding why Head Start is the nation's pride.* Alexandria, VA: National Head Start Association.

Powell, C.G. (1998). *Targeted fiscal investment and quality in preschool intervention programs: Policy lessons learned from the Head Start Expansion and Improvement Act of 1990.* Ann Arbor, MI: UMI Dissertation Services.

Powell, C.G., Brush, L., & Gaidurgis, A. (1998). The effects of Head Start's quality improvement funding, *NHSA Dialog,* 2:1, 20–30.

Rovner, J. (1990). Head Start is one program everyone wants to help. *Congressional Quarterly,* 48(16), 1191–1195.

Schweinhart, L. (1990). Testimony for the subcommittee on Human Resources; Committee on Education and Labor. Washington, DC: U.S. House of Representatives.

U.S. Department of Health and Human Services (DHHS). (1993). *Creating a 21st century Head Start: Final Report of the Advisory Committee on Head Start Quality and Expansion.* Washington, DC: Author.

U.S. Department of Health and Human Services (DHHS), Administration on Children, Youth and Families (ACYF). (1992). *Head Start statistical fact sheet.* Washington, DC: Author.

U.S. Department of Health and Human Services (DHHS), Administration on Children, Youth and Families (ACYF). (1995). *Head Start performance measures: Progress report.* Washington, DC: Author.

U.S. Department of Health and Human Services (DHHS), Administration on Children, Youth and Families (ACYF). (2003). *Head Start statistical fact sheet.* Washington, DC: Author.

U.S. General Accounting Office. (1994a). *Early childhood programs: Local perspectives on barriers to providing Head Start Services* (GAO/HEHS-95-8). Washington, DC: Author.

U.S. General Accounting Office. (1994b). *Early childhood centers: Services to prepare children for school often limited* (GAO/HEHS-95-8). Washington, DC: Author.

U.S. Department of Health and Human Services (DHHS), Office of the Inspector General. (1989). *Dysfunctional families in Head Start.* (OEI-09-90-01000). Washington, DC: Author.

Washington, V., & Greene, S. (1995). *Head Start success stories.* Alexandria, VA: National Head Start Association.

Washington, V., & Oyemade-Bailey, U.J. (1995). *Project Head Start: Models and strategies for the twenty-first century.* New York: Garland Publishing

Zigler, E., & Muenchow, S. (1992). *Head Start: The inside story of America's most successful educational experiment.* New York: Basic Books.

Zigler, E., & Styfco, S.J. (1994a). Head Start: Criticisms in a constructive context. *American Psychologist,* 49, 127–132.

Zigler, E., & Styfco, S.J. (1994b). Is the Perry Preschool better than Head Start? Yes and no. *Early Childhood Research Quarterly,* 9, 269–287.

Zigler, E., & Styfco, S.J. (1997). Preface to the paperback edition. In E. Zigler & J. Valentine (Eds.), *Project Head Start: A legacy of the War on Poverty* (pp. xi–xxxix). Alexandria, VA: National Head Start Association.

Zigler, E., Styfco, S., & Gilman, E. (1993). The national Head Start program for disadvantaged preschoolers. In E. Zigler & S. Styfco (Eds.), *Head Start and beyond: A national plan for extended childhood intervention* (pp. 1–41). New Haven, CT: Yale University Press.

CHAPTER 21

Head Start

A Decade of Challenge and Change

JUDITH A. CHAFEL AND HEATHER L. SUGIOKA

O ver the course of Head Start's nearly 40-year history, the early intervention model has faced many challenges. These challenges have stemmed from controversies that have ranged from finding an appropriate site for the program's administrative structure in the federal bureaucracy to demonstrating cost-effectiveness (Butler & Gish, 2002). Congressional appropriations have never fully resolved issues of quality and access because funding has always been problematic. (Butler & Gish, 2002; Gish & Spar, 1999). To illustrate, at the end of the 20th century only a proportion of economically eligible children had gained entry to the program (see Table 21.1). This chapter provides a 10-year perspective on Head Start by examining authorizations of funding, program quality, and societal change. The inquiry was undertaken with the aim of suggesting directions for future policy.

HEAD START REAUTHORIZATIONS IN THE 1990S

Over the years, a debate over expansion versus quality has accompanied reauthorizations of Head Start. The Head Start Expansion and Quality Improvement Act of 1990 (PL 101-501), considered by some to be "landmark legislation" (National Head Start Association, 1993), authorized funds to serve every eligible child by 1994 (Congressional Quarterly Almanac, 1990). Unfortunately, this worthwhile goal has not been met, although fund-

We express our appreciation to Julia Dadds, Judi Johnson-Stevens, and Nathan Sugioka for their assistance in the preparation of this chapter. Special acknowledgment is given to Guillermo Montes for creating the inflation figure that appears in the chapter.

An earlier version of this chapter was presented at the Fifth International Conference on the Child: Children in Poverty—The Impact of Economic, Social and Political Choices, sponsored by the Organization for the Protection of Children's Rights, Dorval, Quebec, May, 2002. This chapter was submitted for publication in November 2002.

Table 21.1.　Estimates of Head Start populations and percent served, FY 1998
(number in thousands)

Age	Population March 1999	Economically eligible 1998	Enrollment FY 1998	Percent served
Younger than 3	11,456	2,607	28	1%
Age 3	3,944	938	264	28%
Age 4	3,982	892	475	53%
Age 3–4	7,926	1,830	739	40%

ing increased more than four-fold between 1990 and 2002 (Butler & Gish, 2002) and enabled growth in cost per child to outpace inflation (see Figure 21.1) and to steadily increase enrollments (Head Start Bureau, 2001). The full-funding provision was surrounded by a strong political debate (Congressional Quarterly Almanac, 1990; Rovner, 1990). While Congress preferred to focus on quality, the first Bush Administration favored expansion (Congressional Quarterly Almanac, 1990; Hook, 1990; Rovner, 1990). The 1990 bill attempted to achieve a compromise by authorizing enough funds for both purposes (Hook, 1990).

The Head Start Act Amendments of 1994 (PL 103-252) and the Head Start Amendments of 1998 (PL 105-285) effected a gradual transition toward an emphasis on quality. The 1994 legislation addressed a growing concern that quality not be diminished by expansion (S.R. Rep. 103-251, 1994a). Shortly before the 1994 Act was passed, the Committee on Labor and Human Resources stressed growth in enrollments but stated that it "must be undertaken in a planned and orderly fashion" (S.R. Rep. 103-251, 1994a). Therefore, the legislation addressed both expansion and quality but placed conditions on the former. For the first time, the quality of a program and its capability to serve more children were evaluated in granting funds for expansion (Katz, 1994a). The Secretary of Health and Human Services was authorized to grant monies for the extension of services to programs based on a number of considerations that included

1. The quality of a program

2. The need for full-day, year-round child care

3. The number of eligible but unserved children (PL 103-252)

Concerned about quality, the 1998 Amendments curtailed expansion to a certain extent (Gish & Spar, 1999).

Each reauthorization of Head Start reserved funding for quality. The 1990 Act provided that after the first year, 25% of any funds appropriated beyond the appropriation of the previous year (adjusted for inflation) were to be used for quality improvements for

1. Increased salaries and benefits (at least one half of the quality improvement fund)

2. Employment of additional staff

3. Training to enhance staff qualifications

4. An adequate physical environment

Authorizations of funding for quality in the 1994 legislation (again 25% of excess funds) were targeted for similar quality improvements, although half of the funds were no longer

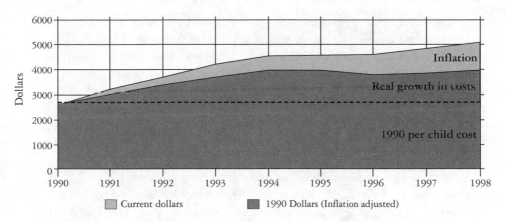

Figure 21.1. Head Start per-child cost, adjusted for inflation

Note: Data on cost per child were obtained from the Head Start Fact Sheets. The authors used the inflation calculator on the Department of Labor web site (http://www.bls.gov) to adjust for inflation. The calculator is based on the average consumer price index, which is a measure of changes in the cost of goods and services bought by urban households. Figure created by Guillermo Montes.

reserved for salaries and benefits. In addition, the legislation designated funds to improve community needs assessments and to meet performance standards regarding the provision of services. With growing acknowledgment of the importance of quality and a concern for long-term educational impact and program performance (Butler & Gish, 2002), the 1998 legislation raised the amount of funds set aside for quality improvements (60% of new funds), a substantial increase from the 25% required by the 1990 and 1994 legislation. The legislation, however, authorized a gradual decrease to 25% by 2003.

Although Head Start legislation in the 1990s authorized "a set-aside" for quality improvements, the approach had limitations because the amount designated depended on the availability of excess funds. If excess funds are guaranteed, then connecting the two may be a wise strategy, but as Verzaro-O'Brien, Powell, and Sakamoto pointed out, this may not always be the case when the political climate makes funding problematic. In *Investing in Quality Revisited,* a report of the National Head Start Association, they called for "a more stable solution" (1996, p. 22).

Demonstrating a growing concern for quality, legislation from 1990 to 1998 created greater monitoring procedures and higher performance standards. The 1990 legislation mandated a review of each agency every 3 years. The Head Start Improvement Act of 1992 (PL 102-401) extended this review to include newly designated programs. The creation of new outcome measures, updated performance standards, and enhanced monitoring and improvement procedures represented important elements of the 1994 Act's focus on quality. The legislation brought about a new expectation that Head Start provide better evidence of its effects on children, and the federal government was to assume a more active role in this process (Katz, 1994b). The Secretary of the United States Department of Health and Human Services (DHHS) was instructed to develop updated quality standards, and each Head Start agency was to undergo a review, as legislated by prior reauthorizations, to ensure compliance with these standards. Agencies failing a review were bound to begin immediate correction or develop an improvement plan, and the DHHS

Secretary was obliged to provide training and technical assistance. In addition, the Amendments required the Secretary to initiate procedures to terminate Head Start agencies that failed to correct any deficiency. To enhance quality and ensure school readiness, the 1998 legislation created standards that required children in Head Start programs to develop a variety of specific skills. The legislation directed the Secretary to see to the design of *results-based* performance measures to assess the attainment of these new standards to ensure that Head Start children had obtained the required skills. The consequences of failure were essentially the same as specified by the 1994 legislation. New priorities for technical assistance focused on school readiness and the new educational performance measures.

Over the years, Head Start Amendments have mandated higher credentials for teachers and, to a lesser degree, enhanced qualifications for family services staff. The 1990 legislation required at least one credentialed teacher for every Head Start classroom by 1994. Accepted credentials included a Child Development Associate (CDA) credential, state-awarded certificate (at least commensurate with a CDA), an associate's, bachelor's, or advanced degree in early childhood education, or a related degree with demonstrated preschool competency. The 1994 legislation extended this mandate to 1996 due to a lack of qualified staff (S.R. Rep. 103-251, 1994b). The 1998 Act strengthened the teacher qualification requirement by mandating that at least 50% of teachers nationwide by 2003 must possess a degree (an associate's, bachelor's, or advanced degree in early childhood education or a related degree combined with preschool teaching experience). *Alternatively,* those without a degree were required to have an appropriate credential. To enhance the qualifications of family service staff, the 1994 legislation mandated the development of qualification standards and model curricula for skill development in family services and supported the creation of a nationally accepted credential.

The design of research on Head Start quality has continued to improve. The 1990 legislation attempted to enhance quality by funding more *extensive* research. The law asked for a report on the status of Head Start children every 2 years, research on approaches to providing comprehensive services to low-income children from birth to age 3 and children in dysfunctional families, and a longitudinal study on the effects of Head Start components on particular subgroups. For methodological rigor, this research was to use a control group consisting of children not participating in Head Start as a basis for comparison.

The 1994 Act improved on previous research methods by requiring a continuing program of research rather than simply conducting specific studies. This program was intended to ensure consistent improvement of Head Start quality and to investigate new methods of serving low-income families and children. The legislation also reflected an awareness that Head Start be a testing ground for best practices in early childhood education (S.R. Rep. 103-251, 1994c). The 1990 legislation's emphasis on longitudinal research continued in 1994 by authorizing studies on 1) improvement of the program as preparation for school and other settings and 2) developmental progress of Head Start children and families during and after participation in Head Start. In the context of disagreement about the long-term benefits of Head Start, Congress asked for increased evaluation in 1998 (Butler & Gish, 2002), bringing a concern for the need for rigorous research to new heights. The 1998 legislation required the use of sound methodological techniques, such as random selection of subjects, consideration of sources of variation, longitudinal designs, standardized measures, and employment of national data sets. The legislation also expanded the breadth of what was to be investigated, mandating a national impact study, and more.

Several initiatives broadened the scope of Head Start's services over the years. The 1990 Act 1) reauthorized the very early childhood intervention programs and Parent-Child Centers for children less than 3 years of age; 2) encouraged the provision of full-day, year-round child care; and 3) created (and evaluated) the Head Start Transition Project to assist children and their families in the passage from Head Start to elementary school. The 1994 legislation also extended services by providing for infant/toddler care, integrating past early child care programs with a new initiative for children from birth to age 3, later called Early Head Start. The Amendments mandated basic activities (e.g., the transfer of Head Start records and parental training in school administrative procedures) to facilitate children's transition to elementary school. The legislation identified the development of full-day, year-round care as one of several training and technical assistance priorities.

Welfare reform inspired an increasing concern about collaboration. Due to the need for full-day, year-round care and the importance of accommodating parents' work schedules (S.R. Rep. 103-251, 1994d), the 1994 Amendments urged the creation of partnerships with community agencies serving low-income children and families. The 1998 legislation encouraged collaboration between local Head Start agencies and state Head Start Associations and instructed the Secretary to eliminate barriers between Head Start and other local, state, and federal child care programs and to provide technical assistance for these purposes. The legislation also authorized technical assistance for the development of collaborative initiatives with states to share ideas on new methods for supplying care full-day, year-round, and to create early childhood professional development systems.

Although no further authorizations since 1998 have been implemented at the time of this writing, the George W. Bush Administration forwarded new funding proposals and designed new initiatives to support as a top priority prereading and numeracy skills (Butler & Gish, 2002). President Bush requested $6.667 billion in funding for 2003. To promote school readiness, the President made a proposal to move Head Start's administrative structure to the Department of Education. He suggested and supported initiatives to ensure that all children in Head Start and other preschool programs be able to read by the third grade. He recommended the creation of a task force to accomplish a number of objectives, such as 1) implementing research on reading and numeracy skills development, 2) reviewing the administration and budget of Head Start and other programs to ascertain effectiveness in reaching the new learning objectives, and 3) developing initiatives based on successful early learning methods in science.

Summary

Appropriations of funding for Head Start rose appreciably throughout the 1990s. Legislation enacted during this time attempted to balance increasing access for children with implementing quality improvements, while extending the services provided by Head Start. Quality was addressed through new performance standards, monitoring procedures, training and technical assistance, staff improvement requirements, strengthening of the program's educational component, research initiatives, and so forth. Despite these emphases, serious challenges continued to confront the early intervention model. By the end of the 20th century, Head Start had strengthened its quality, but shortcomings remained.

HEAD START QUALITY

In 1997, the National Research Council (NRC) commissioned its Committee on Early Childhood Pedagogy "to study a broad range of behavioral and social science research on early learning and development and to explore the implications of that research for the education and care of young children ages 2 to 5" (Bowman, Donovan, & Burns, 2001, p. 3). The report issued by the NRC summarized a large body of literature, some of which concerned "program quality." Ample empirical findings suggested a connection between a number of programmatic attributes and positive effects on children. In summarizing the review, the report emphasized seven interrelated factors grouped into three categories: program structure, processes, and curricula. (See also Frede, 1998, for a brief review.)

The discussion that follows draws on a variety of literature and data, including two sets of Head Start Program Information Reports (PIRs; Administration on Children, Youth and Families, 2001) to examine Head Start's status on these program attributes. The PIR poses questions about program specifics, some of which relate to "quality," and completion is obligatory for every program (DHHS, 1998). In 1996, Verzaro-O'Brien and colleagues reported on the findings of an analysis similar in nature to the one conducted here. The present work extends the time frame for study and employs a somewhat different conceptual framework of quality variables. Data are taken or calculated from PIR National Summaries for the 1990–1991 and 2000–2001 program years. Dates that the data sets closed, number of agencies reporting, and response rates can be found in Table 21.2.

To guide the discussion, Table 21.3 summarizes PIR data related to Head Start program quality for the two sets of years.

Structure

The PIR furnishes information directly bearing on two of the variables shown in Table 21.3 (class size and child–teacher ratio) as well as on others of relevance to service intensity (length of day and length of duration in the program). Service intensity may be addressed in a variety of ways, but as Frede (1998, p. 92) pointed out, it should "be viewed as more than a matter of hours of services." Based on PIR data, as shown in Table 21.3, only small proportions of children were enrolled for 2 years or more in both sets of years, although proportions of the total enrollment were higher in 2000–2001. About twice as many children in the center-based option 5 days per week were provided with full-day services in 2000–2001 compared with 1990–1991, but while the figure is substantial, it still represents only a minority of children. According to Barnett (1998, p. 40), "high-quality, full-day, year-round ECE beginning in infancy and continuing to school entry is likely to produce the greatest cognitive and academic gains for disadvantaged children."

In fiscal year 2000, enrollment was divided among children of these ages: younger than 3 years (6 %), 3 years (33%), 4 years (56%), and 5 years and older (5%) (Head Start Bureau, 2001). The average child–teacher ratio and class size in Head Start classrooms may be compared with guidelines set by the National Association for the Education of Young Children (NAEYC; DHHS, 2001). NAEYC's guidelines have been established for accreditation purposes: For children 3, 4, and 5 years of age, a ratio of at least 1 adult to every 10 children and a maximum class size of 20 (Bredekamp, 1990). Head Start regu-

Table 21.2. PIR national summaries for the 1990–1991 and 2000–2001 program years

PIR	Date data set closed	Agencies reporting	Response rate
1990–1991	December 1991	1,857	Not available
2000–2001	December 2001	2,518	99.3%

lations require two teachers or a teacher and an aide in every classroom, no more than 20 children in a group of 4- and 5-year-olds or 17 in a group of 3-year-olds (smaller for double sessions), and no more than 8 in a group of infants and toddlers (*Federal Register,* 1996; DHHS, 1999). Unfortunately, data broken down by age of group (and double session) are not available from the PIR. So, only a cautious general statement may be offered here. Table 21.3 shows PIR numbers lower than the NAEYC figures for both sets of years. The child–teacher ratios in Table 21.3 compare favorably for 1990–1991 and slightly less favorably for 2000–2001, with the ratios of "successful" interventions that seldom assigned more than seven children to a teacher (United States General Accounting Office [USGAO], 1995, cited by Frede, 1998). Findings from several studies suggest that positive teacher behaviors, positive child behaviors, and positive effects on learning and child development are more likely when teachers are assigned to a smaller number of children (Bowman et al., 2001; DHHS, 2001; Frede, 1998).

Because Head Start concentrates on child and family needs in a variety of areas, it is also important to look at staffing beyond the level of the classroom. A 1994 study by the USGAO analyzed data obtained from a nationally representative sample of programs and found a sizable proportion of Head Start directors (more than 86%) short of qualified staff. The report pointed to noncompetitive salaries as a source of the problem. Yet, Whitebook (1995) reported that average caseloads for some Head Start staff had declined considerably between 1990–1991 and 1994–1995: for example, from 1:305 to 1:178 for parent involvement personnel and 1:161 to 1:91 for social services staff (cited by Verzaro-O'Brien et al., 1996). According to the 2000–2001 PIR, the average number of families served by each family service caseworker was 37.9, a more acceptable figure than those just noted. The PIR does not provide information about other areas of service delivery, although it is possible that these caseloads were high.

Although Head Start throughout its history has offered inadequate compensation to its employees, the extent to which this contributes to staffing problems presently is not entirely clear. The National Summary of the 2000–2001 PIR shows that a teacher earned an average annual salary of $21,000, an assistant teacher $14,000, a parent involvement services expert $28,000, a child development/education services expert $35,000, and a program director $50,000 (the first two figures full-time averages, and all figures rounded to the nearest thousand). Workers with a high school diploma in the U.S. labor force earn more than Head Start teachers: an average of $24,572 per year in 2000 (United States Census Bureau, 2001). To further compare, the federal government defined a yearly income of $17,050 for a family of four as the "poverty line" in 2000 (*Federal Register,* 2000). Though PIR data on number of years in position are not reported for all staff, data that are available for 2000–2001 indicate that some staff remained in their positions for multiple years. The length of time ranged from 6.06 years (family and community partnership expert) to 8.39 years (director). Average turnover rates for teachers (9.7%) and staff

Table 21.3. Head Start quality[1]

Dimension	1990–1991 PIR	2000–2001 PIR
Structure		
Class size	19.24	17.385
Child-teacher ratio	1 to 4.65	1 to 7.815
Service intensity	• 19.2% of children full day* • 36.3% of children part day* • 17.8% of children second year** • .93% of children third year**	• 39.1% of children full day* • 22.2% of children part day* • 26.0% of children second year** • 1.7% of children three or more years**
Processes		
Classroom/Child development or education supervisory staff qualifications	• 82.1 (27.2)% of teachers (aides) with degree in ECE, CDA, or CA preschool certificate*** • 55.5 (23.2)% of teachers (aides) with CDA • 9.6 (22.3)% of teachers (aides) in CDA training • 81.3% of supervisory education staff with degree in ECE, CDA, or CA preschool certificate*** • 31.8% of supervisory education staff with CDA	• 41.1 (7)% of teachers (assistant teachers) with degree in ECE or field related to ECE*** • 3.9 (.85)% of teachers (assistant teachers) with degree in family/child studies or related field**** • 40.9 (21.1)% of teachers (assistant teachers) with CDA credential or state certificate • 6.9 (25.9)% of teachers (assistant teachers) in CDA training • 54.5% of supervisory child development staff with degree in ECE or field related to ECE*** • 12.6% of supervisory child development staff with degree in family/child studies or related field**** • 24.1% of supervisory child development staff with CDA or state certificate
Reflective teaching practices	Not available from PIR	Not available from PIR
Parent involvement	• 36.1% of staff current or former Head Start parents • 77.6% of volunteer hours by current or former Head Start parents	• 28.8% of staff current or former Head Start parents • 61.5% of volunteers current or former Head Start parents or guardians
Curricula		
School–Home connection	Not available from PIR	Not available from PIR

*for centered-based option 5 days per week and based on total funded enrollment
**based on total actual enrollment
***includes associate's, bachelor, and graduate degrees
**** bachelor or graduate degree
[1]The quality variables shown in the table are from Bowman, Donovan, and Burns (2001).

(not excluding teachers; 12.6%) based on 2000–2001 PIR data are relatively low. The average rate of teacher turnover compares quite favorably with other early childhood programs. Whitebook, Howes, and Phillips (1998) arrived at an estimate of 27% for the child care teachers they sampled in 1997.

Nonetheless, inadequate compensation does seem to have a connection with turnover. In a study of the effects of Head Start salaries and benefits on turnover, recruitment, and retention, McKey and Keating (1998) found fairly high levels of employee satisfaction with benefits, made better by the use of "quality improvement funds," but they nonetheless pointed out the inadequacy of salaries. Program directors most often attributed staff turnover (7.6% in the sample overall, although not a high figure) to inadequate salary. Although Head Start legislation in the 1990s attempted to address the issue of employee compensation through quality set asides, better funding is needed. McKey and Keating cited literature (Carnegie Corporation, 1994; NAEYC, 1996; National Center for the Early Childhood Work Force, 1996) that argues that salaries and benefits contribute in important ways to program quality.

Processes

Table 21.3 shows a category of "process" variables (qualifications for teaching, reflective teaching practices, and parent involvement; Bowman et al., 2001). More responsive and sensitive teacher behavior and better classroom quality have been related to higher teacher qualifications (DHHS, 2001; Frede, 1998). Adherence to Head Start's Program Performance Standards is also more likely when teachers are better educated (and remunerated; Whitebook, 1997). Unfortunately, PIR data on teacher qualifications were not reported in the same way in 1990–1991 and 2001–2001, which somewhat limits comparison. Nevertheless, some general inferences can be drawn. In both sets of years, estimates based on PIR data show that the vast majority of teachers (aides/assistant teachers) and supervisors possessed some form of credential. Larger proportions held some type of credential in 2000–2001 than in 1990–1991 (although the difference was small), a finding that seems to suggest that at least some progress was achieved by legislative mandates consistently directed toward this end. Although legislative mandates during the 1990s addressed the need for credentials, they required only 50% of all teachers to have an associate's or bachelor's degree (a requisite for teaching in the public schools). Only about one quarter of all head teachers (26.3%) and about half of all child development supervisors (51.7%) in 2000–2001 (figures not shown on Table 21.3) possessed a bachelor's degree or an advanced degree. Bowman and colleagues (2001, p. 262) stated: "What early childhood teachers know and are able to do is one of the major influences on the learning and development of young children." They concluded from a review of relevant research that a bachelor's degree, with expertise in early childhood education and development, was necessary.

The study by the USGAO (1994) pointed out that minimum educational requirements were not mandated for Head Start's nonteaching staff and suggested that without the necessary know-how, they may not be adequately equipped for the work that they do, especially with dysfunctional families. The development of competency-based credit for family service workers in social services stipulated by the 1994 Head Start reauthorization represented a partial response to this problem (USGAO, 1994). The 2000–2001 PIR shows average education levels for some personnel. On a scale of 1 to 5—with "3" indicating an associate's degree or at least 2 years of college completed, "4" a bachelor's degree, and "5" a graduate degree—the figures are: director (4.3), child development/education services expert (4.1), health services expert (3.5), parent involvement services expert (3.4), and family and community partnership expert (3.7). These staff possessed at least some college education. Unfortunately, the data do not show to what extent their educational backgrounds matched job requirements.

When teachers "reflect," another process variable shown in Table 21.3, they carefully consider their craft, and deliberation of this nature may culminate in better teaching with appropriate mentoring (Bowman et al., 2001; Frede, 1998). The Head Start Program Performance Standards, a mandated set of guidelines and requirements intended for all grantees (Gish & Spar, 1999), describe a variety of activities that necessitate reflection by Head Start's teaching staff:

- Plan for variation in ability levels and individual interests in all activities;

- Observe carefully as children engage in activities, and watch for opportunities to extend their thinking and range of interests, and to develop their problem-solving skills;

- Assist children to develop decision-making skills; and

- Together with parents, identify learning opportunities in the home, including how to adapt activities and household routines in response to children's interests, strengths, and needs (DHHS, 1999, p. 63)

Committees, with parents playing an important role, engage in curriculum review (DHHS, 1999). Head Start regulations also require staff communication and suggest ways of achieving it: for example, by "establishing a supportive climate in which open and frequent staff communication is encouraged and appreciated, so that staff can freely share their ideas and concerns and provide constructive feedback to their colleagues and supervisors" (DHHS, 1999, p. 183). They additionally speak to sufficient opportunity to plan, and impose pre- and in-service training. The federal government also obliges each program to undertake a comprehensive review annually, and the process suggested is not only methodical but also recursive in nature. To what extent reflective teaching occurs in Head Start programs, and how it is associated with positive outcomes for children and families, should become the focus of systematic empirical research.

Head Start has always emphasized parent involvement, another attribute of effective preschool programs shown in Table 21.3. For example, the 1994 amendments required agencies to include parents in decision making and program design. Other modes of parent involvement that characterize Head Start include family assessment, parent education, and program evaluation (DHHS, 1999, 2001). The PIR furnishes a limited amount of information on parent involvement. Estimates in Table 21.3 based on PIR data show that staff were made up of a smaller proportion of current or former Head Start parents in 2000–2001 than in 1990–1991, although current or former Head Start parents or guardians represented a sizable proportion of volunteers in 2000–2001. FACES, the Head Start Family and Child Experiences Survey (DHHS, 2001), provides more detailed data. These national-level data were obtained from 40 randomly selected programs, with 3,200 children and families participating in the study.

Findings confirmed substantial involvement by primary caregivers: for example, 54% and 69.4%, respectively, attended a parent education meeting or volunteered in the classroom. More than three fourths observed in the classroom, attended a parent–teacher conference, or visited with staff in the home. Involvement on Head Start's planning groups was also high, with 33% of parents participating at least once, and 15% more than three times. FACES data also showed full compliance on the part of a sizable proportion of grantees (73%) with Head Start objectives for effective parent participation in decision making about the program. Other results suggested that knowledgeable teachers may be better at fostering parent involvement, which speaks to the significance of adequate preparation for teaching. The study found a positive relationship between higher parent involvement and teacher certification and in-service training for staff, but the report was quick to point out that causality could not be inferred from the data. The study also documented very high levels of parent satisfaction with the program. Parent satisfaction extended to a number of areas, including respect and support for the family's background and culture (87.5%) and openness to parental ideas and participation (78.1%).

Analysis of the relation between family characteristics and parent involvement indicated better involvement on the part of unemployed parents as well as more educated parents. A decline in parent involvement is likely as a result of possible schedule conflicts created by the work requirements of welfare reform. In the future, as enforcement of these requirements continues, many of the activities described previously may become problematic (Joyner, 1998).

Curricula

Bowman et al. made this point about curricula, the third category of program quality shown in Table 21.3:

> While no single curriculum or pedagogical approach can be identified as best, children who attend well-planned, high-quality early childhood programs in which curriculum aims are specified and integrated across domains tend to learn more and are better prepared to master the complex demands of formal schooling. (2001, pp. 7–8)

According to the federal government, Head Start programs construct curriculum from sound child development principles (DHHS, 1999). Acknowledgment is given to every aspect of a child's development (cognitive, emotional, social, and physical) with the aim

> To provide all children with a safe, nurturing, engaging, enjoyable, and secure learning environment, in order to help them gain the awareness, skills, and confidence necessary to succeed in their present environment, and to deal with later responsibilities in school and in life. (DHHS, 1999, p. 58)

The federal government does not prescribe any particular curriculum but does expect an appreciation of diversity, linguistic and developmental appropriateness (Ripple, Gilliam, Chanana, & Zigler, 1999), and strong parent involvement (DHHS, 1999). To ensure school readiness, the 1998 Head Start legislation created standards that required programs to help children develop specific skills. Unfortunately, all Head Start programs do not exhibit the same quality despite the federal government's requirement that they conform to performance standards (Gish & Spar, 1999; Ripple et al., 1999).

FACES found an overall rating of "good" quality in a sample of 498 classrooms on the Early Childhood Environment Rating Scale (ECERS; DHHS, 2001). The instrument assesses numerous dimensions, some of which comprise the "stuff" of early childhood curricula, including learning activities, furnishings and equipment, and teacher–child interaction. Data collected at three different points in time consistently yielded the same finding. The third data set (Spring 1998) showed the largest proportion of classrooms as being at least of "good" quality or higher (87.1%), although a small minority were rated as less than "good" (12.9%). Less favorable data from some of the individual scales showed that only a minority of classrooms attained a score of "excellent" on receptive and expressive language skills (39% and 41%, respectively), and sizable proportions less than "excellent" on activities that encouraged reasoning and thinking (40%) and informal use of language (44%).

The ECERS data were obtained from a sample (not *all*) of Head Start classrooms. Some Head Start observers have commented on differences in quality among Head Start programs (as noted; e.g., Ripple et al., 1999), so guarded interpretation of the overall results on classroom quality is warranted, even though FACES concluded that these and other available findings on center-based preschool programs provided evidence for Head Start's superiority.

FACES also collected data on this question: "Does Head Start enhance children's development and school readiness?" (DHHS, 2001, p. ii). Though the study found them "ready to learn," it pointed out that "despite the progress they made in kindergarten, Head Start graduates continued to score below national norms on most tasks for which norms were available" (p. 93). FACES reported sizable gains in areas such as writing and math skills, letter recognition, and word knowledge. The FACES study also found 1) better vocabulary scores in classrooms having more language learning opportunities and richer teacher–child interaction and 2) less time in noninteractive play and more devoted to pretense or interactive play by children in classrooms scoring better with respect to learning environment materials. While the last set of findings is promising, these results are limited because they are only correlational in nature (e.g., children's abilities on admission into higher-quality classrooms were not taken into consideration; see Bowman et al., 2001).

Summary and Conclusions

With more generous funding during the 1990s, Head Start enrollments steadily increased, a pattern of improved access for children that ought to be continued (Head Start Bureau, 2001). Class sizes and staff–child ratios remained acceptable, the average caseloads and qualifications of some staff improved, sizable proportions of FACES parents indicated being highly satisfied with and actively involved in the program, and the environment of a vast majority of FACES classrooms showed at least "good" quality (although the latter finding may not be generalizable to *all* Head Start classrooms). Nevertheless, serious problems continued to confront the early intervention model. Though a vast majority of teachers were credentialed, a bachelor's degree was not possessed by all, and insufficiently trained staff in many other areas of the program performed their tasks without the expertise required by their specialized and complex positions. Inadequate salaries and benefits may have negatively affected the hiring and retention of qualified personnel and thereby the size of comprehensive services caseloads. Although parent participation was high, the requirements of welfare reform (to be discussed later) render future continuation at such a high rate questionable.

These programmatic shortcomings suggest the need for specific policy changes. Despite persistent legislative mandates directed toward the goal of enhancing teacher qualifications, the credentials of Head Start teachers still do not meet the standards found in the public schools (DHHS, 2001). A minimum of a bachelor's degree with expertise in early childhood education and development should be mandated (Bowman et al., 2001). Making the degree mandatory for every lead teacher would provide a more solid foundation for achieving the goal of school readiness and meeting the new educational performance measures outlined by the 1998 legislation.

Similarly, specific educational credentials should be obligatory for *all* comprehensive services staff and caseloads reduced. Although the 1994 legislation mandated the development of model curricula and qualifications standards for family services staff, a specific degree and area of specialization should be legislated for *all* personnel. Progress made in implementing these mandates should be investigated and deficiencies addressed. The needs of Head Start families and the mandates of welfare reform both suggest that improving the competency and effectiveness of family services staff, especially, should be given top priority. Staff require specialized knowledge to cope with the challenges presented by their positions. Although some progress has been made in lowering caseloads, ratios remain high and should be further reduced. The serious social problems that frequently accompany poverty necessitate that staff work with only a limited number of families.

Raising teacher salaries would facilitate efforts to retain high-quality teaching staff. Past legislation has addressed the issue through "set-asides," but this mode of funding has not resulted in adequate compensation. To make adequate pay a reality, teacher salaries should be considered a priority to be achieved through "specified sums" rather than an objective to be attained through "excess funds" (Verzaro-O'Brien et al., 1996). Head Start's national visibility as a federally funded program places it in a pivotal position to serve as a model for acknowledging the professional status of early childhood personnel. This can be achieved by providing "a fair wage" to all of its employees and thus positively influencing the field of early childhood education as a whole (Whitebook, 1997).

Reflective teaching merits investigation. Federal legislation has mandated reflection in Head Start's administrative structure through regular monitoring and improvement procedures and performance standards. Systematic data on the extent to which reflection actually occurs should be collected. The PIR represents a valuable resource for providing specifics about this quality factor because of the exceptionally high response rate guaranteed by its federal mandate. Beyond that, carefully designed qualitative studies, especially ethnographies, should be conducted. In-depth observations can be designed to yield a holistic picture of the processes involved in reflective teaching and their implications for child development and the improvement of practice.

A CHANGING SOCIETY

Over the course of Head Start's history, American society has witnessed many changes (Joyner, 1998; Kassebaum, 1994; Takanishi & De Leon, 1994; USGAO, 1994). Today, more problems stress the economically disadvantaged: family instability, homelessness, substance abuse, street violence, and so forth. Furthermore, the problems are complex and demand immediate and extensive intervention (USGAO, 1994). In addition, more children younger than age 6 reside in families with single mothers in the workforce, a statistic likely to increase as additional families leave welfare (Joyner, 1998). The welfare system has been radically revised, moving from the goal of supporting low-income mothers in raising their children at home to requiring financial independence.

Legislated by the Personal Responsibility and Work Opportunity Reconciliation Act of 1996 (PRWORA), welfare reform emanated from 1) a concern about the increasing number of out-of-wedlock births, 2) a belief that the welfare system undermined work ethics (Larner, Terman, & Behrman, 1997), and 3) the size and cost of government. Aid to Families with Dependent Children (AFDC) was created in 1935 to protect offspring whose fathers had died or abandoned them. The program provided financial support for full-time mothers to raise their children at home (Blank & Blum, 1997; Larner et al., 1997). By 1993, however, 48% of AFDC recipients were never-married women (United States Department of Commerce, Bureau of the Census 1995, cited by Larner et al., 1997), and as more mothers entered the labor force, public opinion shifted toward disapproval of these nonworking, single mothers (Skocpol, 1996, cited by Larner et al., 1997). A main goal of the most recent legislation was to move welfare recipients into the workforce (Holcomb & Martinson, 2002; Loprest, 1999, 2001).

PRWORA strove to increase financial independence and work ethics by means of several requirements. The legislation eliminated entitlements, enforced work requirements, and imposed a lifetime limit of 5 years for receipt of welfare assistance, replacing the federal entitlement program, AFDC, with a lump-sum capped block grant to each state called Temporary Assistance for Needy Families (TANF; Zaslow, Tout, Smith, & Moore, 1998). With the shift from federal to state control, eligibility requirements and the amount of money allotted to families vary by state (Larner et al., 1997). The amount provided by TANF does not change with shifts in the economy (Larner et al., 1997). This means that funds may not be sufficient to assist additional families falling into poverty during periods of economic downturn. The legislative changes mandated by PRWORA affect many Head Start participants. Estimates based on PIR data show that 24.3% of Head Start families received TANF benefits during the 2000–2001 Program Year.

Zedlewski (2002) indicated that evidence for the impact of welfare reform on the income of low-income families is mixed. Analysis of the findings of several studies showed that although poverty overall has decreased, families with the lowest incomes have been harmed by the changes. For example, the annual disposable income (including means-tested benefits) of most single-mother families increased from 1995–1997, but that of single-mother families in the lowest and second to lowest deciles decreased (Primus, Rawlings, Larin, & Porter, 1999). More than 50% of those who had left welfare had pre-tax incomes below the poverty line, and more than 40% remained below the poverty line when receipt of food stamps and the Earned Income Tax Credit (EITC) were included (Loprest, 2001). Several problems affect families leaving welfare: for example, failure to utilize nontax benefits such as food stamps and child care (Zedlewski, 2002). Furthermore, a low rate of eligible families receive child care assistance due to low funding (Layzer, 2001, cited by Zedlewski, 2002).

Tout, Scarpa, and Zaslow (2002) found that a recent transition from welfare to work (that is, left welfare between 1997 and 1999) neither benefited nor harmed the well-being of children (birth to 17 years of age) on most of the outcomes measured (e.g., school engagement, health, social behavior). They highlighted the negative role of poverty on the well-being of *all* low-income children who fare poorly in comparison to more affluent children (at or above 200% of the poverty line in 1998) regardless of welfare history. While there is a scarcity of research on the effects of welfare reform on infants and toddlers (Child Trends, 2002), research on older children and children of all ages indicates that the mandates of welfare reform could have a positive effect on children if increased income accompanied mandatory parental participation in the work force (Aber, 2002; Child Trends, 2002).

A study by Chase-Lansdale, Coley, Lohman, and Pittman (2002) examined the relationship between welfare participation, welfare sanctions, and child development. Families leaving welfare between 1997 and 1999 (recent leavers) had the highest proportion of preschool children at risk for behavioral and emotional problems compared with families on welfare in 1999, those who left welfare before 1997, and nonentrants. Children in families on welfare with decreased benefits and those with reduced or eliminated benefits who had left welfare recently displayed lower cognitive scores and greater risk of behavioral problems than children in families whose welfare benefits had not been reduced or eliminated, either while on welfare or after recently leaving. According to Chase-Lansdale and colleagues (2002), children from sanctioned families who recently left welfare "show rates of problem behaviors three times higher than national norms" (p. 6). Increased exposure to stress resulting from the transition to work and diminished family income may explain why some groups of children fared worse (Chase-Lansdale et al., 2002).

Immediately after leaving welfare, the ability of mothers to provide economically for their children depends partly on their earnings (Executive Summary, 1997). Although a sizable proportion find employment, the majority have few assets to bring to the labor market (Executive Summary, 1997; Loprest, 2001), which makes the goal of self-sufficiency difficult to achieve. The type of work found tends to be of a low-skilled, low-paying nature (Aber, 2002; Loprest, 1999; Zedlewski, 2002). Most do not receive employer-sponsored health insurance, and more than one quarter work at night, making it challenging to find child care (Loprest, 1999, 2001). Assistance with child care is particularly important, as the average number of children for mothers on welfare is 2.6, and two thirds of them are younger than 6 (Executive Summary, 1997).

Most participants in welfare-to-work programs choose informal care provided by relatives and neighbors (Fuller, Kagan, Caspary, & Gauthier, 2002), a type of arrangement that is less expensive and more flexible than formal child care (Kisker & Ross, 1997) but that generally provides lower quality services (Kontos, Howes, Shinn, & Galinsky, 1995, cited by Zaslow et al., 1998). Fuller and colleagues (2002) reviewed several studies and found that mothers moving from welfare to work are likely to choose formal arrangements when they find a more stable job. Although resources for child care provided by federal and state governments for welfare recipients and low-income families have greatly increased since welfare reform, the supply of high quality formal child care is uneven in low-income neighborhoods (Fuller et al., 2002), and full-time formal care is more difficult to secure in these types of neighborhoods (Kisker & Ross, 1997). Therefore, formal child care arrangements identified are likely to be of low quality (Burchinal, Roberts, Nabors, & Bryant, 1996). Estimates based on PIR data indicate that during the 2000–2001 program year, 49% of all Head Start/Early Head Start (HS/EHS) families needed child care, full-day, year-round. Of these families, 26.3% received child care through a full-year HS/EHS program (using HS funds), 15.4 % through a HS/EHS program (using non-HS funds), and 35.2 % left their children at home or another home with a relative or unrelated adult (no cost).

Summary and Conclusions

The studies just reviewed suggest that families with the lowest incomes have fared worse economically under welfare reform, and children in these families may be more developmentally disadvantaged as a result. To address the developmental issue, Head Start services must be adapted to provide full-day child care for every family requiring this service. If not, parents may enroll their children in alternative care of inferior quality, and these arrangements may increase a child's exposure to risk factors with further negative implications for development (see Schorr, 1988). Inferior care combined with Head Start services part-day may also make the goals of early intervention more difficult to achieve because care of inferior quality may offset any benefits gained.

Lack of full-time child care not only inhibits Head Start's ability to meet the developmental needs of low-income children but also places the program's future at risk. In a needs analysis completed by one of the authors, a Head Start director spoke of unfilled openings for children in her program, a phenomenon that she attributed to the increasing demand for full-day care (Sugioka, Bahamonde, Brackman, Hadley, & Klotz, 1999). Though the administrator spoke only for her site, it is not unreasonable to conclude that the statement pertains to Head Start centers nationwide. The manager of another program used the word "evaporating" to characterize the demand for part-day Head Start (Joyner, 1998, p. 12).

The transformation of Head Start into a full-day, year-round service should proceed quickly. Although past legislation has attempted to address family requirements for a program of this type, need still exceeds supply. Steps should be taken to increase the supply of *high-quality care.* The Cost, Quality, and Child Outcomes in Child Care Centers Study substantiated the value of high-quality care with a diverse sample of children (Executive Summary, 2000). The longitudinal study (from preschool to early elementary school) documented the beneficial effects of high-quality care and the negative effects of poor-quality care persisting through second grade that affected children at risk more than others. Other results indicated that high-quality care was associated positively with behavioral and cognitive skills and readiness for school of a diverse group of children. Both sets of effects continued into elementary school. Additional positive outcomes persisted through early elementary school: better social skills and classroom behavior by children enjoying closer relationships with their teachers and better math and language skills by those experiencing classroom practices of higher quality. The study also found a connection between teacher compensation, specialized early childhood training, and formal educational levels *and* the quality of care. If Head Start rises to the challenge of offering high-quality child care, full-day year-round, the opportunity exists for it to demonstrate exemplary practice.

Collaboration between existing child care and early education programs may increase the supply of care, and states and Congress already have taken steps in this direction (Gish & Spar, 1999). This strategy encompasses other advantages as well (e.g., consolidation of services; see Holmes, 1995). Unfortunately, many impediments exist to achieving it (e.g., inadequate financial support; see USGAO, 1999). In the 1990s, Head Start legislation attempted to promote collaboration by making it a consideration for funding, and in other ways (Gish & Spar, 1999). Given the urgent need for full-time child care, maximizing the advantages of collaboration and minimizing the disadvantages is a necessary and worthwhile endeavor.

Efforts made by Head Start to move in the direction of providing full-day, year-round child care should be systematically studied. Quantitative and qualitative data from policy-relevant inquiries may result in valuable insights about how best to increase the supply of *high-quality care*. Phillips and Cabrera (1996) suggested issues bearing on the provision of care that merit examination (e.g., cost-effective methods). Another very important set of issues must be studied: the effects that full-day, year-round care provided by Head Start may have on children whose parents are becoming economically self-reliant and the mediating processes responsible for these effects. Findings emanating from studies focused on the last set of issues may help to resolve questions about Head Start's effectiveness.

As the mandates of welfare reform were being implemented, legislation enacted in the 1990s attempted to strengthen Head Start's parent involvement component through several mandates: 1) involving parents in educational services (Head Start Expansion and Quality Improvement Act, 1990), 2) providing literacy training and education in child development (either directly or through referral; Head Start Improvement Act of 1992), and 3) facilitating parents' presence in Head Start decision making and educational activities (Head Start Act Amendments of 1994). Although these efforts represent positive steps forward, the requirements of welfare reform imperil parent involvement as it exists today. If Head Start is to continue to involve parents in programming in substantive ways, as it has done in the past, it must develop innovative strategies that take into account work schedules, such as offering more services and opportunities for participation in the evening and providing home visits at more flexible hours.

CONCLUSION

Throughout the 1990s, Head Start met numerous challenges posed by an increasing awareness of the importance of program quality and the complex demands of a changing society. Despite the fact that it has flexibly adapted to many emerging priorities, unresolved issues persist. Some pertain to chronic programmatic weaknesses and others to societal needs yet to be addressed. The problems of contemporary children and families in poverty beg for imaginative and thoughtful solutions. If Head Start is to survive in the era of welfare reform, it must build on its historic strengths, rethink its vision, and seek out innovative strategies to heighten its quality and address new social realities. Numerous challenges lie ahead. They can be met, at least in part, with creative social policy.

REFERENCES

Aber, J.L. (2002). Framing the PRWORA/TANF reauthorization debate. *News & Issues, 12*(2), 1–3.
Administration on Children, Youth and Families. (2001). *Head Start Program Information Report 2000–2001*. Washington, DC: U.S. Department of Health and Human Services.

Barnett, W.S. (1998). Long-term effects on cognitive development and school success. In W.S. Barnett & S.S. Boocock (Eds.), *Early care and education for children in poverty: Promises, programs, and long-term results* (pp. 11–44). Albany: State University of New York Press.

Blank, S.W., & Blum, B.B. (1997). A brief history of work expectations for welfare mothers. *The Future of Children, 7*(1), 28–38.

Bowman, B., Donovan, M., & Burns, M. (Eds.). (2001). *Eager to learn: Educating our preschoolers.* Washington, DC: National Academy Press.

Bredekamp, S. (Ed.). (1990). *Accreditation criteria and procedures of the National Academy of Early Childhood Programs.* Washington, DC: National Association for the Education of Young Children.

Burchinal, M.R., Roberts, J.E., Nabors, L.A., & Bryant, D.M. (1996). Quality of center child care and infant cognitive and language development. *Child Development, 67,* 606–620.

Butler, A., & Gish, M. (2002). *Head Start: Background and funding.* CRS Report for Congress. Available at: http://www2.acf.dhhs.gov/programs/hsb/research/02_hsfs.htm

Carnegie Corporation. (1994). *Starting points: Meeting the needs of our youngest children.* New York: Author.

Chase-Lansdale, P., Coley, R., Lohman, B., & Pittman, L. (2002). *Welfare reform: What about the children?* (Policy Brief 02–1). Available at: http://www.jhu.edu/~welfare/19382_Welfare_jan02.pdf

Child Trends. (2002). *The unfinished business of welfare reform: Improving prospects for poor children and youth.* Available at: http://www.childtrends.org

Congressional Quarterly Almanac. (1990). *Major expansion for Head Start program.* 101st Congress, Second Session (Volume XLVI). Washington, DC: Author.

Executive Summary. (1997). Welfare to work. *The Future of Children, 7*(1), 1–7.

Executive Summary. (February 10, 2000). *The children of the Cost, Quality, and Outcomes Study Go to School.* Available at: http://www.fpg.unc.edu/~NCEDL/PAGES/cqes.htm

Federal Register. (1996, November 5). Washington, DC: US Government Printing Office.

Federal Register. (2000, February 15). Washington, DC: US Government Printing Office.

Frede, E.C. (1998). Preschool program quality in programs for children in poverty. In W.S. Barnett & S.S. Boocock (Eds.), *Early care and education for children in poverty: Promises, programs, and long-term results* (pp. 77–98). Albany: State University of New York Press.

Fuller, B., Kagan, S., Caspary, G., & Gauthier, C. (2002). Welfare reform and child care options for low-income families. *The Future of Children, 12*(1), 97–119.

Gish, M., & Spar, K. (1999). *Head Start: Background and funding.* (Issue Brief for Congress). Washington, DC: Library of Congress (Congressional Research Service).

Head Start Act Amendments of 1994, PL 103-252, 108 Stat. 624-651.

Head Start Amendments of 1998, PL 105-285, 112 Stat. 2703-2727.

Head Start Bureau. (2001). *Fiscal year-2001 Head Start fact sheet.* Washington, DC: Author. (Also available at: http://www2.acf.ddhs.gov/programs/hsb/about/fact2001.htm)

Head Start Expansion and Quality Improvement Act, 1990, PL 101-501, 104 Stat. 1224-1242.

Head Start Improvement Act of 1992, PL 102-401, 106 Stat. 1956–1960.

Holcomb, P., & Martinson, K. (2002). *Implementing welfare reform across the nation.* Available at: http://www.urban.org/Template.cfm?Section=ByTopic&NavMenuID=62&template=/TaggedContent/ViewPublication.cfm&PublicationID=7857

Holmes, M. (1995). Head Start: A key partner in system reform. *NHSA Journal, 13*(4), 18–21.

Hook, J. (1990). 101st Congress leaves behind plenty of laws, criticism. *Congressional Quarterly, 48*(44), 3683–3709.

Joyner, C. (1998). *Head Start: Challenges faced in demonstrating program results and responding to societal changes* (GAO/T-HEHS-98–183). Washington, DC: United States General Accounting Office.

Kassebaum, N. (1994). Only the best for America's children. *American Psychologist, 49,* 123–126.

Katz, J.L. (1994a). Head Start reauthorization. *Congressional Quarterly, 52*(23), 1653–1655.

Katz, J.L. (1994b). Head Start funding nears legislative crossroad. *Congressional Quarterly, 52*(9), 541–547.

Kisker, E.E., & Ross, C.M. (1997). Arranging child care. *The Future of Children, 7*(1), 99–109.

Kontos, S., Howes, C., Shinn, M., & Galinsky, E. (1995). *Quality in family child care and relative care.* New York: Teachers College Press.

Larner, M.B., Terman, D.L., & Behrman, R.E. (1997). Welfare to work: Analysis and recommendations. *The Future of Children, 7*(1), 4–19.

Layzer, J. (2001). *Child care funding: How much is needed and is there enough?* Statement presented at the Brookings Institute Forum, Washington, DC.

Loprest, P. (1999). *Families who left welfare: Who are they and how are they doing?* Washington DC: The Urban Institute.

Loprest, P. (2001). *How are families that left welfare doing? A comparison of early and recent welfare leavers.* Available at: http://www.urban.org/Template.cfm?Section=ByAuthor&NavMenuID=63&template=/TaggedContent/ViewPublication.cfm&PublicationID=7249

McKey, R., & Keating, K. (1998). *Study of benefits for Head Start employees: Final report.* McLean, VA: Ellsworth Associates.

National Association for the Education of Young Children. (1996). *An important bond: Your child and your caregiver.* Washington, DC: Author.

National Center for the Early Childhood Work Force. (1996). *Child care staff profile.* Washington, DC: Author.

National Head Start Association. (1993) *Investing in quality: The impact of the Head Start Expansion and Improvement Act of 1990 in its first year of implementation.* Alexandria, VA: Author.

Personal Responsibility and Work Opportunity Reconciliation Act (PRWORA) of 1996, PL 104-193, 42 U.S.C. §§ 1305 *et seq.*

Phillips, S.A., & Cabrera, N.J. (1996). *Beyond the blueprint: Directions for research on Head Start's families.* Washington, DC: National Academy Press.

Primus, W., Rawlings, L., Larin, K., & Porter, K. (1999). *The initial impacts of welfare reform on the incomes of single-mother families.* Washington, DC: Center on Budget and Policy Priorities.

Ripple, C., Gilliam, W., Chanana, N., & Zigler, E. (1999). Will fifty cooks spoil the broth? The debate over entrusting Head Start to the states. *American Psychologist, 54,* 327–343.

Rovner, J. (1990, April 21). Head Start is one program everyone wants to help. *Congressional Quarterly, 48*(16), 1191–1195.

Schorr, L. (with Schorr, D.). (1988). *Within our reach: Breaking the cycle of disadvantage.* New York: Doubleday.

Skocpol, T. (1996). The politics of American social policy, past and future. In V.R. Fuchs (Ed.), *Individual and social responsibility: Child care, education, medical care, and long-term care in America* (pp. 309–340). Chicago: University of Chicago Press.

S.R. REP. NO. 103-251, at 24-25 (1994a), *reprinted in* 1994 US Code Congressional and Administrative News, 598, 622.

S.R. REP. NO. 103-251, at 45 (1994b), *reprinted in* 1994 US Code Congressional and Administrative News, 598, 643.

S.R. REP. NO. 103-251, at 47 (1994c), *reprinted in* 1994 US Code Congressional and Administrative News 598, 645.

S.R. REP. NO. 103-251, at 25 (1994d), *reprinted in* 1994 US Code Congressional and Administrative News 598, 623.

Sugioka, H.L., Bahamonde, C., Brackman, R., Hadley, K., & Klotz, M. (1999). Final report: 1998 needs analysis of four community agencies serving the poor in Bloomington, Indiana (pp. 3–12). *Proceedings of the Thirteenth Conference on The Small City and Regional Community,* University of Wisconsin-Stevens Point Center for the Small City.

Takanishi, R., & De Leon, P. (1994). A Head Start for the 21st century. *American Psychologist, 49,* 120–122.

Tout, K., Scarpa, J., & Zaslow, M. (2002). *Children of current and former welfare recipients: Similarly at risk.* Available from Child Trends, Washington, DC.

United States Census Bureau. (2001). *Statistical abstract of the United States: 2001.* (121st ed.). Washington, DC: The Bureau (GPO).

United States Department of Commerce, Bureau of the Census. (March, 1995). *Mothers who receive AFDC payments, fertility, and socioeconomic characteristics.* Statistical brief 95–2. Washington, DC: Author.

United States Department of Health and Human Services (DHHS). (1998). *Head Start Program Performance Measures: Second Progress Report.* Washington, DC: Author.

United States Department of Health and Human Services (DHHS). (1999). *Head Start Program Performance Standards and Other Regulations.* Washington, DC: Author.

United States Department of Health and Human Services (DHHS). (2001). *Head Start FACES: Longitudinal Findings on Program Performance: Third Progress Report.* Available at: http://www.acf.hhs.gov/programs/core/ongoing_research/faces/faces_intro.html

United States General Accounting Office (USGAO). (1994). *Early childhood programs: Local perspectives on barriers to providing Head Start services* (GAO/HEHS-95–8). Washington, DC: Author.

United States General Accounting Office (USGAO). (1995). *Early childhood centers: Services to prepare children for school often limited* (GAO/HEHS-95–21). Washington, DC: Author.

United States General Accounting Office (USGAO). (1999). *Early childhood programs and services for low-income families* (GAO/HEHS-00–11). Washington, DC: Author.

Verzaro-O'Brien, M., Powell, G., & Sakamoto, L. (1996). *Investing in quality revisited: The impact of the Head Start expansion and improvement act of 1990 after five years of investment.* Alexandria, VA: National Head Start Association.

Whitebook, M. (1995). *Salary improvements in Head Start: Lessons for the early care and education field.* Washington, DC: National Center for the Early Childhood Work Force.

Whitebook, M. (1997). Looking at salary improvements in Head Start. *Children and Families: The Magazine of the National Head Start Association, 16*(2), 48–52.

Whitebook, M., Howes, C., & Phillips, D. (1998). *Worthy work, unlivable wages: The National Child Care Staffing Study, 1988–1997.* Washington, DC: Center for the Child Care Workforce.

Zaslow, M., Tout, K., Smith, S., & Moore, K. (1998). Implications of the 1996 welfare legislation for children: A research perspective. *Social Policy Report* (Society for Research in Child Development), 12(3).

Zedlewski, S. (2002). Family economic resources in the post-reform era. *The Future of Children, 12*(1), 121–145.

CHAPTER 22

Professional Social Work Involvement in Head Start

Arthur J. Frankel

There is every reason to believe that the social work profession should be integrally involved with Head Start. Social work's mission includes advocating for America's poor, disadvantaged, and disenfranchised communities—all of which are heavily represented in Head Start programs. In fact, because most of the families that are enrolled in Head Start have historically been well below the poverty line, it would be a rare Head Start family indeed that did not have extensive contacts with social workers in a social service or welfare program, such as Welfare-to-Work, mental health programs, or drug and alcohol services.

In social work education, from the 2-year B.S.W. (bachelor's of social work) undergraduate programs, to the 1- or 2-year graduate M.S.W. (master's of social work) programs, the educational curriculum is heavily concentrated in concepts and skills for working with families and children. Required curricula cover intensive classroom and practicum training in case management and approaches to dealing with the many issues that impoverished families face, which, of course, include helping families access necessary child care and early educational opportunities for children.

Head Start, too, has a long history of attempting to provide and facilitate social services for the families in their programs. National *Head Start Performance Standards* (1998) have dictated that every Head Start program develop a comprehensive education/social service model. Not only are there early childhood educational standards for teachers, aides, and curriculum areas, but there are also mandates for a wide range of social services, all of which are familiar to what social workers do as part of their mission. Head Start programs employ a range of coordinators who are responsible for different aspects of their social service support system. The Special Needs Coordinator is responsible for assessing early childhood learning difficulties, including cognitive impairments and delays and indications of behavior disorders, such as attention-deficit/hyperactivity disorder (ADHD). The Health Coordinator organizes health screenings; assesses nutritional, dental, and general health problems; and facilitates the presentations of preventive health programs to children and their families. Although the Special Needs Coordinator and the Health Coordinator are focused on their specialties, they are not necessarily responsible for providing direct services if they should suspect a potential problem. Rather, they are responsible for accessing local resources that can further assess problems related to special needs or health or calling on a consultant hired by the Head Start program. In most cases, Head Start programs have either formal or informal contractual relationships with professionals and/or agencies that provide assessment and treatment for Head Start families. Thus, these coordinators are acting as case managers once a problem is suspected.

Every program also has a Parent Involvement Coordinator who is responsible for encouraging parents to become involved in the Head Start classrooms, as well as a wide scope of parent educational classes, self-help groups, field trips, and other organized events sponsored by each program. Parent involvement is viewed as integral to the Head Start philosophy. In fact, there are those who feel that the remarkable short- and long-term effects in the academic and "life success" indicators documented by Head Start researchers (Haskins, 1989) are heavily related to the high intensity of parental involvement that all Head Start programs demand of their families (Frankel, 1997).

Although all of these coordinators are obviously performing tasks that would be comfortably integrated into any professional social work role, it is the Head Start Social Service Coordinator position in which there is the clearest intersection of traditional social work. In most programs, the Social Service Coordinator supervises one or more Family Service Workers (FSWs) who are responsible for linking the family with the teachers and other coordinating staff, as well as doing comprehensive case management (A Guide for Providing Social Services in Head Start, 1994). It is the FSW's role to monitor that each child and family is getting needed assessments and services, whether Head Start has these readily available or not. Thus, like all social workers, FSWs need to have a good grasp of community resources, excellent case management skills, and a system for following up both Head Start and community social service outcomes. Some types of referrals have become easier for FSWs as numerous Head Start programs around the country have developed special in-house programs to help families with such issues as drug and alcohol treatment, job readiness training and employment support, mental health treatment, literacy training, and family therapy.

Thus, when viewing both the social service profession and the Head Start program, it should be obvious that these two groups would have found each other almost from Head Start's inception and would still be reciprocally supporting each other into the 21st century. Social work offered a comprehensive training program and value system compatible with Head Start's mission. Head Start offered social work many opportunities as well. It is, and always has been, a unique "in-vivo" training ground for social work trainees. Head Start has been one of the few, if not the only, national community-based institutions serving the poor that integrated education, families, social services, and community action. Head Start's continual striving to be a true community-based institution, with required parental involvement in the classroom and on governing boards, is the embodiment of the social work mission. The expanding Head Start program, like the disappearing settlement house movement, could have been an excellent platform for social work to advocate its community mission, while providing needed services for families.

Unfortunately, in the 4 decades since Head Start began, the integration of Head Start and professional social work has not happened—in either academic preparation or in direct practice. Documentation of social work's involvement in Head Start comes from two sources: a very limited data base emanating from too few studies and anecdotal assessments from anyone who has worked with local Head Start social service systems. Both sources of information have indicated, with some sporadic exceptions, that there have been very few professional social workers directly involved in Head Start.

In 1990, the national Head Start Bureau in Washington, D.C., sponsored a case management demonstration project in 67 program sites selected to be representative of the wide variety of Head Start settings. This project, called the Family Services Center Project, provided grants to improve the social services delivery system. Grantees were to hire more highly trained social service staff and lower the worker–family ratio to 1:10 for a 3-year period. The typical FSW–family ratio ranged from 1:40 to 1:120 nationwide. This project also mandated a randomly selected control group in 26 of the funded sites. The independent variable was essentially the differences between the worker–family ratios in regular Head Start social services versus those in the Family Service Center. The dependent variables were to compare three specific outcomes between experimentals and controls: differences in drug and alcohol assessment and treatment; job training and employment; and literacy. Unfortunately, the comparative results from the 26 experimental sites with control groups showed no significant differences in any of the three major dependent variables (*Head Start Research,* 2000). This intensive study showed the difficulties in trying to track the effectiveness of the Head Start social service system. What the results suggested, more than its equivocal dependent variable outcomes, is that much more thinking and planning needs to go into assessing what Head Start social service workers should be doing, what to expect from their work with families, and how to document their work

A lot of time, money, and energy have been expended in Head Start's social service component. The philosophical and theoretical foundation of this work is sound. It is obvious that Head Start is connecting in unique ways with America's impoverished families, and it follows from any systems approach that this organization has a unique opportunity to have an impact not only on the family but also on the community life, social service organizations, and social policy issues relating to poverty. Head Start has appropriately struggled with how to make its social service system more effective and what professional entity should guide it on this journey. Social work has been the one profession singled out for this potential support (*Commissioners Task Force,* 1988).

To assess social work's support in the Head Start social service system, Frankel (1997) surveyed a random sample of the 67 project sites in the Family Services Center Project to assess the degree of professional social work involvement. Because the grants were clearly aimed at improving social services and there were funds allocated that allowed grantees to hire professional social workers at prevailing rates, this survey asked what they did with these staff funds. The survey asked questions about both types of social service workers at each site: those in the regular social service case management system, which was not affected by the grant, and the new social service hires required for the project. Thus, there was an opportunity to compare the degrees and training of a representative cohort of regular Head Start social service staff with the newly hired social service workers for the project.

The results showed that the involvement of professional social workers in both the usual Head Start social service system and in the Family Service Center demonstration project was minimal (Frankel, 1997). Relatively few B.S.W.s or M.S.W.s were represented in either social service group. Out of 227 regular social service workers, only 18 had a professional social work degree; out of 105 workers in the Family Service Centers funded by the grant, only 15 had a professional social work degree. What is also interesting is that 78% of the demonstration grant's workers had college degrees or better, contrasted with only 28% of the regular Head Start workers. What this outcome showed is that even when given the opportunity to hire professional social workers to upgrade their social service system, these Head Start administrators hired many college graduates but were not concerned whether these new workers had been trained in the social work profession. A social work professional viewing the outcomes of this demonstration project might suggest that one reason why the results were not significant was that there were so few social workers in the experimental group. Be that as it may, it is evident that the much higher number of college educated staff in the demonstration project's case management system, with their smaller caseloads, did not have the impact that was hoped for.

Although the evidence does not seem to show that there are many social workers directly involved in Head Start centers, there are indications that some social work schools have become involved. In 1993, the Head Start Bureau sponsored a project in which some social work schools received grant funds to develop social service manuals for Head Start and provide regional technical assistance and training. Although there was no empirical evidence of the effect of these trainings, the project did produce a series of manuals covering family needs assessment instruments, social service guidelines, and parent education guides (Johnson, 1992, 1994).

Given that the values and missions of Head Start and professional social work are similar and that each has so much to offer the other, we must ask the following cogent questions: 1) What historically have been the barriers to more involvement? 2) Is there any *interest* in bringing Head Start and professional social work closer together? 3) What would need to be done to bring these two recalcitrants together? 4) Given the trends in Head Start and social work, what is the likely future for more cooperation between the social work profession and Head Start?

BARRIERS TO INVOLVEMENT

In order to understand why professional social workers and Head Start have historically kept their distance from each other, we need to assess each entity separately. Barriers have arisen from differences in training, workplace culture, salary levels, and advancement opportunities.

The social work profession does not adequately prepare its future professionals to work in child care settings, much less Head Start (Frankel, 1992). This lack of preparation and subsequent involvement in child care is reflected in the social work literature. Social work articles and studies concerning the direct practice of social workers in child care, Head Start, or early childhood education are scarce. There has been some social work interest in social policy related to child care issues (Kamerman & Kahn, 1981). A review of the literature also shows very little interest on the integration or potential interface of social work with child care programs in preschools, child care centers, or family child care homes (Frankel, 1991). In direct practice, there must be many social workers in agencies who have to deal with the problems of child care for their clients. Their work is not well reflected in the literature. Thus, the first significant barrier that social work puts up to Head Start is a demonstrated empirical lack of professional interest.

For 1 year in B.S.W. and M.S.W. programs, students receive a required and concentrated dose of case management theory and skills, both in the classroom and as interns. At the graduate level, they must further concentrate either in a practice concentration and/or a specific client focus, depending on the school. For example, such concentrations can include combinations of generic case work, clinical case work, group work, community organization, administration, families and children, drugs and alcohol, mental health, or developmental disabilities. There is only one concentration that clearly alludes to early childhood educational and child care issues—school social work. This concentration, however, focuses on the K–12 public school system. Therefore, the second barrier that social work has is a serious lack of curriculum content relating to those issues essential for working in early childhood educational settings.

The basic academic training ground for early childhood professionals is in schools of education, which have little or no connection with their academic social work counterparts. It is impossible to work in any early child care setting without comprehensive training in developmental issues, the process and goals of early childhood curriculum, and the complex structural and political context of how child care is organized in this country. Without such professional training, social workers are at an initial disadvantage entering the Head Start arena.

Social workers are at a disadvantage, too, when trying to enter child care in general, of which Head Start is only a part. The child care industry puts up serious barriers to social work involvement. Most American children in child care are in family child care homes, the great majority of which are "underground," taking "under the table" fees for their services (Frankel, 1994). This basically unregulated child care system represents the backbone of child care in this country. Family child care has obviously not been open to much social work involvement, or anybody else's involvement for that matter. The other basic type of child care occurs in child care centers, most of which are independently operated for-profit or in the nonprofit domain. Although these centers have clear connections with early childhood education, their connection to social work is nebulous at best. Thus, with so many structural barriers facing social work as it views early childhood education and child care in general, it is no wonder that social work professionals have focused their efforts elsewhere.

This separation of early childhood education and social work is also clearly seen in the national associations that represent these two constituencies. Social work is represented by two major associations: the Council on Social Work Education (CSWE), its academic accreditation body, and the National Association of Social Workers (NASW), representing practicing professionals. It is rare to find in either group an organized cohort of social work academicians or practicing professionals representing Head Start or child care interests. Similarly, early childhood education and child care professionals have a national association called the National Association for the Education of Young Children (NAEYC). Social work has virtually no representation in NAEYC. Although over the

decades there have been occasional voices in these professional associations paying lip service to the need for better cooperation between social work and early childhood education,
meaningful linkages just have not occurred.

Head Start, in particular, has a workplace culture that can make the integration of
professional social work difficult. One of the wonderful aspects of Head Start has been
how it has captured the hearts and minds of so many former Head Start mothers. Head
Start has a long and proud tradition in hiring former participant mothers as teacher aides,
social service staff, and administrative assistants. As anyone who has been part of Head
Start will tell you, these women are an invaluable and talented part of their center's milieu, helping to build a broader community culture in the program. The survey reported
previously by Frankel (1997) showed that only 28% of the regular social service workers
had college degrees and that an additional 20% of this group did not have a high school
education. When a degreed social worker enters this paraprofessional culture, life is not
always easy. Most of the nondegreed social service workers are quite experienced and
"street savvy" and may not appreciate working side by side with someone with social work
credentials who may be making more money for doing the same work. Social workers, too,
have their own issues related to professional status. In the past 3 decades, almost every
state has passed licensing legislation defining literally who can be called a social worker.
Social workers entering Head Start are working with paraprofessionals who have been
doing exactly what social workers do but may take issue with staff calling themselves social workers. There are obvious reciprocal issues of professional respect that have to be ne-
gotiated before close-working relationships can occur.

Probably the greatest barriers to professional social work involvement in Head Start
are the salary levels available. The child care industry in general pays its staff extremely
low wages, and unfortunately, Head Start follows suit. In the mid-1990s, regular Head
Start social service staff were paid $15,000–$20,000 (Frankel, 1997); while the high end
of this range might be possible for the B.S.W. level social worker, it is a far cry from what
M.S.W. social workers expect when they graduate. Graduating M.S.W.s can usually expect starting salaries from $25,000 to $35,000, depending on the area of the country in
which they live. In addition, experienced social workers over time can expect salaries from
$30,000 to $40,000, and with advancement into administration might expect more. In
Head Start, there is little chance for advancement for social workers. Essentially, there is
no place to go. Although a social worker could become a Social Service Coordinator, it is
unlikely that he or she would advance into a higher Head Start administrative role that
often requires early childhood credentials. Thus, salary levels and opportunities for advancement are additional barriers to social work involvement in Head Start.

INTEREST IN SOCIAL WORK AND HEAD START INVOLVEMENT

More than a decade ago, Head Start formed a national task force to assess the role of social services in their centers (*Commissioners Task Force,* 1988). The results of this national
review showed that Head Start Centers across the country were providing a wide variety
of social services that included working with refugee families, substance abuse, family
abuse issues, teenage pregnancies, family therapy, and public health services. From this
assessment, the Task Force made three recommendations. First, it was acknowledged that

the family service worker caseloads were much too high and should be reduced to at least 1:35. Second, the Task Force suggested that every Head Start program should have a trained Social Service Coordinator. This position was further clarified as "the coordinator having sufficient theoretical as well as practical background to effectively manage and give guidance to social service staff" (*Commissioners Task Force*, 1988, p. 10). Third, it was clear to the Task Force that graduate level social service staff were not applying for social service positions in Head Start programs. Thus, the Task Force recommended raising the salaries for Head Start social service workers and making opportunities for advancement clearer.

This report made the conclusion that the "Head Start Bureau's goal should be to develop a high quality social services component that is comparable to the best practice, as defined by the social work profession" (*Commissioner's Task Force*, 1988, p. 24). Furthermore, the report suggested that workers should develop theoretical foundations for their work, keep pace with new trends and issues in the field of social work, develop case management skills, and follow the social work value system, including showing respect for clients, controlling personal biases, and maintaining confidentiality.

During the 1990s, there were indications that Head Start was attempting to act on some of these recommendations. The Family Service Center Project, which was discussed previously, was one clear attempt to upgrade staff and to demonstrate the need for lower case management ratios. In addition, the national Social Service Training and Technical Assistance Project, which was awarded to a number of social work schools in 1993, also was related to the Task Force's recommendations. There have also been numerous social service grants made for Head Start studies, including the areas of drugs and alcohol services, integrating fathers into the Head Start program, and employment. Some of these grant awards have been given to social work professionals. Thus, although there is very little data concerning how much social work is actually involved in Head Start centers, there is every reason to believe that Head Start is still philosophically committed to the recommendations of the Task Force relating to social work (*Creating a 21st Century Head Start*, 1993).

The same reciprocal degree of interest cannot be said for social work. There are few indications that social work as a profession wishes to become more involved with Head Start to help it with upgrading its social service system. A number of social work academicians are involved in Head Start research. The research by Frankel (1997), if we can extrapolate, suggested that there are also a number of B.S.W./M.S.W.s working in Head Start social services. Nevertheless, what drives social work into particular social service arenas starts with the curriculum offered in schools of social work and is certainly greatly influenced by the social service marketplace.

CSWE mandates most of the curriculum content for B.S.W. and M.S.W. programs. As stated before, there is required content relating to early childhood developmental issues and the necessity of child care, especially relating to employment and child abuse, and support for families in general. In addition, there is a heavy emphasis on learning case management theory and skills, with concurrent required practicums. It is infrequent, however, to find comprehensive content either in required or elective social work courses relating to the child care industry or Head Start. Even in textbooks and articles relating to school social work, discussion of the social work role in child care centers, family child care homes, or Head Start is given very short shrift, if it is mentioned at all.

When social workers graduate from a B.S.W. or M.S.W. program, the jobs they find are in the public agencies and other nonprofit organizations that are dealing with a myriad of America's social problems including: drugs and alcohol, mental health, developmental disabilities, workfare, foster care, public school systems, immigration, and forensics. Although all of these areas are certainly consistent with social work's mission, one important common characteristic is that they offer similar entry-level pay scales and offer opportunities for advancement, if not in a particular agency, at least in the larger field of a particular specialization.

In the chicken-or-the-egg world of developing new employment opportunities, it is not clear to what extent developing new social work curriculum as contrasted to emerging workplace forces guides this process. But on both counts, there does not seem to be much to motivate social workers into Head Start, early childhood education, or other child care arenas for that matter.

BRINGING HEAD START AND SOCIAL WORK TOGETHER

Head Start is clearly interested in improving the process and outcomes of its social service endeavors. If there is going to be more involvement of social work to help in this process, I believe it will have to be initiated by Head Start. I do not think that the field of social work, already overextended into too many social service issues, has the will or motivation to focus on Head Start without some prodding.

The first option might be to extend a Head Start helping hand to some social work schools. This will require a plan that starts with its national and regional staff and then filters down to local Head Start programs. One of the most obvious ways to involve social work schools in Head Start is to offer sites for the B.S.W. and M.S.W. required practicum experiences. Social work schools often have a hard time finding good sites for student internships. The B.S.W. and first-year M.S.W. internship is supposed to have an intensive case management experience, which is exactly what Head Start offers. A basic requirement for all social work internships is that there be a licensed M.S.W. social worker somewhere in the organization to supervise the student. Therefore, this strategy would only work if an M.S.W. were available, and there are certainly some programs that meet this criteria. Head Start Bureau staff could contact CSWE staff (both in Washington, D.C.) to let them know of this interest. Letters could be sent to the Field Directors of schools in the areas in which Head Start centers meet internship criteria, and then local Head Start directors could contact the schools. Student internships not only affect the student involved but also affect their fellow students and social work faculty. Internship experiences are used in class as part of the learning experience, one or more faculty are often assigned to connect with the agency, and students are required to write papers about their work that are shared in class.

In addition, if Head Start wants to bring social work into the process of helping to upgrade its social service system, it is going to have to grapple with the issues of salaries, advancement opportunities, and how to integrate the paraprofessional and professional staff in their social service environment. No matter how wonderful and meaningful the work, qualified social workers are not going to flock to Head Start centers unless competitive pay and benefits are available.

Second, the tradition of hiring former Head Start mothers for social service positions is a good practice but will continue to create staff problems. No one wants to work side-by-side with someone, doing the same work, and getting paid thousands of dollars less. Assuming the funds were potentially available, it might be possible to make pay scales dependent on education as well as on the position. In this way, former Head Start mothers might be encouraged, hopefully with some Head Start subsidy, to get professional social work degrees.

The problem of advancement in Head Start social services is a difficult one. Obviously, a family service worker could advance to a Social Service Coordinator position. There is only one Social Service Coordinator position in most Head Start centers, so this avenue of advancement is rather limited. Head Start is basically an early childhood program with social services as an important adjunct. To bring a social worker into Head Start administration without the prerequisite early childhood credentials may be difficult.

Should a school of social work become seriously interested in an integration of social work with Head Start and early childhood education, there is a way that opportunities for advancement in Head Start could be greatly enhanced. Joint M.S.W. and Ph.D. programs have been available in some social work schools for many years. For example, there are numerous examples of joint social work degrees with departments of psychology, sociology, economics, law, political science, the clergy, and public health. With appropriate motivation, there is no reason why a joint social work degree with a department of education or early childhood education couldn't be developed. Such joint degrees would give social workers better credentials to become administrators in Head Start.

Another way Head Start might consider connecting with social work is to continue offering grants in which social workers can become involved. In the past decade, this approach seems to have worked well. In addition, Head Start might consider offering B.S.W. and/or M.S.W. stipends. These types of stipends usually carry a requirement that the graduated student commit to 1 or 2 years working in the sponsoring agency.

THE FUTURE

The question of whether we will see social work giving significant support to Head Start revolves primarily around funding. There seems to be a national political will to increase Head Start's budget to make it more available for America's eligible families. Even with these additional funds, it is not clear whether salary levels will eventually reach the point that they are competitive with the general social work marketplace. Without such parity, it will be extremely difficult to entice social workers into Head Start centers to spearhead developing a more effective Head Start social service system.

Salary issues aside, there is also the question of whether Head Start is willing to expend the energy and time to push its agenda onto the social work profession. Social work has shown very little interest in Head Start. It is also not clear from the available data that more social work involvement would improve social service outcomes. Research suggests that Head Start is one of the most successful programs ever devised to help poor children longitudinally reverse the cycle of poverty. It has made great inroads toward achieving these important goals without much professional social work help. Although most social workers, including myself, might believe that intensive social work involvement should make Head Start social services more effective, this is more of a philosophical position than one based on demonstrated practice experiences in Head Start. It is surely the case that social services in Head Start need to be continually assessed and improved. It is just not clear how or how much Head Start should actively try to engage the social work profession in this endeavor. It may be possible that a systematic effort to upgrade the theoretical and practice skills of the current cohort of Head Start Social Service Coordinators and FSWs would be a good plan. This might be able to be done through social work sponsored continuing education programs. Head Start could also develop stipend programs for social work B.S.W. and M.S.W. training, or social work sponsored training and technical assistance should be considered.

By whatever means, however, Head Start needs to develop a more focused strategy for systematically upgrading and focusing its social service system nationwide, both theoretically and practically. Waiting for social work to be the profession to longitudinally support this process may be like waiting for Godot. There are few indications that social work's involvement in Head Start will change without concerted national and local strategic interventions by Head Start staff. Should Head Start attempt to plan such strategic interventions, it will find a number of social work academic and practicing friends eager to support such a process. In the meantime, it would be important for Head Start to continue to experiment with its social service system as it has been doing with various grants and better document the short- and long-term outcomes of its social service component.

REFERENCES

Commissioners task force on social services in Head Start. (1988). Washington, DC: U.S. Department of Health and Human Services, Head Start Bureau.

Creating a 21st century Head Start: Final report of the Advisory Committee on Head Start Quality and Expansion. (1993). Washington, DC: U.S. Department of Health and Human Services, Administration on Children, Youth and Families.

Frankel, A.J. (1991). The dynamics of day care. *Families in Society, 72,* 1–10.

Frankel, A.J. (1992). Social work and day care—a role looking for a profession. *Child and Adolescent Social Work Journal, 8,* 53–67.

Frankel, A.J. (1994). Family day care in the United States. *Families in Society, 75,* 550–560.

Frankel, A.J. (1997). Head Start and social work. *Families in Society, 78,* 172–184.

A guide for providing social services in Head Start. (1994). Washington, DC: U.S. Department of Health and Human Services, Administration on Children, Youth and Families.

Haskins, R. (1989). Beyond metaphor: The efficacy of early childhood education. *American Psychologist, 44,* 274–282.

Head Start Performance Standards. (1998). Washington, DC: U.S. Department of Health and Human Services, Head Start Bureau.

Head Start research: Evaluation of the Head Start Service Center Demonstration Projects, Vol. 1. (2000). Commissioners Office of Research and Evaluation and the Head Start Bureau. Administration on Children, Youth and Families, U.S. Department of Health and Human Services. (Available at: http://www.abtassoc.com/reports/ES-40421.pdf)

Johnson, R.H. (1992). *Social services component.* Washington, DC: U.S. Department of Health and Human Services, Head Start Bureau.

Johnson, R.H. (1994). *Social services and parent involvement branch: Activities and accomplishments (1987–1994).* Washington, DC: U.S. Department of Health and Human Services, Head Start Bureau.

Kamerman, S.B., & Kahn, A.J. (1981). *Child care, family benefits, and working parents: A study in comparative policy.* New York: Columbia University Press.

CHAPTER 23

Head Start and Child Care

Programs Adapt to Meet the Needs of Working Families

HELEN BLANK AND NICOLE OXENDINE POERSCH

Head Start's hallmark has always been its ability to meet the varied needs of the families it serves. For a growing number of families, this means providing both high-quality learning environments and programs that are also structured to help parents work. In 2001–2002, about 68% of Head Start families had working parents, and many children (45%) needed full-day, full-year care (Schumacher & Irish, 2003). Traditionally, Head Start classrooms operate morning and/or afternoon classes. For some parents, these time slots may not fit their work, training, or education schedules. Increasingly, Head Start programs are exploring strategies for providing full-day programs that meet the needs of such families. The importance of these efforts is growing with welfare reform expanding the number of families needing full-time (and in some cases, even odd-hour) care for their children. In 1996, at least 30% of Head Start grantees were accessing child care funds or linking with child care programs to provide full-day services for children enrolled in Head Start (Poersch & Blank, 1996). These programs are striving to meet the dual needs of families for quality early learning environments and for full-day care.

When working parents are comfortable with their child care arrangements, they are more productive on the job. When care is inadequate, parents' stress mounts and work performance suffers. Poor quality child care arrangements are more likely to fall apart, causing parents to miss work (Fernandez, 1986; Galinsky, Bond, & Friedman, 1993; Shore, 1998). The quality of child care can make a critical difference in low-income parents' ability to work. Evaluations of GAIN (the job-training program for welfare recipients in California) found that mothers on welfare who were worried about the safety of their children and who did not trust their providers were twice as likely to drop out of the job-training program (Myers, Gilbert, & Duerr-Berrick, 1992).

QUALITY EARLY EDUCATION MAKES AN
IMPORTANT DIFFERENCE FOR CHILDREN

Quality early education experiences help ensure that young children have opportunities to build their language and literacy skills so they can enter school ready to learn (Schulman, Blank, & Ewen, 1999). Research also demonstrates that high-quality early care and education experiences have positive effects on the later academic performance of low-income children. For example, a major study has been following the developmental progress of children in high- and lower-quality child care. Researchers have thus far tracked the children from age 3 through second grade. At the end of the most recent study period, children in high-quality care demonstrated greater mathematic ability, greater thinking and attention skills, and fewer behavioral problems. These differences had particularly significant effects for children at risk (Peisner-Feinberg et al., 1999).

Quality early education experiences are particularly important for low-income children. Several studies have indicated that children living in low-income families are less likely than their peers to enter school with the language skills they need to learn to read. Research suggests that

- Low-income children may have a more limited vocabulary. A study that followed children over a 3-year period found that at age 3, children from families receiving welfare had less than half the number of words in their vocabularies as children from professional families. This gap grew over time, and by first grade the children from families receiving welfare had one quarter as many words as children from professional families (Schulman et al., 1999).

- Low-income children may be read to less often. A study of families in 13 states found that one out of four children ages 1 to 5 living in low-income families (income below 200% of the poverty level) were read to or told stories fewer than 3 days per week. Only 1 of 10 children in families with higher incomes were read to this infrequently (Urban Institute and Child Trends, 1997).

- Low-income households may have fewer books. A study of primarily low-income families found that over half the households had fewer than 10 children's books and almost a quarter of these homes contained fewer than 10 books total (High et al., 1999).

Head Start Offers a High-Quality Early
Learning Experience Including Comprehensive Services

Efforts to provide full-day services are exceedingly important to Head Start parents who work. Affording good quality care can be very challenging for low-income parents because of its high costs. Head Start was developed as a national comprehensive family program to help low-income children enter school ready to learn and succeed. Toward this goal, Head Start is structured to provide high-quality education, health, nutrition, parent involvement, and social services as part of a comprehensive early childhood development program. It is also unique because it offers parents and community residents the opportunity to design, operate, and make decisions about programs that affect their children and families. Key to the ability of Head Start to provide high-quality comprehensive services is the fact that programs are funded through a grant or contact approach that ensures a relatively stable funding stream sufficient to provide mandated services. Although some observers still do not believe their Head Start funding is sufficient to cover the cost of the intensive services that many low-income families need, the investment per child for a part-day program far exceeds the subsidy available to parents who are receiving publicly funded child care assistance. Because Head Start was conceived as a part-day program, however, it is not able to meet the child care needs of all its participants without additional resources.

Child Care May Lack the Resources to Offer High-Quality Care

Although high-quality child care is particularly important to all children, many child care settings are not designed to meet the early learning needs of young children. For example, 30 states allow teachers in child care centers to begin working with children before receiving any training in early childhood (data used in Ewen & Hart, 2002). Thirty-two states allow family child care providers to begin caring for children before receiving such training (data used in Ewen & Hart, 2002).

Although many child caregivers would like to offer higher quality care as well as health and social services and to have more opportunities to involve parents, most lack the resources to do so. Child care providers serving low-income families are particularly constrained by low parent fees and limited public funds. The fee structure for child care is heavily based on the amount that parents can afford to pay, which is not necessarily the actual cost of providing care. Limited family incomes make it difficult for parent fees alone to finance programs that can provide good quality care, much less include other needed services and intensive staff training and support. In fact, estimates show that local market rates (fees charged to parents) cover only about one half of what would be the full cost of quality programming (Blank, Schulman, & Ewen, 1999). Even where government assistance is provided to help low-income parents pay for part of the cost of child care, subsidies are barely adequate to help parents afford even basic services. As of June 1, 2002, more than half the states were paying rates for publicly funded child care that were based on 75th percentile of the current market rate (Ewen & Hart, 2002). Because public child care funding streams generally were created as a tool to help parents work, they are neither funded nor designed to support high-quality comprehensive services for children.

Head Start Moves to Meet Both Needs

In order to meet the important needs of both children and their working parents, Head Start programs across the country have developed a variety of strategies for providing, connecting to, and collaborating with child care services. The most common approaches include *connecting* Head Start children to other child care services after the Head Start day has ended; *wrapping-around* care by accessing child care funding from other sources, which allow the Head Start program to offer extended-day services; and collaboratively *wrapping-in* Head Start services into child care programs serving Head Start–eligible children (Brush, Deich, Traylor, & Pindus, 1995).

Connected Care   In this model, Head Start arranges with a child care program to provide children with care after the Head Start day. Head Start typically provides transportation to the after-school services. The child care program is not required to meet the Head Start Performance Standards for the supplemental care. Although this approach has helped many working families participate in Head Start, some grantees would prefer greater continuity of care by providing uninterrupted full-day care in one site.

Wrap-Around Care   In this model, Head Start programs access public child care funds, the Child Care and Development Block Grant (CCDBG), welfare-related child care funds (TANF), Title XX, United Way, or other private dollars to provide child care before and after the Head Start day and all day when Head Start is not in session. The Head Start program may use the same staff or bring in part-time staff to provide the extended-day care. Programs may or may not meet Head Start Performance Standards for the full day of services.

Collaborative Wrap-In Care Partnerships   In this model, Head Start contracts with a child care program to provide full-day care and education services for Head Start–eligible children. The child care programs are expected to meet relevant Head Start Performance Standards and the Head Start grantee wraps-in Head Start's unique package of comprehensive services and parent involvement.

A CLOSER LOOK AT COLLABORATIVE PARTNERSHIPS

Although many programs continue to use the connected care and wrap-around care models to extend their day, a growing number of innovative Head Start and child care partnerships are forging new program designs that offer a combination of early childhood services. For example, in Ohio, where federal TANF funds allow the state to serve almost 90% of eligible Head Start children, more than 10,000 out of 50,000 children are enrolled in Head Start–child care partnerships.

Because the wrap-in model is growing in popularity and offers many unique benefits to both the partners and the children enrolled, it deserves a closer look. The wrap-in initiatives combine the strengths of each partner and expand the reach and scope of the services they can offer to children and families. In addition, by working together to design compatible services, child care and Head Start partners are contributing to the long-term vitality and success of local early childhood systems. Coordinating services within communities can help get the most out of limited resources and strengthen the short supply of quality early childhood experiences available to low-income families.

The Benefits

In addition to being able to offer full-day care, Head Start and child care partners have realized a number of considerable benefits by combining their strengths and resources.

Increasing Access to Health and Social Services   Head Start and child care partnerships are increasing the availability of critical health and social services for many low-income children enrolled in child care centers and family child care homes. Many of the children receiving Head Start services through a collaborative program would not have had access to such support because their child care programs could not afford to provide it. These children, most of whom are Head Start-eligible but not previously enrolled, can now receive Head Start's comprehensive package. In addition, partnerships are able to increase the resources available within a program, and thus, provide health and social services to low-income children who are not Head Start-eligible.

Maximizing Facility Space and Resources Many new relationships between child care and Head Start have been forged to address the shortage of facility space available for Head Start expansion. With limited increased funding for expansion, grantees have found that the considerable start-up costs of new facility space would greatly restrict the number of children who could be served. By forging partnerships with child care centers or family child care homes, grantees have avoided the challenge of finding new space while also reducing start-up expenses.

Serving low-density rural areas can be challenging for early childhood programs. There are often too few Head Start–eligible children and children in need of child care within a reasonable geographic area to open both a Head Start classroom and a separate child care classroom. At the same time, if the service area is broadened in an effort to fill separate child care and Head Start classrooms, the time and cost of transportation becomes significant for programs and parents. Transportation is particularly a problem for child care providers, as they usually do not receive reimbursement for these expenses. In rural areas, partnerships between child care and Head Start allow programs to offer multiple services to children in one location, even within a single classroom.

Serving a Wider Age Range of Children Child care providers generally serve a combination of age groups, ranging from infants to preschoolers, and often school-age children as well. In contrast, Head Start primarily serves children ages 3–4. Through new Early Head Start partnerships, as well as partnerships between traditional Head Start programs and child care, grantees are able to expand their reach. Providing services for younger childrFen as well as preschoolers in an environment where their siblings are present may improve the early childhood experience for some children, as well as offer the convenience of a single child care arrangement for working parents.

Improving Quality in Early Childhood Settings Partnerships are helping many child care programs access additional resources to improve program quality. By combining child care and Head Start resources, partners have been able to improve staff–child ratios, expand training for child care staff, increase the number of staff with child development credentials, purchase equipment and supplies for children, and improve child care facilities.

Increases in the training available for child care providers have been particularly important. The Head Start statute includes a 2% training set-aside, which supports an extensive regional training network in addition to direct funds to local programs for their individual training needs. Equally important, Head Start programs, unlike child care programs, can hire substitute teachers to replace staff who are attending training or can pay staff overtime for training outside work hours. Head Start can also cover the cost of an obtaining an associates or a child development associates degree. The availability of designated training funds is unique to Head Start and makes it considerably easier for child care staff to take advantage of training opportunities. Family child care providers, who are often the most isolated from training and professional development opportunities, have seen some of the greatest gains in professional development through partnerships.

Providing More Flexible Hours of Service Head Start providers have also understood the need to respond to parents who work odd hours. Some partnerships have enabled programs to offer more flexible hours of service for families. For example, Neighborhood

House Association Head Start in San Diego, California, is collaborating with the San Diego Community College district to help meet both the child development needs and the employment development needs of families. The child development centers at the two college campuses were providing only day services when a community needs assessment showed that families needed late afternoon and evening child care at those sites as well. Therefore, Head Start began collaborating to provide care during that time period. Now, Head Start parents can take vocational or academic courses in the late afternoon or evening while their children participate in a Head Start program on the same campus. The Head Start programs are open from 4 P.M. until 10 P.M. on weekdays and on Saturdays to accommodate parents' class and work schedules. At the same time, the agency is collaborating with about 90 licensed family child care home providers to offer up to 10 hours of high quality, full-day, full-year child care to approximately 300 children and their families. The network of providers offers Head Start parents the opportunity to select among caregivers in their community.

In addition, Neighborhood House Association Head Start offers families care that covers three work shifts Monday through Saturday by using Head Start funds to keep all 60 of its Head Start sites open from 5 A.M. until 8 P.M. for community and parent activities plus child care. Twelve sites including one in a low-income apartment complex are open year-round from 5 A.M. until at least 11:30 P.M. Some centers are also open until midnight.

Toledo-Lucas County Head Start also is working with child care programs to offer extended-day and odd-hour care to families. Head Start and the Toledo Day Nursery have teamed up to offer 4-year-olds a Head Start program from 3 P.M. to 7 P.M. and wrap-around care until midnight. Head Start is also collaborating with two additional child care programs to serve families who need evening care for their infants and toddlers as well as their 4-year-olds. Head Start provides transportation from the Head Start site to the child care program (Finlay, Blank, & Poersch, 1998).

Reaching New Communities   Linkages have helped some Head Start grantees to extend services to new communities and populations. Such linkages have been helpful in providing traditionally underserved groups or areas access to the comprehensive health and social services available through Head Start. For example, the local Head Start grantee in Dallas, Texas, wanted to better serve the Dallas Latino community. Given their limited access to facilities in these communities, they sought a partnership with a community organization with an extensive history serving the area's diverse populations. This allowed community residents to work with an organization they knew and trusted and increased the likelihood that they would use and benefit from the services.

Evaluations of Child Care Partnerships Show Positive Results

Preliminary findings of a 2-year study of Kansas City, Missouri's KCMC's Child Development Corporation's partnership program, Full Start, demonstrate that partnerships can provide high quality services to children. The study looked at 146 three- and four-year-olds enrolled in three centers in 1995 and 182 four-year-olds enrolled in four centers in 1996. Thirteen measures were used to assess program outcomes, including standardized questionnaires and rating scales, extensive on-site observations of children and teacher–child interactions, and interviews with center administrators and parents.

Interim findings from most of the 13 measures demonstrate that the partnership had no adverse effect on Head Start quality and performance measures. Full Start appeared to have positive impacts on teacher behavior, teacher–child attachment, child activity and behavior, and quality of the global classroom and center environments. When average quality ratings of the three Full Start centers in the spring of 1996 were compared with ratings of local full-day, full-year Head Start centers, no statistically significant differences were found (Head Start Bureau, 1997).

How Partnerships Work

Partners include small single-site Head Start agencies, child care centers, and family child care providers, as well as multisite agencies serving one or more counties. They cover urban and rural areas, small communities, and major metropolitan areas. Although most initiatives link the services of two separate organizations, some combine the Head Start and child care programs offered within a single multiservice organization.

Although the partnerships vary in scope and design, all of the initiatives provide comprehensive services to children and families in a child care setting. These include

- A full-day child care and education component that allows children to be safe and secure while their parents are at work, ensuring continuity of care for children by not having them shuttle between multiple providers in a single day, and provides developmentally appropriate activities designed to meet each child's individual learning needs

- A social services component that helps families identify available resources to meet their specific family needs

- A health services component that provides medical and dental screenings and follow-up services to ensure children's healthy development

- A parent involvement focus that enhances parents' ability to nurture and support their children's development by encouraging them to participate as policy makers, volunteers, and training participants

- A commitment to quality that ensures that all program components meet the Head Start Performance Standards, state licensing requirements, and all other appropriate standards

Grantees and their partners have taken a variety of approaches to determine exactly how responsibilities are implemented by each partner. There are, however, some general commonalities in approach across the models. Generally, the family child care provider or child care center teacher is also the Head Start teacher and receives significant support from the Head Start grantee including training, technical assistance, supplies and materials, and access to a provider support group. Head Start grantees work with the families to ensure they receive needed health and social services. Child care programs usually receive some additional compensation for work involved as a Head Start provider above and beyond meeting child care licensing standards, including home visits, curriculum planning, screening, staffing, and record keeping.

Partnerships for providing full-day care have not been limited to child care providers. Some partners include state-funded prekindergarten dollars to create a longer day for Head Start children. For example, Parent and Child Head Start in San Antonio, Texas, has been providing extended day care for many years through its "flip flop" model. Under this model, Head Start collaborates with about half of San Antonio's 18 school districts and several Bexar County school districts to give preschoolers a half-day of Head Start and a half-day of the state preschool program, usually at the same school building. At some locations, Head Start also has room to serve younger siblings of children using the flip-flop services. The school districts give Head Start space at various schools, while Head Start administers the program and collaborates with the school districts on staff training and special student activities. Head Start centers at the schools open at 7 A.M. for families who must drop off their children early and are open until 5:30 P.M. for all participating children. Some children attend Head Start in the morning and switch to a preschool classroom in the afternoon; others do the reverse. The school districts provide transportation for participating children who do not have access to both programs at the same location (Poersch & Blank, 1996).

Sharing Finances and Resources

Partners have developed a variety of methods for sharing and accounting for the costs of services provided in collaborative classrooms. Methods range from completely merging their budgets to not exchanging any funds at all. Regardless of how closely combined the funds are, participating agencies must determine how to divide the costs of services between the budgets of each partner.

Some programs have completely merged their child care and Head Start budgets and allocate costs based on the availability of funds from each funding source for any particular program component. These partnerships provide the same services to all children but sort out the finances for the founders. Child care funds may be claimed for care and education services, whereas Head Start and private funding sources may be used for providing the comprehensive health and social services.

Some partnerships split program costs based on children's eligibility. Some use a cost-per-child basis; programs allocate costs by calculating a per-child cost for services and then pay that cost for each eligible child. In some arrangements, child care funds cover the cost of the basic care and education component, and Head Start provides the funds for the comprehensive services component. In some cases, Head Start may also contribute to the increased service and administrative costs incurred by collaborative classrooms. Such arrangements are particularly common with family child care providers.

Some partnerships do not exchange any money. Each party provides part of the package of services; the total package is coordinated for the children and their families. In these situations, the child care program usually provides the care and education portion of the services, while Head Start provides the comprehensive health and social services.

Special Challenges

The partnership model can bring special challenges. Some of these arise around the basic issues of collaboration and the ongoing communication that it entails. Many service providers are hesitant to collaborate because they fear losing control, funding, or possibly the unique identity of their program. Helping program administrators overcome these fears and recognize the positive opportunities offered by partnerships may take time. Some partnership initiatives have grown out of a history of joint advocacy, planning, and training activities shared by child care and Head Start programs within a community. Other partnerships have sprung up quickly in response to local needs. In fact, many partners have found that focusing on community needs has been the most important catalyst to any collaboration. Program staff have overcome considerable hesitation once they recognized that a partnership could help them to better meet the needs of the children and families they service. At the beginning of a partnership, Head Start and the other providers must build relationships, develop communications system, and learn each other's specific issues, including respective requirements.

A number of challenges also arise around cost allocation. Partners face significant challenges sorting through the varying and sometimes conflicting requirements of multiple funding streams. Each funding stream has its own set of eligibility and reporting requirements. These dilemmas are compounded by the fact that program administrators and auditors may not consider the uniqueness of partnerships when reviewing the fiscal reporting of such programs. Although the U.S. Department of Health and Human Services, which is responsible for both Head Start and CCDBG, has been working to make the cost allocation process less cumbersome for grantees, funding sources are often still viewed in terms of traditional hours and service slots. Partnerships must therefore translate their service packages into the boxes required by their multiple funders.

Addressing Barriers to Providing Full-Day Services

A number of Head Start grantees have discovered challenges to providing full-day services through the wrap-around and partnership models. One issue is the uncertainty of child care funding. There are two facets to this issue. The first involves changes in parents' work status and/or income. In Head Start, once a child enters the program, he or she remains eligible for services regardless of changes in parents' income or work status. This policy recognizes the importance of continuity of care for young children and avoids bouncing them between caregivers. In contrast, child care subsidy eligibility is tied to the work, training, or education status of parents as well as their income and not to the developmental needs of the child. When a parent's income increases or job status changes, he or she may lose eligibility for child care assistance. This is particularly problematic with welfare-related child care funding streams. When a parent moves from training to school or from training to a job, the child may lose eligibility for child care assistance in the process. With no financial support, the provider may not be able to continue serving that child. Most child care programs, because they operate on such limited funds, do not have sufficient cash reserves to cover children when their family becomes ineligible for a subsidy. This means that Head Start children enrolled in partnerships or receiving wrap-around child care funds can still participate in Head Start but are not eligible for child care services. To remedy this gap, some Head Start programs use Head Start dollars to cover child care services for children no longer eligible for assistance.

Some states have attempted to remedy this problem. For example, Ohio will allow state child care funding to continue uninterrupted until the end of the Head Start program year if a child in a joint Head Start–child care slot loses eligibility for assistance. The District of Columbia will allow children who are dually eligible for Head Start and child care subsidies to remain eligible for both programs for a full year without having their eligibility redetermined.

Another issue that affects funding stability is the payment approach that states use to reimburse providers. Head Start operates on a contract-like basis that guarantees a certain amount of funds for a certain number of children. This arrangement gives Head Start programs a fairly stable funding base. In contrast, the majority of child care programs that receive public funding are dependent on certificates or vouchers that do not provide a steady source of funding. If a parent leaves the center, the child's slot may not be refilled because the availability of new vouchers from the state or locality may be frozen. Even if parents can obtain subsidy certificates or vouchers, a center has no guarantee that they will choose their program. This makes it difficult for Head Start programs that combine preschool and child care services either through partnerships or a wrap-around model. For example, if programs are to open a classroom for the second half of a day, they must know how many children to expect in order to hire staff and cover other costs. This is not always possible with a certificate or voucher system.

The low payment level of state-subsidized child care reimbursements is also a barrier for programs. When programs wrap-around care or wrap-in care, a full-day rather than a partial-day reimbursement is often necessary to make this possible. Three states, New Hampshire, South Dakota, and Washington, will provide full-day reimbursements for children who are also enrolled in half-day Head Start programs.

It is also important for Head Start programs that are using the wrap-around model to be able to easily access CCDBG funds or other funds to extend the day. A significant number of states have allocated targeted amounts of CCDBG funds to make it easier for Head Start programs to expand their day. Massachusetts has actually structured its prekindergarten program, the Community Partnership Program, not only to expand prekindergarten opportunities for children but also to help part-day programs such as Head Start provide full-day care. Connecticut, Hawaii, and New Jersey use state Head Start funds to provide full-day, full-year and/or extended day programs. Oklahoma Head Start programs have the option of using state funds to provide extended hours. Some states have also taken broader steps to smooth the way for partnerships. Oregon has held three summits focusing on Head Start–child care partnerships. Maine has merged its Head Start child care offices into a single agency and has given priority to partnerships in distributing child care funds. These efforts have paid off—all Maine Head Start grantees have partnerships. About 16% of the state and federally funded Head Start children are served through the partnerships.

SUMMARY

Head Start, child care, and prekindergarten partnerships are a growing phenomenon. It will become increasingly important to help these new relationships succeed as well as to ensure that Head Start programs have the resources they need to extend their day. Head Start programs using the wrap-around model in particular must have access to additional funds to extend their day. The federal government and states must continue to support policies that promote full-day, full-year Head Start experiences for children through various models. These steps will help to ensure that children receive the early education they need to succeed and that parents have access to the hours of care they need in order to work and be independent of welfare.

REFERENCES

Blank, H., Schulman, K., & Ewen, D. (1999). *Key facts: Essential information about child care, early education, and school-age care.* Washington, DC: Children's Defense Fund.

Brush, L., Deich, S., Traylor, K., & Pindus, N. (1995). *Options for full-day services for children participating in Head Start.* Washington, DC: Office of the Assistant Secretary for Planning and Evaluation.

Ewen, D., & Hart, K. (2002). *State developments in child care, early education, and school-age care.* Washington, DC: Children's Defense Fund.

Fernandez, J. (1986). *Child care and corporate productivity: Resolving work family conflicts.* Washington, MA: Lexington Books.

Finlay, B., Blank, H., & Poersch, N. (1998). *Head Start: Helping families move from welfare to work.* Washington, DC: Children's Defense Fund.

Galinsky, E., Bond, J.T., & Friedman, D.E. (1993). *The changing workforce: Highlights of the National Study.* New York: Families and Work Institute.

Head Start Bureau. (1997). *Head Start bulletin: Enhancing Head Start communication.* Washington, DC: U.S. Department of Health and Human Services.

High, P., Hopmann, M., LaGasse, L., Sege, R., Moran, J., Guiterrez, C., et al. (1999). Child-centered literacy orientation: A form of social capital? *Pediatrics, 103*(4), 55.

Myers, M., Gilbert, N., & Duerr-Berrick, J. (1992). *GAIN: Family Life and Child Care Study.* Berkley: University of California, Family Welfare Research Group.

Peisner-Feinberg, E.S., Clifford, R.M., Colkin, M.L., Howes, C., Kagan, S.L., et al. (1999). *The children of the Cost, Quality, and Outcomes Study go to school.* Chapel Hill: University of North Carolina.

Poersch, N., & Blank, H. (1996). *Working together for children: Head Start and child care partnerships.* Washington, DC: Children's Defense Fund.

Schulman, K., Blank, H., & Ewen, D. (1999). *Seeds of success: State prekindergarten initiatives 1998–99.* Washington, DC: Children's Defense Fund.

Schumacher, R., & Irish, K. (2003). *What's new in 2002? A snapshot of Head Start children and families.* Washington, DC: Center for Law and Social Policy.

Shore, R. (1998). *Ahead of the curve: Why America's leading employers are addressing the needs of new and expectant parents.* New York: Families and Work Institute.

Urban Institute and Child Trends. (1997). *Snapshots of America's families. Children's environments and behaviors: Reading and telling stories to young children.* Washington, DC: Author.

CHAPTER 24

Are There Better Ways to Spend Federal Child Care Funds to Improve Child Outcomes?

Douglas J. Besharov

Thank you for inviting me to testify about the availability of early childhood programs and their impacts on low-income children and families.

Essentially, I recommend that you *courageously* come out in favor of "more careful thought and more research," which, by the way, is how I interpret the GAO (Government Accounting Office) reports that you have received.

You have probably heard the same recommendation many times before, in many different contexts—and usually by researchers. But in this context, it does take courage. For, in order to decide that it is too early to embark on a major expansion of early childhood programs—advocated by many leaders of both political parties—you need to take on a deeply imbedded conventional wisdom about the ability of early childhood programs to improve cognitive and social outcomes for children. The plain fact—undisputed in serious academic circles, by the way—is that past research is inadequate for policy making and that, therefore, most of the rhetoric on the subject is overblown.

I believe that it is important to set the record straight. Vast amounts of public money are being spent on programs that may not be effective. Worse, there is a real opportunity cost involved: A clearer view of the facts might lead policy makers to support other education and antipoverty efforts. But trying to be more realistic about the limited effectiveness of these programs is a thankless, uphill effort—I can tell you from personal experience.

In my testimony today, I first present my estimate of the adequacy of state and federal child care and early childhood expenditures to meet the needs of low-income children. Then, I present cost estimates for transforming our current, family oriented early

This chapter reprints Besharov's statement before the Senate Committee on Health, Education, Labor and Pensions Subcommittee on Children and Families, April 11, 2000.

child care system into a formalized, center-based system (with separate estimates for child care-based and Head Start-based systems). Then, I review the evidence of the effectiveness of both "quality" child care and early childhood programs on child outcomes. Finally, I raise the question of whether the funds being proposed to expand early childhood programs might be better spent on other efforts. In other words, would it be "worth it" to adopt these expansions.

Funding Adequacy

Current Spending   It is actually quite difficult to calculate total state and federal spending on child care and early childhood education programs and impossible to know exactly how many children are served. No unit of the federal government tracks all federal expenditures, let alone those of the states. The 1996 welfare reform law created what is now the Child Care and Development Fund, a semi-block grant that somewhat simplified the programmatic framework, but there are still dozens of federal child care programs, many with overlapping eligibility rules and funding streams. (Efforts now underway within the U.S. Department of Health and Human Services may eventually result in better data, but their completion is some time off.) Thus, examining child care programming is like putting together the pieces of a jigsaw puzzle.

Chart 1, "Child Care Dollars: 1981 through 1999," portrays our estimates for spending between 1981 and 1999. It includes spending on both child care and Head Start, on the ground that child care programs often have an educational and social component, and Head Start provides the equivalent of child care services as well as educational and social services.

As you can see, over the period between 1994 and 1999, combined federal and federal-related state funding rose from $8.7 billion to $14.6 billion (in 1999 dollars). (Excluded from the graph are the myriad of small federal programs under $100 million/year as well as purely state spending that is not collected nationally.) The major components of this increase, as we will see, are increased funding for 1) Head Start and 2) welfare-to-work efforts.

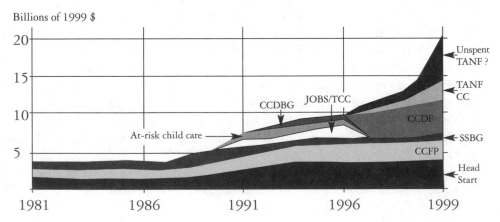

Chart 1.   Child care dollars: 1981–1999.

Head Start Coverage In FY 2000, total federal spending on Head Start exceeded $5.2 billion (Office of Management and Budget, 2000). It is important to note, however, that much of the increase in Head Start funding was earmarked for "quality improvements," which mainly went to salary increases and new buildings. As a result, per-child costs increased dramatically, while the total number of children served did not. For example, in 1992, the per-child cost for Head Start was $3,546 compared with $5,288 in 1998. Per-child costs increased by nearly 50%, while the number of children served increased by only 30% (Head Start Bureau, 2000).

The usual way to assess the adequacy of Head Start funding is to ask what percent of eligible 3- and 4-year-olds are being served by the program. In 1998, only about 53% of income-eligible 4-year-olds and only about 28% of income-eligible 3-year-olds were enrolled in Head Start (Butler & Gabe, 2000). These figures suggest that substantial undercoverage exists. However, this is misleading.

Head Start is predominantly a part-time, part-year program—not suited for families in which the mother works. In fact, only 7% of Head Start programs offer care for 8 or more hours per day; 51% offer care for 4 hours per day or less (Government Accounting Office [GAO], 1998). Most of the mothers whose children are in Head Start do not work full time, and many do not work at all (GAO, 1998). Thus, before deciding that we need to put more disadvantaged children in Head Start, we should ask where they are now. Many are already in some form of child care.

The response to these broader child care figures is usually that the care that these children are in is of such low quality that it compromises their development (Fuller & Kagan, 2000). I will return to that issue in a moment. But for now, I want to make another point: Why should we think that *all* low-income children need the compensatory services of Head Start?

The idea behind compensatory child development programs like Head Start is that low-income parents do not give their children the needed cognitive stimulation, emotional support, and social guidance—and that middle-class parents do. But surely, many low-income parents do an adequate job, and just as surely some do a very bad job. The plain fact is that some poor children do not need Head Start, and some need a double dose, or more. (Social scientists would call this subgroup analysis. A layperson would just call it targeting services on those who need them.)

Coverage for Welfare-to-Work Since 1994, welfare rolls have declined by 50%. And that is the national figure. Fifteen states have had declines of over 60%; three reported declines of 85% or more. A major concern has been the adequacy of child care support for the children whose mothers are now working. (Studies of welfare leavers indicate that about 60% percent are working regularly. Although the caseload decline may also be influenced by fewer entrants, the data to assess these numbers and the reasons for nonentry are not available. Thus, we rely on the leavers studies as a proxy for assessing what is happening as a result of the broader caseload decline.)

The first column of Chart 2, "Estimating TANF-related Child Care Needs—Roughly," displays our analysis of the sufficiency of federal–state child care funding for the children whose mothers left welfare for work. The calculation requires a large num-

In billions of 1999 dollars

Estimates based on:

Number of children leaving TANF whose mothers are working, 1994–1999		Current patterns	Full substitution at market rates	Full substitution at government rates	"High-quality"
0-5 year olds					
Full time	1,096,690	3.000	5.134	5.550	14.781
Part time	365,563	0.370	0.942	1.016	1.826
6-11 year olds					
Full time	636,192	0.715	1.760	1.891	1.447
Part time	212,064	0.043	0.128	0.137	0.065
12-13 year olds					
Full time	184,186	0.207	0.509	0.547	0.419
Part time	61,395	0.012	0.037	0.019	0.019
Total	2,556,091	4.350	8.510	9.161	18.557

Chart 2. Estimating TANF-related child care needs—roughly.

ber of subjective assumptions (laid out in the notes to the chart), and I will not go though them now. I would only mention that we have tried to err on the side of overstating the level of need. For example, the figures you have assume that families leaving welfare will use *the same mix of services as all American families* (predominantly middle class) even though all studies find that low-income families spend less on child care. The only area in which we may have exaggerated the impact of the increased spending is that we treat the increase in Head Start as if it resulted in commensurate increases in Head Start slots. (As noted above, the majority of the funding increase was devoted to quality improvement activities.)

As you will see, we calculate that $4.35 billion per year would be needed to cover the child care needs brought on by the decline in welfare cases between 1994–1999. As discussed above, by 1999, annual child care spending increased by over $6.1 billion from its 1994 level, indicating that there is sufficient funding if our subsidy programs mirror current patterns of child care use. Please do not take these to be precise calculations, but they seem to be in accord with reports from the field that increased funding has covered just about all the children whose parents have sought child care subsidies. That is why a 1999 GAO report, *Education and Care: Early Childhood Programs and Services for Low-Income Families,* stated that "care for preschool children generally was not difficult to find" (p. 11), although parents still face difficulties finding care for infants, children with special needs, and nonstandard hours.

In our calculations, the increased funding is sufficient only because many working mothers do not use paid child care—and Column 1 reflects that reality. Many advocates bemoan this result (Schumacher & Greenberg, 1999) and call for a much greater use of public subsidies. This is a key issue. Columns 2 and 3 present our estimate if all mothers leaving welfare for work paid for the child care they used.

If the mothers used *the same mix* of family and center-based care as all American families, Column 2, the total additional, annual cost for the children of welfare leavers who work would be $8.5 billion. If mothers used the same mix of family day care homes and center-based care as all American families, *but paid as much as the federal government pays under the CCDF,* the total costs would be $9.2 billion.

To meet either scenario, an additional $4 or $5 billion would be needed every year, and the number would rise if there are additional declines in the welfare rolls.

The Cost of an "Early Childhood Education" System   But these are only the costs for child care "as we know it." What if we took the advocates at their word and tried to provide "high quality" early childhood education programs? The Carolina Abecedarian project cost about $15,000 per child. High/Scope Perry Preschool project cost about $12,000 (1999 dollars) for 2 and 1/2 hours per day, 5 days a week, for 9 months of the year. The Public Relations Department of the Department of Health and Human Services estimates that full-time, full-year Head Start would cost about $9,000 per child. This seems to understate costs. Currently, as a part-day, part-year program, Head Start costs over $5,000 per child (not including non-Head Start funding such as Medicaid and the Child and Adult Care Feeding Program). A 1998 GAO report found 12 states with Head Start programs that cost over $10,000 per child per year, with some costing as much as $17,000 per child.

We estimate that full-time, full-year Head Start costs about $14,000 per child per year. (This is the figure we use for our calculations.) On this basis, providing full-time, early childhood services for all the children whose mothers have left welfare and are working would require an additional $18.5 billion—each year. And, if these services were provided full-time, full-year to all children under age 5 with family incomes at or below the federal poverty line, the annual cost would be more than $77 billion.

Impact on Children

These additional costs for either "quality child care" or expanded early childhood programs might be acceptable if they achieved the results claimed by their proponents. Unfortunately, there is only weak evidence that they do and substantial reason to think that they do not.

"Quality" Child Care   The research evidence about the impact of what the experts call "quality child care" on child outcomes is extremely weak. We started our work on this subject with the assumption that the quality of child care matters for child development. And we still believe that. But we discovered that the word *quality* has been defined to mean much more than most would think. Programs cannot be judged as more than "minimal" unless they engage in measurable activities designed to enhance children's social, emotional, and cognitive development. At first blush, this makes sense. But many of the development aspects of care are not measurable using existing methods. As a result, past research studies may not have obtained an accurate picture of care children are receiving. Moreover, almost all studies are also seriously compromised by small samples and selection bias problems.

Our estimate, therefore, is that the regulatable aspects of child care have, at best, only a modest impact on child development—certainly not enough to justify a major increase in per child costs. Many other researchers agree. For example, economist David Blau (1997) examined whether the regulatable aspects of care actually result in better care for children, presumably the first step to achieving better child outcomes. Using data from the National Child Care Staffing Study, Blau estimated the effects of different attributes thought to affect quality (group size, staff–child ratio, teacher training) on the child care environment (the nature of teacher–child interactions, curriculum, activities). Of all the attributes he examined, only group size, staff–child ratios, and recent teacher training were found to affect the child care environment, and their effects were small. Thus, factors typically regulated and typically considered to result in better child outcomes were found to have little influence on the quality of the child care environment, as measured by the nature of teacher–child interactions, curricula, and activities. Blau concluded that "the results of this study could be interpreted as implying that efforts to improve day care quality by regulating and subsidizing the inputs would be ineffective" (p. 383).

The typical response to such criticisms is that child care programs are not intensive enough, and long-term enough, to remedy the deep-seated problems of disadvantaged children. That is undoubtedly true. The problem is, we have very little evidence about what would work.

Early Childhood Programs, "Head Start"   If any government program "works" in the eyes of the American people, it is Head Start. Since its inception in 1965, Head Start has served more than 17 million children at a cost of nearly $47 billion (Head Start Bureau, 2000). Although the program enjoys wide popular and political support, surprisingly little rigorous research has been conducted on the program's impact.

No study has used either a nationally representative sample or an experimental design, two factors that make it difficult to draw any conclusions about programmatic effects. The GAO, in its 1997 review of Head Start research, concluded that "The body of research on current Head Start is insufficient to draw conclusions about the impact of the national program" (p. 8). According to the report, "All of the studies had some methodological problems" (p. 10), and "Until sound impact studies are conducted on the current Head Start program, fundamental questions about program quality will remain" (p. 20).

The usual response to the paucity of sound research on Head Start's effectiveness is to cite the success of two "Head Start-like programs": The High/Scope Perry Preschool and Carolina Abecedarian projects. We examined the research surrounding both programs and found that despite their high cost, the evidence of their success is weak and inconsistent.

In the end, all we know for certain is that they are costly programs run under special circumstances that produced modest positive effects for some children in some areas of development. Rebecca Maynard, of the University of Pennsylvania and Mathematica Policy Research, Inc., in reviewing research on such model early childhood development programs, wrote that

> We have been more careless than we should in reading and interpreting the research. For example, while the results of the Abecedarian and Perry Preschool programs are very encouraging, these programs operated many years ago, targeted particular groups of children, and were not traditional child care programs. (2000, p. 3)

Researchers Robert McCall, Lana Larsen, and Angela Ingram of the University of Pittsburgh were more positive, concluding that "Early childhood programs *can* accomplish many of their short-term and some of their long-term goals," but even they noted that some of these achievements, such as increases in IQ and other indicators of cognitive development, "diminish and may disappear entirely . . . over the three years following the termination of program attendance" (1999, p. 8).

Alternate Priorities

The uncertainty caused by the weakness of current research raises an even larger issue: Given the ambiguous impact of expensive, "quality" child care and early childhood programs on child outcomes, how much money should be spent on them *versus* on other programs for disadvantaged children? That is not a question one often hears in the child care debate, but it should be decisive.

Compare the $18 billion to $77 billion we estimate that it would cost to provide full-time, early childhood education to all children under the poverty line with what we spend on some other programs under the jurisdiction of the Senate Committee on Health, Education, Labor and Pensions: elementary and secondary education—about $15 billion; student financial assistance—about $10 billion; and Older Americans Act—about $1.6 billion.

It may well be that there are better ways to spend $10,000–$15,000 per child to improve child outcomes. Imagine the following: A single mother with two preschoolers working full time at the minimum wage earns $10,300. Then we spend $20,000–$30,000 of taxpayer money to enroll her two preschoolers in an early childhood education program. What if we used part of the money to support basic, decent child care and used the rest to allow her to work part-time, so she could spend more time with her children? Or, what if we used the rest of the money to increase the Earned Income Tax Credit (EITC), so that she could take more money home? Or, what if we used the rest to remove the marriage penalty embedded in the EITC and other quasi-welfare programs?

The failure to be clear about the weak evidence behind claims for the effectiveness of "quality" child care and early childhood education programs prevents policy makers from asking such questions. Does anyone doubt the answer that the mother in my example would give? Doesn't that tell us something very important?

REFERENCES

Blau, D. (1997). The production of quality in child care centers. *Journal of Human Resources, 32,* 354–387.

Butler, A., & Gabe, T. (2000, April 6). (Congressional Research Service.) *Memorandum to the Senate Health, Education, Labor and Pensions Committee, Subcommittee on Children and Families.*

Fuller, B., & Kagan, S.L. (2000). *Remember the children: Mothers balance work and child care under welfare reform.* Growing Up in Poverty Project 2000. Wave 1 findings. Berkley: Graduate School of Education, University of California.

General Accounting Office (GAO). (1997). *Head Start: Research provides little information on impact of current program* (GAO/HEHS-97–59). Washington, DC: Author.

General Accounting Office (GAO). (1998). *Head Start programs: Participant characteristics, services, and funding* (GAO/HEHS-98–65). Washington, DC: Author.

General Accounting Office (GAO). (1999). *Education and care: Early childhood programs and services for low-income families* (GAO/HEHS-00–11). Washington, DC: Author.

Head Start Bureau. (2000). *1999 Head Start fact sheet.* Retrieved April 10, 2000 from http://www.acf.hhs.gov/programs/hsb/research/factsheets/99_hsfs.htm

Maynard, R. (2000, January 10). *Memorandum prepared for the Committee for Economic Development Planning Meeting on Early Childcare and Education,* p. 3.

McCall, R.B., Larsen, L., & Ingram, A. (1999). *The science and policies of early childhood education and family services.* Unpublished paper.

Office of Management and Budget. (2000). *Budget of the United States Government: Fiscal Year 2001.* Washington, DC: U.S. Government Printing Office.

Schumacher, R., & Greenberg, M. (1999). *Child care after leaving welfare: Early evidence from state studies.* Washington, DC: Center for Law and Social Policy.

CHAPTER 25

The "Failure" of Head Start

JOHN MERROW

When this article appeared first in Education Week *on September 25, 2002, it produced a firestorm of criticism from quite a few people in the early childhood education community. Some of the critics who contacted me directly had not read the article closely enough to realize that it is both a criticism of the Bush Administration's policies and an argument for expansion and improvement of early childhood education programs. A few callers saw the headline and reached for the telephone, without pausing either to read the piece or to wonder why* failure *appeared in quotes.*

A few thoughtful critics expressed concern that Head Start's enemies would use the headline as a weapon against the program; if that happens, I will join in Head Start's defense, because, although it needs improvement, it represents (as Ed Zigler noted in our PBS documentary) "America's finest hour."

Head Start has "failed." The federal preschool program for 4-year-olds was supposed to "level the playing field" for poor children, and it has not done that.

Educationally and linguistically, poor children are behind from the beginning. Parents with professional jobs speak about 2,100 words per hour to toddlers, while those in poverty speak only about 600. Not surprisingly, a 5-year-old low-income child has a 5,000-word vocabulary, whereas a middle-class child already knows 20,000 words.

One reason for Head Start's "failure" was the misguided practice at some Head Start centers, where teaching the alphabet was actually banned, in favor of teaching social skills. But the dominant reason for the persistent gap is the fervor with which middle- and upper-middle-class parents have embraced preschool.

These parents enroll their children in preschool because they know that 3- and 4-year-olds are ready and eager to learn. Seventy-six percent of 4-year-olds from households with an annual income of more than $50,000 are enrolled. The National Center for Education Statistics reports that twice as many 3- to 5-year-olds from families with incomes above $75,000 are enrolled, compared with children whose parents make $10,000 a year.

Less than half of children whose families fall below the poverty line attend preschool, not because their parents don't want them to, but because we haven't created enough Head Start programs. To serve all the eligible children, we'd need twice as many as we have. Once again, we're talking the talk when it comes to helping poor children but not walking the walk.

We ought to be embarrassed about our approach to preschool. Most industrialized countries provide free, high-quality preschool for 3-, 4- and 5-year olds, regardless of family income. Almost all 4-year-olds in England, Luxembourg, and the Netherlands go to public school; 70% of German, Danish, and Greek 4-year-olds go to public school; and more than 90% of 4- and 5-year-olds in Italy and Spain are in public school.

We're the opposite: a patchwork nonsystem with weakly trained, poorly paid staff. The quality ranges from excellent to abysmal, the tuition from $15,000 to zero, the teachers' salaries from $45,000 a year with benefits to $8 or $9 per hour.

I've just spent 7 weeks driving around Europe, visiting lots of small towns and villages. Every small town I visited in France had a sign, prominently placed, pointing the way to the local Ecole Maternelle, the town's preschool. Had I stopped to look, I would have found every 3- and 4-year old from the village at the school.

A few months earlier I visited three Ecoles Maternelles in very different neighborhoods in Paris. The school serving poor children was virtually identical to those serving middle-class and upper-middle-class children. All three schools were staffed with well-trained, well-paid teachers because all Ecole Maternelle teachers must have master's degrees, and all are paid at the same rate as elementary school teachers. Today in France, 100% of children ages 3 through 5 attend preschool, most in public programs.

In the United States, preschool is a seller's market, and even well-off parents have to endure "preschool panic" because there's not enough quality to go around. One of the families in "The Promise of Preschool," our PBS documentary,[1] moved from New York City to France while we were filming. In New York, the parents were forced to choose between career opportunities for themselves and a decent preschool for their sons. Today, although both parents are struggling to develop their careers, their children are in sound educational programs.

Today, preschool is on a lot of state agendas. According to the Child Care Action Campaign, 42 states now have some form of "preschool initiative." However, that phrase encompasses everything from legislative proposals to real programs, and only Georgia, New York, Oklahoma, and the District of Columbia have genuine programs that provide free preschool for a substantial number of children.

Georgia is at the head of the preschool class. Its program currently serves more than 63,000 4-year-olds. In all, 70% of Georgia's 4-year-olds are now in some form of publicly subsidized preschool. The Georgia program is the brainchild of former Governor Zell Miller, now a U.S. Senator, who believes that "preschool is more important than the 12th grade in high school." Georgia requires districts to offer prekindergarten and pays the bill—$240 million a year—with money from its lottery and with federal Head Start funds. New York and Oklahoma are leaving it up to school districts to decide whether they will provide such services, with the state paying the bills. But states are hard-pressed

---

[1] It began airing on PBS in October 2002. Copies are available through the PBS web site, http://www.pbs.org/merrow.

for funds these days, and so, for example, New York's legislature has put up less than half of the money needed to establish programs across the state.

Creating high-quality programs is proving to be difficult. No state is starting from scratch, of course, which means that any new program must be grafted onto what exists. And what exists is a hodgepodge of programs—some are run for profit; some are staffed with trained, well-paid teachers; and some are storefront operations where a television set is the caregiver. Some Head Start programs are excellent, but others are woeful. One evaluation of Head Start found that some children began the program knowing just one letter of the alphabet, A, and left 9 months later without having learned B.

President Bush says he wants to change that, but his proposal is flawed. To improve literacy skills, he gave 2,500 Head Start teachers 4 days of training in early literacy instructional techniques, after which they were supposed to pass on what they learned to the other 47,000 Head Start teachers. Critical reaction to the plan was immediate. A spokesman for Rep. George Miller (D, CA) told reporters, "The idea that you would be able to create reading specialists among Head Start teachers with 4 days of training is absurd." Moreover, the President's budget won't allow Head Start to grow, even though the program now misses more than half of eligible children.

I believe that we're operating from the wrong premise. Instead of relying on income-based programs such as Head Start that are supposed to help the poor, we ought to be creating a system that would be good enough for the well off. Create something that's good enough for those with money, but make it available to everyone. Design a preschool system the way we built our interstate highway system. We didn't create separate highways for rich and poor. Instead, we built an interstate system that was good enough for people behind the wheel of a Cadillac or a Lexus, a Corvette, or a Mercedes, and there were no complaints from those driving a Chevy or a Ford.

Creating universal, free, high-quality preschool will be difficult, complicated, and costly: By one estimate, it would cost $30 billion a year to run programs just for those 3- and 4-year olds from families making less that $30,000 a year. For all 3- and 4-year-olds, "The cost could easily be $100 billion," according to Ron Haskins of the Brookings Institute. We know, however, that good preschools have long-term benefits for children, and we ought to recognize that as a nation.

It took 50 years for the United States of America to be able to compete as a peer in Soccer's World Cup with Italy, Mexico, Portugal, France, Germany, Sweden, and other long-established powers. We cannot afford to take that long to catch up in the world of preschool education.

CHAPTER 26

A Head Start for All Children

GWEN MORGAN

B orn in the turbulence and energy of the 1960s, Head Start is a program for some of the children in the United States, but not a policy for all our children. Most of us value Head Start and its accomplishments. It is a treasure we want to preserve; it is a structure that needs to, and does, change and grow. Without change, Head Start could be an obstacle to the development of needed policy for the children of the 21st century.

In the 1960s, the United States was committed to a head start for the poor so that they could catch up to other children in the United States. At the beginning of the 21st century, the concern is to give a head start to all children in the United States so that they can catch up with the children in other countries of the world and so that the United States can maintain its economic leadership. Most of these other countries have had early care and education programs for all children as long as we have had Head Start. If our children are to succeed in school, early childhood programs will be needed to give them a head start on school readiness, in today's popular view.

Bruce Esterline (1976), speaking during the period that incubated Head Start, distinguished between a program approach and a policy approach to issues we want to solve. The program approach so prevalent in the 1960s, he said, has led to such familiar problems as "limited client coverage, gaps in services, fragmented administrative structures." Further, he said, the program approach is inimical to real policy. "It creates an environment that resists the development of true policy by turf-building" (p. 5).

Head Start was and remains a program. It may be the most successful of all the programs our country has generated. We need to think about how this program can fit together with new policies at the changing community level and how to make Head Start a continuing and valued part of implementing our policy goals for all our children.

This chapter presents some of the reasons why comprehensive child development services need to be accessible for all children and their families and explores a vision for a common infrastructure.

A POLICY EXAMPLE

The following story raises some of the issues that are yet to be resolved in U.S. policy. In 1965, filled with the fervor of anti-poverty commitment, I was asked by a manufacturing company to develop a plan to add a child development center for workers at the place of employment. The company already employed and trained workers who were discriminated against in the marketplace: women with young children, men with prison records, African American men and women, and members of minority groups speaking languages other than English. The 600 workers at this relatively small urban workplace spoke 52 different languages.

The plan for the child development center was simple: The company would pay one third of the cost of the center, and the parents would pay one third. It seemed reasonable to suggest that government pay the remaining third. The company would hire 60 welfare mothers and would train them, paying them training wages. On completion of the 3 months of training, the company would hire them and place them on its regular wage scale of stepped increases in pay.

On behalf of the company, I wrote to the newly created Office of Economic Opportunity (OEO) describing this proposal (KLH Research and Development Corporation, Letter from Gwen Morgan to OEO, 1965). The letter that came back was brief and to the point:

> Thank you for your interest in the country's economic opportunity programs. However, the program you suggest would not be an appropriate one for U.S. financial participation. If the company pays the women the amount you suggest, they will cease to be poor and therefore not suitable targets for federal programs.[1] (Letter from OEO to Gwen Morgan, 1965)

Given those ground rules for the economic opportunity programs, it is not surprising that terminology during the 1970s moved from "economic opportunity programs" to "anti-poverty programs" to "poverty programs" (Albelda, 1996). Given the commitment to serve only the "truly needy," advocates and policy makers alike accepted stories like this one as a necessary evil, preferable to mistakenly serving someone who is not permanently poor. If family income were to rise during the intervention, that would be viewed as failure to target, rather than a success of the program. Economic opportunity, and the American dream of success through one's own efforts, were not a part of the assumptions of these decades, the 1960s, the 1970s, the 1980s, and even the 1990s. Times do change, however.

ANOTHER CENTURY, A NEW MILLENIUM

There have been many changes in our country since Head Start was born. The number of children, even infants, whose mothers work is much greater, and three in every five preschoolers are in some kind of early education/care (National Center for Education Statis-

---

[1]There is more to this story. After receiving this federal rebuff, the company approached the local antipoverty agencies in Boston and in Cambridge. The Boston agency, without informing the company, rewrote the proposal to make it fit federal guidelines. In the rewritten version, the company was to pay the women a low "training" wage for several years, indeed indefinitely so that she would remain poor and therefore eligible. The child development center would be available only to these women and not their fellow workers. Outraged by these provisions, the company withdrew its proposal and asked to meet with the community's antipoverty council to explain what had happened. We were cheered up to receive a letter from the secretary of the council that said, "We have had a chance to read your proposal and you were right! We hope you will keep on trying." The child development center was later funded by the U.S. Children's Bureau.

tics, 1996). Quality in these programs is threatened by salaries of the teachers/caregivers, which have decreased in real dollars (Center for Child Care Workforce, 1998). The children in the United States are much more diverse than they were in the 1960s (U.S. Census Bureau, 2002; Washington & Andrews, 2001). By the year 2000, the country was experiencing unprecedented prosperity, and its tax base was never stronger. A major welfare reform resulted in reduction of the welfare rolls, and a large number of families were struggling to support themselves, primarily with marginal employment. They and their children were still poor (Fuller & Kagan, 2000). School reform became a policy priority.

Many of the national organizations that have worked to create policy for all children have long held goals of universally accessible early care and education. The word *universal* is more frequently used now, usually in connection with preschool and the national goal that all children arrive at school ready to succeed. In 2000, as the country neared its first presidential election of the new century, a *USA Today* newspaper poll reported that 68% of the public was in favor of spending on school-age programs and early childhood development programs as a priority more important than reducing taxes.

Milt Akers, former President of the National Association for the Education of Young Children, said early in the 1960s that we could not afford to have separate programs to serve the same children. We do not have separate sets of 4-year-olds, for example, one set in need of education and not care and another in need of care and not education. As Akers put it, all our educational programs for young children have to "double in brass" to provide care for children whose parents are at work.

The most thorny set of issues facing Head Start today includes determining how Head Start as a program for low-income children fits into the nation's goals for all children and what its role is in the overall system of services. Welfare reform has removed a target population of nonworking mothers and replaced it with working parents. Once employment becomes part of the equation, eligibility guidelines become restrictions on earnings. From the parents' perspective, income is the outcome of working, not a definition of their psychological need. There are issues of social justice that justify a universal approach.

The Economic Issues

In today's world, in which welfare mothers are expected to work and most families have working mothers, if Head Start keeps to its previous concepts of eligibility, then the issues of segregation and economic opportunity become too important to ignore.

Income eligibility restrictions have a segregating effect. One important issue for this new era is this: If Head Start were to serve all disadvantaged children in the eligible age groups, then all children who are not disadvantaged will be in other programs. National policy would therefore totally segregate all 3- to 5-year-olds in the United States. If parents' income does not change, their children remain poor. Head Start has no stated goal to help families improve their income. As long as Head Start is viewed as a demonstration project targeted for some 3- to 5-year-olds, most of whose parents do not work, the effect of income eligibility can be acceptable. Head Start can be viewed as serving only those families in which the parent is not able to work and is being supported by welfare. Once employment is part of the picture, income becomes the outcome of the program, and low wages are not a goal that Head Start wants to support. Head Start has certainly helped families to find employment in Head Start and turn their lives around but has never had a stated goal of helping families increase their earnings.

As more families leave welfare, Head Start's relationship with the disadvantaged who remain poor is threatened. Because almost all families are working, there are fewer nonworking poor. Other programs are available for families who earn more than Head Start's eligibility criteria. Families are using other services that are less restrictive of their economic opportunity. The American Dream does not fit well with the hopes for welfare reform.

Hope is a concept strongly incorporated into the American ethos, but little studied in developmental psychology, especially in an economic context. If all the poor could find gold, or strike oil, would their children be disadvantaged? Even in a fully comprehensive service, providing the best possible support for children in low-income families, it is possible that hope is eroded because economic improvement is not even a goal. When children live in neighborhoods where members of their community cannot find employment in positions of leadership, it is hard to conceive that any program, no matter how high in quality, can bring the hope they need for their own futures.

Head Start serves a group of families in extreme poverty, with 10% leeway to include other families not defined by income. Even in the early days of Head Start, many in the general public perceived an injustice in antipoverty programs. A low-income individual may be placed in a job as a trainee in an office, and her child may be attending Head Start. Working in the same office might be another clerk, earning low income, but not eligible for Head Start. The very name "Head Start" rankled, implying that one child would be ahead of the other (conversation with Thomas P. O'Neil, 1966). Since the 1960s, there has been a "gap group" not poor enough to receive publicly funded services and not earning enough to purchase the services on their own.

A single-parent working mother often qualifies by family income as poor or near poor because in our society it usually takes a second job to raise a family's income to the median. Two-parent families, with two low wages, usually fall outside the definition of the working poor. Because they are working, their children need education and care. But their two incomes add up to a level that makes them appear to be middle class. They are the forgotten group, the "gap group" in U.S. policy—A family with two low-income wage earners that use child care as a necessity and are doubly stressed by issues of balancing work and family appears to be the same as a family with one wage earner and a stay-at-home parent at the same family income level. In general, our policies bring help to families only after family breakdown, and they keep children poor.

Broadening the Vision for All Children and Families

This chapter is written with the hope that Head Start will join other national organizations in a commitment to a national policy of universal access to high-quality early care and education for all children, using a fee scale that slides up to point of affordability. Like the scholarship formula used in higher education, this policy would assume that the parents will pay what they can afford.

In this vision, Head Start will have a stated goal to help families escape from poverty through increasing their income whenever that is possible. When families earn more, it should be celebrated as a success, rather than considered irrelevant to Head Start's goals.

Families who are working out of economic necessity should be eligible regardless of what they earn. In the past, Head Start has emphasized only early childhood jobs that pay so little that working families can qualify as poor. If Head Start is to serve working families more broadly, it cannot use low-income (i.e., low-paying job) as a goal. Head Start and other early childhood programs for working parents should adopt a "need for employment" criterion and not use the earnings (outcome) to define eligibility. Earnings are criteria for fees to be paid, not for eligibility to enroll in a program. A family with a "need for employment" is defined as a family in which the income of the primary wage earner is not adequate to support a family without child care and a second income.

This vision assumes that Head Start will continue as a program, with its identity and its name. It will keep its economic opportunity goals but not its poverty requirements. Head Start voices in developing the infrastructure for all programs will assure that what has been learned in Head Start up until now becomes a part of the learning for all programs. A vision for all children requires a policy for all children but it does not require that all children be in the same program.

As of 2003, there are three major delivery systems for publicly funded early care and education: Head Start, the schools, and the purchase of service system supported by parent fees and governmental third-party payments. All of these programs will continue because all of the public and private resources that support them are needed. But we need a single system, rather than three.

The vision is a policy for all children, not a program. It requires changes in systems to make it work, not the creation of something new. In the planning that produced *Not by Chance: The Quality 2000 Initiative*, Kagan and Cohen (1997) provided a simple and useful formula:

$$\text{Programs} + \text{Infrastructure} = \text{System}$$

The *programs* are all of the Head Start programs, all of the child care centers and preschools, and all of the family child care—licensed, nonlicensed, publicly funded or private—that parents use for their children. The *infrastructure* is all of the supports that are necessary to create a system capable of delivering high-quality early care and education to all children in all of these programs.

In order to create a universal system, we need a common infrastructure that supports all programs. We have bits and pieces of infrastructure, some of it relating only to one of the three major funding streams, most of it unconnected. In the past several years, aided by welfare savings and federal CCDF money, most states embarked on a massive expansion of quality initiatives (Abt Associates and the National Center for Children in Poverty, 2000). Without evaluation of their impact on quality, and without an overall vision of how these pieces fit together, we do not yet have a system, but these funding commitments may lead us to create a system.

A COMMON INFRASTRUCTURE FOR A UNIVERSALLY ACCESSIBLE SYSTEM

Infrastructure means the underlying systemic supports that will enable us to take our early care and education programs to universal scale. We speak of roads and bridges as necessary to a transportation system that relies heavily on automotive vehicles. Gallagher and

Clifford (2000) give the examples of the medical practitioner and the infantry soldier, each of whom has a complex support system that enables them to do their jobs. This section will identify elements of the needed infrastructure for early care and education and suggest what existing supports might be expanded and/or connected to provide a common infrastructure across all programs.

The current early care and education set of programs is not a system. It is plagued by fragmentation, turf issues, weak quality control, lack of resources, inaccessibility, and lack of affordability. We need to create a system that will work for all children, to implement a policy that all children are eligible for early care and education at a price their parents can afford.

Visioning can create "castles in the air," that is, imagining an entire new and coherent system to replace all of the current programs and their supports. Or, visioning can "follow the dots," that is, identifying parts of a future system that are already in place and connecting them into a whole. The "follow the dots" type of visioning has the advantage of preserving and making use of the "small wins" and valuable assets created over time (Weick, 1984).

It would make no sense to replace Head Start with another system. In the same way, it would make no sense to replace any good program and throw away any of the assets and resources that have been painstakingly constructed over the past 100 years and more. We need to create a system that incorporates all that is good that we have already achieved.

There are existing pieces of infrastructure that could serve as supports for all programs, but many of them focus on only one of the three major funding systems. Those that are most likely to transcend these funding divisions are 1) higher education, which should prepare teachers and caregivers in all systems at all levels; 2) the Department of Labor's apprenticeship program, which uses higher education coursework and supervised experience to credential teachers in child care; 3) resource and referral organizations, which provide training and other assistance to child care programs but have a perspective of serving all children and families; and 4) state licensing, which sets baseline standards for children in all private programs, whether subsidized or not.

The needed infrastructure at best will support programs across all funding streams, public and private. The elements of this infrastructure should include

1.   A common regulatory system that assures safety from any form of harm, including physical harm or developmental impairment

2.   Recruitment, training, and career counseling to attract needed workers into the field

3.   A higher education system of public and private colleges that offers preparation for career development for all the roles and specializations needed in the field

4.   Scholarship help for current and future practitioners, and direct funding to colleges

5.   Technical assistance and consultative help available locally to all programs

6.   Consumer information to parents that includes specific information about available programs and ratings in addition to parenting information

7.   Data systems

8. Collaborative planning at the local level, met by responsive collaborative funding at the state and or federal level

9. Community health and mental health systems

10. Public and/or private capitalization of facilities

11. Evaluation and research

These infrastructure elements, as conceptualized here, are not invented just to make the early care and education system work. Most of them are existing organizations or systems with broader societal function. Some pieces of infrastructure that have been invented for, or attached to, particular programs rather than supporting all programs could be expanded (The Open Forum, 1999).

As we think about infrastructure to support a system for all children, it should be assumed that the infrastructure would not be the same in every state and community. Different localities will build it differently reflecting differences in history and context. The following discussion suggests some possibilities.

A Common Regulatory System

Currently, there are different systems for regulating the schools, Head Start, and child care. The schools in general have lacked any standards applicable to early childhood programs. Head Start has its own Performance Standards and monitoring system, and some child care is licensed for all children whether publicly funded or not. Coverage by licensing varies, and these are beginning to overlap as a few states have begun to try to license early childhood programs in schools. Funding sources will, in the future as in the past, apply purchase standards to the programs they fund, unless there is some broader infra structure system that defines levels of quality.

We still need a "common set of program standards," as mandated by the Congress in 1968 and never achieved federally. The licensing system applied by the states to private child care, both centers and family child care, also applies to some Head Start programs if they are full day and not operated by public or private schools. Licensing lays down a baseline of protection from harm of all children. The 1968 Congressional mandate was for a common set of funding standards for all federally subsidized child care, set at the Head Start level. These higher standards are not licensing, but they may be applied out of licensing offices, which are broadening their responsibilities. Future licensing offices may give themselves names such as "Office of Licensing and Quality Initiatives." Today's version of a common set of standards may turn out to be accreditation standards developed by professional organizations at the national level and used as funding requirements.

It is probably not politically feasible for a state agency to use police powers to license public schools, which have their own statutory permission to operate. But, state statutes could require that the same standards be applied to schools as those that apply to private child care when the schools offer programs for preschool children. Advocates have long complained that the schools operate programs that do not meet standards that would apply to child care or Head Start.

A strong regulatory system, adequately staffed for inspection, can encourage career progression and stimulate colleges to offer required coursework. It can keep children safe and healthy. It can stimulate change through its periodic democratic standards revision processes. Federal funding for the improvement of licensing could encourage states to apply their basic standards to both full-day and part-day programs for children and to all family child care.

The state departments of education license teachers to work in the public schools. Licensing agencies set standards for teachers to work in child care, a few actually grant a license to the individual. The Head Start Bureau and Congress set standards for teachers to work in Head Start. The field as a whole needs a system that sets qualifications for all roles in all programs at all levels of quality. Some states have begun to develop such a system of qualifications, involving their departments of education with advocacy groups working on career development. A necessary ingredient for salary policy in early care and education is a career lattice and a rational set of qualifications or role progression across the systems.

All of these systems are already in place somewhere, even though not everywhere, and could be modified to support the entire system of early care and education, rather than just parts of it. Divided, they are not as strong as they would be together across all the sectors.

Recruitment, Training, and Career Advising

Severe staffing shortages have undermined the quality of programs for young children. Because salaries are so low, college advisors steer students away from this work, even when the students are attracted to it. These are problems that need to be addressed across the entire system for all programs and for all children. Solving these problems requires an understanding of all the roles in the entire system and an ability to conceptualize the career lattice that exists.

Salaries must be improved before we have quality in our system. All of the components of the infrastructure are necessary to this salary increase (Mitchell & Morgan, 2000), and each of the components will affect the salary issue. Compensation is a systemic issue that will only be solved by changes in the system as a whole.

Already in place is a national network of resource and referral agencies (R&Rs), many of which provide training that is subsidized by state governments and often by business as well. Training must be connected with colleges in the long run, and some of the local R&Rs have begun to form connections with colleges in order that their training can count toward future degrees in the field. Some of the R&Rs have developed career counseling and recruitment services for the child care field.

This network is the only national network that talks to parents and relates to early care and education, and it took many years to put into place. The existence of a nationwide network in all of the states, in touch with the many small and large programs that serve children, enables funding sources, both public and private, to reach the variety of children's programs. This network will need to build much stronger relationships with school districts and with Head Start, as some R&Rs have begun to do in a few states.

The work of recruitment and career advisement should also fall within the functions of professional organizations such as the National Association for the Education of Young Children, the National School-Age Alliance, and the National Association for Family

Child Care, all of which are national membership organizations. There are also career development planning and advocacy groups in almost all of the states. All of these advocates for the profession should be part of the system, developing or using counseling materials, job fairs, and activities to interest high school students and young adults in the field.

Recruitment, training, and credentialing are also done for the Department of Labor's apprentice programs in early care and education. Colleges with early care and education programs recruit for their own programs. If their programs serve the field as a whole, rather than just child care, or just Head Start, or just public school, they will be better able to market them to the future field.

A Higher Education System

The higher education system of colleges is the infrastructure support that prepares those who work in early care and education programs. There are many roles in the field, and role progression both in the same programs and across programs. This fact leads to opportunities for teachers to enter the field in assisting roles and to attain degrees while they are employed.

Low-income individuals can and do attain degrees, but these individuals are unlikely to sign up for a four-year degree or higher all at once or even apply for a scholarship to help them reach their future goals. Low-income individuals are more likely to progress in smaller steps, with benchmark accomplishments along the way—a course, a certificate, a degree, a higher degree.

Head Start's mandate for degreed teachers now brings in higher education as a part of its support system for Head Start, in addition to schools and child care programs. The Head Start mandate has resulted in college programs that build the Child Development Associate credential into an associate's degree. To be responsive to Head Start, colleges will need to ensure success, diversity, and articulation.

Scholarship Help for Staff and Direct Funding to Colleges

Scholarship and funding might be considered components of the higher education infrastructure, except that there needs to be specific support for the early care and education field. The higher education system already has its sources of support, and those sources support the colleges to serve as infrastructure for many fields. Specific support for the early care and education programs in colleges can be realized from higher education authorizations, foundation grants to colleges, and business. Generic scholarship help, such as Pell grants, are used by early childhood staff when counseling is available to them. Specific scholarships for early care and education have been developed in some states, such as New York, and some localities, such as Kansas City.

The T.E.A.C.H. scholarship program, originating in North Carolina, has spread to at least 17 other states and is being considered by many others. This program brings scholarship help specifically to those already employed in the field. There are many advantages to its becoming national in scope. It emphasizes data on its effects so that national data could result. It lends itself well to public and private support because donors can specify their target participants. Like the Department of Labor apprentice programs, it emphasizes the raise in compensation that by any logic must accompany significant increases in qualification.

Related to scholarship help are loan forgiveness programs. Loan forgiveness is appropriate for teachers who work in child care, Head Start, or schools, especially those who work in areas with severe labor shortages or who have competencies that are in short supply, such as infant/toddler programming.

College degrees must be accessible to those already employed, not just those preparing for future employment. Individuals who work as aides and assistants are major targets for preparation for career advancement. Some of the 4-year colleges are not yet fully adapted to the changes in their environment and not yet fully able to recruit already employed individuals into their programs. Their infrastructure support for the child care field is weakened and their own future enrollment is undermined by their preconceived ideas about their student body. Faculty institutes and other incentives for change could speed up this necessary process.

Technical Assistance and Consultative Help

As we try to improve the quality of programs for young children, technical assistance and consultative help are essential to help programs move to higher levels. One source of such help has been the R&R network, described previously as the only national network of local agencies capable of delivering services across the systems and the states.

There have been efforts to create new sources of help. For example, the Office of Special Education Programs provides technical assistance for programs serving young children with disabilities, and the Head Start Bureau established a technical assistance network (QICs) for Head Start on a regional basis, but has phased them out. Efforts like these have not yet succeeded in creating outreach to serve Head Start, the schools, and child care programs, rather than focusing on only part of the system. Funds for technical assistance need to be expanded in scope and outreach as part of an effort to raise the level of quality of all of the programs. Quality will improve if there is a flow of information and communication across all sectors so that organizations can share what they learn.

Consumer Information to Parents

The existence of a national network of R&R agencies presents major opportunities for delivering consumer information to parents. The rationale developed in the 1970s–1990s in the R&R network was that "we do not make recommendations; we only give referrals." Parents, on the other hand, have been asking for expert help from the R&R counselors. "Would you put your child here?" Consumer information is a key factor in improving a system, creating a demand for higher quality, and a valuing that leads to a willingness among purchasers to pay higher salaries to those who provide the care.

Like consumers of any major product or service, parents need specific information on which to base their decisions. The Cost, Quality and Child Outcomes study found that parents define quality much as the experts do but that parents have difficulty in seeing quality and nonquality before their eyes (Cost, Quality and Outcomes Study Team, 1995).

There are no consumer reports or ratings for quality, as there are to help consumers make decisions about buying a car.

The R&R network has begun to add new approaches. There is no liability risk in giving parents accurate objective information. For example, they can, and most do, tell parents which programs are accredited. They can tell parents how a state has rated a program in states with rated licenses or tiered reimbursement. Most now supply this information. Beyond that they can tell parents which programs have 50% of their staff with college degrees. They can tell them which infant programs say they limit the number of infants and toddlers to three or four, even if licensing would permit more. They can tell parents the size of the groups of preschool children that the program says it maintains. R&Rs can even develop criteria and rate programs themselves on their licensing record of compliance. Some licensing offices may be bold enough to supply R&Rs with this summary information or put it on the Internet where parents can find it.

This type of consumer information will become available to parents because they need it, and the system needs for them to have it. If some R&Rs do not provide it now, they will in the future because other competing organizations will make it available.

Data Systems

For some systems, the availability of data is taken for granted, and the general public knows how to interpret what key data mean. For example, we know the unemployment rate for the country as a whole and for localities. When it changes a percentage point or two, we know what might result from the change.

For early care and education, which also fluctuates with the economy, there is an astonishing lack of data given the fact that it is a $700 billion industry. For example, we do not have regular information on

- How much is spent in federal and state dollars across the systems, by state, and by locality

- How much is spent in all, by parents, government, and private sources, on early care and education

- Where the children are, whether in their own homes, other homes, family child care, or centers

- How many children have serious injuries or die, by the type of care including parental, and the categories of harm

- Whether children who were abused were at home or in child care

Many pediatricians do not know whether a child's parents are using a care arrangement, or what it is, when they prescribe treatment for a child. Many of our data systems do not produce the data we need because they were never coded for child care. We need to update all of our public health systems so that we get the information we need in order to make the early education and care system safer and better. We also need to collect, compare, and analyze the data on dollars spent and allocation of those dollars. We need better information on family income to enable us to distinguish between families with two low-wage earners from families with one high wage earner. Finally, we need ongoing updated information on child care prices by locality and data on parent preferences and supply and demand. These data can be regularly supplied from the future R&R network.

Local Collaborative Planning and State Responsiveness

Part of the infrastructure must be cross-program structures that can allocate resources, plan for transitions from one program to another, ensure supportive funding for quality across the system, and envision changes to make the system work better.

It is futile to create local planning groups that have no power to influence funding decisions for their area. Equally futile is to create coordinating structures at the state level that are not connected to the imagination and knowledge of needs that exist at the level of the actual services.

Local councils and local planning structures have been created by legislation and by executive decisions over and over. They are an essential part of Smart Start in North Carolina, for example (Bryant & Smart Start Evaluation Team, 1999). They have been invented and reinvented in the states since the 1970s (Morgan, 1972). These local groups are usually mandated to have a democratically representative structure including parents. Any universal structure would need to meet requirements like this. Currently, most of these bodies have few parents, primarily because funds are no longer available to pay their expenses.

Criticisms of past structures like these have been that they can allocate funds but lack vision to set directions and make policy recommendations. Further, there has been duplication of such structures, creating competing structures.

Another example of local collaborative planning and state responsiveness has been the career development planning. Beginning around 1991, groups began planning to create career paths and lattices and to pull together the planners who affect the systems and standards to make a more coherent system. From the beginning, state licensing agencies and state funding agencies were aware of this planning, and some participated in it. This was an emerging idea in 1991, but by 2001, these groups had had remarkable success in making systemic change (Wheelock College Institute for Leadership and Career Initiatives, 2002).

More than 30 states had identified core knowledge or core competencies in early care and education, which was important for guidance to the higher education sector. Just less than 30 states had identified a "career lattice" (i.e., a progression of roles and levels of qualifications with identified pathways between them). Twenty-two states had computerized registries to track teachers' qualifications, 26 had training approval processes, and 21 had compensation improvements tied to qualifications. Almost every state had a Department of Labor Apprenticeship Program.

Seventeen states had the T.E.A.C.H. scholarship project, a model that brings higher education to the already employed and ties qualifications to compensation. Nineteen states had developed an administrator credential, and 18 states had an infant/toddler credential.

The most astonishing change was in its vision for systemic change. Roughly half the states had developed rated licenses and/or tiered reimbursement systems to identify levels of quality and to pay more for higher quality. Licensing offices, previously committed to maintaining the base life of quality, were now involved in helping to develop levels of quality above the licensed level and working with other agencies to create financial incentives for programs to move to higher levels. Licensing rules themselves began to refer to these innovative changes.

Clearly, the state level agencies were responsive to the career development groups' innovations and responded with their funds from federal "quality" dollars and other sources. The planning groups were advocates and individuals familiar with the system and knowledgeable about how to make it work better.

The Community Health and Mental Health Systems

The health systems today are quite different from the services that existed when Head Start began and are still being reinvented. Head Start tried to ensure health and social services for all eligible children by building them into the Head Start program. Today, these services may exist in the community, and the role of the program is to connect children and families to the services they need and assure that they are covered by Medicaid or other sources of funds to pay for the service. In some communities, however, there are few services available to families. Head Start's comprehensiveness is only as good as the system that can deliver the services.

Knowing this, it is important to recognize that the infrastructure of early care and education includes the delivery of health and social services at the community level. Where this infrastructure is weak, it should be strengthened, not just for Head Start children but for all children. For the poor, there is an effective advocacy thrust occurring to assure that all children are covered by health insurance.

The Maternal and Child Health structures have been in place for many years and have a strong interest in children's health and development. Community Mental Health structures no longer have the commitment to preventive programs for young children they once had, but this commitment may remain strong in certain areas. A model worth reinventing as infrastructure was developed in Cambridge, Massachusetts, by the Cambridge-Somerville Mental Health Center. The center saw itself as infrastructure for all the child care and Head Start programs in its geographic area and sent its staff to those settings to work with teachers and talk to parents. They believed that the staff of a center, with the opportunity to see children everyday and talk to parents briefly every morning and afternoon, was in a better position to deliver mental health services, with support from the center, than could be delivered by 1-hour office visits at the mental health center (Personal communication with the Director of the Cambridge-Somerville Mental Health Center, 1971).

Similarly, over the years, there have been models of delivering health services to children at their early childhood programs, particularly vision screening and other basic screenings and immunizations. The American Academy of Pediatrics advocates a medical home for every child. This piece of infrastructure might unite the different sectors in early child care and education more than any other single component. However, it is a part of health planning, not early childhood planning. Viewing health and social services as a necessary infrastructure support, rather than program components, could lead to a stronger early care and education system.

Facility Capitalization

In the United States, there has been little public support to develop physical facilities for early care and education programs. Both Head Start and child care have been largely dependent on using existing space, in schools, churches, and other building not constructed with young children in mind. At some point, we will need to recognize the need for high-quality facilities for our youngest children. Some method for capitalizing buildings must ultimately be part of the infrastructure.

At present, there are systems in place for capitalizing public school buildings. In some states, these capital funds can be assessed for child care and for preschool, but only if the school district itself is applying for the funds. A few states have developed capital loan programs that can be used by child care and possibly by Head Start as well.

Evaluation and Research

As states develop early care and education systems, they will need to justify their expenditures by measuring results of some kind. For the federally funded Head Start program, this element of the infrastructure has always been important. Yet, there are still many unresolved issues about what to measure, at what level, and how to measure it. Further, research has usually addressed one sector, or possibly two, but seldom all sectors.

Gallagher and Clifford (2000) summarized the North Carolina Smart Start approach as follows

> Each of the counties was responsible for the design of its own early childhood program, and so the goals and program emphasis varied from one county to another. There were no generally agreed upon goals such as one would find in the primary grades, where mastery of reading and arithmetic skills makes broad assessments more interpretable.

In many ways, Head Start has faced the same sort of problems by permitting local programs to pursue their own values, and this variety may characterize our future system as well. The system as a whole does rely on basic research findings in many ways. Licensing standards are influenced by research. Best practice in the field as a whole is developed in an ongoing way, influenced by what research has found.

Much of the research that is applied in these ways has been funded through the National Institute for Child Health and Human Development, the Institute of Education Sciences, the Head Start Bureau, the Child Care Bureau, and the Office of Special Education Programs. In addition, the Census Bureau regularly produces information about the population and its use of early care and education programs. Demonstration programs have been created, especially for children with disabilities, where others can observe good practice and get consultation and advice.

These elements of the infrastructure, if connected and strengthened and conceptualized as supporting all programs, can be the basis for evolving our future system. It does not need to happen all at the same time. It is not a blueprint. But it will require agreement on a common vision of universal service, agreement on the concept of multiple funding sources and multiple programs, and collaboration among all the programs and their infrastructures.

REFERENCES

Abt Associates and the National Center for Children in Poverty. (2000). *Report 1 from Study of Low-Income Child Care.* Washington, DC: Authors.

Albelda, R. (1996). *The war on the poor: A defense manual.* New York: New Press.

Bryant, D., & Smart Start Evaluation Team. (1999). *North Carolina's Smart Start Initiative: 1998 Annual Evaluation Report.* Chapel Hill: University of North Carolina.

Center for the Child Care Workforce. (March 1998). *Current data on child care salaries and benefits in the United States.* Washington, DC: Author.

Cost, Quality, and Outcomes Study Team (1995). *Quality and outcomes study.* Denver: University of Colorado.

Esterline, B. (1976). *Coordination: A conceptual model and practical consideration.* Paper presented at the National Seminar on State Capacity Building, Denver, Colorado.

Fuller, B., & Kagan, S.L. (2000). *Remember the children: Mothers balance work and child care under welfare reform.* Wave 1 findings of a study: Growing up in Poverty Project 2000. Berkeley: University of California, Graduate School of Education.

Gallagher, J., & Clifford, R. (2000). The missing support infrastructure in early childhood. *Early childhood research and practice* (Vol. 2, No. 1). Chapel Hill: Frank Porter Graham Child Development Center, University of North Carolina.

Harbin, G., & McNulty, B. (1990). Policy implementation: Perspectives on service coordination and interagency cooperation. In: S.J. Meisels & J.P. Shonkoff (Eds.), *Handbook of early intervention* (pp. 700–772). Cambridge, MA: Cambridge University Press.

Kagan, S.L., & Cohen, N. (1997). *Not By chance: The Quality 2000 Initiative.* New Haven, CT: Yale University, Bush Center in Child Development and Social Policy.

Mitchell, A., & Morgan, G. (2000). *New perspectives on compensation strategies.* Boston: Wheelock College, Center for Career Development in Early Care and Education.

Morgan, G. (1972). *Evaluation of the 4-C concept.* Washington, DC: Day Care and Child Development Council of America.

Morgan, G. (1999). *Updated summary of local structures created in Massachusetts for child care policy-making and coordination: We keep pulling our infrastructure up to examine its roots to see whether it's growing.* Boston: Wheelock College.

National Center for Education Statistics. (1996). *Child care and early education program participation of infants, toddlers, and preschoolers.* Washington, DC: Author.

The Open Forum. (1999). *The purple book.* Cambridge, MA: Child Care Resource Center.

U.S. Census Bureau. (2002). *Growing diversity of the population of the U.S. between 1990 and 2000.* Washington, DC: Author.

Washington, V., & Andrews, J.D. (2001). *The children of 2010.* Washington, DC: National Association for the Education of Young Children.

Weick, K.E. (1984). Small wins: Redefining the scale of social problems. *American Psychologist, 39,* 40–49.

Wheelock College Institute for Leadership and Career Initiatives. (2002, July). *Report on 2001 Early Childhood/School-age Career Development Survey.* Boston: Wheelock College.

CHAPTER 27

Dosage-Response Effects and Mechanisms of Change in Public and Model Programs

ARTHUR J. REYNOLDS

O f all social programs, early childhood interventions (ECI) in the first years of life have among the greatest levels of support across the nation. In 2002, state and federal expenditures for them totaled $22 billion (White House, 2003), and they have an increasingly important role in school reforms. The key advantage of ECIs is their potential for prevention and cost-effectiveness. This intervention approach is an exemplar of the growing interdisciplinary field of prevention science (Coie et al., 1993; Weissberg & Greenberg, 1998). The high priority of early childhood programs provides a good opportunity to highlight recent advances and discuss three major issues of the field: the optimal timing and duration of participation, the mechanisms by which the effects of program participation are expressed, and the consistency of effects of large-scale and model programs. In this chapter, ECI is broadly defined as the provision of educational, social, and health services to children and families during any of the first 8 years of life who are at risk of poor outcomes because of socio-environmental disadvantages or developmental disabilities.

ADVANCES IN KNOWLEDGE ABOUT EFFECTIVENESS

Three major advances in knowledge about the effects of ECI have occurred over the past decade. First, in contrast to the 1990s, there is substantial support for the short- and long-term impact of a wide variety of well-implemented programs on child development (Barnett, 1995; Barnett & Boocock, 1998; *Future of Children,* 1995; Guralnick, 1997; Karoly

Preparation of this chapter was supported by grants from the National Institute of Child Health and Human Development (No. R01HD34294) and the Office of Educational Research and Improvement, U.S. Department of Education (No. R305T990477).

et al., 1998; Zigler, 1994). Relative to nonparticipation, participation in ECI is consistently associated with higher levels of cognitive development, early school achievement, and motivation in the short term, with lower rates of grade retention and special education services during the elementary grades, and, increasingly, with higher rates of school completion and educational attainment. Some studies also have found that program participation is associated with lower rates of antisocial behavior, delinquency, and crime (Lally, Mangione, Honig, & Wittner, 1988; Reynolds, Chang, & Temple, 1998; Schweinhart, Barnes, & Weikart, 1993) and with employment and economic success in adulthood (Schweinhart et al., 1993). Although these findings generally hold for both model and large-scale programs, the quality of large-scale programs continues to be uneven (Zigler, 1994), and the evidence base for them is weaker relative to model programs, especially for Head Start (Currie & Thomas, 1995; Phillips & Cabrera, 1996; United States General Accounting Office [USGAO], 1997).

A second major advance is that there is increasing evidence that both the timing and duration of intervention matter. Since 1990, empirical support for these characteristics of participation has grown (C.T. Ramey & Ramey, 1998; S.L. Ramey & Ramey, 1992; Yoshikawa, 1995). As reviews by Weissberg and Greenberg (1998) and Yoshikawa (1995) revealed the most effective programs reported in the literature spanning home visitation to center-based preschool education have been those that began during the first 3 years of life, continue for multiple years, and provide support to families. Studies in the Carolina Abecedarian Project (Campbell & Ramey, 1994, 1995) and the Chicago Child-Parent Centers (Reynolds, 1994, 1998) show that children who participate in preschool alone have consistently higher school achievement and lower rates of remedial services than children who participate in school-age intervention alone. Both studies also found that the largest effects accrue to children whose participation continues to second or third grade (Campbell & Ramey, 1995; Reynolds, 1994; Reynolds & Temple, 1998). Nevertheless, the optimal timing and duration of participation remains a major issue, especially with regard to long-term effects. Comprehensiveness (breadth), quality, and intensity of services matter as well (C.T. Ramey & Ramey, 1998; Reynolds, 1998), and these attributes are independent of timing and duration.

A third major advance in the field of early childhood intervention is that a major developmental mechanism of long-term effects of early intervention on child development outcomes is attributable to the cognitive/scholastic advantage experienced in the program. Although the Consortium for Longitudinal Studies (1983; Lazar, Darlington, Murray, & Snipper, 1982) and Berrueta-Clement et al. (1984) provided empirical demonstration for the cognitive advantage hypotheses, more recent studies into adulthood (Barnett, Young, & Schweinhart, 1998; Schweinhart et al., 1993) and contemporary large-scale programs (Reynolds, 2000; Reynolds, Mavrogenes, Bezruczko, & Hagemann, 1996) reinforce the validity of this hypothesis. Program participation is associated with long-term success because children's developed abilities are enhanced and this initiates cumulative advantages in children's school performance. Moreover, there is emerging support for the significant role of the family support hypothesis (e.g., nurturing parenting, participating in children's education) as a major path of long-term effects in impacting school achievement (Lamb, 1998; Reynolds et al., 1996) and in preventing antisocial behavior and delinquency (Reynolds et al., 1998; Yoshikawa, 1995; Zigler, Taussig, & Black, 1992). Evidence for the school support hypothesis is emerging as well (Currie & Thomas, 1998; Lee & Loeb, 1995; Reynolds, 1991). Unfortunately, however, these and other hypotheses (e.g., motivational advantage) have never been considered together or tested for large-scale programs.

ISSUES FOR A NEW AGE IN RESEARCH AND DEVELOPMENT

While recognizing the important advances in knowledge in the past decade, many scholars and policy analysts continue to raise questions about the depth of our knowledge about several fundamental issues. Three recurrent issues stand out and are presaged by the preceding discussion:

1. What is the optimal timing and duration of program participation for affecting child development?

2. What are the causal mechanisms and environmental supports through which the effects of participation lead to long-term success for children?

3. What are the effects of contemporary public programs such as Head Start and other government-funded programs? Can confidence in findings be strengthened for policy decisions?

These questions are consistent with Guralnick's (1997) view that the next generation of research is to address more specific and policy-relevant questions such as who benefits most from which particular programs, what environmental conditions influence effectiveness, and what are the benefits to society of program participation relative to costs. Alternatively, these and other questions have been raised since the early 1970s. Why has more not been accomplished in the past 3 decades? The issue of pathways of effects (post-program conditions and experiences that affect long-term gains) is central to understanding the process of change over time. Until the late 1990s, direct evidence of mechanisms of effects came from the model projects in the Consortium for Longitudinal Studies (1983), primarily the Perry Preschool Program (Schweinhart et al., 1993). Issues surrounding differential effects by child, family, and program characteristics are far from settled (Barnett & Boocock, 1998; Consortium for Longitudinal Studies, 1983). Studies of the comparative effects of program curricula have been limited mostly to model programs. Finally, a clear need exists for more and better evidence of the longer-term effects of large-scale programs such as Head Start. Of the 15 reviews of the effects of early childhood intervention published from 1983 to 1997, 89% of the total number of program citations were for model programs rather than large-scale programs (Reynolds, 2000; Reynolds, Mann, Miedel, & Smokowski, 1997). Given the diversity of programs being implemented at the beginning of the 21st century, more research on public programs is needed.

There are many reasons for the underdeveloped knowledge base on the effects of early childhood programs. Two stand out. First, investments in research and evaluation have been and continue to be low. In 1996, Head Start spent one third of 1% of its federal expenditure on research and evaluation. This proportion is nearly identical to that allocated for all educational and social programs for children and youth in the United States (National Science and Technology Council, 1997). In contrast, the proportion of total expenditures devoted to research and development in the sectors of transportation, energy, and biomedical science is 2% to 3%, 6–10 times greater than for social programs for children and families.

Another explanation is that research methodology remains significantly associated with the tradition of Campbell and Stanley (1966) and Cook and Campbell (1979) in which main effects and internal validity are emphasized over issues associated with generalizability, such as moderators and mediators of effects and program features associated with success (Cronbach, 1982; Lipsey, 1993). The development of theory-driven approaches to evaluation has contributed to a greater appreciation of explanatory and multiple methodologies of evaluation research (Bickman, 1987; Chen, 1990; Chen & Rossi, 1983). It was from this perspective that Reynolds developed Confirmatory Program Evaluation (1998). In this evaluation approach, the explicit theory of the program is highlighted to establish an *a priori* model of how the program is expected to exert its influence. As adapted from Susser (1973) and Anderson et al. (1980), six empirically verifiable criteria strengthen the validity and applicability of research findings: 1) temporality of participation, 2) strength of association (e.g., the larger the association, the more likely it is real), 3) gradient (dosage-response), 4) specificity, 5) consistency, and 6) coherence. In the following sections, I discuss the three criteria most directly relevant to emerging early intervention research.

Gradient (Dosage-Response)

In this criterion, a causal inference is more warranted if, other factors being equal, a monotonic relationship exists between program exposure (e.g., number of days or sessions attended, number of contact hours, number of years of participation) and the program outcome. Outside of public health and medicine, gradient effects are rarely investigated, probably because participation in interventions is not coded as a continuous variable. The gradient (dosage-response) effect was a major criterion for determining that the relationship between cigarette smoking (treatment) and lung cancer is causal (U.S. Department of Health, Education, and Welfare, 1964). The ECI equivalent of gradient effects has been found in studies of the Abecedarian Project (Campbell & Ramey, 1995), the Chicago Child-Parent Centers (Reynolds, 1994; Reynolds & Temple, 1998), and the Infant Health and Development Program (C.T. Ramey, Bryant, & Wasik, 1992). Gradient effects also strengthen an investigator's capacity to draw causal inferences when experiments are not possible, which is often the case in intervention studies.

A major issue in early education is the optimal timing and duration of children's program participation. Although it has long been posited that the earlier program participation begins, the greater and more lasting the impact, the duration of program participation or dosage level also is believed to be an important principle of effectiveness. In the duration perspective, the continuity of children's development from infancy to preschool and beyond is believed to be more crucial than experiences or developmental changes that occur just in infancy. Thus, from this perspective there is an equal balance of influences in the learning environments between infancy and early childhood. This perspective is best represented by the ecological model of development in which children's outcomes are conceptualized as a function of a nested structure of influences emanating from the individual child to the larger systems of family, school, and community (Bronfenbrenner & Morris, 1998).

Consistency

Consistency of association between program exposure and outcome indicates whether the estimated program effect is similar across sample populations; similar at different times and places, under different types of analyses and model specifications; and for similar program theories. The greater the consistency of findings favoring positive effects (or alternatively, absence of effects), the more likely the observed effects are real. There are two dimensions of consistency. Evidence of within-study consistency would be based on the degree to which evaluation data are robust and sensitive (Rosenbaum, 1995; Rosenbaum & Rubin, 1984). For example, if positive findings remained the same under alternative analytic techniques (i.e., regression, ANCOVA, simultaneous modeling, latent variable modeling) and different model specifications (e.g., covariates), confidence about program affect also would increase. Contemporary statistical techniques of bias reduction have rarely been used in research on ECI. Evidence for between-study consistency is based on the correspondence of study findings with previous studies using different samples, social contexts, and program variations. If these studies show a consistent and interpretable pattern of results, causal inferences are more likely. Nevertheless, a critical issue for CPE is to determine whether inconsistent or unexpected findings are due to theory failure, program implementation failure, or to limitations of the research design or data analysis.

Coherence

The coherence criterion is about the hypothesized causal mechanisms (active ingredients) that give rise to the effects of program participation over time. Once a direct relation is established between program participation and an outcome variable, the pathways that produce this estimated effect must be identified. With few exceptions (e.g., Barnett, Young, & Schweinhart, 1998; Consortium for Longitudinal Studies, 1983), little attention in the field of early intervention has been given to the developmental pathways or causal mechanisms that promote long-term effects.

THREE EMERGING THEMES: DOSAGE-RESPONSE EFFECTS, PATHS OF CHANGE, AND CONSISTENCY OF EFFECTS

Dosage-Response Effects

Although there are many reasons why the effects of programs fade over time, the key rationale for extended interventions is that the continuation of programs into the primary grades will not only promote more successful transitions but also help prevent the fading effects of preschool intervention. Most developmental theories indicate that environmental support during the transition to formal schooling is important for children's continued success (Entwisle, 1995; Reynolds, 1991). A longer duration of participation in early childhood programs through either lengthening the years of preschool or by extending preschool programs into the primary grades (continuation programs) may lead to greater and longer-lasting effects than interventions that end in preschool for several reasons. First, longer periods of implementation may be necessary to promote greater and longer-lasting changes in scholastic and psychosocial outcomes. Early interventions are often comprehensive, and they provide many services to children and parents that require significant coordination. They may be more effective if they have more time to work. This is borne out in two reviews of social programs for children and youth (Durlak & Wells, 1997; Weissberg & Greenberg, 1998). Another factor that reinforces the need for longer-lasting interventions is that children in many urban settings are more at risk today than in the past (Wilson, 1996). Thus, programs must last longer and be better in quality to be as effective as in the past.

Second, extended early childhood programs are designed to encourage more stable and predictable learning environments, both of which are key elements in optimal scholastic and social functioning. Participation in extended interventions, for example, may encourage higher rates of school and home stability than would otherwise be expected. Certainly, environmental forces continue to operate after preschool and kindergarten.

A third rationale for extended childhood interventions is that they occur at a time increasingly viewed as a sensitive if not "critical" period in children's scholastic development (Entwisle, 1995; Entwisle & Alexander, 1993; Reynolds, 1991). It is expected that the provision of additional educational and social support services to children and families during this key transition would promote greater success and would help prevent major learning problems by third grade, a primary marker that presages later academic and social development. Since the 1990s, many studies have provided empirical validation for the strong link between early school adjustment and educational success during the entire schooling process (Entwisle & Alexander, 1993; Reynolds et al., 1996).

Pathways of Change from Program Participation

Identification of the pathways through which the long-run effects of early childhood programs are achieved help identify intervening factors and processes that can be the focus of intervention for maintaining or enhancing earlier gains. Identified pathways also aid program design and improvement by highlighting key components or active ingredients that require special attention. If ECI, for example, influenced later school achievement through primarily enhancing children's early cognitive-scholastic skills rather than their social skills, then program content may be optimally directed toward the development of structured language and cognitive enrichment (although not ignoring family of social development). Such a focus can also promote generalizability of findings to other settings and populations.

Figure 27.1 shows five hypothesized pathways through which early childhood intervention may affect social competence behaviors in the years after the program ceases. Derived from the extant literature (see Reynolds, 2000), the hypotheses associated with these pathways provide a foundation for developing the knowledge base on how early childhood programs lead to longer-term effects and the environmental conditions that promote or limit success. The effects of early intervention may be transmitted through

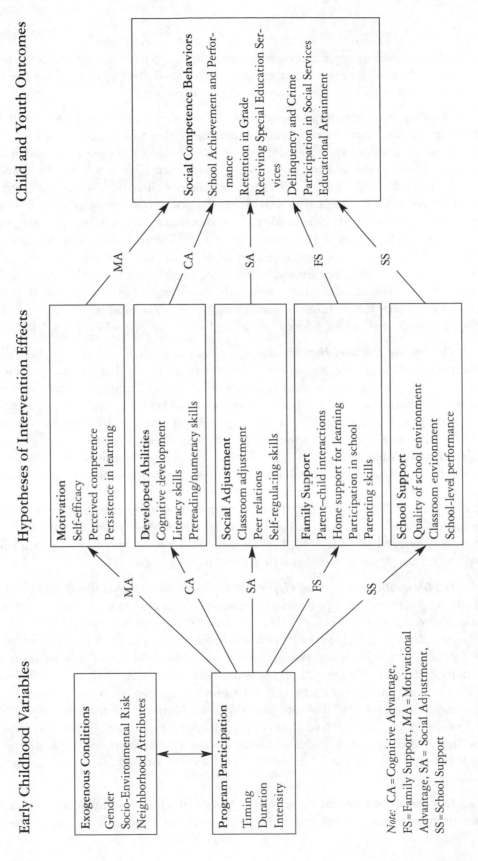

Early Childhood Variables

Hypotheses of Intervention Effects

Child and Youth Outcomes

Exogenous Conditions

Gender
Socio-Environmental Risk
Neighborhood Attributes

Program Participation

Timing
Duration
Intensity

Motivation
Self-efficacy
Perceived competence
Persistence in learning

Developed Abilities
Cognitive development
Literacy skills
Prereading/numeracy skills

Social Adjustment
Classroom adjustment
Peer relations
Self-regulating skills

Family Support
Parent–child interactions
Home support for learning
Participation in school
Parenting skills

School Support
Quality of school environment
Classroom environment
School-level performance

Social Competence Behaviors

School Achievement and Performance
Retention in Grade
Receiving Special Education Services
Delinquency and Crime
Participation in Social Services
Educational Attainment

Note: CA = Cognitive Advantage, FS = Family Support, MA = Motivational Advantage, SA = Social Adjustment, SS = School Support

Figure 27.1. Five hypotheses for explaining the effects of early childhood intervention.

five sets of intervening experiences and environmental supports: the cognitive advantage hypothesis, the family support hypothesis, the motivational advantage hypothesis, the social adjustment hypothesis, and the school support hypothesis.

The Cognitive Advantage Hypothesis   The cognitive advantage hypothesis indicates that the long-term effects of intervention are initiated by improvements in children's developed abilities in early childhood, usually at the end or close to the end of the program. The cognitive and language stimulation experienced in center-based education may directly affect children's cognitive functioning as well as their social and motivational behavior. A major focus of an activity-based educational component is the development of literacy skills through individual and group reading and writing activities, play, and frequent field trips in the community to promote knowledge and understanding of the world. These systematic educational experiences produce cognitive advantages that initiate a positive cycle of performance culminating in more successful adolescent adjustment. The cognitive advantage hypothesis is the most frequent explanation for the long-term effects of early intervention (Consortium for Longitudinal Studies, 1983; Lazar et al., 1982; Reynolds et al., 1996; Schweinhart & Weikart, 1980; Schweinhart et al., 1993).

The Family Support Hypothesis   The family support hypothesis indicates that longer-term effects of early intervention will occur to the extent that program participation enhances the capacities of parents to support children's learning and development. Parenting behavior may include those with or on behalf of children such as home support for learning and school support for learning through participation in school-related activities. A central goal of ECI is to promote family development, often through the provision of family education activities. The family support hyporhesis was offered by Bronfenbrenner (1975) as an explanation for the observed dissipating cognitive effects of participation in Head Start. He noted, for example, that family functioning and parent–child relations must be affected for long-term effects on child development to occur. The family support hypothesis is the central theory of family centered programs and interventions since the 1960s and 1970s (Powell, 1999; Seitz, 1990). It has not been tested in many individual studies, especially in long-term follow ups.

The Motivational Advantage Hypothesis   In the motivational advantage hypothesis, the long-term effects of program participation are due to changes in children's motivational development rather than in their cognitive or language development. Motivation is broadly defined to include self-system attributes such as perceived competence, self-concept of ability, self-efficacy, task persistence, and effort. This hypothesis derives from work by Zigler and colleagues (Zigler, Abelson, Trickett, & Seitz, 1982; Zigler & Butterfield, 1968) indicating that changes in intelligence test scores among low-income children may have a substantial motivational component. Motivational development was one of the original goals of the Head Start program (Zigler & Styfco, 1993). There have been few direct tests of this hypothesis. Using teacher ratings of children's motivation, Schweinhart et al. (1993) and Reynolds (1991) found only limited evidence in support of this hypothesis.

The Social Adjustment Hypothesis   The social adjustment hypothesis indicates that improved social development is the major reason why participation in early intervention leads to long-term program effectiveness. Rather than directly changing children's cognitive status or motivation, participation may enhance children's internalization of social rules and norms as well as peer relations necessary for successful school adjustment and for negotiating social situations. As a result of participation in the organized activities of early educational intervention, children are expected to learn self-regulatory skills such as following directions, working with others, and inhibition of behavior. This hypothesis of the effects of early intervention has rarely, if ever, been directly tested.

The School Support Hypothesis In the school support hypothesis, the effects of program participation would persist to the extent that children attend schools of sufficient quality to maintain or enhance the impact of earlier intervention experiences. This hypothesis is the school-based version of the family support hypothesis. It has never been directly tested as an explanation of long-term effects, although there is evidence that postprogram enrollment in poor-quality schools may reduce the persistence of learning gains (Currie & Thomas, 1998; Lee & Loeb, 1995) and that school instability (i.e., school transfer) and the consequent disruptions it may cause also affects this process (Reynolds et al., 1996; Temple & Reynolds, 1999). One key issue is whether the school support hypothesis explains intervention effects above and beyond that of the cognitive advantage hypothesis and others. Of course, the hypotheses could work in combination. For example, program participation may affect adolescent social competence through early developed abilities and family support experiences or through a combination of early developed abilities, family support, and school support factors.

EXAMPLES FROM THE CHICAGO LONGITUDINAL STUDY

Three examples corresponding to the major questions noted previously are described in this section for data in the Chicago Longitudinal Study (Reynolds, Bezruczko, & Hagemann, 1997). These examples provide a foundation for further investigations of ECI. The first example is of the timing and duration of participation. The second is the investigation of hypotheses associated with long-term effects. The third is the consistency of effects reported in large-scale programs.

The Chicago Longitudinal Study is an on-going investigation of the effects of the Child-Parent Center (CPC) Program. The longitudinal quasi-experimental cohort design included 989 low-income mostly African American children who entered the program in preschool and graduated from kindergarten in 1986 from 20 centers as well as 550 children from similarly disadvantaged neighborhoods who participated in an alternative all-day kindergarten program in the Chicago schools, which was the "treatment as usual" at the time. The groups were well matched on eligibility for intervention, family socioeconomic status, gender, and race/ethnicity. At age 14 (in 1994), 1,164 children (76% of the original sample) were active in the study sample in the Chicago Public Schools. No differential attrition between groups has been detected (Reynolds, 2000), and positive findings for high-school dropout have been detected (Temple, Reynolds, & Miedel, 2000). The Chicago Longitudinal Study is unique in two key respects. First, it is the largest and most extensive longitudinal study ever of the effects of a federally funded early childhood program. Second, children varied considerably in their length of participation from 1 to 6 years, and thus the added value of different lengths of intervention can be assessed.

The CPC program is a Title I funded center-based early intervention that provides comprehensive educational and family support services to economically disadvantaged children from preschool to the early elementary grades (birth to 6 years). It is the second oldest federally funded preschool program (after Head Start) and the oldest extended childhood intervention (see Reynolds, 1994, 1998). Each site is under the direction of a head teacher and is located adjacent to the elementary school or as a wing of the school. Major features of the program include

- A structured and diverse set of language-based instructional activities designed to promote academic and social success: The centers use the Chicago EARLY (Chicago Board of Education, 1988) as a common activity guide; field trips are frequent.

- A multifaceted parent program that includes participating in parent room activities, volunteering in the classroom, attending school events, and enrolling in educational courses for personal development, all under the supervision of the Parent-Resource Teacher

- Outreach activities, such as resource mobilization, home visitation, and enrollment of children most in need, coordinated by the School-Community Representative

- A comprehensive school-age program from first to third grade that supports children's transition to elementary school through reduced class sizes (35 to 25 children), the addition of teacher aides in each class, extra instructional supplies, and coordination of instructional activities, staff development, and parent-program activities organized by the Curriculum-Parent Resource Teacher

Hypothesized Pathways of Program Effects

To provide a foundation for investigating these hypotheses, Reynolds (2000) implemented a confirmatory program evaluation approach. The program theory of the intervention is that children's scholastic readiness for school will be facilitated through the provision of systematic language learning activities in center-based early intervention and opportunities for family support experiences through direct parent participation in the program with and on behalf of their children. The central theory is embodied in this goal statement: "[CPC is] designed to reach the child and parent early, develop language skills and self-confidence, and to demonstrate that these children, if given a chance, can meet successfully all the demands of today's technological, urban society" (cf. Naisbitt, 1968). The key measures to assess this goal include indicators of school achievement, incidence of grade retention and special education placement, and family–school relations. Previous studies have demonstrated that several measures of participation in the program are significantly associated with higher school achievement and performance and lower rates of grade retention, special education, and high school dropout (Reynolds, 1994, 1995; Reynolds & Temple, 1998; Temple et al., 2000).

Results of the structural model of the five hypotheses are illustrated in Figure 27.2. The coefficients are standardized and significant at the .01 level. Structural modeling is particularly appropriate for theory-driven tests of hypotheses of causal mediation. The top half shows the paths of influence for preschool participation versus no participation. The bottom half shows the paths of influence for years of total participation (0 to 6). School achievement at age 14 was defined by the manifest indicators of reading comprehension

Paths from CPC Preschool Participation to School Achievement

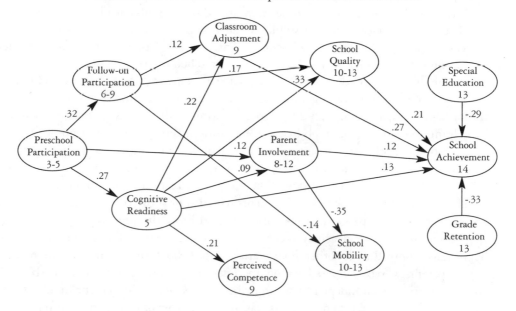

Paths from CPC Preschool Participation to High School Dropout

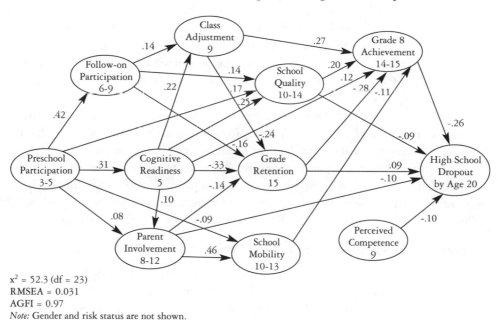

$x^2 = 52.3$ (df = 23)
RMSEA = 0.031
AGFI = 0.97
Note: Gender and risk status are not shown.

Figure 27.2. Paths of influence for preschool participation on school achievement and dropout.

and math achievement scores of the Iowa Tests of Basic Skills. As displayed in Figure 27.2, the cognitive advantage hypothesis, measured by the school readiness battery on the ITBS at age 5, provided the best single explanation for the significant relation between preschool participation and school achievement. Preschool participants started kindergarten more cognitively ready to learn than no-preschool participants (b = .27), and this advantage directly carried over to later school achievement (b = .13) above and beyond the effects of other intervening variables. Apparently, this cognitive advantage diffuses throughout the schooling process by also promoting positive classroom adjustment and by helping to reduce school mobility, grade retention, and special education placement.

Among the other significant pathways contributing to the explanation of preschool effects was the dual mechanism of cognitive readiness and school quality (b = .019 or .27 × .33. × .21). School quality was the number of years children attended schools in which relatively high proportions of students scored at or above the national achievement norms. Parent participation in school also was a pathway through which preschool participation affected school achievement. This provides support for the family support hypothesis. Controlling for other model variables, preschool participants were more likely to have parents who participated in school activities after the end of the program (b = .12), and this participation independently contributed to school achievement in adolescence (b = .12). A similar pattern of findings was found for years of CPC participation.

Table 27.1 summarizes the major contributing pathways to the long-term effects of CPC program participation as a proportion of the total indirect effect. The total indirect effect (standardized) denotes the effect CPC participation through the intervening variables or the hypotheses of program influence.

For the most part, the cognitive advantage hypothesis contributed the most to the explanation of CPC effects on school achievement. For preschool participation, the cognitive advantage hypothesis (measured by cognitive readiness at age 5) accounted for 21% of the total indirect effect. This hypothesis contributed an even larger share to the explanation of years of total CPC participation. To demonstrate the variation by outcome, the second column shows the contribution of the different hypotheses using high-school dropout by age 20 as the dependent variable. Here, the hypotheses of program effects were more balanced, as the cognitive advantage, school support, and family support hypotheses contributed to the total indirect effects of program participation (Reynolds, 1999). These and other hypotheses warrant further tests using a variety of indicators.

Presence and Consistency of Estimated Effects in Large-Scale Programs

In confirmatory program evaluation, emphasis is given to the sensitivity of effects to model specification and method of analysis. Such sensitivity analysis is frequently recommended (Anderson et al., 1980; Rosenbaum, 1995) and can strengthen the validity of findings. This is especially the case for quasi-experimental and nonexperimental designs that are frequently utilized in studies of large-scale programs. To date, research on Head Start programs and other early interventions has not utilized systematic strategies to investigate consistency of estimated effects.

In the Chicago Longitudinal Study, Reynolds (2000) analyzed the effects of preschool participation and duration of program participation (0–6 years) for school achievement at age 14 and prevalence of grade retention under four sequential model

Table 27.1. Total indirect effects of two program indicators

Key pathways	Age 14 school achievement	Age 20 high school dropout
A. Preschool participation	.17	-.13
Percentage of indirect effect due to:		
Cognitive advantage	21	8
Family support	8	6
Cognitive advantage and school support	11	7
Cognitive advantage and social adjustment	9	–
School support	–	12
Cognitive advantage and retention	–	7
B. Years of total participation	.26	-.14
Percentage of indirect effect due to:		
Cognitive advantage	59	36
Family support	5	10
School support	7	14
Cognitive advantage and school support	4	–
Cognitive advantage and retention	–	6

specifications: 1) unadjusted mean group difference, 2) adjustments for sex of child and environmental risk (number of family risk factors such as low parental education), 3) adjustments for parent participation in school as rated by teachers, and 4) adjustments for school site attributes as measured by 20 site dummy variables. The findings indicated that both preschool participation and years of total program participation were significantly associated with child outcomes under all model specifications. Preschool participation was associated with a 5- to 7-month advantage in reading achievement and an 8 to 10 percentage-point reduction in the rate of grade retention. Each additional year of program participation was associated with a 2- to 3-point advantage in achievement and a 3 to 4 percentage-point reduction in grade retention. Coefficients varied by less than 10% in either direction. These findings are consistent with those using psychometric latent variable models and econometric simultaneous equation modeling (Reynolds & Temple, 1995, 1998) and suggest that unmeasured variables do not influence the findings. Such testing of consistency of program effects under different model specifications and analytic techniques is rare in intervention research and shows the value of confirmatory approaches to evaluation.

The consistent evidence of beneficial program effects in this study under many different models and analytic methods adds to the growing body of knowledge that quasi-experimental designs can lead to conclusions that are consistent with those of randomized experiments or that approximate those of randomized experiments (Lipsey & Wilson, 1993; Shadish & Ragsdale, 1996). The keys seem to be that 1) the groups are reasonably well matched, 2) they come from similar populations, 3) the program selection process is well known, and 4) findings are robust to alternative model specifications. Yet, as Popper (1956) noted, research findings—regardless of the design on which they are based—can only corroborate hypotheses, not prove them to be true.

There are two kinds of selection bias to be concerned about in intervention studies. The first is selection bias due to nonrandom assignment to program and comparison groups. Uncontrolled selection may include self-selection, family selection, or administrative selection (e.g., enrolling the most advantaged or the most disadvantaged). The second is selection due to attrition from the study sample, usually during or after implementation of the program. Attrition may occur in all intervention studies, experiments, quasi-experiments, and nonexperiments. Attrition rates of up to 50% have occurred for model and large-scale programs. As demonstrated by Reynolds and Temple (1995, 1998), the influence of both kinds of selection bias can be investigated as part of standard data analysis within existing statistical software.[1]

OTHER UNANSWERED QUESTIONS AND ISSUES

Certainly, there are other questions about early childhood interventions that should also be addressed. One is the efficacy of new and emerging state and local programs. This is the fastest growing area of the early intervention field. Another is designing studies that include samples of sufficient size and variation on key sample attributes, program characteristics (e.g., from curriculum approaches to parent involvement), and neighborhood conditions.

Among the emerging questions are: What is the optimal number of years of preschool for most children? Is 1 year of preschool at age 4 as effective as 2 years beginning at age 3? Is full-day preschool better for children than half-day preschool for federal and state programs? Likewise, what about among half-day, extended-day, and full-day kindergarten programs? What are the crucial environmental supports that have to be in place to maintain or enhance performance advantages? How does child care quality and participation affect children's readiness for Head Start? Is the effect of participation in Head Start greater for children who enrolled in Early Head Start? Are Early Head Start parents more likely to participate in Head Start or other programs? Does improved coordination between early childhood centers and public schools increase effectiveness for children?

Investments in research and evaluation that approximate those devoted to energy, transportation, and biomedicine would help advance knowledge in the field significantly. The National Science and Technology Council (1997) indicated that only 2.8% of the total federal research and development expenditure goes to research on children. "Yet, this amount was aimed at understanding the growth and development of 30% of the nation's population—more than 80 million children and adolescents younger than age 21" (p. 2). Matched with the growing interest in child development and social policy, greater resources for research and evaluation on ECI and other social program may have substantial long-term payoffs.

---

[1]The programs LIMDEP (Greene, 1995) and LISREL (Joreskog & Sorbom, 1996) are prominent. These approaches simultaneously estimate two equations: 1) a sample selection equation predicting program participation or sample recovery (1 = participation or sample retention, 0 = otherwise) and 2) an outcome equation predicting program outcome. The correlation between the error terms of these equations (Rho) is an indicator of selection bias and is taken into account in the estimation of intervention effects (see Reynolds & Temple, 1995; Temple, Reynolds, & Miedel, 2000). This is estimated simultaneously through maximum likelihood rather than in two steps as was common when the approach was developed (Greene, 1995).

CONCLUSION

More than 35 years ago, the planning committee for Project Head Start issued a report that served as the foundation for our country's first federal preschool program. This February 1965 report explained that

> It is clear that successful programs of this type must be comprehensive, involving activities generally associated with the fields of health, social services and education. Similarly, it is clear that the program must focus on the problems of child and parent and that these activities need to be carefully integrated with programs for the school years. (quoted in Richmond, 1997, p. 122)

This forward-looking statement is still the vision for early childhood interventions. As discussed in this chapter, we know more about the effects of programs having these elements, about their magnitude and persistence, but also the difficulties of implementing them well. The issues in this chapter provide some directions for future research and program development and program improvement.

REFERENCES

Anderson, S., Auquier, A., Hauck, W.W., Oakes, D., Vandaele, W., & Weisberg, H.I. (1980). *Statistical methods for comparative studies: Techniques for bias reduction.* New York: Wiley.

Barnett, W.S. (1995). Long-term effects of early childhood programs on cognitive and school outcomes. *The Future of Children, 5*(3), 25–50.

Barnett, W.S., & Boocock, S.S. (Eds.). (1998). *Early care and education for children in poverty.* Albany: State University of New York Press.

Barnett, W.S., Young, J.W., & Schweinhart, L.J. (1998). How preschool education influences long-term cognitive development and school success: A causal model. In W.S. Barnett & S.S. Boocock (Eds.), *Early care and education for children in poverty* (pp. 167–184). Albany: State University of New York Press.

Berrueta-Clement, J.R., Schweinhart, L.J., Barnett, W.S., Epstein, A.S., & Weikart, D.P. (1984). *Changed lives: The effects of the Perry Preschool Program on youths through age 19.* Ypsilanti, MI: High/Scope.

Bickman, L. (1987). The functions of program theory. In L. Bickman (Ed.), *Using program theory in evaluation: No. 33* (pp. 5–18). San Francisco: Jossey-Bass.

Bronfenbrenner, U. (1975). Is early intervention effective? In M. Guttentag & E. Struening (Eds.), *Handbook of evaluation research* (Vol. 2, pp. 519–603). Thousand Oaks, CA: Sage.

Bronfenbrenner, U., & Morris, P. (1998). Ecological processes of development. In W. Damon (Ed.), *Handbook of child psychology: Theoretical issues* (Vol. 1, pp. 993–1028). New York: Wiley.

Campbell, D.T., & Stanley, J.C. (1966). *Experimental and quasi-experimental designs for research.* Boston: Houghton Mifflin.

Campbell, F.A., & Ramey, C.T. (1994). Effects of early intervention on intellectual and academic achievement: A follow-up study of children from low-income families. *Child Development, 65,* 684–698.

Campbell, F.A., & Ramey, C.T. (1995). Cognitive and school outcomes for high risk African-American students at middle adolescence: Positive effects of early intervention. *American Educational Research Journal, 32,* 743–772.

Chen, H., & Rossi, P.H. (1983). Evaluating with sense: The theory-driven approach. *Evaluation Review, 7,* 283–302.

Chen, H.T. (1990). *Theory-driven evaluations.* Thousand Oaks, CA: Sage.

Chicago Board of Education. (1988). *Chicago EARLY: Instructional activities for ages 3 to 6.* Vernon Hills, IL: ETA.

Coie, J.D., Watt, N.D., West, S.G., Hawkins, J.D., Asarnow, J.R., Markman, H.J., et al. (1993). The science of prevention: A conceptual framework and some directions for a national research program. *American Psychologist, 48,* 1013–1022.

Consortium for Longitudinal Studies. (1983). *As the twig is bent: Lasting effects of preschool programs.* Mahwah, NJ: Lawrence Erlbaum Associates.

Cook, T.D., & Campbell, D.T. (1979). *Quasi-experimentation: Design and analysis issues for field settings.* Chicago: Rand McNally.

Cronbach, L.J. (1982). *Designing evaluations for educational and social programs.* San Francisco: Jossey-Bass.

Currie, J., & Thomas, D. (1995). Does Head Start make a difference? *American Economic Review, 85,* 341–364.

Currie, J., & Thomas, D. (1998). School quality and the longer-term effects of Head Start. *NBER Working Paper* (No. 6362). Cambridge, MA: National Bureau of Economic Research.

Durlak, J.A., & Wells, A.M. (1997). Primary prevention mental health programs for children and adolescents: A meta-analytic review. *American Journal of Community Psychology, 25,* 115–152.

Entwisle, D.R. (1995). The role of schools in sustaining early childhood program benefits. *Future of Children, 5*(3), 133–144.

Entwisle, D.R., & Alexander, K.L. (1993). Entry into schools: The beginning school transition and educational stratification in the United States. *Annual Review of Sociology, 19,* 401–423.

Future of Children. (1995). Long-term outcomes of early childhood programs [Special issue], *5*(3). Whole issue.

Greene, W. (1995). *LIMDEP: User's manual* (Version 7). New York: Econometric Software.

Guralnick, M. (Ed.). (1997). *The effectiveness of early intervention.* Baltimore: Paul H. Brookes Publishing Co.

Joreskog, K., & Sorbom, D. (1996). *LISREL 8: User's reference guide.* Chicago: Scientific Software.

Karoly, L.A., Greenwood, P.W., Everingham, S.S., Hoube, J., Kilburn, M.R., Rydell, C.P., et al. (1998). *Investing in our children: What we know and don't know about the costs and benefits of early childhood interventions.* Santa Monica, CA: RAND.

Lally, J.R., Mangione, P.L., Honig, A.S., & Wittner, D.S. (1988). More pride, less delinquency: Findings from the ten-year follow-up study of the Syracuse University Family Development Research Program. *Zero to Three,* April, 13–18.

Lamb, M.E. (1998). Nonparental child care: Context, quality, correlates, and consequences. In W. Damon (Ed.), *Handbook of child psychology: Child psychology in practice* (Vol. 4, pp. 73–133). New York: Wiley.

Lazar, I., Darlington, R.B., Murray, H.W., & Snipper, A.S. (1982). Lasting effects of early education: A report from the consortium for longitudinal studies. *Monographs of the Society for Research in Child Development, 47*(2/3, Serial No. 195).

Lee, V.E., & Loeb, S. (1995). Where do Head Start attendees end up? One reason why preschool effects fade out. *Educational Evaluation and Policy Analysis, 17,* 62–82.

Lipsey, M.W. (1993). Theory as method: Small theories as treatments. In L. Sechrest & A. Scott (Eds.), *Understanding causes and generalizing about them: New directions for program evaluation* (No. 57, pp. 5–38). San Francisco: Jossey-Bass.

Lipsey, M.W., & Wilson, D.B. (1993). The efficacy of psychological, educational, and behavioral treatment: Confirmation from meta-analysis. *American Psychologist, 48,* 1181–1209.

Naisbitt, N. (1968). *Child-Parent Education Centers, ESEA Title I, Activity I.* Unpublished report, Chicago, IL.

National Science and Technology Council. (1997, April). *Investing in our future: A national research initiative for America's children for the 21st century.* Washington, DC: Executive Office of the President, Office of Science and Technology Policy, Committee on Fundamental Science, and the Committee on Health, Safety, and Food.

Phillips, D.A., & Cabrera, N.J. (Eds.). (1996). *Beyond the blueprint: Directions for research on Head Start's families.* Washington, DC: National Academy Press.

Popper, K. (1956). *The nature of scientific discovery.* New York: Basic Books.

Powell, D.R. (1999). Early childhood development. In A.J. Reynolds, H.J. Walberg, & R.P. Weissberg (Eds.), *Promoting positive outcomes: Issues in children's and families' lives.* Washington, DC: Child Welfare League of America.

Ramey, C.T., Bryant, D.M., Wasik, B.H., Sparling, J.J., Fendt, K.H., & LaVange, L.M. (1992). Infant Health and Development Program for low birth weight, premature infants: Program elements, family participation, and child intelligence. *Pediatrics, 3,* 454–465.

Ramey, C.T., & Ramey, S.L. (1998). Early intervention and early experience. *American Psychologist, 53,* 109–120.

Ramey, S.L., & Ramey, C.T. (1992). Early educational intervention with disadvantaged children: To what effect? *Applied & Preventive Psychology, 1,* 131–140.

Reynolds, A.J. (1991). Early schooling of children at risk. *American Educational Research Journal, 28,* 392–422.

Reynolds, A.J. (1994). Effects of a preschool plus follow-on intervention for children at risk. *Developmental Psychology, 30,* 787–804.

Reynolds, A.J. (1995). One year of preschool or two: Does it matter? *Early Childhood Research Quarterly, 10,* 1–31.

Reynolds, A.J. (1998). Confirmatory program evaluation: A method for strengthening causal inference. *American Journal of Evaluation, 17,* 21–35.

Reynolds, A.J. (1999, April). *Pathways of long-term effects in the Title I Child-Parent Center Program.* Paper presented at the biennial meeting of the Society for Research in Child Development, Albuquerque, New Mexico.

Reynolds, A.J. (2000). *Success in early intervention: The Chicago Child-Parent Center Program and youth through age 15.* Lincoln: University of Nebraska Press.

Reynolds, A.J., Bezruczko, N., & Hagemann, M. (1997). *Chicago Longitudinal Study of Children in the Chicago Public Schools: User's guide* (Version 5). Madison and Chicago: University of Wisconsin-Madison and Chicago Public Schools.

Reynolds, A.J., Chang, H., & Temple, J.A. (1998). Early childhood intervention and juvenile delinquency: An exploratory analysis of the Child-Parent Centers. *Evaluation Review, 22,* 341–372.

Reynolds, A.J., Mann, E., Miedel, W., & Smokowski, P. (1997). The state of early childhood intervention: Effectiveness, myths and realities, new directions. *Focus, 19*(1), 3–11. Institute for Research on Poverty, University of Wisconsin-Madison.

Reynolds, A.J., Mavrogenes, N.A., Bezruczko, N., & Hagemann, M. (1996). Cognitive and family-support mediators of preschool effectiveness: A confirmatory analysis. *Child Development, 67,* 1119–1140.

Reynolds, A.J., & Temple, J.A. (1995). Quasi-experimental estimates of the effects of a preschool intervention: Psychometric and econometric comparisons. *Evaluation Review, 19,* 347–373.

Reynolds, A.J., & Temple, J.A. (1998). Extended early childhood intervention and school achievement: Age 13 findings from the Chicago Longitudinal Study. *Child Development, 69,* 231–246.

Richmond, J.B. (1997). Head Start, A retrospective view: The founders; Section 3: The early administrators. In E. Zigler & J. Valentine (Eds.), *Project Head Start: A legacy of the war on poverty* (2nd ed., pp. 120–128). Alexandria, VA: National Head Start Association.

Rosenbaum, P. (1995). *Observational studies.* New York: Springer-Verlag.

Rosenbaum, P., & Rubin (1984). From association to causation in observational studies: The role of tests of strongly ignorable treatment assignment. *Journal of the American Statistical Association, 79,* 41–48.

Schweinhart, L.J., Barnes, H.V., & Weikart, D.P. (1993). *Significant benefits: The High/Scope Perry Preschool study through age 27.* Ypsilanti, MI: High/Scope Educational Research Foundation.

Schweinhart, L.J., & Weikart, D.P. (1980). *Young children grow up: The effects of the Perry Preschool Program on youths through age 15.* Ypsilanti, MI: High/Scope Educational Research Foundation.

Seitz, V. (1990). Intervention programs for impoverished children: A comparison of educational and family support models. *Annals of Child Development, 7,* 73–103.

Shadish, W.R., & Ragsdale, K. (1996). Random versus nonrandom assignment in controlled experiments: Do you get the same answer? *Journal of Consulting and Clinical Psychology, 64,* 1290–1305.

Susser, M. (1973). *Causal thinking in the health sciences, concepts and strategies of epidemiology.* New York: Oxford University Press.

Temple, J.A., & Reynolds, A.J. (1999). School mobility and achievement: Longitudinal findings from an urban cohort. *Journal of School Psychology, 37,* 355–378.

Temple, J.A., Reynolds, A.J., & Miedel, W.T. (2000). Can early childhood intervention prevent high school dropout? Evidence from the Chicago Longitudinal Study. *Urban Education, 35,* 31–56.

U.S. Department of Health, Education, and Welfare. (1964). *Smoking and health: Report of the advisory committee to the surgeon-general of the Public Health Service* (Public Health Service Publication No. 1103). Washington, DC: Author.

U.S. General Accounting Office (USGAO). (1997). *Head Start: Research provides little information on impact of current program* (Report GAO/HEHS-97-59). Washington, DC: Author.

Weissberg, R.P., & Greenberg, M.T. (1998). School and community competence-enhancement and prevention programs. In W. Damon (Ed.), *Handbook of child psychology: Child psychology in practice* (Vol. 4, pp. 877–954). New York: Wiley.

White House. (2003, February). *Head Start policy book.* Washington, DC: Office of the President. Retrieved July 11, 2003 from http://www.whitehouse.gov/infocus/earlychildhood/hspolicybook/hs_policy_book.pdf

Wilson, W.J. (1996). *When work disappears: The world of the new urban poor.* New York: Knopf.

Yoshikawa, H. (1995). Long-term effects of early childhood programs on social outcomes and delinquency. *The Future of Children, 5*(3), 51–75.

Zigler, E. (1994). Reshaping early childhood intervention to be a more effective weapon against poverty. *American Journal of Community Psychology, 22,* 37–48.

Zigler, E., Abelson, W., Trickett, P.K., & Seitz, V. (1982). Is an intervention program necessary in order to improve economically disadvantaged children's IQ scores. *Child Development, 53,* 340–348.

Zigler, E., & Butterfield, E.C. (1968). Motivational aspects of change in IQ test performance of culturally deprived nursery school children. *Child Development, 39,* 1–14.

Zigler, E., & Styfco S. (1993). *Head Start and beyond: A national plan for extended childhood intervention.* New Haven, CT: Yale University Press.

Zigler, E., Taussig, C., & Black, K. (1992). Early childhood intervention: A promising preventive for juvenile delinquency. *American Psychologist, 47,* 997–1006.

CHAPTER 28

The Transition to School

Building on Preschool Foundations and Preparing for Lifelong Learning

Sharon Landesman Ramey,
Craig T. Ramey, and Robin Gaines Lanzi

U ndeniably, entering the world of school is a major, highly valued, and memorable life transition. Just as certainly, the transition to school is a time of remarkable opportunity, setting the stage for many years of formal education in a societal institution that itself is constantly changing. Until the early 1990s, views about transitioning to school were primarily child-focused; that is, the child's intelligence and/or school-related skills were seen as the primary determinants of how well he or she adjusted to school. At the beginning of the 21st century, there is a new perspective that a child's successful transition to school represents multiple factors, including what parents and educators expect, the quality of both the preschool learning opportunities and the classroom teaching practices, the extent to which parents fulfill their role as children's first and foremost teachers, and peer and community support for the well-being and academic progress of young children in the elementary school years (Caldwell, 1991; Crnic, 1994; Erwin, 1996; Kagan, 1991a, 1991b, 1994; S.L. Ramey & Ramey, 1992, 1994). And yes, children's own skills and propensities still are part of the equation because children themselves can bring forth more (or less) positive opportunities by their own actions and reactions and are more (or less) able to take advantage of what their teachers and peers have to offer in the school setting.

The increasing concern that many children do not come to school adequately prepared was expressed clearly in the first of our country's education goals for the year 2000: namely, that "All children will arrive at school ready to learn" (National Education Goals Panel, 1991). A concurrent concern is that many teachers and administrators are not prepared to meet the increasingly diverse needs of the children and families they serve (Adelman, 1996; Bowman, 1994; Graue, 1993; Holtzman, 1992; Kagan, 1991a, 1991b; Montgomery & Rossi, 1994; Pianta & Walsh, 1996; Powell, 1995; S.L. Ramey, Ramey, & Phillips, 1997). This especially affects children who enter school with below-average skills, special educational or health care needs, and linguistic and cultural differences, as well as those from multirisk or deeply troubled families.

In this chapter, we present new findings about the transition of thousands of former Head Start children into public schools, based on the largest national study ever conducted on the transition to school (S.L. Ramey et al., 2001). Head Start represents a valuable platform from which to study the passage to school for several reasons. The program's mission is to prepare low-income children for school; it has experimented with transition activities since shortly after it began; and its focus on children, families, and communities coincides with current thinking on the process of transition.

The national study, initiated by the United States Congress via legislation passed in 1990, built on years of demonstration programs conducted by Head Start and elementary schools and on university-based research about what contributes to more or less successful early school experiences among low-income, at-risk children. This study, formally titled the National Head Start-Public School Early Childhood Transition Demonstration Project, was designed specifically to test the hypothesis that providing comprehensive, Head Start–like activities from kindergarten through third grade could help former Head Start children "maintain the gains" they may have realized in preschool (S.L. Ramey & Ramey, 1992; S.L. Ramey et al., 2001). The study provided a unique opportunity to compare the transition to school experiences of children and families in very diverse communities with different levels of support for children, parents, teachers, principals, and other community-based service providers.

The findings are directly germane to future policy and to educational practices because they provide compelling evidence that schools and families working together can dramatically boost the performance of Head Start children from kindergarten through third grade. At the same time, this study reaffirms two well-established tenets: first, that children's school entry skills in terms of language, reading readiness, and basic awareness of numbers and math concepts do matter for future academic attainment; and second, that low-income children from families with relatively greater resources and strengths and fewer risk factors are the most likely to be among the very competent.

DEFINING THE TRANSITION TO SCHOOL

A generation or two ago, kindergarten was viewed as a year of preparation for school—with first grade identified as the beginning of formal education. Presently, kindergarten plays a greater role in a child's academic education and is close to universal—more than 98% of American children have at least 1 year of kindergarten before entering first grade (Zill, Collins, West, & Hausken, 1995). As a result, families, educators, and communities more actively prepare children for the kindergarten year—now considered part of "real school" (Crnic, 1994; Kagan, 1991a, 1991b; S.L. Ramey & Ramey, 1998).

Beyond kindergarten, however, each year in school represents a somewhat new set of expectations with corresponding adjustments and procedures (Alexander & Entwisle, 1988; Caldwell, 1991; Kagan, 1991a, 1991b; Montgomery & Rossi, 1994). Why then, demarcate the transition to school years as distinct from the annual transitions through-out all of the elementary school years? The research evidence is clear: There are important distinctions in both the magnitude and the type of adjustments that occur in the first major transition into school, relative to subsequent yearly transitions (S.L. Ramey & Ramey, 1999). The identification of an initial transition-to-school period in no way di-minishes the fact that subsequent education and experiences also matter. Instead, recog-nizing that the developmental needs of young children differ from older ones and that early emotional and social adjustment reflects on later academic success (S.L. Ramey & Ramey, 2000) help to inform educators and parents about the value of addressing needs of the child as a whole. This is highly consistent with the philosophy and policies that have guided the Head Start program from its inception (Zigler & Styfco, 1993).

Three prominent features distinguish the transition to school from the general ad-justment to school thereafter. *First, school itself represents a new culture that is not the same as that of the family.* School thus represents a major new force in a child's life—with distinct and consequential expectations that will be part of the child's everyday world for many years (Bronfenbrenner, 1979; Bronfenbrenner, Moen, & Garbarino, 1984; Haines, Fowler, Schwartz, & Rosenhoetter, 1989; Ladd, 1989; Love, Logue, Trudeau, & Thayer, 1992; Stipek, 1993). Although there will be variations over the school years, children will learn the essential features of the school culture during the transition phase. *Second, there is a very high need for participants to become acquainted, exchange information, and hopefully reach consen-sus about how to promote children's learning and school adjustment.* In many ways, all transitions throughout life are characterized by greater-than-average uncertainty, an increased need for information, the acquisition of new skills, and the ever-present possibility of failure in the new situation (Landesman, Jaccard, & Gunderson, 1991; C.T. Ramey & Ramey, 1998). Even young children know that the transition to school—the first universal transi-tion in our society—has high importance and visibility attached to its success (or failure).

Third, transitions are assumed to be especially important because early experiences can set the stage for and significantly influence subsequent events. That is, what occurs during the school transition is likely to affect what occurs in the next few elementary school years and set into motion multiple forces that may enhance (or hinder) a child's ultimate school attain-ment and success in life. This assumption is supported, in part, by longitudinal studies (Alexander & Entwisle, 1988; Pianta & McCoy, 1997), with extensive endorsement for its importance deriving from anecdotal and personal observations by educators and individ-uals (Comer, 1988; Entwisle & Hayduk, 1978; Entwisle & Stevenson, 1987; Huston, 1991; S.L. Ramey & Ramey, 1998; Zigler & Styfco, 1993). Well-controlled, experimental studies of learning also show the primacy of early successes and failures (Guralnick, 1997; C.T. Ramey & Ramey, 1998). Undeniably, extremely negative early experiences may con-tribute to a pattern of altered expectations, attitudes, behavior, and critical decisions for a given child that may be difficult or impossible to overcome in later years.

Why Is There So Much Interest in the Transition to School?

The vigorous interest in the topic of transition can be attributed to several social and ac-ademic changes. Demographically, the diversity of children and families served by schools is greater than at any time in history. This presents many practical challenges and demands increased resources and teacher skills, compared with times when schools served young children who mostly spoke the same language, came from intact families, had mothers at home when school was out, and whose parents had grown up in the same community. Diversity among the student body has also increased since schools were mandated to serve all children with disabilities through federal legislation. Prior to 1975, children with major health, behavioral, and intellectual differences were often excluded from school. Today, the majority are in inclusive educational settings.

Many other legislative and judicial mandates have contributed to diversity in classrooms. Issues of equity in education, for example, have led to busing, school redistricting, and lawsuits about distribution of resources. Together, such social factors have heightened awareness of the early transition to school—simply because the children who come to school are expected to graduate and will be tested for their academic competence (the results of which will be used to judge the quality of the schools). Interestingly, the largest literature on transition concerns those at risk and in special education (Olson & Hoza, 1993; Reynolds, 1994, 2000).

On the academic front, shifting paradigms in early childhood education and developmental psychology have redefined the process of transition. Historically, most theories about success in school have been child-centered and strongly endorsed the dual assumptions that 1) development progresses in an orderly, stage-like manner, dependent largely on a child's individual maturation; and 2) a child's school readiness is determined mostly by his or her own intellectual and social skills. Within these traditional views of child development, research on elementary school–age children concentrated on identifying variables associated with individual differences in performance on standardized tests of achievement and the degree to which children's early academic and social competence predicts their subsequent school performance. Increasingly, scientific inquiry has considered the effects of so-called "nonacademic" variables on children's school progress, including academic self-esteem, academic expectations, and peer relationships (Eccles, 1993; Entwisle & Hayduk, 1978; Entwisle & Stevenson, 1987; Stipek, 1993; Stipek & Gralinski, 1996; Stipek & MacIver, 1989; Weiner, 1992; Wessels, 1996). These studies affirm that multiple forces contribute to enhancing (or hindering) academic achievement. Probably the most influential shift in conceptualizing child development derives from social ecology (Bronfenbrenner, 1979; Landesman, Jaccard, & Gunderson, 1991; Magnusson, 1988; Sameroff, 1983). Social ecology places the child within a social context that can be evaluated at multiple levels, ranging from the child's everyday transactions to more distal ones that affect other systems or ecologies. Social ecology is particularly valuable in identifying likely elements in a complex process such as the transition to school, including influences at many levels, such as teacher–child interactions, dynamics among school personnel and between school personnel and other constituencies, how educators interact with families, and the overall community and political context in which schools exist. The perspectives from elementary and early childhood education, sociology, psychology, economics, anthropology, pediatrics, and child psychiatry, to name a few, all have information relevant to creating and sustaining more successful transitions for a greater number of children.

A final cause of the new interest in transition is an expansion in the techniques available to study the process and new ways of estimating children's gains and adaptation (Love, Logue, Trudeau, & Thayer, 1992; S.L. Ramey, Ramey, & Phillips, 1997; Reid &

Landesman, 1988a, 1988b; Reid, Ramey, & Burchinal, 1990; Stipek & MacIver, 1989). These include tools for measuring children's opinions about schools, their perceptions of their competencies in academic and other situations, qualitative ways of reviewing their school achievements, strategies for measuring the school climate, new observational techniques for documenting classroom practices, and new rating tools for measuring developmentally appropriate practices. These methodological advances, however, often require a major investment of time and training to collect reliable and valid information. Quick, easy, inexpensive ways of measuring all of the hypothesized important aspects of the transition to school are not available, and probably never will be, given the complexity and variability of what happens in schools.

A Modern Definition of Transition

As of 2004, there is emerging agreement that the transition to school involves multiple transactions among key participants in understanding the relevant cultures of the child's family, the new school, and the community at large. These extend far beyond the classroom and the child's primary teacher for a given year. The transactions include communication about values, policies and procedures, opportunities, and the expectations for *who* should do *what* and *when* to maximize a child's successful school outcome.

The evolving conceptualization of the transition to school thus underscores the importance of collaboration, communication, and a shared vision for what education can and should be—from the very first day of school and beyond (Crnic, 1994; Erwin, 1996; Kagan, 1991b; S.L. Ramey & Ramey, 1998; S.L. Ramey, Ramey, & Phillips, 1997). We define *transition to school* as follows:

> A process that starts when families, educators, and communities engage in activities to prepare for the school entry of a child or children. The transition process ends when the child, family, teachers, and other key individuals perceive that equilibrium has been achieved or when they have a mutual agreement regarding expectations, roles, and actions to ensure that a given child will make good progress in (i.e., benefit from) the school setting.

Using this definition, the start of the transition to school cannot be delineated simply by chronological age or enrollment in kindergarten or first grade in school. Similarly, the end of the transition process cannot be equated with completion of a particular grade in school. This definition of transition thus emphasizes two points: 1) there is variation and individuality in the transition to school experience, and 2) the processes of mutual adjustment and accommodation are crucial to the outcome of this major life transition. At a practical level, however, we recognize the usefulness of identifying a general time frame that captures the transition process for the majority of children, families, and schools. Accordingly, we consider the period from 3 through 8 years as capturing the transition to school process for most children (S.L. Ramey & Ramey, 1999).

AN OVERVIEW OF THE NATIONAL HEAD START-PUBLIC SCHOOL EARLY CHILDHOOD TRANSITION DEMONSTRATION PROJECT

This national study, which began in 1991 and ended in 1998, involved 31 sites in 30 states and one American Indian nation, with 31 teams of local investigators collaborating with the National Study Team at the Civitan International Research Center at the University of Alabama at Birmingham. We gathered longitudinal information from kinder-garten through third grade on two cohorts of former Head Start children and families in more than 450 schools in more than 85 school districts. (See S.L. Ramey, Ramey, & Phillips, 1997, for a detailed overview of this project.) The general study design involved random assignment of schools to one of two treatment conditions: 1) the Transition Demonstration condition in which additional resources (averaging $500,000 to $1,000,000 per site per year for each of 8 consecutive years, with additional funding for the national evaluation) were provided to facilitate providing comprehensive, Head Start–like supports to children, families, schools, and communities; or 2) the comparison condition, in which transition activities (if any) were those typically provided by the schools and communities. Note that schools in the comparison condition were not prevented from offering similar types of transition supports. In the final analysis, the data set yields a rich empirical basis for analyzing what combinations of supports are most strongly associated with more (or less) successful transition to school experiences and outcomes, rather than a straightforward answer to the question "How well did this particular Transition Demonstration Project work?"

The Transition Demonstration Project provided a common framework and set of objectives (see next section) for all 31 programs but did *not* prescribe exactly how the programs would operate. This resulted in 31 distinct Transition Demonstration programs, which varied tremendously in terms of their approach, quality, intensity, and consistency over the 8 years of planning, implementation, and evaluation. Further, these 31 programs occurred in a wide range of community and school contexts, from inner-city neighborhoods to relatively affluent suburban school districts to isolated rural settings. Some schools served children from highly similar family and linguistic backgrounds, while others served children from literally dozens of different types of families in the same classroom setting. The teachers and principals also differed in terms of their prior experience in providing additional supports to low-income families, such as health and social services and parent involvement activities, and their endorsement of what is referred to as developmentally appropriate practices (DAP) as promoted by the National Association for the Education of Young Children (Bredekamp, 1998; Bredekamp & Copple, 1997). Despite the fact that this site-by-site variation complicates statistical analyses and limits certain types of conclusions, the project as a whole affords an extraordinary opportunity to document, in considerable detail, the natural history of school adjustment for more than 8,000 former Head Start children and their families.

Program Components

This program was ambitious from the start. Each local Transition Demonstration Program was required to include the following:

- A social services component to help strengthen families and to link families to school (including hiring Family Service Coordinators, with caseloads not to exceed 35 families)

- A parent involvement component to increase parents' participation in their children's education

- A focus on providing good health and nutrition for every child and family

- The promotion of both excellence and continuity in the curriculum, along with the use of DAP in the kindergarten through third-grade classrooms

Other required components included an emphasis on parent involvement in program governance, with each local program establishing a Governing Board comprised of at least 51% former Head Start parents; ensuring a multicultural component of the curriculum and cultural appropriateness of the intervention and the school program; annual evaluation of each participating child and the development of an individualized transition plan; and the inclusion of children with disabilities in general classrooms. All of these components represent an extension of the ideal, comprehensive Head Start program and were designed to foster a long-term partnership between the local Head Start centers and the public schools, with other community agencies and programs collaborating as well.

Key Findings

The results provide new and compelling evidence about 1) the challenges faced in implementing and sustaining community-based partnerships and evaluations and 2) the academic achievement of low-income children from kindergarten through third grade. In addition, concerns about family well-being, high rates of maternal depression, and tremendous diversity among poverty level families in terms of their strengths and risks are strongly affirmed in this national study. (See Phillips et al., 2000, for more details about the statistical strategies and analyses of these key findings.)

Collectively, the results of this study refute the long-standing impression that the benefits of Head Start fade out when children attend public schools. Exceptionally encouraging is the fact that across these diverse local sites, former Head Start children demonstrated large and early gains in the areas of reading and math achievement—*bringing them to national averages.* Further, former Head Start parents generally had favorable impressions of their children's schools and school progress and reported that they engaged in a wide variety of parent support activities at home and school. Of course, the local sites differed greatly in the quality, intensity, and consistency of program implementation, and many of the so-called comparison (control) schools often engaged in similar vigorous efforts to improve children's transition experiences. Because the national study included repeated visits to local sites by a multidisciplinary team, qualitative data (with ethnographic studies at a number of local sites), and self-evaluations from local leaders and participants at the 31 sites, many valuable lessons about what facilitates and hinders successful program implementation have been learned. The findings are detailed in the next sections.

CHALLENGES AND SUCCESSES IN PROGRAM IMPLEMENTATION

This National Transition Demonstration Project was conducted in a manner consistent with the Head Start Bureau's philosophy of maximizing local planning and local control of programs. There were no clear performance standards (similar to the early history of Head Start itself) or mechanisms in place to monitor program performance, other than a heroic and conscientious effort by the one Federal Program Officer assigned to oversee and provide support for all 31 programs and local evaluations. In fact, all 31 sites did enact some activities in all of the required program components of social services, health, parental involvement, and educational enhancements in the schools, and each established the required Local Governing Boards that included parents and strove to maximize inclusion of children with disabilities in inclusive classrooms. How well the local programs achieved at least minimal compliance with the many goals of the program, however, differed dramatically. Some sites had already been enacting community partnerships and already had many of the elements in place when they began, along with tremendous support from superintendents and principals. Other local sites struggled to even get their programs fully staffed, or staffed with stability in the first year or two, and encountered much more difficulty in gaining full cooperation from participating schools, school districts, and/or agencies. Further, the local sites were free to decide how far to stretch their federal dollars—with some sites choosing to serve only a handful of schools and others eagerly sharing the external resources with dozens of schools.

In the final analysis, relying on multiple types of data gathered over the course of the national study, we concluded that only about 20% (6) of the local sites implemented very strong programs—of the kind envisioned in the original legislation. These six sites were rated as very good to excellent in all features of their programs. Not unexpectedly, the majority of sites (17, or 55%) showed a combination of strengths and weaknesses in their programs, including annual fluctuation in what types of supports and education were provided for participating children, families, and schools. Disappointing was the fact that eight local sites were rated as weak or fair in their implementation of all aspects of the Transition Demonstration Program.

Acknowledging this large variation in the success with which this program was realized is crucial because this means that any simplistic analyses that combine all sites and seek to test the difference between "treated" and "untreated" (control) children are inherently limited. That is, although this was a study with randomized assignment related to treatment condition, it was not a randomized *controlled* study—the type conducted in the early intervention research that has shown positive long-term gains (and the type that represent the "gold standard" for biomedical research). In a randomized *controlled* study, the treatment itself is standardized and carefully controlled in terms of its content, intensity, and delivery. In contrast, in this study there was no single treatment being evaluated. Rather, 31 different multipronged local programs designed to help children and families were studied.

The variances across local sites contributed to our data analytic approach that involved a systematic series of analyses of the outcomes, starting with analyses of the local sites (treating each site as a study unto itself, sometimes even further dividing the site by the participating school districts, schools, and even classrooms). We then proceeded to meta-analyses or combined site analyses that took into account a variety of factors such as the quality and intensity of program implementation and the types of children and families served.

Most Successful Sites

We also concentrated on understanding what happened at the six most successful local sites. Three characteristics distinguished these local programs:

1. *Highly competent, dedicated, and locally respected leadership:* Without a doubt, the program leaders in these six sites were at the heart of their programs' multiple achievements. This leadership was not always limited to the local program "director" or "coordinator," nor was the leadership invariably stable over the course of this project. Rather, the programs overall had leaders whose various combinations of charisma, knowledge, control over local resources, community connections and respect, and unwavering commitment to this program were readily visible and acknowledged. This observation derives from the annual site visit team reports; our own evidence at the biannual meetings of the consortium of program directors, public school and Head Start representatives, and local evaluators; ratings of the submitted progress reports; and extended interactions with local personnel in the course of conducting the national study.

2. *Very strong and positive working relationships between the public schools and the local Head Start programs:* These working relationships affected the day-by-day and year-by-year integrity of the Transition Demonstration Program. Both project staff and local evaluators were welcomed in these school and Head Start settings, and, often, additional community resources were obtained because of the ease of communication and trust among program and school personnel. (*Note:* In this national project, some of the grantees who received the federal funds were the school districts, others were the Head Start programs, and some were school districts that currently were Head Start grantees as well.)

3. *A successful track record of creating strong partnerships to implement and evaluate large-scale programs:* Although the exact nature of these prior partnership experiences varied, in none of the most successful sites was the launching and management of this ambitious Transition Demonstration Program a brand new endeavor. The local educators, Head Start directors and teachers, social and health service agency leaders, and evaluators tended to be program savvy about partnerships and how they needed to be nurtured in an ongoing, highly professional and collegial manner. These successful partnerships are promoted, in part, by an awareness of the political and pragmatic realities that each of the partners faced. These include the facts that public schools already have their own highly complex and legal systems in place for their administration and accountability (and almost everywhere, these are in flux themselves); that Head Start and other community programs also have their own reporting structures and operating guidelines; and that the many other partners, including university-based researchers, involved in a successful Transition Demonstration Program also have their own priorities and accountability needs.

Rarely was the Transition Demonstration Program a brand new idea or goal for these communities. More typically, in these successful sites, this program was another promising opportunity for expanding, funding, and evaluating the types of collaborative efforts that they already endorsed. This is not to say that there were not, in fact, many new innovations and activities associated with these local site programs. Instead, the prior experience with partnerships and complex projects facilitated more timely and high-quality enactment of the joint plans of the partners. Similarly, these sites valued careful evaluation and research and often clearly benefited en route from the active participation of the local evaluation team in the overall partnership.

An interesting and unexpected finding about these most successful sites is that they were quite likely to have vigorous competition from the control schools in their study. That is, the comparison schools often launched programs that were remarkably similar in their goals, scope, and content to those of the Transition Demonstration Program. In fact, sometimes the comparison schools raised additional funds, both public and private, to enact these efforts. Where the local Transition Demonstration Program occurred in only one or two school districts, there sometimes was vigorous exchange of ideas and even training in all participating schools, as well as movement of teachers and other key staff over the 8 years of the project—further facilitating the treatment spread effect and eroding the differences between the treated and supposedly untreated schools.

BARRIERS TO SUCCESSFUL PROGRAM IMPLEMENTATION

Concerning the least successful sites, there were multiple obstacles that seemed to limit the strength of their programs. In six of these sites, there were strong and multiple local conflicts, including both personality and agency clashes. In general, the local leadership for these sites also was less involved, less experienced, and/or less successful in training and supervising the program staff and in working closely and effectively with school and community agency personnel. These least successful sites tended to have extremely high rates of poverty in their local school districts, although it is noteworthy that several of the most successful sites had equally high rates of poverty. Regrettably, a few of these programs had early and serious problems identified in the planning year or even in the process of initial award of the grant—especially major conflicts among the participating partners and failure to develop even minimally adequate required plans (thus potentially jeopardizing their continuation)—and despite the Head Start Bureau's hopes and outreach efforts, these programs never surfaced as strong.

There were many hypothesized features that did not reliably distinguish which sites would be the most or least successful. These included the location or type of school districts (rural, suburban, urban, or inner city); the per pupil average expenditures by the school districts; the proportion of federal, state, and local funding to the local schools; whether the program was administered primarily by a Head Start grantee, the public school district, or jointly; the amount of annual funding for the Transition Demonstration Program (this was not the same for all programs); the size of the local demonstration program (measured by the number of participating children and families, schools, or school districts); or the quality of the original grant application (which was not always written by the individuals who assumed responsibility for the program).

One significant feature of this national effort warrants singling out because of its deviation from most federal poverty programs. From the start, this program contained a vigorous effort to ensure that former Head Start children and families were not stigmatized by their participation. Accordingly, the Transition Demonstration Program was to be provided for entire classrooms, ideally affording benefits to all the classmates and their families. In reality, this aspect of the program—like all other aspects of this intervention—varied considerably in terms of how well the ideal was realized.

Overall, the greatest difficulties in program implementation for all sites occurred in the educational arena. The program goals were to ensure that all children received a developmentally appropriate and individually tailored education. The obstacles to making this happen were many and not unlike what school districts face nationwide. These included reluctance and ambivalence from many of the teachers or principals to adopt the proposed classroom practices and the fact that many schools had already and recently implemented what they considered to be DAP or enhanced instruction in the elementary grades. In some schools, the educational leaders viewed DAP as being of uncertain merit and not yet proven to be effective; accordingly, they were not willing to make certain types of changes in classroom organization and instructional approaches. One of the strongest findings was that even within the same site, the classroom-to-classroom variation in educational practices—even in the same grade level—was very large. The importance of individual teachers' skills and commitment to meeting the needs of all the children in the classroom cannot be overstated. Similarly, principals' commitment to this project had an early and continuous effect on the strength of the educational aspect of this intervention. In retrospect, we wonder whether the administration of this program solely by the Head Start Bureau in some way limited the engagement of public schools—rather than forging at the federal and state levels the types of partnerships that the local programs were supposed to develop. In the planning year, the Head Start Bureau invited participation from the federal Department of Education, but this did not continue in any strong way thereafter.

EFFECTS ON ACADEMIC ACHIEVEMENT AND EARLY SCHOOL ADJUSTMENT

Since the 1960s, the most discouraging set of findings about early intervention programs—often mentioned in public policy circles—is that the benefits of early intervention seem to fade out. In the past 10 years, a number of studies that have followed large samples of former Head Start children or children receiving similar services (Currie & Thomas, 2000; Reynolds, 1994, 2000; Reynolds, Mavrogenes, Buzruczko, & Hagemann, 1996) have shown that fade-out occurs especially when children enter poor-quality public schools and/or do not continue to receive high-quality educational and other supports (Entwisle, 1995). Indeed, two longitudinal studies that followed children who received specially tailored, high-quality preschool educational programs—the Abecedarian Project (C.T. Ramey, Campbell, Burchinal, Skinner, Garner, & Ramey, 2000) and Perry Preschool Project (Schweinhart, Barnes, Weikart, & Barnett, 1993)—have documented long-term benefits into adulthood. These, however, were not Head Start programs; they provided services that were more intensive and educationally focused than typical Head Start programs of that era.

In the National Transition Demonstration Project, the educational outcomes for children were positive, to a greater extent than many would have predicted. Specifically, these former Head Start children showed good academic progress during each of the first 4 years in public school, with their largest gains occurring in the first 2 years. When they entered kindergarten, they scored below national averages in both reading and math. By the end of the second and third grades, however, they performed at essentially the national average in both areas. An important finding was that this pattern of achievement occurred in both the Transition Demonstration and comparison conditions. Not only did former Head Start children "maintain the gains" that they might have realized during their Head

Start experience, but they also showed acceleration in the two skill areas that are actively taught in virtually all early elementary grades. These findings from standardized assessment provide strong support for a new perspective on the school performance of former Head Start children: They buttress the conclusion that Head Start children are "ready to learn" when they enter school and can perform at nationally competitive levels.

The findings about positive transition to school experiences were not limited to achievement scores. Both the parents and the children reported highly positive perceptions of the transition to school and the children's general academic and social adjustment. Across both treatment conditions, parents and children indicated that they highly valued doing well in school—contrary to negative stereotypes. The children, in the spring of each year, overwhelmingly reported that they had positive experiences in school. The vast majority liked school, valued doing well, tried hard, reported getting along well with teachers and peers, and said they "learned a lot" from their teachers (S.L. Ramey, Lanzi, Phillips, & Ramey, 1998). Once again, the news headlines of pervasive failure of public schools to meet the needs of low-income, at-risk children were not confirmed in this large-scale national study.

A particularly encouraging finding was that the highest achieving among the former Head Start children were, in fact, highly capable and competitive. The top 3% earned reading and math achievement scores that placed them in the 98th percentile nationally. These children were more likely to have families with somewhat higher resource levels (e.g., as measured by family income and parent education), fewer stressors, and parents who endorsed more positive and nonrestrictive parenting styles than did other former Head Start families. (See Robinson, Weinberg, Redden, Ramey, & Ramey, 1998, and Robinson, Lanzi, Weinberg, Ramey, & Ramey, 2002, for a more complete report of these academically talented children.) Among children who fared the worst in public schools were those living with factors such as maternal depression, overly restrictive parenting practices, limited parent education, homelessness, and multiple moves.

Findings About Families

From early in this study, we identified distinctive subgroups or clusters of family types within the former Head Start population (C.T. Ramey, Ramey, & Gaines-Lanzi, 1998). Recognizing this and developing strategies for meeting the remarkably diverse needs and life situations of these families warrants greater attention, for both theoretical and practical programmatic reasons. Although we affirmed that generally the very lowest income families are facing the greatest number and severity of risks, even profoundly challenged families have strengths, and some families were distinguished by their lack of either strengths or risks. In this sample, however, the most prevalent problem in these former Head Start families that was likely to affect the extent to which the families were supportive of learning activities at school and home was maternal depression.

Specifically, more than 40% of the primary caregivers (mostly mothers) of these former Head Start children reported signs of clinical depression when their children entered kindergarten. Even more alarming, about 19% of the caregivers suffered from chronic depression throughout the first 4 years their children were in elementary school. Maternal depression is not independent of one's life situation, but poverty may be a barrier to proper identification and treatment of depression. School and Head Start personnel may need better guidelines for detecting the presence of this mental health problem in the families they serve.

Despite the alarmingly high rates of parental depression, these former Head Start families as a group showed steady improvements in terms of their family earnings and decreased dependence on forms of public assistance. This trend occurred in both the Transition Demonstration and comparison families, perhaps because the community collaborations often extended to both the treatment and control schools and families. In fact, at the completion of the national evaluation, a majority of the local sites showed signs of sustaining or had institutionalized at least some of the valued components of the Transition Demonstration Program.

WAS THE TRANSITION PROGRAM SUCCESSFUL?

The most obvious question, concerning this highly favorable report is whether the Transition Demonstration Program was unnecessary or a failure. We conclude that the variation in program implementation and the presence of strong local competition and enactment of transition support-like programs in the supposed control condition make such a conclusion virtually impossible to entirely support or refute. Based on the annual site visits to these programs, it is clear that they did *not* comprise a nationally representative sample of all public schools serving former Head Start children. In fact, the processes involved in applying for the federal grants and the selection of the best applicants from each applying state were factors that led to the identification of highly competent and committed school districts willing to enact such programs. Given that this was to be a randomized trial, all schools participating agreed in advance to enact the program if they were selected. In the process, many of the school administrators may have become even better informed about promising strategies to increase parent involvement, enhance early childhood instruction, and provide needed social and health services to low-income children and their families. Information about transition supports continued to be available to almost all of the schools over the course of this project, including newly funded efforts by the Head Start Bureau to disseminate what appeared to be "best practices" during the transition year, even before results of this project were available. At many sites, there appeared to be a general spirit of collaboration that extended to the control schools and to in-service training for teachers.

At the same time, we recognize that even with this high level of commitment, many of the public schools in the study were far from ideal and fell below the school districts' own definition of optimal performance. The analyses from a few sites with highly detailed program implementation data from classrooms indicate that children in the "best" classrooms within the site showed the greatest academic acceleration. However, in these sites, some of the outstanding classroom teachers were in the control condition. We have concluded that, on average, the education provided in these classrooms represented a positive learning opportunity for former Head Start children who had sufficient entry skills in both the social and preacademic areas to benefit from what their schools offered.

Two of the most fascinating questions generated by the national study are 1) Will these former Head Start children continue to perform well as they enter later grades, when the academic standards become more demanding, peer influences are likely to increase, and educators may not have either the same level of resources or commitment to helping these children succeed? and 2) To what extent are transition-like supports now in place nationally to facilitate positive early school transitions? Both the Transition Demonstration and comparison school principals and teachers reported multiple kinds of outreach and assistance efforts, at levels much higher than reported by Love and colleagues (1992) when this project was launched. We cannot help but wonder whether these now are becoming standard practice so that children and families rarely arrive at public school with no advance preparation and with little or no communication between school and Head Start staff.

The 1998 Performance Standards for Head Start now require transition planning. This planning encompasses contact between Head Start and the children's elementary schools, as well as activities to engage families in registering their children for kindergarten and becoming acquainted with key school expectations, practices, and policies. This requirement, even in the absence of strong empirical support, can be justified because of its apparent value for families with limited knowledge about the school their child will attend and who themselves may have had few if any positive, firsthand experiences with today's American elementary schools. Beyond the introduction phase, however, it appears that school instruction and transition services (whether or not in a formal program) can enable Head Start graduates to achieve at national norms.

REFERENCES

Adelman, H.S. (1996). Restructuring education support services and integrating community resources: Beyond the full service school model. *School Psychology Review, 25,* 431–445.

Alexander, K.L., & Entwistle, D.R. (1988). Achievement in the first two years of school: Patterns and processes. *Monographs of the Society for Research in Child Development, 53*(Serial No. 218).

Bowman, B.T. (1994). The challenge of diversity. *Phi Delta Kappan, 76,* 218–224.

Bredekamp, S. (1998). Defining standards for practice: The continuing debate. In C. Seefeldt & A. Galper (Eds.), *Continuing issues in early childhood education* (pp. 176–189). Columbus, OH: Merrill.

Bredekamp, S., & Copple, C. (Eds.). (1997). *Guidelines for developmentally appropriate practices: Early years are learning years.* Washington, DC: National Association for the Education of Young Children.

Bronfenbrenner, U. (1979). *The ecology of human development.* Cambridge, MA: Harvard University Press.

Bronfenbrenner, U., Moen, P., & Garbarino, J. (1984). Child, family, and community. In R.D. Parke (Ed.), *Review of child development research, Volume 7: The family* (pp. 283–328). Chicago: University of Chicago Press.

Caldwell, B. (1991). Continuity in the early years: Transitions between grades and systems. In S.L. Kagan (Ed.), *The care and education of America's young children: Obstacles and opportunities: Vol. 15. Ninetieth yearbook of the National Society for the Study of Education* (pp. 69–90). Chicago: University of Chicago Press.

Comer, J.P. (1988). *Maggie's American dream: The life and times of a black family.* New York: New American Library.

Crnic, K.A. (1994). Reconsidering school readiness: Conceptual and applied perspectives. *Early Education and Development, 5,* 91–105.

Crnic, K.A., & Lamberty, B. (Eds.). (1994). School readiness: Scientific perspectives (special issue), *Early Education and Development, 5.*

Currie, J., & Thomas, D. (2000). School quality and the longer-term effects of Head Start. *Journal of Human Resources, 35*(4), 755–774.

Eccles, J. (1993). Age and gender differences in children's self- and task- perceptions during elementary school. *Child Development, 64,* 830–847.

Entwisle, D.R. (1995). The role of schools in sustaining benefits of early childhood programs. *The Future of Children, 5,* 133–144.

Entwisle, D.R., & Hayduk, L.A. (1978). *Too great expectations.* Baltimore: Johns Hopkins University Press.

Entwisle, D.R., & Stevenson, H.W. (1987). Schools and development. *Child Development, 58,* 1149– 1150.

Erwin, E.J. (Ed.). (1996). *Putting children first: Visions for a brighter future for young children and their families.* Baltimore: Paul H. Brookes Publishing Co.

Graue, M.E. (1993). *Ready for what? Constructing meanings of readiness for kindergarten.* Albany: State University of New York Press.

Guralnick, M.J. (Ed.). (1997). *The effectiveness of early intervention.* Baltimore: Paul H. Brookes Publishing Co.

Haines, A.H., Fowler, S.A., Schwartz, I.S., & Rosenhoetter, S. (1989). A comparison of preschool and kindergarten teacher expectations for school readiness. *Early Childhood Research Quarterly, 4,* 75–88.

Holtzman, W.H. (Ed.). (1992). *School of the future.* Austin, TX: American Psychological Association and Hogg Foundation for Mental Health.

Huston, A.C. (1991). Antecedents, consequences, and possible solutions for poverty among children. In A.C. Huston (Ed.), *Children in poverty: Child development and public policy* (pp. 282–313). New York: Cambridge University Press.

Kagan, S.L. (1991a). Moving from here to there: Rethinking continuity and transitions in early care and education. In B. Spodek & O. Saracho (Eds.), *Yearbook in early childhood education* (Vol. 11, pp. 132– 151). New York: Teachers College Press.

Kagan, S.L. (Ed.). (1991b). *The care and education of America's young children: Obstacles and opportunities: Vol. 15.* Chicago: University of Chicago Press.

Kagan, S.L. (1994). Readying schools for young children: Polemics and priorities. *Phi Delta Kappan, 76,* 226–233.

Ladd, G. (1989). Children's social competence and social supports: Precursors of early school adjustment. In B.H. Schneider, G. Attili, J. Nadel, & R. Weissberg (Eds.), *Social competence in developmental perspective* (pp. 277–291). New York: Kluwer Academic Publishers.

Landesman, S., Jaccard, J., & Gunderson, V. (1991). The family environment: The combined influence of family behavior, goals, strategies, resources, and individual experiences. In M. Lewis & S. Feinman (Eds.), *Social influences and socialization in infancy* (pp. 63–96). New York: Plenum Press.

Love, J.M., Logue, M.E., Trudeau, J.V., & Thayer, K. (1992). *Final report of the National Transition Study: Transitions to kindergarten in American schools.* Portsmouth, NH: Regional Medical Center Research Corporation.

Magnusson, D. (1988). *Individual development from an interactional perspective.* Mahwah, NJ: Lawrence Erlbaum Associates.

Montgomery, A., & Rossi, R. (1994). *Educational reforms and students at risk: A review of the current state of art.* Washington, DC: U.S. Government Printing Office.

National Education Goals Panel. (1991). *The National Education Goals report: Building a nation of learners.* Washington, DC: National Association of State Boards of Education.

Olson, S.L., & Hoza, B. (1993). Preschool developmental antecedents of conduct problems in children beginning school. *Journal of Clinical Child Psychology, 22,* 60–67.

Phillips, M., Ramey S., Ramey, C., Lanzi, R.G., Katholi, C., & Brezausek, C. (2000). *Technical appendices for the National Head Start/Public School Early Childhood Demonstration Study.* Washington, DC: Administration on Children, Youth and Families.

Pianta, R.C., & McCoy, S.J. (1997). The first day of school: The predictive validity of early school screening. *Journal of Applied Developmental Psychology, 18,* 1–22.

Pianta, R.C., & Walsh, D.J. (1996). *High-risk children in schools: Constructing sustaining relationships.* New York: Routledge.

Powell, D.R. (1995). *Enabling young children to succeed in school.* Washington, DC: American Educational Research Association.

Ramey, C.T., Campbell, F.A., Burchinal, M., Skinner, M.L., Gardner, D.M., & Ramey, S.L. (2000). Persistent effects of early childhood education on high-risk children and their mothers. *Applied Developmental Science, 4,* 2–14.

Ramey, C.T., & Ramey, S.L. (1996). Early intervention: Optimizing development for children with disabilities and risk conditions. In M. Wolraich (Ed.), *Disorders of development and learning: A practical guide to assessment and management* (2nd ed., pp. 141–158). Philadelphia: Mosby.

Ramey, C.T., & Ramey, S.L. (1998). Early intervention and early experience. *American Psychologist, 53,* 109–120.

Ramey, C.T., Ramey, S.L., & Gaines-Lanzi, R. (1998). Differentiating developmental risk levels for families in poverty: Creating a family typology. In M. Lewis & C. Feiring (Eds.), *Families, risk, and competence* (pp. 187–205). Mahwah, NJ: Lawrence Erlbaum Associates.

Ramey, S.L., Lanzi, R.G., Phillips, M., & Ramey, C.T. (1998). The transition to school: The perspectives of Head Start children and their parents. *Elementary School Journal, 98,* 311–327.

Ramey, S.L., & Ramey, C.T. (1992). Early educational intervention with disadvantaged children: To what effect? *Applied and Preventive Psychology, 1,* 131–140.

Ramey, S.L., & Ramey, C.T. (1994). The transition to school: Why the first few years matter for a lifetime. *Phi Delta Kappan, 76,* 194–198.

Ramey, S.L., & Ramey, C.T. (1998). The transition to school: Opportunities and challenges for children, families, educators, and communities. *Elementary School Journal, 98,* 293–295.

Ramey, S.L., & Ramey, C.T. (1999). *The transition to school: Concepts, practices, and needed research.* Commissioned paper for the American Institutes for Research. Washington, DC: U.S. Department of Education, OERI.

Ramey, S.L., & Ramey, C.T. (2000). Early childhood experiences and developmental competence. In J. Waldfogel & S. Danziger (Eds.), *Securing the future: Investing in children from birth to college* (pp. 122–150). New York: Russell Sage Foundation.

Ramey, S.L., Ramey, C.T., & Phillips, M. (1997). *Head Start children's entry into public school* (Research report no. 1997-02). Washington, DC: U.S. Department of Health and Human Services, Administration for Children and Families.

Ramey, S.L., Ramey, C.T., Phillips, M.M., Lanzi, R.G., Brezausek, C., Katholi, C.R., et al. (2001). *Head Start Children's Entry into Public Schools: A Report on the National Head Start/Public School Early Childhood Transition Demonstration Study* (contract no. 105–95–1935). Washington, DC: Commissioner's Office of Research and Evaluation; Administration on Children, Youth and Families; U.S. Department of Health and Human Services.

Reid, M., & Landesman, S. (1988a). *What I think of school.* Seattle: University of Washington.

Reid, M., & Landesman, S. (1988b). *Your child's adjustment to school.* Seattle: University of Washington.

Reid, M., Ramey, S.L., & Burchinal, M. (1990). Dialogues with children about their families. In I. Bretherton & M. Watson (Eds.), *Children's perspectives on their families: New directions for child development* (pp. 5–28). San Francisco: Jossey-Bass.

Reynolds, A.J. (1994). Effects of a preschool plus follow-on intervention for children at risk. *Developmental Psychology, 30,* 787–804.

Reynolds, A.J. (2000). *Success in early intervention: The Chicago Child-Parent Centers.* Lincoln: University of Nebraska Press.

Reynolds, A.J., Mavrogenes, N.A., Buzruczko, N., & Hagemann, M. (1996). Cognitive and family-support mediators of preschool effectiveness: A confirmatory analysis. *Child Development, 67,* 1119–1140.

Robinson, N.M., Lanzi, R.G., Weinberg, R.A., Ramey, S.L., & Ramey, C.T. (2002). Family factors associated with high academic competence in former Head Start children at third grade. *Gifted Child Quarterly, 46,* 281–294.

Robinson, N.M., Weinberg, R.A., Redden, D., Ramey, S.L., & Ramey, C.T. (1998). Family factors associated with high academic competence among former Head Start children. *Gifted Child Quarterly, 41,* 148–156.

Sameroff, A. (1983). Developmental systems: Contexts and evolution. In P.H. Mussen (Series Ed.) & E.M. Hetherington (Vol. Ed.), *Handbook of child psychology: Vol. 1. History, theory, and method* (4th ed., pp. 237–294). New York: Wiley.

Schweinhart, L.J., Barnes, H.V., Weikart, D.P., & Barnett, S.W. (1993). *Significant benefits: The High/Scope Perry Preschool Study through age twenty-seven.* Monographs of the High/Scope Educational Research Foundation 10. Ypsilanti, MI: High/Scope Press.

Stipek, D.V. (1993). *Motivation to learn: From theory to practice.* Englewood Cliffs, NJ: Prentice-Hall.

Stipek, D.V., & Gralinski, J.H. (1996). Children's beliefs about intelligence and school performance. *Journal of Educational Psychology, 88,* 397–407.

Stipek, D., & MacIver, D. (1989). Developmental change in children's assessment of intellectual competence. *Child Development, 60,* 521–538.

Weiner, B. (1992). *Human motivation: Metaphors, theories and research.* Newbury Park, CA: Sage.

Wessels, M.R. (1996). All children must know and learn from one another. In E.J. Erwin (Ed.), *Putting children first: Visions for a brighter future for young children and their families* (pp. 257–256). Baltimore: Paul H. Brookes Publishing Co.

Zigler, E., & Styfco, S.J. (Eds.). (1993). *Head Start and beyond: A national plan for extended childhood intervention.* New Haven, CT: Yale University Press.

Zill, N., Collins, M., West, J., & Hausken, E. (1995). *Approaching kindergarten: A look at preschoolers in the United States (National Household Education Survey).* Washington, DC: U.S. Department of Education, Office of Educational Research and Improvement.

CHAPTER 29

Early Head Start, Child Care, Family Support, and Family Policy

SHEILA B. KAMERMAN AND ALFRED J. KAHN

T he Early Head Start (EHS) program, serving infants and toddlers and their families, was established in 1994 as an addition to Head Start, the primary program serving 4-year-olds. In this chapter, we argue that rather than a modest supplement, EHS should be the model for Head Start in the 21st century. We begin with a brief description of the EHS program and then discuss the need for Head Start to adapt to the social changes that have occurred since it was established and the new knowledge that has emerged. We conclude with a recommendation.

EARLY HEAD START

The Administration for Children and Families (ACF) reports in its 1998 EHS Fact Sheet, "in recognition of the powerful research evidence that the period from birth to age three is critical to healthy growth and development and to later success in school and in life," President Clinton signed the Head Start Act Amendments of 1994, establishing a new EHS program, expanding the benefits of early childhood development programs to low-income families with children younger than age 3. The purpose of EHS is to

- Enhance children's physical, social, emotional, and cognitive development

- Enable parents to be better caregivers of and teachers to their children

- Help parents meet their own goals, including that of economic independence

The program provides "early, continuous, intensive, and comprehensive child development and family support services" to low-income families with infants and toddlers. The services provided are designed to reinforce and respond to the unique strengths and needs of each child and family. Services include "quality" early education in and out of the home; home visits; parent education, including parent–child activities; comprehensive health services, including services to women before, during, and after pregnancy; nutrition; and case management and peer support groups for parents.

The Fact Sheet further notes that EHS was designed with the advice of the Advisory Committee on Services to Families with Infants and Toddlers, a committee established by the Secretary of the Department of Health and Human Services. Committee members included leading academic and program experts in early childhood development and support. The program builds on both the latest research and the experiences of earlier demonstration programs and focuses on what are described as the "four cornerstones" essential to quality programs: child development, family development, community building, and staff development.

In 1995, when the program was first launched, there were 68 successful applicants for the new initiative who served about 5,000 children and families in 34 states and the District of Columbia and Puerto Rico, at a total federal cost of $47.2 million. In 1996, 74 new applicants were selected to serve an additional 5,000 children and their families in 8 additional states, at a cost of $40 million. In fiscal year (FY) 1998, funding for EHS totaled $279 million, or more than 5% of the total Head Start budget, and served about 39,000 children and their families. In FY 1999, funding totaled nearly $340 million, almost 8% of the total Head Start budget, to support more than 600 EHS projects in 50 states and the District of Columbia. More than 40,000 children and their families participated. As part of President Clinton's Child Care Initiative, the Administration announced plans to double the number of children served over the next 5 years. By 2003, there were 708 community-based EHS programs serving 61,500 children. The total budget for EHS for 2003 was $654 million (ACF, 2003).

Clearly, "if you build it, they will come." The response has been enthusiastic and the demand is far greater than can be met. In this chapter, we argue that this is, in fact, where Head Start should be concentrating its efforts: on infants and toddlers. It is this group that has the greatest need now, and it is with regard to this group that the benefits will be greatest as well.

THE NEED FOR HEAD START TO ADAPT

It does not diminish the accomplishments of Head Start to note, more than 35 years after its first development, the need for adaptation to social change and to acknowledge that Head Start is not necessarily the model for all preschool-age children in the 21st century. Head Start was never conceived as a static, uniform, rigidly designed program but rather an "evolving concept . . . that illuminated new pathways leading toward the goals of better serving children and families" (Zigler & Styfco, 1993, p. 6). It has already played a role in developing programs for very young children (e.g., Parent and Child Centers; Parent Child Development Centers) as well as school-aged children (e.g., Follow Through, Transition Project).

Moreover, at a time when political and popular support for Head Start are strong but experts are raising questions about quality, outcomes, and impacts, it may be useful to recall Head Start's original target and to address it in ways now better understood than in 1965.

Head Start began with the concept that for children to enter primary school ready to learn, they required an earlier preschool experience that would offer: the stimulation and enrichment provided by an excellent nursery school; compensation for earlier social and cognitive deprivation; access to health care, good nutrition, and social services; and the active involvement of parents in their children's experiences. Moreover, recent research continues to underscore the importance of providing more in the way of cognitive stimulation and support for deprived and disadvantaged children of this age.

If child development experts have taught us anything since then, it is that waiting until ages 3 and 4 to provide children, especially poor children, with such an experience, is too late. The real need is for a program "designed to meet the developmental needs of poor children in order to optimize their competence in social and school settings" from birth to age 3 (Zigler & Styfco, 1993, p. 5).

Regardless of the debate about early brain development and whether the first 3 years are a "critical" period determining subsequent outcomes (see Chapter 30; Carnegie Task Force on Meeting the Needs of Young Children, 1994; Hamberg, 1992), clearly these years are important and provide an essential foundation for later development. Head Start was established on this premise, too, but at a time when the first years of life were thought of as beginning at age 3. Now we recognize that children learn from birth onward.

The case for re-focusing Head Start, however, goes beyond the new understanding. All of the Head Start experience since 1990 is pointing that way as well. And, all of the changes in the experience of very young children and their parents are pointing in the same direction.

Thus, our second argument would stress the need for a high-quality early childhood program for infants and toddlers, one that provides cognitive and social stimulation that is usually absent or less developed in family child care—the dominant form of child care for infants and toddlers. Such an experience is especially important for children coming from poor and disadvantaged backgrounds, as a foundation for subsequent learning (see Karoly et al., 1998).

Third, we note the growing interest in supporting comprehensive community initiatives (CCIs), which are defined as initiatives seeking "to strengthen all sectors of neighborhood well-being including social, educational, economic, physical, and cultural aspects, and in so doing seek to achieve a level of synergy among them" (Fulbright-Anderson, Kubisch, & Connell, 1998, p. 2). These initiatives are increasingly viewed as the "principal building blocks of adult cognitive and emotional functioning" (Berlin, Brooks-Gunn, & Aber, 2001, p. 4). EHS is among the very few early intervention programs that explicitly identify community development as a central component of effective intervention (ACF, 2003). Given the growing conviction concerning the value of CCIs, expanding coverage to all disadvantaged infants and toddlers would seem especially important. As a caveat: EHS has its own validity and is not dependent on the unknown future expansion of CCIs and the evidence as to their actual impact.

Fourth, we argue that Head Start should target children younger than 3 years because a part-day program is no longer adequate for 3- to 5-year-olds given current family lifestyles (and not even adequate for many toddlers as well, given current welfare policies); and, because if parent involvement is an essential component, sustained active involvement is possible only for the mothers of infants (and not always for these either).

By the time children reach age 3, almost two thirds of their mothers are in the labor force. Moreover, given the policy embedded in the 1996 welfare legislation, defining women with children ages 1 and older as employable and permitting states to require women with infants ages 3 months and older to engage in employment related activities, it should not surprise us to see almost two thirds of the mothers with 1- and 2-year-olds now in the labor force and close to 60% of those with infants younger than 1 year. This both underscores the need for a full-day program, going beyond what Head Start has traditionally provided, and further constrains mothers' interest in—and ability to use—a part-day program such as Head Start (U.S. Bureau of Labor Statistics, 2003).

Given that most of the children in Head Start before 1996 came from families receiving Aid to Families with Dependent Children (AFDC) and AFDC served, overwhelmingly, families with children younger than age 3 rather than those ages 3–5, if the TANF pattern is similar (which we would assume), the only mothers who *might* be available to be active program participants are likely to be those with infants, or at most those with toddlers (USHR, 1998).

Our fifth argument has to do with the changes that have occurred over time with regard to the age group served by Head Start. When Head Start was first launched in 1965, it was a summer program only, but by 1996, it had already been extended to its current major model, a half-day program for the 9- to 10-month school year. It began with a primary focus on 5-year-olds but shortly after focused primarily on 4-year-olds. Indeed, between 1980 and 1991, the percentage of 5-year-olds in the program declined by 67%—from 21% in 1980 to 7% in 1991—while the proportion of 3- and 4-year-olds grew by about 15% (from 24% to 27% and from 55% to 63%, respectively, during these same years); and children younger than 3 years emerged from 0% in 1980 to 3% in 1991. About 67% of the children served in Head Start in 1991 were 4 years old, 27% were 3 years old, 7% were 5 years old, and an insignificant 3% were younger than age 3 (USHR, 1992). In 1998 and 1999, 5-year-olds continued to decline as a portion of the Head Start participants, first to 6% and then to 5%. Four-year-olds began to reflect a declining share as well, from 63% to 58% in 1999 and 52% in 2002 (but still the dominant group). Three-year-olds constituted one third of the group (33% in 1999 and 36% in 2002); the proportion younger than age 3 has increased by still more, to 7% in 2002 (see Table 29.1).

Sixth, in effect, just as kindergarten has already taken over a significant component of Head Start's initial target population, prekindergarten is likely to take over another group. As of 2004, universally available kindergarten serves 5-year-olds, and, as public prekindergarten expands—and, according to Mitchell, Seligson, and Marx (1989), two thirds of the programs were for children viewed as at risk of problems in primary school—the 4-year-olds are almost inevitably likely to transfer to these programs, leaving Head Start to the 3-year-olds and younger children.

Indeed, we see that already. Ninety-five percent of 5-year-olds were already attending kindergarten or first grade in 1994 (Bruno & Curry, 1996), and more than half (55.6%) were attending school full day. Two thirds of 4-year-olds were enrolled in preschool in 1998, and 38% of 3-year-olds, as compared with 60% of the 4-year-olds and 34% of 3-year-olds, just 4 years earlier. More than half the 3- and 4-year-olds were enrolled in a preschool program as of 2000 (U.S. Census Bureau, 2001), as compared with 40% in 1991 and 44% in 1994.

Table 29.1. Characteristics of children enrolled in Head Start, selected fiscal years (in percentages)

Fiscal year	Disabled	Age of children enrolled				Enrollment by race				
		5 and older	4	3	Younger than 3	Native American	Hispanic	Black	White	Asian
1980	12	21	55	24	0	4	19	42	34	1
1982	12	17	55	26	2	4	20	42	33	1
1984	12	16	56	26	2	4	20	42	33	1
1986	12	15	58	25	2	4	21	40	32	3
1988	13	11	63	23	3	4	22	39	32	3
1990	14	8	64	25	3	4	22	38	33	3
1991	13	7	63	27	3	4	22	38	33	3
1992	13	7	63	27	3	4	23	37	33	3
1993	13	6	64	27	3	4	24	36	33	3
1994	13	7	62	28	3	4	24	36	33	3
1995	13	7	62	27	4	4	25	35	33	3
1996	13	6	62	29	4	4	25	36	32	3
1998	13	6	59	31	4	3	26	36	32	3
1999	13	5	58	33	4	3	27	35	31	3
2002*	13	5	52	36	7	3	30	33	28	2

Source: Head Start Bureau, U.S. Department of Health and Human Services; Green Book 2000.
Source: ACF Head Start Bureau.

Seventh, another program development that has emerged in the last two decades appears to be a potential catalyst for shifting Head Start's focus from the 3- to 4-year-olds to the children younger than 3. Here, we refer to the development of a variety of family support services targeted at children younger than age 3 and their families. These programs are designed to serve vulnerable and high-risk, very young children and their families, overwhelmingly their mothers, through a range of individualized and group services delivered in community centers, at the children's homes, or both. Despite an emphasis on targeting what could be characterized as children and families "in need," none of these programs has income criteria for eligibility, and so at least hypothetically, can serve children from different socioeconomic classes as well as a diverse racial and ethnic population. These family support programs, funded since 1993 as part of an amendment to the federal child welfare legislation, provide parent education, counseling, information and referral services, drop-in child care services, and close linkages with health care services. Most of these programs, however, are missing what we view as an essential solid child care core component. This is what Head Start could and should provide. As of 2004, the family support services are seen as belonging before Head Start, with the expectation that the families who use them will subsequently place their children in Head Start, but it often does not work out that way. Places are not available, or the families do not meet the income criterion. Moreover, the children and their parents need the early childhood program experience while participating in the family support program, not later. Even most of the health care services provided by or through Head Start, such as immunizations, should be provided before age 3 rather than later. Indeed, we have seen very effective programs that link family support and child care services in England and Italy.

Finally, as our comparative child and family policy research documents, by the time children are 3 years old, they should be in a universal preschool program, not in a program that is segregated by income or by other special needs. Belgium, France, and Italy cover almost all 3-, 4-, and 5-year-olds in free, public school related preschool programs covering the full school day, with supplementary services available at income-related fees to cover before and after school services (Kamerman, 2001). The Nordic countries guarantee children a place in a high-quality program from the age of 1 at low-cost, income-related fees and in programs covering the full work day.

As Head Start is refocused on younger children, places in decent quality preschool/prekindergarten programs need to be guaranteed to all 3- and 4-year-olds. To ensure adequate preparation for such programs, however, an earlier experience in a program that serves parents and children and provides a part-day or part-week experience, in particular for the deprived and disadvantaged very young and their mothers and caregivers, is absolutely essential. An integrated Family Support/Head Start experience would prepare poor and disadvantaged children and their parents for a preschool that would include all children; such programs exist in Italy, for example (Kamerman & Kahn, 1994, 1995). The two together would enable the more disadvantaged children as well as all other children to be ready for more formal learning when they enter primary school. Moreover, by involving mothers in a Head Start/Family Support program from their pregnancy on, the potential for enhancing parenting capacities and skills and empowering these parents would be much greater. Furthermore, special needs would more likely become visible and intervention more likely initiated early through such a program.

Head Start, which began as a separate and idiosyncratic program that provided nutrition, health care, and social services but has been having difficulties lately in ensuring access to many of these services, could now be more closely linked to the other services within an explicitly designed "comprehensive child and family service."

CONCLUSION

Child development experts stress the importance of stimulation and enhanced developmental experiences during the first 3 years of life. The growing conviction regarding the impact of community-based initiatives underscores the importance of launching these initiatives early in a child's life. Mothers emphasize their desire for such programs and their availability to participate in them during the first 3 years after birth rather than later. The expansion of prekindergarten programs is likely to draw a growing group of 4-year-olds out of Head Start. Linking Head Start with family support programs would provide the framework for an integrated and holistic child and family service and the key component for an effective early intervention program. Finally, focusing Head Start "downward" to serve infants and toddlers, along with providing a guarantee of a place in prekindergarten for all 3- to 4-year-olds, would go a long way to achieving the goals of universal preschool and school readiness in the United States, and the structure and function of Head Start clearly would fit best with the younger group.

A refocus on the earliest years would make the most sense for the future development of Head Start. This would require a phased shift from the 3- to 4-year-olds who now dominate the program to the 3-month to 2-year-olds and their mothers who now are in greatest need of the program, could benefit from it most, and would constitute the best "individual/consumer" for such a program, in particular if it included both full-workday and part-day programs.

If a phased transition from the current to the future Head Start model were needed, we would recommend beginning by guaranteeing the 4-year-olds a place in a public prekindergarten, with wrap-around services available for the 4- and 5-year-olds for a full workday and work year. Focus Head Start on the 2- and 3-year-olds while expanding prekindergarten for the 3-year-olds and planning what an appropriate Head Start program for infants and toddlers would look like.

REFERENCES

Administration for Children and Families (ACF). (1998). *Early Head Start fact sheet.* Washington, DC: Author.

Administration for Children and Families (ACF). (2003). *Early Head Start information folder.* Washington, DC: Author.

Berlin, L., Brooks-Gunn, J., & Aber, J.L. (2001). Promoting early development through comprehensive community initiatives. *Children's Services: Social Policy, Research, and Practice, 1–24.*

Bruno, R., & Curry, A. (1996). *School enrollment—social and economic characteristics of students: October 1994.* Washington, DC: U.S. Government Printing Office.

Carnegie Task Force on Meeting the Needs of Young Children. (1994). *Starting points.* New York: Carnegie Corporation.

Fulbright-Anderson, K., Kubisch, A.C., & Connell, J.P. (Eds.). (1998). *New approaches to evaluating community initiatives.* New York: Aspen Institute.

Hamberg, D. (1992). *Today's children.* New York: Random House.

Kamerman, S.B. (Ed.). (2001). *Early childhood education and care: International perspectives.* New York: Columbia University Institute for Child and Family Policy.

Kamerman, S.B., & Kahn, A.J. (1994). *A welcome for every child.* Washington, DC: ZERO TO THREE National Center for Infants, Toddlers and Families.

Kamerman, S.B., & Kahn, A.J. (1995). *Starting right: How America neglects its youngest children and what we can do about it.* New York: Oxford University Press.

Karoly, L.A., Greenwood, P.W., Everingham, S.S., Houbé, J., Kilburn, M.R., Rydell, C.P., et al. (1998). *Investing in our children: What we know and don't know about the costs and benefits of early childhood interventions* (MR-898). Santa Monica, CA: RAND.

Mitchell, A., Seligson, M., & Marx, F. (1989) *Early childhood programs and the public schools.* Dover, MA: Auburn.

U.S. Bureau of Labor Statistics. (2003, July). *Employment characteristics of families.* Available at http://www.bls.gov/news.release/fame.toc.htm

U.S. Census Bureau. (2001, June). *School enrollment data.* Available at http://www.census.gov

USHR, Committee on Ways and Means. (1992). *The green book.* Washington, DC: U.S. Government Printing Office.

USHR, Committee on Ways and Means. (1998). *The green book.* Washington, DC: U.S. Government Printing Office.

USHR, Committee on Ways and Means. (2000). *The green book.* Washington, DC: U.S. Government Printing Office.

Zigler, E., & Styfco, S.J. (Eds.). (1993). *Head Start and beyond.* New Haven, CT: Yale University Press.

CHAPTER 30

The Brain and Child Development
Time for Some Critical Thinking

JOHN T. BRUER

S ince the mid-1990s, a flood of policy reports, conference proceedings, and professional and popular articles have proclaimed that "new" discoveries in brain science will revolutionize how we think about children, parenting, and early education. We have at our disposal, enthusiasts claim, a neuroscientific basis for an action and policy agenda on behalf of young children. Advocates of a brain science/child policy link cite evidence that they claim shows that certain early childhood experiences are necessary for optimal brain development.

This claim has support in high places—the White House, the National Governors' Association, private foundations, children's advocacy groups—and has immense popular appeal. However, there are also good reasons to temper our enthusiasm and to take a more critical, skeptical view of this claim. Among them is that the neuroscience advocates cite in support of their claim is hardly new; that the neuroscience is selective, oversimplified, and interpreted incorrectly; and that these claims and interpretations are emanating primarily from policy advocates, not from neuroscientists or even developmental psychologists. Indeed, to get from the brain science to the supposed policy implications requires some mighty leaps of faith and interpretation. These leaps are so long and perilous that we might do more for children by questioning than by accepting this popular claim.

THE BRAIN AND EARLY CHILDHOOD: THE BACKGROUND AND THE ARGUMENT

Interest in the brain is not new among educators and policy makers. Many of the same ideas about and discussions of how brain science might inform policy, practice, and parenting have been around for at least 30 years (Chall & Mirsky, 1978; Friedman, Klivington, & Peterson, 1986; Healy, 1986, 1987; Ibuka, 1977; "The Infant," 1985).

This chapter is reprinted from Bruer, J. (1998). The brain and child development: Time for some critical thinking. *Public Health Reports, 113,* 388–397, by permission of Oxford University Press.

Interest in brain and child development most recently surged in the early 1990s. In 1991, the Carnegie Corporation of New York formed its Task Force on the Needs of Young Children to address the "quiet crisis" afflicting children from birth through age 3. The task force's report, *Starting Points: Meeting the Needs of Our Youngest Children,* is justifiably hailed as the seminal document of the heightened interest in brain science and child development (Carnegie Corporation of New York, 1994). As stated in the report, the task force's mission "was to develop a report that would provide a framework of scientific knowledge and offer an action agenda to ensure the healthy development of children from before birth to age 3" (Carnegie Corporation of New York, 1994, p. viii). The report pointed to the wide gap between scientific knowledge and social policy, a gap that is particularly wide—the report noted—between brain science and early childhood policy. Yet, *Starting Points* contained only a limited, superficial, and poorly documented discussion of brain research. For a foundation policy report, *Starting Points* received unprecedented, positive media coverage. Oddly, though, given the little brain science in the report (1½ pages of 132), the media coverage emphasized what the new brain science meant for parenting, child care, and early education.

In February 1996, *Newsweek* helped bring the discussion of brain science and early childhood into the mainstream with its cover story, "Your Child's Brain" (Begley, 1996). In June 1996, the Carnegie Corporation along with several other foundations sponsored a conference in Chicago, which served as the basis for the publication *Rethinking the Brain: New Insights into Early Development* (Shore, 1997), released in conjunction with an April 1997 White House conference (titled the White House Conference on Early Childhood Development: What New Research on the Brain Tells Us about Our Youngest Children). The sponsors of the Chicago conference intended *Rethinking the Brain* to provide a more complete account than did *Starting Points* of the neuroscience that parents, educators, and Congress should use to reformulate policies and priorities.

The arguments made by the advocates of a brain science/child policy link rely on three relatively well-established findings from developmental neuroscience as a basis for their policy recommendations. First, neuroscientists have known since the late 1970s that in various species including rats, cats, and primates there is a period of rapid synapse formation in the brain cortex. This period, during which connections rapidly form among nerve cells, starts prior to or shortly after birth, depending on the species (Cragg, 1975; Goldman-Rakic, Bourgeois, & Rakic, 1997; Huttenlocher & Dabholkar, 1997; Huttenlocher, de Courten, Garey, & van der Loos, 1982; Lund, Boothe, & Lund, 1977).

Second, neuroscientists have also known since the early 1970s that there are critical periods of experience-dependent development in some sensory and motor systems. The best-known example is that of critical periods in the development of the cat and monkey visual systems, as discovered by David Hubel and Torsten Wiesel (1977; Hubel, Wiesel, & LeVay, 1977). Animals deprived of visual stimulation to one eye early in development remain permanently blind in that eye.

Third, studies have shown that at least in rats, complex or enriched environments increase brain size and weight as well as the number of synapses per cortical neuron. This work dates back to the 1960s. Beginning in the late 1970s, William Greenough and his colleagues have published some of the most rigorous and widely cited work in this area (Greenough, Withers, & Anderson, 1992).

None of this brain science, dating back as it does 20–30 years, could be accurately described as "new" in such a rapidly developing field. These three ideas, alone or in various combinations, appear in arguments to explain the importance of early childhood experiences and to encourage policies that assure children will have the experiences necessary for optimal brain development. These arguments, as they are popularly understood, can be distilled into a single sentence: In humans, the period of rapid synapse formation, which ends at around 3 years of age, is the critical period in brain development during which enriched environments can have permanent and unique beneficial effects on children's brain development.

However, if we look critically at the neuroscience, the arguments, and the claims, we have good reason to be skeptical. The popular understanding of how brain science relates to early childhood is highly inaccurate and misleading. What follows is a brief description of the basic brain science and some examples of how it is used (and abused) to support specific claims about early child development.

EARLY SYNAPSE FORMATION

Building on work that began in the 1970s (Cragg, 1975; Lund et al., 1977), Pasko Rakic, Jean-Pierre Bourgeois, and Patricia Goldman-Rakic (1994) studied synaptic development over the life span in rhesus monkeys. Peter Huttenlocher and his colleagues have done similar, human neuroanatomical studies using autopsy material (Huttenlocher & Dabholkar, 1997; Huttenlocher, de Courten, Garey, & van der Loos, 1982). Although there are some unresolved differences between the monkey and human data, in both species synaptic densities—the number of synapses per unit volume of brain tissue—vary following an inverted-U pattern. At birth, synaptic densities in the human brain are approximately the same as those found in adults. In the months following birth, synapses form rapidly. In all areas of the brain, by age 3 years, synaptic densities peak at levels 50% higher than those found in adults. Synaptic densities remain at these elevated levels until puberty, when they decline to adult levels. Synaptic densities in adults are approximately the same as in newborns.

These neuroanatomical findings provide the basis for claims in the policy and popular literatures on early childhood about the unique importance of children's first 3 years. The first 3 years are important, the argument goes, because during those years, synapse production outpaces synapse elimination and the vast majority of synapses are produced (Clinton, 1996; Shore, 1997). The Education Commission of the States (1998), a nationwide alliance for educational improvement affiliated with the National Governors' Conference, tells us that this time is developmentally crucial because

> Brain connections develop especially fast the first 3 years of life in response to stimuli, such as someone talking to, singing to, reading to, or playing with the infant or toddler. Such experiences significantly influence brain development and enhance central nervous system connections that define the capacity to learn.

Brain development is so rapid during this period, advocates of the brain science/policy link claim, that by the time a child enters school at age 5, the most crucial learning years are past and he or she may have already irretrievably lost some crucial learning opportunities (Newman, 1997). Rapid postnatal synapse formation is given as the reason why we should sing, talk, and read to infants, invest in high-quality early child care, and exploit this optimal learning period that augments intelligence and learning skills throughout life.

Although there may be excellent reasons to do all these things, what we know about early, rapid synapse formation does not by itself provide any justification for doing them. Although it is true that during these early years synapse formation outpaces synapse elimination, it is not accurate to say that during this period synapses form rapidly in response to environmental stimulation. Given what we know from animal studies, both deprivation and stimulation experiments, it appears that this process of exuberant synaptic growth is primarily under genetic, not environmental, control. Monkeys raised in darkness, monkeys deprived of vision before birth, and monkeys delivered prematurely and visually overstimulated show the same pattern of rapid synapse formation as normal monkeys (Rakic et al., 1994). In monkeys, and no doubt in humans, experience after birth does affect brain development and neural circuitry, but it does so primarily by eliminating synapses formed during the period of rapid formation, not by causing them to form in the first place. Given what we know about what controls rapid synapse formation in animals including humans, there is little reason to think that *more* singing, talking, and reading to infants will cause *more* synapses to form.

We should also be skeptical of claims that the period of rapid synapse formation is the optimal time for learning and that when this period ends a child's most crucial learning years are over. If we look at the temporal relationships between the period of rapid synaptic proliferation and when sensory, motor, and memory skills emerge, it appears that the skills supported by a specific brain area first appear in rudimentary form when synaptic densities peak. However, these skills continue to improve during and after that time and continue to improve even as synaptic densities fall to final adult levels. For some short-term memory skills, we reach final adult levels of performance only at puberty, when synaptic densities fall to adult levels. At infancy and adulthood, synaptic densities are approximately the same, but our sensory, motor, and memory skills are obviously much more highly developed in early adulthood than in infancy. Thus, there is no known simple, linear relationship between synaptic densities and synaptic numbers on the one hand, and intelligence, the maturation of our sensory, motor, and memory skills, and the ability to learn on the other. In fact, some neuroscientists and developmental psychologists argue that it is only after our neural machinery has matured at puberty that we are ready to engage in high-level learning and intellectual development (Goldman-Rakic et al., 1997; Rakic et al., 1994).

We often read in the policy and popular literatures that a child's ability to learn and function in society is largely determined by age 3. In fact, the entire discussion of the implications of brain science for child development occurs under the umbrella of this assumption. Although some developmental psychologists and child psychiatrists, in the attachment theory tradition, believe that childhood experiences before age 3 determine a child's future cognitive, emotional, and social well-being, there are others who question this notion of "infant determinism," the assumption that as the twig is bent so grows the tree. Those who question the assumption can also point to a substantial research corpus for support (Kagan, 1998). This is a complex issue that cannot be addressed in detail here.

However, in evaluating the claims about the life-long significance of early experience on brain and cognitive development, readers should be aware that the claim is not universally accepted within the social and behavioral sciences. One sometimes gets the impression that early synapse formation figures centrally in the early childhood literature only because it happens to be a neural event that coincides with a developmental period some researchers deem important for other reasons.

CRITICAL PERIODS

The second neurobiological idea used to link brain science with early childhood policy is that of critical periods. Frequently cited is the example of Hubel and Wiesel's kittens, which, deprived of visual input to one eye during the first months after birth, remained permanently blind in that eye. There is a tendency in the early childhood literature to identify "the critical period" in brain development with the period of rapid synapse formation in the brain, the first 3 years of life. Critical periods are a bit more complicated than that.

Appeals to critical periods are used to support claims about the life-long impact of early experiences and the permanent damage that can be done if critical periods are "missed." One use of this idea is to attempt to explain why the cognitive gains Head Start participants make are short-lived rather than long-lasting. The explanation is that Head Start begins for most children at 3 years of age, too late to fundamentally rewire the brain. Early child care experts have been quoted as saying that according to our "new" knowledge about infant brain development, Head Start may be too little, too late; to make a significant, lasting impact on children's development, enrichment programs are needed for children from birth to 3 (Begley, 1996; Blakeslee, 1997). We should note that there is a 20-year history of using whatever current brain theory is at hand to explain why Head Start is not all that its advocates might have hoped. For example, in the late 1970s, Herman Epstein's (1978) theory of growth spurts in the brain figured in such arguments (Healy, 1986).

There certainly are critical periods in development. Some kinds of learning and skill acquisition are constrained within maturational windows. Common examples are newborn geese following the first moving object they encounter, male birds learning to sing, and the development of binocular vision in primates, including humans. For humans, we should also add aspects of social-emotional development and language acquisition. We must have the appropriate experiences at the right developmental moments to acquire certain social, language, sensory, and motor skills. One of Hubel and Wiesel's great contributions was to initiate a research program to identify the neural mechanisms underlying critical periods. They studied the visual system, as have many other neuroscientists since. Thus, we know much more about critical periods for vision than we do about those for other sensory and motor systems. Yet even for vision, neuroscientists are still not certain what causes critical periods to end.

Neuroscientists now understand that critical periods are not simply "windows" that slam shut. For human visual functions, such as visual acuity, critical periods appear to have at least three phases: a phase of rapid maturation of the function to near mature levels; a phase during which deprivation can result in degradation of the function; and a phase during which therapy or compensatory experiences can repair some damage due to deprivation (Daw, 1995). Neuroscientists and clinicians also know that critical periods are complex in a second way. For any one sensory system, such as vision, there are different critical periods for specific functions—for example, visual acuity, stereopsis, binocular vision. When these periods occur and how long they last depend on when the specific brain areas supporting the function mature. For humans, critical periods for some visual functions extend well beyond age 3, until 8 or 9 years of age. For some aspects of language acquisition, critical periods appear to extend at least through puberty. Thus, although some critical periods do occur before age 3, critical periods in humans do not in general map neatly onto the period of rapid synapse formation, that is, onto the first 3 years of life.

Claims about critical periods should also be assessed with a second caveat in mind. Although these claims often give the impression that there are critical periods for all kinds of learning, we have firm evidence for the existence of critical periods only for component functions within sensory and motor systems and, in humans, for components of language such as phonology and syntax. We do not know if critical periods exist for culturally transmitted knowledge, including reading, math, and music—often cited as examples. Reading and mathematics educators are generally skeptical that critical periods limit skill acquisition in these and other school subjects. For the present, we might best share their skepticism.

Some neuroscientists also argue that critical periods are limited to certain kinds of neural systems and functions. Some neural systems—vision is a good example—rely on environmental stimuli to prune synapses and fine-tune highly sensitive neural circuits. Environmental tuning allows us to have much more sensitive sensory systems than we could possibly have if the systems were hardwired at birth. Relying on the availability of specific kinds of environmental stimuli at just the right time would seem to be a highly risky way to develop the circuitry we need for survival. Of course, the risk diminishes to zero if the kinds of stimuli needed are overwhelmingly likely to occur in any even remotely normal environment. Over the course of evolutionary history, William Greenough argues, species have come to "expect" that the necessary stimuli will be present. Greenough talks about the "experience-expectant" plasticity of sensory and motor systems (Greenough, Black, & Wallace, 1987). The expected experiences must be present at the appropriate developmental time, but the needed experiences are of a very general kind that are ubiquitous for the species—pattered visual input, the opportunity to move and manipulate objects, presence of speech sounds. Based on what we know about critical periods from a neuroscience and evolutionary perspective, we can safely conclude that critical periods are unlikely to depend on highly specific experiences in highly specific social and cultural environments.

Children could be expected to acquire such skills, and they almost always do, in a range of environments—at home with a parent, with siblings or grandparents, with other child care providers, or in Head Start. Infants do not need highly specific, carefully tailored experiences for this kind of species-typical development to occur. For this reason, critical periods do not really speak to how we should design preschool or Head Start programs, choose toys, time music lessons, or establish early child care policies, with one important exception. Neuroscience and what we know about critical periods do tell us that it is extremely important to identify and treat sensory problems in children—for example, cataracts, eye misalignments, chronic ear infections—as early as possible. Normal, species-typical fine-tuning, even in a normal environment, cannot occur if the child cannot see, hear, or feel the ubiquitous environmental stimuli.

ENRICHED OR COMPLEX ENVIRONMENTS

Early childhood advocates claim that stimulation matters and that early stimulation matters most. In their view, research on the effects of enriched, or more accurately complex, environments on brain development supports these claims. They argue as follows: during the "critical period" of rapid synapse formation, "early experiences can have a dramatic impact on brain wiring, causing the final number of synapses in the brain to increase or decrease by as much as 25 percent" (Ounce of Prevention Fund). Although, they admit, this finding is based primarily on rodent studies, people who care for children should take heart from the animal studies because "research bears out that an enriched environment can boost the number of synapses that children form" (Shore, 1997). This research, they claim, underscores the importance of early enrichment programs, especially for socially and economically disadvantaged children. An example commonly cited in the policy and popular literatures is the North Carolina Abecedarian Project, a program that provided enriched child care to at-risk children, starting in the first year of life and continuing through school entry (Campbell & Ramey, 1995; As is shown in the sections that follow, this project had a rigorous experimental design that has allowed long-term follow-up of participants). Indeed, Colorado Governor Roy Romer actually told the *Rocky Mountain News,* "brain research showed that early childhood education could increase adult intelligence by a third" (Seebach, 1998).

As much as we might want to believe Governor Romer, it takes several mighty leaps to get from rats to children to dramatic increases in adult intelligence, leaps that defy both logic and brain science.

Let's start with the rats. First, many neuroscientists who study how rearing environments affect brain development prefer the descriptor "complex" to "enriched." They see raising rats in groups in large cages filled with objects and obstacles as a laboratory simulation of the animals' normal, wild environment. It is enriched only with respect to lab rearing in single cages. In policy discussions, the term "complex" is also preferable. It prevents us, when we begin to think about how this research might relate to children, from too quickly defining enriched environments as culturally preferred ones. It reminds us that we should not identify complex rodent environments with human middle-class neighborhoods—we should be careful in leaping from rats negotiating obstacles to children learning chess or taking music lessons. We have no reason to infer that the environs of Harvard Square or Palo Alto are complex or enriched while those of Roxbury or East Palo Alto are deprived. Complex for rats does not readily translate into culturally enriched for humans.

Raising rats in complex environments does affect brain development. Neuroscientists have known since the 1960s that such rearing increases the size and weight of certain brain areas. More recent electron microscopic studies found that young rats raised in complex environments starting at 10–12 days of age had synapse-per-neuron ratios 20%–25% higher than their littermates that were raised in isolation (Turner & Greenough, 1985). However, differences of this magnitude occur primarily in the visual area, not throughout the entire brain. The result is the source of the "25% more synapses in children" claim we see in the policy and popular articles.

Neuroscientists have also known since the mid-1960s, although this is never mentioned in the policy and popular literatures, that complex environments have the same effects on brain structure (although to gradually lesser extents as animals age) throughout the animals' lifetimes. Research on complex environments does not point to the unique importance of early stimulation for this kind of brain plasticity. In fact, one of the most exciting discoveries of neuroscience in the past 30 years is that the adult brain remains highly plastic throughout the life span. Even in adulthood, changes in patterns of stimulation due to amputation or nerve damage, new experiences, or training and learning result in relatively rapid and substantial cortical reorganization (Green, Greenough, & Schlumpf, 1983; Merzenich et al., 1983; Pons, 1995; Ramachandran, 1995). This is what enables us to learn throughout our lives. In short, the research on complex environments is often distorted, misinterpreted, and oversimplified in the early childhood literature. Early stimulation might matter and it might even play an exceedingly important role in early child development, but the research on complex environments and adult brain plasticity does not provide the evidence.

Extrapolating from synapse-per-neuron ratios in rats to children requires another leap. It is a leap because we have no data to support a claim that early educational experiences increase synapse-per-neuron ratios by 20% to 25% in children's brains. The argument proceeds by assuming that what is good for the rats is good for the rugrats, suggesting that the effects of early intervention programs must have something to do with synaptic change. For example, it is easy to assume that measured changes on intelligence tests must result from some commensurate change in synapse-per-neuron ratios.

We should be concerned about children at risk for school and life failure. We should applaud and encourage longitudinal studies like that of the Abecedarian Project. But, as we move into policy, we should be clear about what the research does and does not say. The Abecedarian Project is a fine example of behavioral science. In the follow-up studies done on Abecedarian participants at age 15 (7–10 years after the intervention ended), the participants did show improved school achievement that was related to the time and intensity of their participation (Campbell & Ramey, 1995). However, the study design does not allow one to conclude that it was early intervention, as opposed to the duration of the intervention, that contributed to the improvements. The measured intelligence part of the story is less encouraging. Children in the study did show early gains in IQ scores, but they declined over the course of the follow-up. The largest gains in IQ scores appeared at age 36 months, with a 16.4-point differential between the intervention and control groups. But by age 15, children in the intervention group had IQ scores only 4.6 points higher than the children in the control group, a difference that would hardly be perceptible in classroom performance. (Here is where Governor Romer made his error: 4.6 IQ points represent an improvement of one third of a standard deviation in IQ score, not a one third increase in adult intelligence.) Furthermore, children in the intervention group had IQ scores in the low to mid-90s, still below the national mean of around 100. The effect of early intervention on measured intelligence is not as robust as many people had hoped and many still believe. Brain research provides no direct evidence of a unique, life-long impact of early childhood education.

CONCLUSION

The "new" brain science does not appear to offer much in terms of a scientific framework for an action agenda to improve social policies for young children. When we see how advocates of a brain science/policy link misinterpret and oversimplify the science, we have reason to be skeptical, at least. Infants do undergo a period of rapid synapse formation, but it does not appear to be under environmental control. There are critical periods in development, but they operate to fine-tune our specieswide neural systems in an experience–expectant way. The stimuli required for this fine-tuning are available in any normal environment. "Complex" environments do, at least in rodents, affect brain connectivity, but they appear to do so throughout the lifetime of the animal. Attempts to extrapolate from rodent studies to the importance of early childhood intervention programs are logically, methodologically, and substantively dubious.

Policy makers and child care advocates are the most vocal at invoking brain science as a guide for policy. Generally, neuroscientists are more cautious. In 1992, Carla Shatz observed that although we know infants who suffer gross neglect develop abnormally, such observations do not support the view that enriched environments will enhance development or that extra stimulation is helpful. "Much research remains to be done," she wrote, "before anyone can conclusively determine the types of sensory input that encourage the formation of particular neural connections in newborns" (p. 61). In a more recent review of the evidence, Charles Nelson and Floyd Bloom (1997) concluded that "it may be useful to question the simplistic view that the brain becomes unbendable and increasingly difficult to modify beyond the first years of life," noting that even at the end of adolescence, "the brain is far from set in its trajectory" (p. 983). Similarly, William Greenough (1997), whose work is widely cited by the brain science/child policy advocates, has stated that neuroscience does not support a selective focus of interest and resources on the first 3 years of life.

There are two positive outcomes of this intense interest in child development and the brain. First, the advocates have heightened interest in child development among parents, educators, and policy makers. Second, it has caused neuroscientists to reflect on what they do and do not know about brain development. Thoughtful brain scientists realize— and they are saying publicly—that they do not know nearly as much as the public and some policy makers claim they know. Reading the popular and policy literature on early brain development, they find themselves asking, "Do we really know that?" Their reflection promises to accelerate research in fields such as developmental cognitive neuroscience and neurobiology.

All of us interested in good science and sound science-based policy might be best advised to share the neuroscientists' caution and reflection. When we see in a policy document or popular article the assertion that "New research on the brain shows . . .," we should stop and ask ourselves, "Does it?"

REFERENCES

Begley, S. (1996). Your child's brain. *Newsweek, 127*(8), 55–62.

Blakeslee, S. (1997, April 17). Studies show talking with infants shapes basis of ability to think. *New York Times,* p. A21.

Campbell, F.A., & Ramey, C.T. (1995). Cognitive and school outcomes for high-risk African-American students at middle adolescence: Positive effects of early intervention. *American Educational Research Journal, 32,* 742–772.

Carnegie Corporation of New York. (1994). *Starting points: Meeting the needs of our youngest children.* New York: Author.

Chall, J.S., & Mirsky, A.F. (1978). The implications for education. In S. Chall & A.F. Mirsky (Eds.), *Education and the brain* (pp. 371–378). Chicago: University of Chicago Press.

Clinton, H.R. (1996). *It takes a village.* New York: Touchstone.

Cragg, B.G. (1975). The development of synapses in the visual system of the cat. *Journal of Comparative Neurology, 160,* 147–166.

Daw, N.W. (1995). *Visual development.* New York: Plenum.

Education Commission of the States. (1998). *Brain research and education: Neuroscience research has impact for education policy.* Policy Brief. Available from http://www.ecs.org/clearinghouse/11/96/1196.htm

Epstein, H.T. (1978). Growth spurts during brain development: Implications for educational policy and practice. In S. Chall & A.F. Mirsky (Eds.), *Education and the brain* (pp. 343–370). Chicago: University of Chicago Press.

Friedman, S.L., Klivington, K.A., & Peterson, R.W. (1986). *The brain, cognition and education.* Orlando, FL: Academic Press.

Goldman-Rakic, P.S., Bourgeois, J.P., & Rakic, P. (1997). Synaptic substrate of cognitive development: Synaptogenesis in the prefrontal cortex of the nonhuman primate. In N.A. Krasnegor, G.R. Lyon, & P.S. Goldman-Rakic (Eds.), *Development of the prefrontal cortex: Evolution, neurobiology, and behavior* (pp. 27–47). Baltimore: Paul H. Brookes Publishing Co.

Green, E.J., Greenough, W.T., & Schlumpf, B.E. (1983). Effects of complex or isolated environments on cortical dendrites of middle-aged rats. *Brain Research, 264,* 233–240.

Greenough, W.T. (1997). We can't just focus on ages zero to three. *APA Monitor, 28,* 19.

Greenough, W.T., Black, J.E., & Wallace, C.S. (1987). Experience and brain development. *Child Development, 58,* 539–559.

Greenough, W.T., Withers, G.S., & Anderson, B.J. (1992). Experience-dependent synaptogenesis as a plausible memory mechanism. In I. Gormezano & E.A. Wasserman (Eds.), *Learning and memory: The behavioral and biological substrates* (pp. 209–229). Mahwah, NJ: Lawrence Erlbaum Associates.

Healy, J. (1986). Brainpower! You can make smarter babies. *Parents, 61,* 100–105.

Healy, J.M. (1987). *Your child's growing mind: A parent's guide to learning from birth to early adolescence.* Garden City, NY: Doubleday.

Hubel, D.H., & Wiesel, T.N. (1977). Functional architecture of macaque monkey visual cortex. *Proceedings of the Royal Society of London - Series B: Biological Sciences, 198,* 1–59.

Hubel, D.H., Wiesel, T.N., & LeVay, S. (1977). Plasticity of ocular dominance columns in monkey striate cortex. *Philosophical Transactions of the Royal Society of London-Series B: Biological Sciences, 278,* 307–409.

Huttenlocher, P.R., & Dabholkar, A.S. (1997). Regional differences in synaptogenesis in human cerebral cortex. *Journal of Comparative Neurology, 387,* 167–178.

Huttenlocher, P.R., de Courten, C., Garey, L.J., & van der Loos, H. (1982). Synaptogenesis in human visual cortex—evidence for synapse elimination during normal development. *Neuroscience Letters, 33,* 247–252.

Ibuka, M. (1977). *Kindergarten is too late!* New York: Simon and Schuster.

The infant: Ready and able to learn. (1985). *Children Today, 14,* 19.

Kagan, J. (1998). *Three seductive ideas.* Cambridge, MA: Harvard University Press.

Lund, J.S., Boothe, R.G., & Lund, R.D. (1977). Development of neurons in the visual cortex (Area 17) of the monkey (Macaca nemestrina): A Golgi study from fetal day 127 to postnatal maturity. *Journal of Comparative Neurology, 176,* 149–188.

Merzenich, M.M., Kaas, J.H., Wall, J.T., Nelson, R.J., Sur, M., & Fellman, D.J. (1983). Topographic reorganization of somatosensory cortical areas 3b and 1 in adult monkeys following restricted deafferentation. *Neuroscience, 8,* 33–55.

Nelson, C.A., & Bloom, F.E. (1997). Child development and neuroscience. *Child Development, 68,* 970–987.

Newman, F. (1997). Brain research has implications for education: Is 1st grade too late? *State Education Leader, 15,* 1–2.

Ounce of Prevention Fund. *Starting smart: How early experiences affect brain development.* Available from http://www.bcm.tmc.edu/cintas/lines/ounce/html

Pons, T.P. (1995). Lesion-induced cortical plasticity [abstract]. In B. Julesz & I. Kovacs (Eds.), *Maturational windows and adult cortical plasticity* (pp. 175–178). Reading, MA: Addison-Wesley.

Rakic, P., Bourgeois, J.P., & Goldman-Rakic, P.S. (1994). Synaptic development of the cerebral cortex: Implications for learning, memory, and mental illness. In J. van Pelt, M.A. Corner, H.B.M. Uylings, & F.H. Lopes da Silva (Eds.), *Progress in Brain Research, 102,* 227–243.

Ramachandran, V.S. (1995). Plasticity in the adult human brain: Is there reason for optimism? In B. Julesz & I. Kovacs (Eds.), *Maturational windows and adult cortical plasticity* (pp. 179–197). Reading, MA: Addison-Wesley.

Seebach, L. (1998, April 5). "Brain research" may lead education astray. *Rocky Mountain News,* p. B2.

Shatz, C.J. (1992, September). The developing brain. *Scientific American,* 61–67.

Shore, R. (1997). *Rethinking the brain: New insights into early development.* New York: Families and Work Institute.

Turner, A.M., & Greenough, W.T. (1985). Differential rearing effects on rat visual cortex synapses I: Synaptic and neuronal density and synapses per neuron. *Brain Research, 329,* 195–203.

CHAPTER 31

Critical Periods in Central Nervous System Development

PAUL J. LOMBROSO AND KYLE D. PRUETT

Neuroscientists have long been fascinated by the rich diversity of human personalities, their unique behaviors, and their varied abilities. A central question is whether these differences result from the way the central nervous system (CNS) is constructed or from individual experiences. To discover the exact mechanisms by which the CNS develops, matures, and maintains itself over the human life span, much neuroscience research has been devoted to identifying the molecular basis for neuronal birth, the formation of major axon tracts, and the growth of synaptic contacts between interconnected cells. In this chapter, we review what is known about the role that environmental factors play in these events. Particular attention will be given to research that addresses the validity of the concept of critical periods. This is an area fraught with contemporary controversies and varied opinions and has been represented in previous chapters.

NATURE VERSUS NURTURE

We begin with a discussion of the nature–nurture controversy. Over the years, clinicians, researchers, and policy makers have debated the relative importance of genetic or environmental factors in guiding the development of the CNS. One side argues the importance of genetic factors while the other emphasizes the importance of the environmental factors. Entrenched camps interpret the available data as supporting their particular point of view. Advocates from both sides point to one particular study or another to explain how the CNS develops and how disruptions in the normal developmental process are etiologically related to many psychiatric disorders.

One example of this debate emerges from the history of research on autism. Autism is a severe developmental disorder that appears in the early years of life. The cardinal features of the disorder are a markedly abnormal development in social interactions. Children with autism have impaired communication and social skills and have a restricted repertoire of activities and interests (American Psychiatric Association, 1994). Repetitive or stereotyped patterns of behaviors and movements are commonly found among children with autism.

When Leo Kanner (1943) first described the syndrome, he wondered whether the core symptoms were based within the genetic blueprint of these children. He also noted in his original paper that some of the parents of children with autism had distinct personality traits. This seemingly innocuous statement launched a debate over whether genetic or environmental factors were the primary causes of the disorder. The term *refrigerator mother* was coined to characterize the alleged aloofness and distance of the biological mother. The inadequacies of the parents and how they related to their children were believed by many to be the underlying reasons as to why these children withdrew from the world.

Research on autism since the 1990s has made it clear that genetic factors are the predominant etiological factor. The evidence for this comes from a number of carefully controlled genetic studies in which both monozygotic and dizygotic twins were compared for the frequency of the disorder (Bailey et al., 1995; Folstein & Rutter, 1977; Steffenburg et al., 1989). Monozygotic twins share nearly identical genes, while dizygotic twins share approximately half the number of genes, but both share nearly identical environments. This design has been used to study many disorders because it controls both genetic and environmental factors and elucidates whether one or the other plays an etiological role.

A significantly higher concordance rate is consistently found among monozygotic twins worldwide. These results strongly support the hypothesis that genetic factors are more important than environmental ones in the pathophysiology of autism. A number of laboratories are searching for mutated gene(s) that contribute to the expression of autism or related disorders. Three groups have now published their findings from genomewide scans in autistic families (International Molecular Genetic Study of Autism Consortium, 1998; Jamain et al., 2003; Philippe et al., 1999; Risch et al., 1999; Veenstra-VanderWeele et al., 2003; Yonan et al., 2003).

Additional support comes from the recent isolation of a gene that causes a related disorder, Rett syndrome (Amir et al., 1999). This disorder is quite rare, and it was initially difficult to establish its genetic basis. Females are almost exclusively affected and develop typically for the first year. Milestones are reached on time with no abnormalities apparent early in life followed by a rapid regression. These children lose purposeful hand movements and often show growth retardation, loss of speech, microcephaly, ataxia, and a striking absence of cognitive progression.

Early researchers sought the chromosomal location for the mutated gene. Because of the high frequency of the disorder among female children, investigators focused on the X chromosome and then an area within that chromosome (Xq28). Many of the genes present in this region were carefully screened for mutations, leading to the isolation of one gene in particular that was altered among several affected children. The gene encodes the methyl CpG-binding protein 2 (MeCP2), and mutations in two critical domains of the protein were discovered in some of the affected probands. This protein normally regulates the expression of other genes that are critical to the normal growth and development of the CNS (Nan, Campoy, & Bird, 1997). Researchers in this area expect to find other genes that cause disorders related to autism. The characterization of these genes will help in determine exactly what types of disruptions in normal CNS developmental result in these devastating illnesses.

Neuroscientists no longer question whether genetic or environmental factors play a critical role in CNS development. Both are vitally important in a dynamic interchange that changes our perspective on causative factors. At the beginning of the 21st century, research strategies address the interplay of nature and nurture during normal development. Nonetheless, it is important to recognize that there are times when genetic factors will disrupt CNS development no matter how supportive and nurturing the environment. This is what happens when a gene that is absolutely necessary for normal cellular function is mutated, as with Rett syndrome. Similarly, there are times when the environment is so severely deprived through poverty, neglect, abuse, or malnutrition that brain development suffers despite perfectly normal genes. Together, a stable environment and adequate genetic factors allow our brains to develop normally.

The next question is whether genetic and environmental factors play an equal role throughout development or whether there are times when one or the other has a more predominant effect. Research findings from the last decade suggest that genetic factors predominate during the earliest stages of CNS development and are overtaken by environmental factors with the birth of the infant.

Most of the 100 billion neurons that form the adult brain are produced during a few months early in embryonic life by an exquisitely small population of progenitor cells. The birth of these neurons occurs in the ventricular zone—so called because it is near the fluid filled ventricles of the brain. This zone contains the progenitor cells that give rise both to other progenitor cells that will divide again and to postmitotic cells that will differentiate and mature into neurons and glia. Once the progenitor population has expanded to a certain size, only postmitotic neurons remain and must migrate into the surrounding areas to further develop the nervous system.

These earliest events are largely determined by two factors. The first is the expression of certain "master control genes," or transcription factors, that regulate the orderly expression of other genes throughout the brain. The second factor is the expression of growth factors and other signaling proteins secreted in gradients along the developing neuraxis (Leckman & Lombroso, 2001). A consequence of this changing pattern of signaling molecules and transcription factors is that developing cells vary their patterns of gene expression, which determine exactly where, when, and which cells will be born.

That said, we also know that while genetic factors guide many of these early events, environmental factors may interfere at times. It is well appreciated that malnutrition, alcohol, drugs, and certain viral illnesses can disrupt CNS development. They often do so by disrupting the normal expression of regulatory genes and growth factors.

An example of this comes from work with a medication called Accutane, often used for dermatological problems (Adams, 1996). Severe developmental CNS abnormalities may occur when a woman takes this medication during the first trimester of pregnancy. It is now known that Accutane interferes with the normal expression of a specific growth factor called retinoic acid. This growth factor is critically involved in patterning the developing limbs and neural tube. Accutane causes a disturbance in the retinoic acid gradient within the developing embryo, which in turn, disrupts the expression of key transcription factors. Alcohol, nicotine, and other drugs cause similar disruptions. These drugs have more of an effect during periods of CNS development when the expression of these genes is absolutely required for normal brain development. Ingestion at other times may not result in congenital malformations but may cause other deleterious effects on neuronal function.

The growth and consolidation of synaptic connections are among the final events to occur as the brain matures. Although synaptogenesis begins *in utero,* some synapses are pruned away and others are strengthened during postnatal life. During this later phase of CNS development, the effects of environmental factors become increasingly evident. This does not mean that gene expression is no longer important. Obviously, the production of new synapses and strengthening of older ones requires the concerted efforts of many newly expressed proteins, but the balance between genetic and environmental influences is shifted.

A tremendous amount of brain remodeling occurs after birth. The majority of neurons are born by this time, but the size of the brain more than doubles over the first several years of life. This increase is largely due to the dramatic increase in synaptic connections occurring throughout the brain. Neuronal activity in response to sensory stimulation is required for the postsynaptic growth and proliferation of synaptic connections (Shatz, 1990). (Earlier, during prenatal development, spontaneous neuronal activity that occurs in the absence of sensory stimulation is required for the initial production of synaptic contacts established *in utero.*)

Birth initiates a tremendous increase in the amount of sensory input, and a large increase in neuronal activity is generated throughout the CNS as a consequence. This additional neuronal activity stimulates new synaptic connections as the infant begins to interact with the world. This environmental input is necessary for normal growth and maturation of the brain. The process of discriminating sensory information, learning motor skills, and laying down new memories and retrieving old ones all require neuronal activity, which in turn, leads to structural changes between and within the neurons engaged in this activity. Both environmental input and the expression of genes are required, as many genes must be expressed and others repressed for the proper growth of axons and elaboration of synaptic connections as the infant matures. Thus, the environment of the newborn and older child is critically important, and considerable research is devoted to understanding the interplay between environmental factors and gene expression during early learning.

CRITICAL PERIODS

The classical work of Hubel and Wiesel during the 1960s and 1970s fostered the concept of critical periods (reviewed in Hubel & Wiesel, 1970). These are periods of neural development when the substrate for behavior is irrevocably established. These investigators focused on the influence of early experience on visual cortex organization during postnatal development. What emerged from their work and many research groups that followed is the notion of a brief period during which normal environmental stimulation is required for proper development of permanent circuitry in the visual system. Neuroscientists are now devoting considerable research efforts to determine the exact molecular and cellular events that occur as the visual cortex organizes itself in response to the environment.

The visual cortex encompasses more than one third of the cortex when all the visual areas are included. A distinctive feature of the primary visual cortex, which receives direct input from the eye via the thalamus, is the modular ocular dominance column. Vertically arrayed columns of neurons that span the six horizontal layers of the visual cortex respond predominantly to visual input from one or the other eye. Left and right eye columns alternate across the visual cortex making a pattern of stripes that are each about half a millimeter wide.

Although ocular dominance columns have been observed in human cortex, most of what we know comes from work in cats and monkeys. More primitive forms of columns are present *in utero,* and over the first months of postnatal life they become more distinct. Most visual cortex neurons in a newborn cat or monkey respond equally well to input from both eyes at first. Gradually over the next several months, influences from the right and left eye segregate into alternating columns that are driven predominantly by one or the other eye. Methods of visualizing this excitation pattern exist and show thin alternating stripes of excitation and quiescence across the visual cortex when one eye is diffusely illuminate while the other is kept in the dark.

Many investigators have demonstrated that this process does not proceed without normal visual experience and normal synaptic activity. Hubel and Wiesel made the striking observation that the precise timing of this experience is also critical. Animals that are deprived of normal visual experience during specific and relatively brief periods of time are never able to obtain normal vision. They showed this conclusively in experiments in which one eye was kept closed throughout early postnatal development. Irreversible changes occurred in the visual cortex. Ocular dominance columns failed to develop, and stimulation to the previously closed eye could not excite many neurons in the visual cortex. Subsequent experiments in which eye closure occurred over successively shorter and shorter periods defined the window of time during which visual inputs are absolutely required for proper cortical development. This type of plasticity is not present later in life. Eye closure in older animals has no effect on the visual cortex. When the closed eye is reopened, the normal compliment of neurons and ocular dominance columns are excited by that eye.

These research studies clearly demonstrate that sensory input associated with neural activity is required for normal development of the visual cortex during a brief, postnatal critical period. No amount of stimulation later will correct the abnormal development that results from the absence of proper stimulation during the critical period. "Catch up" is not possible, and the damage is permanent.

Humans with cataracts provide the setting for natural experiments of this kind. An infant born with a congenital cataract that remains undetected during the first years of life remains permanently blind in the affected eye, even when the cataract is removed. This is in stark contrast to what happens later in life in the mature visual system. Many older individuals have cataracts removed after prolonged periods of time of diminished visual input and their vision returns to normal.

It is important to emphasize what this body of research tells us and what it does not. It does demonstrate that several factors are absolutely required for the normal development of the visual system. First, one must have a full range of natural stimuli to develop a full range of neuronal connections, and second, it must be present during a particular period of time when the cortex is particularly plastic and responsive to synaptic activity associated with sensory input. It does not suggest that an increase in visual input beyond the natural stimuli typically available early in life will make any difference in terms of future intelligence or abilities. The absence of visual input during this critical period will produce an impairment. In the presence of normal visual input, the visual cortex will develop normally. Extra visual input will not necessarily improve cortical development or produce a brilliant artist or creative architect.

What other regions of the developing cortex show this type of dependence on environmental input? What are the other critical periods during which environmental stimulation and neuronal activity must be present for the nervous system to develop normally?

Functional magnetic resonance imaging (fMRI) is a noninvasive technique by which investigators can visualize the human brain while subjects are involved in certain tasks, from the mundane to the sophisticated. As a result, researchers are now asking questions of human development that were never possible before. A report addressed whether the developing auditory cortex has requirements similar to those observed in the visual cortex. Pantev and colleagues (1998) looked at fMRIs of the brains of musicians and compared them with controls who had never played an instrument. They found that the age at which musicians begin to play their instruments is related to the size of the cortical structures devoted to these skills. Also, the degree of cortical reorganization and the extent of cortical activity in response to musical notes are significantly different among musicians compared with controls. These results replicate earlier findings that show a similar enlargement of structures in the left hemisphere in musicians compared with nonmusicians (Schlaug, Jancke, Huang, & Steinmetz, 1995). These observations are consistent with the idea that environmental factors have an impact on cortical development.

These results should not be interpreted as suggesting that newborns should be given Mozart compact discs on leaving the nursery or that all 2- to 3-year-old children should receive expensive musical training. First, the findings must be replicated. Moreover, several possible explanations for the observed correlations can be put forward. It is possible that only children with a particular type of cortical response are capable and interested in playing an instrument at such an early age. It is also possible that children who begin to play at that age are brought up in musical families and hear more music at an earlier age, inducing greater cortical reorganization. These alternative hypotheses are testable, and the initial results must be replicated with suitable controls. These studies on the cortical representations for music, however, do support the idea that the cortex is a plastic organ that responds to environmental input by reorganizing relevant structures. Moreover, the studies suggest that the earlier one exposes children to musical training, the more significant the reorganization of the auditory cortex.

The ability of humans and other animals such as songbirds to develop vocalizations has been studied for many years (Doupe & Kuhl, 1999). It is well established that the time for learning either spoken language or birdsong is easiest accomplished when one is very young. A critical period for any behavior is defined as a period of time in which there is an enhanced sensitivity of the cortex to environmental inputs. It also refers to a failure of the cortex to develop normally in the absence of such experiences. The term *critical period* derives from the early work on visual experiences described previously, during which the time period for the impact of visual inputs are relatively short, end abruptly, and are absolutely necessary. After the window of opportunity has passed, no amount of visual input will allow the visual cortex to develop normally.

Some critical periods have less abrupt endings, and many investigators now prefer the term *sensitive period*. For example, the window of opportunity to learn a foreign language is never really closed. As many of us remember from personal experience, it is possible to learn a new language after the first decade of life. Nonetheless, it is much easier to learn a first or a second language as a toddler, and the skill with which one learns the new language is not equivalent across all ages. After puberty, second languages are often spoken with a significant accent, suggesting that the phonetics, intonation, and patterns of speech are established by different neural mechanisms that operate when a language is learned during childhood.

A number of studies have suggested that a sensitive period exists during childhood when language acquisition is most readily accomplished. It is considerably easier for children to recover from limited cerebral damage than it is for adults, and the prognosis for ultimate language recovery is more likely when the cortical damage occurs early in life than when it occurs after puberty (Bates, 1992). Finally, the ease with which very young children learn a second language is reflected in the speed and accuracy by which they speak compared with learning that occurs later in life.

An interesting series of studies looked at what happens to the cortex when adults learn language compared with what happens when children learn language (Kim, Relkin, Lee, & Hirsch, 1997). fMRIs in adults who learned a second language as adults compared with those who learned as children show that late-learners develop a new language center distinct from the one dedicated to their first language (Broca's area). This is in marked contrast to individuals who learned the second language early, whose native and second languages are both represented in the same cortical region. This suggests that early on, the neurons and connections within the language area are flexible enough to accommodate a second language, but after a sensitive or critical period, its connections are established and the circuitry needed for an additional language must come from somewhere else.

Related studies addressed long-term outcomes in children born with congenital deafness but provided with early intervention strategies (Downs & Yoshinaga-Itano, 1999). Children with hearing impairments are usually identified by the time they are 2½ years old, but screening tests can now detect congenital hearing loss by the age of 2 months. If there is a critical period of time during which the auditory cortex must receive auditory input in order to develop normally, it might be apparent in children with hearing impairments who were identified early and treated early compared with those detected later and treated later.

Yoshinaga-Itano, Sedey, Coulter, and Mehl (1998) looked at this question in deaf children who were diagnosed by the time they were 6 months old and received appropriate interventions and compared them with children who received similar services at a later age. Ninety percent of the children with early interventions developed vocabulary skills in sign language within the normal range compared with only 25% of those who received the later interventions. Those diagnosed late achieved vocabulary skills equivalent to the bottom 10% of children with normal language development. The authors concluded that there is a very short period of time when normal language develops in children and that a universal screening for hearing loss can prevent an absence of later communication skills in these children.

Taken together, these studies suggest that learning to speak and sign is more readily accomplished during the first years of life. They do not indicate, however, the absolute closing of a "window," as was seen with the development of the visual system. It is possible with effort to learn other languages after puberty, although different cortical regions appear to be involved, and the process is not as seamless and effortless as when a young child learns the same skills.

THE HEAD START DEBATE

As our understanding of critical periods deepens, national policy should be adjusted accordingly. But because this area of study is still developing, we must be careful to avoid misunderstandings that could influence policy decisions. The very idea of a critical period often raises parental concern. The notion of sensitive periods for cortical development raises the fear that we might miss a window of opportunity and leave our children wanting. Early childhood intervention programs might miss these sensitive periods in terms of early identification or intervention, wasting valuable assets and resources. Some suggest that a backlash is coming to research in developmental neuroscience as the timing and value of many early intervention paradigms are being questioned.

Backlash or not, we are experiencing some leavening of what has been a productive period of consciousness raising regarding the significance of the early years to a child's well-being across his or her life span. As child psychiatrists, neuroscientists, and developmentalists, we are now more keenly aware than ever of the interplay between the genes and environmental factors that shape healthy development. Social networks, economics, and physical habitat shape the well-being of children on a daily basis.

The state also influences the well-being of its children with its laws and policies. Because such laws and policies are shaped by politics, they are eroded and then rebuilt depending on who is in power and who the visionaries are at the time. *Explicit* policies, such as child protective services, may powerfully influence a child's well-being. *Implicit* policies can be equally powerful, such as the presence, or absence, of an organized paid parental leave policy. Policies of *omission* might include the lack of a national policy toward universal health insurance, particularly for young children.

At the same time, Head Start, Early Head Start, and Healthy Start compete for finite financial resources. Their relative success depends on local politics, regional politics, and family values above or below the Mason Dixon Line and east or west of the Mississippi. A recent trend toward focusing on the child as independent of the context in which he or she is being raised is of limited value because it disregards an important set of environmental influences.

Large disparities exist between the services provided to children at risk from one state to the next and will continue to persist. Some states are notoriously neglectful, others are benign, and still others are helpful and supportive. This situation was even more extreme in the earlier years of ZERO TO THREE: National Center for Infants, Toddlers and Families, which was founded in 1977. The idea that anyone might be interested in the early years outside of a few small bands of far-flung zealots seemed remarkable. At that time, only a small group of pediatricians, child psychiatrists, psychoanalysts, developmental psychologists, social workers, policy makers, philanthropists, nurses, and early childhood educators wanted to think together about the importance of the early years. At the beginning of the 21st century, the early years of child development are cover stories for the leading national news magazines. Happy as we are to have their attention, media coverage of these scientific issues is often oversimplified and leads to misunderstandings and misrepresentations.

There is no simple way to describe what the early years are about. Most of what is known is still in its own early years of development. We try to be cautious with what is presented in the news media, but this is often the only source of information for America's parents.

Some parents recoil at the idea that science might have something important to tell us. Others are too eager to take up the latest fad about sleep, toilet training, or discipline and buy all of the related products. They need authoritative and understandable information that can convey the importance of the early years without oversimplifying, or overstating its significance. So far, our efforts in this area have fallen short.

One of the firsts signs of potential backlash to ideas about critical periods appeared in a *Newsweek* editorial regarding the Comprehensive Child Development Project (Samuelson, 1998). This was a closely watched demonstration project designed to test certain ideas about early intervention. The editorial concluded that all publicly supported programs designed to help children and their families in poverty were a waste of money. This was based on the lack of positive findings in an initial report on the project: No differences were found between the served and the unserved groups of children and their parents. This fundamental misunderstanding of how science advances left the public with the false impression that the money and effort were wasted. When activist Bill Harris got an advance copy of this editorial, he said, with ashen expression and hand shaking, "It's over, it's just over." This strong advocate was, however, already mobilizing his own conviction that it certainly was far from over, and he was already planning his response.

A more scholarly analysis of the Child Development Project was conducted by Walter Gilliam and Ed Zigler (Gilliam, 2000; Gilliam, Ripple, Zigler, & Leiter, 2000). They engaged in a dialectic about what was right and what was wrong with the timing and nature of the initial evaluation and presented exactly what we need to know about how the firestorm of criticism started.

Another example of backlash came with the publication of *The Myth of the First Three Years: A New Understanding of Early Brain Development and Lifelong Learning* (Bruer, 1999). The author, a foundation director with no training in child development or neuroscience, set out to debunk current research about the relationship between early learning and early experience. He was apparently distressed at the "overselling" of this connection by the then First Lady Hillary Clinton and actor and producer Rob Reiner. The author suggested that most early intervention programs are ill advised because there is "little if any science" to prove that they are needed. Although the author's own ideas and his distress with Hillary Clinton's advocacy take up more space than any useful discussion of the research on critical periods, this publication did succeed in opening a lively debate.

Malcolm Gladwell talks about this book in the *New Yorker* (January 10, 2000) and comes to some remarkable conclusions. He describes Bruer as being distressed about the scientific irresponsibility of the claims made by the I Am Your Child campaign, which was put together by Rob Reiner and supported by Hillary Clinton. The central point of the campaign is that the first years of life are the most important years according to brain and developmental research, and we, as a society, should be focusing far more energy and resources on these earliest years. Indeed, one particularly damaging oversimplification that came out of the campaign implied that significant brain growth is over by the end of the first 3 years when it assuredly is not.

Unfortunately, Bruer used his criticism of this particular campaign to put forward his own hyperbole: that we don't know much of anything that *really* matters about the early years. He depends on the opinion of Steve Peterson, a neuroscientist from Washington University, to say that neuroscience offers such weak support for the significance of the early years, that the only real advice to parents should be "don't raise your children in a closet, starve them, or hit them in the head with a frying pan" (cited in Bruer, 1999, p. 188). Whatever else you do won't really make that much difference. He refers to Romanian orphanage studies suggesting that infants who spent their first years severely deprived tended to recover. Of course this statement is itself an oversimplification.

Bruer began well when he wrote a scholarly piece in the *Educational Researcher* called "Education and the Brain: A Bridge Too Far" (Bruer, 1997). In it he provided an examination of the ways in which findings in the scientific literature are blown out of proportion when we imply that we know how to increase the neural connections of the child's brain and ultimately the child's intelligence. Take the so-called Mozart effect. The notion is that playing classical music to infants boosts a child's IQ score. Bruer rightly pointed out that this idea was popularized in the press, as Mozart CDs for infants and parents appeared, although no clear foundation in science existed in the first place.

The journal *Nature* published two critical articles on the Mozart effect (Rauscher, Shaw, & Ky, 1993). The original authors were able to clarify that they had found some effects, but these were not in infants and not permanent (Rauscher, 1999). Rather, their work had been performed with elementary students and the short-lived effects were in spatial-temporal task performance, not in intelligence quotients per se.

Bruer's book is written for an antiscience, antimedicine audience. But although the neuroscience of early childhood is in many ways in its own infancy, it is not irrelevant or ill-motivated. It is simply not finished. Far too soon, Bruer comes to the extreme conclusion that what happens to a child in the early years is of little consequence to subsequent intellectual, moral, or social development. He suggests that intervening in the lives of very young children at risk for poor school adaptation has little or no effect. We are concerned that parents are now confused about what infants need and what they can do to encourage healthy development. We are equally concerned that certain predisposed policy makers will see these arguments as an excuse to ignore the growing interest and demand for policies and services to support developing children, particularly those with special needs.

This much is true. Neuroscientists have only begun to sort out how trillions of cellular connections among billions of neurons in the child's brain get organized during the first 3 years of life to allow a child to learn, speak, feel, and reason. The early and exciting research has sometimes been exaggerated, particularly by the media. It has also been used prematurely to make claims about what parents, educators, and policy makers should or should not be doing. Every graduate student knows that work published in scientific journals is often too new to be reliable—it's not true yet—not until scientists have had time to replicate, expand, and refine the early findings.

Much confusion centers on the incorrect notion that the first 3 years are *the* sensitive period, or window of opportunity, for neural circuitry to be established in the child's brain and that at the end of 3 years, that window is shut tight. As we saw earlier in this chapter, there are indeed several periods when various sensory and motor skills are best learned, but a child's brain is not even close to being completely wired by the time the third candle is placed on the birthday cake.

In fact, research suggests just the opposite. Important parts of the brain are not fully developed until well past puberty as the brain changes and continues to produce new architecture. The human brain is capable of learning and laying down novel circuitry until old age. Nonetheless, there is no doubt that something about the first 3 years of life has a critical impact on intelligence and personality.

The importance of the first 3 years is hardly exaggerated. Parents and policy makers must not be misled. Critical issues and eras in the first 3 years of life include the origins of trust in relationships, the bedrock of self-image and self-regard, the earliest structures in the management of one's impulses and self-control, the earliest manifestations of competence, and the emergence of desire for mastery. Intelligence and achievement in school do not depend solely on the young child's fund of factual information or her or his ability to read or recite the alphabet and be familiar with numbers and colors.

An example of an emerging skill that appears around 9–11 months is what happens when the parent points to an object to direct the infant's attention. The infant begins to look not at the end of the finger but at *what* the parent is showing him or her. When we point, we don't mean to direct the infant to the end of our finger but to the object of interest. This is shared attention, courtesy of a critical period. This is a tidy example of the emergence of a skill by the end of a sensitive period and the capacity of parents to respond appropriately. This is not something we teach children to do. Their brains have matured sufficiently with the appropriate synaptic connections to perform this task, and it shows up right on time.

But what if no one was there to participate in shared attention? Would it develop? Or does it require that curiosity be shared and jointly enjoyed to flourish? When no one is there to respond, it happens far less often. We don't know what happens to that child's intelligence or interest in the outside world, but he or she apparently becomes less interested in simply being curious for its own sake, and pointing has far less relational value.

Successful learning requires that children of whatever background come to school curious, confident, and aware of what is expected of them. All aspects of development affect one another, and children cannot learn or display their intelligence effectively if they have been deprived of a natural sensory, motor, and social environment.

Some members of our society may be offended by Bruer's assertion that middle-class families provide the best model for secure emotional attachment:

> One thing we do know from research on attachment is that mothers who behave in acceptable, American, middle-class fashion tend to have securely attached children. The challenge is to get more noncompliant, mostly minority and disadvantaged mothers to act in this way. (1999, p. 195)

We know that there are many poor minority parents who raise children with securely attached relationships. Stigmatizing minority, racial, and ethnic groups by defining them as the exception to the rule is hardly a model for a good public policy.

If policy makers come away from Bruer's book with the misconception that all efforts to help young children are a waste of money and time, it is because this appears to be Bruer's intention. While attacking the very modest funding provided to such programs as Early Head Start, a desperately needed initiative, where is the balanced treatment of the ample evidence of the value of early intervention gathered long ago? Instead, we are supplied with notions of infant determinism—a straw man turned to dust decades ago. Lost on opponents of Head Start is the profound implication that infants as well have an impact on the nurturing transaction. Early experience is an interaction that is profoundly shaped by the transactions between caregiver and infant (Sameroff & Fiese, 1990).

Pioneering work done in the 1970s by Sally Provence describes a very different picture. Provence studied two groups of families with young children over a period of several years. Both were at risk for poor outcomes in school and adulthood. One group was offered free medical care and high-quality child care. In addition, they received health care and parental support and assistance in learning how to be more responsive parents to their particular children. The other group was simply observed (Provence & Naylor, 1983).

Provence found that, by the time the children of both groups were school age, those who had received the interventions missed far less school, were able to learn and retain information more easily, were more easily motivated, and their mothers had fewer children that were spaced farther apart.

Our infants come to us so vulnerable and capable of growth at astonishing speed. They are simply amazing in their capabilities, yet so needing of us for their very lives. What do they arrive with and what are we to do? Our bewilderment easily gives rise to myths, but Wordsworth reassures us

> *Not in entire forgetfulness,*
> *And not in utter nakedness,*
> *But trailing clouds of glory do we come* (Wordsworth, *Ode: Intimations of Immortality from Recollections of Early Childhood*)

REFERENCES

Adams, J. (1996). Similarities in genetic mental retardation and neuroteratogenic syndromes. *Pharmacology, Biochemistry & Behavior, 55,* 683–690.

American Psychiatric Association. (1994). *Diagnostic and statistical manual of mental disorders* (4th ed.). Washington, DC: Author.

Amir, R.E., Van den Veyver, I.B., Wan, M., Tran, C.Q., Francke, U., & Zoghbi, H.Y. (1999). Rett syndrome is caused by mutations in X-linked MECP2, encoding methyl-CpG-binding protein 2. *Nature Genetics, 23,* 185–188.

Bailey, A., Le Couteur, A., Bottesman, I., Boulton, P., Simonoff, E., Yuzda, E., et al. (1995). Autism as a strongly genetic disorder: Evidence from a British twin study. *Psychological Medicine, 25,* 63–77.

Bates, E. (1992). Language development. *Current Opinion in Neurobiology, 2,* 180–185.

Bruer, J.T. (1997). Education and the brain: A bridge too far. *Educational Researcher, 41,* 123–139.

Bruer, J.T. (1999). *The myth of the first three years: A new understanding of early brain development and life-long learning.* New York: Williams and Wilkins.

Doupe, A.J., & Kuhl, P.K. (1999). Birdsong and human speech: Common themes and mechanisms. *Annual Review of Neuroscience, 22,* 567–631.

Downs, M.P., & Yoshinaga-Itano, C. (1999). The efficacy of early identification and intervention for children with hearing impairment. *Pediatric Clinics of North America, 46,* 79–87.

Folstein, S., & Rutter, M. (1977). Infantile autism: A genetic study of 21 twin pairs. *Journal of Child Psychology and Psychiatry and Allied Disciplines, 18,* 297–321.

Gilliam, W.S. (2000). On over-generalizing from overly-simplistic evaluations of complex social programs: In further response to Goodson, Layzer, St. Pierre, and Bernstein. *Early Childhood Research Quarterly, 15*(1).

Gilliam, W.S., Ripple, C.H., Zigler, E.F., & Leiter, V. (2000). Evaluating child and family demonstration initiatives: Lessons from the Comprehensive Child Development Program. *Early Childhood Research Quarterly, 15,* 41–59.

Hubel, D.H., & Wiesel, T.N. (1970). The period of susceptibility to the physiological effects of unilateral eye closure in kittens. *The Journal of Physiology, 206,* 419–436.

International Molecular Genetic Study of Autism Consortium. (1998). A full genome screen for autism with evidence for linkage to a region on chromosome 7q. *Human Molecular Genetics, 7,* 571–578.

Jamain, S., Quach, H., Betancur, C., Rastam, M., Colineaux, C., Gillberg, I.C., et al. (2003). Mutations of the X-linked genes encoding neuroligins NLGN3 and NLGN4 are associated with autism. *Nature Genetics, 4,* 27–29.

Kanner, L. (1943). Autistic disturbances of affective contact. *Nervous Child, 2,* 217–250.

Kim, K.H.S., Relkin, N.R., Lee, K.M., & Hirsch, J. (1997). Distant cortical areas associated with native and second languages. *Nature, 388,* 171–174.

Leckman, J.F., & Lombroso, P.J. (2001). Genes and developmental neurobiology. In M. Lewis (Ed.), *Child and adolescent psychiatry: A comprehensive textbook* (2nd ed., pp. 1–9). New York: Williams & Wilkins.

Nan, X., Campoy, J., & Bird, A. (1997). MeCP2 is a transcriptional repressor with abundant binding sites in genomic chromatin. *Cell, 88,* 471–481.

Pantev, C., Oostenveld, R., Englien, A., Ross, B., Roberts, L.E., & Hoke, M. (1998). Increased auditory cortical representation in musicians. *Nature, 392,* 811–814.

Philippe, A., Martinez, M., Guilloud-Bataille, M., Gillberg, C., Rastam, M., Sponheim, E., et al. (1999). Genome-wide scan for autism susceptibility genes. *Human Molecular Genetics, 8,* 805–812.

Provence, S., & Naylor, A. (1983). *Working with disadvantaged parents and their children: Scientific and practice issues.* New Haven, CT: Yale University Press.

Rauscher, F.H. (1999). Reply to: Prelude or requiem for the 'Mozart effect'? *Nature, 400,* 827–828.

Rauscher, F.H., Shaw, G.L., & Ky, K.N. (1993). Music and spatial task performance. *Nature, 365,* 611.

Risch, N., Spiker, D., Lotspeich, L., Nouri, N., Hinds, D., Hallmayer, J., et al. (1999). A genomic screen of autism: Evidence for a multilocus etiology. *American Journal of Human Genetics, 65,* 493–507.

Sameroff, A.J., & Fiese, B.H. (1990). Transactional regulation and early intervention. In S.J. Meisels and J.P. Shonkoff (Eds.), *Handbook of early childhood intervention* (pp. 119–149). Cambridge, MA: Cambridge University Press.

Samuelson, R.J., (1998). Investing in our children. *Newsweek, 131,*(8), 45.

Schlaug, G., Jancke, L., Huang, Y., & Steinmetz, H. (1995). In vivo evidence of structural brain asymmetry in musicians. *Science, 267,* 699–701.

Shatz, C.J. (1990). Impulse activity and the patterning of connections during CNS development. *Neuron, 5,* 745–756.

Steffenburg, S., Gillberg, C., Hellgren, L., Andersson, L., Gillberg, I.C., Jakobsson, G., et al. (1989). A twin study of autism in Denmark, Finland, Iceland, Norway and Sweden. *Journal of Child Psychology and Psychiatry and Allied Disciplines, 30,* 405–416.

Veenstra-VanderWeele, J., Kim, S.J., Lord, C., Courchesne, R., Akshoomoff, N., Leventhal, B.L., et al. (2003). Transmission disequilibrium studies of the serotonin 5-HT2A receptor gene (HTR2A) in autism. *American Journal of Medical Genetics, 114,* 277–283.

Yonan, A.L., Alarcon, M., Cheng, R., Magnusson, P.K., Spence, S.J., Palmer, A.A., et al. (2003). A genomewide screen of 345 families for autism-susceptibility loci. *American Journal of Human Genetics, 73,* 886–897.

Yoshinaga-Itano, C., Sedey, A.L., Coulter, D.K., & Mehl, A.L. (1998). Language of early- and later-identified children with hearing loss. *Pediatrics, 102,* 1161–1171.

CHAPTER 32

The Environmental Mystique

Training the Intellect
versus Development of the Child

EDWARD ZIGLER

This chapter is an adaptation from a classic paper published in 1970. It was written in response to wild swings in the nature–nurture pendulum that were occurring at the time. Behavioral scientists had abandoned their long-held belief that child development is a maturational process governed mainly by genes and biology. They had jumped to the opposite extreme, proclaiming that a child's potential is almost unlimited if the proper environmental nutrients are fed during circumscribed magical periods in development. Such claims inspired great expectations for the new Head Start program, making the disappointment that much stronger when it failed to meet unattainable goals. Public sentiment gravitated toward the opposite extreme again, when dashed hopes led many to concede that little could be done to improve the life's chances of children born and raised in poverty. By the end of the 20th century, neuroscientific studies of early brain development rekindled dreams that proper environmental stimulation during critical periods of cognitive development could produce a nation of geniuses. "The Environmental Mystique" is reprinted here to lend a sense of balance to the current reincarnation of the nature–nurture controversy, the same purpose it had when originally written.

Not too many years ago, in the heyday of John Dewey and his adherents, education in general was very much concerned about the emotional development of the child; emphasized were the child's personal adjustment and overall contribution to a democratic society. Acceptance of this popular point of view eventually fell into disfavor, however, due in part to excesses by those who did not comprehend it fully. The falling away had nothing to do with children intrinsically or with the inherent nature of a good education. It had

From a paper by the same title that appeared in *Childhood Education*, 1970, 46, 402–412. Adapted by permission of Edward Zigler and the Association for Childhood Education International, 17904 Georgia Avenue, Suite 215, Olney, MD 20832. Copyright © 1970 by the Association.

more to do with the spirit of the time, a *zeitgeist* that had a tremendous impact especially on early childhood education.

Our attitudes were seriously jolted with the launching of Sputnik. It appeared that the entire American populace panicked—"My Lord, the Russians are ahead of us!" The critics arose in swarms to attack the education system. A cry went up: "The Russians are training children in mathematics, scientific concepts and engineering, while we are training our children in finger-painting. We must do something! Enough of this adjustment nonsense!" Shortly thereafter, the nation witnessed a super-swing of the pendulum toward the three R's. Reading, writing, and arithmetic were *in.* Concern for the adjustment of the child gave way to concern for cognitive development. The always implicit and sometimes explicit question here was: "How do we make our children smarter so that we may build bigger and better Sputniks than the Russians?"

APOSTLES OF THE ENVIRONMENTAL MYSTIQUE

Simultaneously, there developed in this country an emphasis that actually has rather long historical roots, a viewpoint with great appeal because of our nation's particular philosophy concerning the nature of man. This point of view I have referred to in a previous work as the "environmental mystique." In its simplest form, the environmental mystique holds that intelligence is essentially trainable: The intellect (that collection of cognitive processes—memory, concept formation, the formal structures of cognition and intelligence) is essentially the result of environmental input and, in essence, that intelligence is an environmental product. This viewpoint, this environmental mystique, is sweeping the country just as it did in the post-Sputnik era. Back then, Hunt's (1961) book, *Intelligence and Experience,* became the credo, almost the Bible, of the environmental mystique. The very title, *Intelligence and Experience,* many interpreted to mean that if we could just get the right experiences into children, they would all be brilliant.

I found Hunt's book a healthy theoretical treatise, but the implications as they were spelled out to the layperson I considered *not* so healthy. For example, *Reader's Digest* published an interview with Dr. Hunt, advertising it on a flier attached to the cover that provocatively read, "How To Raise Your Child's IQ by 20 Points." Other spokespersons for the environmental mystique had no trouble finding reporters who would listen. In articles in both *Harper's* and *The New York Times Magazine,* "eminent child-development specialist" Maya Pines told the world, "What we need for the poor children of this country is a pressure-cooker education." I encountered people who were actually persuaded by a *Time* magazine report of a particular remedial program to believe that shouting loudly at children makes them smarter.

Life carried a feature article on the work of Professor Burton White and his colleagues with infants of Harvard-MIT personnel. Cited was the "finding" that putting mobiles and other moving objects over cribs of young infants caused them to do better on certain developmental tasks than infants who weren't exposed to these objects. What was not emphasized was that the correlation between the developmental abilities measured and later intelligence is about zero.

Actually, I always thought well of White's research efforts; what I objected to were the popularized implications of this work. Mothers, anxiety-laden because they didn't put mobiles over their infants' cribs, often asked me what they could do to rectify the tragic error they didn't realize they made until their children were 17 or 18 years old. Someone must finally stand and say, "Look, these are hypotheses, theories, and preliminary findings. We actually know little about changing the formal structure of the intellect. Experiments have been promising, but it is much too early to speak in terms of those specific events that produce intelligence. It's just not that simple."

Another whose work was used to support the environmental mystique was Professor Bruner of Harvard, for whom I had great respect but with whom I would take issue on views concerning the plasticity of the intellect. He was fond of talking of technology. The notion was that with the right technology, we could increase both the rate and the final level of cognitive achievement.

All this was reminiscent of reports in New York papers concerning the work of the Deutsches in New York, reports that certainly were not the fault of the investigators. The Deutsches found an increase of approximately 10 IQ points in children attending their nursery school—an observation reported in the paper as indicative of "A Point a Month IQ Increase." Thus, all you have to do is send your child to this particular nursery school and his or her IQ will be raised a point a month. If true, many of us would like to send our own children there for 40 to 50 months' worth.

Limitations of the Research

We are all indebted to the researchers mentioned, for the work needs doing; I was long engaged in much the same sort of research myself. What I object to is the naïve acceptance of the environmental mystique without a careful analysis of what the research actually shows, the limitations of the research, and the implications of this work for our understanding of the development of cognitive processes. Findings are seized on to support the view that all differences in cognitive functioning are due solely to differences in environmental input—a point of view I cannot accept. The mysteries of cognitive development have not been resolved sufficiently to allow for a comprehensive educational technology. The gimmicks and gadgets being used with young children are not the optimal means of producing intelligence. Many of these devices have been built on theoretical efforts that have not been developed to the point that would allow such technological derivations.

Much more is involved here than profits (from sales of the gimmickry) and the quality of the theoretical papers. Actually, the papers of Hunt, White, Bruner, and the Deutsches are good, provided their impact is made on people who understand them and can build on them. The concern is with the increasing adherence to a point of view about children, especially economically disadvantaged children, which in the long run may be potentially harmful to them.

HEAD START AND THE ENVIRONMENTAL MYSTIQUE

The environmental mystique permeated our views concerning Head Start programs from the beginning. It has been found that in many of the programs the children's IQ scores do rise initially, but they do not permanently become more intelligent. For those who have accepted the environmental mystique, the only logical conclusion is that something is lacking either in the children or the individuals attempting to teach them. Some feel that the poor child is beyond help.

Lessons from the Mental Orthopedics Movement

In an earlier era in the history of education in this country, the environmental mystique also held sway, albeit with a somewhat different type of child. I refer to a period in the training of children with mental retardation when the notion of mental orthopedics was in ascendancy. The idea was that, given the right kind of experience and training, intellectually retarded children could be made "normal." State schools were originally set up in the country with this idea in mind.

Early in the 20th century, children with mental retardation did not live in state schools but instead participated in special training programs. (Interestingly, many of the practices involved in these programs, in vogue a century ago, are being rediscovered as "enrichment programs.") Did people with mental retardation become normal as a result? They did not. The professional became negative about children with mental retardation, asserting that the best that could be done for them was assignment to state institutions. This point in time, when the state schools became custodial institutions, was when the treatment of people with mental retardation entered its darkest phase. If we are not realistic in our expectations for children, if we expect too much, demand too much, the pendulum seems to pull us in the opposite direction. Reaction to overoptimism seems to be undue pessimism in which we assert that little can be done for at-risk children. This conclusion, of course, is not valid.

We are far from understanding the nature of cognitive development. We can certainly all agree that experience interacts with the child's genetic endowment in the production of intelligence. We have not discovered any sure-fire experiences that invariably make the individual wind up at an intellectual level higher than that which he or she could have attained without them. A common view is that intelligence is furthered by whatever it is that modal middle-class parents do. I, for one, would certainly object to any extreme environmental position. Anyone who denies the fact of native endowment is ignoring a convincing body of evidence.

Points of View About Cognitive Development

Answers that have been offered to this question of the role of environment have varied tremendously. At one extreme are the neo-Gesellians, whose views represent a strong nativistic, antienvironmentalist position that still has many followers. Within such a position, cognitive development is seen as being, in many ways, an unfolding process. Thus, if you guarantee the child a normal environment, defined in relatively broad limits, the child's cognitive abilities will naturally develop, a supposition that reminds us of the preformationistic or predeterministic views of cognitive development. At the other extreme are the advocates of the environmental mystique, to whom all differences in cognitive development are viewed as the result of differences in experiences.

Falling somewhere between these extremes are others who assert that the child is not influenced equally by every experience. These thinkers have emphasized such phenomena as critical experiences, viewing the impact of an experience as determined by the particular point in cognitive development in which the child happens to be. Several other possibilities of cognitive development present themselves, but no theorist has yet, to my satisfaction, totally illuminated the nature of intellectual development. It must be admitted that both experiences and endowment are important. However, exactly how experience interacts with the inherent characteristics of the individual remains far from clear.

The formal intellect of the child is not as plastic as the supporters of the environmental mystique would have us believe. The notion that we will produce a homogeneous race of geniuses through the programming of experiences is a daydream, a daydream I find contrary to a very basic biological law; namely, the law of human variability. We are not going to repeal that law. The very nature of the gene pool of our population will always guarantee variability in cognitive development.

I take exception to another aspect of the environmental mystique and the teaching methods to which it has given rise; namely, the inherent view of the child's learning process as contained in Pines's request for a pressure-cooker approach to children and held by many others who speak to us of the mass acceleration of intellectual growth. These individuals basically mistrust and misunderstand the nature of the child in his or her development. Buried in their hurry-up efforts is the question, "How do we make the child learn?" In my opinion, learning is the natural condition of the child.

The child learns for the same reason that birds fly. You do not need to force learning on the child. Learning is an inherent feature of being a human being. The only meaningful question, therefore, is not "*Why* do children learn?" but, "Why is it that some children do not learn?" Approached in this way, the problem is not one of getting intelligence into nonlearners but rather of determining the conditions and attitudes that interfere with the natural process of learning. We are all aware that children learned before cognitive theorists told us how and before the invention of talking typewriters and computers. Indeed, children learned before schools of any sort existed. How could this learning have been possible without the formal programming of experiences that we have come to associate with the formal education process? The answer, I think, is that in the natural state the child is a much more autonomous learner than adherents of the pressure-cooker approach would believe. I am convinced children do most of their learning on their own and often the way to maximize it is simply to let them alone. They accomplish some of the most significant learning in their everyday interactions with the environment. Learning for the child is, thus, a continuous process and not one limited to the formal instruction and whizbang remedial efforts that have recently captured our attention.

This point of view is not particularly unique. It can be found readily in the theoretical statements of Montessori and other early childhood workers who have profound respect for the importance of play, curiosity, the natural give-and-take between the child and his or her environment. If we were to put these views into practice and diligently structure situations so that the child could have maximal commerce with the environment and utilize the constructive aspects of play and other natural features of development, we would in the long run develop more intelligence than would evolve from Pines's pressure cookers. Unfortunately, proponents of this philosophy are only voices in the wilderness.

Whatever the nature of cognitive development might be, such development has been overemphasized in our society. Too many leaders view the child, whether in a crib or in a

Head Start center, as a small computer that adults must program. What is not emphasized is that cognitive development and/or intelligence does not equal social competence.

IQ MYTHOLOGY

Why are we that concerned about intelligence anyway? Is it that great a predictor of the
way someone behaves? A substantial amount of literature on children with mental retardation speaks to this point. Workers once thought that the prognosis for children with
metal retardation who were institutionalized could be determined by giving an intelligence test, a simple and appealing view. If the child had a relatively high IQ score, he or
she would be socially competent when released from the institution; if the IQ score was
low, so would competence be. It eventually became evident there is little relation between
IQ and the ability to function in our society for children whose IQ scores are in the mild
and moderate ranges. Even in children of normal intellect, the relation between intelligence and a variety of social competence indices is not striking. On school achievement
measures that should be highly related to intelligence, the typical correlation between IQ
score and achievement is about .50, which means that intelligence can account for about
25% of the variation in achievement. Behavior is not determined solely by the formal
computer between the individual's ears. Furthermore, our society must be concerned with
more than just producing geniuses. Our society would hardly advance if everyone was
Einstein.

Intelligence and Alienation

The major crisis confronting our nation is not solely one of intelligence or the lack thereof.
The violence and drug dealings in our cities do not have a great deal to do with formal
characteristics of the intellect. It really makes little difference if the individual who sells
the drugs or the individual who shoots down the dealer has an IQ score of 55 or 155. More
important than intellectual level is the fact that many of these individuals have had experiences that have alienated them from our society. The attitudes of these people toward
themselves and others are such that they find it difficult to contribute to society and actualize themselves within its framework. We should all be aware that part of the problem
here is due to faults inherent in our society, such as failures in the education system, pervasive violence in television programming, and diminished respect for others.

We must be just as concerned with the development of positive attitudes and motives as with the development of the intellect. Failure to appreciate how much a child's
values, motives, and general psychological orientation determine his or her social competence as an adult has led to misunderstanding of what optimal child development is all
about and to interacting with the child in an erroneous fashion.

"What's Your Name?"

In the case of a child who is economically disadvantaged, error has often been made in
that, instead of approaching him or her as a whole child, as a dynamic ongoing system,
we think only in terms of cognitive input-output. We ask a little boy, "What's your
name?" and what we sometimes get is, "I don't know." Such a response is likely to be
judged as a direct reflection of the poor quality of the child's cognitive system.

Let us look at this matter, not as cognitive theorists, but from the perspective of the child being questioned. When do you ask the child to tell you his name? Typically, on the first day of school. He arrives at school, knowing only the culture of the inner-city housing projects. A woman he knows nothing about asks him to tell her his name. The problem such a child has at this point has little to do with the formal cognitive system and much with the attitudes toward strangers that he has developed during a formative period in his life.

When asked his name by the teacher, his thoughts are probably concerned with the following doubts, unworded but partly formed concepts: "Why does she want to know? Is she a police lady? Something to do with welfare? She looks friendly—maybe I should tell her . . . no, it might cause trouble—don't tell strangers anything—keep your mouth shut." What the teacher gets out of him is, "I don't know." The teacher whose orientation is a cognitive one concludes that this child is so stupid he does not know his own name. He knows his name as well as you know yours.

Something *is* wrong with this child, but it is not a cognitive defect. He is defective in the sense that he is interacting with the teacher in a way that is self-defeating. His psychological stance, his orientation, is overly cautious to the extent that it takes him out of the mainstream of an educational system as it is typically structured. If the teacher wishes to help, the answer is not careful teaching of the child's own name, but giving him those experiences that will lead to his interacting with a strange adult in a trusting way.

IQ Tests and Effective Behavior

Failure to appreciate the importance of motivational and emotional factors in the child's performance has led us to overemphasize, misinterpret, and misunderstand the implications of those findings that have reported increased IQ scores in poor children following a nursery school experience. As is the case for any behavior, performance of the child on an IQ test essentially reflects three factors:

1. *Formal cognitive ability*—a factor studied at great length by such workers as Piaget, Bruner, and Hunt.

2. *The child's achievements*—determined in large part by idiosyncratic experiences. It is possible to separate formal cognition from the child's achievements. Thus, a child may have a formal cognitive system adequate to the task of storing information concerning the definition of the word *gown,* but if he has never heard the word *gown* and you ask him what it is, his answer must be that he does not know. The problem is the lack of particular achievement caused by the nature of the child's experiences. To consider this child stupid would be just as erroneous as to consider a middle-class child stupid who has not experienced that particular set of events that includes the definitions of *chittlings* and *wino.*

3. *The motivational and emotional system*—It is possible to get an "I don't know" response from a child whose formal cognitive system and achievements are both adequate to the task at hand. Competing motivational responses may result in performance far below that dictated by his or her cognitive and achievement abilities.

Earl Butterfield and I (Zigler & Butterfield, 1968) once examined the nature of changes in poor children's IQ performance following a nursery school experience. We discovered that the improvement in IQ score, averaging about 10 points, was due not to changes in the formal intellectual functioning of the child but rather to changes in the motivational system. These Head Start children enter the program with 10 more points of intelligence than they are capable of using in the standard test or, for that matter, in standard school situations. The Head Start experience doesn't make the children inherently brighter. The extremely worthwhile thing that it does do is to give them those experiences that, by the end of the year, allow them to use, in a standard testing situation, all of their intelligence.

My purpose is not to belittle the role of experience in the development of formal cognition. By all means, let us continue to work on how and when particular experiences influence the development of specific cognitive process. But my bet is that a considerably larger pay-off would result if we spent as much time in our Head Start centers getting children to use the 10 points of intelligence that motivational factors cause to lie dormant as we do trying to add 10 more IQ points to the child's potential. If we work directly on those motivational and emotional factors that often constitute the roots of a child's ineffectual behavior, the entire IQ issue falls into proper perspective. As long as we worship cognition, remedial efforts such as Head Start will be evaluated in terms of IQ score changes, which will be misinterpreted as the inexorable reflection of changes in the child's formal cognitive system. We can appreciate the importance of cognition, while at the same time attending to those other aspects of the child's development that are clearly important in determining what type of adult the child will become.

Again, the proper goal of education is not the production of intellectual paragons but rather the production of adjusted individuals representing a wide spectrum of intellectual ability, who actualize themselves as human beings given whatever intellectual potential they have.

Those of us who believe in the importance of emotional and motivational factors in a child's development must do more than engage in polemics; we must demonstrate through sound empirical research the important role played by motivational factors. We must isolate experimentally the specific emotional and motivational variables that interfere with the child's competence across a wide variety of tasks. We must discover which particular experiences give rise to self-defeating motives. And, most important for educators, we must discover those experiences that ameliorate the effects of such negative factors. My colleagues and I for many years engaged in just such efforts at Yale. We uncovered a number of motivational variables that characterize the nonlearning child, and we demonstrated that motivational effects can be manipulated experimentally in just as rigorous a fashion as other types of variables. For example, we found that the child's history of deprivation or failure, motivation for attention and affection, wariness of adults, views of self, and expectancy of success are just as important determinants of behavior as formal cognition.

The question is not really one of being tough-minded or tender-minded but simply of being committed to a view that motivational and emotional development are just as important as intellectual development. If we are going to fulfill our obligations to the children in our care and to the society in which both they and we are members, we must be equally concerned with both the cognitive and the personal development of the child. Little chance exists that our current theorists will allow us to forget the cognitive system.

But, regardless of the current theoretical emphasis, it behooves each and every one of us to direct considerable effort to the proper emotional, social, and motivational adjustment of a child. The oft-heard truism that the early years are highly important for child development firmly applies to emotional and social development as well as cognition. Only by consciously directing our efforts to the development of *both* of these aspects of human growth will we be producing the kinds of individuals who can shape a better world.

REFERENCES

Hunt, J. McV. (1961). *Intelligence and experience.* New York: Ronald Press.

Zigler, E., & Butterfield, E.C. (1968). Motivational aspects of changes in IQ test performance of culturally deprived nursery school children. *Child Development, 39,* 1–14.

CHAPTER 33

Coordinating
Head Start with the States

WADE F. HORN

W elfare reform, as codified through the Personal Responsibility and Work Opportunity Reconciliation Act of 1996 (PRWORA), seeks to move millions of previously welfare-dependent heads of households, primarily single mothers, into the paid labor force. Doing so will require that we put their children somewhere. In many cases, that somewhere will be out-of-home child care.

To help states with this task, more than $52 billion has been spent in state and federal funding for child care over the first 6 years of welfare reform (including the required state match, maintenance of effort, and fiscal year 1997 2002 appropriated funding). Still, some worry that there are not enough funds available for child care, particularly if stronger work requirements are included in the next re-authorization of the welfare reform program, known as Temporary Assistance to Needy Families (TANF). One place to look for additional child care opportunities is Head Start.

In fact, Head Start and the TANF program have overlapping target populations and overlapping goals. Slightly less than half (46%) of the parents of Head Start children are unemployed, and 21% receive benefits under TANF (Head Start Bureau, 2002), making many Head Start families eligible for the welfare-to-work programs under PRWORA. In addition, consistent with the goals of PRWORA, a significant amount of Head Start's resources are devoted to helping the parents of children enrolled in Head Start acquire the educational and job preparation skills necessary to escape long-term welfare dependency, primarily through its social services and parent involvement components. Given this overlap in goals and target population, there is a compelling need to coordinate these two programs.

Wade F. Horn, Ph.D., is Assistant Secretary for Children and Families at the U.S. Department of Health and Human Services. From 1994 to 2001 he was President of the National Fatherhood Initiative, an organization whose mission is to improve the well-being of children by increasing the number of children growing up with involved, committed, and responsible fathers. This chapter is adapted from testimony Dr. Horn provided before the United States House of Representatives Subcommittee on Early Childhood, Youth and Families, Committee on Education and Workforce on June 9, 1998. The opinions represented herein are the sole possession of the author and do not necessarily reflect the views of the U.S. Department of Health and Human Services or the Bush Administration.

POSSIBILITIES FOR COORDINATION

Coordinating different government programs is never easy, but coordinating child care, Head Start, and welfare-to-work programs has proven particularly difficult because of idiosyncratic and sometimes contradictory programmatic requirements. For example, under TANF, states must guarantee child care for parents who are required to work under welfare reform. But, because most Head Start programs provide only part-day services totaling 20 hours or less per week, it is likely that the work schedules of many TANF participants will not correspond exactly with that of a Head Start program.

In addition, some welfare-to-work participants will obtain employment or enroll in training or education programs that exceed 20 hours per week, making access to a part-day child care arrangement even less relevant. To make matters worse, Head Start is typically a 9-month program, leaving the need for child care unanswered for those who work year-round.

There are two possible solutions to this problem. First, Head Start funds could be used to expand Head Start from a part-day, part-year program, to a full-day, full-year program. This solution has the advantage of ease of administration. For example, if Head Start funds are used to expand the hours of the program to full-day, full-year, program administrators could be certain of space requirements and staffing needs. The big disadvantage would be cost. Although exact estimates of the cost of Head Start are hard to come by, it appears that a full-day, full-year Head Start program can cost upwards of $10,000 per child, nearly twice as much as ordinary child care.

An alternative would be to require Head Start programs to provide extended day services through wrap-around child care arrangements. Wrap-around child care entails using other funding sources to keep the Head Start center open for those children for whom full-day child care is a necessity. Thus, Head Start would be able to provide child care for families in which caregivers are employed full time outside the home, without having to transport the child to a different location in order to satisfy their child care needs. Those children who do not require full-time child care would be sent home after the delivery of the 3- to 4-hour core Head Start services. The primary disadvantage to wrap-around child care arrangements is the burden it places on program administrators to seek out, procure, and coordinate different funding streams.

The most obvious source of funds for wrap-around child care arrangements is the child care development block grant (CCDBG). The Head Start grantee and the state agency administering the CCDBG could make various arrangements for paying for wrap-around child care, but the best arrangement would be "purchase of service" contracts. Such an arrangement allows Head Start administrators to know in advance the amount of space and the number of child care providers necessary to fulfill the contract. In contrast, after-the-fact reimbursement arrangements could place financial burdens on the Head Start program because of unexpected absences.

CCDBG is by no means the only source of funds for wrap-around child care arrangements. Other sources of funding include the Title I program within the Department of Education, the Job Training Partnership Act (JTPA), the Community Development Block Grant, the TANF block grant, and the Social Services Block Grant (Title XX).

BARRIERS TO EFFECTIVE COORDINATION

Whether one expands Head Start through Head Start expansion funds or through wrap-around child care arrangements, several additional barriers to effective coordination exist. One such procedural barrier has already been discussed, differences in hours of operation. Relatedly, many half-day Head Start programs employ double shifts in which separate morning and afternoon classes are conducted utilizing the same classroom space. The use of double shifts most commonly occurs in communities lacking adequate space for Head Start classrooms. Thus, in many communities, it may be impossible to extend the day for children of parents enrolled in welfare-to-work programs because the available classroom space is already being fully utilized.

In addition, welfare-to-work programs enroll participants throughout the year, whereas Head Start primarily enrolls children during the spring and summer preceding the Head Start school year. This means that families enrolled in welfare-to-work programs after the beginning of the Head Start school year will most likely be unable to enroll their child in Head Start; all the available slots will have been filled. The fact that Head Start enrolls children only part of the year and welfare-to-work programs enroll families continuously throughout the year can result in welfare administrators becoming frustrated with the inability of Head Start to satisfy the child care needs of their clients. Such frustration naturally leads to reluctance to continue to refer welfare-to-work participants to the Head Start program.

The need for child care by welfare-to-work participants may also change over time. During an education and training period there may be less of a need for full-time child care because of the flexibility and limited hours of many education and training programs. Once employed, however, welfare-to-work participants may have a greater need for full-time child care. Unfortunately, part-day Head Start programs may not be able to accommodate to changing child care needs over time. As a result, children of parents enrolled in welfare-to-work programs may experience multiple disruptions in their child care arrangements as they are transferred back and forth from Head Start to other child care arrangements.

Even more concerning is the possibility that some parents may actually turn down bona fide, and otherwise attractive, employment opportunities in order to keep their child enrolled in Head Start. Conversely, some children may be denied the Head Start experience altogether because the program cannot accommodate the child care needs of the parent.

A third barrier to effective coordination is the difference in culture and mission between Head Start and welfare-to-work programs. Despite the explicit focus in many welfare-to-work programs on the chronically unemployed, many local programs are held accountable for expeditiously moving participants into jobs. This has led at least some observers to feel that welfare-to-work programs tend to focus on the recently, rather than the chronically, unemployed.

In contrast, Head Start's mission has always been to focus on the "poorest of the poor." There are few, if any, expectations for Head Start programs to move families expeditiously off welfare and into self-sufficiency. Indeed, it is not uncommon to hear Head

Start staff talk of using a full year of Head Start simply to get the parents comfortable with the idea of accepting help through the Head Start program.

A second difference in missions between these two programs is that welfare-to-work programs see the parent(s) as their primary client, whereas Head Start sees the child as its primary client. Given this difference in perspective, welfare-to-work program administrators and frontline staff often lack the background and expertise to know how to meet the needs of the children in participant households.

In addition, the adult focus of welfare programs frequently leads welfare-to-work case workers to view child care arrangements as acceptable so long as that child care setting provides a safe, healthy, and sanitary environment for the child while the child's parent(s) is in an education or training program or at work. Little emphasis in welfare-to-work programs is given to addressing the individual needs of a particular child while in that child care setting. Head Start, in contrast, sees as its primary mission the enhancement of the child's developmental status. To Head Start administrators and frontline staff, a safe environment is not adequate; the setting must also be developmentally appropriate and designed to meet each child's individual needs.

In addition, Head Start staff themselves may be reluctant to shift from a part-day, part-year program to a full-day, full-year program. Research suggests that one reason individuals are attracted to employment in child care settings is that such employment may not be full time, allowing the provider time to be with one's own children or the freedom to pursue other education or career goals (Fuchs & Coleman, 1991). In fact, when a summer Head Start program was contemplated in 1993, there were reports of Head Start staff raising objections to having to work during the summer and disrupt family vacation plans (Besharov, 1993).

Turf battles among different constituent groups also have hampered collaboration efforts. Rather than using the different categories of federal funding of child care to develop a seamless system of child care services, each child care grant program has developed its own constituents who have a rather proprietary view of the monies made available through "their" particular grant program. For example, when the CCDBG was implemented in 1989, representatives from the Head Start community often were specifically not invited to attend statewide planning meetings because of the feeling that Head Start had its own source of funds, and the CCDBG monies were for the non–Head Start child care community.

A final barrier to effective coordination is that Head Start and the CCDBG have entirely different funding mechanisms. From its inception, Head Start has been a direct federal-to-local grant program. Funding levels for specific Head Start programs are based on a determination as to what it will cost to operate an effective early childhood intervention program. Although it is possible to calculate a per-child cost in Head Start, funds are not generally awarded based upon such a calculation.

CCDBG, however, frequently awards funds through contracts and vouchers based upon a unit cost per-child calculation. Head Start program operators are not accustomed to administering programs in which funding is tied so explicitly to an individual child. Conversely, CCDBG administrators seldom have the luxury of thinking programmatically when it comes to child care arrangements because funds are tied so explicitly to individual children. This difference in funding mechanisms can make it difficult for these two programs to coordinate with each other.

TWO ROUTES TO MORE EFFECTIVE COORDINATION

As the previous discussion illustrates, coordination between Head Start, welfare-to-work programs, and child care funding streams has proven difficult, to say the least. In fact, according to the data collected by the Head Start Bureau in the 2001–2002 program year, 447,294 (48%) of Head Start enrollees were in need of full-time, full-year child care, but only 232,564 (25%) of enrollees actually received full-time, full-year child care through the Head Start program. This does not mean there are no effective models of coordination and collaboration, but coordination has proven to be difficult—and the exception, rather than the rule.

Might there be a better way? Let me suggest two possibilities. One possibility is to strengthen the current Head Start State Collaboration Grants Program by providing governors with the authority to seek waivers from Head Start programmatic requirements in order to more effectively coordinate Head Start with welfare reform and other funding mechanisms. For example, governors could petition for a waiver to relax the income guidelines so as to allow participation of more of the working poor in the Head Start program than is currently the case. Alternatively, governors could petition to ensure that welfare-to-work participants are given preference in terms of entry into the Head Start program, a decision that is currently left up to the local grantee.

A second possibility is to allow states greater administrative authority and oversight of the Head Start program. Although controversial, this possibility deserves serious consideration for several reasons.

First, Head Start has grown too large; there is simply no precedent for a direct federal-to-local grantee arrangement for a program with a budget of more than $6 billion and annual participants exceeding 900,000. Why should states have so little (if any) input into the oversight and administration of a program that touches so many of its citizens?

Second, over the past decade, the federal government has been downsizing, both at the federal level and in its regional offices. This downsizing makes oversight of an *expanding* program ever more difficult. Allowing states some measure of administrative control over Head Start would allow for better oversight of the program.

Third, coordination is made especially difficult by the fact that Head Start is a federally administered program, whereas both welfare-to-work programs and most child care funding streams have been devolved to the states. Allowing states some degree of administrative control over Head Start would provide program planners and policy makers at the state level an increased ability to coordinate all three programs which, after all, do share a common target population and common goals.

Finally, there are many lessons learned from Head Start about providing developmentally appropriate settings and experiences for children. Allowing states to better coordinate Head Start with pre-K programs would allow more effective cross-pollination of the lessons learned from Head Start into the broader child care and state-administered preschool communities.

I know that any proposal to allow states some measure of administrative control over Head Start will be controversial—especially within the Head Start community. So it should not be done impulsively and certainly not simply because I say so. Rather, my purpose in offering this idea is to stimulate a discussion about the rationale for continuing Head Start as a strictly federally administered program.

Perhaps there are very good reasons to do so, but one of them should not be "because that's the way we've always done it." Instead, we should look more comprehensively at the needs of low-income families and their children, especially within the context of welfare reform, and develop even more effective systems for supporting them.

EVALUATING THE IMPACT OF HEAD START

We do know something about the impact of Head Start. We know, for example, that parents who are actively involved in Head Start show immediate treatment effects—they have higher self-esteem and provide more language stimulation in the home. We also know that communities with Head Start programs evidence increased use of paraprofessionals, greater attention to the needs of poor students, and more mental health.

Most important, we know that Head Start can have significant and positive effects on a host of child variables including: achievement, aptitude scores, achievement motivation, self-concept, and measures of physical health. We also know, however, that most of the superiority shown by Head Start children on these measures, when compared with non–Head Start peers, fades by the third grade (Haskins, 1989; McKey et al., 1985; White, 1985–1986).

Critics of Head Start point to this fade-out effect and conclude that Head Start is of little value. Some perspective, however, is in order here. I come from a profession (clinical psychology) that throws wild parties if we can demonstrate that the effect of a particular psychotherapeutic intervention lasts for more than 6 months. Hence, a program that has demonstrated positive outcomes for several years is, in my judgment, a success, not a failure. Indeed, it is ludicrous to expect Head Start—or any other preschool intervention program—to overcome the devastating effects of crime-ridden neighborhoods; communities without fathers; and ineffective, and even dangerous, schools.

But, while congratulating ourselves on Head Start's short-term effectiveness, we must at the same time focus on strengthening Head Start's long-term effectiveness. There are at least two possibilities for doing so:

1. Giving more years of Head Start before school entry

2. Transforming the system into which the Head Start child goes, most especially the schools

The first possibility is part of the rationale for Early Head Start. Unfortunately, there is little empirical evidence that multiple years of Head Start, or any other preschool intervention program, yield substantially better effects than 1 year. The highly touted Perry Preschool Project, for example, specifically compared the effectiveness of 1 year versus 2 years of its program and found no differences as a function of length of time children were enrolled.

A much more promising approach is to fundamentally transform the schools into which the Head Start child graduates. This was the idea behind the Head Start Transition grants, which I helped to implement during my tenure as Commissioner of ACYF. (For the results of the effectiveness of this program, see Chapter 28.)

Today, I recommend a much bolder idea. I see little evidence that public schools within low-income communities are capable of transforming themselves. Rather, I now champion the use of school choice as the impetus for fundamental school reform.

Here's my idea. Congress should authorize a demonstration program in which a randomly selected sample of Head Start graduates would receive tuition vouchers for use in the public or private school of their choice. The outcome of these children could then be compared with the outcome of Head Start graduates who do not receive vouchers to determine whether the fade-out effect is diminished, if not eliminated, through school choice.

CONCLUSION

Head Start has been operating as an exemplary program since 1965. I offer these ideas for reform not because I believe Head Start to be a failure but because I believe that to remain exemplary, Head Start must change with changing conditions. Better coordination of Head Start with welfare reform and education reform, and especially school choice, offers the potential for doing just that.

REFERENCES

Besharov, D. (1993, June 14). Fresh start: What works in Head Start? *The New Republic,* 14–16.

Fuchs, V.R., & Coleman, M. (1991, Winter). Small children, small pay: Why child care pays so little. *The American Prospect,* 74–80.

Haskins, R. (1989). Beyond metaphor: The efficacy of early childhood education. *American Psychologist, 44*(2), 274–282.

Head Start Bureau. (2002). *2001–2002 Program Information Report.* Washington, DC: U.S. Department of Health and Human Services.

McKey, R.H., Condelli, L., Gamson, H., Barrett, B., McConkey, C., & Plantz, M. (1985). *The impact of Head Start on children, families and communities: Final report of the Head Start Evaluation, Synthesis and Utilization Project.* Washington, DC: U.S. Department of Health and Human Services.

Personal Responsibility and Work Opportunity Reconcilliation Act (PRWORA) of 1996, PL 104-193, 42 U.S.C. §§ 1305 *et seq.*

White, K.R. (1985–1986). Efficacy of early intervention. *Journal of Special Education, 41,* 401–416.

CHAPTER 34

Maintaining Federal to Local Management of Head Start

SARAH M. GREENE

"More than just an educational program, Head Start provides family services, dental care, and health care. Head Start provides the opportunity for a young girl to have a book read to her for the first time; for a young boy to have his first check-up; and for a mother or father to understand nutrition, the early signs of lead poisoning and the right treatment, or how to encourage learning at home."
—Hillary Clinton, U.S. Senator (1947–), July 29, 2003

The Head Start program has developed some exciting new service directions, and the expectation grows among the Head Start community that the program will finally attain the level of quality and responsiveness we have worked toward over the past decades. Further Head Start success would be jeopardized if Head Start is transferred to the Department of Education or if Head Start funds are block granted to state management. The National Head Start Association (NHSA) maintains that the Head Start program should remain as a federal-to-local program, with funding, oversight, and technical assistance being delivered directly from the federal Administration for Children and Families (ACF)—specifically the Head Start Bureau, ACF's 10 geographic regional offices, and its two population-specific regional offices. NHSA is vehemently opposed to any attempt to make Head Start a block grant program.

Head Start is *not* child care. Head Start is a comprehensive child development program designed to address the needs of the "whole" child. Unlike basic child care, it is not defined as a care service for working parents. Guided by the Head Start Program Performance Standards, it has an operational framework that extends far beyond a standard child care system. Head Start's structure addresses the developmental domains that increase a child's learning potential and school success. By addressing child and family needs, such as health, nutrition, dental, mental health, and social services—in addition to cognitive development—Head Start is positioned to achieve the best possible outcomes for low-income children. With Head Start's approach, low-income children have an increased chance of starting school with the essential building blocks for learning.

To magnify its effects, Head Start has a strong parent involvement component. Parent involvement is a pivotal part of Head Start. Head Start recognizes parents' roles in child development and seeks to maximize their value by providing training opportunities that improve parenting skills, literacy skills, and employment skills. Parents are encouraged and are given the opportunity to participate in important decisions affecting their child's Head Start program. Head Start's approach allows parents, children's first and primary teachers, to understand their value and encourages opportunities that lead to Head Start children having increased chances for school success.

Head Start's approach consists of a two-variable system: processes and outcomes. Due to this system, Head Start is able to provide quality services that promote future school success. Head Start processes include

- Providing children with educational, health, and nutritional services

- Having well-managed programs in which parents are active in the decision-making process

- Linking children and families to needed community services

Head Start outcomes include

- Enhancing children's growth and development

- Strengthening families as the primary nurturers of their children

- Promoting children's overall social competence (Administration on Children, Youth and Families, 1997)

Children need many things in order to enter kindergarten ready to do their best: safe and supportive homes, sufficient nutrition, health care, and the preparation that quality prekindergarten programs can provide. There are many children, of all income levels, who start school ill prepared for the challenges that await them. With kindergarten teachers estimating that one in three children enters the classroom unprepared to meet the challenge of school (Blank, Schulman, & Ewen, 1999), the need for quality child development programs, which incorporate Head Start's whole child approach, is even greater now than it has been in the past.

The school readiness problem is not a problem specific to low-income children. The Economic Policy Institute reported data that indicated that middle-class children enter kindergarten with skill levels closer to those from the poorest families rather than the most affluent (The Trust for Early Education, 2003). This data may suggest that while attention should be given to a child's cognitive development, attention needs also to be given to various other factors (e.g., health, nutrition, social, family) that stimulate and increase a child's learning ability.

BACKGROUND

"History repeats itself, and that's one of the things that's wrong with history."
                                    —Clarence Darrow, American lawyer, writer (1857–1938)

The idea of altering the management of Head Start is not a new one, and we expect it will continue surfacing in the future. The failure to understand history causes these types of recommendations to reappear as leadership changes. During the original discussions in

1964, the founders of Head Start came to the logical conclusion that communities had to be empowered to administer the program. States were not in a position to give communities the authority or autonomy to do so, and NHSA's view on this has not changed.

In 1968, the first attempt surfaced to place Head Start into the federal Office of Education. Lawmakers wanted to give a lump sum of federal funds to the states to be used for early childhood education. This attempt took place only 3 years after the Head Start program was founded, and the Head Start community took action. The national Director of Head Start, Richard Orton, alerted a telephone network, and the House of Representatives was flooded by calls from Head Start constituents. The attempt was halted—the first successful movement to maintain Head Start's federal-to-local funding (Zigler & Muenchow, 1992).

In 1974, then Governor Jimmy Carter brought up the idea of managing Head Start in his state, after the OMB published Circular A-95, giving the states an opportunity to take a larger role in federally managed programs. His idea was blocked by opposition from the Head Start community. When Carter became president, he again made plans to include Head Start in his newly created Department of Education. The Head Start community again rallied successfully as Carter tried twice to remove the program from federal management (Zigler & Muenchow, 1992).

Head Start's constituents prepared for President Reagan's defunding of federal human services programs even before he came into office. They found ways to protect the program through public support and positive research. Yet, during the Reagan Administration, Head Start still faced a struggle to maintain quality standards, partly because of Reagan's plan to increase the number of children served without providing additional funds (Zigler & Muenchow, 1992). During the first Bush administration, Head Start received support in the White House, and in 1989, the nation's governors and former President Bush set national education goals. The first goal was having "every child enter school ready to learn." Access to good-quality early childhood programs was considered key to meeting this goal (Blank et al., 1999). Throughout the most recent administrations, Head Start has prospered and expanded to serve even more children and families, although we have not yet met the goal to serve all those eligible. NHSA is prepared to continue Head Start's expansion throughout future administrations and to protect the advances Head Start has made on reaching its program goals.

THE STATES' ROLE IN EARLY CHILDHOOD EDUCATION

The states' role in education has changed since Head Start began. Many states now have an active part in early childhood education, and a majority administer preschool programs. Child care has become an issue of urgency with recent welfare reform that has placed a strain on a child care system that has historically been on overload. State child care programs are dissimilar to the Head Start program. They have few regulations other than basic safety and health requirements. They have no national standards for quality and no progress measurement structure. Head Start takes pride in its national performance standards and its ability to measure how well they are being administered. The Head Start Program Performance Standards allow the program to maintain the highest level of quality throughout the entire nation; regardless of what state you live in, the same quality is assured. State child care programs offer no guarantee that any services will be the same as in a neighboring state.

The Head Start program has seen numerous increases in federal funding. It is important to ensure that these funds are being used for their original purpose of providing a quality child development program. It is essential that all efforts are made to ensure that the Head Start program is not entangled in state bureaucracy and state level deficiencies. Ripple, Gilliam, Chanana, and Zigler (1999) identified the following possible problems and consequences with state management of Head Start:

- States are not equipped to meet the needs of low-income families; communities are more aware of local community needs.

- State programs will have varying goals, target populations, and political and financial support.

- States are unlikely to offer comprehensive services and/or incorporate a strong parent involvement component.

- The Head Start Program Performance Standards may not be maintained and/or monitored.

Head Start was designed to fight the conditions and implications of poverty by providing services that would mediate the hardships of poverty. By providing services and opportunities that are commonly neglected or not provided, Head Start helps economically disadvantaged children to not fall victim to poverty but to be better prepared to start school ready to learn.

It would be a contradiction in purpose to have a program designed to fight the disadvantages of poverty in the educational system and turn the management of that program to those who systemize inequalities. It cannot be disputed that the educational system across the nation has various levels of quality. The educational system in the United States does not enforce national standards and has fallen victim to the inequalities that the Head Start program was founded to alleviate. Some schools are wealthy with seemingly endless resources, while others in poor districts have very few resources. Children are supposed to be guaranteed equal opportunities to education, and this goal could never be accomplished with such a variance in the educational system. To add Head Start to the U.S. Department of Education and make it a part of that system would be disastrous for the entire low-income community.

If Head Start were given to school districts, it is likely that those would be the districts least capable of effectively managing the program. Head Start would be added to a system wherein opportunities and quality are often defined and determined by income and race. Regrettably, it is a system whereby minority, low-income children are strapped with the pitfalls associated with larger class sizes, poorer facilities, limited resources, and less-qualified teachers. An examination by Valerie E. Lee and David T. Burkam (2002), *Inequality at the Starting Gate,* revealed that

- Minority children are typically enrolled in larger kindergarten classes than white children.

- Children with more economic need are enrolled in larger kindergarten classes.

- Children in urban areas are in much larger kindergarten classes.

- Minority kindergartners attend schools with teachers who are less prepared and less experienced.

- Kindergartners with more educated parents attend schools with teachers who are more experienced.

- Low-income kindergarten children are more likely to attend schools that have teachers with less than positive attitudes.

Those who support moving Head Start from the Department of Health and Human Services (DHHS) to the Department of Education suggest that it should be integrated with more state education programs. Some lawmakers stress the fact that Head Start is such an important educational tool that it should be removed from DHHS and moved directly into the Department of Education. These lawmakers do not realize that the Head Start program would be lost if it were integrated into state management. They do not recognize that Head Start was founded to alleviate the hardships associated with poverty. They are not acknowledging that what our low-income children need are resources, services, and support systems to combat the disabling realities of poverty. Head Start's success depends on an approach rooted at the community level that can identify and meet the needs of children living in poverty. It is an approach dependent on meeting the developmental needs to make cognitive development possible. Moving Head Start to the Department of Education would direct the focus to cognitive development and would ignore the critical domains that make learning possible. Such a shift would jeopardize the futures of many low-income children.

CONSOLIDATING FEDERAL PROGRAMS

There are several reasons why lawmakers want to consolidate federal programs: administrative cost savings, decentralized decision making, and providing greater state discretion with the use of federal funds. Administrative cost savings of block granting categorical funds is very controversial: Dividing Head Start into individual state programs could prove to be a costly endeavor. A U.S. General Accounting Office (USGAO) report issued in January 1998, *State and Federal Efforts to Target Poor Students,* found that federal funds are eight times more likely than state funds to target disadvantaged students.

Former U.S. Secretary of Education, Richard Riley, stated, "Any legislation that just dumps federal money into general state operating funds is not serving the needs of the children. It would be a diversion and would likely lead to less money going to schools and students most in need" ("Riley Says No to Education Block Grants," 1998). The assumption that block granting Head Start will save money is erroneous. If states could administer the program for 6% of the current Head Start budget, it would require an additional $407 million to maintain funding for the current number of Head Start children. The children and families will be the ones to suffer if Head Start becomes part of the Department of Education. With the increased costs of administering the program, many families would lose services, and enrollment would decrease across the nation. Legislators' goal for Head Start is full enrollment of all eligible children. With a drastic change in funding, this goal could never be reached.

In addition, there is a fear that states will use Head Start money for child care programs. This would be harmful because state-managed child care programs generally do not offer the same level of training and staffing requirements and typically provide a lesser-quality program than Head Start provides. While many child care and early education programs are subject to federal, state, and/or local licensing or quality standards that provide basic health and safety protections, there is not one set of quality standards that govern all child care and early education programs nationwide (Children's Defense Fund [CDF], 2002). Child care has extreme variability from state to state. Head Start, however, is more uniform. Head Start programs follow the Federal Performance Standards and are subject to the same set of federal rules, regulations, and guidelines. The child care system is of concern because

- Only 10 states require child care centers to have child/staff ratios that meet any regulations. Thirty-one states allow a single caregiver to be responsible for more than six 2-year-olds.

- Many states do not require providers to have even a basic knowledge of child development issues, and many states require little or no training before providers can work with children. (CDF, 2002)

Providing a "care service" while parents work is not the goal of Head Start. Head Start's goal relates more to providing an opportunity for low-income children to have the best preparation for school success. Good early care and education are essential in helping low-income children to be ready for school. Research clearly demonstrates that children who participate in high-quality early education programs score higher on cognitive, reading, and math test than their peers who did not participate in a quality early education program (CDF, 2002). Further, children who participate in quality programs are less likely to require special or remedial education and are more likely to graduate from high school and have higher earnings as adults (CDF, 2002). Without Head Start, with its current structure, low-income children will be less likely to have access to a quality early care and education program.

Another goal of consolidation of federal programs is to decentralize decision making. The Omnibus Budget Reconciliation Act of 1981 created nine block grants from about 50 categorical programs. Its design was to consolidate federal programs and to broaden program flexibility among states. There are many conclusions to be drawn from studying the results from this Act. Some of the programs that were block granted had a smooth transition, but others that were previously entirely federally funded or had local service providers dealing with federal agencies had patchy transitions (USGAO, 1995).

States are given broad discretion under block grant programs to determine what services and programs to provide, as long as they relate to the grant program. States also become responsible for monitoring programs and accountability of federal funds. Accountability became a problem with the categorical programs consolidated in the Act. States developed their own program reporting formats. It made it impossible to measure results throughout the entire nation with varying programs and measurements. Congress received little information on use of federal funds and program activities, services delivered, and clients served (USGAO, 1995). The current Head Start federal administration has no problem complying with the Government Performance Results Act that states that every federal program will be judged on whether its ideas and approaches produce real, tangible results for the taxpayers' dollar. Head Start's current federal administration is able to prove that their program produces good results for the money spent. If Head Start was broken down into individual state operations, it would be difficult to prove overall results nationwide, and a lack of nationwide results may negatively influence further funding increases and could cause a decrease in federal funding. Of the categorical programs consolidated in the Omnibus Budget Reconciliation Act of 1981, there was a 12% decrease in funding for the next fiscal year, which equaled about $1 billion (USGAO, 1995). Again, quoting former Secretary Riley, "Proposals to collapse federal education funds into block grants to states would be a step in the wrong direction. We've been down this road before and the result was lack of focus and accountability" ("Riley Says No to Education Block Grants," 1998). NHSA and the Head Start community have worked hard to maintain and expand Head Start funding and we will not let a devolution of the entire program occur.

NHSA applauds any effort to improve Head Start's ability to serve children and families. We do not contest the concept of personal responsibility. In fact, that is what parent involvement in Head Start is all about. In a spirit of cooperation, NHSA makes the following recommendations regarding the program issues: fulfill the promise to children and families, fulfill the promise to local communities, fulfill the promise on quality, and fulfill the promise on collaboration.

Fulfill the Promise to Children and Families

- Achieve full enrollment of all Head Start–eligible children. This will not be inexpensive, but nothing worthwhile is. Let's meet the challenges of the new millennium by fulfilling the promise to children and families.

- Head Start should revise the income eligibility policy to enable families who are above the federal poverty line to participate in the program. The cost of living for families varies across the states. With some exceptions, all Head Start programs must currently deny enrollment to any family above the federal poverty guidelines. This guideline is arbitrary, too low, and completely unrealistic. If Congress really wants to be fair to citizens of each state, then eligibility should be based on state and local cost of living.

Fulfill the Promise to Local Communities

- Head Start must maintain its unique federal-to-local identity and not be regulated by the states through block grants or other strategies for devolution. Local communities must have greater input to the policy-making process and must have options for implementing programs based on their own unique circumstances.

Fulfill the Promise on Quality

- All disadvantaged children and those with disabilities must have access to high-quality and developmentally appropriate preschool programs that will help prepare them for school.

- Every parent in America should be considered their child's first teacher and be able to devote time each day to helping his or her child learn; parents should have access to training and support they need.

- Children should receive the nutrition and health care they need to arrive at school with healthy minds and bodies; the number of low birthweight infants should be significantly reduced through enhanced prenatal health systems.

Fulfill the Promise on Collaboration

- Head Start should model and disseminate a wide variety of program and resource partnerships, with federal and state agencies as well as corporations, private foundations, and nonprofit organizations to increase local Head Start programs' access to financial and other resources and supplement federal dollars (NHSA, 2000). Although there have been problems in some states, NHSA supports the concept of state collaboration projects. This is the appropriate way to encourage state involvement with Head Start. We suggest Congress look at successful state collaboration projects and work with the administration to expand these partnerships.

- Head Start should explore additional strategies for collaboration with other child care agencies and providers and replicate successful partnership models. These partnerships should form the foundation for an integrated system of care for children ages birth to 5, with specialized training and staff (NHSA, 2000).

CONCLUSION

"It was once said that the moral test of government is how that government treats those who are in the dawn of life, the children; those who are in the twilight of life, the elderly; and those who are in the shadows of life—the sick, the needy, and the handicapped."
—Hubert H. Humphrey, Statesman, U.S. Vice President (1911–1978)

There are some issues that are too important to the nation to be left to the management of individual states. It is the position of NHSA that the needs of low-income children are a national concern deserving national attention with direct local input taking precedence over state concerns. By reinventing Head Start as a block grant program, all guarantees of minimum standards of services will be lost. No individual state should have the right to decide what level of safety or well-being is appropriate for low-income children because these children belong to all of us; they are the children of this nation. Why change a program that works? The often quoted old African proverb reminds us that "it takes an entire village to raise a child," not a state.

REFERENCES

Administration on Children, Youth and Families (ACYF). (1997). *First progress report on the Head Start Program Performance Measures.* Washington, DC: U.S. Department of Health and Human Services.

Blank, H., Schulman, K., & Ewen, D. (1999). *Key facts: Essential information about child care, early education, and school-age care.* Washington, DC: Children's Defense Fund.

Children's Defense Fund (CDF). (2002). *State developments in child care, early education, and school age care.* Washington, DC: Author.

Lee, V.E., & Burkam, D.T. (2002). *Inequality at the starting gate.* Washington, DC: Economic Policy Institute.

National Head Start Association (NHSA). (2000). *Fulfilling the promise: Report of the Head Start 2010 National Advisory Panel.* Alexandria VA: Author.

Ripple, C.H., Gilliam, W.S., Chanana, N., & Zigler, E. (1999). Will fifty cooks spoil the broth? The debate over entrusting Head Start to the states. *American Psychologist, 54,* 327–343.

The Trust for Early Education. (2003). *The foundations for high quality pre-kindergarten: What all children need.* Washington, DC: Author.

U.S. General Accounting Office (USGAO). (1995). *Block grants: Characteristics, experience, and lessons learned* (GAO No. GAO/HEHS-95-74). Washington, DC: Author.

U.S. General Accounting Office (USGAO). (1998). *State and federal efforts to target poor students* (GAO No. GAO/HEHS-98-36). Washington, DC: Author.

Zigler, E., & Muenchow, S. (1992). *Head Start: The inside story of America's most successful educational experiment.* New York: Basic Books.

CHAPTER 35

What Can Be Learned from State-Funded Prekindergarten Initiatives?

A Data-Based Approach to the Head Start Devolution Debate

Walter S. Gilliam and Carol H. Ripple

Since the mid-1990s, policy analysts and decision makers have debated whether Head Start should be devolved from federal to state control. Devolution presumably would be accomplished by block granting Head Start to the states, in a manner similar to, for example, the Child Care Development Block Grant. Proponents of Head Start devolution, such as former Administration on Children, Youth and Families (ACYF) Commissioner Wade Horn (see Chapter 33), suggest that states could more efficiently blend Head Start and child care funds and could provide superior vision and oversight due to their more geographically proximal administrative seat. Some proponents of devolution have bolstered their argument with null findings from other federal programs (see Gilliam, Ripple, Zigler, & Leiter, 2000).

As social scientists interested in informing social policy, we approached the devolution debate by using extant data to shed light on possible outcomes of a shift from federal to state control over Head Start. Because many states have already implemented their own prekindergarten programming, we examined these efforts as a potential indicator of how states might fare in implementing Head Start. This means of predicting future state performance in administering a block-granted federal program is predicated on a study by the U.S. General Accounting Office (USGAO, 1995). In examining the implementation and effectiveness of block-granted programs, the USGAO found that some states were

The authors acknowledge Steven Abramovitz for his assistance in the collection and organization of the data for updating this survey, as well as the many state officials who provided the information.

able to smoothly transition from federally administered categorical programs to state-administered block grants, whereas others struggled. The difficulties were associated with a lack of preexisting infrastructure in some states, leading to an inability to assume appropriate state-level authority.

The USGAO noted other concerns as well. First, they found that Congress and the federal officials responsible for the appropriated funds could not easily track their appropriate and efficient use at the state level. Second, the state flexibility that was promised by the move from federal categorical programs to block grants often diminished over time as funding constraints were added. Finally, although state officials reported that the block-granted programs were administratively easier to manage, the change was difficult to quantify in cost savings. Regarding one particular block grant that was intended to provide states with funds to support low-income communities and families, the USGAO (1994) questioned whether states were faithful to the mandate to serve these populations.

Based on the USGAO's findings regarding already block-granted programs, we were interested in determining how states might fare in the administration of a block-granted Head Start. Many states are already in the business of early care and education, so an examination of these initiatives should shed light on how states might conduct Head Start programs under devolution. We begin by presenting a brief updated summary of our earlier survey of state-funded preschool programs (Ripple, Gilliam, Chanana, & Zigler, 1999). Then, we draw on the results of this survey and empirical findings from other sources to consider possible benefits, limitations, and challenges of devolving Head Start. Finally, we end with some general conclusions about the potential effects of Head Start decentralization.

DESCRIPTION OF STATE-FUNDED PRESCHOOL PROGRAMS

In an earlier paper, we reported results of a comprehensive survey of all 50 states plus the District of Columbia regarding state-funded preschool programs (SFPPs; Ripple et al., 1999). Data were obtained by mail survey, with a telephone update, from state-level program administrators. The survey addressed program structure and administrative authority, oversight and quality control mechanisms, teacher qualifications, eligibility and accessibility, duration and intensity, class size and staff–child ratios, curricula, health and social support services, and parent involvement efforts. Based on fiscal year (FY) 1996 data, 31 SFPPs met our criteria for inclusion.[1] These data were updated in early 2000 by follow-up contact with state program administrators, which resulted in the identification of three new SFPPs and the elimination of one we had previously reported.[2] Results of this update are summarized in Tables 35.1, 35.2, and 35.3.

---

[1]To meet our definition of a "state-funded preschool program," the program must 1) target or be accessible to children from low-income families; 2) provide at least some form of classroom-based, educational service directly to preschool-age children; 3) be implemented and administered at the state level (not state aid for low-income parents to purchase their own preschool services); 4) be primarily state-funded (not state supplementation to programs funded primarily at the federal or local level); and 5) not serve exclusively children with disabilities. For the purposes of this survey, the District of Columbia was treated as a state. Descriptions of additional state-funded programs for young children that do not meet these criteria are available (Cauthen, Knitzer, & Ripple, 2000; Schulman, Blank, & Ewen, 1999; Smith, Fairchild, & Groginsky, 1997).

[2]Although some Pennsylvania school districts do have preschool programs, there is no state mandate for them to do so, and the decision is left to local districts and individual schools. In addition, there are no statewide program standards or quality controls.

Two caveats offered for our original survey still apply. First, some states had so few guidelines for their SFPPs that they were more a funding stream than a discernible program. Second, some programs were changing even as data were being collected. Most often, new programs were introduced, and funding and/or eligibility requirements were expanded for extant programs. In light of these caveats, we suggest that the broader patterns in implementation are of greater import to our discussion than individual program specifications. In the sections that follow, we present our observations of several programmatic domains, discussing each in comparison with Head Start. (For more detailed study rationale and data, see Ripple et al., 1999.)

Program Structure

Aspects of program structure or governance include the administrative seat of the state system, the program venues that are utilized, and the ways in which program regulations are established and monitored.

Administration and Location   All but two SFPPs were administered through state departments of education. All programs located at least some of their classrooms in public school buildings; and in seven states, classrooms were only located in the public schools (Table 35.1). In most states, however, programs were delivered in a variety of locations, typically through subcontracting arrangements under the local public school system, which served as the primary grantee. Interestingly, nearly two thirds of all states reported that at least some of their classrooms were located in Head Start centers. Other providers included multiservice community agencies, religious organizations, and private for-profit child care programs. The implementation of SFPPs in multiple agencies suggests the likelihood of highly variable quality and philosophical differences within individual state programs.

Guidelines and Oversight   Many states reported having few or even no program guidelines, instead leaving it to local providers to decide what if any types of services and curricula to offer. About half of the states reported requiring (or at least requesting) program providers to adhere to nationally accepted guidelines for high-quality early childhood care and education (e.g., National Association for the Education of Young Children [NAEYC] guidelines or Head Start Program Performance Standards). About 20% only required providers to meet their state's rules for child care licensure, a standard aimed more at preventing unsafe or negligent care than at facilitating child development and school readiness. Unfortunately, these licensure requirements have such large interstate variability as to render them useless as an indication of quality (Young, Marsland, & Zigler, 1997). Finally, about 30% of states applied state elementary school guidelines to preschool services without attention to developmentally appropriate practices for these youngest of students.

We examined levels of program oversight and quality control from reported in-service training, technical assistance from the authorizing state agency, and formal program evaluations aimed at documenting program quality and specific measurable outcomes. As shown in Table 35.2, 28% of the SFPPs had no in-service training requirements, and 16% did not offer technical assistance to local programs.

Table 35.1. State-funded preschool initiatives: Program profiles (FY 2000)

State	Children served	Program locations	% served	Age	Eligibility requirements Other
Arizona[1]	~3,600	**	**	4	Low income (1.85 FPL)
Arkansas	~10,000	PS, CA, CC, IH, O	**	3–5	Low income (1.85 FPL), low parental education, teen parent, familial substance abuse, LBW, child abuse/neglect, DD, or ESL
California	49,213	PS (PV, CA, HS, CC), PV, CA, CC, IH	**	3–4	Priority to children in protective services; then low income, ESL, DD, or other risk factors
Colorado	9,950	PS (PV, CA, HS, CC)	80	4–5	Child abuse/neglect, ESL, or low parental education
Delaware	843	PS, CA, HS, CC	**	4	Head Start criteria
District of Columbia	3,664	PS	**	3½–4	NONE
Florida	~29,000	PS, CA, CC	**	3–4	≥ 75% shall be low income (1.3 FPL) 4-year-olds, welfare-to-work or migrant families; rest shall be child abuse/neglect, prenatal exposure to drugs/ alcohol, foster placement, or DD
Georgia	~46,000	PS (PV, CA, HS, CC), HS, CC, O	40	4	NONE
Illinois[2]	~53,000	PS (CA, CC)	**	3–5	Locally determined criteria
Iowa	1,800	PS (CA, HS, CC), CA, HS	85	3–4	Low income (1.85 FPL) plus secondary risk factors
Kansas	~1,800	PS	**	4	Low income (1.85 FPL), low parental education, ESL, teen parent, DD, or welfare
Kentucky	15,577	PS (PV, CA, HS, CC)	79	3–4	(1) 4-year-olds: low income (1.3 FPL) or DD; (2) 3-year-olds: DD only
Louisiana	~2,600	PS	~5	4	Low income or DD, plus locally determined criteria
Maine	1,020	PS (PV, HS)	**	4	Locally determined criteria
Massachusetts	19,100	PS (PV, CA, HS, CC), HS, CC	20	2¾–5	Low income (1.25 state median income), plus locally determined criteria
Maryland[3]	~11,000	PS, CA, HS	50	4	Must reside in attendance area of Title 1 eligible school, plus locally determined criteria chosen from list of state-approved risk factors
Michigan	21,085	PS (PV, CA, HS, CC), PV, CA, HS, CC; IH	60	4	(1) Low income, plus 1 of 24 identified risk factors; (2) > 50% must be low income (1.3 FPL) or unified child day care eligible

State	Enrollment	Agencies	%	Ages	Eligibility criteria
Minnesota[4]	44,889	PS	46	3½–5	50% low income (1.3 FPL)
Missouri	3,080	PS	**	3–4	Reside in a high need district, with districts chosen based on need and application date
Nebraska	~275	PS (CA, HS, CC), O	**	3–4	70% either Head Start criteria, low income (1.5 FPL), LBW, ESL, teen parent, parent with disability, or Department of Social Service client
New Jersey[5]	9,410	PS (CA, HS, CC)	**	4	Reside in one of 128 high needs districts chosen based on percent of low income families
New York[6]	47,300	PS (CA, HS, CC)	90	4	Priority to low income (1.85 FPL); NONE starting FY 2004
Ohio	20,881	PS (HS), HS	75	3–4	Low income (1.85 FPL) or receiving welfare benefits
Oklahoma	20,984	PS, HS, CC, O	46	4	NONE (Contingent on district offering program and available space)
Oregon	3,600	PS (HS), CA, HS, CC, O	50	3–5	Head Start criteria
South Carolina	~15,000	PS (HS)	32	4	Locally determined criteria
Tennessee	~600	PS (CA), HS	**	3–4	Priority to welfare-to-work families, then low income (1.85 FPL) or language delay
Texas	138,429	PS (HS, CC)	**	3–4	Low income (1.3 FPL), ESL, or homeless
Vermont	1,094	PS, CC, O	35	3–4	DD (6 month delay), child abuse/neglect, low income (1.85 FPL), ESL, domestic violence, familial substance abuse, or other specified high-risk indicator
Virginia	5,926	PS (PV, CA, HS, CC), O	78	4	Locally determined criteria (subject to state approval)
Washington	7,034	PS (CA, CC), CA, HS, CC, IH, O	60	3–4	Both low income (FPL) and risk of school failure (e.g., child abuse/neglect, homeless, ESL)
West Virginia	2,346	PS	6	3–5	Contingent on district offering program and available space
Wisconsin	12,300	PS	40	4	Contingent on district offering program and available space

Notes: ** State did not provide data. PS = public schools; PV = private schools; CA = various community agencies; CC = private child care centers; IH = in-home programs; O = other facilities; HS = Head Start centers. Agencies in parentheses indicate a subcontracted or a mandated collaborative arrangement under the preceding agency. FPL = federal poverty level; LBW = low birth weight or prematurity; DD = developmental delay; ESL = English as a second language or non-English-speaking family.

[1] Preschool in Arizona is funded as part of the Early Childhood Block Grant that funds programs serving children in preschool to third grade.
[2] Preschool is funded as part of the Early Childhood Block Grant that funds all Illinois programs for children younger than 6 years old.
[3] Maryland's SAFE block grant funds preschool as well as other early childhood programs.
[4] Minnesota has several early childhood programs, but only the preschool program is described here.
[5] New Jersey's Early Childhood Program Aid is implemented in 128 districts where at least 20% of students are low income.
[6] New York funds two preschool programs: Experimental Prekindergarten (serving ~20,000 children) and Universal Prekindergarten (serving 47,300). Statewide implementation of the Universal program is slated for FY 2004.

Table 35.2. State-funded preschool initiatives: Teacher training and quality control mechanisms (FY 2000)

State	Teacher qualifications	Teaching certificate required	In-service training required	Technical assistance	Collaboration with other providers
Arizona	**				
Arkansas	BA		√	√	√
California	BA(ECE); O		√	√	√
Colorado	O		√	√	√
Delaware	BA(ECE); CDA		√	√	√
District of Columbia	BA(ECE)	√	√	√	√
Florida	BA(ECE); CDA; O			√	√
Georgia	BA(ECE or EL); CDA; O		√	√	√
Illinois	BA(ECE)	√	√	√	√
Iowa	BA; CDA; O		√	√	√
Kansas	BA	√	**	**	√
Kentucky	BA; CDA; O		√	√	√
Louisiana	BA(ECE or EL)	√		√	
Maine	BA(ECE)	√	√	√	√
Massachusetts	BA(ECE or EL); CDA; NC		√	√	√
Maryland	BA(ECE)	√		√	√
Michigan	BA(ECE); CDA; O		√	√	√
Minnesota	BA(ECE or EL)	√			√
Missouri	BA(ECE); CDA		√	√	√
Nebraska	BA(ECE)		†	√	√
New Jersey	BA(EL)	√	√	√	√
New York	BA(ECE or EL)	√	√	√	√
Ohio	BA(ECE); O		√	√	√
Oklahoma	BA(ECE)	√	√	√	(√)
Oregon	CDA		√	√	√
South Carolina	BA(ECE)		√	√	√
Tennessee	BA(ECE); CDA		√	√	√
Texas	BA(ECE)				
Vermont	BA(ECE); CDA; NC		√	√	√
Virginia	O		√	√	√
Washington	BA(ECE)		√	√	√
West Virginia	BA(ECE)	√			
Wisconsin	BA(ECE)	√			

Notes: √ = implemented statewide; (√) = implementation varies from site to site; † = planned but not yet implemented; ** = no data available.

BA = bachelor's degree in any field; BA(ECE) = bachelor's degree in early childhood education or child development; BA(EL) = bachelor's degree in elementary education; CDA = Child Development Associate credential; NC = no college degree but some early childhood courses; EXP= appropriate work experience; O = other.

Program Accessibility   Accessibility is a function of eligibility requirements and the provision of services that reduce participation barriers (e.g., fees structure, transportation, language services for non–English-speaking families).

Eligibility Requirements   On the whole, SFPPs have eligibility requirements far more liberal than Head Start, which serves children living at or below 100% of the federal poverty level (FPL). All but four states restrict eligibility to at-risk children, with about two thirds of SFPPs using some measure of financial disadvantage as their primary criterion (see Table 35.1). Most typically, this criterion was set at 185% FPL, which corresponds to eligibility for reduced-price meals from the National School Lunch Program. In Georgia, Oklahoma, the District of Columbia, and New York (slated to be statewide by FY 2004), eligibility is based on age alone. Of these, Georgia provides the fullest access to age-eligible children. Although programs in the other three states claim universal eligibility, either space limitations, inadequate funding, or partial implementation limit access in each state to some degree.

Participation Barriers   One of the most obvious barriers to participation for low-income families is paying tuition or attendance fees. Unlike Head Start, which is free to all eligible children and families, some SFPPs charge families for at least part of their services. Massachusetts, for example, has implemented a sliding-fee scale. Another salient barrier is a lack of transportation. Most states reported that they did not provide free transportation to all children who needed it, and Louisiana, where only about 5% of the eligible children are served, reported that a lack of transportation was one of the main barriers to participation. One way to circumvent transportation problems is to provide in-home services. Four states offered home-based programs (Table 35.1), a strategy that Head Start also uses (Head Start Bureau, 1999a). A third barrier to participation is language. Although an increasing number of low-income families are non-native English speakers, only about half of the states reported having English as a second language (ESL) services that were as comprehensive as Head Start's.

Differences across states in approaching common participation barriers surely contribute to the wide variability in the percentage of eligible children served. Of the states that collected data on the percentage of eligible children served, a median of 50% were served by state preschool programs during FY 2000, up from a median 43% reported for FY 1996 (Ripple et al., 1999) and about the same as the 50% currently in Head Start. There was wide variability among states, however. Louisiana and West Virginia reportedly served only 5% and 6% of their eligible children, respectively, whereas Colorado, Iowa, and New York each reportedly served 80% or more of those eligible.

Because the proportion of eligible children served is tied closely to available funds, inadequate program funding can be a powerful barrier to participation. Lack of adequate funding for all eligible children is a well-known problem for Head Start, and many SFPPs struggle with this as well. Some states, however, have taken positive steps toward full funding. These include the states currently or soon to be providing universal access to their SFPPs and Delaware, which has recently pledged full funding to serve all 4-year-olds across an array of programs.

Program Duration and Intensity

All states providing data in this area reported that their SFPPs operated on a schedule similar to the public schools, with 150–180 service days per year. State programs (58%) were typically part-day (2½ to 4 hours per day), with only a few (18%) providing services that approximate a school day (6 to 6½ hours per day). The remaining 24% reportedly had no mandated minimum duration, leaving this to local providers. During FY 1998, Head Start provided full-day services beyond the typical school day in about half of its programs nationwide (Head Start Bureau, 1999a). Although Head Start (excluding Early Head Start) is technically a 2-year program, funding restrictions limit participation to a single year for over half of participating children nationwide. Similarly, only about half of the SFPPs offer more than 1 year of preschool.

Classroom Characteristics

Structural variables of classroom characteristics are reflected in mandates regarding the maximum class size, minimum teacher–child ratios, and minimum level of teacher credentials.

Class Size   Head Start is mandated to serve no more than 20 children in predominantly 4-year-old classrooms and no more than 17 where most children are 3 years old (Head Start Bureau, 1999b).[3] Similarly, NAEYC (1998) recommended no more than 20 children in classrooms serving 3- to 5-year-olds. Mirroring Head Start and NAEYC, most states (78%) mandate that their programs serve 20 or fewer children per classroom. Three states, however, exceeded these guidelines (Texas with 22, California with 24, and New Jersey with 25). Three additional states (Florida, Maine, and Wisconsin) reported having no state-mandated limits on class size. Of these six states, three serve children as young as 3 years old.

Teacher–Child Ratios   Head Start mandates two teachers (plus one volunteer when possible) per classroom, resulting in a maximum teacher–child ratio of 1:10 for classes of mostly 4-year-olds and 1:8.5 for classes of mostly 3-year-olds[4] (Head Start Bureau, 1999b). On the one hand, most states (77%) met or bettered Head Start's mandated ratios; Washington's ratio of 1:6 was by far the best. On the other hand, six states had no mandated teacher–child ratios, and New Jersey only recommended that classrooms have at least one teacher for every 15 children, allowing higher ratios at each site's discretion.

Teacher Qualifications   In the area of teacher training, SFPP requirements were generally more stringent than Head Start. In Head Start, all lead teachers must possess a degree in early childhood education, or at minimum a Child Development Associate (CDA)[5] credential or similar state certificate. All SFPPs had teacher qualifications that met or surpassed this level. Most states (55%) required their preschool teachers to possess a bachelor's degree, typically specific to the field of early childhood education or development. Recognizing Head Start's need in this area, Congress mandated that by FY 2003 at least half of all Head Start teachers must hold a college degree (at minimum a 2-year associates degree) in early childhood education or in a related field with preschool teaching experience (Head Start Amendments, Coats Human Services Reauthorization Act of 1998).

Comprehensive Services

As reflected in Goal 1 of the Goals 2000: Educate America Act of 1994 (PL 103-227), school readiness is a comprehensive construct that encompasses children's physical and mental health, as well as familial well-being and parental involvement. Head Start's compre-

---

[3]In practice, Head Start classrooms may be considerably smaller than the federal mandate. Head Start's Family and Child Experiences Survey (FACES), an ongoing nationally representative study of Head Start quality, reported that classrooms during the spring of 1997 averaged 13.6 students, with 50% of the classrooms having 11.2 to 15.9 children (Zill et al., 1998).

[4]The average teacher–child ratio in the FACES sample of Head Start classes was a far better 1:5.6, with 50% of the classrooms ranging from 4.3 to 6.7 children per adult (Zill et al., 1998).

[5]The CDA requires teachers to possess at least 1) a high school diploma or equivalent; 2) 480 clock hours of appropriate preschool experience; 3) 120 clock hours of specific formal early childhood education; 4) documented competency through formal observation of their teaching, satisfactory confidential evaluations from parents, and an approved professional resource file; and 5) passing scores on the CDA written and oral examinations (Council for Early Childhood Professional Recognition, 1996).

hensive services are recognized as one of the program's greatest strengths. Whereas Head Start programs are mandated to provide comprehensive services to all enrolled children and families, SFPPs are inconsistent in their delivery of these services (see Table 35.3).

As Figure 35.1 demonstrates, only five of the eight services listed in Table 35.3 are mandated by even half of the SFPPs: physical health referrals, immunizations, vision and hearing tests, mental health referrals, and meals that meet minimum nutritional guidelines. (Head Start mandates the provision of all eight of these important services.) These five most common services are mandated in between half and three quarters of all SFPPs, with physical health referrals being the most widely offered. On-site family caseworkers and required home visits were the least commonly provided services. Head Start may be directly responsible for much of the family caseworker services being provided by SFPPs: All but 2 of the 18 states that provide these services subcontract to Head Start.

Parent Involvement Efforts

Overall, SFPPs are less likely than Head Start to provide services to promote parent involvement in their children's education and to enhance family functioning and economic self-sufficiency. About 35% of the states reported *requiring* local preschool programs to involve parents in the governance or implementation of the program, and an additional 26% reported having mechanisms for *encouraging* parent involvement. Only four states offered a full range of parent involvement activities (e.g., participation on advisory councils, opportunities to volunteer in the classroom, regularly scheduled conferences, parent education programs)—three of them because they adhered to the Head Start Program Performance Standards (Head Start Bureau, 1999b).

STATE COMMITMENT TO EARLY CHILDHOOD PROGRAMS

Several potential arguments exist for devolving Head Start to state control, each based on assumptions about the desire and ability of state governments to implement and sustain comprehensive early childhood education programs for children and their families. We consider several of these underlying assumptions in light of extant data regarding the level of commitment and programmatic success states have shown.

Assumption 1: States have the desire to address children's developmental and school-readiness needs.

Before expecting that states can and would implement comprehensive preschool programs, one must assume that they have the desire to do so. One way to ascertain this desire is to examine states' historical interest in providing early childhood programs, both before and after federal funds were made available for this purpose. This inquiry revealed that only 10 states provided preschool or child care services before federal funds were allocated (Ripple et al., 1999). During the 1980s and 1990s, however, when federal funds from a variety of sources were made available to states,[6] the number of SFPPs tripled.

---

[6]For example, the Individuals with Disabilities Education Act (IDEA) of 1990 (PL 101-476) mandated the provision of special education preschool services to children 3–5 years old and created a framework for states to provide services to low-income preschoolers by relaxing the eligibility criteria. In the 1990s, the Child Care Development Fund (CCDF), Temporary Assistance for Needy Families (TANF) program, and Social Services Block Grant (SSBG) also funneled a significant amount of money to states for child care programs for low-income families.

Table 35.3. State-funded preschool initiatives: Comprehensiveness of services (FY 2000 updated)

State	Meals provided	Physical health referrals	Dental referrals	Mental health referrals	Vision and hearing tests	Immunizations provided/ referred	On-site family case workers	Home visits required
Arizona								
Arkansas	√*	√	√		√	√		
California	√*	√	√			√		
Colorado[1]								
Delaware	√*	√	√	√	√	√	√	√
District of Columbia		√						
Florida[2]	√	√			√			
Georgia[3]	√	√		√	√		(√)	
Illinois		√	√	√	√	√		†
Iowa	√*	√	√	√	√	√	(√)	√
Kansas	√*	√	√	√	√	√	(√)	√
Kentucky	√*	(√)	√		√	√	(√)	
Louisiana[4]		(√)		(√)				
Maine		√	(√)	√	(√)	√	(√)	(√)
Massachusetts		(√)	(√)	(√)	(√)	(√)	(√)	
Maryland	√(*)	√	(√)	√	√	√	(√)	(√)
Michigan	√*	√	√	(√)	√	√	(√)	√
Minnesota	√*	√		√				√
Missouri	√*	√		√	√	√	(√)	(√)

486

State									
Nebraska	√*	√	√	√	√	√	√		(√)
New Jersey	√	√	√	(√)	√	√	(√)		(√)
New York	√*	√	√	√	√	√	√		(√)
Ohio	√*	√	√	√	√	√	√		(√)
Oklahoma	√(*)	√	(√)	(√)	(√)	(√)	√		(√)
Oregon	√*	√	√	√	√	√	√		√
South Carolina	√*	(√)	(√)	(√)	√	√	√		√
Tennessee	√*	√	√	√	√	√	√		(√)
Texas⁵	(√)	√	(√)	(√)	(√)	√	√		
Vermont	√	√	√	√	√	√	√		√
Virginia⁶	√*	(√)	√	√	√	√	√		√
Washington	√*	√	√	√	√	√	√		√
West Virginia									
Wisconsin	√*	√	√	√	√	√	√		√

Notes: √ = implemented statewide; (√) = varies from site to site; † = planned but not yet implemented; * = state reported that a minimal nutritional requirement exists for meals; (*) = state reported that nutritional requirements vary from site to site.

¹All health and dental services and home visits are encouraged/recommended but not required in Colorado.

²All Florida program plans must describe developmental/health screening and referral services for each child and must assure that needed services will be provided through interagency coordination.

³Georgia providers must ensure that children have hearing, vision, and dental examination certificates on file within 90 days of the start of program and evidence of age-appropriate immunizations within 30 days of start of program.

⁴In Louisiana, mental and physical health services are not required, but many local programs do provide them. Programs housed in public schools receive same services as K-12 students.

⁵In Texas, all programs are housed in public schools and follow school service provision guidelines.

⁶Ninety percent of Virginia programs are based in the public schools and have the same health services that the school provides. Other programs follow the services of the local grantee, but the state does not have a physical/mental health service mandate.

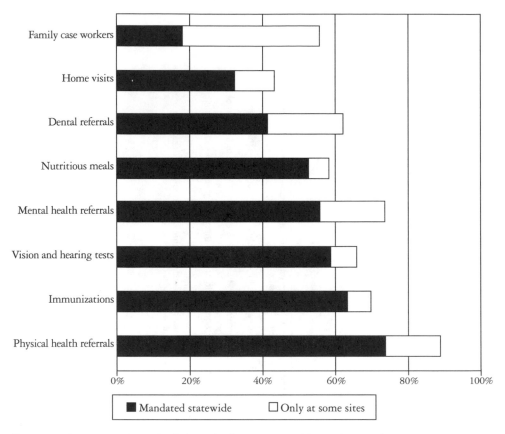

Figure 35.1 Percentage of state-funded preschool programs providing various services.

Despite this dramatic increase in SFPPs, however, many states chose not to use these funds to implement their own statewide preschool programs. Furthermore, one fifth do not even provide supplementary funding to Head Start or other preschool programs and express no plans to implement or supplement programs in the future. A relatively low level of state commitment is also evident in state funding for child care. Indeed, only an estimated 10% of children eligible for child care services under the state-administered Child Care and Development Fund (CCDF) received services during FY 1998 (USGAO, 1999). Our review demonstrates that some states are significantly less committed than others to providing preschool programs. The fact that some states did not choose to fund either preschool or child care programs even when federal funds were available raises concern about their political will to provide these services.

Regarding state financial commitment, a large interstate discrepancy exists between the level of funding for all forms of early childhood care and education, with the 10 most committed states securing $4\frac{1}{2}$ times the level of funding *per child* than the 10 least committed states (Adams & Poersch, 1996). Two hypotheses can be used to explain this discrepancy: 1) States with fewer children and families in need of services can spend less than states with greater need, and 2) some states simply have less money to spend on children. Adams and Poersch (1996), however, reported evidence that suggests that neither of these hypotheses holds. First, states with the highest proportion of child poverty allocated somewhat less money per child relative to states with less child poverty. Second, some states with relatively high 1994 per capita tax revenue allocated significantly less money for early childhood programs compared with tax poorer states.

In sum, although some states have shown a historic desire to provide quality pre-kindergarten programs, the evidence suggests that many states have not demonstrated a similar commitment. Most states did not provide these programs before the allocation of federal funds, and some still do not implement them or meaningfully support existing programs, even with federal funds available. When states do provide programs, many serve only a small percentage of the eligible children. Finally, the provision of state-funded early childhood care and education does not appear to be significantly related to either the needs of their children and families or the amount of state funds available. Rather, there appears to be a philosophical and political divide between states that are committed to the care and education of their young children and those that are not.

Assumption 2: States will maintain Head Start standards of quality and comprehensiveness.

The issue of devolution should rest on whether Head Start could be better administered by state governments at a level of quality consistent with the Performance Standards. After all, high variability Head Start quality is widely acknowledged, leaving room for improvement. As demonstrated by the findings from our survey, however, quality and comprehensiveness of SFPPs also vary significantly among states. For example, minimum teacher–child ratios in state programs ranged from 1:6 in Washington to 1:15 in New Jersey. Likewise, three states (Delaware, Oregon, and Washington) mandated all eight of the comprehensive services offered by Head Start, whereas twice as many states required programs to provide *none* of these services. (The average number of comprehensive services required by states was four.) Also, four states mandated a comprehensive array of parent involvement activities, whereas nearly 40% of the states reported neither mandating nor even recommending ways to involve parents.

When compared with Head Start, SFPPs on the whole appear to do well in some areas and poorly in others. For example, many SFPPs require their lead teachers to possess a level of training that greatly exceeds current Head Start mandates, and no state requires less. Also, the eligibility requirements of most state programs are more liberal than Head Start's, giving more children living above the poverty line the opportunity to attend. Yet, states in general provide far fewer services aimed at promoting children's overall health and well-being, supporting caregivers, increasing family stability and economic self-sufficiency, and facilitating caregiver involvement in their children's education.

Overall, the pattern of strengths and weaknesses for SFPPs, in comparison with Head Start, may be related to their typical placement in state departments of education. That is, the relative strength of classroom quality and weakness of comprehensive services may reflect the differential value placed on these items by public schools in their K-12 mission. Whereas the emphasis on the classroom is not surprising, the de-emphasis on comprehensive services raises concerns that the most basic school-readiness needs, particularly of low-income young children, are not met in many state programs.

In sum, several states provide preschool programs that rival Head Start's quality in some areas. Some programs appear to be quite good overall, but this does not appear to be true for many of the SFPPs: Some provide far fewer services to a much smaller proportion of their eligible children. Although the evidence suggests that some states might use Head Start money to implement or expand their own high-quality programs, it also suggests that many may not.

Assumption 3: States will design and implement programs that most closely meet the unique needs of their children and families.

One might assume that variability across state-funded preschool programs is good, reflecting services tailored to the unique needs of each state's population. The pattern of service differences between states of similar need, resources, and geography, however, does not necessarily support this assumption. Consider Alabama and Mississippi. During FY 1998, these two neighboring states both ranked in the top third of all states in child poverty rates (Alabama ranked 6th, Mississippi tied for 12th) and in the bottom third in fourth-grade reading skills (of 39 participating states, Alabama ranked 28th, Mississippi tied for 37th; Bennett & Lu, 2000; Donahue, Voelkl, Campbell, & Mazzeo, 1999). Despite the apparent need for comprehensive preschool programs aimed at addressing both the effects of poverty and associated deficits in school readiness and subsequent achievement, neither Alabama nor Mississippi has passed SFPP legislation. They remain among 10 states that neither fund their own preschool programs nor supplement existing federal preschool programs operating in their state.

Conversely, the five states that border Alabama and Mississippi (Florida, Georgia, Tennessee, Arkansas, and Louisiana) all provide some level of state-funded preschool programs. Beyond geographic proximity, these five border states also all fall in the bottom one third in fourth-grade reading skills, and three of them are in the top third in child poverty (Louisiana, Georgia, and Florida). In addition to similar need, these five border states are apparently similar to Alabama and Mississippi in the funds they might tap to pay for preschool. Based on FY 1994 per capita tax revenue data, two of the five states had more available state funds than Alabama and Mississippi, two had less, and one state fell between the two (Adams & Poersch, 1996).

The service discrepancies between these states with apparently similar needs and resources are further exacerbated when one considers the comprehensiveness and inclusiveness of the programs in these bordering states. For example, preschool-age children in Alabama and Mississippi do not have access to any SFPP services. Across the state line in Tennessee, however, low-income preschoolers are eligible for a wide variety of comprehensive services but are unlikely to receive them because the program can only accommodate 600 children per year. Whether low-income or not, a child in neighboring Georgia would be practically assured access to state-funded preschool, albeit one that is less comprehensive than Tennessee's (Raden, 1999).

Many examples from across the nation could be cited to highlight differences in service provision among states with similar needs and resources. Even in states that do provide preschool, no apparent relation can be seen between the level of children's needs and the quality, comprehensiveness, or inclusiveness of the programs. Therefore, it seems likely the rationale for state decisions regarding preschool services for low-income children rests in something other than the educational needs of their children, the service needs of their low-income families, or the fullness of their tax coffers.

Assumption 4: States will provide better oversight, leading to higher quality services.

Proponents of devolution believe that moving administrative control of Head Start to the states will afford better oversight and guidance to individual program sites. Although we found that the scope and quantity of mandated services varied widely among states and in comparison to Head Start, the actual *quality* of the services is quite another matter. The former can be measured by reading the states' authorizing legislation and program guidelines and by surveying program administrators. The latter, however, is best measured by the direct observations of outside raters using objective measures of the quality of services actually being delivered.

Considerable evidence has linked the overall quality of preschool programs to their effectiveness at improving children's school readiness (Berlin, O'Neal, & Brooks-Gunn, 1998; Bryant, Burchinal, Lau, & Sparling, 1994; CQO Study Team, 1995, 1999; Frede, 1995; Howes, Galinsky, & Shinn, 1998; Love, Schochet, & Meckstroth, 1996). Furthermore, ineffective child and family programs may be associated with poor implementation and weak quality assurance (Bickman, 1997; Gilliam et al., 2000). The link between program quality and school readiness has been documented in SFPPs in both Michigan (Florian, Schweinhart, & Epstein, 1997) and South Carolina (South Carolina Department of Education, 1987).

Concerns about the quality of Head Start programs around the nation (Zigler & Styfco, 1993) have led to an evaluation of Head Start quality and its bearing on effectiveness. In a nationally representative sample of 40 Head Start classrooms, the Family and Child Experiences Survey (FACES; Zill et al., 1998) has shown that 78.5% of the classes obtained a rating of "good" or better on the Early Childhood Environment Rating Scale (ECERS; Harms & Clifford, 1980), with the remaining classrooms scoring in the "minimal" range. Comparing their results to data from other studies of preschool and child care quality, Zill and colleagues found Head Start's ECERS ratings to be comparable or better than those of preschool classrooms in other types of programs.

Statewide evaluations of quality have only been reported in 3 of the 33 state-funded preschool programs described in this chapter (Kentucky, Michigan, and South Carolina), and only the study in Kentucky used the same instrument employed in the FACES study. Therefore, direct comparison of classroom quality between SFPPs and Head Start is not possible. In Kentucky (Hemmeter et al., 1997), ECERS scores for a representative sample of their SFPP was nearly identical to those for Head Start.

Although most SFPPs are administered through state departments of education, services often are provided by a range of agencies. Fully 64% of SFPPs provide at least some of their services through Head Start centers, a venue second only in frequency to the public schools. The tendency of many states to contract out preschool programs and to provide little or no service guidelines and weak program oversight may contribute to a high degree of variability in service quality both between and within states. Many recent initiatives, such as the FACES evaluation, quality-enhancement funds, and the revision of the Program Performance Standards, have begun to address the issue of unevenness in Head Start quality. Devolving Head Start may be a step in the opposite direction.

Assumption 5: State programs will be more effective than Head Start at enhancing children's school readiness.

Considerable evidence suggests that Head Start can be highly effective at improving comprehensive school readiness among low-income preschoolers (Barnett, 1998; McKey et al., 1985). These findings, however, have been criticized because differences between Head Start participants and contrast children are difficult to find after third grade and because the evidence is not based on randomized experiments. Concerns over "fade-out" have led to questions regarding whether the extant research on Head Start is sufficient to establish its effectiveness (USGAO, 1997). Some researchers have argued that the lack of demonstrable, lasting effects was associated with the quality of elementary schools typically attended by Head Start graduates (Lee & Loeb, 1995). It has also been suggested that fade-out is a methodological artifact due to differential study attrition resulting from Head Start's positive impacts on reducing grade retention (Barnett, 1992). Regardless of the reasons for the dearth of convincing evidence, pressure for accountability has led lawmakers to demand a national, randomized evaluation of Head Start effectiveness (not yet completed at the time of this writing).

Head Start and nearly all SFPPs report that their primary goal is to increase school readiness. Because nearly all SFPPs are administered by state departments of education, one might hypothesize that the states might be more effective than Head Start in supporting children's academic school readiness. The best way to test this hypothesis is to examine the results of formal evaluations of SFPPs. Less than one third of all SFPPs have been formally evaluated. Gilliam and Zigler (2000) identified 10 SFPPs that have been the subject of outcome evaluations that use at least minimally rigorous research methods, although none was randomized. As can be seen in Table 35.4, several SFPPs have evidence to support their effectiveness in promoting school readiness and reducing subsequent grade retention. Overall, effects in the area of school readiness were similar to what has been demonstrated for Head Start, though in many cases the research was not as rigorous and the findings were often mixed. In the areas of child health and parent involvement in their children's education, in which ample evidence exists to suggest Head Start's effectiveness (Hale, Seitz, & Zigler, 1990; Parker, Boak, Griffin, Ripple, & Peay, 1999), SFPPs may not fare as well. In fact, many evaluations did not focus on these outcomes, and those that did typically did not find any significant impacts. This might be expected, given these programs' spotty provision of comprehensive services in these areas as described earlier.

Assumption 6: States will combine funding sources to implement full- and extended-day programs that benefit working families.

Proponents of devolution suggest that states will be able to combine Head Start funds with the currently block granted CCDF, TANF, and SSBG, leading to more efficient service delivery. Blending disparate funding streams that benefit similar populations is

Table 35.4. Statistically significant effects of state-funded preschool programs through grade 4

	End of preschool	K	1	2	3	4
Cognitive/Language development						
District of Columbia		Mixed	Mixed			
Florida	Yes	Yes				
Georgia			No			
Kentucky	Yes	Mixed	Mixed	No		
Maryland		Yes				
Michigan		Yes				
New York	Yes	Mixed			No	
South Carolina			Yes			
Washington	Yes					
Behavior problems						
Florida						Yes
Kentucky	Mixed	No	No	No	No	No
Washington			No	No	No	
Child health						
Washington			No	No	No	
Attendance						
Florida		Mixed	Mixed	No	Mixed	
Georgia		Yes	Mixed			
Kentucky		No	No	No	No	No
New York		Yes	Yes	Yes	Yes	Yes
Grades (reading and math)						
District of Columbia		Mixed	No		No	No
Florida		No	No	No	No	No
Washington			Mixed	No	No	
Achievement tests (reading and math)						
District of Columbia					No	
Florida		Yes	No	No	No	No
Georgia			Mixed			
Maryland					Yes	
New York					Mixed	
South Carolina			Mixed	No	No	
Texas					Yes	
Grade retention						
Florida		Yes	No	No	Yes*	Mixed
Georgia		Yes	No			
Maryland					Yes*	
New York		No	Yes	No	No	No
South Carolina			Yes	No	No	
Texas				Yes		
Special ed referral/Placement						
Georgia		No	No			
Florida		No	No	No	No	No
New York		No	No	No	No	No
South Carolina			Yes			
Texas				Yes		
Washington		No				
Parent involvement						
Georgia		No	No			
Texas			Yes			
Washington			No	No	No	

Note: *Indicates that data were analyzed cumulatively (e.g., grade retention up to and including third grade); *Yes* indicates that significant effects were found for all cohorts studied; *No* indicates no significant effects found; mixed indicates inconsistent findings across cohorts.

praised as a way to reduce both competition among programs and gaps in services. Because many of these programs have similar eligibility criteria, and because families that meet these criteria tend to cluster geographically, there are areas that are oversaturated with services, while other families go unserved. Without blending, or at least coordination between programs at the state or local level, agencies may end up competing for funds, facilities, staff, and even for children.

Despite the advantages, concerns about blended funding at the state level arise from basic differences in mission between Head Start and the goals of CCDF, TANF, and SSBG. Head Start provides a comprehensive array of services aimed at improving low-income children's school readiness, overall health and well-being, and family functioning. Whereas Head Start centers may also provide child care to meet the needs of participating families, child care in its simplest terms[7] is not, nor has it ever been, the program's primary goal (Zigler, 1999). Child care subsidies associated with CCDF, TANF, and SSBG, however, are provided with the primary purpose of increasing the availability of safe and affordable care. Although affordable child care is inarguably essential, simply providing a safe place for children while their parents work is not necessarily the same thing as enhancing children's health and school readiness. The promotion of school readiness in these child care programs would be fortunate, but there are neither effective mechanisms for facilitating these benefits nor methods for determining whether they have occurred (Shaul, 2000). By devolving Head Start in order to co-mingle these funds at the state level, Head Start might become no more than child care for the poor, especially in states that have invested little in promoting comprehensive school readiness.

This is not to say that the states and Head Start cannot work together toward mutual goals. In fact, recognizing the need for increased collaboration to extend hours of service, ACYF's Request For Proposals for 1997 grantees attached financial incentives to the formation of Head Start–child care partnerships. These arrangements have been successful in increasing the supply of full-day, full-year care (see Chapter 23; Kagan, Verzaro-O'Brien, Kim, & Formica, 2000). Further, many states are using block-grant funds to provide wrap-around child care services to Head Start's working families.

CONCLUSIONS

Our review of SFPPs reveals a high level of variability in states' commitment to funding, implementing, and conducting comprehensive preschool programs. We found high variability on nearly every level we examined: guidelines, oversight and regulation, accessibility, classroom quality, comprehensive services, and in the very existence of programs. Some have implemented high-quality programs with state funds, while others have not even accepted available federal funds. When states have implemented SFPPs, the range and quality of services vary considerably—sometimes rivaling Head Start but often falling short. These differences in scope and quality have no apparent relation to either the needs of state populations or states' available financial resources. Our analysis raises two particular concerns associated with Head Start devolution: first, the evident variability across programs; and second, their particular weakness in comprehensive services.

---

[7]We use *child care* in this section to describe the simple provision of care in a safe place for young children outside of their homes, with no intention to suggest that child care programs cannot effectively facilitate children's development.

This evidence suggests that states can implement good, comprehensive prekindergarten programming, and on an individual basis, some states appear to be doing a good job of promoting school readiness. The variability across states, however, is most relevant. The success of a few states does not support the devolution of a federal program to state control. Even with Head Start's own problems with quality assurance, the federal nature of the program ensures that even in states with no SFPP, the most needy children have a chance of access to a program.

Given that SFPPs tend to be under the aegis of public schools, it is not surprising that their greatest strength lies in classroom-related programming. However, it is equally unsurprising that comprehensive services are their weakness, as these services tend to be in the domain of social services agencies and not departments of education. If Head Start is devolved to state authority, children may stand to lose the most in terms of services that promote physical and mental health and parent involvement in their education.

Head Start is more than just child care. It is a program aimed at improving the comprehensive school readiness of low-income children through an array of educational, health, and social services. If the goal of devolution is to better integrate child care programs, America risks losing Head Start's unique contribution to helping close the gap between children in poverty and their more advantaged peers. Indeed, past experience with other block-granted programs suggests that whereas some states would do very well, many would struggle or abandon the effort altogether.

When the National Governor's Association endorsed Goal 1 of what became Goals 2000, we as a nation and each state individually promised all children access to "high-quality and developmentally appropriate preschool programs that help prepare children for school." We promised to infuse these programs with an array of comprehensive services, specifically mentioning health care, nutrition programs, physical education, and parent training and support programs. The target date has come and gone, but the aims remain essential to improving the outlook for all children. If more states deepen their commitment to providing good prekindergarten programs, then the Head Start devolution debate will need revisiting. Indeed, the day may come when all states, or at least most, will have the will and the infrastructure necessary to implement, maintain, and evaluate the success of a comprehensive child and family program such as Head Start. Unfortunately, that day has not yet dawned.

REFERENCES

Adams, G., & Poersch, N.O. (1996). *Who cares? State commitment to child care and early education.* Washington, DC: Children's Defense Fund.

Barnett, W.S. (1992). Benefits of compensatory preschool education. *Journal of Human Resources, 27,* 279–312.

Barnett, W.S. (1998). Long-term effects on cognitive development and school success. In W.S. Barnett & S.S. Boocock (Eds.), *Early care and education for children in poverty* (pp. 11–44). Albany: State University of New York Press.

Bennett, N.G., & Lu, H.H. (2000, August). *Child poverty in the states: Levels and trends from 1979 to 1998* (Research Brief 2). New York: National Center for Children in Poverty, Columbia University. Retrieved August 22, 2000 from http://www.nccp.org/media/cpr00b-text.pdf

Berlin, L.J., O'Neal, C.R., & Brooks-Gunn, J. (1998). What makes early intervention programs work? The program, its participants, and their interaction. *Zero to Three, 18*(4), 4–15.

Bickman, L. (1997). Resolving issues raised by the Fort Bragg evaluation. *American Psychologist, 52*, 562–565.

Bryant, D.M., Burchinal, M., Lau, L.B., & Sparling, J.J. (1994). Family and classroom correlates of Head Start children's developmental outcomes. *Early Childhood Research Quarterly, 9*, 289–309.

Cauthen, N.K., Knitzer, J., & Ripple, C.H. (2000). *Map and track: State initiatives for young children and families, 2000 edition.* New York: National Center for Children in Poverty.

Coats Human Services Reauthorization Act of 1998, PL 105-285, §§ 115 *et seq.* Also available at http://web.lexis-nexis.com/universe/

Council for Early Childhood Professional Recognition. (1996). *The child development associate assessment system and competency standards: Preschool caregivers in center-based programs.* Washington, DC: Author.

CQO Study Team. (1995). *Cost, quality, and child outcomes in child care centers: Technical report.* Denver: University of Colorado.

CQO Study Team. (1999). *The children of the cost, quality, and outcomes study go to school.* Denver: University of Colorado. Executive summary retrieved April 21, 2000 from: http://www.fpg.unc.edu/~ncedl/pages/cqes.htm

Donahue, P.L., Voelkl, K.E., Campbell, J.R., & Mazzeo, J. (1999, March). *The NEAP 1998 reading report card for the nation and the states.* Washington, DC: National Center for Education Statistics, Office of Educational Research and Improvement, U.S. Department of Education. Retrieved August 22, 2000 from: http://nces.ed.gov/naep/pdf/main1998/1999500.pdf

Florian, J.E., Schweinhart, L.J., & Epstein, A.S. (1997). *Early returns: First year report of the Michigan School-Readiness Program Evaluation.* Ypsilanti, MI: High/Scope Press.

Frede, E.C. (1995). The role of program quality in producing early childhood program benefits. *The Future of Children, 5*(3), 115–132.

Gilliam, W.S., Ripple, C.H., Zigler, E.F., & Leiter, V. (2000). Evaluating child and family demonstration initiatives: Lessons from the Comprehensive Child Development Program. *Early Childhood Research Quarterly, 15*, 41–59.

Gilliam, W.S., & Zigler, E.F. (2000). A critical meta-analysis of all evaluations of state-funded preschool from 1977 to 1998: Implications for policy, service delivery and program evaluation. *Early Childhood Research Quarterly, 15*, 441–473.

Goals 2000: Educate America Act of 1994, PL 103-227, §§ 102 *et seq.*

Hale, B.A., Seitz, V., & Zigler, E. (1990). Health services and Head Start: A forgotten formula. *Journal of Applied Developmental Psychology, 11*, 447–458.

Harms, T., & Clifford, R.M. (1980). *Early childhood environment rating scale.* New York: Teachers College Press.

Head Start Bureau. (1999a). *1999 Head Start fact sheet* [online]. Retrieved August 14, 2000 from: http://www2.acf.dhhs.gov/programs/hsb/research/factsheets/99_hsfs.htm

Head Start Bureau. (1999b). *Head Start program regulations* (45 CFR, Parts 1301–1311). Retrieved August 16, 2000 from: http://www.acf.hhs.gov/programs/hsb/performance/index.htm

Hemmeter, M.L., Wilson, S.M., Townley, K.F., Gonzalez, L., Epstein, A., & Hines, H. (1997). *Third party evaluation of the Kentucky Education Reform Act Preschool Programs.* Lexington: College of Education & College of Human Environmental Studies, University of Kentucky.

Howes, C., Galinsky, E., & Shinn, M. (1998). *The Florida child care quality improvement study: 1996 report.* New York: Families and Work Institute.

Individuals with Disabilities Education Act (IDEA) Amendments of 1986, PL 99-457, §§ 303 *et seq.*

Kagan, S.L., Verzaro-O'Brien, M., Kim, U., & Formica, M. (2000). *Head Start-child care partnership study.* New Haven, CT: Yale University, Bush Center in Child Development and Social Policy.

Lee, V.E., & Loeb, S. (1995). Where do head start attendees end up? One reason why preschool effects fade out. *Educational Evaluation and Policy Analysis, 17*, 62–82.

Love, J.M., Schochet, P.Z., & Meckstroth, A.L. (1996). *Are they in any real danger? What research does and does not tell us about childcare quality and children's well-being.* Princeton, NJ: Mathematica.

McKey, R., Condelli, L., Ganson, H., Barrett, B., McConkey, C., & Plantz, M. (1985). *The impact of Head Start on children, families, and communities: Final report of the Head Start Evaluation, Synthesis, and Utilization Project.* Washington, DC: U.S. Department of Health and Human Services.

National Association for the Education of Young Children (NAEYC). (1998). *Accreditation criteria and procedures of the National Association for the Education of Young Children: 1998 edition.* Washington, DC: Author.

Parker, F.L., Boak, A.Y., Griffin, K.W., Ripple, C., & Peay, L. (1999). Parent-child relationship, home learning environment, and school readiness. *School Psychology Review, 28,* 413–425.

Raden, A. (1999, August). *Universal prekindergarten in Georgia: A case study of Georgia's lottery-funded pre-k program* (Working Paper Series). New York: Foundation for Child Development. Retrieved from: http://www.ffcd.org/prek.pdf

Ripple, C.H., Gilliam, W.S., Chanana, N., & Zigler, E. (1999). Will fifty cooks spoil the broth? The debate over entrusting Head Start to the states. *American Psychologist, 54,* 327–343.

Schulman, K., Blank, H., & Ewen, D. (1999). *Seeds of success: State prekindergarten initiatives 1998–1999.* Washington, DC: Children's Defense Fund.

Shaul, M.S. (2000, April). *Preschool education: Federal investment for low-income children significant but effectiveness unclear.* Testimony before the Subcommittee on Children and Families, Committee on Health, Education, Labor, and Pensions, U.S. Senate (GAO/T-HEHS-00-83). Washington, DC: United States General Accounting Office. Retrieved from: http://www.access.gpo.gov/su_docs/aces/aces160.shtml

Smith, S.L., Fairchild, M., & Groginsky, S. (1997). *Early childhood care and education: An investment that works* (2nd ed.). Washington, DC: National Conference of State Legislatures.

South Carolina Department of Education. (1987). *Executive summary of the evaluation of South Carolina half-day programs for four-year-olds.* Columbia: Office of Research, South Carolina Department of Education. Available: State Documents, South Carolina State Library, Columbia.

U.S. General Accounting Office (USGAO). (1994). *Community Development Block Grant: Economic development activities reflect local priorities* (GAO/RCED-94-108). Washington, DC: Author. Retrieved from: http://www.access.gpo.gov/su_docs/aces/aces160.shtml

U.S. General Accounting Office (USGAO). (1995). *Block grants: Characteristics, experience, and lessons learned* (GAO/HEHS-95-74). Washington, DC: Author. Retrieved from: http://www.access.gpo.gov/su_docs/aces/aces160.shtml

U.S. General Accounting Office (USGAO). (1997). *Head Start: Research provides little information on impact of current program* (GAO/HEHS-97-59). Washington, DC: Author. Retrieved from: http://www.access.gpo.gov/su_docs/aces/aces160.shtml

U.S. General Accounting Office (USGAO). (1999). *Education and care: Early childhood programs and services for low-income families* (GAO/HEHS-00-11). Washington, DC: Author. Retrieved from: http://www.access.gpo.gov/su_docs/aces/aces160.shtml

Young, K.T., Marsland, K.W., & Zigler, E. (1997). The regulatory status of center-based infant and toddler child care. *American Journal of Orthopsychiatry, 67,* 535–544.

Zigler, E. (1999). Head Start is not child care. *American Psychologist, 54,* 142.

Zigler, E.F., & Styfco, S.J. (1993). Using research and theory to justify and inform Head Start expansion. *Social Policy Report of the Society for Research in Child Development, 7,* 1–25.

Zill, N., Resnick, G., McKey, R.H., Clark, C., Connell, D., Swartz, J., et al. (1998). *Head Start Program Performance Measures: Second progress report.* Washington, DC: Administration on Children, Youth and Families, U.S. Department of Health and Human Services.

CHAPTER 36

Caveat Emptor
The Head Start Scam

JOHN HOOD

I t is safe to say that America's public schools are not exactly basking in the glow of achievement and approbation. While the education establishment continues to block fundamental state and federal reform efforts, public disaffection with the country's system of public education is at an all-time high. Business leaders are increasingly vocal in their criticism of public schools. Journalists are not as eager as they used to be to parrot the National Education Association's line on school reform. Activists across the country have won important victories—from privately funded voucher plans to local and state choice initiatives—against sloth and bureaucratic intransigence. Students in a widening swath of towns can take advantage of vouchers from businesses and foundations to attend local private schools. Private firms are managing public schools in several states.

But even as public elementary and secondary schools increasingly draw fire from every side, one government-run education program continues to attract substantial political and public support: Head Start. Both liberal Democratic and conservative Republican governors tout it. Even disgruntled, frustrated business leaders—willing to back revolutionary change in K-12 education—sing the praises of Head Start, a Great Society program that spends billions of dollars per year to provide educational, developmental, medical, and nutritional services to poor preschoolers.

Head Start's impressive public relations triumph should surprise no one. The program's boosters base their appeal on a sensible-sounding premise: If we can intervene early in poor children's lives, give them a "head start" on developing into good students and well-educated teens, then many of them will not grow up to be welfare mothers, deadbeats, or criminals. With every social catastrophe averted, we'll save ourselves a lot of worry, trouble, and money. That is the essence of "fiscal conservatism," advocates say, be-

---

This chapter is adapted with permission from the original published by the Cato Institute in 1992.

cause a little "public investment" now will pay huge dividends in tax revenues and forgone social spending later.

Head Start's sales pitch works wonderfully. Business leaders like the investment rhetoric. Journalists love all the photo opportunities with cute, smiling kids. Teachers' union officials and other leaders of the education establishment relish the chance to extend their reach beyond kindergarten into the preschool years. Big-spending politicians enjoy touting a program that actually appears to work. Fiscal conservatives prefer Head Start's relatively low price tag (in comparison with the rest of the education establishment's agenda: higher teachers' salaries, smaller class sizes, bigger buildings, equalization of spending for small or rural school systems, and so forth).

The pitch works, despite the fact that Head Start's major selling point—early intervention can prevent future dependence and delinquency—rests on several shaky foundations. First, it assumes that policy makers can draw sweeping national conclusions from studies of a few unique (and non–Head Start) preschool programs. Second, it assumes that children's futures are fundamentally malleable, that a brief outside intervention can make an indelible impact on most children's lives despite the continuing influence of both heredity and environment. And third, the Head Start thesis assumes not only that successful early intervention is possible but that government is an appropriate and effective provider of it.

All three of these propositions are false. Head Start's hucksters, all smiles and promises, have sold the public on a shiny prototype that bears little resemblance to what will actually be provided and, on closer examination, is an empty shell with nothing under the hood. Before American policy makers sign anything, they'd better take a good look at what they're getting.

FOUR DECADES OF HEAD START

Head Start was a linchpin of President Lyndon Johnson's Great Society and it is one of the few programs created during the mid-1960s that has not only survived basically intact but also retains a good reputation outside the insular circles of Johnson Administration alumni. Since its inception in 1965, the program has served more than 18.5 million preschool children, the vast majority of whom have come from poor households. The Head Start Bureau (2000) reported that more than 826,000 children were enrolled in Head Start in fiscal year (FY) 1999, 55% more than in 1989.

A few years ago, numerous press accounts and public statements by Head Start boosters made the claim that the program was "falling short" of its potential as the result of federal neglect and budget cuts (e.g., "Funds for Head Start," 1992). It is certainly true that Congress never appropriated the amount of funds authorized in 1990 Head Start legislation, which was the first time money was targeted to improve quality; for example, the bill authorized $4.3 billion in Head Start spending in 1992, whereas the actual appropriation was approximately $2.2 billion. Still, that 1992 figure represents a real increase of about 70% over Head Start's 1981 budget, and FY 2001's $6.2 billion is nearly a whopping 400% hike.

Although Head Start does serve poor children, one common stereotype of the program beneficiaries—that they are mostly black children of single mothers—is untrue.

Only about half of the children in Head Start come from single-parent families; 30% of Head Start children are white, 35% are African American, and 28% are Hispanic (Head Start Bureau, 2000).

TELLING HEAD START WHOPPERS

The efficacy of preschool programs hasn't been ignored by academic and government researchers. During the past 3 decades, researchers have published hundreds of studies focused on the Head Start program itself, though only about half of them provided detailed information about samples and results (Haskins, 1989; U.S. General Accounting Office [USGAO], 1997). The distinction between studies of Head Start and those of other preschool programs is crucial—all preschool programs are not created equal.

Policy makers have gotten the wrong impression about Head Start by listening to enthusiastic boosters who cite the success of model preschool programs as though it proved the efficacy of Head Start. But you don't judge the quality of a Ford Escort by test driving a Lincoln Continental. Similarly, Head Start must be judged on its own merits, not by a sort of "fleet averaging" gimmick that hypes the successes of one or two unique projects that aren't Head Start programs at all.

Perhaps the most famous preschool in the United States is the Perry Preschool in Ypsilanti, Michigan. In 1962, researchers selected 123 poor children to take part in an experiment. Half the group was given 2 years of preschool instruction and services, $2\frac{1}{2}$ hours per day, 5 days per week. The other half took part in no preschool program. Both groups of children were then tracked throughout their academic careers and into adulthood. The Perry students demonstrated not only significant short-term gains—higher IQ scores 1 year into the program, for example—but also long-term gains on some important social indicators. About two thirds of the Perry group graduated from high school, compared with 50% of the control group. Similarly, whereas members of the control group had been arrested an average of 4.6 times by age 27, the average was exactly half that among the Perry graduates (Schweinhart, Barnes, & Weikart, 1993).

Studies of the long-term effects of the Perry program, many conducted by the operators of the program itself, made a big splash when they were first published in the 1980s. Suddenly, there was "hard evidence" for the notion that universal preschool for poor children might significantly reduce crime, increase employment and graduation rates, and lessen the dependency on public services. The Perry studies even generated a useful factoid for advocates of preschool education: Every dollar spent on "quality preschool education" saves about $5 in future economic, education, welfare, and crime costs (e.g., Children's Defense Fund, 1991).

Policy makers at the beginning of the 21st century should keep in mind the atmosphere in which those findings were made public. When Ronald Reagan was elected, Washington, D.C., bureaucrats still running Great Society programs got a big scare. Most believed their programs were doomed. Even though Head Start enjoyed strong support from Reagan Administration officials such as budget director David Stockman and Caspar Weinberger, former secretary of Nixon's Department of Health, Education and Welfare, program boosters sought to cement their loyalty. They made a calculated effort to link the long-term benefits of the Perry Preschool with Head Start. In fact, while the researchers who studied Perry believed their results wouldn't generate much national interest, Head Start supporters engineered a highly successful public relations effort that created a boomlet of positive press coverage. As Edward Zigler, one of the creators of Head Start in the 1960s, wrote, program boosters believed that "if the research had implications for Head Start funding, reporters would be interested" (Zigler & Muenchow, 1992, p. 192). They were.

The problem is that the studies of the Perry project actually don't tell us very much about the efficacy of Head Start. For openers, the Perry project and Head Start are not interchangeable. Perry was a special experiment conducted under near-laboratory conditions. "These intervention programs were conducted under ideal circumstances," wrote Ron Haskins, a staff member of the House Ways and Means Committee. They had "skilled researchers, capable staffs with lots of training, ample budget. . . . It seems unwise to claim that the benefits produced by such exemplary programs would necessarily be produced by ordinary preschool programs conducted in communities across the United States" (1989, p. 277).

The difference between studies of the Perry experiment and studies of Head Start programs couldn't be more striking. A 1985 synthesis of Head Start studies to that date showed that ambitious claims for Head Start's long-term effects were exaggerated. "Children enrolled in Head Start enjoy significant immediate gains in cognitive test scores, socioemotional test scores, and health status," the authors noted. "In the long run, cognitive and socioemotional test scores of former Head Start students do not remain superior to those of disadvantaged children who did not attend Head Start" (McKey et al., 1985, p. 1). More recent summaries confirm their conclusion. Short-term gains in intelligence scores and learning skills disappear for most Head Start students after 2 or 3 years at school, and copious evidence that Head Start has a long-term effect on graduation rates, teen pregnancy, crime, or unemployment simply doesn't exist (Haskins, 1989; USGAO, 1997).

Another major difference between Perry and Head Start is obvious: Studies of the Perry project track only a relative handful of students, 100 or so, through their academic and early adult lives. Studies of Head Start, on the other hand, involve hundreds of preschool programs and thousands of children. When dealing with complex issues such as child development, researchers and policy makers must seek out a consensus—not simply hype a few best cases. To any fair-minded observer, the evidence available to date on Head Start suggests only temporary academic benefits. A few studies of Head Start programs show limited benefits extending until about junior high, but most do not. Grandiose claims about Head Start being an antipoverty program, or an anticrime program, or a welfare-reform program exhibit little regard for truth or reason.

THE PROBLEM WITH EARLY INTERVENTION

Policy makers should seek a consensus among researchers and academic literature when devising new policies or evaluating old ones. Yet, in the case of Head Start, as in so many others, elected officials, bureaucrats, and opinion leaders have mistaken a few special cases for "proof" of a general thesis: Early intervention by the federal government can keep poor children from growing up into poor adults or criminals. The reason elected officials and others swallow the Head Start hype hook, line, and sinker is that they believe in "early intervention" as an article of faith, not as a proposition to be proven or disproven with facts.

That is ironic, given that the early intervention fad in child development and education circles, which began in mid–20th century and gained momentum during the 1960s, is starting to fade. Liberal social workers, development specialists, educators, and others who graduated from college in the 1950s and 1960s were convinced that a child's social and intellectual development was infinitely malleable. Jerome Kagan, a Harvard developmental psychologist who has studied human behavior for more than 3 decades, explained in an interview,

> In 1950, when I graduated from college, there was much more optimism over the ability of the social sciences, especially developmental psychology, to solve social problems like crime, delinquency, and psychosis. Psychology was very confident then for it believed that some combination of learning theory and psychoanalysis constituted the truth; hence most social problems were learned rather than genetic. Therefore, if one could discover the learning experiences of children during their first five or six years that produced these undesirable outcomes, we could tell parents in America what they should and should not do, and we would have no crime and no more psychoses. (Ellis & Robbins, 1990, p. 623)

But after years of research in developmental psychology, as well as years of experience in running the new social programs of the Great Society, many experts began to change their minds. It became apparent that children's minds are so unique, and personal traits so determined by heredity and idiosyncratic relationships between particular parents and children, that researchers could no longer defend their limitless faith in the efficacy of intervention. Again, Kagan explained,

> It is improbable that I would be working on temperament because temperament implies the inheritance of styles of behavior and moods that are hard to change. I am politically liberal, trained in the 1950s to be an environmentalist who, for the first twenty years of my career, wrote essays critical of the role of biology and celebrated the role of the environment. I am now working in the opposite camp because I was dragged there by my data. (Ellis & Robbins, 1990, p. 624)

Kagan's research revealed significant differences in the way children develop at very early ages, before parenting environments can really make a difference. For example, studies showed that even in the first week of life, middle-class Chinese-American infants displayed different personality traits than did middle-class Caucasian-American infants (Kagan, Kersley, & Zelazo, 1978). Other studies using twins separated at birth showed that heredity has an important influence on future behavior (e.g., Scarr, 1989). Similarly, psychologists found that "general rules" about the success of particular parenting styles or environments were hard to come by (Rowe, 1990). Research showed that the relationship between care providers (parents, therapists, and teachers) and children matters more than the type of care provided. Because children exhibit different personalities—due largely to heredity—they require different types of care, therapy, and education.

For decades, those currents of thought flowed through the psychological literature without having a great deal of impact on policy. But in the 1980s and 1990s, psychologists and child development experts began to speak out against some of the main assumptions of the therapeutic state—and against the idea that preschool education is a "silver bullet" against social problems (Bruer, 1999). In an important 1990 article in *Science*, a number of experts told reporter Constance Holden of their doubts about Head Start's success. Kagan, for example, told Holden that early intervention programs have traditionally been spelled out like recipes: administer the treatment, measure the outcome. But the crucial aspect, he said, may be the relationship between the person doing the intervening and the child. And, unfortunately, "we don't know how to measure relationships," he told Holden (1990, p. 1402).

Kagan's point has great relevance to the Head Start debate. If he is right, not only is it unwise to assume that a few unique projects prove the need for universal preschool education but also it is a fundamental misunderstanding of the data. Personal talents of staff, not design, explain the success of a few projects. So a mandatory universal preschool program for poor children, even one based on the model of the Perry Preschool, will not enjoy the success its boosters assume.

Several other noted developmental psychologists and education experts have questioned the assumptions behind the Head Start myth. Russell Gersten of the University of Oregon told Holden that early intervention research "is not a very intellectually rigorous field" (p. 1402). He said the field was highly politicized and had therefore produced "mushy findings" such as those on the Perry Preschool project. Child development specialist Craig Ramey also blamed the problem on political influence. Ramey said that in order to support Head Start, an idea everyone in the field instinctively thought was good, research on early intervention "got pushed prematurely into looking at long-term consequences"—the purported findings that research data support the least (Holden, 1990, p. 1402).

It is important to remember that many of the experts still believe in the efficacy of government programs; they simply do not buy Head Start's claim to be a "silver bullet." Most, in fact, favor even more government spending on new "Head Start plus" programs that would continue to provide special attention and services to youngsters throughout their school careers. For example, *Newsweek*—breaking a virtual "code of silence" once common among the major media—trumpeted the results of a study on the long-term impact of a large intervention project in Chicago with the headline, "A Head Start Does Not Last" (Kantrowitz, 1992). The study was conducted by J.S. Fuerst of Loyola University School of Social Work. Fuerst traced the performance of 684 Chicago kids who attended not only 2 years of preschool but also, during their elementary school years, 2–7 additional years of what Fuerst called "Head Start to the fourth power." Although his initial study—published in 1974 when most of the students were age 13 and younger—found significant reading and math gains, his later study told a different story. Only 62% of the participating students graduated from high school, compared with the then national average of 80%. Continuing studies of the project by Arthur Reynolds (Chapter 27) show that measures of school success remain improved relative to control groups of poor children, but the long-term impact of the intensive Chicago program is nevertheless disappointing in absolute terms.

Fuerst himself contends that his results only prove the need for special education programs that last as long as 9 years, which shatters the notion that a small early investment heads off bigger costs down the road. It also begs an obvious question: Why not fix the school system itself, rather than devise new and expensive federal supplements to it?

Furthermore, if children can avoid the ravages of poverty, dependency, and delinquency only if they receive a quality education throughout their school career, then why spend the extra money on Head Start in the first place? Early intervention could never make as much of a difference to a child as 13 years of quality education could, as even the most vocal Head Start booster admits. The authors of a large longitudinal study, which is generally favorable to Head Start, wrote,

> Policy decisions that support the expansion of preschool programs without addressing the more fundamental question of trying to alter what happens to disadvantaged children in our nation's public schools are short-sighted. Research such as this, which provides evidence of some success of preschool education for disadvantaged children, could be used to support arguments for what might be politically expedient and even short-sighted "solutions" to a pervasive problem. Inducing sustained and successful academic experiences for children of poverty *throughout* their educational careers, rather than focusing on efforts to "fix" the problem with one-year preschool programs (however successful they may be), is absolutely essential. (Lee, Brooks-Gunn, Schnur, & Liaw, 1990, p. 505)

A similar point is made by Edward Zigler and Susan Muenchow in their book, *Head Start: The Inside Story of America's Most Successful Education Experiment* (1992). As you can tell by its title, the book is full of praise for Head Start. The authors exaggerate the evidence of Head Start's long-term benefits and ignore some of the evidence against the benefits of early intervention generally. But even Zigler and Muenchow resist the notion that Head Start is a "silver bullet." They wrote,

> We must also guard against the impression that any one- or two-year program can, by itself, rescue a whole generation of children and families. Early childhood educators are rediscovering what was really clear from the outset of Head Start: the program is far more effective when it is followed up by projects designed to ease the child's transition to elementary school. (p. 207)

International evidence would tend to support the view that early intervention is not a panacea for learning problems. Indeed, in such countries as Japan and Korea, no "Head Start" types of program exist for the vast majority of children. In general, Asian parents simply do not believe that formal instruction during a child's preschool years provides a boost in educational achievement. Instead, wrote Harold Stevenson and James Stigler, "Asian mothers believe that whatever teaching they do with their preschool children should be as informal as possible" (1992, p. 76). Japanese preschools have no relations to elementary schools; they exist primarily to help children "learn to enjoy group life and to participate effectively in it," Stevenson and Stigler continued (p. 78).

In keeping with the pattern discussed previously, American children do at first exhibit academic benefits from formal preschool experiences. American kindergartners hold their own, or even outscore their Asian peers, on various tests of academic performance. But those benefits are purely short-term. "Only a year separates the ages of kindergartners and the first-graders, but during this time the performance of the American children deteriorates relative to that of the Chinese and Japanese children," Stevenson and Stigler concluded (pp. 79–80), and they went on to identify explanatory factors in schooling and home environments. In other words, even though we already give American children a "head start" in academic competitions with Asians, our children still fall behind fairly quickly.

The dilemma posed for proponents of the Head Start myth by modern psychological research is perhaps best summarized by the comments of Sandra Scarr, who has served as president or board member of some of the most prestigious professional associations in psychology during her academic career. She is no conservative hack; she believes in an activist role for government in day care and other areas. Yet she, too, questions many of the assumptions implicit in the Head Start hype. She believes that heredity plays a crucial role in development, that children's natures are not infinitely malleable by outstanding forces, and that parenting environments need not be uniformly "perfect" for the children to succeed. "Fortunately, evolution has not left development of the human species, nor any other, at the easy mercy of variations within environments," she said in her 1991 presidential address to the Society for Research in Child Development. "We are robust and able to adapt to wide-ranging circumstances . . . . If we were so vulnerable as to be led off the normal developmental track by slight variations in our parenting, we should not long have survived" (1992, pp. 15–16).

Scarr is blunt about Head Start. "There is quite a mystique in our culture about the importance of early intervention," she told Holden (1990, p. 1402), yet "there is no evidence [for it] whatever." Scarr and other child development experts may favor a significantly different approach to education reform than do free-market thinkers, but they clearly reject the notion that "investing" our hopes and our tax dollars in preschool education programs such as Head Start will make our social ills go away. It is the public schools that must change. Head Start is neither a necessary nor a sufficient condition for helping poor children succeed.

HEAD STARTS, GOVERNMENT STUMBLES

Despite the paucity of evidence that Head Start has a long-term impact on children, there is no doubt that Head Start's medical, nutritional, and (to some extent) educational services provide immediate benefits to poor children. But it does not follow that a federal government program is needed to provide those services to preschoolers. A mix of private-sector, nonprofit, church, community group, and extended-family providers is a better way to provide such care for children, poor or not.

There is plenty of evidence to suggest that an ever-increasing number of employers provide help to their employees in finding quality child care and preschool programs. Some large corporations, such as Campbell Soup Company, Corning Glass Works, and Richardson-Vicks U.S.A., provide their employees on-site or near-site child care centers for a low weekly fee. Other corporations are forming consortia to make child care available to all employees who live in a particular city or metropolitan area (Nollen, 1989).

Still, the number of companies that can actually provide programs on site will always remain rather small; a 1989 survey of employers by Developmental Child Care, Inc., of Connecticut found that only 600 firms—of 3,700 firms that provided employees with some help with child care—had centers on site. The remaining firms provided financial assistance, information, referral, and flexible personnel policies to help employees find the care best suited to their children (Werther, 1989). There is no need for government to force further action on this front because competitive pressures will continue to drive many large and medium-sized firms toward helping employees find appropriate care for their children (Rodgers & Rodgers, 1989).

Given those trends, it should come as no surprise that America's education establishment covets the huge, lucrative market for providing preschool care. That's one reason (blame-shifting is another) the National Education Association (NEA), state and federal education bureaucrats, and education researchers and consultants, and their legislative allies in Washington, D.C., and the state capitals all spend so much time attributing current education problems to lack of a comprehensive federal Head Start program. Indeed, the education establishment would like to take it one step further and base virtually all Head Start and preschool programs at public schools. They view the prospect of a dynamic, private marketplace for preschool care with much disdain. By masterminding further government intervention in preschool programs, the establishment hopes to broaden and strengthen its power over American education. If you think I exaggerate their intentions, consider the remarks of Keith Geiger, then president of the NEA, in a March 1991 editorial in the association's in-house magazine:

> Might not our reluctance to open our public schools to children younger than age five be one reason our nation faces such a stern economic challenge from foreign competitors? I think there's something to that analysis. And so does our NEA Board of Directors. That's why the Board has formally adopted a position that "public schools should become the primary providers of preschool education for three- and four-year-olds." . . . . Right now, early childhood education is a hodgepodge of public and private day-care centers, nursery schools, child-care homes, and baby sitters of widely differing quality and huge cost variations. All of us know what this hodgepodge means. It means failure. (1991, p. 2)

Geiger's barely concealed contempt for diversity and competition demonstrates a bureaucratic conceit of the highest order: Unless one institution the public school—controls the entire preschool sector and imposes uniformity, children will fail. Given public education's record—national reading scores were essentially flat from 1992 to 2003, for example, despite dramatic increases in funding and reform initiatives—it would be hard for anyone unaffiliated with the NEA not to burst out laughing at Geiger's preposterous thesis.

A HEAD START WON'T WIN THE RACE

America's leaders and policy makers need to think more strategically about how best to improve the lives and prospects of poor children.

First, there is the issue of child care costs. In 1998, full-time care for a 4-year-old cost an average of $4,000 to $6,000 per year (Mitchell, Stoney, & Dichter, 2001). Some church-run centers provide lower cost care, although private, selective preschools and centers can cost up to $200 or more per week.

Government is one major cause of such high costs. Local and state regulations of employees, staff–child ratios, services, insurance, and amenities all increase the per child cost of preschool and child care significantly (Hood & Merline, 1990; Lehrman & Pace, 1985).

Zoning is another major culprit; it forces child care centers into business or industrial areas and raises building costs (Postrel, 1989). Numerous studies confirm that effect.

One study of child care regulation in North Carolina found that every increase of 1 year in training mandates for caregivers increased the annual fee per child by $71 (in 1992 dollars). The average fee increased another $429 for every increase of one caregiver per day care group (Walden, 1992). Even researchers who are sanguine about the impact of government regulations nonetheless advocate lifting some of the costliest rules, such as child–staff ratios, and reducing the regulatory burden on informal home-care arrangements that provide adequate, low-cost services for most families—especially for poor families who may find formal centers or preschools beyond their means even after deregulation (Gormley, 1991).

There is no evidence that formal centers or preschools necessarily provide better care for children than informal centers and homes (indeed, there is quite a bit of evidence to the contrary; Siegel, 1990). Many psychologists counsel that preschoolers, disadvantaged or not, should not be pushed precipitously into formal education, anyway. As Lilian Katz, a professor of early childhood education at the University of Illinois, Urbana-Champaign, wrote in *Parents* magazine,

> The fact that preschoolers *can* learn basic academic skills through formal instruction does not mean that they should: The issue is not simply whether it can be done but rather what the immediate and long-term effects of early academic pressures might be. Recent research indicates that for many children, early academic pressures produce anxiety, doubts about parents' acceptance of them, and less positive attitudes toward school. (1990, p. 206)

Relieving preschools, child care centers, and informal child care arrangements of regulatory burdens would do much to help poor families provide for their children. Radically altering the federal government's current role in preschool programs—by ending the Head Start program—would help even more. The amount of federal funds appropriated for Head Start in FY 2000—$5.2 billion—represents a per child expenditure of around $5,400 (Head Start Bureau, 2000), surely a sum large enough to provide care for a child in the private or nonprofit sector. Policy makers should at least convert Head Start funds into direct grants to families, thus allowing poor parents to choose among care providers. For all the same reasons that choice and competition could improve public schools, Head Start–like services would be better provided in the already competitive marketplace for child care and preschool programs.

An even better approach would be to convert federal money now committed to Head Start into vouchers or tax relief to give parents the opportunity to send their children to private or parochial schools in their communities. If the federal government converted the amount of money spent on Head Start in 2000 into $2,000 vouchers—which would significantly defray the cost of attending most private schools—each year as many as 2.6 million poor children would have the chance to get a decent education in a local school of their parents' choice. As argued previously, helping poor children to attend quality elementary and secondary schools would be a much better "public investment" than extending the federal government's reach further into the lives of preschool children.

Head Start's popularity is due more to slick salesmanship and superficial thinking about child development than to proven success. The immediate benefits Head Start confers on poor children—by improving their nutrition, providing a safe and stimulating environment, and helping teach their parents basic parenting skills—could be made available to poor families more efficiently through a competitive, deregulated marketplace of private centers, nonprofit organizations, and church- and community-run programs. More important, early intervention by any outside institution is not a panacea for the long-term ravages of poverty. The money spent on Head Start, if converted into vouchers for poor children to attend the schools of their parents' choice, offers a much better prospect of ending the poverty cycle and its immense public costs than does increased government control of and intervention in the lives of American preschoolers.

REFERENCES

Bruer, J.T. (1999). *The myth of the first three years: A new understanding of early brain development and life-long learning.* New York: Free Press.

Children's Defense Fund. (1991). *The state of America's children yearbook.* Washington, DC: Author.

Ellis, M.V., & Robbins, E.S. (1990). In celebration of nature: A dialogue with Jerome Kagan. *Journal of Counseling and Development, 68,* 623.

Funds for Head Start. (1992, July 9). *Christian Science Monitor,* 20.

Geiger, K. (1991, March). An idea whose time has come. *NEA Today,* 2.

Gormley, W.T., Jr. (1991). State regulations and the availability of child-care services. *Journal of Policy Analysis and Management, 10,* 91.

Haskins, R. (1989). Beyond metaphor: The efficacy of early childhood education. *American Psychologist, 44,* 274–282.

Head Start Bureau. (2000). *Project Head Start 2000 fact sheet.* Washington, DC: Administration on Children, Youth and Families, U.S. Department of Health and Human Services.

Holden, C. (1990). Head Start enters adulthood. *Science, 247,* 1400–1402.

Hood, J., & Merline. J. (1990). What consumers should know about day care. *Consumers' Research,* 21–26.

Kagan, J., Kersley, R.B., & Zelazo, P.R. (1978). *Infancy: Its place in human development.* Cambridge, MA: Harvard University Press.

Kantrowitz, B. (1992, January 27). A Head Start does not last. *Newsweek,* 44–45.

Katz, L.G. (1990). Should preschoolers learn the three R's? *Parents, 65*(10), 206.

Lee, V.E., Brooks-Gunn, J., Schnur, E., & Liaw, F. (1990). Are Head Start effects sustained? A longitudinal follow-up comparison of disadvantaged children attending Head Start, no preschool, and other preschool programs. *Child Development, 61,* 495–507.

Lehrman, K., & Pace, J. (1985). *Day-care regulation: Serving children or bureaucrats?* Cato Institute Policy Analysis, no. 59.

McKey, R.H., Condelli, L., Ganson, H., Barrett, B.J., McConkey, C., & Plantz, M.C. (1985). *The impact of Head Start on children, families and communities: Executive summary. Final Report of the Head Start Evaluation, Synthesis and Utilization Project.* Washington, DC: CSR.

Mitchell, A., Stoney, L., & Dichter, H. (2001). *Financing child care in the United States. An expanded catalog of current strategies, 2001 edition.* Kansas City, MO: Ewing Marion Kauffman Foundation.

Nollen, S.D. (1989). The work-family dilemma: How HR managers can help. *Personnel, 66*(5), 27.

Postrel, V. (1989, June). Who's behind the child care crisis? *Reason,* 20–27.

Rodgers, F.S., & Rodgers, C. (1989). Business and the facts of family life. *Harvard Business Review, 67,* 122–123.

Rowe, D.C. (1990). As the twig is bent? The myth of child-rearing influences on personality development. *Journal of Counseling and Development, 68,* 606–611.

Scarr, S. (1989). Award for distinguished contributions to research in public policy: 1988. *American Psychologist, 44,* 652–653.

Scarr, S. (1992). Developmental theories for the 1990s: Development and individual differences. *Child Development, 63,* 1–19.

Schweinhart, L.J., Barnes, H.V., & Weikart, D.P. (1993). *Significant benefits: The High/Scope Perry Preschool study through age 27.* Ypsilanti, MI: High/Scope Press.

Siegel, C.N. (1990). The brave new world of child care. *New Perspectives Quarterly 7, 34–45.*

Stevenson, H.W., & Stigler, J.W. (1992). *The learning gap: Why our schools are failing and what we can learn from Japanese and Chinese education.* New York: Summit Books.

U.S. General Accounting Office (USGAO). (1997). *Head Start research provides little information on impact of current program* (Report GAO/HEHS-97–59). Washington, DC: Author.

Walden, M.L. (1992). The cost of care. *Carolina Journal 1*(6), 16.

Werther, W.B., Jr. (1989). Child care and eldercare benefits. *Personnel, 66*(9), 42.

Zigler, E., & Muenchow, S. (1992). *Head Start: The inside story of America's most successful educational experiment.* New York: Basic Books.

CHAPTER 37

The Wisdom of a Federal Effort on Behalf of Impoverished Children and Their Families

EDWARD ZIGLER AND SALLY J. STYFCO

Although uneven quality is found among Head Start programs, it is much more so in the mixed system of child care that John Hood (Chapter 36) concludes could better serve families. By child care, he is referring to supplemental care of children while their parents work, although he occasionally interchanges this term with "preschools," probably meaning nursery school programs. To conclude a critique of early childhood intervention with a recommendation for parental choice of child care is a *non sequitur.*

MISCONCEPTIONS ABOUT CHILD CARE

Hood is not alone in confounding early childhood intervention programs with the provision of child care. His chapter also advances some popular but factually wrong notions about the child care industry. In this chapter, we discuss what we see as errors in common knowledge brought out in Hood's chapter by treating him as spokesman for those views.

First, Hood seems to believe that the supply of child care is sufficient to meet demand. Although this may be the case in some geographic areas, most analysts agree that parents often have difficulty finding affordable, convenient care, particularly for infants and school-age children (Helburn & Bergmann, 2002). Hood believes that employers will take up the slack, although he acknowledges that only a small fraction of them currently help workers with child care needs. This argument overlooks the facts that employees in entry-level or part-time positions (typically women paid at minimum wage) are not al-

This chapter is condensed from our original reply to John Hood. The entire manuscript is available from Edward Zigler or Sally J. Styfco, Yale Center in Child Development and Social Policy, Yale University, 310 Prospect St., New Haven, CT 06511.

ways eligible for this assistance; that the "help" is most often referral services to child care providers who may or may not have slots available and may or may not charge fees affordable to the worker; and that one has to have a job to take advantage of an employer's child care benefits, if there are any. Three quarters of Head Start families earn less than $15,000 per year, making it exceedingly difficult for them to pay for good child care. (Relatively few Head Start centers provide full-day care.) A main reason for the dismal success of the Job Opportunities and Basic Skills Training (JOBS) program, part of welfare reform legislation preceding Temporary Assistance for Needy Families (TANF) that required welfare recipients with preschoolers to work or enter job training, was the lack of affordable child care (Children's Defense Fund, 1992).

Hood would have us believe that child care is provided at bargain-basement prices by nonprofit groups. He notes that church and community child care tend to be less expensive. Expensive or not, families who earn $15,000 per year will have to devote a significant percentage of their income to child care tuition. Hood speaks for many in claiming that government regulations that require staff training and limit group sizes drive prices up and that informal arrangements provide better care for children. What is his definition of "better"? Untrained staff caring for large numbers of children? His argument completely avoids the importance of quality caregiving.

A great deal of research proves the obvious: Good care is good for children; poor care is not. Good care is more likely to be provided by caregivers with some training in child development or early education. Hood himself concludes, "Personal talents of staff, not design, explain the success of a few projects" (p. 504, Chapter 36). Yet, he decries regulations governing staff qualifications because they increase fees. He cannot have it both ways. Good care is necessarily more expensive than poor care (because there are more and better-trained staff), and states with stronger rules for training and other quality indicators have, in fact, been found to house better child care centers (Phillips, Mekos, Scarr, McCartney, & Abbott-Shim, 2000; Phillipsen, Burchinal, Howes, & Cryer, 1997; Whitebook, Howes, & Phillips, 1989). We would like to see the "considerable evidence" Hood alludes to that supposedly proves that informal settings provide the best care. There are little data about these arrangements, precisely because they are informal and out of the public eye. We do not even know how many of them meet minimal health and safety standards, regulations meant to prevent children from dying while their parents work.

Switching the discussion to nursery school programming, Hood correctly asserts that formal instruction in academic skills is not appropriate for young children. But just because a program is formally organized does not mean that it has a structured academic curriculum. For example, Head Start's program guides specify that although curricula be planned and written, learning should be prompted through play and opportunities for creative and social experiences. An informal, " developmentally appropriate" curriculum is also one of the criteria used by the National Association for the Education of Young Children (NAEYC) to accredit child care settings. Hood also has the wrong impression that organization means there is a rigid program to which children must conform. He argues that this is inappropriate: "Because children exhibit different personalities . . . they require different types of care, therapy, and education" (p. 503, Chapter 36). Both Head Start and NAEYC specify individualized programming that accommodates children's unique needs and rates of development. Good, regulated settings thus strive to deliver the type of program that Hood and experts agree can help to optimize development. We do not know what is delivered in the informal arrangements he promotes, except that in some of them, children watch more television (Goelman & Pence, 1987).

COMPREHENSIVE PROGRAMMING

Whether good or poor, regulated or not, child care and preschool programs do not offer the broad range of services that Head Start provides to children and families. Preschool education is the only component common to all three systems, with the exception of low-quality child care settings. Health and dental care are available only in Head Start. Nutrition may be provided in child care—although in many programs children bring their own breakfasts and lunches—but is generally not found in the typical half-day nursery school. Parental involvement is minimal in most child care and preschool programs; at the level of planning and decision making, it is nonexistent. And, only in Head Start can parents obtain jobs and family support services.

All of Head Start's services are provided at no cost to parents. Low-income families may be able to obtain subsidized child care at no or reduced fees. The tuition at nursery schools is generally set, although many states offer free prekindergarten to a limited group of children as part of their public school programs. Like Head Start, the majority of the public preschools enroll income-eligible children who are at-risk of eventual school failure. Like most nursery schools, however, the curricula are limited to school readiness skills. Only half of the state programs are required to provide services that go beyond education; few do so, and none approaches the level of services in Head Start (see Chapter 35). Although we do not share Hood's disdain for the education establishment, we believe that "readiness to learn" entails good health, motivation, social skills, a supportive family, and a functional home environment.

The value of Head Start's comprehensive program lies not just in the range of services but in the fact that they are available or made available in one place. Hood believes that a "competitive marketplace" and a "mix of private-sector, nonprofit, church, community group, and extended-family providers is a better way to provide such care for children, poor or not" (p. 506, Chapter 36). He fails to understand that poor individuals often feel isolated from the community and betrayed by social institutions. They may not know about services available to them or how to gain access. On a practical level, they many not have transportation or child care to enable them to visit service agencies. The frustration of having to "carry their life stories around to several places" to obtain help for "multiple problems, or to receive help with multiple pieces of one problem" ("New Beginnings," 1990, pp. v, vii) can make them give up trying.

Family service coordinators in Head Start work to understand the needs of individual families and to link them with appropriate services. Although their caseloads are currently too high and services in the community too strained by increased need and reduced resources, Head Start's commitment to families remains strong. Eventually, parents come to trust the staff and become more open to the possibility of bettering their lives. If anyone doubts that a bond develops between parents and staff, they might not know that in 2002 alone, more than 867,000 parents, or most participating families, volunteered in Head Start classrooms (Head Start Bureau, 2003). Parents were the ones who saved the program when they heard rumors that the Nixon Administration was developing a plan to phase it out. Parents also get the most credit for preventing Head Start's transfer to the Department of Education in the late 1970s, a move many feared would jeopardize the program's comprehensive nature.

Hood's failure to appreciate the value of coordinating family services stems partly from his misconception that Head Start directly provides these services and partly from his lack of acquaintance with social services delivery. The Silver Ribbon Panel recommended that Head Start strengthen its ties to local service agencies, not usurp their roles (National Head Start Association, 1990). Collaboration of this type was also called for by the Educational and Human Services Consortium, a group of 22 prominent national organizations serving children and families, whose members realized they could better do their jobs working together rather than in a "competitive marketplace." A U.S. General Accounting Office (USGAO; 1992) report concluded that programs that link clients with existing services are far more successful than efforts to create new services or delivery mechanisms. To paraphrase the USGAO, attempts to eliminate fragmentation of services in Hood's "free marketplace" have generally not developed a comprehensive care system, for reasons such as agencies' protecting their own identities and resistance to combining personnel and resources (p. 4). The USGAO suggested that, "Congress may wish to consider promoting service-orientated efforts like Head Start" (p. 6). As Hood surely knows, the USGAO is notoriously hardheaded when it comes to recommending expenditures for social programs.

Hood's belief that the community and private sector will meet the needs of poor children is thus idealistic and naïve. C. Arden Miller, a physician and professor of public health, wrote of the need to expand programs that promote good health in children, including Head Start, but his observations are applicable to all types of child and family services:

> We seem content to demonstrate program effectiveness and then to hope that in some misguided and underfinanced way other responsible parties—maybe "communities" or public/ private interaction—will act on the wisdom displayed by successful demonstrations and will spontaneously replicate them wherever there is need. It doesn't much happen. (1992, p. 4)

A similar verdict was reached at a 1992 ZERO TO THREE/National Center for Clinical Infant Programs forum, which called for increased regulatory and voluntary strategies to improve child care services "because the goodness in people's hearts is not enough to protect children" (p. 45).

Hood admonishes policy makers to "seek a consensus among researchers and academic literature when devising new policies or evaluating old ones" (p. 502, Chapter 36). Where is the research consensus that providing poor parents with vouchers to purchase child care or schooling of their choice will improve their children's futures? There is plenty of evidence to show that the child care they find may not be of very good quality. There is ample evidence to show that without a formal program such as Head Start, their children are not likely to obtain the dental or health care they need in a timely manner. And, while we await evidence to substantiate Head Start's long-term effects on social competence and family functioning, we have a genuine, data-based consensus that the program has immediate benefits to children's health, socialization, and school readiness. The Bush Administration and Congress should heed Hood's advice and listen to the child development experts (not those conservatively sitting on the sidelines). The experts have agreed that upgraded and modernized, Head Start is a sound social investment that has immense potential to enhance the life space of every poor child in the United States of America.

REFERENCES

Children's Defense Fund. (1992). *Child care under the Family Support Act: Early lessons from the states.* Washington, DC: Author.

Goelman, H., & Pence, A. (1987). Effects of child care, family and individual characteristics on children's language development: The Victoria Day Care Research Project. In D.A. Phillips (Ed.), *Quality in child care: What does research tell us?* (pp. 89–104). Washington, DC: National Association for the Education of Young Children.

Head Start Bureau. (2003). *Fact sheet.* Washington, DC: Author.

Helburn, S.W., & Bergmann, B.R. (2002). *America's child care problem.* New York: Palgrave.

Kisker, E.E., Hofferth, S.L., Phillips, D.A., & Farquhar, E. (1991). *A profile of child care settings: Early care and education* (Vol. 1). Washington, DC: U.S. Department of Education.

Miller, C.A. (1992, February). *Making a difference in the health of children.* Paper commissioned for the conference, Medical Care and the Health of Poor Children. Cornell University Medical Center, New York.

National Head Start Association. (1990). *Head Start: The nation's pride, a nation's challenge.* Report of the Silver Ribbon Panel. Alexandria, VA: Author.

New Beginnings: A feasibility study of integrated services for children and families. (1990). Final report. Available from the office of the Deputy Superintendent, San Diego City Schools, San Diego, CA.

Phillips, D., Mekos, D., Scarr, S., McCartney, K., & Abbott-Shim, M. (2000). Within and beyond the classroom door: Assessing quality in child care centers. *Early Childhood Research Quarterly, 15,* 475–496.

Phillipsen, L.C., Burchinal, M.R., Howes, C., & Cryer, D. (1997). The prediction of process quality from structural features of child care. *Early Childhood Research Quarterly, 12,* 281–303.

U.S. General Accounting Office (USGAO). (1992). *Integrating human services.* (Report No. GAO/HRD-92–108). Washington, DC: Author.

Whitebook, M., Howes, C., & Phillips, D. (1989). *Who cares? Child care teachers and the quality of care in America.* Final report, National Child Care Staffing Study. Oakland, CA: Child Care Employee Project.

ZERO TO THREE: National Center for Clinical Infant Programs. (1992). *Finding and funding quality child care and Head Start services for infants and toddlers.* Arlington, VA: Author.

CHAPTER 38

Head Start as a National Laboratory

CHRISTOPHER C. HENRICH

In 1969, the Nixon Administration moved Head Start from the Office of Economic Opportunity to the newly founded Office of Child Development (OCD) in the Department of Health, Education and Welfare (HEW). Edward Zigler, one of the original founders of Head Start, was appointed the first director of the OCD. He came to Washington, D.C., from his professorship at Yale eager for the opportunity to run the program he helped create. Within months, however, Zigler found himself fighting for Head Start's very existence. Soon after his appointment, Zigler learned that the Nixon Administration was planning to phase out Head Start over the course of 3 years. He had not been hired to run Head Start, he had been hired to dismantle it.

This book is a testament to the fact that not only was Head Start never dismantled but also it has continued to grow and expand for the past 35 years and is one of the most popular federal programs. How was Head Start rescued from an early demise and transformed into one of the country's most successful pieces of federal social policy? Zigler (Zigler & Muenchow, 1992) recounted going to Elliot Richardson, then Secretary of HEW, soon after hearing about Nixon's phase-out plan and threatening to resign if the Head Start budget were cut by a single dollar. Richardson conveyed this message to Nixon and persuaded the President to shelve the phase-out plan. However, the introduction of the plan exemplifies the precarious position of Head Start in 1970. In coming up with a strategy to save the program and ensure its continued existence, Zigler and his staff at the OCD developed Head Start as a national laboratory for innovative children's programs and policy.

In order to understand how the national laboratory saved Head Start, one must understand the factors that led to the Nixon Administration's initial phase-out plan. The biggest factor working against Head Start was the first federally commissioned research evaluation of the program's effectiveness, conducted by the Westinghouse Learning Corporation. The results of this evaluation were released in the spring of 1969 and were primarily negative, indicating that Head Start did not have any effect on children's achievement in elementary school (Cicirelli, 1969). These negative findings were widely disseminated and embraced by the Nixon Administration. Nixon and his advisors interpreted the report's findings as evidence that Johnson's War on Poverty had failed. Even the members of the administration who supported the efforts of the War on Poverty, such as Patrick Moynihan, took the findings to mean that early childhood education was not an effective approach and that Project Head Start should be terminated.

There were, however, a number of flaws in the evaluation's design that led many, including Zigler, to question the validity of its conclusions. Furthermore, not all of the results were negative. For example, most Head Start programs in the sample were summer programs. The school-year programs included in the sample did show positive effects of elementary school achievement. Plus, parents in the sample almost unanimously supported Head Start (Zigler & Muenchow, 1992).

Zigler and many other social scientists at the time were influenced by the writings of D.T. Campbell, who advocated for an "experimenting society." Campbell's idea was to try out programs, evaluate them, and discard what did not appear to work and refine what did (Campbell, 1969). Accordingly, the lesson to be learned from the Westinghouse Report was not to dismantle Head Start, but rather to refine it and use it as a laboratory for developing, testing, and improving federal programs and policies for children and families in poverty. Furthermore, to keep Head Start from being terminated, the OCD had to keep a high profile in the Administration and build momentum, showing that it could produce benefits.

One of Zigler's first actions as the director of OCD was to coordinate all federal programs for young children through his office. This synergistic effort was well received by the Nixon Administration and bolstered the OCD's momentum and visibility. As a next step, Zigler and his staff used this momentum and visibility to engage in the development of innovative efforts on behalf of children and families. Head Start played an integral role in these activities, and this wedding of Head Start with the office's broader efforts helped solidify its role as a national laboratory to devise and test programs and policies.

This chapter describes the initial program and policy development during the early years of the OCD, discusses how these "laboratory experiments" have evolved and continue to do so today, and speculates on the future of Head Start as a national laboratory.

THE EARLY YEARS

Soon after Head Start's inception, the OCD used it to model the development of additional programs for low-income families and children. In its early years, Head Start was also used as a model for federal policy pertaining to the care of young children.

Programs

Head Start was initially conceptualized as a 6- or 8-week program for low-income children the summer before they started kindergarten. Yet, even its founders knew that more comprehensive and ongoing support for children and families was needed to combat the deleterious effects of poverty. Whether for this reason or to build on the project's immense popularity, President Johnson announced that Head Start would be expanded to a school-year program as soon as the first summer was over (it took several years for all centers to comply). This might be considered the first of a series of efforts to extend the length of services provided by Head Start. Over the next few years, the Head Start model continued to expand in several directions via a series of pilot programs. It was *extended upward* into elementary school with programs such as Projects Developmental Continuity and Follow Through; it was *extended downward* to reach infants and toddlers with Parent and Child Centers (PCCs); programs such as Home Start and the Family and Child Resource Programs were developed to provide more *extensive family outreach and support;* and the *health* goal of Head Start was expanded via Health Start. As discussed in the next few sections, all of these programs were piloted before going to scale, and many never made it to scale. Nevertheless, they propelled innovation in Head Start.

Upward Extensions The first off-shoot of Head Start was Project Follow Through, which originated in 1967. The original purpose of Follow Through was to extend Head Start services into elementary schools. Follow Through was unique from the other programs discussed in this chapter because it was housed in the Department of Education, not OCD. In the fall of 1967, it began as a pilot program in 40 school districts; it was implemented at scale 1 year later. Follow Through never garnished the success of Head Start, and its relative failure was due to several problems in its initial conceptualization. Although it was first designed to introduce the Head Start model of comprehensive services to elementary schools, this goal was altered in 1968 when Congress failed to allot the anticipated budget. Due to this financial shortfall, instead of emulating the Head Start model, Follow Through was farmed out to 12 universities and corporations, each of which designed its own model. The pilot, however, had already begun with the original Head Start model. When the program was implemented at scale, schools had their choice of 13 models instead of the initial Head Start model that was piloted the previous year.

A national evaluation of Follow Through also began in 1968. This evaluation was plagued by problems caused by the program's rushed and unfocused beginnings. Because the program had no clear goals and was being implemented through a number of models, and because there was no set criteria for comparisons groups across sites, it is not surprising that it showed lukewarm effects (see Doernberger & Zigler, 1993, for more details).

Follow Through continued to exist into the 1990s, but only as a small Department of Education program that primarily experimented with new elementary school curricula. For all intents and purposes, it failed as an extension of Head Start. Several causes for this failure were 1) the pilot was too short; 2) the program changed dramatically in concept between the pilot and its implementation and evaluations; and 3) it was evaluated as a diffuse, hastily conceived initiative without clear goals. In short, Follow Through grew too big, too fast.

Seven years after the introduction of Follow Through, the OCD began its own initiative to bridge the transition from Head Start to elementary school. Project Developmental Continuity was initiated as a demonstration project in 1974. The project was manifested through two models. In the Preschool Linkage model, connections were formed between Head Start centers and schools. Teachers from both institutions would agree on and coordinate a continuous curriculum over the transition to elementary school, and both institutions encouraged parent involvement during the transition. In the Early

Childhood School model, Head Start and elementary schools were merged into one facility, and a sequential curriculum was developed for children ages 4–8. Although Project Developmental Continuity only existed as a pilot program and was never evaluated, it was one of a continuing series of efforts to bridge the transition from Head Start to elementary school. (The most recent incarnation, the Head Start/Public School Early Childhood Transition Project, is described by Ramey, Ramey, and Lanzi in Chapter 28).

Downward Extensions   Another early program to evolve from Head Start was the implementation of PCCs, which began in 1968. These centers aimed to reach children early in life to prevent the cognitive and emotional problems many already evidenced by the time they entered Head Start. Thus, the PCCs targeted children from birth to age 3 and their families.

The PCCs were not regulated by specific standards or requirements, so the programs they offered could and did differ substantially from one another. The only criteria specified for the PCCs were that they include 1) health care; 2) activities to stimulate physical, cognitive, and emotional development; 3) activities to help parents in their relationships with their children, spouse, and so forth; 4) social services for families; 5) programs designed to increase families' community involvement; and 6) training programs (Valentine, 1997). With such vague directions, the initial 36 centers approached their charge in a variety of ways. No systematic research was conducted to assess the variation among programs or to determine their effectiveness. Regardless, the PCCs received continued congressional support. Until 1994, when some began to be phased into Early Head Start, these centers continued to exist without any real accountability for what they were doing (see p. 524 for a discussion on Early Head Start).

Family Outreach and Support   Two early OCD initiatives attempted to extend the reach of Head Start services to low-income families who did not participate in the traditional Head Start model. In Home Start, paraprofessionals provided Head Start services in families' homes. In 1972, the OCD funded 16 programs for 3 ½ years. The rationale behind Home Start was threefold: 1) In a center-based program, the skills learned may not be carried home; 2) in many sparsely populated communities, center-based programs were not feasible; and 3) learning at home could be transferred to siblings through diffusion (Valentine, 1997). The program's effectiveness at providing services was evaluated compared with the traditional Head Start model. These evaluations showed that Home Start programs and Head Start programs were equally effective, with the one exception that Home Start did not provide the same quality of health services (Valentine, 1997). The Home Start model continued to evolve after the end of the pilot phase; the current home-based programs are discussed on pages 524–526.

The OCD's other model of extended outreach, the Child and Family Resource Program, was the nation's first federally sponsored family support program. It offered a panoply of services to families with children from birth to age 8. In 1973, the OCD founded 11 demonstration programs. The programs' mandates were broad, including individual assessments of need; medical, dental, and mental health screenings; prenatal care; education services; and family support services. These mandates fell under the rubrics of early childhood education, parental involvement, and health and medical services—the same conceptual foundation behind Head Start. The goal was to coordinate families' access to these services while facilitating continuity of care. The key players in the program were home visitors who worked with and advocated for families, providing direct counseling, assistance, and crisis intervention as well as community referrals for child and parent education and health services. The program was terminated in 1983, and unfortunately, little research was conducted to evaluate its effectiveness (Zigler & Styfco, 1993). The research that was conducted, however, indicated that the Child and Family Resource Programs showed promise because they were individually tailored interventions for each family rather than a "one size fits all" intervention (Zigler & Seitz, 1982). The flip side of this promise is that the nature of individually tailored interventions makes evaluation of program effectiveness more difficult.

Health Health Start was a summer medical screening program for low-income children who were not served by other programs such as Head Start. In 1971, 29 Health Start demonstration projects were funded. In addition to summer medical and dental checkups and referrals, the programs were also charged with continuing follow-ups over the course of the year.

Health Start operated for 2 years, providing services to roughly 10,000 children (Valentine, 1997). Its success was limited due to confusion about how to coordinate the referral and follow-up services. Although Health Start was not an ultimately successful program, the story behind its inception is an important lesson in how policy is guided by the interaction of research and politics. In 1970, Zigler was called to testify before the House Education and Labor Committee about the Westinghouse findings indicating that Head Start produced no academic benefits. In his testimony, he recommended that summer funding be redirected to the full-year program. Zigler (personal communication, January 17, 2000) recalled that the Committee Chair, Representative Carl Perkins, a strong supporter of Head Start, got furious at this recommendation and refused to consider redirecting any summer funding. Zigler was confused by this reaction because the research clearly showed that 6 weeks of Head Start in the summer had no long-term benefits. After the hearing, he privately asked one of the committee members, Representative John Brademus, to explain what had happened. Brademus replied by asking Zigler two questions:

Question 1: In the Perkins's district, who works in the summer Head Start programs?

Answer: School teachers.

Question 2: When Perkins runs for re-election, who mans the telephones for his campaign?

Answer: School teachers.

As director of the OCD, Zigler thus had to conceive a way to budget the summer Head Start money so that it would not be wasted on an ineffective program. It was decided that medical screenings would be an efficient use of the summer budget, and Health Start was born. This story of Health Start's conception highlights the role played by politics in the development of Head Start as a national laboratory. Many of the innovative initiatives arose from political necessity. The next section discusses how this mixture with politics influenced Head Start's evolution as a national laboratory for children and family policy.

Policies

In the early 1970s, Head Start became another type of national laboratory, this one for federal children's policy. The project served a role in the development of two major pieces of legislation, the Comprehensive Child Development Act of 1971 and the Family Assistance Plan of 1970. Neither of these bills was ultimately passed into law, but their introductions did focus federal attention on child care for the first time.

The Comprehensive Child Development Act, introduced by Senator Walter Mondale and Representative Brademus, would have provided access to quality child care for all working mothers. Low-income families would have access to free care, and other families would pay on a sliding scale based on income. Head Start centers would serve as a model for and the nuclei of this new child care system.

Before the introduction of the bill, there had been no systematic government effort to define child care quality. To determine the criteria of quality, the OCD held a conference at the Airlie House in Washington, D.C. Eighty-five child development experts from across the country attended the conference. They produced a series of manuals for infant and toddler, preschool, and school-age care. They also drafted a statement of purpose in support of quality child care.

At the same time, the Nixon administration was working on its welfare reform package, the Family Assistance Plan. The goals of the plan were to get women off the welfare rolls and into jobs, which meant providing them with job training and child care. Two agencies vied for control over the child care component of the plan—the Labor Department and the OCD. The Labor Department was only interested in the child care components because it was housing most of the other components as well. Its focus was on getting adults into the labor force, and it proposed providing only custodial child care. The OCD proposed a more expensive type of developmental child care, which is defined as care adequate for facilitating children's optimal developmental trajectory (Zigler, personal communication, January, 17, 2000). Understanding the importance of having experts in child development run the child care component of the bill, the Secretary of HEW, Elliot Richardson, advocated for developmental care, and through his influence the child care component of the Family Assistance Plan wound up being developed by the OCD.

As a next step in supporting the Family Assistance Plan and the Comprehensive Child Development Act, the OCD needed to articulate the specific criteria constituting quality developmental child care. Before Zigler had come to the OCD, Acting Director Jule Sugerman had proposed a list of Federal Inter-Agency Day Care Requirements (FIDCR). The requirements, however, were not specific enough to be adequately assessed or enforced. Zigler and his staff set out to draft a revised set of federal standards that were specific, realistic, and enforceable. The new standards were then sent to Secretary Richardson, who fine-tuned and approved them.

Because the welfare and child care bills failed to become law, the OCD's revised standards were never federally implemented. However, they were eventually adapted by the National Association for the Education of Young Children (NAEYC) as their voluntary standards for child care licensing, and the NAEYC retains versions of the standards to this day. Ironically, these standards are now adopted by many Head Start centers seeking NAEYC accreditation.

The work of the OCD on the Comprehensive Child Development Act and the Family Assistance Plan exemplify the ways in which Head Start played a role in much broader initiatives to reform this country's child care system. With the newfound emphasis on quality in child care, Zigler realized that it was also necessary to ensure that child care providers had adequate training to implement good care. He conceived of the Child Development Associate (CDA), a performance-based certificate of competence. He convened a task force of experts in child development to work out the specific criteria for the CDA. Under the direction of Barbara Biber of the Bank Street College of Education, the task force decided to base the CDA on six observable competencies and six personal characteristics of providers (Bouverat & Galen, 1994). Qualifications for the CDA included some classroom training in child development plus detailed observations of candidates. The CDA became the first collaborative effort to operationalize and evaluate quality in child care provider performance.

The story behind the conceptualization of the CDA is again based in Head Start. According to Zigler (Zigler & Muenchow, 1992), he conceived of the CDA during a visit by Betty Johnson, an early childhood educator who trained Head Start teachers in American Samoa where her husband was governor. Her Samoan trainees would begin by observing the work in the centers and then gradually start to work with the children. Johnson and her fellow trainers would observe the trainees interacting with the children and decide whether they were qualified based on these observations. Zigler asked her how she came to conclusions about trainees' qualifications based on observations, and she replied by nudging him and saying, "Oh, you know!" (Bouverat & Galen, 1994). Zigler interpreted this comment as meaning that there were observable competencies apparent in quality child care providers and that there should be a systematic way to measure these competencies through an observation-based assessment. Thus, this conversation about the training of Head Start teachers in American Samoa resulted in the birth of the CDA.

CURRENT ISSUES

Head Start is not the same program that it was when initiated 35 years ago; it is an evolving concept (Zigler, 1997). The programs spawned by Head Start have evolved as well. They have expanded to meet the changing needs of children and families, and increased emphasis has been placed on evaluating their effectiveness. Head Start also continues to play an integral role in federal policy for children and families. This section describes the current initiatives of Head Start as a national laboratory for programs and policy, discussing how the current initiatives have evolved from the previous generation already described.

Programs

In recent years, congressional reauthorizations of Head Start plus initiatives out of OCD's successor, the Administration on Children, Youth and Families (ACYF), have funded a new generation of demonstration projects, all of which have evolutionary roots in the demonstration projects funded during the office's early years. These programs, which follow the same directions discussed previously, include upward extensions of Head Start, such as the Transition Project; downward extensions of Head Start, such as Early Head

Start and Home-Based Programs; and family outreach and support programs, such as the Comprehensive Child Development Program (CCDP). Most of these demonstrations are accompanied by comprehensive evaluations that are substantially more sophisticated than the ones conducted during the early years of Head Start. In terms of health, there has been new focus on providing mental health services through the Head Start model (see Chapter 12).

Upward Extensions The Head Start Transition Project evolved from Project Developmental Continuity. The Transition program funded partnerships between Head Start centers and elementary schools for coordinating Head Start services during the transition to school. The project mandated coordination across four components: 1) a developmentally appropriate and continuous curriculum, 2) health services, 3) encouragement and facilitation of parental involvement, and 4) social services to families.

Initially funded in 1991, the Transition Project was implemented in 32 sites across the nation. An evaluation followed children through third grade (see Chapter 28). Although strong transition efforts undertaken in the control sites made it difficult to discern the effects of participating in the program itself, this attention to transition enabled children in both groups to achieve national norms. While the transition demo is over, the 1998 Head Start reauthorization mandates that all Head Start centers take steps to coordinate with local schools to ease children's transition to kindergarten, and the new performance standards mandate that all centers work on transition activities.

Downward Extensions Early Head Start is a downward extension of Head Start designed to serve low-income pregnant women and families with infants and toddlers. The model evolved from the PCCs, and some PCCs have been incorporated into Early Head Start. Like Head Start, Early Head Start provides comprehensive early child development, health, and family support services. These services can be provided in center- or home-based programs.

Early Head Start was established in 1994. In 1995, 3% of the Head Start budget went to Early Head Start. By 2002, this amount was increased to about 10% and the number of programs to 650 nationally (Head Start Bureau, 2003). ACYF has funded a nationally representative evaluation of 17 of these programs, which is being conducted by Mathematica Policy Research, Inc. (1999). This comprehensive evaluation is thus far showing very positive results. Early Head Start has positive effects on children's cognitive, language, and social-emotional development at age 3; it also has a broad array of effects on parents (Love et al., 2002). The evaluation is continuing to follow children and families after they exit the program to see whether these effects are maintained. The follow-up will be completed in 2004.

In addition, the establishment of Early Head Start served as an impetus for a 1998 overhaul of the 20-year-old Head Start quality standards. The initial standards applied only to preschool-age children. The new standards are applicable to infants and toddlers as well.

Family Outreach and Support Over the years, home-based programs have become a standard alternative model for delivering Head Start services to some families, such as those in rural communities, who do not have easy access to Head Start centers. The ACYF continues to invest in training and support for these programs The current Home-

Based Programs, which originated with Home Start, aim to facilitate parental participation in their children's learning and in their community by offering families Head Start services in their homes. Home-Based Programs are implemented by home visitors who provide multifaceted support services ranging from direct instruction of parent and children to facilitation of referrals to other services. There are four key elements to Home-Based Programs:

1. Weekly home visits with parents and children, which can occur in a variety of settings, provide individualized instruction for both parents and children that promotes the generalization of learning in the home, even in the absence of the home visitor.

2. Group social activities for parents and children help children develop peer social skills and provide parents with the opportunity to form relationships with other parents in their community.

3. There is a focus on parent education about child development, encouragement for parents to seek out other educational opportunities, and facilitation of leadership skills by including parents in the administrative structure of Head Start.

4. In addition to providing direct services, Home-Based Programs provide community outreach services by establishing links with other community agencies and also helping parents coordinate access to these additional resources.

CCDP evolved from the Child and Family Resource Programs and from subsequent Family Services Centers, which were a scaled-back version of the Child and Family Resource Programs funded by ACYF during the first Bush Administration (Zigler & Muenchow, 1992). The CCDP was a 5-year national demonstration project. The goals of the CCDP were to enhance the development of children from birth to age 5 directly by providing quality child care, early education, and health care, and indirectly by providing parent education, job training, and additional family support services (Gilliam, Ripple, Zigler, & Leiter, 2000). The CCDP was designed to coordinate existing services rather than create new ones. This program was implemented by assigning families case managers who would make referrals or provide services directly in cases in which referral services were not available.

The CCDP was implemented and evaluated in 21 sites across the country over its 5-year life span. The evaluation concluded that the program was not effective in terms of improving children's developmental trajectories (St. Pierre, Layzer, Goodson, & Bernstein, 1997). This conclusion, however, does not indicate that the demonstration project was a failure. On the contrary, the findings provided valuable lessons for improving both the evaluation and implementation of comprehensive family support efforts. First, it was difficult to compare the intervention group with the control group because the controls also had access to many of the same referral services (Gilliam et al., 2000). Also, the program was evaluated before many sites had enough experience to implement it well (Gilliam et al., 2000).

One of the 21 sites was effective, indicating that the CCDP could be effective at improving children's developmental trajectories. This site differed from the rest in that it was already well established at the commencement of the evaluation, it had little staff turnover, and it was the only site located in the public schools (Gilliam et al., 2000). Another implementation issue was that, in spite of CCDP's evolution from Head Start, quality child care and early education services were underutilized. Less then one quarter of the children in the programs attended child care or preschool, and the quality of the institutions that were attended was not assessed (Gilliam et al., 2000). Although research from the previous generations of Resource Programs highlighted the difficulties of evaluating such individually tailored interventions, the evaluation of the CCDP suggests a number of ways—including professional development, coordination with the community institutions such as public schools, and referral to high-quality child care and education—that the impact of comprehensive family support programs could be bolstered by making general adjustments in implementation. In short, effective programs work directly with children as well as with parents.

Health Provisions for the prevention and treatment of mental health problems have become an integral part of Head Start's health goals. As of 2004, every Head Start center must have access to at least one mental health professional to provide training for teachers and parents and screening for children. The U.S. Department of Health and Human Services (1999) has also identified Head Start as an integral component of efforts to prevent the development of mental health problems in children.

Although the mental health potential of Head Start has long been recognized (e.g., Scherl & Macht, 1972), the program's mental health component is still hampered by a lack of clarity and knowledge pertaining to how early intervention workers should go about screening, treating, and preventing mental health problems in young children (Forness, Serna, Kavale, & Nielsen, 1998; Knitzer, Chapter 12). Hopefully the current focus on mental health in Head Start will spawn a new generation of research to determine how the program can effectively promote mental as well as physical well-being among low-income children.

Policy

Child care policy in this country has made little progress since the failures of the Comprehensive Child Development Act and the Family Assistance Plan in the early 1970s. Since then, only one subsequent attempt has been made to federally regulate child care. In 1980, the Carter Administration attempted to revise and enforce the FIDCR standards. Patrice Harris, then Secretary of Health and Human Services, sent the proposed standards to Congress, but the bill failed to pass before Carter was replaced by Reagan, and the quality standards effort was abandoned.

It seems highly unlikely that enforceable federal child care standards will be passed into law in the near future. The current political zeitgeist is for devolution to the states in the form of block grants with few federal strings attached. States prefer to make decisions regarding child care standards autonomously. Also, there is an increasingly powerful for-profit child care industry lobby that is opposed to standards because, among other things, high-quality child care can be more costly to deliver.

Without a model of federal standards, let alone enforceable standards, the quality of child care in this country is in a precarious state. The quality of care has not improved over the past 30 years (National Council of Jewish Women, 1999). Regulation has been delegated to the states, and these standards are highly variable (Hayes, Palmer, & Zaslow,

1990; Ripple, Gilliam, Chanana, & Zigler, 1999). Alarmingly, most programs are of substandard quality, particularly those for infants and toddlers (Cost, Quality, and Child Outcomes Study Team, 1995; Young, Marsland, & Zigler, 1997). Despite the overall low quality of child care in this country, two of the initial efforts to promote quality in child care and early child education—Head Start and the CDA—continue to expand, reach more children, and set the benchmark for high-quality care.

Head Start–Child Care Partnerships   The Head Start Performance Standards are the only federally enforced quality requirements. As part of a federal initiative to increase the quality of child care, ACYF offers financial incentive to Head Start grantees for building partnerships with child care providers. Through these partnerships, the combined centers can provide full-day and full-year care that meets the Head Start Performance Standards to children and families from a broader socioeconomic range. There are three arrangements for these partnerships: 1) Head Start contracting with family child care providers; 2) child care centers providing Head Start services to their children; and 3) Head Start programs expanding to full-day, full-year care (Bancroft, 1997; Blank & Poersch, Chapter 23). In the first arrangement, the child care provider (who must be licensed) is not a Head Start employee but serves as a Head Start teacher. Even though the provider is in this way independent, Head Start grantee staff provide support in the form of training, materials, technical assistance, and help with the comprehensive services associated with Head Start. The provider also receives a small amount of Head Start money in addition to his or her child care income. In the second arrangement, staffing models vary. For example, center employees may provide child care while Head Start employees provide home visitation and family outreach services, or both sets of staff may work in collaboration at the center. The third arrangement operates by using other sources of child care monies to supplement and expand Head Start services. This arrangement provides the most control over child care quality standards because all care must meet the federal performance standards, but it is the least commonly implemented model because of the issues and complications that arise when multiple funds are pooled (Bancroft, 1997).

Evaluations of Head Start–Child Care Partnerships indicate that they can effectively serve more children than traditional Head Start centers without sacrificing the quality of the Performance Standards. An evaluation by KMC Child Development Corporation of three Full Start Head Start–Child Care Partnership programs showed that the Full Start centers met the same quality standards as a comparison Head Start program (Crompton, 1997). In addition, an ACYF-funded evaluation of 18 Head Start–family child care demonstration projects found that the family child care partnerships met the same quality standards of Head Start centers. This finding is impressive in light of other research showing that family child care for low-income children is typically of substandard quality (Galinsky, Howes, Kontos, & Shinn, 1994). These evaluation results from center- and family-based child care partnerships demonstrate the potential of these arrangements to raise the bar of child care quality across the socioeconomic spectrum, reaching a broader scope and larger number of children.

CDA   In the past 30 years, the CDA program has expanded considerably. To date, more than 100,000 CDAs have been conferred (Council for Professional Recognition, 1998). The training standards and assessment have also grown more stringent. The initial six competency goals have been more than doubled to 13. Furthermore, CDA applicants must now go through a five-step assessment process before they can earn their degree. In addition, training requirements have been substantially expanded. As of 2000, 480 hours of formal training and work experience are prerequisite for eligibility. This is up from 120 hours of informal training, prior to 1992. There is also greater focus on professional development once child care providers have received their degrees. Candidates for CDA renewal must be a member of a professional organization in the field of early child development/education and must take college-level courses to maintain their CDA status.

As the CDA program has expanded and evolved more rigorous training and assessment standards, it has become a benchmark for quality in child care and early childhood education. For example, the CDA currently plays a critical role in Head Start quality improvement efforts. In 1998, 88% of Head Start teachers had at least a CDA. The 1998 Head Start Reauthorization Bill mandates that there be one teacher with at least a CDA in each Head Start and Early Head Start classroom. The CDA credential is also recognized in most states for early childhood workers. In these ways, the CDA continues to be at the forefront of national quality improvement in Head Start and other early care and education programs.

FUTURE

The future of Head Start as a national laboratory for the development of innovative programs and policies serving children and families has its foundation in the early initiatives spearheaded by the Office of Child Development. The founders and early administrators of Head Start conceived of it as an evolving effort to meet the changing needs of children and families. This chapter has shown how, through a commitment to coordination and experimentation, Head Start services have evolved and expanded over the past 3 decades. It has also highlighted the key roles that evaluation (e.g., the Westinghouse Report) and legislative action (e.g., the Comprehensive Child Development Act and the Family Assistance Plan) have played in propelling the development of Head Start as a national laboratory. Recent evaluation and legislative initiatives continue to challenge the future evolution of Head Start as a national laboratory.

Evaluation

In 1998, Congress authorized the first national evaluation of Head Start effectiveness in 30 years. This evaluation was designed to be more rigorous and robust than earlier research, such as the Westinghouse study, which was plagued with methodological problems. The ongoing evaluation employs a random assignment experimental design and uses a large battery of exhaustively developed performance measures. These performance measures assess an operationalization of school readiness that includes factors such as children's social competence and mental health and parents' involvement in education, in addition to standardized measures of academic achievement (ACYF, 2001).

Congress authorized the evaluation because it did not feel that previous research had answered the question, "Does Head Start work?" Not only will the evaluation answer the question more definitively than it predecessors were able to but also it will be able to identify the ways in which Head Start works as well as the role that quality and comprehensive implementation of the Head Start model plays in determining program effectiveness. These results will potentially give rise to a whole new generation of demonstration projects seeking to address the weaknesses and capitalize on the strengths identified by the evaluation.

The authorization of the evaluation and the development of performance measures has a broader potential impact on quality child care and early childhood education as well. The performance measures contain the most robust assessments of quality early childhood education and school readiness to date. In tandem with the Performance Standards, these performance measures provide a strong federal model for what comprises quality child care and early education, how programs can assess whether they meet these standards, and tools for determining whether programs are adequately preparing children for elementary school. As with the standards drafted by the OCD in the early 1970s, these performance measures and standards can be adopted by private licensing associations and states, even if they are never enforced federally beyond Head Start.

Legislation

Two recent legislative trends have changed the nature of early childhood educational policy in this country. The first is the devolution of program funding and responsibility to the states. As a federally regulated program for young children, Head Start must continue to forge partnerships with state and local agencies. This focus on partnership is illustrated by many of the initiatives described previously in this chapter in which Head Start programs are partnering with schools, child care providers, and social service agencies to provide comprehensive, quality services to children and their families. Head Start continues to experiment with new ways to form partnerships. For example, since 1990, ACYF has funded a growing number of Head Start–State Collaboration grants. These grants aim to coordinate states' delivery of early education, child care, and health care. Head Start needs to continue its experimentation with these partnerships, expanding its scope of coordination.

In addition, Head Start grantees continue to explore new models of bolstering the upward extension of Head Start services into elementary school. These models experiment with the pooling of Head Start funds, federal block grants, and private grants, as well as state and local funding, to reform educational institutions. Another model is the School of the 21st Century program developed at Yale University (Zigler, Finn-Stevenson, & Marsland, 1995). The Schools of the 21st Century provide expanded Head Start–like services to children and families and are administered by elementary schools. These services include on-site preschool, before- and after-school care, community child care, and family outreach and support. The program implementation varies from school to school, as do funding sources. Schools can combine a variety of private, federal (including Head Start), state, and local monies to fund changes in their infrastructure and service delivery.

The Department of Education funded an evaluation of the Schools of the 21st Century as implemented in five school districts across the country. This evaluation, conducted by the Yale Bush Center in Child Development and Social Policy, explores how program variation across sites affects impact, in addition to determining the effectiveness of the program overall (Fedoravicius & Henrich, 2002). The results will hopefully provide Head Start programs and schools with a host of data on the most effective ways to bridge transitions for children entering elementary school.

A related trend in children's policy is the recent proliferation of state preschool initiatives. A growing number of states are moving toward providing universal access to preschool education (Ripple et al., 1999). This trend is tied to Head Start in two ways. First, Head Start is a long-established national model for future state and federal efforts to emulate in terms of comprehensive service delivery and quality standards. Second, this trend could potentially result in direction competition between state preschools and Head Start programs for funds and for children. In 1998, ACYF directly addressed this issue through new initiatives in early education partnerships. Quality in Linking Together (QUILT) seeks to promote partnerships between Head Start and other early education programs. ACYF-funded Head Start-State Collaboration grants seek ultimately to promote systematic coordination of Head Start with state early education initiatives. These initiatives potentially could carve out a niche for Head Start within state preschool initiatives, thereby bolstering the quality of state-sponsored early childhood education.

If and when universal preschool becomes a reality, the future of Head Start may lie in providing services more exclusively to infants and toddlers. The national laboratory has a long tradition of developing innovative downward extensions of Head Start services, the most recent and ambitious of which is Early Head Start. The future prospects of Early Head Start were recently given a boost by the results of its evaluation by Mathematica Policy Research, Inc. If the follow-up evaluation continues to show promising results, Early Head Start will probably consume an increasingly larger percentage of the overall Head Start budget. As with the national impact study of Head Start, the results of the Early Head Start evaluation will also potentially launch a new generation of downward extension projects. These experiments will address the weakness and capitalize on the strengths identified by the evaluation, thereby providing future directions for Head Start both as a national laboratory and as a unique niche of services for very young low-income children and their families.

REFERENCES

Administration on Children, Youth and Families (ACYF). (2001). *Head Start FACES: Longitudinal findings on program performance. Third progress report* (Document # 2001–615–032/24251). Washington, DC: U.S. Government Printing Office.

Bancroft, J. (1997). Strategies for Head Start-Child Care Partnerships. *Head Start Bulletin, 62,* 3–4.

Bouverat, R.W., & Galen, H.L. (1994). *The Child Development Associate National Program: The early years and pioneers.* Washington, DC: Council for Early Childhood Professional Recognition.

Campbell, D.T. (1969). Reforms as experiments. *American Psychologist, 24,* 409–429.

Cicirelli, V.G. (1969). *The impact of Head Start: An evaluation of the effects of Head Start on children's cognitive and affective development.* Athens: Ohio University, and New York: Westinghouse Learning Corporation.

Cost, Quality, & Child Outcomes Study Team. (1995). *Cost, quality, and child outcomes in child care centers.* Denver, CO: Department of Economics, University of Colorado at Denver.

Council for Professional Recognition. (1998). *The Child Development Associate (CDA) national credentialing program* [brochure]. Washington, DC: Author.

Crompton, D.A. (1997). Full Start: The results are in! *Head Start Bulletin, 62,* 13.

Doernberger, C., & Zigler, E. (1993). Project Follow Through: Intent and reality. In E. Zigler & S.J. Styfco (Eds.), *Head Start and beyond* (pp. 43–71). New Haven, CT: Yale University Press.

Fedoravicius, N., & Henrich, C.C. (2002, June). *Preliminary findings from year 1 of the national evaluation of the School of the 21st Century.* Poster presented at Head Start's Sixth National Research Conference, Washington, DC.

Forness, S.R., Serna, L.A., Kavale, K.A., & Nielsen, E. (1998). Mental health and Head Start: Teaching adaptive skills. *Education and Treatment of Children, 21,* 258–274.

Galinsky, E., Howes, C., Kontos, S., & Shinn, M. (1994). *The study of children in family child care and relative care: Highlights of findings.* New York: Families and Work Institute.

Gilliam, W.S., Ripple, C.H., Zigler, E.F., & Leiter, V. (2000). Evaluating child and family demonstration initiatives: Lessons from the Comprehensive Child Development Program. *Early Childhood Research Quarterly, 15,* 41–59.

Hayes, C.D., Palmer, J.L., & Zaslow, M.J. (1990). *Who cares for America's children? Child care policy for the 1990's.* Washington, DC: National Academy Press.

Head Start Bureau. (2003). *2003 Head Start fact sheet.* Washington, DC: Author.

Love, J.M., Kisker, E.E., Ross, C.M., Schochet, P.Z., Brooks-Gunn, J., Paulsell, D., et al. (2002). *Making a difference in the lives of infants and toddlers and their families: The impacts of Early Head Start. Executive summary.* Princeton, NJ: Mathematica Policy Research.

Mathematica Policy Research, Inc. (1999). *Overview of the Early Head Start research and evaluation project.* Princeton, NJ: Author.

National Council of Jewish Women (NCJW). (1999). *Opening a new window on child care: A report on the status of child care in the nation today.* New York: Author.

Ripple, C.H., Gilliam, W.S., Chanana, N., & Zigler, E. (1999). Will fifty cooks spoil the broth? The debate over entrusting Head Start to the states. *American Psychologist, 54,* 327–343.

Scherl, D.J., & Macht, L.B. (1972). An examination of the relevance for mental health of selected antipoverty programs for children and youth. *Community Mental Health Journal, 8,* 8–16.

St. Pierre, R.G., Layzer, J.I., Goodson, B.D., & Bernstein, L.S. (1997). *The effectiveness of comprehensive case management interventions: Findings from the national evaluation of the Comprehensive Child Development Program.* Cambridge, MA: Abt Associates.

Tarullo, L. (1997). Evaluation of Head Start family child care. *Head Start Bulletin, 62,* 14.

U.S. Department of Health and Human Services (DHHS). (1999). *Mental health: A report of the Surgeon General.* Rockville, MD: Author.

Valentine, J. (1997). Program development in Head Start: A multifaceted approach to meeting the needs of families and children. In E. Zigler & J. Valentine (Eds.), *Project Head Start.* Alexandria, VA: The National Head Start Association.

Young, K.T., Marsland, K.W., & Zigler, E. (1997). The regulatory status of center-based infant and toddler care. *American Orthopsychiatric Association, 67,* 535–544.

Zigler, E. (1997). Head Start: Not a program but an evolving concept. In E. Zigler & J. Valentine (Eds.), *Project Head Start.* Alexandria, VA: The National Head Start Association.

Zigler, E., Finn-Stevenson, M., & Marsland, K.W. (1995). Child day care in the schools: The School of the 21st Century. *Child Welfare, 74,* 1301–1326.

Zigler, E., & Muenchow, S. (1992). *Head Start: The inside story of America's most successful educational experiment.* New York: Basic Books.

Zigler, E., & Seitz, V. (1982). Social policy and intelligence. In R. Sternberg (Ed.), *Handbook of human intelligence* (pp. 586–641). New York: Cambridge University Press.

Zigler, E., & Styfco, S.J. (1993). *Head Start and beyond.* New Haven, CT: Yale University Press.

CHAPTER 39

The Future of Head Start

BARBARA T. BOWMAN

I n the 21st century, how we care for and educate young children is gaining public attention as Americans recognize that the out-of-home care and education delivery systems are not serving children and families as well as they should or could (Kagan &
Cohen, 1997). Many children are not receiving the quality of services they need to develop
optimally and succeed in school. To remedy this will require careful and systemic planning that takes into account past, current, and future social and economic constraints and
opportunities. Inevitably, Head Start, our largest and most important national program
for children, has a critical role to play. As we are now in a new millennium, it is a good
time to review the contribution Head Start has made and consider how it can be adapted
to the challenges of tomorrow.

THE ORIGINS OF HEAD START

The original mission of Head Start was to foster the development of children from low-
income families. A history of limited health, social service, education, and employment
opportunities compromised the development of many such children, and they were ill
prepared for school. Head Start was to provide the human and material capital necessary
to assure their healthy development and school readiness.

Support for the Head Start mission came from three directions: developmental research, governmental activism, and the civil rights movement. Research provided evidence
that children's intelligence is malleable, the environment is critical in shaping it, and
early childhood is an important period for development (Bloom, 1964; Hunt, 1961). This
research suggested that young children from low-income families needed a range of social, psychological, health and nutrition, and educational services to enhance their development and, consequently, their school achievement. Pilot programs demonstrated the
feasibility of this approach (Beller, 1979).

Governmental activism, spurred during the depression and war years, resulted in a
number of 20th-century initiatives to redress social problems. During the first half of

the 20th century, health, labor, welfare, and education legislation was passed to promote children's well-being. For example, public schools required vaccinations for school attendance, child labor laws limited the number of hours children could work, financial assistance was made available to families with dependent children, and Work Projects Administration and Lanham Act nurseries provided care and education during national emergencies.

The civil rights movement, led by African Americans after the Second World War, agitated for the end to racial segregation. The greater economic and social security of middle-class and white Americans undoubtedly contributed to the public willingness for government to address social inequities and the needs of children. Finally, in the 1960s, there was sufficient political will to pass the civil rights and economic opportunity bills, which energized national efforts on behalf of low-income and minority groups.

Against this backdrop, Head Start was born as one of a number of programs making up the War on Poverty. The Office of Economic Opportunity (OEO) administered the program directly from Washington, D.C., and under its aegis, low-income people were encouraged to make decisions about how funds were to be used, thus combining political, economic, and social service objectives. Because OEO was a federal agency, it was able to make a commitment to social justice and community empowerment, even though these goals were not favored in some of the states and localities where programs were opened.

Head Start was infused with these goals. It reflected the understanding that children's development is tied to their families and communities. To effect change, parents and community members needed to be educated and supported, so Head Start encouraged, indeed required, parents to make their own decisions about Head Start goals and objectives, curricula, staff, and budgets. There was no single model of Head Start. At various times and places, its purposes included empowering parents, employing community members, registering voters, redressing caste and class discrimination, arranging health care, providing social services, supporting children's cognitive development, and/or teaching children academic skills.

Despite its community action orientation, Head Start's central mission was to provide comprehensive services for children. The expectation was that Head Start interventions could be accomplished quickly and would have great benefits for children. For example, in communities where health services were not available through public or private means, Head Start contracted and paid for medical and dental care. Head Start's educational program was to be brief—summer-long, then year-long. At that time, few American children were enrolled in preschool, and in some states, even public kindergarten was not available. Therefore, the short educational program would confer an advantage on low-income children, giving them a head start on school. Parents, by volunteering in the center and attending parent meetings, would learn new child-rearing practices, which would enhance children's development.

Staff training was an early focus of Head Start. In the late 1960s, there were few well-trained professionals skilled in working with low-income families and preschool-age children. Not only did the Head Start program include a strong in-service education program, but it also provided college and graduate school tuition for staff interested in formal education. Head Start staffs included teachers, administrators, social workers, nurses, and psychologists, while physicians and dentists were often retained to provide direct services. Professionals were regularly engaged to monitor, assess, and report on the quality of the programs. It was a time of social activism, and volunteers—parents, professionals, and community members—were encouraged to be involved.

The first summer programs were housed (and largely staffed) by public schools. There was, however, considerable reluctance to formally lodge the new program in schools (the primary agency for children in localities) because politicians and administrators saw local educational bureaucracies as cumbersome and expensive, early childhood specialists considered traditional school practice (formal instruction) inappropriate for young children, and schools were disinclined to take on an age cohort with which they had no experience. Thus, outside of the big cities, public schools were less and less involved as Head Start developed. The majority of programs were located in small, not-for-profit agencies and religious institutions, and articulation between Head Start and public schools became tenuous.

The first few years of Head Start were a time of almost frenetic activity, excitement, enthusiasm, and hope, with new initiatives going off in almost every conceivable direction. Within a few years, however, controversies arose. Was Head Start effective? In what way? What were the desirable components? How should they be organized? How should Head Start balance its mission and means between community action and early childhood education?

A robust research agenda was soon undertaken, funded by government and private foundations, which eagerly tracked both Head Start's successes and failures. The broad sweep of Head Start objectives made it a complex organization to administer. Variation was the norm, and administrative control, necessarily loose, unfortunately often led to programs with little educational benefit for children. Order was gradually established in programs, largely through the efforts of Edward Zigler and the Office of Child Development (OCD) in the Department of Health, Education and Welfare. Gradually, Head Start became a leader in the field of early childhood education, and Head Start components, monitoring, and performance standards defined the leading edge for good early childhood practice.

WHAT HAS CHANGED?

Life in the United States at the beginning of the 21st century is vastly different in many respects from the 1960s. To be sure, children from low-income families continue to be at risk. Impoverished communities are still beset by a host of problems, including political powerlessness, economic disinvestment, community disorganization, and poorly delivered social and health services. Of particular concern is the intransigence of the achievement differential between low- and middle-income children, which places low-income children at increasing disadvantage in school and in life.

Nevertheless, many changes have occurred in child development knowledge, resource systems, and social attitudes and beliefs. Research and experience with Head Start and other early intervention programs over the past 35 years have added to our understanding of what it takes to provide a "head start." Following are my observations about these changes and some questions and options I think we might consider as we work to improve developmental and educational opportunities for low-income children.

The Goals of Head Start Are Complex and Have Proven Difficult to Implement

As noted previously, Head Start began as one of a number of OEO programs designed to empower low-income people to take control of their communities and improve their lives. It did not take long for an inherent conflict to become evident: The strategies of community action and those of early education were often at odds. Community action programs generally focused on system change, which eventually might have a long-term salutary effect on children's lives. In the short term, however, agitation and disruptions were inimical to the institutional consistency and stability essential for young children. Within a few years of its inception, Head Start was moved from OEO to OCD and performance standards were established and oversight increased.

Despite the switch in administration, Head Start continued to balance its legacy of conflicting goals regarding community change and child achievement. For example, one tension has been between hiring professionally educated staff and employing low-income community residents, who have little education and often are not well-prepared to teach. The advantage of employing teachers who know the community and need employment is pitted against the need for well-trained teachers. Another pressure, that of increasing enrollment of children, mitigates against upward economic mobility for staff because wages and expenditures for teacher training must be kept low. Even efforts to increase education and mobility have been undermined because there were few rewards for getting the child development associate (CDA) certificate.

These conflicts in goals raise a number of questions: Does the very flexibility and community embeddedness that is the legacy of Head Start's community action roots interfere with accountability for child outcomes? What should be the priority? More specifically, can Head Start employ minimally educated residents of low-income communities and still effectively prepare children for school? Is a much more robust commitment to staff education more important than increasing the number of children enrolled?

Health and Social Service Delivery Systems Have Changed

The dearth of health care and social services in low-income communities was a major problem in 1966, and Head Start provided or contracted for otherwise unavailable services. Over the past 3 decades, however, with leadership from Head Start, public systems have expanded. Further, new resources have developed as violence, drug addiction, employment, and single parenting have complicated family life and created a need for much more sophisticated services. As a consequence, Head Start's role has largely shifted from direct service and contracting to monitoring services provided by other delivery systems.

As the health and social services delivery systems change, the new danger is not as much resource deprivation as system confusion. For example, there are a variety of specialized services—preventing child abuse, housing the homeless, counseling troubled families, and treating substance misuse. These services are offered by multiple agencies—with different funding requirements, waiting periods, treatment strategies, and administrative structures—making obtaining services complicated and difficult. To determine client or patient eligibility requires specialized knowledge, which Head Start's largely untrained staff often does not have.

What seems to be needed is a more comprehensive approach to arranging services for low-income children: to find what is needed, figure out the most economical funding strategies, work out accountability agreements, and monitor services. How can we do this? Do we need to design a new system in which the responsibility for providing and monitoring services for all low-income children is lodged in public health clinics and departments of family services? Other possible models include lead agency case management, one-stop shopping, and collaboration between institutions and agencies. Public schools in some communities are taking over as the center for coordinating services for families. Are they a better location than Head Start for this task? Or should Head Start restructure its health, psychological, and social services delivery system to include children who are not enrolled in Head Start? This question becomes more cogent as Head Start engages in collaborative agreements with child care centers, some of whose children would ordinarily not be eligible for Head Start services. Rethinking the delivery of health and social services needs to be high on the list of considerations as we develop new systems to serve young children.

Developmental Competence Doesn't Necessarily Guarantee School Achievement

Early research on Head Start effectiveness focused on whether programs improved children's cognitive skills and academic achievement. Considerable evidence has accrued to show that children attending Head Start and Head Start—type programs performed better on cognitive measures after 1 year in preschool (Barnett, 1995). However, benefits have been short-term and generally have not overcome the cumulative effects of living in a low-income community. After 35 years of Head Start, low-income children continue to perform less well in school than do middle-class children, indicating that the problem of low achievement has not been solved.

Promoting school learning has turned out to be much more complex than was thought when Head Start began. Then, there was considerable hope that if we made sure low-income children had the basic ingredients for healthy development, they would learn well in school. Head Start, therefore, directed attention to ensuring these requirements—healthy bodies, adequate nutrition, help for families with problems, and socialization for children. When these conditions are met, we believed, children would be developmentally competent. They would know how to care about others, talk and understand speech, and know about the different objects in their environment. They would be ready for school.

Head Start has, by and large, accomplished the goal of ensuring developmental competence so that children arrive at school healthy in bodies and minds. Unfortunately, healthy development is not enough. Developmental competence, it turns out, is only one of the conditions necessary for school achievement. Children may be quite capable in their homes and communities and still not have the skills, knowledge, attitudes, and behavior necessary to succeed in school (Bowman & Stott, 1994). The other requirement is a "knowledge-centered" environment (Bransford, Brown, & Cocking, 1999), one that enables children to make sense of the various intellectual disciplines that define our world. A knowledge-centered environment directs children's attention to the specific concepts and procedures that underlie school subjects: literacy, math, science, and the humanities. It builds on ideas children learn on their own and in informal interactions with others—natural learning—but focuses on the particular skills and knowledge necessary for school success. For instance, learning a language, any language, is indicative of developmental competence; thus children who speak a dialect or a language other than English are developmentally on target. School competence requires more; simply knowing a language is not enough. A large vocabulary, phonemic awareness, alphabetic knowledge, and facile use of Standard English are highly correlated with academic achievement. In math, most developmentally competent children acquire informal knowledge of numbers and the ability to recite number tags fairly easily. But to succeed in school, children need to build on this knowledge, to explicitly grasp mathematical ideas, such as one-to-one relationships, patterning, and symbols. When children are not exposed to the broad set of cognitive tools, their knowledge remains superficial and places them at a disadvantage for building a strong understanding of school subjects.

School also requires specific social skills (e.g., don't hit or push in the classroom), patterns of emotional expressiveness (e.g., try to please the teacher), physical skills (e.g., highly developed small motor ability), and motivation to learn school subjects (e.g., enjoy reading and writing). Environments may be supportive of development but still not teach these particular social, emotional, physical, and motivational underpinnings of school learning.

As schools set higher standards, the misfit between what some low-income children know and can do and what is expected of them in school is likely to grow, and children will fail unless preschools provide, and help parents provide, the necessary foundation for schooling.

Teachers Need More and Better Training

Since the inception of Head Start, increasingly persuasive research has shown teacher education is a critical variable in determining achievement outcomes for children (Bowman, Donovan, & Burns, 2001). Model programs demonstrated that low-income children could learn school-related knowledge and skills if, in addition to strong developmental supports, they had well-educated and well-supported teachers (Campbell & Ramey, 1995). In general, Head Start has not provided a sufficiently powerful program to accomplish the same task, primarily because Head Start teachers do not have the necessary education nor is the system in place to provide it for the current teachers. Although Head Start's new requirement for the associate of arts (AA) degree for teachers is a step in the right direction, it will take a considerable time to raise the level of teacher training in Head Start to that found in model programs. It is also worth noting that many Head Start teachers are not enrolled in AA degree programs but in associate of applied science (AAS) programs that do not articulate with the requirements of many 4-year colleges. Thus, Head Start teachers often spend more time and money to obtain a bachelor's degree than students who enroll in 4-year institutions.

It is to Head Start's credit that concern about the quality of the education program led to steps to shore it up. There is now an emphasis on degrees, CDA certification, increasing wages, and providing clearer curriculum guidelines. Yet, the dilemma remains: how teachers can achieve high standards for children when they are poorly prepared for the task. Despite numerous initiatives designed to help, the history of Head Start is punctuated with new in-service programs—silver bullets—designed to overcome the lack of teacher education. The new training for literacy continues this tradition. It provides short, methods-oriented training in a pass-along model. The hope, of course, is that by simplifying the curriculum and giving clear directions, relatively untrained teachers can implement it. Regrettably, when poorly understood concepts are integrated into teachers' own beliefs and practices, the result is often an educational travesty. A brush with a recently trained teacher who had the children chant the letters in their names—without knowing the form of the letters or the sounds they make—again convinced me of the wrongheadedness of the dictum that teachers of young children do not need to know much because the children do not.

The disparity between quality in Head Start and quality in model programs is profound. Given the funding level and turnover rates, can Head Start provide additional education for a sufficient number of teachers to increase program quality? Can Head Start garner the resources to add enough quality to achieve more positive gains for children? If not, should we match more carefully the quality and quantity of intervention children need with what Head Start can provide? Perhaps it is time to think more carefully about whom Head Start should serve and what it will take to serve those children well.

The Early Care and Education Delivery System Has Expanded

When Head Start began, there were few educational or child care programs available for preschool-age children, much less for children from low-income families. Today, this is no longer the case. Programs have mushroomed, especially since the early 1990s. Federal government programs, such as those funded under the Child Care and Development Block Grant, Even Start, and early childhood resource and referral agencies, are widely available. In most states, public schools are engaged in early childhood activities, from screening children to funding programs for at-risk and special needs children, and a few have initiated systems of universal access. In addition to government-supported services, many private agencies and corporations sponsor programs, including child care, early literacy, and recreation, which serve some low-income children. Infants and toddlers, once viewed as too young for out-of-home programs, are now being enrolled in child care and Early Head Start. Most preschool-age children are in out-of-home programs some part of the day, and school is no longer as new an experience for young children as it was a generation ago. The proliferation of programs, however, has led to overlap, competition for clients, conflicting funding requirements, differing standards, and poor communication across systems.

Head Start has attempted to promote collaboration with public schools, encouraging and supporting transition activities. It is not surprising, however, that the gulf between them has been difficult to overcome, given that Head Start and public schools have different teacher education standards, unequal resources, and owe their loyalties to different professions. Both recognize there is often a misfit between the two systems, although when preschool programs are actually located in a public school, there seems to be greater communication among teachers and coherence in expectations (Love, Logue, Trudeau, & Thayer, 1992).

The question of retaining Head Start and public schools as distinct and separate systems is worthy of revisiting. The case for locating early education in public schools was originally outlined in the early 1970s and was based on the public schools' potential for funding, higher educational requirements for teachers, and economies provided by using school buildings, administrative infrastructures, and other support services. At that time, I was reluctant to support such a move. Public schools had little experience with young children and families, a history of poor service to low-income families and children of color, and no experience providing comprehensive services (Bowman, 1976).

Many of my 1976 criticisms no longer apply. As of 2004, all states have some form of early education, and several are beginning universal preschool. In fact, in some communities, Head Start and state-funded prekindergartens compete for the same children, often leaving both underenrolled. Family and community involvement and counseling are now components of many school programs, and public school teachers increasingly not only have a college degree but also specific training and experience in early education. There is now much more synchrony between Head Start and public school agendas. How can they forge a tighter connection?

A similar set of issues pertains to Head Start and child care. Perhaps the most profound change in the lives of low-income children and families is welfare reform. As more middle-income mothers joined the workforce in the 1980s and 1990s, attitudes changed regarding public assistance for parents with dependent children. Low-income mothers must work, too. Unfortunately, working has resulted in only small increases in family income and diminishes the amount of time mothers have to help educate their young children. The new work requirements mean that many potential Head Start parents are unable to use part-day programs, and others are unable to take advantage of parent education and volunteering opportunities even if their children are enrolled.

Head Start has responded to the need of families for full-day care by encouraging collaboration between Head Start and child care programs. These alliances, however, come at some cost to local programs that must negotiate funding with several agencies, that have differing guidelines and standards. For instance, state licensing standards, which determine teacher education requirements for child care, often make it difficult for Head Start to raise standards in collaborating programs. Unless Head Start uses some of its resources to upgrade the quality of child care, quality suffers. Should Head Start concentrate on upgrading the educational programs in child care and pay less attention to the other components? Should child care be an income-targeted program if it receives Head Start dollars? Does meeting performance standards, especially for parent involvement, place an unachievable burden on programs serving working mothers?

Earlier Intervention Is Effective

Child development research has continued to support the malleability of children's intelligence and provided evidence of the benefits of earlier intervention. Recent research on the brain suggests that learning is complex and subtle, and although this research does not give explicit direction about how best to structure learning environments for young children, it does make its importance clear. Although the timetable for the development of various capabilities and behavioral representations shows considerable individual and cultural variation, learning potential can be expanded or compromised quite early in life. Head Start recognized this by establishing Early Head Start.

The expansion of the Head Start mission, however, brings new difficulties. How will Head Start design programs and prepare staff to work with infants and toddlers? Will Early Head Start opt for numbers over quality, as did Head Start, or can it mount a comprehensive plan for personnel that include higher levels of education and better training? Can Head Start raise the educational standards for Early Head Start at the same time it raises the bar for teachers of 3- to 5-year-olds?

Family Education and Support Are Difficult to Implement

The tradition of parent education is long-standing in the early childhood education field and has been an important component of Head Start from the beginning. Over the years a number of research studies have shown the benefits of parents' involvement in their children's education (Bowman, 1994). Yet, although there is an indisputable connection between parent involvement and children's school success, it is far from clear that involvement causes achievement, especially when participation is required. Apparently, most parent support and involvement programs are unable to produce meaningful changes in parenting behavior (Barnes, Goodson, & Layzer, 1995; St. Pierre, Layzer, Goodson, & Bernstein, 1997).

Conflicts between goals and priorities for parents and children arise because family values and practices are related not just to the needs of children but to a variety of other considerations in family life, including income, housing, culture, and their own and other family members' needs. When these factors do not change, it is difficult to stimulate meaningful changes in child-rearing practices. Halpern wrote the following:

> Parent support and education programs cannot be expected to alter basic parenting capacities and styles, acquired through a lifetime of experience in a particular familiar and social world, and often continually reinforced in the present. Nor can they alter families' basic life situation. (1990, p. 305)

Another difficulty is that the crises facing families are more pervasive and more severe than in the past; substance abuse, violence, adolescent parenting, foster child placements, and high unemployment are endemic in many communities. Families' needs often are more acute and/or require more skilled intervention than Head Start programs are able to provide.

As Head Start moves into the new millennium, questions about the parent program include the following: What skills do staff need to have an effective parent program? Should Head Start make training the same priority for social service staff as it now is for teachers? How should Head Start gauge the success of its parent program when many parents either do not have time or do not want to be involved? As more families reach the limit of their eligibility for public assistance and more move into the low-wage workforce, how can Head Start respond to their continuing poverty?

POLICY ISSUES TO CONSIDER

Many challenges and options face Head Start as it continues to provide leadership in the care and education of low-income children. I see four critical issues on its agenda, which can lead to a number of different policy and program options. A brief summary of these issues and some of the questions and choices they evoke follow.

1. Should Head Start continue to provide both basic developmental supports and educational services? The necessity for low-income children and families to receive basic support services if children are to develop and learn well should no longer be a policy question. The problem I see is that only the low-income children who are enrolled in Head Start are guaranteed to receive supportive services. Children in child care, state prekindergartens, and in homes often do not, yet many of them need them, too. How do we ensure that all low-income children and families have access to the supports taken for granted in Head

Start—comprehensive services that are monitored and service providers that are held accountable? Can Head Start join with the various public and private service programs to create a comprehensive system that provides basic services to all low-income families?

The most efficient and cost-effective system may not be the traditional Head Start design. State and local health and/or social service organizations may be better lead agencies than Head Start if all low-income children were included in the same plan. If this were the case, Head Start would be in a position to devote more of its energy toward the education of children and families.

2. *Should Head Start continue its educational program exclusively for low-income children?* Has the time come to end the mandatory segregation of low-income children in Head Start? Is keeping low-income children separate increasing the differences between them and their peers? Conventional wisdom suggests that inclusion is more socially responsible and educationally beneficial than isolating children by disability or disadvantage.

Head Start is moving toward inclusion as it makes contracts with child care agencies to enroll Head Start children. This makes it possible for low-income children to enroll in programs serving a broader socio-economic mix. Are there other collaborations that could lead more children into mainstream settings? As long as Head Start standards continue to guide our understanding of what low-income children and families need, Head Start may not need to be the direct service provider.

Placing greater emphasis on including low-income children in more diverse settings does not mean that there would no longer be a need for educational programs solely for low-income children. Given the income segregation of much American housing, it is likely that most low-income children will continue to be served in segregated programs. Nevertheless, it seems an important principle that children are not intentionally segregated by their parents' income. Whether in Head Start or other programs, however, making sure that all children have the same educational opportunities and success will continue to be a challenge.

3. *How much education do teachers of low-income children need?* Considerable research has shown that teachers with more years of education provide higher quality school-related learning experiences for children (Bowman, Donovan, & Burns, 2001). The connection between child outcomes and the number of years of education a teacher has mirrors the relationship between children's academic achievement and mothers' years of schooling. If Head Start is to improve low-income children's school readiness, teachers need formal education as well as training in early care and education. Recently, Head Start recognized the relationship between teacher education and child outcomes and increased the educational requirements for teachers. It will be many years, however, before it has a cadre of highly educated teachers able to plan and implement a more effective program. What can we do about increasing the educational level of Head Start teachers without attenuating the commitment to educate community members? More scholarships, tuition forgiveness, tutoring, and better counseling are just a few possibilities.

There is also the problem of retaining better-educated teachers. Ending the pay differentials between public school and Head Start for teachers with equal amounts of education and early childhood training would go a long way toward solving this problem. Where could the money to do this come from? Are there activities that Head Start pays for that could be provided more cheaply by other agencies and organizations? Are there economies of scale and administrative practices that would free up resources? Can Head

Start and other government agencies and programs find innovative ways to combine money (e.g., contracts between child care and Head Start) that can diminish overlapping administrative costs? Should Head Start temporarily decrease the number of children enrolled while building a cadre of better educated teachers? This would mean cutting the number of children being serviced, but not to do it means more children will enter school unprepared to succeed.

4. How should Head Start collaborate with other state and local early childhood programs? When Head Start began, state and local governments assumed little responsibility for delivering or coordinating early childhood services. As of 2004, many states and localities are deeply involved in planning, funding, coordinating, and monitoring programs. In most instances, programs are funneled through state and local agencies for planning and oversight. Head Start's complicated structure—national planning and local implementation—often short-circuits the planning and oversight process, leading to overlaps and redundancies. Valuable time and effort is used trying to collaborate in the face of conflicting plans, guidelines, and evaluation. Can we design a more robust coordinating mechanism to fully integrate Head Start into statewide planning, funding, implementation, and evaluation efforts? Head Start can have considerable influence in assuring high-quality services for low-income children by leveraging its resources with others. Such a move would go a long way toward building a unified system of early care and education.

What Other Roles Could Head Start Play?

If Head Start were to alter some of its current activities, are there other ways it might influence the learning of young children from low-income families? Following are some possibilities:

- Head Start might fund new model programs that explore more efficient ways to achieve positive learning outcomes for children.

- Head Start might focus on the neediest children, providing them with a higher-quality program than most children need. This would mean serving fewer children, rather than trying to serve such children in a large, mediocre-quality program.

- Head Start funds might stimulate state and local governments to raise licensing standards.

- Head Start might switch more of its funding to child care, leaving the half-day option to state-funded prekindergarten programs where they exist.

- Head Start might shift more of its focus from the preschool age (3- to 5-year-olds) to younger children. The years between birth and age 3 are increasingly viewed as an important time for intervention.

- Head Start might play a larger role coordinating other early childhood initiatives, such as employment training for parents, family literacy, family networks, and rehabilitation.

CONCLUSION

Over the years, Head Start has been a beacon of hope for many children and families. As a long-term admirer of the contribution of Head Start parents, teachers, and administrators, I share with others a reluctance to change it. Head Start has contributed not only to the education of low-income children, but, through research and demonstration programs, it has also made a lasting contribution to our understanding of children's development and learning. Few in our field will forget Head Start's emphasis on the whole child and comprehensive services. Nevertheless, as we go forward it is important to continue Head Start's tradition of adaptation and improvement. Much can be gained if Head Start continues to analyze the changes in society and considers policy and program alternatives. Head Start has served well in the past. I am certain that the Head Start heritage will live on no matter what its future directions.

REFERENCES

Barnes, H., Goodson, B., & Layzer, J. (1995). *Review of research on supportive interventions for children and families.* Two volumes. Cambridge, MA: Abt Associates.

Barnett, S. (1995). Long-term effects of early childhood programs on cognitive and school outcomes. *The Future of Children, 5,* 25–50.

Beller, K. (1979). Early intervention programs. In J. Osofsky (Ed.), *Handbook of infant development* (pp. 852–94). New York: Wiley.

Bloom, B.C. (1964). *Stability and change in human characteristics.* New York: Wiley.

Bowman, B. (1976). Early childhood education in the public schools. In J.D. Andrews (Ed.), *Early childhood education: It's an art, it's a science* (pp. 109–119). Washington, DC: National Association for the Education of Young Children.

Bowman, B. (1994). Home and school: The unresolved relationship. In S. Kagan & B. Weissbourd (Eds.), *Putting families first* (pp. 51–73). San Francisco: Jossey-Bass.

Bowman, B., Donovan, S., & Burns, M. (Eds.) (2001). *Eager to learn: Educating our preschoolers.* Washington, DC: National Academy Press.

Bowman, B., & Stott, F. (1994). Understanding development in a cultural context: The challenge for teachers. In B.L. Mallory & R.S. New (Eds.), *Diversity and developmentally appropriate practices: Challenges for early childhood education* (pp. 119–133). New York: Teachers College Press.

Bransford, J., Brown, A., & Cocking, R. (Eds.). (1999). *How people learn.* Washington, DC: National Academy Press.

Campbell, F., & Ramey, C. (1995). Cognitive and social outcomes for high-risk African-American students at middle adolescence: Positive effects of early intervention. *American Educational Research Journal, 32*(4), 743–772.

Halpern, R. (1990). Parent support and education programs. *Children and Youth Service Review, 12,* 285–308.

Hunt, J. (1961). *Intelligence and experience.* New York: Ronald Press.

Kagan, S.L., & Cohen, N. (1997). *Not by chance: Creating an early care and education system for America's children.* New Haven, CT: Yale Bush Center, Yale University.

Love, J., Logue, M., Trudeau, J., & Thayer, K. (1992). *Transitions to kindergarten in American schools.* Portmouth, NH: RMC Research Corporation.

St. Pierre, R., Layzer, J., Goodson, B., & Bernstein, L. (1997). *The effectiveness of comprehensive care management interventions: Findings for the national evaluation of the Comprehensive Child Development Program.* Cambridge, MA: Abt Associates.

Index

Page numbers followed by *f, t, n,* and *tn* indicate figures, tables, footnotes, and table footnotes, respectively.